CALVIN'S POLITICAL THEOLOGY AND THE PUBLIC ENGAGEMENT OF THE CHURCH

This book explores a little-appreciated dimension of John Calvin's political thought, his two kingdoms theology, as a model for constructive, Christian participation in liberal society. Widely misunderstood as a proto-political culture warrior, due in part to his often misinterpreted role in controversies over predestination and the heretic Servetus, Calvin articulated a thoughtful approach to public life rooted in his understanding of the gospel and its teaching concerning the kingdom of God. He staked his ministry in Geneva on his commitment to keeping the church distinct from the state, abandoning simplistic approaches that placed one above the other, and rejecting the temptations of sectarianism or separatism. This revealing analysis of Calvin's vision offers timely guidance for Christians seeking a mode of faithful, respectful public engagement in democratic, pluralistic communities today.

Matthew J. Tuininga holds a Ph.D. in Religion, Ethics and Society from Emory University and is Assistant Professor of Moral Theology at Calvin Theological Seminary. He formerly taught politics and core studies at Oglethorpe University in Atlanta, Georgia, and he has also taught at Emory University and at Sewanee, the University of the South. He previously worked as a congressional aide in Washington D.C. and as a counterterrorism intelligence analyst for the Federal Bureau of Investigation.

The Law and Christianity series publishes cutting-edge work on Catholic, Protestant, and Orthodox Christian contributions to public, private, penal, and procedural law and legal theory. The series aims to promote deep Christian reflection by leading scholars on the fundamentals of law and politics, to build further ecumenical legal understanding across Christian denominations, and to link and amplify the diverse and sometimes isolated Christian legal voices and visions at work in the academy. Works collected by the series include groundbreaking monographs, historical and thematic anthologies, and translations by leading scholars around the globe.

Books in the series

Calvin's Political Theology and the Public Engagement of the Church

CHRIST'S TWO KINGDOMS

MATTHEW J. TUININGA

Calvin Theological Seminary

CAMBRIDGE
UNIVERSITY PRESS

CAMBRIDGE
UNIVERSITY PRESS

University Printing House, Cambridge CB2 8BS, United Kingdom

One Liberty Plaza, 20th Floor, New York, NY 10006, USA

477 Williamstown Road, Port Melbourne, VIC 3207, Australia

4843/24, 2nd Floor, Ansari Road, Daryaganj, Delhi – 110002, India

79 Anson Road, #06–04/06, Singapore 079906

Cambridge University Press is part of the University of Cambridge.

It furthers the University's mission by disseminating knowledge in the pursuit of education, learning, and research at the highest international levels of excellence.

www.cambridge.org
Information on this title: www.cambridge.org/9781107171435
DOI: 10.1017/9781316760000

© Matthew J. Tuininga 2017

First published 2017

A catalogue record for this publication is available from the British Library.

ISBN 978-1-107-17143-5 Hardback

To my parents, Cal and Ellen Tuininga, to whom I owe so much.

Contents

Acknowledgments

This book arose from a dissertation I wrote while studying at Emory University in Atlanta, Georgia. It is the culmination of five years of doctoral work and many more years of research and conversation with teachers, colleagues, students, family members, and friends. I have accumulated more debts than I can possibly acknowledge here: library staff at the Robert W. Woodruff and Pitts Theology libraries at Emory University; staff at Emory Law School's Center for the Study of Law and Religion (especially Amy Wheeler); colleagues and friends who attended presentations of the work and offered their critical feedback; students and other conversation partners in seminars, classes, online forums, and other informal settings; and teachers who challenged and encouraged early attempts to work out my thoughts in various assignments or papers. I am grateful for opportunities to present summaries of the work at the Third Refo500 Conference in Berlin in May 2013 and at the Second Annual Convivium Calvinisticum, sponsored by the Davenant Trust, in South Carolina in June 2014. I am thankful for funding I received through the Faculty Heritage Fund at Calvin Theological Seminary during the final stages of putting this book together.

I owe a special debt of gratitude to Michael S. Horton and David VanDrunen of Westminster Seminary California, who first guided me into the field of political theology and drew my attention to the Reformed two kingdoms tradition. Both Mike and Dave helped me begin to explore the field through directed studies, while Dave gave me the opportunity to serve as his research assistant and work with him on multiple projects on Reformed political theology and ethics.

I am very thankful to the four individuals who graciously served as my doctoral committee: Timothy P. Jackson, John Witte, Jr., Elsie Anne McKee, and Steven M. Tipton. Steve gave me the opportunity to teach the sociology of religion with him while helping me to take a sociological perspective on religion and politics into proper account. Elsie offered her excellent historical theological expertise to the project from Princeton Seminary, despite having never met me personally beforehand. Tim guided me through my doctoral program as a teacher, advisor, and friend, beginning with the day he went above and beyond the call of duty by allowing me, my wife, and our one-month-old son to stay indefinitely at his home in Atlanta until we could find our own place to live. He has always challenged me to wrestle with the implications of Christian *agape* in social, political, and ecclesiastical contexts. Even where we have our disagreements, he has cheered me on as a friend and colleague.

To John I owe an enormous debt; he was the one who first believed in me as a graduate student and made me excited about the prospect of coming to study at Emory. John and I hit it off as soon as we realized that we both grew up in the same Dutch Reformed immigrant community in southern Ontario and attended the same school (at different times of course!). He made me his research assistant and introduced me to the immense field of Calvin studies, driving me to Calvin's commentaries, sermons, and letters to scour everything he wrote relating to law, an effort that proved to be an invaluable foundation for my own research. He likewise introduced me to the nexus between religion and contemporary law by graciously including me in Emory Law School's Religion and Law group, which is affiliated with the Center for the Study of Law and Religion. John has the gift of encouragement, and where I faltered, even when his own plate was piled high with challenges, he always helped me see the big picture of what I was doing and how it was thoroughly worth pursuing. Needless to say, without John, this project never would have happened.

I am also grateful for a number of individuals who graciously read the whole of the manuscript and offered their encouragement and advice: Nicholas Wolterstorff, John L. Thompson, David Little, Barbara Pitkin, William R. Stevenson, David VanDrunen, Brad Littlejohn, John Bolt, and Herman Selderhuis. These impressive scholars saved me from numerous mistakes, helped me to clarify key arguments where necessary, and offered invaluable encouragement. It should go without saying – but I must say it anyway – that I alone am responsible for the mistakes and weaknesses that remain.

In addition, I have benefited tremendously from conversations with teachers, colleagues, family members, and friends who've helped me to work out the arguments and perspectives found in this book. They include Jay Green, Richard Follett, Ellen Marshall, Elizabeth Bounds, Stefan Losel, Dianne Stewart, Jimmy McCarty, Justin Latterell, Iwan Baamann (who also helped check some of my translations), David Alenskis, Davey Henreckson, Mika Edmondson, Ron Prins, Jeremy and Janine Huntington, Mark and Carla Van Essendelft, Eric Tuininga, Calvin and Ellen Tuininga, and many others.

I am grateful to my children, Joel, Katherine, and Sarah, who were faithful in prayer and encouraging in spirit while I worked on this book. They always make sure

I keep the bigger picture in perspective, and not infrequently, they have been the inspiration that kept me going.

My greatest debt, without question, is to my wife Elizabeth, who has been my primary conversation partner and best friend from the beginning to the end of this project. She has been gracious, patient, and encouraging far beyond my deserving. As my first and most supportive critic, she faithfully read the early drafts of my work before anyone else and almost always anticipated their best criticism and suggestions. She has kept our family running remarkably smoothly even amid the most stressful of times. Her commitment to me is the bedrock of my life. My gratitude for her love is far beyond what words can express.

Note on Citations of Calvin's Works

Calvin wrote his scholarly works in Latin, but he ordinarily published a French translation as well. He gave his academic lectures in Latin, while he preached his sermons in French. The majority of these primary sources can be found in the *Ioannis Calvini Opera Quae Supersunt Omnia, Corpus Reformatorum* (volumes 29–87; eds. Johann Wilhelm Baum, August Eduard Cunitz, and Eduard Reuss; 1863–1900), hereafter *Calvini Opera* or CO, while the rest of the sources I used can be found in the *Supplementa Calviniana: Sermons Inédits* (eds. Hanns Rückert et al.; Neukirchen: 1936–2006), hereafter SC, or at the Post-Reformation Digital Library (www.prdl.org/). Nearly all of Calvin's works, including most of his sermons, have been translated and published in English. In such cases I have used the English translations while checking key terminology and wording against the original Latin or French. Occasionally I have altered the translation or wording, either for stylistic or substantive clarity. Thus when referring to Calvin's writings, I have used the following method:

- When citing Calvin's *Institutes of the Christian Religion*, I usually cite parenthetically according to book, chapter, and paragraph from the 1559 edition, a form of citation that works for both English translations and the original Latin. When I cite the 1536 edition, however, I cite according to chapter, subchapter, and paragraph. Both these forms of citation work for both the English translations and the original Latin. The English translations I have used are:
  - *Institutes of the Christian Religion*. 1559 Edition. Edited by John T. McNeill et al. Translated by Ford Lewis Battles. Louisville: Westminster John Knox, 1960.
  - *Institutes of the Christian Religion*. 1536 Edition. Translated by Ford Lewis Battles. Grand Rapids: Eerdmans, 1975.
- When citing Calvin's occasional writings, I directly cite the English translation, along with the Latin or French original.

- When citing Calvin's letters, I provide the receiver and date of the letter, along with the original source. The English translations I have used come from:
  - *Selected Works of John Calvin: Tracts and Letters.* 7 Volumes. Edited by Henry Beveridge and Jules Bonnet. Grand Rapids: Baker, 1983.
- When citing Calvin's commentaries and sermons, I provide the passage on which Calvin is commenting, along with the date and the original source. With the commentaries, this is always a citation from the *Calvini Opera*, except in the case of the 1540 commentary on Romans, in which case I have used T. H. L. Parker's *Iohannis Calvini Commentarius in Epistolam Pauli ad Romanos* (Leiden: Brill, 1981), which shows the variants between the 1540 and 1557 editions. The English translations I have used are as follows:
  - *Calvin's Commentaries.* 22 volumes. Translated by John King et al. Grand Rapids: Baker, 2003.
  - *John Calvin's Sermons on 2 Samuel: Chapter 1–13.* Translated by Douglas Kelly. Carlisle, PA: Banner of Truth, 1992.
  - *John Calvin's Sermons on Ephesians.* Revision of the translation by Arthur Golding. Carlisle, PA: Banner of Truth, 1973.
  - *John Calvin's Sermons on Galatians.* Translated by Arthur Golding. Carlisle, PA: Banner of Truth, 1997.
  - *John Calvin's Sermons on Genesis: Chapters 1:1-11:4.* Translated by Rob Roy McGregor. Carlisle, PA: Banner of Truth, 2009.
  - *John Calvin's Sermons on the Acts of the Apostles: Chapters 1–7.* Translated by Rob Roy McGregor. Carlisle, PA: Banner of Truth, 2008.
  - *John Calvin's Sermons on the Beatitudes.* Taken from the *Gospel Harmony*. Delivered in Geneva in 1560. Translated by Robert White. Carlisle, PA: Banner of Truth, 2006.
  - *John Calvin's Sermons on the Ten Commandments.* Translated by Benjamin W. Farley. Grand Rapids: Baker, 1980.
  - *Men, Women, and Order in the Church: Three Sermons* (Sermons on 1 Corinthians). Translated by Seth Skolnitsky. Dallas, TX: Presbyterian Heritage Publications.
  - *Sermons from Job.* Translated by Leroy Nixon. Grand Rapids: Eerdmans, 1952.
  - *Sermons on Deuteronomy.* Translated by Arthur Golding. Edinburgh: Banner of Truth, 1987.
  - *Sermons on Jeremiah.* Translated by Blair Reynolds. Lewiston, NY: Edwin Mellen Press, 1990.
  - *Sermons on the Book of Micah.* Translated by Benjamin Wirt Farley. Phillipsburg, NJ: Presbyterian and Reformed Publishing, 2003.
  - *Sermons on the Epistles to Timothy and Titus.* Translated by Arthur Golding. Edinburgh: Banner of Truth, 1983.

- *Sermons on the Saving Work of Christ.* Translated by Leroy Nixon. Grand Rapids: Eerdmans, 1950.
- *Songs of the Nativity: Selected Sermons on Luke 1 and 2.* Translated by Robert White. Carlisle, PA: Banner of Truth, 2008.
- *The Gospel According to Isaiah: Severn Sermons on Isaiah 53 Concerning the Passion and Death of Christ.* Translated by Leroy Nixon. Grand Rapids: Eerdmans, 1953.

An excellent and thorough guide to Calvin's works is Wulfert De Greef's *The Writings of John Calvin, Expanded Edition: An Introductory Guide* (trans. Lyle D. Bierma; Louisville: Westminster John Knox Press, 2008).

Abbreviations

CO   *Ioannis Calvini Opera Quae Supersunt Omnia, Corpus Reformatorum* (volumes 29–87; ed. Johann Wilhelm Baum, August Eduard Cunitz, and Eduard Reuss; 1863–1900).

LW   *Luther's Works* (55 volumes; eds. Jaroslav Pelikan, et al.; St. Louis: Concordia Publishing House, 1955–).

SC   *Supplementa Calviniana: Sermons Inédits* (ed. Hanns Rückert et al.; Neukirchen: 1936–2006).

Introduction

The premise of this book is that John Calvin's political theology should be an important source of guidance for Christians as they participate in the politics of contemporary pluralistic liberal democracies. In contrast to the common portrayal of Calvin as a revolutionary or socio-political transformationalist (a portrayal which helps explain the popular caricature of Calvin as a theocratic tyrant), my thesis is that, much more than is typically appreciated by scholars, Calvin's conception of Christian political engagement was an expression of his two kingdoms doctrine, by which the reformer distinguished the eternal kingdom of Christ from Christ's lordship over the temporal (i.e., secular) affairs of this life. This in turn led the Genevan reformer to articulate a much sharper distinction between church and political society than did the papacy or the other magisterial reformers, even as he avoided the Anabaptist rejection of politics. It led him to conceive of politics not as a means of transforming society into the kingdom of God according to the dictates of Christian scripture, but as an endeavor to secure temporal order and civil right-eousness in accord with reason, natural law, and the virtues of charity and prudence. While Calvin argued that both kingdoms are Christ's, he insisted that the two should never be confused. The ultimate nature of the eternal kingdom brooks no compro-mise with evil, but the penultimate character of secular politics calls for forms of virtue and justice appropriate for sinful human beings in a fallen world.

Interpreted on its own terms, this political theological perspective is as relevant to Christians in twenty-first-century liberal democracies as it was to those who lived in sixteenth-century Protestant city-states. It offers us the theological resources to reject the ideal of Christendom, in which all citizens are expected to worship and live as Christians, on the one hand, and to affirm the value of political liberalism and principled Christian participation in pluralistic democratic societies, on the other.

Calvin argued that the kingdom of Christ is a fundamentally spiritual (or eschatolo-gical) reality, one that inaugurates the restoration of the entire creation through the

1

regeneration of human beings by Christ's word and Spirit. The location where this restoration has begun is the church, and Calvin sharply distinguished the church, as such, from the temporal and political affairs of life. To be sure, these are not two hermetically sealed realms. On the contrary, for Calvin, the righteousness of Christ's kingdom places its demands on every area of life. But in contrast to that kingdom and its righteousness, Calvin argued, the political affairs of this age will pass away. Temporal civil institutions cannot establish true piety, justice, charity, or peace, let alone save human beings from sin. Calvin thus sharply differentiated a "twofold government in man": one government that has the power to restore humans to spiritual righteousness, true virtue, and eternal life, and one that can only establish outward, civil, and temporal versions of the same. He placed substantive restrictions on the spiritual authority and prerogatives of the church's pastors, limiting them to the ministry of Christ's word and sacraments, while correspondingly binding the powers and intentions of political rulers in accord with their temporal limits.

Calvin thus condemned the persecution of non-Christians, such as Muslims and Jews, and he maintained that it is unjust to punish heretics or apostates in societies with religious diversity. He denied the assumption (of Aristotle and Christian theologians alike) that it should be the goal of magistrates to make people pious or just, hazarding his career on a decisive distinction between civil punishment and spiritual discipline. He rejected the claim that Christian societies must conform to the Old Testament's civil law, favoring the rigorous use of reason, experience, and the laws of nations, in addition to scripture, as sources of political wisdom. He endorsed something like republicanism (or aristocratic democracy), and he insisted that the power of government is limited by God's law, supporting legal and constitutional structures designed to hold magistrates accountable for their actions. He constantly invoked the language of rights (i.e., *ius*), especially with reference to the poor and the vulnerable, and he encouraged the Protestant tendency to locate the responsibilities of the Christian life in secular vocations such as trade, government, and family.

To be sure, Calvin was no liberal. He did not ground political authority in a social contract; he placed God's law above subjective human rights; and he denied that rights to freedom of speech, association, or religion are absolute. Nor did he draw the lines between church and civil government in ways that can be simply transferred to contemporary democracies. Calvin lived, thought, and wrote five centuries ago, when the differentiated complexities of modern society were only beginning to emerge. Like the pagan philosopher Plato and the Christian theologian Augustine, he assumed that government is obligated to make the truth, the honor of God, and the care of religion its chief concern. In (very) rare cases, he supported the death penalty for individuals judged by all Christendom to be heretical teachers. His political views explicitly presupposed the existence and legitimacy of Christendom, with all of its practical similarities to Old Testament Israel.[1]

Thus it may seem ironic to find in Calvin the resources for the abandonment of Christendom in favor of a commitment to secular political liberalism. But in my view Calvin's political theological orientation nevertheless makes his work relevant to contemporary Christians. Calvin had no dog in the fight over liberal democracy, so to speak; he wrote neither as the critic nor the apologist of any particular form of government. Yet his political theology accurately captures commitments central to the Christian faith and thoroughly conducive toward thoughtful Christian participation in twenty-first-century liberal democratic societies.

In this book, therefore, I presuppose a conceptual distinction between Calvin's practical politics and his political theology. By the term *practical politics*, I refer to Calvin's political actions and commitments, such as his support for the capital punishment of Servetus. By *political theology*, I mean Calvin's theological and ethical account of human life and society, with its consequent implications for the nature of the church, civil government, and other social institutions. My premise is that the value of Calvin's thought does not lie in his practical politics, which reflect the unique context of a time and place far different from our own (with a vastly different "social imaginary"![2]), but in the degree to which it offers Christians a coherent model for thinking about the implications of the gospel for Christian political engagement. Context is crucial for a clear understanding of Calvin's work, and for that reason I take his practical politics seriously. But my primary interest is in Calvin's theology, including its useful set of distinctions between the church and politics, Israel and contemporary political societies, natural law and the Torah, the spiritual use of the law and its civil use, and true righteousness and civil righteousness.[3]

In fact, I believe that most of Calvin's practical political judgments were not derived from his theology. Rather, they were Calvin's best efforts at interpreting the

---

[1] See John T. McNeill, "Calvin and Civil Government," *Readings in Calvin's Theology* (ed. Donald McKim; Grand Rapids: Baker, 1984), 274. Cf. Susan Schreiner, "Calvin's Use of Natural Law," *A Preserving Grace: Protestants, Catholics and Natural Law* (ed. Michael Cromartie; Grand Rapids: Eerdmans, 1997), 61.

[2] Charles Taylor defines our social imaginary as "the way that we collectively imagine, even pre-theoretically, our social life in the contemporary Western world." See Charles Taylor, *A Secular Age* (Cambridge: Harvard University Press, 2007), 146.

[3] As the French scholar Marc Chenevière put it so well, "the politico-religious thought of Calvin does not concern us, Protestants of the twentieth century, except in so far as it rests on a Biblical foundation ... It is Calvin's fidelity to Scripture that gives so much value to his teaching; it is this that *a priori* inspires our confidence in him." Marc Chenevière, "Did Calvin Advocate Theocracy?" *Evangelical Quarterly* 9 (1937): 160–168, 161.

practical implications of natural law for his own time and place based on reason, the laws of nations, and pagan political philosophy. This reflected Calvin's political theological method, which spurned the simplistic drawing of political conclusions from biblical exegesis in favor of careful reasoning about natural law. But what it means is that Calvin's political theology should be distinguished from his own attempts at such careful reasoning. Calvin himself distinguished between the authority of arguments drawn from natural reason (which could be challenged and rejected) and the authority of scripture (which, if interpreted correctly, could not be rejected). To embrace his political theology and method, therefore, is not necessarily to accept his illiberal conclusions. On the contrary, informed by different interpretations of reason, the laws of nations, and philosophy, we might readily find in Calvin's political theology substantial reasons for Christians to embrace liberal democracy.

By the term *liberal democracy*, I refer to constitutional systems of democratic or representative government designed to protect basic human and civil rights, including rights to life, speech, association, property, religion, and political participation, in accord with the rule of law under a system of checks and balances that includes the separation of church and state.[4] I suggest that Calvin's theology offers helpful guidance for Christians wrestling with how they should participate in liberal politics both *in good faith* to their non-Christian neighbors and in *faithfulness* to their Lord.

Such a perspective, I believe, is much needed in a time when prominent Christian pastors and theologians, not to mention liberal philosophers, are questioning the compatibility of orthodox Christianity with political liberalism. That so many Christians are questioning this compatibility in increasingly pluralistic societies, where fewer and fewer citizens hold to traditional Christian moral commitments, is unsurprising. Yet it is ironic, given the traditional tendency of Protestants to claim credit for the emergence of modern democracy. As Timothy P. Jackson maintains, while Christianity may not have invented political liberalism, political liberalism is certainly Christianity's stepchild. If the child has gone

---

[4] By liberal democracy, I therefore do *not* mean a comprehensive philosophical worldview such as that articulated by John Rawls in *A Theory of Justice* (Cambridge: Harvard University Press, 1971) or traced by Robert P. Kraynak to Immanuel Kant in *Christian Faith and Modern Democracy: God and Politics in the Fallen World* (Notre Dame: University of Notre Dame Press, 2001). I refer to a constitutional and practical liberalism that might be rooted in various comprehensive doctrines, such as that described by John Rawls in his later work, especially "The Idea of Public Reason Revisited," a 1997 essay printed in John Rawls, *Political Liberalism: Expanded Edition* (New York: Columbia University Press, 2005), 440–490, and such as that defended more thoroughly and consistently by Jeffrey Stout in his *Democracy and Tradition* (Princeton: Princeton University Press, 2004).

prodigal in certain respects, Christians should be about the business of reforming rather than abandoning it.[5]

Take, for instance, the widespread dismay among some Christians at the state's retreat from the defense of traditional sexual morality over the past half century (a retreat that culminated in the Supreme Court's declaration in 2015 that same-sex marriage is a fundamental right). This is a phenomenon that bears fascinating similarities to the way in which many Christians experienced the state's abandonment of the care of religion in preceding centuries. As happily as most Christians accept the separation of church and state today, the church's disestablishment was bitterly resisted by many Christians in the eighteenth century. Calvin himself believed that government should punish heresy and sexual immorality alike.

From that perspective it might seem that Calvin has little to say to modern Christians other than to further their disillusionment with liberal politics. But such is not the case, for Calvin understood that, in the real world, magistrates must often tolerate both heresy and sexual immorality. The civil law, he maintained, cannot establish spiritual righteousness. It must tolerate sin due to the hardness of human hearts, and sometimes it must even regulate sinful practices so as to mitigate their most destructive consequences. Thus while liberal societies appropriately fall under criticism for a host of moral failings with respect to fostering community, promoting virtue, protecting life, defending the rights of the poor, caring for the environment, and more, these failings should not come as a surprise, let alone discourage Christians from political involvement. Civil government is not the kingdom of Christ, Calvin would remind us, nor should we try to make it so. The state does not lose its legitimacy when it fails to meet the highest moral standards of the law of God (even though it does nullify its authority at the point that it requires its citizens to violate justice or piety).

The implications for the political involvement of the church are significant. The church is called prophetically to preach the righteousness of God, but that does not mean the church has the authority to dictate the way in which the laws of the state should reflect that righteousness. Unlike Judaism or Islam, as John Locke pointed out, Christianity recognizes no political or legal system as demanded by divine law; it offers no blueprint for a Christian state.[6] Theologians have tried to bridge the gap between the divine word and its political implications through what

---

[5] Timothy P. Jackson, "The Return of the Prodigal? Liberal Theory and Religious Pluralism," in *Religion in Contemporary Liberalism* (ed. Paul J. Weitman; Notre Dame: University of Notre Dame Press, 1997), 182–217.

[6] John Locke, "A Letter Concerning Toleration," in *Two Treatises of Government and a Letter Concerning Toleration* (ed. Ian Shapiro; New Haven: Yale University Press, 2003), 238–239. Cf. Kraynak, *Christian Faith and Modern Democracy*.

John Bennett called "middle axioms."[7] But Calvin's two kingdoms theology warns against any overextension of the church's authority in the cause of politics, clearly differentiating the law of God from the human law of the state and the ministerial authority of the church from the magisterial authority of civil government. To be sure, divine and civil law may never be entirely separated, let alone opposed to one another. Calvin agreed that a civil law that violates God's law is no law at all. But this does not make it an easy task, a simple process of translation, to determine how the laws of the state should best accomplish the purposes of piety and justice in any given context. Christians are called to exercise political judgment in service to their neighbors according to the virtues of love and prudence (which is to say, practical wisdom that seeks to achieve the purposes of love, not self-serving pragmatism).

If Calvin called sixteenth-century Christians to thoughtfully navigate between the Scylla and the Charybdis of political dogmatism and moral relativism, such a task remains all the more daunting in a twenty-first century characterized by multiple forms of pluralism. In addition to the religious pluralism that Calvin could have imagined, contemporary Christians experience the pluralism that arises from the ever-increasing differentiation of society and its institutions into multiple spheres of life, each with its own purpose, rationality, and moral logic.[8] Long gone are the days when the clergy could dictate the will of God for the minutiae of ethical questions that arise in fields as diverse as economics, agriculture, industry, information technology, medicine, law, science, education, art, sports, and many more, let alone the complex policy questions that arise with respect to each of these fields. Christians might be tempted to ignore the moral nuance required to skillfully negotiate such a plurality of spheres, but the gospel calls us to practice wisdom and discernment in a spirit of charity, humility, and reasonableness, not to lord it over one another as the Gentiles do. Calvin's two kingdoms theology grounds the need for moral nuance in a healthy respect for general revelation, and it grounds the need for political compromise in a recognition of human sin and of the multifaceted nature of God's law (natural and biblical; moral, ceremonial, and civil; theological, civil, and spiritual, etc.). It calls Christians not only to appreciate the enormous complexities associated with virtually any matter of public policy, but also to exercise a healthy skepticism toward politicians, pastors, or denominations that claim to proclaim the authoritative will of God for such matters.[9]

---

[7] John Bennett, *Christian Ethics and Social Policy* (New York: Charles Scribner's Sons, 1946), 76–85.
[8] Steven M. Tipton, "Social Differentiation and Moral Pluralism," *Meaning and Modernity: Religion, Polity, and Self* (ed. Richard Madsen, et al.; Berkeley: University of California Press, 2001), 15–40.
[9] Paul Ramsey, *Who Speaks for the Church?* (Nashville: Abingdon Press, 1967), 148–157.

On the other hand, what of the argument offered by the growing number of Christian theologians who are tapping into disillusionment with the modern liberal state by taking up what has come to be called the neo-Anabaptist critique?[10] If neither America nor political liberalism are particularly Christian, so the argument runs, we would do well to return to the example of the early church, which had the good fortune of recognizing that it inhabited a pagan world. In hindsight it appears that the church took a seriously wrong turn with Constantine and Christendom, allying the church with the state, and it is long past overdue for Christian political theology to repent of that turn. The true expression of the kingdom of God and its socio-political ethic, the neo-Anabaptists point out, is the church. The only faithful way to involve ourselves with politics, then, is to center politics in the true community of virtue that is the church, to make our political objectives explicitly Christian, and to abandon any sort of political logic that presupposes liberal neutrality or public reason. Christians should not, in any case, be complicit in the state's violence. Faithful witness, rather than the stewardship of American culture, should be our goal.

There is much that is true in the neo-Anabaptist critique, I believe, especially with respect to its critique of Christendom. Still, I am not prepared to dismiss well over a thousand years of the Christian tradition's teaching regarding the legitimacy of coercive government and the importance of faithful Christian participation in it, let alone to give up on political liberalism. Christians cannot afford to reject liberal politics if we are to take seriously the command to love and serve our neighbors. If such disengagement is attractive to Christians disoriented by the religious, cultural, political, and legal changes of the past few decades, there is a desperate need to reground Christian political convictions in the church's rich theological tradition, while reevaluating the implications of that tradition (as well as its missteps) in light of the passing of Christendom. We will not be in good shape if our theology apes that of Augustine, Aquinas, Luther, or Calvin, but neither will we be better off if we disregard them.

There are prominent criticisms of liberalism that are firmly embedded in church tradition, including those associated with communitarians like Alasdair MacIntyre, advocates of "radical orthodoxy" like John Milbank, and liberation theologians like

---

[10] Here I have in mind especially the prominent works of John Howard Yoder, including *The Politics of Jesus* (2nd ed.; Grand Rapids: Eerdmans, 1994), *For the Nations: Essays Public and Evangelical* (Grand Rapids: Eerdmans, 1997), and *The War of the Lamb: The Ethics of Nonviolence and Peacemaking* (ed. Glen Stassen et al.; Grand Rapids: Brazos Press, 2009); and Stanley Hauerwas, *A Community of Character* (Notre Dame: University of Notre Dame Press, 1981), *The Peaceable Kingdom: A Primer in Christian Ethics* (Notre Dame: University of Notre Dame Press, 1983), and *The Hauerwas Reader* (ed. John Berkman and Michael Cartwright; Durham: Duke University Press, 2001); and Daniel M. Bell, Jr., *Just War as Christian Discipleship: Recentering the Tradition in the Church Rather than the State* (Grand Rapids: Brazos Press, 2009).

Gustavo Gutierrez.[11] These theologians, while avoiding the neo-Anabaptist turn to pacifism, offer just as vigorous a critique of the modern liberal state in favor of what they regard as a more faithful (or orthodox) Christian political ethos. In comparison to a comprehensive Christian political vision that provides a foundation for a true community of virtue, such writers argue, the institutions of liberalism – including the constitutional state, free market capitalism, the separation of church and state, and the language of human and civil rights – are impoverished and corrosive. These criticisms also have their merits, but I think they sorely underestimate the extent to which Christian moral commitments are embedded in political liberalism. Though liberalism is certainly no utopia, it may well be, to echo Winston Churchill, the best political system human beings have yet devised. Too often Christians dwell on what is wrong with the liberal state rather than what is good about it. They fail to wrestle adequately with how Christians can be constructively engaged in service to our neighbors in the political society in which we actually live.

Furthermore, while these criticisms of liberalism are often insightful, all too often they assume the hegemonic normativity of Christianity for politics and hence require the abandonment of pluralistic liberalism as a matter of principle. All too often they write as if the kingdom of God should be expected to take substantive socio-political expression in this age. Their over-realized eschatology inevitably forces us to choose between withdrawing from worldly politics or seeking the establishment of an illiberal theocracy (albeit one that purports to be gentle and gracious in its use of force).

A major reason why it is worthwhile to return to Calvin's two kingdoms theology, then, is because it enables us to recover the traditional Christian conviction that civil government is ordained by God as a temporal institution charged with restraining evil for the common good, while nevertheless providing us with the resources for a substantive Christian critique of the ideal of Christendom. To put it another way, there is a need for a "realist" response to the over-realized eschatology of so much contemporary Christian ethics, one that teaches us how to participate faithfully in the politics of a pluralistic society rather than to withdraw from it or require that it be Christian. As a powerful critic of both the social gospel and pacifism, Reinhold Niebuhr has long been the face of Christian realism.[12] But Niebuhr's theology is too

---

[11] Alasdair MacIntyre, *After Virtue: A Study in Moral Theory* (3rd ed.; Notre Dame: University of Notre Dame Press, 2007); John Milbank, *Theology and Social Theory: Beyond Secular Reason* (2nd ed.; Oxford: Blackwell Publishing, 2006); Gustavo Gutierrez, *A Theology of Liberation* (Maryknoll, NY: Orbis Books, 1973), 150. A more nuanced view, but one that is nevertheless sharply critical of liberalism, can be found in William T. Cavanaugh, *Migrations of the Holy: God, State, and the Political Meaning of the Church* (Grand Rapids: Eerdmans, 2011).

[12] See especially Reinhold Niebuhr, *Moral Man and Immoral Society: A Study in Ethics and Politics* (New York: Charles Scribner's Sons, 1932); *The Nature and Destiny of Man: A Christian Interpretation* (2 vols.; New York: Charles Scribner's Sons, 1941–1943).

often only tenuously rooted in Christian scripture, his critics unable to escape the sense that a virtuous pragmatism plays a greater role in his ethics than does scriptural teaching regarding the love and justice of Christ.[13] There is a need, therefore, for a form of Christian realism more deeply rooted in Christian theology, scripture, and tradition. Recognizing this need, ethicists such as Paul Ramsey and Timothy P. Jackson have attempted to ground a realist approach in the theological virtue of love. Others, including Nicholas Wolterstorff and Eric Gregory, seek resources for an affirmation of political liberalism in the theological tradition of the church.[14]

This book is not constructive in the sense that these works are. I focus almost entirely on describing Calvin's theology in its own context and on its own terms, postponing my own critical and constructive proposals until the conclusion. My goal, however, is to recover Calvin as a relevant voice for contemporary Christian political theology. Calvin's two kingdoms theology offers contemporary Christians a rigorously orthodox and scriptural foundation for Christian realism, even as it embraces some of the central concerns of neo-Anabaptism regarding the importance of the church as the only truly restorative community of virtue. Here Ernst Troeltsch has insightfully identified Calvin's genius as his synthesis of the Anabaptist "sect-type" of Christian social engagement, in which the church is a distinct community of the faithful, with the medieval "church-type," in which

---

[13] See, for example, the critique in Richard B. Hays, *The Moral Vision of the New Testament: A Contemporary Introduction to New Testament Ethics* (New York: HarperOne, 1996), 215–225. Calvin is neither a realist nor a pragmatist in this Niebuhrian sense. For instance, while Niebuhr would argue that in an emergency Christians must sometimes act unjustly, getting their hands dirty, so to speak, Calvin insists that Christians must act justly regardless of the consequences. Likewise, while Niebuhr argues that love is a personal virtue inappropriate for the complexities of life in "immoral society," Calvin declares the law of charity to be the rule for politics.

[14] Jackson prefers the term "prophetic liberalism" because it stresses the positive function of Christian love. See Timothy P. Jackson, *Political Agape: Christian Love and Liberal Democracy* (Grand Rapids: Eerdmans, 2015). I maintain the term "realism" both because it is relevant to societies liberal and illiberal alike, and because it properly accentuates the limits of temporal politics. Cf. Paul Ramsey, *Basic Christian Ethics* (Louisville: Westminster John Knox Press, 1993); Timothy P. Jackson, *The Priority of Love: Christian Charity and Social Justice* (Princeton: Princeton University Press, 2003); Eric Gregory, *Politics and the Order of Love: An Augustinian Ethic of Democratic Citizenship* (Chicago: University of Chicago Press, 2008); Nicholas Wolterstorff, "The Wounds of God: Calvin's Theology of Social Injustice," *Reformed Journal* 37.6 (June 1987): 14–22; *Justice: Rights and Wrongs* (Princeton; Princeton University Press, 2008); *Justice in Love* (Grand Rapids: Eerdmans, 2011); *The Mighty and the Almighty: An Essay in Political Theology* (Cambridge: Cambridge University Press, 2012). Oliver O'Donovan takes a somewhat more critical yet ultimately constructive approach, seeking to ground Christian political participation in liberal democracies in classic Christian understandings of justice, authority, and judgment. Oliver O'Donovan. *The Desire of the Nations: Rediscovering the Roots of Political Theology* (Cambridge: Cambridge University Press, 1996); *The Ways of Judgment* (Grand Rapids: Eerdmans, 2005); *Resurrection and Moral Order: An Outline for Evangelical Ethics* (2nd ed.; Grand Rapids: Eerdmans, 1994).

the church remains committed to seeking and serving the social good of all persons.[15] It offers the theological basis for the model that Martin Marty, Robert Bellah, and Steven M. Tipton call a "public church," a church that conceives of its mission in relation to the restoration of all things, not simply in relation to the deliverance of the elect who are "only passing through."[16] Thus Calvin's political theology provides the foundation for a form of Christian realism in which the motive and guide for Christian political participation is always the gospel of Christ, but in which neither the gospel nor the kingdom of God are confused with what politics can accomplish.[17]

INTERPRETING CALVIN

The vast scholarship on Calvin has spawned numerous interpretations of the reformer's social-political thought and legacy. I would suggest that these interpretations can be grouped as five general types:

1) Calvin as a catalyst for modernity
2) Calvin as a socio-political transformationalist
3) Calvin as a dialectical theologian
4) Calvin as a political actor
5) Calvin as a pastor and teacher of scripture

I present these as types, but in reality they overlap to one degree or another, and the work of many scholars could readily be assigned to multiple types. Each offers helpful insight into Calvin's thought and legacy, but some of these interpretations also contain serious problems. Let me briefly consider each in turn.

---

[15] Ernst Troeltsch, *The Social Teaching of the Christian Churches* (trans. Olive Wyon; 2 vols.; Louisville: Westminster/John Knox Press, 1992 [1912]), 2:579, 593, 597, 602, 623, 627.

[16] Robert N. Bellah, et al., *Habits of the Heart: Individualism and Commitment in American Life* (Berkeley: University of California Press, 2008), especially 243–248; Robert N. Bellah, et al., *The Good Society* (New York: Vintage Books, 1992), especially 179–219; Martin Marty, *The Public Church: Mainline-Evangelical-Catholic* (New York: Crossroad, 1981); and Steven M. Tipton, *Public Pulpits: Methodists and Mainline Churches in the Moral Argument of Public Life* (Chicago: University of Chicago Press, 2007), especially 399–442.

[17] As Schreiner puts it, Calvin believed Christians must "take responsibility for that world" of which they are a part while holding "an unrelenting realism" about the effects of sin. Such realism seeks to "distinguish carefully between the spiritual and civil realms and to take seriously the fallen nature of the latter." Susan E. Schreiner, *The Theater of His Glory: Nature and the Natural Order in the Thought of John Calvin* (Grand Rapids: Baker Academic, 1995), 84–85. Cf. Schreiner, "Calvin's Use of Natural Law," 74. On Calvin as a realist in the tradition of Augustine, see Derek S. Jeffreys, "'It's a Miracle of God That There Is Any Common Weal among Us': Unfaithfulness and Disorder in John Calvin's Political Thought," *The Review of Politics* 62 (2000): 107–129, 125–126.

Calvin as a Catalyst for Modernity

For the past two centuries there has been no shortage of attempts to find in Calvin or Calvinism some key to understanding the modern world. Inspired by the Whig interpretation of history, scholars have seen in Calvin's Geneva the cradle of the Puritan state, in which in turn lay the seeds of modern democracy.[18] Max Weber launched a world of scholarship, one that has not yet run its course, when he claimed that the roots of the spirit of capitalism lay in Calvin's doctrine of predestination.[19] More recent historians such as John McNeill, Robert M. Kingdon, and John Witte, Jr., have identified in Calvin key concepts that shaped modern theories of law, government, democracy, marriage, poor relief, and human rights.[20] Historians, theologians, and sociologists continue to rework and repackage such theses in volume after volume, essay after essay, to this day.

The most plausible of these works see in the Reformation and in Calvin the intensification of a process of secularization and differentiation that has its roots in

---

[18] Herbert Darling Foster, "Calvin's Programme for a Puritan State in Geneva, 1536–1541," *Harvard Theological Review* 1 (1908): 391–434. Cf. Abraham Kuyper, *Lectures on Calvinism* (Grand Rapids: Eerdmans, 1931).

[19] Max Weber, *The Protestant Ethic and the Spirit of Capitalism* (trans. Talcott Parsons; New York: Scribner's 1958). Cf. R. H. Tawney, *Religion and the Rise of Capitalism* (New York: Mentor Books, 1926); Quentin Skinner, *The Foundations of Modern Political Thought, Volume 2: The Age of Reformation* (Cambridge: Cambridge University Press, 1978); On Troeltsch's incorporation of Weber's thesis, see *The Social Teaching of the Christian Churches*, 2:604–611. Michael Walzer argues that Calvinism spawned the type of individual, the activist revolutionary determined to remake society, that has so left its mark on the modern world. Michael Walzer, *The Revolution of the Saints: A Study in the Origins of Radical Politics* (Cambridge: Harvard University Press, 1965). For criticism of Weber's thesis, see Mark Valeri, "Religion, Discipline, and the Economy in Calvin's Geneva," *Sixteenth Century Journal* 28 (1997): 123–142; W. Stanford Reid, "John Calvin, Early Critic of Capitalism: An Alternative Interpretation," *Reformed Theological Review* 43–44 (1984–1985): 74–81, 9–12. David Little has modified Weber's thesis, arguing that it was in Calvin's concept of order, specifically his differentiation between spiritual and political institutions, within which the seeds of modern differentiation lay. David Little, *Religion, Order, and Law* (New York: Harper and Row, 1969). Ralph C. Hancock argues that Calvin's theology made God and his sovereign purpose so transcendent as to be unknowable to human beings. By emphasizing the importance of actively living for the glory of a God whose *ultimate* will could not be known, Calvin redirected religious energies into *secular* life and its *temporal* purposes. The result was a radical secularization of politics, but one in which the secular takes on a thoroughly religious significance to the believer. Ralph C. Hancock, *Calvin and the Foundations of Modern Politics* (Ithaca: Cornell University Press, 1989.

[20] John T. McNeill, "The Democratic Element in Calvin's Thought," *Church History* 18 (September 1949): 153–171; McNeill, "Calvin and Civil Government," 274. John Witte, Jr., *The Reformation of Rights: Law, Religion, and Human Rights in Early Modern Calvinism* (Cambridge: Cambridge University Press, 2007); Robert M. Kingdon, "Calvinism and Democracy: Some Political Implications of Debates on French Reformed Church Government, 1562–1572," *American Historical Review* 69 (1964): 393–401; Robert M. Kingdon, "Was the Protestant Reformation a Revolution? The Case of Geneva," *Transition and Revolution: Problems and Issues of European Renaissance and Reformation History* (ed. Robert M. Kingdon; Minneapolis: University of Wisconsin, 1974), 53–76.

Christianity itself. Weber rightly identified the tendency of Christianity to differentiate the salvation of the kingdom of God from life in this world, and various scholars point to Augustine's concept of the two cities, the medieval theology of natural law, and Luther's and Calvin's theologies of vocation as further intensifications of a general process by which the natural world was disenchanted and social life was increasingly differentiated into a multiplicity of institutions and spheres, each of which functions according to its own purpose, rationale, and ethic. To recognize that this has taken place is not to be a secularist. The modern differentiated world can be interpreted through either a secularist or a theistic lens, as Charles Taylor has demonstrated.[21] The "spheres" might be conceived as the autonomous invention of human beings, as for Weber and Walzer, or as creation ordinances of God revealed in scripture and in history, as for Kuyper and Herman Dooyeweerd.[22] Either way, Steven M. Tipton argues, the result is "moral pluralism," with the multiple spheres giving rise to multiple forms of moral meaning that consist together uneasily in the lives of individuals and communities.[23]

This book is informed by analyses of Calvin's legacy for secularization, democracy, and modernity insofar as it explores resources in Calvin for a thoughtful Christian response to secularity and social differentiation. But whether or not Calvin was a catalyst for modernity in one way or another is far beyond my scope. My objective is not to demonstrate how Calvin influenced history but to explore his political theology with an eye to how Christians might appropriate it for guidance today.

Calvin as a Socio-Political Transformationalist

Perhaps the most prominent popular interpretation of Calvin's political theology is that which makes the reformer a socio-political transformationalist. H. Richard Niebuhr played no small role in popularizing this view in his 1951 classic *Christ and Culture*, which described Calvin as a representative of Niebuhr's preferred type of Christian cultural engagement, "Christ the Transformer of Culture." Niebuhr placed Calvin's model in contrast to that of Martin Luther, whose two kingdoms doctrine he identified with the type "Christ and Culture in Paradox." Calvin let his

---

[21] Taylor, *A Secular Age*.
[22] See the various essays on vocation by Max Weber in *From Max Weber: Essays in Sociology* (ed. C. Mills and Charles Wright; New York: Oxford University Press, 1946); Michael Walzer, *Spheres of Justice: A Defense of Pluralism and Equality* (New York: Basic Books, 1983); Abraham Kuyper, "Sphere Sovereignty," in *Abraham Kuyper: A Centennial Reader* (ed. James D. Bratt; Grand Rapids: Eerdmans, 1998), 461–490; Herman Dooyeweerd, *A New Critique of Theoretical Thought: The Necessary Presuppositions of Philosophy* (4 volumes; trans. David H. Freeman and William S. Young; Philadelphia: Presbyterian and Reformed, 1953–1958).
[23] Tipton, "Social Differentiation and Moral Pluralism," 15–40.

doctrine of God's sovereignty drive his work, Niebuhr argued, arriving at the conclusion that "what the gospel promises and makes possible . . . is the transformation of mankind in all its nature and culture into a kingdom of God."[24] On this analysis the implications of Reformed political theology seem obvious. Because Jesus Christ is lord of all, there can be no neutrality with respect to the state or to politics. Christians should devote themselves to zealous political activism because, in the popular words of the Dutch Reformed theologian Abraham Kuyper, "there is not a square inch in the whole domain of our human existence over which Christ, who is Sovereign over *all*, does not cry, Mine!"[25] As Troeltsch put it, Calvinism "sought to make the whole of Society, down to the smallest detail, a real expression of the royal dominion of Christ."[26]

Following this general line of interpretation is a myriad of scholars who claim that for Calvin Christians and the church are God's instruments in the renewal or transformation of society into the kingdom of God. One of the most influential such interpretations is that of André Biéler, who describes Calvin as the founder of a new socio-economic order characterized by continual transformation on the part of Christians acting according to divine standards of social justice.[27] Building on Biéler's work, W. Fred Graham presents Calvin as "the leader of a revolution which disturbed Western society not only in the religious sector, but along the total spectrum of human thought and action."[28]

It is true that some Calvinists have viewed the complete transformation of society as a fundamental part of their gospel mission. Far too often this belief has inspired what Max Stackhouse calls "imperial Calvinism,"[29] what John De

---

[24] H. Richard Niebuhr, *Christ and Culture* (New York: HarperCollins, 2001 [1951]), 217–218. Niebuhr admits that this picture is heavily qualified by Calvin's eschatological distinction between the temporal and the eternal. Cf. Thomas G. Sanders, *Protestant Concepts of Church and State* (New York: Holt, Rinehart and Winston, 1964), 223–229. Jürgen Moltmann likewise characterizes Protestant political theology in terms of two chief streams, the "Lutheran doctrine of the two kingdoms" and the "Reformed doctrine of the lordship of Christ." The two doctrines, he simplistically claims, led to contrasting forms of engagement with the Nazi German state during 1933–1945. Jürgen Moltmann, *The Politics of Discipleship and Discipleship in Politics: Jürgen Moltmann Lectures in Dialogue with Mennonite Scholars* (ed. Willard M. Swartley; Eugene: Cascade Books: 2006), 3.

[25] Abraham Kuyper, "Sphere Sovereignty," in *Abraham Kuyper: A Centennial Reader* (ed. James D. Bratt; Grand Rapids: Eerdmans, 1998), 461–490, 488.

[26] Troeltsch, *The Social Teaching of the Christian Churches*, 2:622.

[27] André Biéler, *Calvin's Economic and Social Thought* (ed. Edward Dommen; trans. James Greig; Geneva: World Alliance of Reformed Churches, 2005 [1961]), 218, 265–268.

[28] W. Fred Graham, *The Constructive Revolutionary: John Calvin and His Socio-Economic Impact* (Richmond, VA: John Knox Press, 1971), 11 (Cf. 19). Cf. John Tonkin, *The Church and the Secular Order in the Theology of the Reformers*, 128–129; Benjamin Milner, Jr., *Calvin's Doctrine of the Church* (Leiden: Brill, 1970), 195; Schreiner, *The Theater of His Glory*, 108; Peter Iver Kaufman, *Redeeming Politics* (Princeton: Princeton University Press, 1990), 105–124.

[29] Max L. Stackhouse, *Creeds, Society, and Human Rights: A Study in Three Cultures* (Grand Rapids: Eerdmans, 1984), 56.

Gruchy identifies as Calvinism's "self-righteous triumphalism,"[30] and what Wolterstorff describes as "that most insufferable of all human beings, the triumphalist Calvinist."[31] There has been no shortage of Calvinist theologians who have claimed that the reformer's theology spawns a systematic worldview rooted in the sovereignty of Christ that must be brought to bear authoritatively on culture and politics through the systematic application of scripture.[32] Such attempts span the social and political spectrum. In the hands of Graham, Calvin looks like a 1970s liberal democrat,[33] whereas read through the lens of C. Gregg Singer, the very same Calvin resembles a 1950s conservative.[34] For Paul Chung, Calvin was a proto-liberation theologian.[35]

Such perspectives not only tend to exaggerate the passivity of other Christian traditions, especially Lutheranism, which also had a revolutionary impact on law and society.[36] They also overemphasize certain strands of Calvinism, such as English Puritanism, at the expense of other strands, such as those of Hungary or France. While it is true that Calvin's two kingdoms doctrine differs from Luther's, especially to the extent that Calvin worked it out in institutional terms, two kingdoms theology remains central to Calvin's thought and that of the Reformed tradition.[37] Though Christ's kingdom will one day restore all things, according to Calvin, in the present

[30] John W. De Gruchy, *Liberating Reformed Theology: A South African Contribution to an Ecumenical Debate* (Grand Rapids: Eerdmans, 1991), 21. Cf. William R. Stevenson, Jr., *Sovereign Grace: The Place and Significance of Christian Freedom in John Calvin's Political Thought* (New York: Oxford University Press, 1999), 79.

[31] Nicholas Wolterstorff, *Until Justice and Peace Embrace* (Grand Rapids: Eerdmans, 1983), 21.

[32] See Gordon J. Spykman, "Sphere-Sovereignty in Calvin and the Calvinist Tradition," *Exploring the Heritage of John Calvin* (ed. David E. Holwerda; Grand Rapids: Baker, 1976), 163–208.

[33] Graham, *The Constructive Revolutionary*. Cf. Biéler, *Calvin's Economic and Social Thought*.

[34] C. Gregg Singer, "Calvin and the Social Order; or, Calvin as a Social and Economic Statesman," *John Calvin: Contemporary Prophet* (ed. Jacob T. Hoogstra; Grand Rapids: Baker, 1959), 227–241.

[35] Paul (Sueng Hoon) Chung, *Spirituality and Social Ethics in John Calvin: A Pneumatological Perspective* (New York: University Press of America, 2000), 121–122, 157–158.

[36] See John Witte, Jr., *Law and Protestantism: The Legal Teachings of the Lutheran Reformation* (Cambridge: Cambridge University Press, 2002); Harold J. Berman, *Law and Revolution II: The Impact of the Protestant Reformations on the Western Legal Tradition* (Cambridge: Harvard University Press, 2003).

[37] See Oliver O'Donovan and Joan Lockwood O'Donovan, *From Irenaeus to Grotius: A Sourcebook in Christian Political Thought* (Grand Rapids: Eerdmans, 1999), 662–664; Witte, *The Reformation of Rights*; David VanDrunen, *Natural Law and the Two Kingdoms: A Study in the Development of Reformed Social Thought* (Grand Rapids: Eerdmans, 2010); Thomas F. Torrance, *Kingdom and Church* (Edinburgh: Oliver & Boyd, 1956), 155–160. For examples of scholars who simplistically contrast Calvin with the Lutheran two kingdoms doctrine see Herman Bavinck, "Common Grace," (trans. Raymond C. Van Leeuwen; *Calvin Theological Journal* 24:1 (1989): 35–65, 50; Willem Van't Spijker, "The Kingdom of Christ According to Bucer and Calvin," *Calvin and the State* (ed. Peter De Klerk; Grand Rapids: Calvin Studies Society, 1993), 109–132, 121; Willem Van't Spijker, *Calvin: A Brief Guide to His Life and Thought* (trans. Lyle D. Bierma; Louisville: Westminster John Knox Press, 2009), 143; Wolterstorff, *The Mighty and the Almighty*, 145–147.

age it is manifest only in the church's pilgrimage under the cross.[38] Nor did Calvin develop a transformationalist political theology as the systematic outworking of a central doctrine, such as the sovereignty of God or predestination, as Troeltsch so influentially argued. (Indeed, Troeltsch's claim notwithstanding, the doctrine of predestination hardly shaped Calvin's social thought at all![39]) To be sure, Calvin decisively affirmed the lordship of Christ over every area of life, and this affirmation did lead to a zeal for private and public righteousness, but Calvin's two kingdoms realism preserved him from the sort of zealous socio-political transformationalism that characterized some of his followers.

[38] See John Bolt, "'A Pearl and a Leaven': John Calvin's Critical Two-Kingdoms Eschatology," *John Calvin and Evangelical Theology: Legacy and Prospect* (ed. Sung Wook Chung; Louisville: Westminster John Knox, 2009), 242–265, 252. Cf. P.F. Theron, "The Kingdom of God and the Theology of Calvin: Response to the Paper by Prof. J. H. Van Wyk," *In die Skriflig* 35.2 (2001): 207–213.

[39] Troeltsch, like many early twentieth-century scholars, viewed Calvinism as a system of thought "logically constructed" on "the idea of predestination, the famous central doctrine of Calvinism" (579, 581). The gospel was no longer viewed primarily as a means to the salvation of sinners, but as a means to the greater end of the glory of God. Election freed Christians to look outward and devote themselves to the transformation of society into the holy community of Christ (588–589). This is to take place "in every aspect of life: in Church and State, in family and in society, in economic life, and in all personal relationships, both public and private" (591). Calvinism "transformed the whole conception of the Bible into an infallible authority for all the problems and needs of the Church" (587). Troeltsch's interpretation confuses Calvin's orthodox teaching on predestination with the idea that the elect are a spiritual elite called to transform the world for God. Calvin treated the doctrine as a source of pastoral comfort for believers while warning against speculation about the "terrible decree," including about who is or is not elect. He emphasized love for *all* human beings, bearers of the image of God, as fundamental to Christian obedience. Other scholars have also interpreted Calvin's work as a system of deduction from a central doctrine such as the sovereignty of God. See Foster, "Calvin's Programme for a Puritan State in Geneva," 395–396; Gregg, "Calvin and the Social Order," 228; McNeill, "The Democratic Element in Calvin's Thought," 155; Spykman, "Sphere-Sovereignty in Calvin and the Calvinist Tradition," 186–189; Margaret R. Miles, "Theology, Anthropology, and the Human Body in Calvin's *Institutes of the Christian Religion*," *Harvard Theological Review* 74 (1981): 305; Harro Höpfl, *The Christian Polity of John Calvin* (Cambridge: Cambridge University Press, 1982), 52, 71 (though see 227–229). Recent Calvin scholars have decisively refuted such interpretations. See Richard A. Muller, *The Unaccommodated Calvin: Studies in the Foundation of a Theological Tradition* (New York and Oxford: Oxford University Press, 2000); François Wendel, *Calvin: The Origins and Development of his Religious Thought* (trans. Philip Mairet; London: Collins, 1963 [1950]), 263–284; Wilhelm Niesel, *The Theology of Calvin* (trans. Harold Knight; London: Methuen, 1956), 159–181; John Tonkin, *The Church and the Secular Order in Reformation Thought* (New York: Columbia University Press, 1971), 103–104. Cf. David E. Holwerda, "Eschatology and History: A Look at Calvin's Eschatological Vision," in *Readings in Calvin's Theology* (ed. Donald K. McKim; Grand Rapids: Baker, 1984), 311–342, 313. Anthony Hoekema writes, "The very idea that Calvin took one doctrine as the fundamental principle of his theological system is misleading, because it suggests that Calvin's primary concern was to construct a logically consistent system – one built up by deduction from some original first premise comparable to Descartes' *cogito, ergo sum*. This was not at all his intent. Calvin was concerned to be a theologian of the Word of God – to reproduce as faithfully as he could the teachings of Scripture." Anthony Hoekema, "The Covenant of Grace in Calvin's Teaching," *Calvin Theological Journal* 2 (1967), 133–161, 134.

Calvin as a Dialectical Theologian

The interpretation of Calvin as a dialectical theologian has been carefully articulated in one of the most stimulating and sophisticated analyses of Calvin's political theology to date, that of William R. Stevenson, Jr.'s *Sovereign Grace*. Stevenson presents Calvin's theology as a dialectic arising out of the doctrines of Christian liberty and the sovereignty of God. On the one hand, he claims, Calvin's doctrine of Christian freedom was "a 'goad' to social action" and "social activism," freeing believers to "concentrate their energies on social renewal" through "positive service in God's developing kingdom."[40] On the other hand, Calvin's doctrine of providence called Christians humbly and patiently to submit to the circumstances and vocation within which they found themselves. The powerful tension created by the interplay between these two doctrines helps explain why Calvin's theology could be taken in such different political directions by his followers, but Stevenson judges that in the final analysis Calvin's own "accent falls on 'service' more than [transformative] 'action.'"[41]

Stevenson's dialectical interpretation faithfully captures the tension of Calvin's two kingdoms theology and provocatively explores its potential as a foundation for political liberalism. This book therefore complements Stevenson's perspective of Calvin, but it differs from Stevenson's approach insofar as the latter tends to treat Calvin's thought as a logical system constructed around the doctrines of human liberty and divine sovereignty.[42] It is true that Calvin's biblical theology gave rise to a system of doctrine that in turn informed his exegesis, but in my view, Calvin's political theology is better understood as the product of his biblical eschatology, and it is from this perspective that his account of Christian political engagement should be understood.

Calvin as a Political Actor

Some historians argue that key elements of Calvin's political theology and ecclesiology were shaped by his political experience rather than the other way around.[43] These writers remind us to place Calvin's theology in its historical context. Just as importantly, they remind us that Calvin did not simply apply his theological principles to the institutions of church and civil government as if in a vacuum. His practical efforts with respect to the functioning of the office of elder, the diaconate,

---

[40] Stevenson, *Sovereign Grace*, 60. Cf. 64, 74–75, 77, 124–126, 128–129.

[41] Stevenson, *Sovereign Grace*, 103. Cf. 84, 89, 93–94, 145.

[42] Stevenson, *Sovereign Grace*, 64–69, 149, 151–152.

[43] See William G. Naphy, *Calvin and the Consolidation of the Genevan Reformation* (Manchester: Manchester University Press, 1994); Robert M. Kingdom, "Social Welfare in Calvin's Geneva," *The American Historical Review* 76.1 (February, 1971): 50–69.

or the punishment of crimes were deeply influenced by the time, place, and circumstances in which he lived. I build on this work by seeking to observe the important distinction between Calvin's practical politics and his political theology, as outlined above.

At the same time, I am concerned that some of these interpretations sell the significance of the reformer's exegesis and biblical theology somewhat short. For instance, Harro Höpfl claims that in his early years Calvin's two kingdoms concept was "verbatim Luther's 'two-fold regiment' conception of politics," but that Calvin moved away from such a conception when it failed to meet his practical needs.[44] Calvin thus came to identify the civil government as cooperating with the spiritual government in a common project of edification and sanctification, and the two kingdoms distinction was left "insecurely based in Calvin's theology."[45] But Höpfl does not analyze Calvin's political theology through the lens of the reformer's eschatology or his exegesis of scripture, as would be necessary to warrant such a judgment. Rather, he leverages Calvin's political practice in order to question the consistency and relevance of his theology.[46]

Some scholars evaluate Calvin's two kingdoms doctrine first and foremost as a *political* or *sociological* theory of institutions rather than as *theology*. For instance, Nicholas Wolterstorff criticizes Calvin for identifying the church as a governance-authority structure rather than a community, and for reducing the rest of society to the realm of the state.[47] Gordon Spykman, for his part, reduces Calvin's two kingdoms doctrine to a failed attempt to distinguish church and state. He therefore proposes Abraham Kuyper's doctrine of sphere sovereignty as a superior route to the same end.[48] But whereas sphere sovereignty is a sociological concept that reflects on the modern phenomena of social differentiation, Calvin's

---

[44] Höpfl, *The Christian Polity of John Calvin*, 44. Cf. 66–67, 152, 172. Cf. Harro Höpfl, "The Ideal of Aristocratia Politiae Vicina in the Calvinist Political Tradition," *Calvin and His Influence, 1509–2009* (ed. Irena Backus and Philip Benedict; New York: Oxford University Press, 2011), 46–66.

[45] Höpfl, *The Christian Polity of John Calvin*, 187. Cf. 75, 122–123, 190, 193, 211. Cf. Harro Höpfl, *Luther and Calvin on Secular Authority* (Cambridge: Cambridge University Press, 1991), xxiii, xxi.

[46] Höpfl's goal is "to uncover the relationship between Calvin's practical experience as a political actor and his political theology." Admitting that Calvin's practice was not simply the application of his theological principles, he maintains that Calvin's "political theology did not adequately assimilate his practice." Höpfl, *The Christian Polity of John Calvin*, 1.

[47] Wolterstorff, *The Mighty and the Almighty*, 135–136, 141. Wolterstorff simplistically contrasts Calvin's 'two rules' theology with Luther's two kingdoms, identifying Calvin with the tradition going back to Pope Gelasius that views the church and commonwealth as coterminous and that therefore requires a distinction between a twofold government (134–147, 150–151).

[48] Spykman, "Sphere-Sovereignty in Calvin and the Calvinist Tradition," 191–194. Cf. I.W.C. Van Wyk, "The Political Responsibility of the Church: On the Necessity and Boundaries of the Theory of the Two Kingdoms," *Hervormde Teologiese Studies* 61.3 (September, 2005): 647–664; John T. McNeill, "John Calvin on Civil Government," *Calvinism and the Political Order* (ed. George L. Hunt; Philadelphia: Westminster, 1965), 41; Wendel, *Calvin*, 308–310; Jeong Koo Jeon, "Calvin and the

two kingdoms arise out of a theological doctrine of biblical eschatology. For Calvin the two kingdoms are fundamentally *eschatological* categories. They correspond primarily to the concepts of the eternal and the temporal and only secondarily to the institutions of church and state.

This eschatological emphasis explains why in the title of this book I refer to Calvin's doctrine as a doctrine of two *kingdoms* rather than of a twofold *government*. Calvin used both terms, and each has its advantages and disadvantages. The primary advantage of the language of a twofold government is that it clarifies that there is ultimately only one eternal kingdom of Christ, though the lordship of Christ extends to distinct forms of government, including the institutions of church and state (as Calvin worked out more clearly than did Luther). It reflects the fact that Calvin preferred the terminology of the "political order" or "civil government" to that of a "political kingdom." The advantage of the language of two kingdoms, however, is that it communicates more clearly Calvin's insistence that the "spiritual kingdom" *is* the eternal "kingdom of Christ" (both of which terms Calvin did use consistently), while the political order is not. It clarifies that as an eschatological category the political kingdom encompasses *all* temporal authorities and institutions, not just the state, even as the spiritual kingdom of Christ transcends the institutional church. In short, while the language of a twofold government highlights the *institutional implications* of Calvin's political theology for church and state, the language of two kingdoms highlights its fundamental *eschatological orientation*, and it is the latter that is most foundational to Calvin's thought.

Calvin as a Pastor and Teacher of Scripture

Yet another approach to Calvin's work interprets the reformer's significance in light of his self-identified role as a pastor and teacher of scripture. This perspective views Calvin's *Institutes*, sermons, and commentaries primarily as attempts to articulate the teaching of scripture, as Calvin himself saw them, rather than prioritizing the *Institutes* as the authoritative expression of a deductive theological system. It likewise evaluates Calvin's political and ecclesiastical involvement in the context of his work as a pastor and teacher of the church. To be sure, Calvin was not unique in his devotion to the pastoral call. But one of the reasons why Calvin's theological works continue to be widely published, read, and taught 450 years after his death is that they demonstrate virtually unparalleled levels of energy, skill, and exegetical discipline. Calvin was not interested in inspiring Calvinists or building a Calvinist

Two Kingdoms: Calvin's Political Philosophy in Light of Contemporary Discussion," *Westminster Theological Journal* 72.2 (Fall, 2010): 299–305.

movement, but in establishing churches whose fundamental mark was the faithful proclamation of the word of God.[49]

No one has reengaged the scriptural roots of Calvin's ecclesiology more extensively than Elsie Anne McKee. Her two excellent studies of Calvin's concept of elders and the plural ministry and of the diaconate evaluate the significance of Calvin's interpretation of key texts in light of the history of Christian interpretation. She situates Calvin's perspective as an interpreter in the context of his struggle to maintain the spiritual autonomy of the church from the state.[50] David VanDrunen's recent analysis of Calvin's two kingdoms theology (which he situates in the broader tradition of Reformed two kingdoms theology) complements McKee's work. VanDrunen argues that Calvin emphasized the authority of scripture alone when it came to the spiritual kingdom, the church, redemption, and the soul, while he highlighted the important role of natural law with respect to the political kingdom, civil government, creation, and the body.[51]

This book accepts the view of Calvin as a teacher of scripture and a pastor of the church, but it explores the roots of the two kingdoms in Calvin's theology and exegesis in ways that none of these scholars have. Indeed, none of the writers who prioritize Calvin's role as a teacher of scripture have devoted more than a chapter to his two kingdoms doctrine. My objective is to explore Calvin's two kingdoms doctrine in all of its dimensions, from its foundation in the reformer's eschatology to its practical expression in his politics.

---

[49] See Wendel, *Calvin*, 360. Cf. McNeill, "John Calvin on Civil Government," 24–25; Marc-Edouard Chenevière, *La pensée politique de Calvin* (Geneva and Paris: Labor and Fides, 1937), 181–190; Emil Brunner, "Nature and Grace," in Emil Brunner, *Natural Theology* (trans. Peter Fraenkel; London: Geoffrey Bles: Centenary, 1946), 35–45; Willem Balke, *Calvin and the Anabaptist Radicals* (trans. Willem Heyner. Grand Rapids: Eerdmans, 1981), 267, 277–278; Philip Benedict, *Christ's Churches Purely Reformed: A Social History of Calvinism* (New Haven: Yale University Press, 2002), 533–546; Heiko Oberman, *John Calvin and the Reformation of the Refugees* (Geneva: Droz, 2009); I. John Hesselink, "Calvin on the Kingdom of Christ," *Religion without Ulterior Motive* (ed. E. A. J. G. Van Der Borght. Leiden: Brill, 2006), 139–158; Holwerda, "Eschatology and History," 335–336; Torrance, *Kingdom and Church*; Schreiner, *The Theater of His Glory*; Milner, *Calvin's Doctrine of the Church*; Stephen J. Grabill, *Rediscovering the Natural Law in Reformed Theological Ethics* (Grand Rapids: Eerdmans, 2006); Tonkin, *The Church and the Secular Order in Reformation Thought*.

[50] Elsie Anne McKee, *Elders and the Plural Ministry: The Role of Exegetical History in Illuminating John Calvin's Theology* (Geneva: Librairie Droz, 1988); Elsie Anne McKee, *John Calvin On the Diaconate and Liturgical Almsgiving* (Geneva: Librairie Droz, 1984).

[51] VanDrunen, *Natural Law and the Two Kingdoms*. Witte and Kingdon show how Calvin's teaching and application of scripture were applied to a host of questions revolving around sex, marriage, and the family. John Witte, Jr., and Robert M. Kingdon, *Sex, Marriage, and Family in John Calvin's Geneva: Courtship, Engagement, and Marriage* (Grand Rapids: Eerdmans, 2005); Witte, *The Reformation of Rights*.

THE PLAN OF THIS BOOK

The danger for any study that seeks the contemporary relevance of a theologian such as Calvin is that we find in the reformer those things we want to find, searching his work anachronistically for the answers to questions he could not have asked. Yet this danger is one that we must face, for the only alternative is to dismiss Calvin as a figure of mere historical interest. The solution is to ensure that we have first understood Calvin's work in its historical context and on its own terms as best we can before subjecting it to our critical-constructive engagement. I have attempted to do this by devoting substantial attention to Calvin's historical context (Chapters 1–2) and to the foundations of his theology (Chapters 3–4, 7). Only then do I turn to Calvin's theology of church and civil government (Chapters 5–6), which in turn sets the stage for my evaluation of the more practical political implications of his work (Chapters 8–9) and for reflection on its potential implications today (Conclusion). Thus most of this book is descriptive rather than evaluative or constructive. Such thick description is essential if we are to understand Calvin's political theology in its own right.

It is also important to stress that my focus in this book is on Calvin, not Calvinism, and it is on Calvin's theology, not his legacy. Regardless of how Calvinists have claimed the heritage of their hero, and regardless of how that heritage has played itself out in history, I seek to engage Calvin's work independent of such concerns. I pay attention to what came before Calvin and the circumstances and ideas that shaped his outlook; I pay little attention to what came later. My goal is to describe Calvin's political theology in clearer and more comprehensive terms than has heretofore been done.

The first two chapters of this book place Calvin in his historical and political theological context and describe the immediate impact of his work. In Chapter 1, I outline the late medieval and early Reformation context for Calvin's two kingdoms theology, focusing in particular on the various versions of the hotly contested medieval two swords doctrine, on the political theologies of the leading magisterial reformers, and on their Anabaptist critics. This chapter enables me to show that Calvin's two kingdoms paradigm was indeed a serious alternative to the predominant political theologies in the sixteenth century. In Chapter 2, I turn to Calvin himself, describing the early development of his ecclesiology, his struggle for the spiritual autonomy of the church in Geneva, and his influence on the Reformed churches struggling under the cross in France. This chapter highlights the clear institutional implications that Calvin associated with his two kingdoms theology, as well as the flexibility with which it could be applied to very different political circumstances.

Chapters 3–4 show how Calvin's eschatology grounds the two kingdoms doctrine. Chapter 3 describes Calvin's doctrine of the kingdom of Christ in relation to his concepts of creation, nature, the fall into sin, and the kingdom's restoration of the world. I show that when Calvin maintained that the kingdom of Christ is spiritual he essentially meant that it is eschatological. In Chapter 4, I show how this claim about the eschatological nature of the kingdom underlay the various layers of the two kingdoms doctrine. Calvin used the doctrine to distinguish the spiritual kingdom of Christ that is eternal, which breaks into the present age through the regeneration of believers, from the temporal (and political) affairs of this world, which are destined to pass away.

Chapters 5–6 turn to Calvin's theologies of church and civil government. Chapter 5 shows how closely Calvin identified the church with the kingdom of Christ. He identified kingdom and church alike by the spiritual marks of the ministry of the word and sacraments, to which he closely related faithful church discipline. Against Rome Calvin insisted that the church's spiritual authority is purely ministerial and must be sharply distinguished from all political authority. Chapter 6 then turns to Calvin's early political formulations, showing how decisively the two kingdoms doctrine shaped Calvin's understanding of civil government and its purpose. Calvin viewed the state as a secular institution called to preserve civil righteousness and order subject to the principles of the natural moral law.

Chapters 8–9 turn to Calvin's practical political arguments on the magisterial care of religion, civil law, forms of government, and resistance to tyranny, but Chapter 7 first offers a brief excursus on key elements of Calvin's covenant theology. Calvin meticulously differentiated areas of continuity and discontinuity between the old and new covenants, and this chapter lays the foundation for the analysis of Calvin's use of the Old Testament in Chapters 8–9. Chapter 8 describes Calvin's arguments in defense of the magisterial care of religion. I show that Calvin's arguments rely more on his interpretation of reason, experience, the laws of nations, and classic philosophy than they do on his exegesis of scripture (or even his use of the Old Testament). I also show how Calvin limited the application of his argument to contexts quite different from what we find in modern pluralistic democracies. Finally, Chapter 9 turns to the positive legal and political implications of Calvin's two kingdoms theology with respect to the nature of civil law, forms of government, and resistance to tyranny. This analysis demonstrates the usefulness of Calvin's political theology as a guide for Christian engagement in liberal democratic contexts.

In the conclusion, I tie these various threads together in the form of a constructive proposal regarding the way in which Calvin's two kingdoms theology might be helpful as a guide for contemporary Christians. My proposal is necessarily critical, rooted in Calvin's underlying political theology rather than in his practical politics. It is also brief and suggestive. No doubt readers will find some of my suggestions lacking in one way or another, but the further development of my constructive argument must be the task for another book. Here I beg the reader's indulgence toward comments that are not intended as definitive answers but as the beginning of a new conversation.

1

Two Swords, Two Powers, or Two Kingdoms

Spiritual and Political Authority in Early Modern Europe

Calvin viewed his two kingdoms theology as an expression of the classic Christian distinction between the spiritual and the secular (or temporal). A distinction between the kingdom of God and earthly political power is anticipated in the New Testament and in early Christian writings such as the Epistle of Diognetus. And Augustine argued that although the city of God and the city of man are to be categorically distinguished from one another, the citizens of the two cities are mixed together in the present earthly life, sharing common society and politics. However, when Calvin described his two kingdoms distinction in the *Institutes* he presented it as a version of the traditional medieval distinction between spiritual and temporal jurisdiction that was articulated by the decretists and decretalists during the twelfth and thirteenth centuries. Calvin rearticulated that distinction in ways that built upon the various Protestant political theologies developed during the early years of the Reformation.

In this chapter, therefore, I outline the historical context for Calvin's two kingdoms doctrine, presenting the various Christian understandings of spiritual and temporal power to which Calvin's political theology emerged as an alternative. Beginning with the late medieval era, I describe how the papacy claimed full power over both the spiritual and temporal jurisdictions, while noting the effective opposition such claims received from advocates of secular power. On the eve of the Reformation, I suggest, the civil magistracy was the most plausible authority to which the reformers could appeal to counter that of the papacy. I then describe Luther's development of his two kingdoms doctrine, noting that despite its radical early statement of sharp separation between the power of the word and that of the sword, Luther and Melanchthon eventually adapted the doctrine to justify substantial magisterial control over religious matters. The next part focuses on the origins of the Reformed tradition, arguing that Zwingli's model of the *corpus christianum*, in which church and commonwealth are coterminous, facilitated an unprecedented degree of magisterial control over the church. The fourth part focuses on the

Anabaptist movement that offered the magisterial Reformation its most formidable political theological challenge through its assertion of the sharp difference between civil government and the church and between the Old and New Testaments. In the fifth part of the chapter, I turn briefly to Bullinger, the preeminent theologian of the Zurich Reformed tradition, who strengthened Zwingli's magisterial model by conceptualizing the godly commonwealth through the lens of God's eternal covenant and the continuity between the Old and New Testaments. I conclude by introducing Bucer's early attempts to establish church discipline independent from that of the civil government, an effort that anticipated Calvin's more successful institutional outworking of the Reformed two kingdoms doctrine in Geneva.

THE TWO SWORDS

The canon lawyers of the twelfth and thirteenth centuries presented the distinction between spiritual and temporal power in relation to the classic fifth-century formula of Pope Gelasius I. In 494 Gelasius wrote to Emperor Anastasius, "Two there are, august emperor, by which this world is chiefly ruled, the sacred authority of the priesthood and the royal power. Of these the responsibility of the priests is more weighty in so far as they will answer for the kings of men themselves at the divine judgment."[1] Widely accepted as authoritative, the significance of Gelasius' statement, like that of Augustine's *City of God*, would nevertheless be contested and disputed throughout the medieval period. Whatever Gelasius' intentions, the kings and emperors that emerged in the early medieval period considered themselves to be the vicars of Christ. Sacral rulers were believed to administer Christ's kingship even as the pope, the vicar of St. Peter, represented his priesthood. Christian rulers protected and governed the church within their territories, maintaining substantial control over appointments to clerical offices.[2] Pious reformers within the church complained that popes and bishops were manipulated by political powers who fostered a culture of clerical immorality, worldliness, and simony.

The papacy began to push back as Pope Leo IX assembled an ambitious group of reformers from around Europe to serve as cardinals in Rome. These men rejected the practice of lay investiture, through which secular authorities invested bishops with the pastoral staff and ring that symbolized their spiritual office and the temporal feudal estates and jurisdictions attached to that office, on the basis of the principle that "just as the soul excels the body and commands it, so the priestly dignity excels the royal."[3] Reform kicked into full gear when Hildebrand, one of the youngest

---

[1] Brian Tierney, *The Crisis of Church and State 1050–1300* (Toronto: University of Toronto Press, 1988), 13.
[2] Harold J. Berman, *Law and Revolution: The Formation of the Western Legal Tradition* (Cambridge: Harvard University Press, 1983), 49–84.
[3] Tierney, *Crisis of Church and State*, 35, 41–42.

reformist cardinals, became Pope Gregory VII in 1073. Under the rally cry of the freedom of the church Gregory and his followers launched what has become known variously as the Gregorian Reformation or the Papal Revolution, securing the independence and autonomy of the papacy from lay rulers and centralizing control over the clergy and ecclesiastical institutions. They modernized and bureaucratized the administration of papal government by means of a central court with officials and bureaucrats (the Curia). They gradually built up a legal system that regulated church property, the life and morals of the clergy, education, care for the poor, and a sacramental system that shaped the lives of all in Christendom from the cradle to the grave (incorporating even the social institution of marriage). Canon law became the most reliable, systematic, and comprehensive body of law in Western Europe, and ecclesiastical courts became the arbiters of choice in all sorts of disputes pertaining to property, crime, and morality.[4]

Gregory and his followers succeeded in establishing the independence, autonomy, and spiritual authority of the church, but the vast properties of the church and the extensive temporal lordships of bishops, including that of the papacy in Italy, continued to provoke conflicts with emperors, kings, and other secular powers. Overlapping territorial jurisdictions and legal systems spawned an endless tug-of-war between princes and priests, with both sides offering extensive, conflicting theological and legal arguments to bolster their particular claims. What emerged was a spectrum of positions ranging from the hierocratic papal claim that all power – spiritual and temporal – belongs to the pope, on one extreme, to the caesaropapist secular argument that supreme power – even over spiritual matters – belongs to the emperor or to the king, on the other.[5] While there were always those seeking to maintain a balance, the extremes defined the debate.[6]

The hierocratic theory made use of arguments drawn from both tradition and scripture. It was famously characterized in terms of the "two swords" the disciples offered Jesus in Luke 22:38.[7] The two swords were interpreted allegorically as

---

[4] Both the papacy and its system of canon law became models of governance and law for secular institutions in Europe. See Berman, *Law and Revolution*; Cf. John Witte, Jr., *Law and Protestantism: The Legal Teachings of the Lutheran Reformation* (Cambridge: Cambridge University Press, 2002), 33–50.

[5] J.A. Watt, "Spiritual and Temporal Powers," in *Cambridge History of Medieval Political Thought: c. 350-c.1450* (ed. J. H. Burns; Cambridge: Cambridge University Press, 1988), 367–423. Cf. Tierney, *Crisis of Church and State*; Berman, *Law and Revolution*.

[6] Watt argues, "Each was a theory wherein a unity was founded upon the supremacy of one or other of the powers. Each ... postulated one authority to control both swords. Dualism ... was not that logic which was most characteristic of the later middle ages." Watt, "Spiritual and Temporal Powers," 422–423.

[7] The most famous argument from tradition appealed to the Donation of Constantine, in which the emperor allegedly gave the pope temporal authority over lands in Italy and the west. Steven E. Ozment, *The Age of Reform 1250–1550: An Intellectual and Religious History of Late Medieval and Reformation Europe* (New Haven: Yale University Press, 1980), 140.

representing spiritual and temporal power (or jurisdiction). Christ's decisive answer to the disciples, "It is enough," was thought to confirm the sufficiency of the two kinds of power while establishing that he himself possessed both. Advocates of papal monarchy therefore argued that God had given both the spiritual and temporal swords to the pope, because the pope was not only the vicar of St. Peter – Christ's priestly representative on earth – but the vicar of Christ himself. True, they consistently admitted, the pope was not ordinarily to *use* the temporal sword but to *delegate* its use to temporal powers. But the pope nevertheless maintained absolute power and authority, and he could command the temporal power, if necessary, for the good of the church.

During the crucial papacies of Innocent III (1198–1216) and the former canonist Innocent IV (1243–1254), the proponents of papal supremacy solidified their claims. Innocent III argued that the priesthood is to kingship as the soul to the body: distinct, but obviously superior. Christ made the pope his vicar as the successor of St. Peter, to whom had been given "not only the universal church but the whole world to govern," and therefore "the Roman church has full power in both temporal and spiritual affairs."[8]

> To [the pope] is said in the person of the prophet: "I have set you over nations and over kingdoms, to root up and to pull down and to waste and to destroy and to build and to plant." [Jer. 1:10] To me also is said in the person of the apostle: "I will give you the keys of the kingdom of heaven ..." Thus, others were called to a part of the care, but Peter alone assumed the plenitude of power. You see then who is this servant set over the household, truly the vicar of Jesus Christ, successor of Peter, anointed of the Lord, a God of Pharaoh, set between God and man, *lower than God but higher than man*, who judges all and is judged by no one.[9]

Whereas Gratian's authoritative and systematic book of canon law, the *Decretum* (c. 1140), did not clarify the precise nature of papal power, in 1234 the updated body of canon law that included Innocent III's decretals was promulgated as the *Decretales*, and by this time. the canon lawyers had established the general consensus that the pope held both swords.[10]

At the same time, the canon lawyers were also working out a theory of the plenitude of papal power *within* the church. This theory also made use of arguments from custom and tradition, but its primary defense was Jesus' granting of the "keys of

---

[8] Cited in Tierney, *Crisis of Church and State*, 132.   [9] Quoted in Ozment, *The Age of Reform*, 143.

[10] This consensus is reflected, for example, in Thomas Aquinas's *Commentary on the Sentences* of Peter Lombard, 2.44 and 4.37. See Thomas Aquinas, *On Law, Morality, and Politics*, 2nd edition (trans. Richard J. Regan; ed. William P. Baumgarth and Richard J. Regan; Indianapolis: Hacket Publishing, 2002), 196. Tierney claims that Aquinas's rhetoric should be interpreted narrowly to refer to papal temporal rule in Italy, but Morrall and Aveling argue for a broader interpretation. See Ozment, *The Age of Reform*, 148.

the kingdom" to his apostles in Matthew 16:18–19: "And I tell you, you are Peter, and on this rock I will build my church, and the gates of hell shall not prevail against it. I will give you the keys of the kingdom of heaven, and whatever you bind on earth shall be bound in heaven, and whatever you loose on earth shall be loosed in heaven." This text was closely associated with a similar text in Matthew 18:18, and with John 20:23, where Jesus authorized his apostles, "If you forgive the sins of anyone, they are forgiven; if you withhold forgiveness from anyone, it is withheld." Central to the consensus of the Decretists regarding these texts were the conclusions that 1) Christ granted the sacerdotal power to administer the sacraments to all the apostles (and so immediately to all priests), but 2) he granted supreme "jurisdiction" and "administration," the power to govern, to legislate, and to decide specific cases, solely to Peter, and hence to the pope.[11]

One canonist summarized the consensus when he wrote,

> [The pope is] the vicar of God, Jesus Christ, because he has the fullness of power on earth ... He changes the substance, the quantity, or the nature of things ... He makes a secular canon from a monk ... and just like the emperor, he changes the nature of an action ... and like the emperor he makes two things one, as 'legatum' and 'fideicommissum' ... The pope makes two churches one ... By binding and loosing, he holds the office of God on earth ... The pope is above the law ... dispenses from the rules of the Apostle ... he is above any council.[12]

To be sure, the pope's power of jurisdiction was not absolute. His decisions could not contradict the doctrines of faith, nor could they violate reason or morality. But the pope did have discretionary power over ecclesiastical law, sometimes even when that law came from scripture. He could offer dispensations from vows or oaths, he could depose bishops, and he had supreme authority, the *plenitudo potestatis*, to adjudicate doctrinal and ecclesiastical disputes.[13] All of this authority he could enforce with the powers of excommunication and interdiction. Even here, of course, practice did not conform simply to theory. Popes had to choose wisely when to issue mandates, and they had to work hard to ensure that those mandates were obeyed. But in

---

[11] Brian Tierney, *Origins of Papal Infallibility 1150–1350: A Study on the Concepts of Infallibility, Sovereignty and Tradition in the Middle Ages* (Leiden: E. J. Brill, 1972), 33 (Cf. 14–57). Cf. Brian Tierney, *Foundations of the Conciliary Theory: The Contribution of the Medieval Canonists from Gratian to the Great Schism* (Cambridge: Cambridge University Press, 1955), 31 (Cf. 25–33); Kenneth Pennington, *Pope and Bishops: The Papal Monarchy in the Twelfth and Thirteenth Centuries* (Philadelphia: University of Pennsylvania Press, 1984), 15–72.

[12] Cited in Pennington, *Pope and Bishops*, 28–29.

[13] The pope had the authority to "create and innovate in the sphere of positive canon law." Tierney, *Origins of Papal Infallibility*, 27. But the canonists applied the fullness of power to the papacy "only by carefully delimiting the sphere within which juridical sovereignty could be exercised" (30). They always viewed scripture as the supreme authority (17–25).

principle the pope's jurisdiction was seen as being grounded in the direct authorization of Christ rather than in tradition or positive law.[14]

The hierocratic theory of papal power received its most impressive statement in the papal bull *Unam Sanctum*, promulgated by Pope Boniface VIII (1294–1303) during a conflict with King Philip IV of France. Appealing to the two swords of Luke 22:38, Boniface declared,

> Both then are in the power of the church, the material sword and the spiritual. But the one is exercised for the church, the other by the church, the one by the hand of the priest, the other by the hand of kings and soldiers, though at the will and sufferance of the priest. One sword ought to be under the other and the temporal authority subject to the spiritual power. For, while the apostle says, "There is no power but from God and those that are ordained of God" (Romans 13:1), they would not be ordained unless one sword was under the other and, being inferior, was led by the other to the highest things.

Boniface's final claim made the matter of jurisdiction and appeals clear: "Therefore if the earthly power errs, it shall be judged by the spiritual power, if a lesser spiritual power errs it shall be judged by its superior, but if the supreme spiritual power errs it can be judged only by God not by man ... Therefore we declare, state, define and pronounce that it is altogether necessary to salvation for every human creature to be subject to the Roman Pontiff."[15]

In fact, Boniface VIII was defeated in his struggle with Philip IV of France, and the claims of *Unam Sanctum* amounted to more of a "last-ditch stand against state control of national churches" than a high-water mark of papal power.[16] The rediscovery of Aristotle's works (the *Politics* finally appeared in 1260) rendered possible a more positive view of secular society and civil government than were permitted by hierocratic views of nature and grace. Accordingly, the fourteenth and fifteenth centuries witnessed some of the most impressive intellectual arguments against the supremacy of the papacy.[17]

The University of Paris became especially noted for its defense of royal prerogatives in ecclesiastical matters. Most famously, the Aristotelian Dominican John of Paris defended a two swords dualism in which the two swords were mutually corrective and in which heretical or scandalous popes could be opposed, either through an ecclesiastical council or by the intervention of a lay ruler.[18]

---

[14] Pennington, *Pope and Bishops*, 33, 45, 54.   [15] Cited in Tierney, *Crisis of Church and State*, 189.

[16] Ozment, *The Age of Reform*, 138.

[17] Ozment writes, "The rising nation-states of Europe, in quest of full secular independence and autonomy, acted decisively to curtail the traditional pre-eminence of Peter and, so far as possible, to transform the medieval church into a docile department of the inchoate sovereign state." Ozment, *The Age of Reform*, 138.

[18] Watt, "Spiritual and Temporal Powers," 407–410.

As for the argument that corporeal beings are ruled by spiritual beings and depend on them as on a cause, I answer that an argument so constructed fails ... because it assumes that royal power is corporeal and not also spiritual and that it has charge of bodies and not also of souls, which is false ... [Royal power] is ordained, not for any common good of the citizens whatsoever, but for that which consists in living according to virtue. Accordingly, the Philosopher says in the *Ethics* that the intention of a legislator is to make men good and to lead them to virtue, and in the *Politics* that a legislator is more to be esteemed than a physician, since the legislator has charge of souls, the physician only of bodies.[19]

The Englishman William of Ockham, protected by Ludwig of Bavaria, articulated perhaps the most consistently dualistic argument among medieval philosophers, defending radical Franciscan arguments that Christ has called the church to poverty. Ockham rejected the notion that secular rulers received their authority from, or were in any way responsible to, the papacy.[20] The Italian Marsilius of Padua, also protected by Ludwig, went so far as to challenge the divine origin of the papacy. Rather than articulate a subtle dualism of spiritual and temporal power, he defended the caesaropapist position that the secular power possesses exclusive authority in temporal matters and ultimate authority in matters of church doctrine or scriptural interpretation. He rejected the right of the church to use coercive punishments such as excommunication, limiting it to spiritual, other-worldly functions that were largely sacramental, pedagogical, and moral. Marsilius was the original expositor of the caesaropapist theory that in Protestant circles became associated with the Zurich model of ecclesiastical and political power, a model most famously embodied in Henry VIII's claim to the royal supremacy in the Church of England.[21]

Through the fourteenth and fifteenth centuries the power of the papacy was drastically weakened amid the scandals that became known as the Babylonian Captivity of the Church and the Great Schism. Secular powers increased their control over their respective territorial churches. Half of Europe rendered its support

---

[19] Cited in Ozment, *The Age of Reform*, 148. For an English translation of the work see John of Paris, *On Royal and Papal Power* (trans. J. A. Watt; Toronto: Pontifical Institute of Medieval Studies, 1971).

[20] See Arthur Stephen McGrade, *The Political Thought of William of Ockham* (London: Cambridge University, 1974); David VanDrunen, *Natural Law and the Two Kingdoms: A Study in the Development of Reformed Social Thought* (Grand Rapids: Eerdmans, 2010), 36–42. Another Englishman, John Wyclif, made even more radical arguments defending the absolute right of temporal rulers over Church property. Both Ockham and Wyclif were excommunicated by the papacy. Janet Coleman, "Property and Poverty," *Cambridge History of Medieval Political Thought: c. 350-c.1450* (Ed. J. H. Burns; Cambridge: Cambridge University Press, 1988), 645–647.

[21] Ozment, *The Age of Reform*, 149. Cf. Watt, "Spiritual and Temporal Powers," 415–422. Another Italian, Dante Alighieri made an argument nearly as radical, advocating the universal lordship of the emperor without reference to any authority or interference from the papacy. Watt, "Spiritual and Temporal Powers," 411–415.

to the papacy relocated at Avignon, while the other half rejected that papacy in favor of a line of popes reestablished at Rome. The result was the emergence of the conciliarist movement, as theologians and bishops searched for a means by which the church as a whole, the congregation of the faithful, could bring erring popes back into line. Although the movement was not monolithic, Tierney points out, its unity lay in its "appeal to the underlying authority of the Church, understood as the *congregatio fidelium*"; papal authority was decisively affirmed, but "even the Pope . . . was held to possess only a derivative and limited right of government conferred on him by the Church."[22]

The inspiration for conciliarism came from the canon law. The canon lawyers had always insisted that a pope was not above judgment if he strayed from the true faith into heresy, and the canonist Huguccio had even extended the claim to any case of notorious immorality.[23] Resting on such legal claims and backed by secular rulers, in 1417 the Council of Constance proclaimed that as a general council it "has its authority immediately from Christ; and that all men, of every rank and condition, including the pope himself, are bound to obey it in matters concerning the Faith, the abolition of the schism, and the reformation of the Church of God in its head and its members."[24] The council succeeded in ending the Great Schism by choosing a new pope, Martin V (1417–1431), and it mandated regular meetings of a general council in the future. The Council of Basel (1431–1449) later restricted traditional papal privileges, limiting ecclesiastical appeals to Rome and removing papal rights to annates of benefices.[25]

But the conciliarist movement did not succeed in its ultimate objectives. When the Council of Basel deposed Pope Eugenius and sought to establish a new pope, the credibility of the movement was shattered. By 1447 it had yielded to papal authority. Conciliar theory was never established in canon law, and in 1460 the papal bull *Execrabilis* explicitly rejected any right of appeal over the papacy to a council. It was a modified conciliarism that continued to shape the opinions of intellectuals, reformers and secular authorities into the sixteenth century, ultimately taking expression in the counter-reformation Council of Trent.[26]

The real balance of power was shifting toward temporal rulers. When Pope Leo X (1513–1521) reaffirmed *Unam Sanctum* at the Fifth Lateran Council in 1516, only

---

[22] Tierney, *Foundations of the Conciliar Theory*, 4–5.

[23] Tierney, *Foundations of the Conciliar Theory*, 8–9.   [24] Cited in Ozment, *The Age of Reform*, 156.

[25] It also negotiated significant (and largely permanent) concessions of power over the church to the temporal rulers of France, Germany, and even to the Hussites in Bohemia. Between 1427–1436 papal revenues declined by almost two thirds. Ozment, *The Age of Reform*, 172–174.

[26] Ozment, *The Age of Reform*, 156, 174–181; John A. F. Thomson, *Popes and Princes 1417–1517: Politics and Polity in the Late Medieval Church* (Boston: Allen & Unwin, 1980), 3–28; Diarmaid MacCulloch, *The Reformation: A History* (New York: Penguin Books, 2003), 26–52; Charles F. Briggs, *The Body Broken: Medieval Europe 1300–1520* (New York: Routledge, 2011), 179–199.

a few short months before Luther's posting of the 95 Theses, its doctrine was widely regarded as a mere fiction. The papacy was at the height of its corruption and the nadir of its reputation. Everywhere the church was becoming increasingly national in character as kings and other secular authorities established legally recognized control over their respective churches. Even in the decentralized Holy Roman Empire, where papal power remained strong and where prince-bishops and prelates governed almost half of the 364 registered polities authorities, cities like Nuremburg and Augsburg eliminated clerical privileges and immunities and appropriated traditional ecclesiastical functions such as education and poor relief.[27]

On the eve of the Reformation, therefore, neither council nor bishop nor priest offered a sufficient basis of authority for ecclesiastical reform in opposition to the papacy. Yet clearly some kind of authority was necessary if the Reformation was not to devolve into anarchy. To whom could the reformers turn but the secular authorities who were already eagerly asserting their control over the church? Many of these secular authorities were more than willing to take up the religious authority for which the reformers offered theological warrant. As Diarmaid MacCulloch writes,

> With the trend in late medieval central Europe for local secular rulers to take more and more power and responsibility away from leading churchmen, it was not surprising that the first reformers in the 1520s looked to princes rather than bishops or abbots to undertake a new round of reforms in the Church, or that much of the Reformation continued to develop with the assumption that the godly prince was the natural agent of religious revolution.[28]

The Dutch humanist Desidarius Erasmus, who spent the prominent part of his career in what would become the Reformed city of Basel, encouraged this tendency

---

[27] In England, the king won control over high ecclesiastical appointments, appeals beyond the king's court to the pope were forbidden, and clerical immunity from civil courts was challenged, all long before Henry VIII's establishment of the royal supremacy in the 1530s. In France, the Pragmatic Sanction of Bourges (1438) deprived the pope of traditional rights of appointment, jurisdiction, and taxation in France, and the right of France to choose its own clergy, deny annates to the pope, and restrict appeals from French courts to the pope were declared to be fundamental Gallican Liberties. The Spanish monarchy had incorporated the inquisition as a tool of the state in 1479, and in the following years it won rights of patronage to all major ecclesiastical appointments. Ozment, *The Age of Reform*, 182–190. Thomson, *Popes and Princes*, 29–53; MacCulloch, *The Reformation*, 43–52; Briggs, *The Body Broken*, 91–116. The classic argument about the imperial cities is found in Bernd Moeller, *Imperial Cities and the Reformation: Three Essays* (Philadelphia: Fortress Press, 1972), 41–115; Steven E. Ozment, *The Reformation in the Cities: The Appeal of Protestantism to Sixteenth-Century Germany and Switzerland* (New Haven: Yale University Press, 1975), 1–46; Witte, *Law and Protestantism*, 33–34, 42–46, 177–182. Witte observes, "these fifteenth-century legal reformations laid important groundwork for the massive shift of jurisdiction from the Church to the state in the sixteenth century." Witte, *Law and Protestantism*, 179.

[28] MacCulloch, *The Reformation*, 51.

in his 1516 classic *The Instruction of a Christian Prince*. Erasmus argued that it is the responsibility of a prince not simply to rule justly or even merely to exercise the sword cooperatively with the church, but to rule as a Christian prince responsible for the spiritual welfare of his subjects. Echoing classical figures like Plato and Aristotle, Erasmus described the territorial state or city as a distinctively religious institution in which the prince is responsible for establishing education, wise civic discipline, and ecclesiastical stability conducive of peace, order, and virtue. True, only priests could perform the crucial spiritual tasks associated with the spiritual sword, but princes were also the servants of Christ and were therefore of preeminent importance. Erasmus was by no means the originator of these ideas, but he was one of their most persuasive and prominent advocates. Most of the prominent early reformers, including Zwingli, Melanchthon, and Bucer, were influenced by Erasmus through years of formative humanist education.[29] The great exception was Martin Luther.

LUTHER'S TWO KINGDOMS

The foundation for Martin Luther's assault on the Roman Catholic Church during the early years of the Reformation was his contrast between the inward and spiritual nature of the gospel and the outward and temporal character of the Roman church. Luther argued that there are two kinds of righteousness, an alien righteousness that comes from God and purifies the sinner inwardly, and the righteousness that believers practice outwardly in this world.[30] "Man has a twofold nature, a spiritual and a bodily one. According to the spiritual nature, which men refer to as the soul, he is called a spiritual, inner, or new man. According to the bodily nature, which men refer to as flesh, he is called a carnal, outward, or old man."[31] The problem with

---

[29] "In short," Estes writes, "Erasmus' definition of the relationship between prince and clergy means that for all practical purposes the church is absorbed into the state. The state has been turned into something so overwhelmingly religious in nature that the church is left with no separate, distinct goal or identity." James M. Estes, "*Officium Principis Christiani*: Erasmus and the Origins of the Protestant State Church," *Archiv fur Reformationsgeschichte* 83 (1992): 49–72 [62–63]. Estes argues that this was basically the pattern later enacted in the Protestant territories during the Reformation. Both Zwingli's right-hand man in Zurich, Leo Jud, and one of Luther and Melanchthon's allies in Saxony, Georg Spalatin, produced German editions of *The Instruction of a Christian Prince* in 1520–1521. In his first published work of 1523, the Strasbourg reformer Martin Bucer borrowed from *The Instruction of a Christian Prince* extensively.

[30] Martin Luther, "Two Kinds of Righteousness," in *Martin Luther's Basic Theological Writings*, 2nd ed. (ed. Timothy F. Lull; Minneapolis: Fortress Press, 2005), 134–140. Torrance Kirby argues that this distinction is the foundation for the entire two realms trajectory of orthodox Reformation theology. See W. J. Torrance Kirby, *Richard Hooker's Doctrine of the Royal Supremacy* (Leiden: Brill, 1997).

[31] Martin Luther, "The Freedom of a Christian," in *Martin Luther's Basic Theological Writings*, 2nd ed. (ed. Timothy F. Lull; Minneapolis: Fortress Press, 2005), 386–411, 393

Roman piety and worship was that it pandered entirely to the latter. Only true faith in Christ could establish true, inward righteousness, and along with it a liberty that defined the Christian no matter what her state of service or subjection in this world. As he famously put it in his 1520 treatise on the freedom of the Christian, "A Christian is a perfectly free lord of all, subject to none. A Christian is a perfectly dutiful servant of all, subject to all."[32]

These distinctions between the inward and the outward, the spiritual and the temporal, divine righteousness and human righteousness, soul and body, and the new and the old combined with a range of anthropological, soteriological, and eschatological distinctions in Luther's thought to form what John Witte calls "the broad umbrella of the two-kingdoms theory."[33] Luther articulated this umbrella of distinctions in a myriad of dialectical formulations in response to various challenges as they arose. He did not always clarify how one formulation corresponded to another, nor was he always consistent in his terminology or application. This has made the precise meaning of his two kingdoms theology a matter of continuous scholarly analysis and debate.[34] Here I focus on Luther's application of the dialectic to questions of spiritual and secular power, but it is important to remember that Luther approached such questions from within this broader theological context.

By 1520 Luther had become disillusioned with the likelihood of papal support for reformation. Categorically rejecting claims of papal supremacy by divine right, he argued that within the community of believers, there is an equality before God. By virtue of this equality, any believer can take the necessary steps within his power to reform the church if the clergy fails to do so. In his *Address to the Christian Nobility of the German Nation Concerning the Reform of the Christian Estate*, Luther therefore called the nobility and the emperor to intervene to save Christendom by summoning a council. But he was careful to clarify the nature of the authority secular powers had over the church. Over matters of property and morality, such as control over ecclesiastical benefices and the conduct of the clergy, he argued that secular government has direct authority. Regarding spiritual matters, on the other hand, secular powers have no such authority. The nobility's right to call a council to address spiritual matters was rooted not in the prerogatives of their secular offices but in their equality as believers responsible for the welfare of the church. Just as any citizen, regardless of office, is obligated to sound the alarm and

---

[32] Luther, "The Freedom of a Christian," 408.   [33] Witte, *Law and Protestantism*, 89.

[34] Witte, *Law and Protestantism*, 87–117. Wright argues that Luther was influenced by the strand of Renaissance Humanism that embraced skepticism but rejected Neoplatonism. This informed his skepticism regarding human righteousness and the affairs of this world. William John Wright, *Martin Luther's Understanding of God's Two Kingdoms: A Response to the Challenge of Skepticism* (Grand Rapids: Baker Academic, 2010).

mobilize the city when there is a fire or an attack by enemies, so any Christian must, when necessary, take action necessary for the preservation of the church.[35]

The nobility did not respond as Luther hoped. Although the Elector Frederick of Saxony protected him, the emperor supported the pope's excommunication of Luther with his own imperial ban and outlawed Luther's works and supporters. Luther's response was to emphasize the power of the word to do its own work of reforming. He defended the right of local congregations of Christians to call their own pastors and enact reforms where secular and clerical authorities failed to do so. He attacked secular authorities for interfering with the dissemination of the gospel.[36] Such rhetoric inspired his supporters, led by Andreas Karlstadt, to inaugurate a series of radical reforms in Wittenburg in 1521–1522 while Luther was in hiding. The Eucharist was celebrated, images were removed and destroyed (sometimes violently), and a series of further reforms were initiated, all without authorization from the Elector of Saxony. Though agreeing with the reforms in substance, Luther was horrified because of the lack of authority for the actions. He defended the Elector when he restored the status quo, breaking with Karlstadt by insisting that radical reforms had to be conducted with the approval of the proper authorities and with respect for weaker consciences. At the same time, he tried to persuade the Elector to abolish the Mass.

The compounding confusion was the context for Luther's attempt to clarify his views of the relation between the church and secular authority in his classic *On Secular Authority: To What Extent it Should be Obeyed*. Luther began his argument by invoking Augustine's eschatological distinction between the city of God and the city of man: "We must divide the children of Adam and all mankind into two classes, the first belonging to the kingdom of God, the second to the kingdom of the world. Those who belong to the kingdom of God are all the true believers who are in Christ and under Christ ... All who are not Christians belong to the kingdom of the world and are under the law."[37] Believers and nonbelievers, he made clear, are two mutually exclusive bodies of people. No person can be in both

---

[35] Martin Luther, "An Appeal to the Ruling Class of German Nationality as to the Amelioration of the State of Christendom, 1520" in *Martin Luther: Selections From His Writings* (trans. John Dillenberger; New York: Anchor Books, 1961), 403–485. Already in his *Treatise on Good Works* (1520) Luther argued that temporal government "has nothing to do with the preaching of the gospel, or with faith, or with the first three commandments." Cited in James M. Estes, *Peace, Order and the Glory of God: Secular Authority and the Church in the Thought of Luther and Melanchthon 1518–1559* (Leiden: Brill, 2005), 11 (Cf. 17–30). See *Luther's Works* (55 vols.; ed. Jaroslav Pelikan, et al.; St. Louis: Concordia Publishing House, 1955-), 44:88, 90–91.

[36] Estes, *Peace, Order and the Glory of God*, 30–36.

[37] Martin Luther, "Temporal Authority: To What Extent it Should Be Obeyed," in *Martin Luther's Basic Theological Writings*, 2nd ed. (ed. Timothy F. Lull; Minneapolis: Fortress Press, 2005), 429–459, 435–436. See Johannes Heckel, *Lex Charitatis: A Juristic Disquisition on Law in the Theology of Martin Luther* (trans. Gottfried G. Krodel; Grand Rapids: Eerdmans, 2010 [1973]), 25–38, 145–215.

kingdoms at the same time. Luther then went on to argue, now moving beyond Augustine, that in relation to these two groups of people, God has established two governments. "For this reason God has ordained two governments: the spiritual, by which the Holy Spirit produces Christians and righteous people under Christ; and the temporal, which restrains the un-Christian and wicked so that – no thanks to them – they are obliged to keep still and to maintain an outward peace."[38] Christ governs the first group of people by exclusively non-coercive means (the word and Spirit), producing in them external righteousness consistent with their justification. The second group of people is governed by the only means possible for the rebellious: coercive force.

Luther affirmed that believers must also submit to temporal authority as an expression of love for their unbelieving neighbors. He likewise affirmed that Christians could serve in positions of temporal authority and was emphatic that temporal authority "is to be exercised in a Christian and salutary manner."[39] Indeed, he offered a lengthy analysis of what this meant "for the sake of those very few who would also like very much to be Christian princes and lords."[40] But here Luther was not optimistic:

> Who is not aware that a prince is a rare prize in heaven? I do not speak with any hope that temporal princes will give heed, but on the chance that there might be one who would also like to be a Christian, and to know how he should act. Of this I am certain, that God's word will neither turn nor bend for princes, but princes must bend themselves to God's word.[41]

At a most basic level, Luther argued, a Christian who occupies political office must know how to distinguish the tasks of temporal government from those of spiritual government, "lest it extend too far and encroach upon God's kingdom and government."[42] Temporal rulers must leave the government of souls to God and focus their attention on life, property, and external affairs. "Heresy can never be restrained by force ... Here God's word must do the fighting. If it does not succeed,

---

[38] Luther, "Temporal Authority," 436.   [39] Luther, "Temporal Authority," 444.

[40] Luther, "Temporal Authority," 452. Thus Luther could say that he need not address the "temporal dealings and laws of the governing authority" because the writings of the jurists could be consulted on that point, and because a prince was to use his own reason, prudence, and judgment. On the other hand, no one should "think it sufficiently praiseworthy merely to follow the written law or the opinions of jurists." Following Christ shaped a prince's perspective and principles. "I know of no law to prescribe for a prince; instead, I will simply instruct his heart and mind on what his attitude should be toward all laws, counsels, judgments, and actions" (453). "He should picture Christ to himself, and say, 'Behold, Christ, the supreme ruler, came to serve me; he did not seek to gain power, estate, and honor from me, but considered only my need ... I will do likewise, seeking from my subjects not my own advantage but theirs ... In such manner should a prince [conduct himself] ... For this is what Christ did to us; and these are the proper works of Christian love" (453–454).

[41] Luther, "Temporal Authority," 454.   [42] Luther, "Temporal Authority," 444.

certainly the temporal power will not succeed either, even if it were to drench the world in blood. Heresy is a spiritual matter which you cannot hack to pieces with iron, consume with fire, or drown in water."[43] It is a constant strategy of the Devil to confuse the two kingdoms, Luther observed, and he succeeded in doing so any time popes and bishops ruled over temporal affairs or magistrates sought to interfere with the gospel.[44]

Despite such powerful early arguments in favor of religious liberty, frustration with disorder and the pace of reform quickly tested Luther's commitment to a restrained magistracy. The rejection of Roman worship was giving way to liturgical and doctrinal anarchy. Ecclesiastical wealth was being appropriated by secular authorities for their own use at the expense of education, relief for the poor, and provision for pastors. Matters came to a head with the outbreak of the Peasants' Revolt in 1524 when prominent peasant leaders justified their rebellion with the language of Christian liberty, invoking the authority of Luther. Horrified, Luther was adamant that the peasants were not justified in using violence to defend their temporal concerns on the basis of Christian freedom. He charged that neither temporal concerns nor violence had anything to do with the affairs of the kingdom of Christ, a kingdom of love, forgiveness, peace, and suffering. "Suffering! Suffering! Cross! Cross! This and nothing else is the Christian law!"[45] The earthly concerns of the peasants placed them in the realm of the temporal government and that was a realm in which magistrates must be obeyed. "Now he who would confuse these two kingdoms ... would put wrath into God's kingdom and mercy into the world's kingdom; and that is the same as putting the devil in heaven and God in hell."[46]

Against this backdrop of anarchy and rebellion, Luther sought to articulate grounds for magisterial intervention in ecclesiastical affairs. He claimed that the Mass was an idolatry and blasphemy that the secular authority was obligated to

---

[43] Luther, "Temporal Authority," 450.

[44] In 1524 in his *Letter to the Princes of Saxony Concerning the Rebellious Spirit*, he argued that the secular powers should not use coercive force against heretics who preach falsely but do not engage in rebellious activity. Estes, *Peace, Order and the Glory of God*, 37–41; LW 40:49–59. Emphasizing the difference between the two governments led to some of Luther's most radical rhetoric about the nature of the church. "What kind of authority can there be where all are equal and have the same right, power, possession, and honor, and where no one desires to be the other's superior, but each the other's subordinate?" Luther, "Temporal Authority," 452.

[45] Martin Luther, "Admonition to Peace," in LW 46:29.

[46] Martin Luther, "An Open Letter on the Harsh Book," in LW 46:70. Luther challenged the radicals' assumptions about the normativity of the Mosaic law. In between the two kingdoms "still another has been placed in the middle, half spiritual and half temporal. It is constituted by the Jews." The Mosaic law was only binding insofar as it coincides with natural law and the New Testament. Luther, "How Christians Should Regard Moses," *Martin Luther's Basic Theological Writings*, 2nd ed. (ed. Timothy F. Lull; Minneapolis: Fortress Press, 2005), 124–132 [126]. Cf. LW 35: 161–174.

suppress as part of his responsibility to secure peace and order in external matters.[47] He reasserted his claim that as a Christian a temporal ruler could intervene in ecclesiastical affairs just like any other believer. This did not mean the secular authority should impose a church order from the top down, a step Luther successfully persuaded the Landgrave Philip of Hesse not to take in 1527. Instead, Luther called for the Elector to authorize an ecclesiastical consistory of theologians and lawyers to prescribe a church order for Wittenburg. As he wrote in his preface to the *Instructions of the Visitors to the Parish Pastors* in 1528, the church order would have no binding authority, but the clergy were to embrace it voluntarily. Then, if they refused to do so, the Elector could intervene to enforce the church order by virtue of his obligation to establish peace and order.[48]

Luther also began to defend the obligation of secular authorities to suppress the heresy, blasphemy, and sedition with which he associated radicals and Anabaptists. That Luther was abandoning the position he had advocated so persuasively in *On Secular Authority* was not lost on his opponents and critics, some of whom included civil officials and evangelical pastors. In 1530, Georg Frolich, a clerk in the Nuremburg city chancellery, submitted an (until recently) anonymous memorandum to the secretary of the city council.[49] Frolich argued that, contrary to the arguments of Luther and others, religious toleration is actually more conducive of peace and order than is religious uniformity, and he pointed to the kingdom of Bohemia as an example. He observed that while the Lutherans claimed that religious persecution was in accord with scripture, their arguments came exclusively from the Old Testament. Yet Galatians 5 taught that Christians are no longer bound by the Old Testament law, for "if we are bound in one matter on the ground that it is commanded in the Old Testament, how shall we avoid being bound in other such matters [i.e., circumcision]?"[50] He then argued that the two kingdoms distinction, as originally articulated by Luther, is

---

[47] LW 36:311–328; Estes, *Peace, Order and the Glory of God*, 42–45. Estes points out that Luther made use of two old distinctions here. "One was that a community divided in religion is ungovernable. The other was that the wrath of God" falls on a people "whose ruler tolerates idolatry and blasphemy ... Luther was also giving expression to the idea ... that personal freedom of faith does not include freedom of public worship" (44–45).

[48] See W. D. J. Cargill Thompson, *The Political Thought of Martin Luther* (Totowa, NJ: Barnes & Noble, 1984), 145–150; James M. Estes, "The Role of Godly Magistrates in the Church: Melanchthon as Luther's Interpreter and Collaborator," *Church History* 67.3 (September 1988): 463–483 [472–473]; LW 40:269–320.

[49] That the memorandum was taken so seriously is evidenced by the fact that no fewer than three leading reformers, in addition to Luther, responded to it. See Estes, *Peace, Order and the Glory of God*, 101–111.

[50] For a translation and commentary, see James M. Estes, "Whether Secular Government Has the Right to Wield the Sword in Matters of Faith: An Anonymous Defense of Religious Toleration From Sixteenth-Century Nurnberg," *Mennonite Quarterly Review* 49.1 (January 1975): 22–37 [29]. Cf. Estes, *Order, Peace and the Glory of God*, 104.

taught in the New Testament. Each kingdom has its own distinct king, scepter, goal, and end; in all their actions and teachings, both Christ and the Apostles demonstrated that the kingdom of Christ operates by the power of the word alone. To seek by the sword either to advance the cause of the kingdom, or to persecute those who oppose or reject it, is therefore to rebel against Christ's kingship. Secular authorities had the right to appoint pastors to preach true Christianity, Frolich conceded, but they must allow dissenters, whether papists, Anabaptists, Turks, or Jews, to choose their own pastors and to regulate their own religious affairs.

Luther responded vigorously. In his 1530 commentary on Psalm 82, he insisted that secular authorities "shall honor God's Word above all things and shall further the teaching of it."[51] They were to ensure that sects and false teachers were given no opportunity to mislead the people, whether openly or covertly. The magistrates were thus responsible to suppress not only seditious teachings, but also heretical teachings about the nature of Christ and eternal life. Where there was division in a community over the nature of the gospel, they should refuse to tolerate the party not in agreement with scripture. Radicals should not be permitted to teach privately or in secret because such covert practices were precisely what had caused the Peasants' Revolt.[52] By 1532 Luther even agreed that the Anabaptists should face capital punishment. Yet he continued to insist that his position was consistent with the two kingdoms distinction, claiming that blasphemy and false teaching were matters that affected external order and therefore fell within the prerogative of the magistrate.[53] He stressed that all outward affairs – including public teaching and worship – lay within the realm of the secular kingdom and were therefore subject to some sort of secular control.[54]

Nevertheless, the tension between Luther's two kingdoms distinction and his teaching about the obligations of magistrates was evident. Luther attempted to sort out the matter in his commentary on Psalm 101, published in 1535. On the one hand, he declared, it was by the inspiration of the Devil that secular leaders sought to "be Christ's masters and teach him how he should run His Church and spiritual

[51] LW 13:57.   [52] Estes, *Peace, Order and the Glory of God*, 181–188. LW 13:41–72.
[53] Cargill Thompson, *The Political Thought of Martin Luther*, 159–162. Cf. Luther's *On Infiltrating and Clandestine Preachers*, published in January 1532, in LW 40:383–394.
[54] His increasing reliance on the inward/outward distinction appears in his commentary on the Sermon on the Mount (1532). Seeking an interpretation that avoided both the medieval view that elements of Jesus' teaching were spiritual counsels not binding on all Christians and the Anabaptist tendency to take Christ's commands literally, Luther insisted, "every human being on earth has two persons: one person for himself, with obligations to no one except to God; and in addition a secular person, according to which he has obligations to other people." Christ "is not talking about the way a secular person should work and live, but about the way you should live uprightly before God as a Christian." LW 21:171.

government."[55] Secular government, as such, "is to have no jurisdiction over the welfare of souls or things of eternal values but only over physical and temporal goods."[56] When pastors sought to dictate or dominate the civil law or when princes "want to change and correct the Word of God in a dictatorial and dominating fashion," the kingdoms were inappropriately mixed.[57] On the other hand, Luther pointed to King David's oversight of doctrine and worship as a model for princes inspired by God. When a godly prince calls people to the obedience of God, he insisted, he is being an obedient servant, not a domineering master. Here Luther's rhetoric revealed the limits of his two kingdoms dialectic:

> For with respect to God and in the service of His authority everything should be identical and mixed together, whether it be spiritual or secular – pope as well as emperor ... All should be identical in their obedience and should even be mixed into one another like one cake, every one of them helping the other to be obedient. Therefore in service or submission to God there can be no rebellion among the spiritual or the secular authorities.[58]

Try as he might, Luther was never able consistently or clearly to sort out the relationship between political and ecclesiastical power. During his later years he continued to complain about the heavy-handedness of secular authorities in interfering with ecclesiastical matters. He argued that the consistories of theologians and lawyers established to oversee the church order should be viewed as ecclesiastical institutions, and that while a prince could serve as an "emergency bishop" (*Notbischof*) in overseeing this procedure, he could assume no permanent ecclesiastical authority over the church. At the same time, Luther continued to view the ecclesiastical order of the visible church as part of the earthly kingdom rather than the spiritual.[59] While he therefore opposed the sort of civil control over the church that came to characterize later Lutheranism, he never developed a normative theological model of church government, nor did he find a way to establish church discipline (though he seems to have found it desirable).[60]

In any case, Luther's direct influence was waning. In part because of the increasingly *ad hoc* and tortuous nature of his political theology and in part because of his public solidarity with Melanchthon, by the mid-1530s it was Melanchthon, not Luther, to whom virtually all Lutheran theologians looked for guidance regarding

---

[55] LW 13:194.   [56] LW 13:198.

[57] LW 13:196. Cf. Estes, "The Role of Godly Magistrates in the Church," 474–483.

[58] LW 13:195–196.

[59] Witte, *Law and Protestantism*, 97–99. He even supported the use of canon law as a source for ecclesiastical ordinances (72–74).

[60] With respect to the distinction between the temporal and the spiritual, Höpfl notes, for Luther "the worldly order of the church seems to occupy the interstices." Höpfl, *The Christian Polity of John Calvin*, 26. Luther was "extremely loath to make organizational matters into doctrinal ones" (27).

questions of ecclesiastical and political power.[61] Melanchthon argued that spiritual government consists in the preaching of the word and pertains to matters of eternal righteousness and the Spirit, while corporal government administers external things. Significantly, he placed ecclesiastical traditions and ceremonies firmly in the realm of external matters under the authority of the magistrate: "Ecclesiastical traditions are civil laws and a means of instruction, pertaining not at all to spiritual government."[62] Furthermore, unlike Luther, Melanchthon followed Erasmus in characterizing the office of secular authority as involving responsibility for both the physical and spiritual welfare of its subjects. Promoting godliness by ensuring good instruction for the people through preachers and teachers was conducive of peace and order in a Christian commonwealth.[63]

As the Lutheran movement solidified, Melanchthon systematized his account of spiritual and temporal authority and bolstered its exegetical support. In response to the practical argument that religious persecution was not necessarily conducive of peace and order, he shifted to more principled ground, claiming that magistrates were obligated to enforce both tables of the Ten Commandments for the purpose of maintaining the glory of God, a higher obligation than that of peace. He began to array a plethora of Old Testament texts that described the religious character and obligations attached to the office of civil magistrate, arguing by way of 1 Timothy 1:9 and 1 Timothy 2:2 that these obligations applied in the Christian era, not just under the old covenant.[64] His arguments for the magisterial care of religion were so "clear and persuasive," James Estes concludes, "that it is difficult to find a German Protestant theologian from 1535 onward (until well into the following century) who did not take them over virtually unchanged."[65]

---

[61] See Estes, *Peace, Order and the Glory of God*, 183–184, 208–212.

[62] Quoted in James M. Estes, "Erastus, Melanchthon, and the Office of Christian Magistrate," *Erasmus of Rotterdam Society Yearbook* 18 (1998): 21–39 (31). Melanchthon had articulated his version of the two kingdoms doctrine in his *On the Double Magistracy* in July 1522.

[63] Melanchthon defended the suppression of the Anabaptists on this ground. Estes, *Peace, Order and the Glory of God*, 53–92.

[64] He first articulated this more mature conception of the obligations of magistrates in a letter to Martin Bucer in 1534, and he published his developed arguments in the 1535 *Loci Communes*. See Estes, *Peace, Order and the Glory of God*, 114–128. The texts he invoked include Daniel 3:28–29, Psalm 2, Psalm 82, Proverbs 25:5, and 1 Samuel 2:30. Of particular importance was a shift, in his interpretation of 1 Timothy 2:2, from an emphasis on "peaceful and quiet lives" as the objective of the care of religion to an emphasis on fostering "godliness and holiness" as the higher priority for magistrates, a move that would be followed by Calvin (126–128).

[65] Estes, *Peace, Order and the Glory of God*, 177. Cargill Thompson argues that Luther was opposed to the increasing magisterial character of the churches in Germany, and that what Luther viewed as a temporary emergency measure, Melanchthon turned into a permanent state of affairs. Cargill Thompson, *The Political Thought of Martin Luther*, 150–154. "Luther was in no sense an Erastian" (154). In its final version "his thought is much closer to that of Calvin than is often recognized – indeed, Calvin's doctrine of the Two Kingdoms is clearly derived from Luther's and represents a development

Because neither Luther nor Melanchthon ever developed a vigorous theological paradigm for the institutional church (beyond the tasks of preaching and the administration of the sacraments), in the Lutheran tradition matters such as discipline, ecclesiastical government, and even worship were increasingly subject to civil control.[66] Luther's early two kingdoms doctrine notwithstanding, the form that the Reformation ultimately took in Lutheran territories looked a lot like the caesaropapism that had been advocated in the thirteenth century by Marsilius of Padua, which in Protestant circles came to be known as erastianism.[67]

ZWINGLI'S CORPUS CHRISTIANUM

In the same years that Luther was working out the thorny questions of ecclesiastical and political power through the rubric of his two kingdoms distinction, the priest Huldrych Zwingli was taking a somewhat different approach to the problem as he sought to reform the church in the Swiss city of Zurich. Zwingli quickly came to share Luther's convictions regarding justification by faith alone, the difference between divine and human righteousness, and the necessity of distinguishing between inward and outward realms.[68] Like Luther, Zwingli insisted on the right of the church to follow the teachings of scripture in breaking with the tyranny of ecclesiastical authorities. He rejected the ecclesiastical infrastructure of the Catholic Church with all of its temporal properties, jurisdictions, and laws, becoming even more radical than Luther in his rejection of the Mass and the various ceremonies of medieval worship. Unlike Luther, however, Zwingli was deeply influenced by the communal culture of the Swiss cities, as well as by Erasmus, maintaining a commitment to the unity of city and church in one Christian commonwealth under the guidance of a pious magistracy. While Luther refused the turn to a more radical reformation because of his concern for order and authority, Zwingli broke

from it" (153). Estes agrees that Luther was anxious about the abuse of magisterial authority in the church and "he continued to dream of a church with a greater degree of administrative independence than circumstances allowed." Estes, "The Role of Godly Magistrates in the Church," 481. Luther "never tired of emphasizing that the state ... is not something intrinsically Christian and that secular authority per se is *secular*" (467). But Melanchthon was also concerned about magisterial domination of the church. It was Melanchthon who argued that it was ideal for theologically educated bishop to oversee ecclesiastical matters. Estes, *Peace, Order and the Glory of God*, 174. But Estes argues that the difference was one of emphasis, "one of rhetoric and tone rather than of substance" (205).

[66] Although Melanchthon hoped to see the church unified under bishops, he insisted that magistrates must bring this to pass. Cargill Thompson, *The Political Thought of Martin Luther*, 131–132; Estes, *Peace, Order and the Glory of God*, 128–133, 163–176.

[67] See Witte, *Law and Protestantism*, 119–303.

[68] Gordon argues that the relationship between the spiritual and the material constituted "the absolute nucleus of Zwingli's thought." See Bruce Gordon, *The Swiss Reformation* (Manchester: Manchester University Press, 2002), 80.

with his more radical followers primarily because of his commitment to the unity and integrity of the Christian commonwealth.[69]

Like Luther, Zwingli offered a definitive early statement of the relationship between civil and spiritual power. His 1523 sermon, *Divine and Human Righteousness*, may have been influenced by Melanchthon, but it took a different approach from that of Luther's *On Temporal Authority*.[70] The foundation of the sermon was Zwingli's distinction between "divine righteousness and our miserable human righteousness."[71] Zwingli characterized divine righteousness as the perfect righteousness God demands of human beings: to forgive freely; never to be angry, engage in lawsuits or quarrels, or swear oaths; to give away all our possessions to the poor; to do good to our enemies; and more. Yet no one can attain this kind of righteousness, so God has also given human beings commandments regarding external or human righteousness. Based on these two kinds of righteousness, Zwingli distinguished between two types of law:

> One type of law looks only to the inward person, such as how one is to love God and neighbor. These laws no one is able to fulfill. Just as there is no one who is righteous except for the one God and the one who by grace, of which Christ is the guarantor, is made righteous through faith. The other type of law looks only to the outward person.[72]

It prohibits theft, but not coveting. It allows divorce under certain circumstances.

Zwingli argued that pastors are called to preach pure divine righteousness without compromise, pointing to the gospel as the only means of salvation. They must also teach God's commandments regarding human righteousness, but beyond this they may not seek authority over temporal matters.[73] The primary obligation of temporal authority, on the other hand, is to give the clergy freedom to preach the gospel and abandon old superstitions. "One ought not appeal to the magistrate in such matters; for it has not been set over God's word and Christian freedom as over temporal goods."[74] But Christians are to obey the magistrates in all matters not pertaining to conscience, even though their laws fall far short of divine righteousness, and

---

[69] See Moeller, *Imperial Cities and the Reformation*, 75–103. Cf. Ozment, *The Reformation in the Cities*, 131–138.

[70] It may have been influenced by Melanchthon's *On the Double Magistracy*, a copy of which Zwingli had received. Robert C. Walton, *Zwingli's Theocracy* (Toronto: University of Toronto Press, 1967), 23–24, 168–170.

[71] Huldrych Zwingli, "Divine and Human Righteousness," in *Huldrych Zwingli Writings*, vol. 2 (ed. Dikran Y. Hadidian; trans. H. Wayne Pipkin; Allison Park, Pa: Pickwick Publications, 1984), 1–41 [5].

[72] Zwingli, "Divine and Human Righteousness," 12. Cf. Walton, *Zwingli's Theocracy*, 158–170.

[73] Criticizing the temporal jurisdiction of the Catholic hierarchy, he declared, "Human righteousness or authority is no more than orderly authority which we call temporal power; for so-called spiritual authority has no basis in Scripture for its rule." Zwingli, "Divine and Human Righteousness," 22.

[74] Zwingli, "Divine and Human Righteousness," 32.

magistrates are obligated to govern in accord with scripture, the ultimate standard even for human righteousness. They must therefore submit to the faithful preaching of the clergy.

It is noteworthy that in this sermon Zwingli did not speak directly of the church, but of the offices of magistrate and pastor. In his corporate conception of society there was no such thing in Zurich as a congregated church separate from the body of the city's inhabitants. He emphasized the complete identity of church and city. He thus declared pointedly, "when the gospel is preached and all, including the magistrate, heed it, the Christian man is nothing else than the faithful and good citizen; and the Christian city is nothing other than the Christian church."[75] While Zwingli agreed with Luther that true Christians would always be a minority, even within Christendom, he believed the church encompassed all those who were baptized, professed faith in Christ, and lived consistently with this profession. Where this was true of an entire political community the office of magistrate became an office of the church.[76]

Zwingli thus argued that although the church needed its own elders and deacons in the early centuries, once civil governments were converted to Christ magistrates fulfilled those functions according to the example of Old Testament Israel. "Seeing, then, that there are shepherds in the church, and amongst these we may number princes ... it is evident that without civil government (*magistratu*) a church is maimed and impotent .... we teach that authority (*magistratum*) is necessary to the completeness of the body of the church."[77] Even crucial matters of doctrine and worship were to be under the oversight of the civil government. To be sure, in Zwingli's view it was not a matter of the church submitting to civil government per se; rather, the civil government was the authoritative body *within* the church. As Stephens puts it, "[Zwingli] does not envisage a separate gathering of the church to make decisions in church matters, but sees the church making these decisions through its civic assemblies and leaders."[78] The relation was akin to that of the soul

---

[75] Walton, *Zwingli's Theocracy*, 169. Oakley argues that Zwingli tended "to detect reverberations of harmony where Luther had heard only discord, to move towards reuniting what Luther had put asunder, and, having discriminated so sharply the invisible church from the visible, to identify the latter with the assembled civic community itself." Francis Oakley, "Christian Obedience and Authority, 1520–1550," *The Cambridge History of Political Thought 1450–1700* (ed. J.H. Burns and Mark Goldie; Cambridge: Cambridge University Press, 1991), 159–192, 184.

[76] Höpfl concludes, "Zwingli's thought ... was inherently communal. The 'particular churches' were for Zwingli communities which he without question equated with the secular political unit: its agents were the secular authorities acting on behalf of their citizens/congregations, and reformation was a political activity, with the magistrates acting as 'school-masters' over faith, worship and morals of clergy and laity alike." Höpfl, *The Christian Polity of John Calvin*, 24–25.

[77] Quoted in W. P. Stephens, *The Theology of Huldrych Zwingli* (Oxford: Oxford University Press, 1986), 269–270.

[78] Stephens, *The Theology of Huldrych Zwingli*, 289.

and the body. "For just as a man must consist of both soul and body, though the body is the humbler and lesser part, so the church cannot exist without the magistracy, even though it should take care to only dispose of the more worldly matters which have less to do with the spirit."[79]

The image of soul and body corresponding to the prophetic and magisterial offices came to define the structure of the Christian commonwealth in Zurich. There were two complementary bodies of authority, one dominated by the council with oversight over the laity and the other administered by the clergy with oversight over the clergy. The moral discipline of Christians was separated from the question of access to the Lord's Supper and distanced from the authority of the clergy.[80] Zwingli endorsed the need for the magistrate to suppress those who disturbed the church by preaching or practicing false doctrine. He endorsed a law enacted by the Zurich city council that authorized capital punishment for Anabaptist leaders, and with his approval, Zurich executed the capital sentence by drowning four Anabaptists in 1526.[81]

By 1528 Zwingli's model of reform was coming under criticism from Lutheran circles for conflating the two kingdoms. Zwingli responded to such criticism in a fascinating letter he wrote that year to Ambrosius Blarer, the reformer of Constance. He challenged Luther's statement that "Christ's kingdom is not from without [i.e., external]." He pointed out that Luther and his followers loved to emphasize texts in which Christ spoke of the freedom of believers, but they ignored passages such as his command to the apostles to travel with simplicity and moderation, "entirely a matter of external provision."[82] Zwingli then went on to explain that the example of the early church in Acts 14 demonstrates that it is within the right of the church to regulate external matters. If in the New Testament that task fell to elders and apostles, now it falls to those who fulfill their role in the contemporary church, the civil magistrates. "For it is clear enough that those who in this passage are called presbyters were not ministers of the word but venerable men of substance, prudence and faith who in directing and carrying on business were to the church

---

[79] Quoted in Gordon, *The Swiss Reformation*, 78.

[80] Gordon, *The Swiss Reformation*, 251. With Zwingli's support, in 1525 the city council established the *Ehegericht*, a marriage court made up of pastors and council members and exercising wide-ranging jurisdiction over matters that had formerly been within the realm of the church's canon law. In 1528 the council established a synod made up of clergy to oversee and discipline the clergy.

[81] For a comparison of Zwingli's view of the Anabaptists to Calvin's, see Akira Demura, "From Zwingli to Calvin: A Comparative Study of Zwingli's *Elenchus* and Calvin's *Briève Instruction*," *Zürcher Beiträge zur Reformationsgeschichte* (ed. Alfred Schindler and Hans Stickelberger; Bern: Peter Lang, 2001), 87–99.

[82] See the translation and commentary in George Richard Potter, "Church and State, 1528: A Letter from Zwingli to Ambrosius Blarer (4 May 1528)," in *Occasional Papers of the American Society for Reformation Research* 1 (December, 1977): 108–124 [113].

what the Council is to the city."[83] Why should the common voice of the church be represented in anything other than the leadership of the city? Associating Luther's position with that of the Anabaptists, Zwingli suggested that the riots and disorder plaguing Germany were "caused by Luther's word, [that] 'the Kingdom of Christ is not of this world.'"[84]

Zwingli's model of ecclesiastical authority was challenged by one of his own Reformed colleagues within the Swiss Confederation. In 1530 Johannes Oecolampadius (1482–1531), pastor of Basel, argued to the Basel city council that ecclesiastical and secular power were essentially different from one another and that the church should therefore administer its own system of discipline and excommunication. Whereas civil discipline involved punishment, he argued, ecclesiastical discipline was restorative, an expression of the gospel, and vital to the integrity of the Lord's Supper. Oecolampadius was convinced that some of the Catholic and Anabaptist complaints about the Reformation were legitimate: "we are not a Christian church, [for] we have no keys [with which] to lock up, nor any ban."[85] After Zwingli's death Oecolampadius complained that Zwingli's successor Heinrich Bullinger misunderstood the nature of the word "Christian" as well as the nature of the church and the Lord's Supper, thereby confusing the kingdom with civil government. Before his death in 1531 he participated in the establishment of disciplinary ordinances in Basel and Ulm, although in both cases his proposals were watered down by city councils unwilling to surrender control of excommunication.[86]

Zwingli believed that while the magistrate was in the place of the Old Testament Israelite king, the pastor stood in the authoritative position of the Old Testament Israelite prophet. When the pastor proclaimed the word of God on a given matter, the magistrate was obliged to obey it. This led Zwingli to become deeply involved in

---

[83] Potter, "Church and State, 1528," 114.   [84] Potter, "Church and State, 1528," 117.

[85] J. Wayne Baker, "Church Discipline or Civil Punishment: On the Origins of the Reformed Schism, 1528–1531," *Andrews University Seminary Studies* 23.1 (Spring, 1985): 3–18 [9]. Cf. Akira Demura, *Church Discipline According to Johannes Oecolampadius in the Setting of His Life and Thought* (PhD diss., Princeton Theological Seminary, 1964). Demura argues that Oecolampadius's extensive ties and familiarity with Anabaptists makes their influence on his views of discipline and the church plausible but not certain (291–337). It is important to note that Oecolampadius entirely shared Zwingli's view of the city as a Christian commonwealth (247, 250). Cf. Kenneth R. Davis, "No Discipline, No Church: An Anabaptist Contribution To the Reformed Tradition," *Sixteenth Century Journal* 13 (1982): 43–58.

[86] Oecolampadius nearly persuaded Zwingli of his views. Baker, "Church Discipline or Civil Punishment," 7–13. McKee identifies Oecolampadius as the first Reformed theologian clearly to develop an understanding of multiple ecclesiastical orders distinct from secular authority on the basis of Romans 12:8, though he did not articulate a clear theory of the various orders as offices in the church. Elsie Anne McKee, *John Calvin on the Diaconate and Liturgical Almsgiving* (Geneva: Librairie Droz S.A., 1984), 191–193.

civil matters. Eventually he used his prophetic authority to push Zurich into an aggressive and militant foreign policy that led to a disastrous defeat. Zwingli himself was killed after taking up the sword in the Battle of Kappel on October 11, 1531. The fallout was dramatic, Luther observing that "those who live by the sword, die by the sword."[87] The backlash against clerical interference in the affairs of civil government spread to all of the Swiss Reformed cities. In Zurich, the Meilen Articles prescribed new limits to the office of pastor, declaring, "Let the clergy ... not undertake or meddle in any secular matters either in the city or the countryside, in the council or elsewhere, which they should rather allow you, our lords, to manage."[88] When Heinrich Bullinger was brought in to succeed Zwingli as pastor he was required to agree that ministers should avoid making political comments in their sermons.[89] In cities like Bern and Basel – in whose sphere of influence Calvin's Geneva fell – the clergy preserved even less authority over spiritual affairs than they did in Zurich, where Bullinger managed to preserve some clerical autonomy. In general, the model among the Swiss Reformed became that of direct magisterial control over ecclesiastical affairs, including both doctrine and the life of the clergy. Gordon concludes, "The Reformation had survived, barely, but the bill had now to be paid, and the price was full subordination to the state."[90]

Once the Reformation was "politicized," Steven Ozment observes, the differences between reformers were often "more theoretical than practical." In that respect the legacies of Luther and Zwingli were not so different.[91] Each emphasized the importance of the inward, spiritual realm, while leaving the outward order of the church largely to the magistrates. For their part, magistrates were loath to give up the authority over ecclesiastical affairs that they had won from the church, nor did

---

[87] Gordon, *The Swiss Reformation*, 144. My account of Zwingli's political legacy is drawn from Gordon, *The Swiss Reformation*, 119–144, as well as from Philip Benedict, *Christ's Churches Purely Reformed: A Social History of Calvinism* (New Haven: Yale University Press, 2002), 19–48. Cf. Gordon, "Toleration in the Early Swiss Reformation: The Art and Politics of Niklaus Manuel of Berne," in *Tolerance and Intolerance in the European Reformation* (ed. Ole Peter Grell and Bob Scribner; Cambridge: Cambridge University Press, 1996), 128–144.

[88] Zurich, Bern, and other cities were forced to pay massive reparations, while parts of the Confederation were recovered for Catholicism or barred to Reformed expansion. Gordon, *The Swiss Reformation*, 139.

[89] Bern adopted a series of articles drafted by Wolfgang Capito giving the magistrates full authority over ecclesiastical matters, including discipline, and limiting the freedom of pastors to express their political views. The *Berner Synodus*, adopted in 1532, appealed to the teaching of a twofold government but interpreted it in distinctly Zwinglian terms. Michael W. Bruening, *Calvinism's First Battleground: Conflict and Reform in the Pays de Vaud, 1528–1559* (Dordrecht: Springer, 2005), 63–72.

[90] Gordon, *The Swiss Reformation*, 142; Cf. p. 255.

[91] Ozment, *The Reformation in the Cities*, 137. Yet he goes too far when he writes, "Both Lutheran and Reformed Protestants maintained a basic separation of church and state within the basic unity of religion and society." This is misleading. Neither Lutherans nor Zwinglians separated church and state in any meaningful sense of the term, and while the Lutherans at least distinguished the two, the same could hardly be said of the Zwinglians.

they view the church as body independent of the commonwealth. It would be up to another reformer to challenge this state of affairs.[92]

RADICAL REFORMATION

Despite the trend within Lutheran and Reformed territories toward greater power of the civil magistrates over religion, the early teaching of Luther and Zwingli spawned a plethora of radical movements and individuals that challenged the magisterial character of the Reformation. Radical critics of the magisterial Reformation became known after 1525 as Anabaptists because they rejected infant baptism. But Anabaptism was never a unified movement except in the rhetoric of its opponents, for whom it offered a convenient foil. Even relative to the relationship between church and civil government Anabaptists were all over the map, some with theocratic and revolutionary tendencies, others turning toward spiritualized sectarianism or pacifism.[93]

One of the most significant intellectual fathers of the Anabaptists was Luther's early colleague in Wittenburg, Andreas Karlstadt.[94] Karlstadt pressed Luther's two kingdoms distinction to increasingly radical conclusions in line with his experience. Initially he argued that government should reform the church and even exile heretics, but when the governments under which he resided rejected the gospel as he understood it, he aligned them with the Devil. In this mode he spoke in terms of two kingdoms radically opposed, one consisting of those who serve God and the other of those who follow the Devil.[95] Although in the late 1520s Karlstadt recanted some of these radical ideas, made amends with Zwingli and became a professor in Basel, his early works remained widely influential within the radical movement.

---

[92] With respect to church order, as Höpfl puts it, "the Reformation was in the first instance negative and destructive." Höpfl, *The Christian Polity of John Calvin*, 24 (Cf. 23–31). Foster concludes, "The way was therefore open in 1536 for a new conception of church and state as two distinct and balanced organisms, each co-operating with the other." Herbert Darling Foster, "Calvin's Programme for a Puritan State in Geneva, 1536–1541," *Harvard Theological Review* 1 (1908):391–434, 403–404.

[93] The broad details of my account of Anabaptism are taken from the following: William R. Estep, *The Anabaptist Story* (Grand Rapids: Eerdmans 1975 [1963]); Hans Jürgen-Goertz, *The Anabaptists* (trans. Trevor Johnson; New York: Routledge, 1996 [1980]); James M. Stayer, *The German Peasants' War and Anabaptist Community of Goods* (Montreal: McGill-Queen's University Press, 1991); Gordon, *The Swiss Reformation*.

[94] Unlike Luther, Karlstadt did not believe the reformation of the Mass or the removal of images should be delayed in deference to either the magistrates or weaker consciences. He rejected infant baptism and insisted on the importance of church discipline and excommunication. See Calvin Augustine Pater, *Karlstadt as the Father of the Baptist Movements: The Emergence of Lay Protestantism* (Toronto: University of Toronto Press, 1984).

[95] Pater, *Karlstadt as the Father of the Baptists*, 84.

In Zurich the Anabaptist movement arose when Konrad Grebel and others became disillusioned with the pace of magisterial reform. Claiming to follow Zwingli's own early teachings, they embraced a conception of the church as a self-governed body of the faithful preserved by vigorous church discipline and mutual provision of material needs. They began to agitate for the abolition of the tithe, the establishment of popular control in the churches, and the practice of excommunication. The city expelled them in 1525, and they spread out establishing congregations in the Swiss countryside just as the Peasants' Revolt in southern Germany was spilling across the Swiss frontier.[96]

Accusations regarding who was to blame for the Peasants' Revolt of 1524–1525 flew around as soon as the revolt began, and the debate has continued to this day. The rhetoric of *sola Scriptura*, of the supremacy of divine law over canon law, and of the liberty of the Christian was easily applied by lay pamphleteers and radical preachers to the concerns of peasants and commoners frustrated with the system of tithes and benefices that they believed exploited the people for the well-being of corrupt clergy and self-interested political elites. The peasants appealed confidently to the authority of Luther and Melanchthon, claiming simply to be applying their teachings on matters like usury and the Old Testament law.[97]

The most infamous radical preacher implicated in the Peasants' Revolt was Thomas Muntzer, an early follower of Luther and Karlstadt. Muntzer came to view property as a result of sin and as part of a system of unjust exploitation. Claiming that an uprising against tyranny was morally justified, his advocacy of violence was sharpened by his proclamation of an apocalyptic judgment that would soon fall upon the establishment, separating the elect from the wicked. Although Muntzer's views were extreme, to many of the reformers, Muntzer and the Peasants' Revolt became symbols of the need for suppressing radicalism of any sort. The fact that a significant portion of the Anabaptist leadership, including many from Grebel's circle, were sympathetic toward the peasants' cause, or even directly involved in the revolt, permanently associated Anabaptism with disorder and rebellion in the minds of European elites. Radical teachings regarding the sacraments, the church, and the

---

[96] They continued to seek the reformation of the broader society, reflecting popular demands for justice in the manner of a "popular church." Jurgen-Goertz, *The Anabaptists*, 12–13. Stayer, *The German Peasants' War and Anabaptist Community of Goods*, 61–62. While Zwingli agreed with Grebel and Reublin that the tithe was not required by divine law, he defended it on the basis of human law. Stayer writes, "The obvious link between the radicals' agenda of reconstituting the church through local direct action and the desire of the 1525 rebels to free local communities from the heavy hand of territorial authority explains how the proto-Anabaptists anticipated Articles 1 and 2 of the [rebels'] Twelve Articles" (62).

[97] Stayer, *The German Peasants' War and Anabaptist Community of Goods*, 46. Cf. 19–60.

authority of civil government seemed inseparable from the spirit of disorder.[98] As will be seen, these fears were not entirely groundless.[99]

Nevertheless, in contrast to the activities of figures like Muntzer, after the Peasants' War a number of Anabaptist leaders began to articulate a very different theological vision, one committed to non-violence and separation from both civil government and popular protest. Particularly prominent were the Swiss Brethren, who endorsed the Schleitheim Confession written by the German monk Michael Sattler.[100] Sattler's Schleitheim Confession called for the separation of the Christian community from the world due to the absolute conflict between the kingdom of Christ and the kingdom of darkness.

> Separation should be made from the wickedness that the Devil has sown in the world and from evildoers, lest by associating with them we sink into the same abominations ... From all of this we should learn that everything which is not united with our God and with Christ is nothing other than an abomination which we should shun and flee. By this we mean all papist and anti-papist works and services, assemblies, church-going, taverns, unbelievers' alliances and treaties and

[98] Gordon writes, "The radical circle in Zurich found itself aligned with the aspirations of the rural communities, where sympathy for the demands of the German peasants was rife. As the first acts of rebellion began to take place ... it was virtually impossible to distinguish between the rebellious peasants and those who would emerge as Anabaptists in 1525." Gordon, *The Swiss Reformation*, 196. Stayer, *The German Peasants' War and Anabaptist Community of Goods*, 107–113. Balthasar Hubmaier was a case in point. He was the pastor of Waldshut when he was re-baptized by Reublin in 1525. In his preaching he supported many of the key demands of the peasants and encouraged Waldshut in an alliance with the rebels (63–71; Cf. 139–142; Jurgen-Goertz, *The Anabaptists*, 22–25). Yet he was a unique Anabaptist, affirming the legitimacy of Christian involvement in civil government. Estep, *The Anabaptist Story*, 51–69; Walter Klaassen, *Anabaptism in Outline: Selected Primary Sources* (Waterloo, ON: Herald Press, 1981), 244–264; Gordon, *The Swiss Reformation*, 198–2005. For Karlstadt's debates with Muntzer and Luther, see Pater, *Karlstadt as the Father of the Baptists*, 284–289.

[99] Several of Muntzer's followers, such as Hans Hut, escaped and continued to preach his apocalyptic message. While publicly preaching pacifism, Hut taught his closest followers that Christ's return would follow three and a half years after the war was over, and after Europe had suffered the tribulation of a Turkish invasion. At that time, believers had to be ready to take up the sword for the judgment of the wicked. Stayer, *The German Peasants' War and Anabaptist Community of Goods*, 77–86, 113–114; Jurgen-Goertz, *The Anabaptists*, 16–18.

[100] Sattler was among the radicals expelled from Zurich in 1525. He won the respect and friendship of Capito and Bucer, who described him as a faithful witness and martyr for Christ. Robert S. Kreider, "The Anabaptists and the Civil Authorities of Strasbourg, 1525–1555," *Church History* 24.2 (June 1955), 99–118 [103]. Cf. Estep, *The Anabaptist Story*, 40–47; Demura, "From Zwingli to Calvin," 87–90. The Anabaptist Hans Denck argued that while civil government is appointed by God, the world's understanding of how government should operate – specifically its use of the sword – makes Christian participation practically impossible. He maintained a friendship with Oecolampadius. See Estep, *The Anabaptist Story*, 72–79; William Klassen, "The Limits of Political Authority As Seen By Pilgram Marpeck," *Mennonite Quarterly Review* 56.4 (October 1982): 342–364 [346–347]; Kreider, "The Anabaptists and the Civil Authorities of Strasbourg," 102–103.

anything else which the world greatly values and yet which is carried out directly against God's command ... We will therefore discard unchristian, devilish weapons of violence, including swords, armour and the like, and any employment of them, whether it be for our friends or against the enemy – just as Christ said: 'do not resist one who is evil' (Matthew 5, 39).[101]

The document endorsed believer's baptism, excommunication, and the free election of church leaders. It rejected oaths and the use of the sword, both foundational elements of civic life in sixteenth-century Europe. "The sword is ordained by God outside the perfection of Christ. It punishes and kills the wicked and protects and assists the good ... In order to exercise it, the temporal authorities are instituted. However, in the perfection of Christ the ban is only used to admonish and exclude a sinner."[102] In response to the question of "whether a Christian too could and should use the sword against the wicked, out of love and in order to protect and assist the good," the confession pointed to Christ's refusal to condemn the woman taken in adultery in John 12:50, to his refusal to judge between disputing brothers, and to his refusal to be made king by the Jews. It then concluded that believers cannot serve in government because of the absolute contrast between flesh and spirit, the world and heaven. "The rule of government is according to the flesh, that of the Christians according to the spirit. Its homes and abodes are planted in this world; those of the Christians are in heaven."[103]

In contrast to apocalyptic radicals like Muntzer and Hut, the Swiss Anabaptists resisted using the Old Testament as an authority for church life. The Schleitheim Confession marked a new emphasis on discontinuity between the two testaments that only grew over time. Other Anabaptists also embraced discontinuity between the testaments, even when they did not follow the Schleitheim call for radical separatism. For example, Pilgram Marpeck argued that the common error underlying the Peasants' Revolt, Zwingli's tragic policy in the Kappel Wars, and the later Anabaptist revolution at Munster was the failure to distinguish between the Old and New Testaments. The New Testament is the authority for Christians, he insisted, and the New Testament highlights the spiritual and inward nature of the kingdom of Christ. "There need be no external power or sword, for the kingdom of Christ is not of this world."[104] He appealed to Luther's two kingdoms to

---

[101] Cited in Jurgen-Goertz, *The Anabaptists*, 153–155. The prominence of the Schleitheim Confession gives plausibility to Robert Friedmann's claim that a version of two kingdoms theology lay at the heart of Anabaptist thought. See his *The Theology of Anabaptism: An Interpretation* (Eugene, OR: Wipf and Stock, 1998), 36–48.

[102] Cited in Jurgen-Goertz, *The Anabaptists*, 153–155.

[103] Cited in Jurgen-Goertz, *The Anabaptists*, 153–155.

[104] Klassen, "The Limits of Political Authority As Seen By Pilgram Marpeck," 357–358.

demonstrate that magistrates should not use the sword in matters of religion. "To allow the external authority to rule in the kingdom of Christ is blasphemy against the Holy Spirit, who alone is Lord and Ruler without any human assistance."[105]

But as far as many of the magisterial reformers were concerned, the true nature of the Anabaptist movement was revealed by the Munster Revolution of 1534. The Munster Revolution was an indirect legacy of the apocalyptic preaching of Melchior Hoffman, whose followers were known as the Melchiorites. Hoffman had predicted the imminent return of Christ at Strassbourg, but when Bernhard Rothmann succeeded in launching a magisterial Anabaptist reformation in the city of Munster, many Melchiorites interpreted the feat as a miracle. The Dutch prophet Jan Matthijs declared Munster to be the New Jerusalem and called believers to take up arms (breaking with the pacifist-minded teaching of Hoffman). The events in Munster turned into a fiasco when Easter 1534 passed without Christ's return and Jan Matthijs died in battle. In the months that followed, his successor, King Jan of Leyden, seized control of economic and social affairs in the city, attempting to establish the community of goods and polygamy. His government proscribed a long list of crimes and sins with accompanying Old and New Testament texts, decreeing excommunication and death as the penalty for all of them. Imperial forces finally ended the experiment when they captured the city in August 1534.[106]

The events in Munster were crucial for the legacy of Anabaptism because they seemed to prove the movement's complicity in the sort of apocalypticism that could, if only occasionally, turn even pacifist-minded Anabaptists into violent revolutionaries. If not all Anabaptists were susceptible to such apocalypticism, it seemed impossible to distinguish those who weren't from those who were. For the magisterial reformers, as well as Catholic leaders throughout Europe, the Anabaptist insistence on complete separation between the kingdom of Christ and established civil authorities threatened the very foundations of social order.

---

[105] Klassen, "The Limits of Political Authority As Seen By Pilgram Marpeck," 353–354. "For none can serve two masters: Caesar, king in the worldly office, and Christ in the spiritual, heavenly kingdom (Matthew 6)" (356–357).

[106] The events at Munster are well known, but other examples include a plot to seize control of the city of Erfurt and sporadic violence and uprisings in the Netherlands. See Jurgen-Goertz, *The Anabaptists*, 19–22. Hoffman predicted the imminent coming of Christ following the establishment of the New Jerusalem at the city of Strasbourg in 1533. See Pater, *Karlstadt as the Father of the Baptist Movement*, 175–253. Melchiorite apocalypticism survived into the 1540s until the movement came under the leadership of Menno Simons, at which point apocalypticism was abandoned in favor of the Schleitheim emphasis on radical separation from the world, pacifism, and church discipline. See Stayer, *The German Peasants' War and the Community of Goods*, 123–131; Jurgen-Goertz, *The Anabaptists*, 31–33, 156–158.

BULLINGER'S COVENANTAL COMMONWEALTH

When he arrived in Zurich as Zwingli's successor in 1532, Bullinger quickly agreed to minimize the involvement of the pastors in the political affairs of Zurich, and he recognized the right of the magistrates to step in if the pastors were guilty of excessive political meddling. At the same time, in the ordinances adopted in October 1532, he managed to preserve and solidify the autonomy of the pastors in preaching – including the right to criticize the magistrates when they clearly acted against scripture – as well as over the synod responsible for overseeing the pastors' life and work. Bullinger thus managed to reassure the Zurich magistrates while at the same time solidifying the intertwined character of civil and ecclesiastical power that had been promoted by Zwingli. In the years to come he strengthened the foundation of that model through his careful development of a covenant theology that stressed the unity and continuity of the Old and New Testaments, of Israel and the church.[107]

At the heart of Bullinger's model was his conviction that the authority of the Old Testament was the key to defeating the Anabaptists and spiritualists like Caspar Schwenckfeld.[108] In his *Difference between the Old and New Testaments* (1531), Schwenckfeld argued that while the Old Testament was concerned with temporal promises contingent on Israel's obedience to the Mosaic law, the New Testament is concerned with spiritual promises attained by faith. He maintained that Old Testament teachings concerning war and the coercion of the heathen did not pertain to New Testament believers obligated to live in love and forgiveness according to the kingdom of Christ. As he wrote to the reformer Leo Jud in early 1533, "one must correctly distinguish between ... the spiritual and the

---

[107] See Andreas Mühling, "Heinrich Bullinger as Church Politician," in *Architect of Reformation: An Introduction to Heinrich Bullinger, 1504–1575* (ed. Bruce Gordon and Emidio Campi; Grand Rapids: Baker Academic, 2004), 243–253; Gordon, *The Swiss Reformation*, 251–257; Baker, "Church Discipline or Civil Punishment," 13–17; J. Wayne Baker, "Church, State, and Dissent: The Crisis of the Swiss Reformation, 1531–1536," *Church History* 57.2 (June, 1988): 135–152; J. Wayne Baker, *Heinrich Bullinger and the Covenant: The Other Reformed Tradition* (Athens, OH: Ohio University Press, 1980), 107–163; W. J. Torrance Kirby, *The Zurich Connection and Tudor Political Theology* (Leiden: Brill, 2007), 25–41.

[108] Gordon, *The Swiss Reformation*, 207–208; Jurgen-Goertz, *The Anabaptists*, 51–56; Heinold Fast and John H. Yoder, "How to Deal with Anabaptists: An Unpublished Letter of Heinrich Bullinger," *Mennonite Quarterly Review* 33.2 (April 1959): 83–95. Schwenckfeld rejected infant baptism and the right of civil magistrates to regulate religion, and he called for the establishment of excommunication. On the other hand, he argued that believers should not separate themselves from the official churches, and he affirmed the government use of the sword. See R. Emmet McLaughlin, *Caspar Schwenckfeld, Reluctant Radical: His Life to 1540* (New Haven: Yale University Press, 1986); Klaus Deppermann, "Schwenckfeld and Leo Jud on the Advantages and Disadvantages of the State Church," in *Schwenckfeld and Early Schwenkfeldianism: Papers Presented at the Colloquium on Schwenckfeld and the Schwenkfelders September 17–22, 1984* (ed. Peter C. Erb; Pennsburg, PA: Schwenkfelder Library, 1986): 211–236; Baker, "Church, State, and Dissent," 143–147.

temporal, so that one does not mix together the two different kingdoms or regiments – the world and the kingdom of Christ."[109] Schwenckfeld made his argument about the discontinuity between the testaments the foundation for his case for religious toleration. Israel was not the model for civil government, nor was the Mosaic law binding on Christians.[110]

Bullinger was convinced that the decisive Reformed response had to be to emphasize the unity and continuity of the covenant.[111] In 1533 he published his classic *Treatise on the Unity of the Old and New Testaments*, arguing that the Old and New Testaments contain one continuous covenant of grace covering the period from Adam all the way to Christ and the church. The following year he published *The One and Eternal Testament*, arguing that although the promise of the land of Canaan was intended to foreshadow spiritual promises for the people of God, similar promises of earthly blessing remain for the church. For this reason, even the civil laws of the Old Testament are binding on all ages, including the laws specifying capital punishment for dozens of crimes. As he put it, "in respect to the Decalogue and civil laws, no difference at all has arisen regarding the covenant and the people of God."[112]

Bullinger argued that the prophetic office of pastor and the kingly office of magistrate are necessary in the church, which he identified as the covenantal community that constitutes the commonwealth, just as they were in Old Testament Israel. Indeed, he argued, the very character of the prophetic office is wrapped up with the covenant community as governed by the magistrate. God had given the magistracy as spiritual gift for the government of the church, Bullinger argued from 1 Corinthians 12:28,[113] and the magistrate is therefore responsible for

---

[109] Cited in Baker, "Church, State, and Dissent," 144.

[110] Schwenckfeld's argument temporarily persuaded Leo Jud. Baker, "Church, State, and Dissent," 144. In 1532 Jud wrote a letter to Bullinger criticizing the lack of ecclesiastical discipline at Zurich. Arguing that the church and commonwealth are not coterminous, he wrote, "there remains to each kingdom its own sound, intact, and uninjured jurisdiction. The magistrate has his own laws, his own courts for the state, over which he presides; and the church has its own laws, the word of God, the sacraments, exhortation, discipline, excommunication." Baker, "Church, State, and Dissent," 142. Cf. Deppermann, "Schwenckfeld and Leo Jud on the Advantages and Disadvantages of the State Church," 227; McLaughlin, *Caspar Schwenckfeld, Reluctant Radical*, 146–159.

[111] When asked by Berchthold Haller how to deal with the Anabaptists at the upcoming Disputation of Zofingen in 1532, he stressed that the Old Testament as well as the New Testament had to be established as the basic authority to adjudicate all disagreements. Fast and Yoder, "How to Deal with Anabaptists," 86.

[112] See a translation with commentary in Charles S. McCoy and J. Wayne Baker, *Fountainhead of Federalism: Heinrich Bullinger and the Covenantal Tradition* (Louisville, Ky: Westminster John Knox Press, 1991), 99–138 [122, 128].

[113] "So we may understand those who have been established in command, and therefore the magistracy itself, which is in the church and . . . is necessary for the church." Cited in Elsie Anne McKee, *Elders and the Plural Ministry: The Role of Exegetical History in Illuminating John Calvin's Theology*

religion within his covenanted community. In fact, bishops ordinarily have no right to reform the church, he wrote to Henry VIII of England in 1538, because "first and above all it belongs to the ruler to look after religion and faith."[114] He put the point succinctly in his *Decades* years later:

> For I know that many are of the opinion that the things of religion and their ordering belong to the bishops alone and not to the kings, princes, and other magistrates. But the catholic truth teaches that the things of religion especially belong to the magistracy and that the same not only may but also should and ought to order and promote religion.[115]

The prince is to his realm, in both its civil and ecclesiastical elements, as the soul to the body.[116]

Given such a view it makes sense that Bullinger adamantly rejected excommunication, arguing that baptism and the Lord's Supper are to remain open to all members of the covenantal society in good social standing. The civil government could require outward obedience to the covenant, using capital punishment to free the commonwealth of false teachers, blasphemers, adulterers, or other offenders. It would also be responsible for care for the poor.[117] These civil responsibilities were to be fulfilled in obedience to the word as proclaimed by faithful pastors exercising the prophetic office. For while ministers should not interfere with the affairs of civil government, they must preach the whole counsel of God even when that requires rebuking civil government on matters like morality, ecclesiastical property, marriage, or usury. Just as pastors had to submit to the magistrates in their direction

---

(Geneva: Librairie Droz, 1988), 199. McKee writes with respect to the exegesis of this text, "Among the Zurich theologians . . . there seems to be no clear sense of the *gubernationes* or *opitulationes* functions being distinctly ecclesiastical offices, as opposed to offices of the Christian community. This is in accord with the Zwinglian understanding of ecclesiastical-civil relationships, and it becomes plain in later 'Zwinglian' exegetes." McKee, *Elders and the Plural Ministry*, 74.

[114] Cited in Biel, *Doorkeepers at the House of Righteousness*, 34.

[115] Cited in Biel, *Doorkeepers at the House of Righteousness*, 20.

[116] Kirby, *The Zurich Connection and Tudor Political Theology*, 27. Bullinger believed that God brings most people into his kingdom through the conversion of magistrates, who then lead their people into the faith. See Pamela Biel, *Doorkeepers at the House of Righteousness: Heinrich Bullinger and the Zurich Clergy 1535–1575* (Bern: Peter Lang, 1991), 33. "Our disputation tendeth not to the confounding of the offices and duties of the magistrate and ministers of the church . . . The church of Christ hath, and retaineth, several and distinguished offices (*officia distincta*)." Cited in Kirby, *The Zurich Connection and Tudor Political Theology*, 33, from *Decades* 1:329.

[117] This was a point of some conflict in Zurich over the years, but eventually the system fused together the tasks of magistrate and pastor. As Biel puts it, "When the clergy ministered to the sick, adjudicated marital problems, or aided in the distribution of poor relief, they distinguished themselves both as pastors and as functionaries of an increasingly centralized government." Biel, *Doorkeepers at the House of Righteousness*, 137. Cf. pp. 137–165; Baker, *Heinrich Bullinger and the Covenant*, 107–120.

of temporal and ecclesiastical affairs, so magistrates were obligated to submit to the teaching of pastors in their prophetic ministry. When they submitted to the word in this way, the magistrates fulfilled Old Testament prophecies about kings entering the kingdom of Christ.[118]

While Bullinger distinguished between two kinds of power, therefore, he rejected any distinction between two kingdoms in the context of a Christian commonwealth.

> As long as the rulers of the temporal kingdom remain under the prince of the world and of darkness, not believing in Christ, . . . then certainly the kingdom of the world and the kingdom of Christ should not at all be drawn together. But if the rulers of the temporal kingdom abandon the prince of darkness and cling to the Prince of light, Christ Jesus, in whom they have faith, whom they worship and honor, and also if they further and protect the Christian faith, then they are no longer in the kingdom of this world but in the kingdom of Christ and therefore no longer temporal but Christian princes.[119]

Torrance Kirby rightly observes that Bullinger's covenantal commonwealth, the "Zurich model," was the great alternative to the "Geneva model" established by Calvin and that the two models were counterpoised in repeated ecclesiastical and political controversies during the second half of the sixteenth century. Although Bullinger supported Calvin's determined efforts to establish ecclesiastical discipline in Geneva, he did so only to preserve unity among Reformed churches. When debates over Geneva-style ecclesiastical discipline arose during the 1560s at Heidelberg between Thomas Erastus, who opposed it, and Caspar Olevianus, who favored it, Bullinger advocated for Erastus. Bullinger likewise vigorously defended the royal supremacy in England from the time of Henry VIII through the Elizabethan settlement.[120] When the Calvinist disciplinarians claimed that the royal supremacy challenged Christ's sole headship over the church, Bullinger and the other defenders of the magisterial care of religion retorted that the disciplinarian

---

[118] Kirby, *The Zurich Connection and Tudor Political Theology*, 25–41; Baker, *Heinrich Bullinger and the Covenant*, 149–151.

[119] Baker, *Heinrich Bullinger and the Covenant*, 150.

[120] Kirby, *The Zurich Connection and Tudor Political Theology*, 25–41. For an outline of the development of two kingdoms political theology in England before the establishment of the "Zurich connection" see Oakley, "Christian Obedience and Authority, 1520–1555," 175–182. Cf. J. Wayne Baker, "Erastianism in England: The Zurich Connection," *Die Zürcher Reformation: Ausstrahlungen und Ruckwirkungen* (ed. Alfred Schindler and Hans Stickelberger; Bern: Peter Lang, 2001), 327–349. Baker writes, "By the 1550s, there were two approaches: the doctrine of the single sphere in Zürich and the two kingdoms theory in Geneva ... By the late sixteenth century, the two kingdoms theory of Calvinism had won victories in most of the Reformed churches – in France, Germany, the Netherlands, and Scotland – but not in England" (328).

model amounted to a Protestant version of the old papal two swords theory.[121] The Zurich model of a covenantal commonwealth thus represented much of mainstream Reformed practice in the early sixteenth century. It was the great alternative to the model that was already being worked out during the 1530s by Martin Bucer in Strasbourg and John Calvin in Geneva.[122]

BUCER AND CHURCH DISCIPLINE

Although Bucer was originally committed to the Zurich model of ecclesiastical and political power, he gradually embraced the necessity of a system of ecclesiastical discipline and excommunication distinct from the magistrate's enforcement of the civil law, in part because of his interaction with many Anabaptist leaders passing through Strasbourg during the 1520s and 1530s.[123] At the same time, Bucer continued to maintain the ideal of a unified Christian society under the authority of the magistrate (although he wavered in that commitment as well, especially during his years in Strasbourg). Bucer's attempt to maintain the ideal of the Christian society while establishing church discipline administered by the clergy increasingly led him to use language reminiscent of Luther's two kingdoms theology. His development is crucial for an understanding of Calvin's two kingdoms doctrine because it was within the context of Bucer's influence that Calvin worked out his own views.[124]

---

[121] Bullinger summarized the Geneva model as claiming that "the Civil Magistrate can have no authority in ecclesiastical matters and, moreover, that the Church will admit no other government than that of presbyters and presbyteries." Such views, he argued, were "held in common with the papists, who also displace the magistrate from the government of the Church, and who substitute themselves [i.e., the papacy and the church hierarchy] in his place." Kirby, *The Zurich Connection and Tudor Political Theology*, 37. Bullinger came to view the Royal Supremacy as analogical to the two natures of Christ, a position that was systematically developed by Peter Martyr Vermigli and later by John Whitgift and Richard Hooker in their disputes with Calvinist disciplinarians (40–41). "From the standpoint of Bullinger's unique covenantal interpretation of history, it is certainly arguable that the Old Testament exemplar is more completely realised under England's monarchical constitution than under the republican conditions of Bullinger's own city and canton of Zurich" (41).

[122] See J. Wayne Baker, "Christian Discipline and the Early Reformed Tradition: Bullinger and Calvin," *Calviniana: Ideas and Influence of Jean Calvin* (ed. Robert V. Schnucker; Kirksville, MO: Sixteenth Century Journal, 1988), 107–119; Baker, "Erastianism in England," 327–349.

[123] Davis, "No Discipline, No Church," 43–58. As late as 1531 Bucer continued to support Zwingli's position that church discipline was unnecessary where there was a Christian magistracy. Around this time, however, his views began to change. He worked with Oecolampadius and Blarer to draft a proposal for church discipline for the city of Ulm, a proposal that the city council found went too far in removing such discipline from its own oversight. See Martin Greschat, *Martin Bucer: A Reformer and His Times* (trans. Stephen E. Buckwalter; Louisville: Westminster John Knox Press: 2004 [1990]), 107–109.

[124] The following paragraphs draw on Amy Nelson Burnett, *The Yoke of Christ: Martin Bucer and Christian Discipline* (Kirksville, Mo: Sixteenth Century Journal, 1994); Willem Van't Spijker, *The Ecclesiastical Offices in the Thought of Martin Bucer* (trans. John Vriend and Lyle D. Bierma;

In Strasbourg, Bucer's efforts to establish a system of discipline were tied up with his equally strident attempts to get the city council to take a more proactive role in advancing and enforcing the true religion. In 1533 the city council agreed to hold a synod for the purpose of establishing a church order and confession. The basis for the meetings was to be a document of sixteen articles written by Bucer that called for a mild form of church discipline that fell short of the full separation and ostracism practiced by the Anabaptists, excommunication only in the case of refusal to repent after grave sin, and the use of the sword for the advancement of Christ's kingdom and the suppression of false teaching and worship. The articles were vigorously opposed by a group led by the pastor Antonius Engelbrecht. Engelbrecht advanced objections quite similar to those offered by Frolich in Nuremburg a few years earlier. He argued that while the sword was legitimately used to protect true worship in the Old Testament, in the New Testament, Christ had established a spiritual kingdom governed by the word alone. Thus civil magistrates should never use the sword either to defend the gospel or to impose church discipline. Appealing to Luther's *On Secular Authority*, Engelbrecht insisted that the two kingdoms must be kept separate.[125]

Bucer's response to Engelbrecht is noteworthy because it echoed the arguments of Melanchthon and other Lutheran leaders at virtually every point, except that Bucer refused either to affirm or reject the two kingdoms distinction. When Engelbrecht challenged him to reexamine Luther's *On Secular Authority*, Bucer responded by insisting on a distinction between inward faith and external religious worship and teaching, appealing to Luther's later writings in support. Invoking Romans 13:4 and 1 Timothy 2:2, he argued that the magistrate is to preserve public order by establishing peace and godliness. Finally, he maintained that the Old Testament law clearly reveals that false teaching should be punished with the sword. Around this time Melanchthon wrote to Bucer, articulating his mature view of the responsibilities of secular authorities to enforce both tables of the Ten Commandments and assuring Bucer that he was entirely in agreement with his views, as were the theologians at Wittenburg, including Luther.[126]

In the end the Strasbourg council endorsed Bucer's Sixteen Articles, but it declined to enact the policies he proposed.[127] Over the next few years, Bucer

Leiden: Brill, 1996); Lorna J. Abray, *The People's Reformation: Magistrates, Clergy, and Commons in Strasbourg, 1500–1598* (Ithaca, NY: Cornell University Press, 1985).

[125] Bucer's constant encounters with various Anabaptists and with Schwenckfeld convinced him both of the need for the city council to suppress dissent and of the need for the church to have its own discipline as a response to the dissenters' criticism. See Estes, *Peace, Order and the Glory of God*, 111–114; Greschat, *Martin Bucer*, 116–121; Demura, *Church Discipline According to Johannes Oecolampadius*, 153.

[126] Estes, *Peace, Order and the Glory of God*, 114–119; Greschat, *Martin Bucer*, 121–127.

[127] When news arrived of the Anabaptist takeover of Munster in March 1534, the council adopted Bucer's Sixteen Articles. Soon after Bucer proposed a city ordinance that carefully distinguished between the

continued to develop his ecclesiology in conversation and debate with Catholics, Anabaptists, Lutherans, and Reformed alike. He began to theorize about ecclesiastical offices other than that of pastor, including offices designated for government and care for the poor. He began to distinguish between the offices of apostle, teacher, helper, and ruler, though not as clearly and definitively as Calvin later would.[128] In his classic *On the True Care of Souls*, published in 1538, Bucer explicitly rejected the argument of Zwingli and Bullinger that the New Testament office of elder was abolished when civil authorities became Christian. "Even when the civil authority fulfills its office of warning against and punishing wrong with the greatest diligence, it is still necessary for the church to have its own discipline and correction, which are practiced in the name of Christ and by his Holy Spirit in accordance with his command about the keys."[129] He charged that those who suggest that it is enough for the magistrates to administer discipline "do not sufficiently know or consider how great a difference there is between the government of rulers and the care of souls by the elders in the Christian congregation."[130] He began to describe church discipline as one of the keys of the kingdom that was exercised by the ministers of the church, not under the authority of the magistrates, but as commanded by Christ, a development crucial for his later claim that church discipline is the third mark of the true church. Bucer increasingly described the keys of the kingdom in jurisdictional terms, comparing the church to a republic or city and calling for it to establish its own offices of elder and deacon.[131]

work of civil government and spiritual government in the process of church discipline. However, this Ordinance of 1534 was revised by the city council so as to shift the balance of power and control to the magistrates. Burnett notes, "As in Ulm, the Strasbourg city council had little understanding of or appreciation for Bucer's distinction between the responsibilities of the church and those of the magistrate." Burnett, *The Yoke of Christ*, 71.

[128] McKee, *Elders and the Plural Ministry*, 51, 75–76, 193–194; Greschat, *Martin Bucer*, 149.
[129] Martin Bucer, *Concerning the True Care of Souls* (trans. Martin Beale; Edinburgh: Banner of Truth, 2009), 143.
[130] Bucer, *Concerning the True Care of Souls*, 140. He also continued to affirm that magistrates also had a responsibility to care for souls by establishing discipline and requiring attendance at religious meetings.
[131] Throughout this time, Bucer continued to engage in discussion with Anabaptists and to be influenced by them. In 1538 he went to Hesse to debate some of the followers of Melchior Hoffman and to advise the authorities on the establishment of church discipline. Greschat, *Martin Bucer*, 153–156. He wrote to Philip Landgrave of Hesse, "the most obvious objection of these people, unfortunately, is that we administer [the church] so badly, and with this argument they lead many people astray. May the Lord help us to eliminate this argument of the Anabaptists and the papists, and even of our own consciences and of the Lord." He made it clear in the same letter that he hoped "to achieve reformation of the church, for the sake of the Anabaptists and others." Burnett, *The Yoke of Christ*, 114 (Cf. 91–92). The effort was a success. Franklin Littell, "What Butzer Debated with the Anabaptists at Marburg: A Document of 1538," *Mennonite Quarterly Review* 36 (1962): 256–276. The church ordinance called for discipline to be administered by pastors and elders elected by the church. McKee, *Elders and the Plural Ministry*, 98. Van't Spijker argues that later Bucer's views were also influenced by his

That same year John Calvin arrived in Strasbourg, having already failed in an attempt to establish church discipline in Geneva. He became the pastor of the French refugee church in Strasbourg, where he was able to establish elder-administered church discipline. For the next three years, Calvin and Bucer established a close working relationship that would endure even after Calvin returned to Geneva in 1541.[132] But if in the 1530s Bucer was optimistic that he could persuade the magistrates and lay population of Strasbourg to enact church discipline, by the 1540s he was losing that optimism. Bucer complained that while people used the fear of papal tyranny and the doctrine of Christian freedom to justify their lack of discipline, the real cause was their hypocrisy and their refusal to see the kingdom of Christ established in its fullness.[133] During these later years Bucer shifted from his early commitment to the ideal of the *corpus Christianum* with its organic union of church and state to a growing emphasis on the difference between the kingdom of Christ and civil power. In the early 1540s he changed tactics, calling for voluntary "Christian fellowships (*christliche Gemeinschaft*)" in which devout Christians could submit themselves to discipline administered by the pastors with the assistance of elected elders.[134] But the city council rejected Bucer's arguments and outlawed the fellowships just prior to Bucer's exile as a result of the Augsburg Interim in 1549.[135]

correspondence with leaders of the Bohemian Brethren. Van't Spijker, *The Ecclesiastical Offices in the Thought of Martin Bucer*, 339. Bucer permitted the Bohemians to publish a Czech translation of *On the True Care of Souls* that omitted references to the obligation of the civil magistrates. Greschat, *Martin Bucer*, 204–205. Calvin would also write admiringly to the Bohemian Brethren. Höpfl, *The Christian Polity of John Calvin*, 101.

[132] The influence ran both ways. Calvin's establishment of church discipline in the French congregation in Strasbourg and in Geneva preceded any similar template proposed by Bucer. See Van't Spijker, *The Ecclesiastical Offices in the Thought of Martin Bucer*, 339–343; Willem Van't Spijker, "Calvin's Friendship with Martin Bucer: Did It Make Calvin a Calvinist?," *Calvin Studies Society Papers, 1995, 1997: Calvin and Spirituality, Calvin and His Contemporaries* (ed. David Foxgrover; Grand Rapids: CRC Product Services, 1998), 169–186; Willem Van't Spijker, "Bucer's Influence on Calvin: Church and Community," *Martin Bucer: Reforming Church and Community* (ed. D. F. Wright; Cambridge: Cambridge University Press, 1994), 32–44. Throughout this time Capito was moving in step with Bucer and Calvin in terms of the distinction between the "two regiments" and its implications for discipline. Demura, *Church Discipline According to Johannes Oecolampadius*, 157, 159.

[133] As he wrote in *On the True Care of Souls*, "We need to decide once and for all whether we really want to be Christians." Bucer, *Concerning the True Care of Souls*, 145–146. Cf. Greschat, *Martin Bucer*, 143.

[134] Greschat, *Martin Bucer*, 149–150; Cf. 217. In these later years "his entire line of thought is controlled by the fundamental dissimilarity between ecclesiastical and secular power. Everything depends on 'learning to rightly distinguish the two governments.'" Van't Spijker, *The Ecclesiastical Offices in the Thought of Martin Bucer*, 318. Bucer's thinking increasingly implied that "The church community is severed from the structure of the civil community. The government exercised in the Body of Christ is purely spiritual" (330; Cf. 160–161, 172). Cf. Burnett, *The Yoke of Christ*, 108.

[135] Greschat, *Martin Bucer*, 144, 211–217.

For all of Bucer's efforts in Germany, Strasbourg, and later England,[136] it was Calvin who would insist most sharply and systematically on the distinction between the two kingdoms and its necessary implications for the spiritual autonomy of the church. It was Calvin who would vigorously reject magisterial claims to headship and supremacy within the church, and it was Calvin who would articulate an enduring theological basis for spiritual-ecclesiastical offices oriented toward discipline and care for the poor.[137] Ultimately it was Calvin's two kingdoms theology that would emerge as the alternative to caesaropapism and the Zurich model of the *corpus Christianum.*

---

[136] After his exile and arrival in England, Bucer sought to synthesize a two kingdoms approach with the ideal of a Christian society. In his classic *On the Kingdom of Christ*, he clearly distinguished between the kingdom of Christ and the kingdoms of this world, using the distinction to structure and outline the book, and he explicitly identified the kingdom of Christ with the church. See Martin Bucer, *De Regno Christi* (trans. Wilhelm Pauck) in *Melanchthon and Bucer* (ed. Wilhelm Pauck; Louisville: Westminster John Knox Press, 1969). Cf. Van't Spijker, *The Ecclesiastical Offices in the Thought of Martin Bucer*, 61. In the second part of the book, he explains in extensive detail what it means for the king to establish the kingdom of Christ in his land and to allow its influence to permeate society, its institutions, and its laws. He follows Bullinger in maintaining that magistrates are responsible for leading their people in a covenant relationship with God along the lines of the Israelite covenant in scripture. Calvin never emphasized social and political reform in the sustained, detailed, and even utopian way that Bucer did in *On the Kingdom of Christ*, and he distinguished more sharply than did Bucer between the spiritual and political jurisdictions. Van't Spijker, "The Kingdom of Christ According to Bucer and Calvin," 117; Van't Spijker, "Bucer's Influence on Calvin," 42–44. Cf. Thomas F. Torrance, *Kingdom and Church* (Edinburgh: Oliver & Boyd, 1956), 87. Cf. Thomas Dandelet, "Creating a Protestant Constantine: Martin Bucer's De Regno Christi and the Foundations of English Imperial Political Theology," *Politics and Reformations: Communities, Polities, Nations, and Empires: Essays in Honor of Thomas A. Brady, Jr.* (ed. Christopher Ocker, et al.; Leiden: Brill, 2007), 539–550; Basil Hall, "Martin Bucer in England," *Martin Bucer: Reforming Church and Community* (ed. D. F. Wright; Cambridge: Cambridge University Press, 1994), 144–160; Greschat, *Martin Bucer*, 240–243; Martin Greschat, "Church and Civil Community," *Martin Bucer: Reforming Church and Community* (ed. D. F. Wright; Cambridge: Cambridge University Press, 1994), 17–31.

[137] As Oakley puts it, "Among the theological initiators of Reformed Protestantism, indeed, it was left to Calvin to sound a clear note of reserve about the role of the temporal authority in matters religious, to emphasize in such matters the independence and superiority of the clerical authority, and to do so in so forceful a manner as to make that emphasis henceforth a distinguishing feature of the Reformed tradition." Oakley, "Christian Obedience and Authority, 1520–1550," 185–186

2

Calvin, Geneva, and the French Reformed Churches

Calvin articulated the two kingdoms doctrine before he ever arrived in Geneva as a young French refugee fleeing the persecution in his native land. In the following years, through his first stint in Geneva (1536–1538), his exile in Strasbourg (1538–1541), and his permanent return to Geneva (1541–1564), he progressively worked out the doctrine's institutional implications for church and commonwealth. Until 1555 Calvin's time in Geneva was characterized by his struggle for the church's autonomy from civil government with respect to its discipline and order. Even after 1555 Calvin was not always pleased with the state of affairs, and he never claimed that the forms and practices adopted in Geneva were to be normative for other Reformed churches. What he *did* claim to be normative was the basic structure of the spiritual government of the church as he presented it in the *Institutes* – including the functions and associated offices of the word and sacraments, discipline, and poor relief.

In this chapter I outline Calvin's involvement in political and ecclesiastical affairs in Geneva and France. It is important to do this before turning to Calvin's theology for several reasons. First, whether Calvin advocated, tolerated, or opposed particular practices and institutions reveals a great deal about Calvin's priorities: what he thought was crucial to his two kingdoms theology, what he thought was consistent with it (if not necessarily ideal), and what he thought blatantly contradicted it.

Second, although scholars often assume that mid-sixteenth-century Geneva represents Calvin's model society, the reality is more complicated. Not only was Calvin often in conflict with Geneva's civil government, but during his time there, he nurtured a body of French Reformed refugees who maintained their ties with the burgeoning Reformed churches in France. The forms of discipline and order favored by these French Reformed Christians were distinct from Genevan practice, but they were clearly approved, and sometimes even preferred, by Calvin himself. The result, as Heiko Oberman suggests in his *John Calvin and the Reformation of the Refugees*, is that we have not one but two distinct models of how a Calvinist two kingdoms political theology might be worked out, one in the context of a consolidated *corpus Christianum* in which church and commonwealth were coterminous, the other in a context of religious diversity, where the church was persecuted by the civil authorities.

Third, paying attention to the nature of Calvin's involvement in Geneva and France highlights Calvin's greatest concern and his greatest legacy: the autonomy and integrity of the spiritual kingdom of Christ, which is to say, the church. For all of the attention that has been devoted to Calvin's economic, social, and political legacy, Calvin devoted the balance of his impressive energies to the establishment of the church with its word, sacraments, discipline, and diaconate. His interaction with political affairs was decisively controlled by his desire to see the church independently established and vigorously defended, regardless of the attitudes and preferences of the magistrates in power.

CALVIN'S FIRST STINT IN GENEVA (1536–1538)

The Reformation came to Geneva just as the city's decades long struggle for independence from foreign and ecclesiastical rule was coming to a climax.[1] In fact, in Geneva, reform was thoroughly political in its origins. It followed the pattern of reformation in Zurich, Berne, and the other Swiss cities, with whom Geneva's economic and military ties were significant and with whose help Geneva's independence had been secured. The Bishop and the foreign clergy were the greatest obstacle to Genevan independence, and many Genevans resented the church's powerful control over the city's wealth and revenue. Already in 1527, before the Reformation had touched the city, the Petit Conseil (Small Council) began to assert greater control over the city's temporal and ecclesiastical affairs. When Geneva's ally Berne embraced the Reformation in 1528, it made it inevitable that the movement would come to Geneva. In the early 1530s evangelical preachers, including Guillaume Farel, began to stirring up religious dissent, disorder, and even violence in the already anti-ecclesiastical atmosphere. When the Bishop attempted to intervene he was forced to leave the city, Geneva's Council of Deux Cents (Two Hundred) declaring that in its struggle to maintain its rights and independence

---

[1] Geneva had long been ruled by a bishop and his appointed representative, the Vidomne, but the city's ultimate master was Savoy, from whose family most of the bishops came. On the general details of the Genevan reformation, see William G. Naphy, *Calvin and the Consolidation of the Genevan Reformation* (Manchester: Manchester University Press, 1994), 12–25; E. William Monter, *Calvin's Geneva* (New York: John Wiley & Sons, 1967), 29–59; E. William Monter, *Studies in Genevan Government (1536–1605)* (Geneva: Librairie Droz, 1964); Philip Benedict, *Christ's Churches Purely Reformed: A Social History of Calvinism* (New Haven: Yale University Press, 2002), 78–81; Robert M. Kingdon, "Calvin and the Government of Geneva," *Calvinus Ecclesiae Genevesis Custos* (ed. Wilhelm Neuser. Frankfurt: Peter Lang, 1984), 49–67.

"we have had little help from our Bishop and Prince, from the members of the Cathedral Chapter, and from the other priests."[2]

By now the politics of the Reformation were thoroughly intertwined with the city's conflict with the Bishop. In October 1534 the Petit Conseil deposed the Bishop, who retaliated by excommunicating 250 leading Genevans. The Deux Cents issued a decree provisionally suspending the Mass, and the city government began to confiscate church property and take control of formerly ecclesiastical functions. After fending off a besieging army led by the Duke of Savoy and Geneva's own Bishop, the citizens unanimously ratified the Deux Cents' decision to abolish the Mass and the canon law in a meeting of the Conseil General (General Council) on May 21, 1536. Up to this point the Reformation in Geneva was thoroughly magisterial in character, much like the reformations of other Swiss cities.[3] The city had purged itself of the old clergy and the church was under the administration and control of the civil government, which in turn was beholden to the military power of Berne for its survival. But while the old ecclesiastical regime had been torn down, little had been accomplished in the way of positive reformation.

It was at this time that John Calvin arrived, having fled persecution in his native France, and he was quickly persuaded by Farel to become one of the city's pastors.[4] His first edition of the *Institutes of the Christian Religion* had just been published that year. The work contained the Frenchman's classic statement of the two kingdoms concept, but it said very little about the institutional form a reformed church should take, and it did not say much about the role civil magistrates should play in the process of reformation.[5] Nevertheless, Calvin's practical predilections can already be detected during these first few years in Geneva. In early 1537, Calvin and the other pastors presented to the Petit Conseil a series of articles for the

---

[2] William C. Innes, *Social Concern in Calvin's Geneva* (Allison Park, PA: Pickwick, 1983), 70 (65–70).

[3] Philip Benedict writes, "During these same months, many of the pieces of an austere civic reformation along Swiss lines were put in place." Benedict, *Christ's Churches Purely Reformed*, 81. Geneva's consolidation of its hospital system reflected broader trends in sixteenth century Europe toward laicization, secularization, centralization and rationalization. See Robert M. Kingdon, "Social Welfare in Calvin's Geneva," *The American Historical Review* 76.1 (February, 1971): 50–69; Robert M. Kingdon, "The Deacons of the Reformed Church in Calvin's Geneva," *Melanges D'Histoire Du XVIe Siecle* (ed. Henri Meylan; Geneva: Librairie Droz, 1970), 82–83. Cf. Robert M. Kingdon, "Calvin's Ideas about the Diaconate: Social or Theological in Origin?" in *Piety, Politics and Ethics: Reformation Studies in Honor of George Wolfgang Forell* (ed. Carter Lindberg; Kirksville: Sixteenth Century Journal, 1984), 167–180; Robert M. Kingdon, "Calvin and Social Welfare," *Calvin Theological Journal* 17.2 (1982): 212–230.

[4] For reflections on the potential significance of Calvin's stay in Basel see Akira Demura, "Calvin's and Oecolampadius' Concept of Church Discipline," *Calvinus Ecclesiae Genevesis Custos* (ed. Wilhelm Neuser; Frankfurt: Peter Lang, 1984), 187–189. Cf. J. Wayne Baker, "Christian Discipline, Church and State, and Toleration: Bullinger, Calvin, and Basel 1530–1555," *Das Reformierte Erbe: Festschrift für Gottfried W. Locher zu seinem 80. Geburtstag* (vol. 1; ed. Heiko A. Oberman, et al.; Theologischer Verlag Zürich: 1992), 35–48, 37.

[5] During these early years Calvin viewed the church almost purely in the "invisible" sense that Luther emphasized, but he was already talking about church discipline. See Willem Balke, *Calvin and the Anabaptist Radicals* (trans. Willem Heyner; Grand Rapids: Eerdmans, 1981), 49–51.

organization of the church. They called for monthly celebration of the Lord's Supper, the affirmation by oath of the Geneva *Confession of Faith* by all inhabitants of Geneva as a condition of participation in the Supper, and the establishment of a system of church discipline through which the ministers could bar the unrepentant from the Supper.[6] The articles declared it to be the magistrates' obligation to establish the church along these lines.[7] The document clarified that the pastors did not seek the kind of discipline the popes turned into "tyranny," declaring that such abuse took place because bishops confiscated the right of excommunication from "the assembly of the faithful."[8] To prevent this evil, they called the magistrates "to ordain and elect certain persons of good life and witness from among the faithful" to exercise oversight among the people. Upon witnessing faults of note, these persons would discuss them with some of the ministers and admonish and exhort those at fault. If this failed, the matter would be reported to the church, and if the accused still did not repent, the minister would declare a sentence of excommunication. The excommunicated persons would be refused communion and "intimate dealings" but would be required to continue attending the sermons.[9] Those who rejected such discipline would be dealt with by the magistrates.[10]

The magistrates accepted most of the articles, but they followed the example of the Swiss cities in limiting the celebration of the Supper to four times a year. They also issued a decree clarifying that no one should be barred from the Lord's Supper due to a failure to swear the oath.[11] It would become clear soon enough

---

[6] The Geneva Confession of 1536 outlined the two marks of the church as the preaching of the gospel and the observance of the sacraments (Article 18). It described "the discipline of excommunication to be a thing holy and salutary among the faithful, since truly it was instituted by our Lord with good reason" (Article 19). But the only ecclesiastical office it recognized was that of the "pastors of the Word of God," who are "to conduct, rule, and govern the people of God committed to them by the same Word" (Article 20). See "Confession of Faith Which All the Citizens and Inhabitants of Geneva and the Subjects of the Country Must Promise to Keep and Hold (1536)," in *Calvin: Theological Treatises* (trans. J.K.S. Reid; Philadelphia: Westminster Press, 1954), 26–33.

[7] It called the councilmen to consider its importance "for the maintenance of the honor of God in this State and the conservation of the Church in its integrity." "Articles concerning the Organization of the Church and of Worship at Geneva Proposed by the Ministers at the Council: January 16, 1537," in *Calvin: Theological Treatises* (trans. J.K.S. Reid; Philadelphia: Westminster Press, 1954), 55. The Lord's Supper was to be a weekly celebration. Discipline was said to be necessary to ensure that the body of Christ was not "contaminated by those ... who declare and manifest by their misconduct and evil life that they do not at all belong to Jesus." Those who refuse to repent "should be expelled from the body of the Church" (50–51). Christopher Elwood notes that in contrast to the Swiss Reformed, Calvin "did not view the body of Christ created by the eucharist as coextensive with society at large." Christopher Elwood, *The Body Broken: The Calvinist Doctrine of the Eucharist and the Symbolization of Power in Sixteenth-Century France* (Oxford: Oxford University Press, 1999), 148.

[8] "Articles concerning the Organization of the Church and of Worship," 51.

[9] "Articles concerning the Organization of the Church and of Worship," 52.

[10] The articles also called for the establishment of a court consisting of magistrates and ministers to handle conflicts pertaining to marriage. "Articles concerning the Organization of the Church and of Worship," 55.

[11] Calvin never did get his way on the oath. Adrianus D. Pont, "Citizen's Oath and Formulated Confession: Confession of Faith in Calvin's Congregation," *Calvinus Sacrae Scripturae Professor:*

that they did not understand the distinction between the commonwealth and the church in the same terms as did Calvin. At the heart of the problem was Calvin's desire to establish a relatively autonomous church distinct – though not separate – from the commonwealth. To be sure, it is misleading to reduce the tumult of these years to a conflict over the appropriate relationship between church and state, or even over church discipline. Factionalism robbed Geneva's politics of any sense of continuity or stability, and Berne, the city's more powerful ally, was constantly trying to influence affairs in accord with Berne's own interests.[12] Calvin and Farel became increasingly associated with those citizens who wanted to distance the city from Bernese control. When the council ordered the pastors to reintroduce Bernese practices with respect to the Lord's Supper, baptism, and feast days, Farel and Calvin preached sermons denouncing the council's actions, Calvin referring to it as a "council of the devil." The council responded by forbidding the pastors to preach on political matters and informing them that their continued ministry in Geneva would require them to conform to Berne's demands. Yet Calvin and Farel were insistent that the magistrates did not have the authority to dictate church practice. When they refused to administer the Lord's Supper that Easter, they were removed from office and banished from the city.[13] For Calvin it was a matter of loyalty to Christ over loyalty to the state. "If we served men, we would be badly rewarded. But we serve a great master, who will recompense us."[14]

Calvin as Confessor of Holy Scripture (ed. Wilhelm H. Neuser; Grand Rapids: Eerdmans, 1994), 237–239; Balke, *Calvin and the Anabaptist Radicals*, 92–93.

[12] The 1536 treaty gave Berne significant control over Geneva's foreign relations, and Geneva was involved in continual negotiations with Berne over shared jurisdictions and disputed properties. In addition, Bernese authorities wanted to maintain a degree of religious influence over Geneva. Like the other Swiss cities, Berne did not allow its pastors to exclude persons from the Lord's Supper. Naphy, *Calvin and the Consolidation of the Genevan Reformation*, 29–41. Naphy provides evidence that there was no clear correlation between opposition to church discipline and a reluctance to preserve and enforce moral order. Calvin's personal interaction with the Bernese magistracy was rocky from the start. When Pierre Caroli accused Calvin of failing to hold to the orthodox doctrine of the Trinity, the council of Berne summoned Calvin and Viret to explain themselves. Bruening argues that Calvin's disgust at the Bernese magistrates played a significant role in shaping his suspicion of magisterial control over the church. Bruening, *Calvinism's First Battleground*, 162–165.

[13] Bruce Gordon, *Calvin* (New Haven: Yale University Press, 2009), 72–77, 78–81; Benedict, *Christ's Churches Purely Reformed*, 93–95; Balke, *Calvin and the Anabaptist Radicals*, 93–94. Although Geneva council told a different story, three days after his expulsion Calvin told the Bernese authorities that the problem was not with indifferent ceremonies and feast days but with the lack of discipline: "for without any punishment meted out publicly, there would be a thousand derisions of the Word of God and the Supper." Bruening, *Calvinism's First Battleground*, 162–165.

[14] Cited in Bernard Cottret, *Calvin: A Biography* (trans. M. Wallace McDonald; Grand Rapids: Eerdmans, 2000 [1995]), 131. Cf. Harro Höpfl, *The Christian Polity of John Calvin* (Cambridge: Cambridge University Press, 1982), 77–78. Naphy agrees that for all the international politics involved, the central issue in 1538 was "whether or not the magistracy had the power to order changes to the religious practices of Geneva without consulting the ministers or getting their approval." Naphy, *Calvin and the Consolidation of the Genevan Reformation*, 33.

The reality is that it would have been a hard sell for any city in mid-sixteenth-century Europe, having finally overthrown the despised rule of a bishop and won control over ecclesiastical functions and property, to agree to cede that control to a new ecclesiastical body, and one made up of Frenchmen at that. Calvin's proposals smacked of the ecclesiastical tyranny from which Geneva had just liberated itself, and few Protestants were eager to turn back the clock. All Protestant cities maintained magisterial control over ecclesiastical affairs, including the Lord's Supper and discipline. Geneva had little reason to try something different. The leading Swiss churches addressed the Geneva crisis at a synod in Zurich. They agreed that Calvin and Farel had acted improperly. But at least one delegate judged differently. Although Martin Bucer agreed that Calvin had acted without tact or wisdom, he was sympathetic to the young reformer's view of the church. He invited Calvin to pastor the French refugee congregation in his own city of Strasbourg.

CALVIN IN STRASBOURG (1538–1541)

Calvin arrived in Strasbourg shortly after Bucer had finally succeeded in drafting an ordinance of ecclesiastical discipline that was approved by a Protestant government, the German principality of Hesse. The two reformers agreed that church discipline was a fundamental expression of Christ's spiritual government. Calvin was able to implement church discipline in a congregation of French refugees in Strasbourg, free from the jealous eyes of civil magistrates. Here he had a willing congregation, one that had given up possessions, home, and country in order to practice the true faith. In the meantime he had steady interaction with Anabaptists (he ended up marrying Idelette de Bure, the widow of one of the Anabaptists he converted).[15]

The effect of Bucer and the Strasbourg years on Calvin's understanding of the church is evident from the development of Calvin's *Institutes* over the course of the first three editions, appearing in 1536, 1539, and 1543. The 1536 edition clearly

---

[15] Martin Greschat, *Martin Bucer: A Reformer and His Times* (trans. Stephen E. Buckwalter; Louisville: Westminster John Knox Press: 2004 [1990]), 147–148, 153–156. Balke argues that the Anabaptists were attracted to Calvin because he sympathized with them on discipline. Balke, *Calvin and the Anabaptist Radicals*, 123–143, 153. When supporters from Geneva asked for advice on whether to participate in the worship of the flawed Genevan church, Calvin answered in the affirmative, observing that the city maintained the true marks of the church. Heiko Oberman, *John Calvin and the Reformation of the Refugees* (Geneva: Droz, 2009), 27. He emphasized the centrality of these marks and of discipline in his famous refutation of the Roman Catholic Cardinal Sadoleto. Gordon, *Calvin*, 96–98. On Calvin's efforts to raise international support for church discipline, see Oberman, *Reformation of the Refugees*, 26; Gordon, *Calvin*, 99. Oberman thinks that Calvin's experience pastoring a congregation of refugees permanently altered his perspective, such that when he returned to Geneva his vision was international, rather than urban, and his conception of the church was that of a congregation of refugees under the cross, rather than a *corpus christianum* under the direction of magistrates. Cf. Glenn S. Sunshine, *Reforming French Protestantism: The Development of Huguenot Ecclesiastical Institutions, 1557–1572* (Kirksville, MO: Truman State University Press, 2003), 20.

articulated Luther's two kingdoms doctrine, but it said very little about its potential institutional implications.[16] The 1539 edition added relatively little to this, with one important exception. In the 1536 edition Calvin had followed Reformed precedent and identified the gift of "ruling" in Romans 12:8 as referring to civil government. In 1539 he broke with that tradition, adding a sentence clarifying that the gift of "ruling" given to the church refers primarily to "a council of sober men, who were appointed in the primitive church to preside over the ordering of public discipline (which office is called in the letter to the Corinthians [12:28], 'governments')." Only by extension, "because we see the civil power serving the same end," could it be applied to "every kind of just rule" (4.20.4). This shift of emphasis suggests that Calvin was beginning to break with the political theology of Zwingli and Bullinger.[17]

Calvin developed this interpretation of the passage in his commentary on Romans, which appeared in 1540. He distinguished between the "church" and the "whole community," declaring the functions described in Romans 12:8 to be permanent and prescriptive for the church. The gift of "ruling," he said, refers to "presidents, to whom was committed the government of the church, and they were the

---

[16] Calvin did identify the offices of pastor and deacon, but what he said about them was essentially a reaction to medieval abuses rather than part of a constructive plan for church order. He described the importance of church discipline, but he assigned its exercise rather vaguely to the church.

[17] On Bucer's influence see Willem Van't Spijker, "Calvin's Friendship with Martin Bucer: Did It Make Calvin a Calvinist?," *Calvin Studies Society Papers, 1995, 1997: Calvin and Spirituality, Calvin and His Contemporaries* (ed. David Foxgrover; Grand Rapids: CRC Product Services, 1998), 169–186; Willem Van't Spijker, "Bucer's Influence on Calvin: Church and Community," *Martin Bucer: Reforming Church and Community* (ed. D. F. Wright; Cambridge: Cambridge University Press, 1994), 32–44. See McKee's description of the development of Calvin's ecclesiology, with rich attention to the reformer's exegetical work, in Elsie Anne McKee, *Elders and the Plural Ministry: The Role of Exegetical History in Illuminating John Calvin's Theology* (Geneva: Librairie Droz, 1988) and Elsie Anne McKee, *John Calvin on the Diaconate and Liturgical Almsgiving* (Geneva: Librairie Droz, 1984). McKee identifies Calvin as part of a tradition that interpreted Romans 12:8 as describing an ecclesiastical office, in contrast to another tradition, carried on by Zwingli and Bullinger, which interpreted it with reference to a magistrate and associated it with 2 Chronicles 19:6. McKee, *Elders and the Plural Ministry*, 49–50. Zwinglian theologians used the latter text "to establish the office of moral discipline as properly pertaining to the civil rulers in a Christian state ... In keeping with his insistence that the judicial regulations of Israel do not apply to Christians, Calvin bases the elder's office only, and apparently deliberately, on New Testament texts. The eldership is an office of the church as distinct from the Christian society, even though civil rulers are established by God and directly responsible to God, even though cooperation with the Christian magistracy is appropriate and some of the latter may also be elected as elders" (53–54). A similar dynamic is in play with respect to 1 Corinthians 12:28 (74). Cf. Richard R. De Ridder, "John Calvin's Views on Discipline: A Comparison of the Institution of 1536 and the *Institutes* of 1559," *Calvin Theological Journal* 21 (1986): 223–230; R. E. H. Uprichard, "The Eldership in Martin Bucer and John Calvin," *The Evangelical Quarterly* 61.1 (January, 1989): 21–37; Robert White, "Oil and Vinegar: Calvin on Church Discipline," *Scottish Journal of Theology* 38 (1985): 25–40; Cornelis Augustijn, "Calvin in Strasbourg," *Calvinus Sacrae Scripturae Professor: Calvin as Confessor of Holy Scripture* (ed. Wilhelm H. Neuser; Grand Rapids: Eerdmans, 1994), 166–177; Höpfl, *The Christian Polity of John Calvin*, 31–35, 41–43, 79–89. For arguments that Calvin read his ecclesiology into scripture, see Thomas F. Torrance, "The Eldership in the Reformed Church," *Scottish Journal of Theology* 37 (1984): 504–509; Höpfl, *The Christian Polity of John Calvin*, 54–55, 105–107, 126, 138–140. Cf. Ernst Troeltsch, *The Social Teaching of the Christian Churches* (trans. Olive Wyon; 2 vols.; Louisville: Westminster/John Knox Press, 1992 [1912]), 2:592.

elders, who presided over and ruled others and exercised discipline." Only by extension could the text be taken as a reference to "all kinds of governors ... who ought to watch day and night for the well-being of the whole community."[18] Here again was a clear break with the Zwinglian conviction that Christian magistrates hold an office in the church.

Calvin's concept of the office of deacon developed similarly. In the medieval church the diaconate had become little more than a step on the way to the priesthood, with largely liturgical functions. The early reformers saw evidence for the office in Acts 6 and 1 Timothy 3, but they regarded it as a temporary office now occupied by the civil magistrate. It was Bucer and Calvin, perhaps independently, who described the diaconate as a permanent ecclesiastical office devoted to care for the poor.[19] Calvin first mentioned it in his 1536 *Institutes*, but in his 1540 commentary on Romans he developed a distinction between two kinds of deacons virtually identical to that drawn by Bucer in his 1536 commentary on Romans. He noted Paul's reference to one office that "presided in dispensing the public charities of the church" and another that included "widows and other ministers who were appointed to take care of the sick."[20] Unlike Bucer Calvin would go on repeatedly to reference the twofold diaconate as a prescriptive element of biblical church order.[21]

Bucer's influence on Calvin's ecclesiology is clear, but while Bucer had ambiguously described a fourfold office in the church, Calvin clarified and systematized the concept, bolstered its exegetical support, applied it consistently, and eventually realized its implementation. In particular, he systematically presented the four offices of teacher, pastor, deacon, and elder as permanent offices within a biblical church order.[22] Calvin's emphasis on the enduring prescription of ecclesiastical

---

[18] Commentary on Romans 12:8 [1540]; CO 49:239–240. Cf. McKee, *Elders and the Plural Ministry*, 52.
[19] McKee, *John Calvin on the Diaconate and Liturgical Almsgiving*, 139–158.
[20] Commentary on Romans 12:8 [1540]; CO 49:239–240. Kingdon argues that the distinction of two kinds of deacons came from Calvin's observation of poor relief in Geneva, which Calvin merely sacralized. Kingdon, "Social Welfare in Calvin's Geneva," 59–61. But McKee shows that Calvin had sufficient exegetical warrant to render such assumptions about the role of his Genevan experience unnecessary. McKee, *John Calvin on the Diaconate and Liturgical Almsgiving*, 193–200. Cf. Innes, *Social Concern in Calvin's Geneva*, 115.
[21] McKee, *John Calvin on the Diaconate and Liturgical Almsgiving*, 195–197. Cf. Josef Bohatec, *Calvins Lehre von Staat und Kirche* (Breslau: Marcus Verlag, 1937), 469–470. For my fuller analysis of Calvin's theology of the diaconate, see Matthew J. Tuininga, "Good News for the Poor: An Analysis of Calvin's Concept of Poor Relief and the Diaconate in Light of His Two Kingdoms Paradigm," *Calvin Theological Journal* 49:2 (November, 2014): 221–247.
[22] McKee, *John Calvin on the Diaconate and Liturgical Almsgiving*, 133–137; McKee, *Elders and the Plural Ministry*, 75–76, 123–222. Calvin brings "his characteristic marks of lucidity, coherence, and theological integration," a clearer appreciation for the distinction between elders and the magistracy, and a clarification of the relationship between elders and pastor (76). McKee shows that before the Reformation the various functions described in Romans 12:6–8 and 1 Corinthians 12:28 were viewed as belonging to the clergy as secondary functions, given that the clergy were to be devoted to spiritual matters. The Zwinglians recognized that these texts gave religious significance to temporal functions, but assigned them to secular magistrates. Calvin and his heirs then identified the functions as "lay

offices devoted to poor relief and discipline is significant because, arising out of his unique two kingdoms theology, it became the focal point for early Reformed struggles over the appropriate relationship between the church and civil government. By challenging the claim of Zwingli and Bullinger that in a Christian society the functions of poor relief and discipline are to be yielded to civil government, he launched a new tradition of Reformed political theology dedicated to establishing the autonomy of the church from the political order.[23]

THE CONSOLIDATION OF CHURCH GOVERNMENT IN GENEVA (1541–1546)

In 1541 Calvin was invited back to Geneva after yet another shift in the city's factional politics.[24] Despite nearly five years having passed since Geneva embraced the Reformation, ecclesiastical and civil affairs remained in disarray. Calvin was assigned the task of reorganizing the church, and in fact, he only returned under the condition that the city would establish church discipline along the lines proposed in 1537–1538. Although his fuller theological account of church government would not appear until the 1543 edition of the *Institutes*, its basic outline appears in the 1541 *Ecclesiastical Ordinances* that he submitted to the council. The heading of the document situates ecclesiastical government within the context of Christ's spiritual government: "it appeared good to us that the spiritual government such as our Lord showed and instituted by his Word should be reduced to good order and have place and be observed among us. Hence we have commanded and established to be followed and observed in our city and territory the Ecclesiastical Constitution which follows, seeing that it is taken from the gospel of Jesus Christ." Whereas the 1537 Articles spoke vaguely about discipline and said nothing about elders or deacons, the *Ecclesiastical Ordinances* reflect the clarity gained during Calvin's time in Strasbourg, specifying the four distinct offices of pastor, doctor, elder, and deacon that have been "instituted by our Lord for the government of his Church."[25]

---

offices in the church as a body distinguishable from Christian society" (193). Cf. Uprichard, "The Eldership in Martin Bucer and John Calvin,"21–26.

[23] As McKee puts it, "For sixteenth-century Protestants, the question of ecclesiastical autonomy is bound up with the theory of the plurality of permanent ecclesiastical ministries because the customary second office, the diaconate responsible for poor relief, and the most critical additional office, the ministry of discipline, were both functions disputed between civil and ecclesiastical authorities." McKee, *Elders and the Plural Ministry*, 190.

[24] Naphy, *Calvin and the Consolidation of the Genevan Reformation*, 38–41; Monter, *Calvin's Geneva*, 67–69.

[25] "Draft Ecclesiastical Ordinances: September and October 1541," in *Calvin: Theological Treatises* (trans. J. K. S. Reid; Philadelphia: Westminster Press, 1954), 56–72, 58. For discussion of the *Ecclesiastical Ordinances*, see Höpfl, *The Christian Polity of John Calvin*, 90–96. I discuss Calvin's mature ecclesiology as appears in the 1543 *Institutes* in Chapter 5. On the 1543 *Institutes*, see Höpfl, *The Christian Polity of John Calvin*, 103–127.

The pastors are called to preach and teach the word, administer the sacraments, "and to enjoin brotherly corrections along with the elders and colleagues."[26] The doctors are responsible to teach theology and related subjects in "the order of the schools," which includes a college established for the young "to prepare them for the ministry as well as for civil government."[27] The elders are to exercise oversight over the people through admonition and correction. Unlike the pastors, who are to be selected by the Company of Pastors, the elders are to be nominated by the Petit Conseil in consultation with the pastors.[28] Their task is to meet weekly with the pastors as a body known as the Consistory "to see that there be no disorder in the Church and to discuss together remedies as they are required." The Consistory is charged to use discussion and admonition to discipline people who challenge church teaching, fail to attend church, or commit notorious sins. Where there is no repentance, the elders and pastors are authorized to excommunicate the person from the Lord's Supper. But the ordinances also clarify that although the elders come from the ranks of the governing councils, when serving in the Consistory they "have no compulsive authority or jurisdiction." As a result, the Consistory is to be assisted by a government official who will ensure procedural cooperation on the part of recalcitrant Genevans.[29]

The ordinances distinguish between two kinds of deacons. The "procurators" are described as those who "receive, dispense and hold goods for the poor, not only daily alms, but also possessions, rents and pensions." The "hospitallers" are to "tend and care for the sick and administer allowances to the poor."[30] Both are to be elected according to the same procedure as the elders. The deacons have oversight of the

---

[26] "Draft Ecclesiastical Ordinances," 58. They are to be elected by the Company of Pastors and presented to the Council. When certified by the Council they are to be presented to the people to be received by their consent. "Draft Ecclesiastical Ordinances," 59. Cf. Robert M. Kingdon, "Calvin and 'Presbytery': The Geneva Company of Pastors," *Pacific Theological Review* 18 (1985): 43–55, 48–49. Note that in the *Institutes* Calvin does not promote a magisterial role in the selection of pastors. Höpfl, *The Christian Polity of John Calvin*, 111–112. If the pastors fall into an intractable theological dispute, or if a pastor commits a serious sin, the matter is to be addressed with the assistance of the elders, and, that failing, "referred to the magistrate." "Draft Ecclesiastical Ordinances," 60–61.

[27] They are to be selected with the approval of the pastors and are subject to the same discipline. "Draft Ecclesiastical Ordinances," 62–63.

[28] They are to be selected proportionally from the various governing bodies of the city, and representatively from its various quarters, and approved by the Deux Cents. "Draft Ecclesiastical Ordinances," 63–64. The selection of elders and deacons took place at the same time as the elections for Geneva's civil government. Robert M. Kingdon, "Calvin's Socio-Political Legacy: Collective Government, Resistance to Tyranny, Discipline," in *The Legacy of John Calvin* (ed. David Foxgrover. Grand Rapids: CRC Product Services, 2000), 112–123, 120.

[29] "Draft Ecclesiastical Ordinances," 70–71. In addition to the discussion of the four offices the ordinances call for the establishment of a court of city representatives and pastors to handle matters pertaining to marriage, but they specify that marriage "is not a spiritual matter but involved with civil affairs" (67).

[30] Innes, *Social Concern in Calvin's Geneva*, 114–115. Whereas Calvin's writings tend to assign the dispensing of material needs to the first group, the ordinances associate it equally with the second.

public hospital, which employed a doctor and surgeon and was funded by the city, to ensure the care of the sick, the elderly, widows, orphans, visitors and "other poor creatures." They are to operate under the general oversight of the pastors, who are to visit the hospital every three months, and where there is a problem, the Council is to be notified.[31]

The Council enacted the *Ecclesiastical Ordinances*, but only after making several significant changes. With respect to the discipline of pastors, it added a note specifying that where civil crimes are in view, the pastors must be reported to the magistrates for punishment.[32] Where Calvin's initial draft implied a sharper separation between the spiritual authority of the elders and the civil authority of the magistrates than the Council desired, the latter amended the ordinances to specify that the elders are "to be sent or deputed by the Seigneury to the Consistory."[33] And the Council added several sentences emphasizing the spiritual nature of the Consistory's authority: "All this is to take place in such a way that the ministers have no civil jurisdiction, nor use anything but the spiritual sword of the Word of God, as Paul commands them; nor is the Consistory to derogate from the authority of the Seigneury or ordinary justice. The civil power is to remain unimpaired."[34] Thus the final law blurred Calvin's sharp distinctions between the church's ministry and the civil magistracy, ensuring that Genevan practice would be somewhat more complicated than Calvin's two kingdoms theology implied.[35] Most ominous for the future was the fact that the *Ecclesiastical Ordinances* never actually addressed the fundamental question of whether the Council or the Consistory had the final word on the excommunication of a particular individual. Given the compromise nature of the document, it was no doubt a deliberate omission.

The key to Calvin's eventual success in Geneva was the gradual establishment of a unified Company of Pastors and a unified Consistory, all committed to Calvin's vision of the church. Yet neither existed as such in 1542.[36] Some of the pastors were seeking to to persuade the magistrates to reject Calvin's model of discipline, secretly "exhorting them not to lay at our feet the power which was in their own hands

---

[31] "Draft Ecclesiastical Ordinances," 64–66.   [32] "Draft Ecclesiastical Ordinances," 61.

[33] "Draft Ecclesiastical Ordinances," 63. Cf. Gordon, *Calvin*, 127; Monter, *Calvin's Geneva*, 71. The elders were said to be *commis* (representatives) of the magistrates.

[34] "Draft Ecclesiastical Ordinances," 70–71. Eventually an oath was attached to the ordinances, through which the pastors promised to "to guard and maintain the honor and welfare of the Seigneury and the City" (72).

[35] Gordon, *Calvin*, 128. Naphy, "Calvin's Church in Geneva," 107–108, observes that "there was still much in the structure that developed in Geneva that was very 'Swiss.'" It "certainly was not a full realization of the 'sphere of independence' that Calvin sought for the church."

[36] Calvin testified to Oswald Myconius, the pastor of Basel: "Our other colleagues are rather a hindrance than a help to us: they are rude and self-conceited, have no zeal, and less learning. But what is worst of all, I cannot trust them, even although I very much wish that I could." Letter to Oswald Myconius, March 14, 1542; CO 11:377. Cited in Naphy, *Calvin and the Consolidation of the Genevan Reformation*, 54–55.

(as they said), not to abdicate the authority which God had intrusted to them, and not to give occasion to sedition." Yet while Calvin was not satisfied with the Consistory or the method of discipline as it was established in the *Ecclesiastical Ordinances*, it was the best he could hope for at the time. "We at length possess a Presbyterial Court [*presbyterorum iudicium*], such as it is, and a form of discipline, such as these disjointed times permit."[37]

During the next five years Calvin devoted himself to consolidating his influence on Geneva's pastors and elders. By 1545 his efforts began to bear fruit. The new pastors, men like Nicolas Des Gallars, Reymond Chauvet, Francois Bourgoing, and Michel Cop, were wealthier (and thus less dependent on the provision of the magistracy), better educated, more talented at preaching (and thus better equipped to challenge the magistrates), and zealously committed to reform. Crucially, all except one were French rather than Genevan, and they were devoted to the welfare of the church beyond the city-state.[38] Calvin also consolidated his control over the Consistory. This was a much more impressive achievement, because while the Company of Pastors was permitted to choose its own members, the Consistory's twelve elders were nominated by the Council and were themselves members of the city's various governing councils. They included one syndic, who was the presiding officer of the Consistory, and two other members of the Petit Conseil.[39] There is no evidence that they were strong supporters of Calvin when they were appointed as elders, but over time they became deeply committed to Calvin's vision of what church discipline should look like. By the late 1540s it was not easy for the magistrates to confront a body so unified that it could (and eventually did) threaten to resign *en masse* if necessary to protect its prerogatives.[40]

Although historians used to portray the Consistory as harsh, invasive, and even tyrannical, Robert Kingdon and others have revised that picture by studying the institution's extensive records.[41] In the early 1540s the Consistory focused on

---

[37] Letter to Oswald Myconius, March 14, 1542; CO 11:379. White is correct that Calvin's vision for discipline is best understood from the *Institutes*, because only there is it "untrammeled by the reality of Genevan politics (the church which he describes is independent of the apparatus of government)." White, "Oil and Vinegar," 35.

[38] Naphy, *Calvin and the Consolidation of the Genevan Reformation*, 72 (Cf. 59–68). The Council wanted to ordain Sebastien Castellio, but Calvin and the Company of Pastors refused.

[39] Of the other elders, four were to be drawn from the Soixante and six from the Deux Cents. In addition to the civil officer responsible to make sure people responded to the Consistory's summonses, the city provided a professional notary or secretary. Robert M. Kingdon, *Adultery and Divorce in John Calvin's Geneva* (Cambridge: Harvard University Press, 1995), 13–15.

[40] While the syndics and senators had a high turnover rate, the other elders served longer. By 1546–1547 the Consistory possessed eight elders who would serve for the next six years. Naphy, *Calvin and the Consolidation of the Genevan Reformation*, 75–79.

[41] Kingdon's work is summarized in numerous essays, many of which overlap in their content. See Kingdon, *Adultery and Divorce in Calvin's Geneva*; Kingdon, "Calvin and 'Presbytery'"; Robert M. Kingdon, "Anticlericalism in the Registers of the Geneva Consistory 1542–1564," in *Anticlericalism in Late Medieval and Early Modern Europe* (ed. Peter A. Dykema and Heiko

eliminating Catholic practices regarded as superstitious or idolatrous and ensuring the population's intelligent participation in worship and catechism. This entailed memorization of the Lord's Prayer and the Apostles' Creed and the regular attendance of children at catechism sessions. The Consistory also disciplined those who openly contradicted the teaching of the pastors, turning intransigent opponents over to the Council. In later years the elders and pastors devoted more attention to interpersonal conflict, violence, sexual immorality, and marital problems.[42] The records suggest that the Consistory was fairly effective in resolving disputes and bringing Genevans to repentance. Most cases ended with mere admonition or exhortation, though in some the Consistory required public displays of reconciliation or repentance. While a significant number of persons were temporarily barred from the Lord's Supper, hardly anyone was permanently excommunicated. Excommunicants could not marry, have their children baptized, or act as

A. Oberman; Leiden: Brill, 1993), 617–624; Robert M. Kingdon, "Social Control and Political Control in Calvin's Geneva," *Archive for Reformation History* (special volume, 1993), 521–532.; Robert M. Kingdon, "The Geneva Consistory in the Time of Calvin," *Calvinism in Europe, 1540–1620* (ed. Andrew Pettegree, Alastair Duke, and Gillian Lewis; Cambridge: Cambridge University Press, 1994), 21–34; Robert M. Kingdon, "A New View of Calvin in the Light of the Registers of the Geneva Consistory," *Calvinus Sincerioris Religionis Vindex: Calvin as Protector of the Purer Religion* (ed. Wilhelm H. Neuser and Brian G. Armstrong; Kirksville, MO: Sixteenth Century Journal, 1997), 21–33; Robert M. Kingdon, "Calvin and the Establishment of Consistory Discipline in Geneva: The Institution and the Men Who Directed It," *Nederlands archief voor kerkgeschiedenis* 10 (1990): 158–172; Kingdon, "Calvin's Socio-Political Legacy," 120–123; John Witte, Jr., and Robert M. Kingdon, *Sex, Marriage, and Family in John Calvin's Geneva: Courtship, Engagement, and Marriage* (Grand Rapids: Eerdmans, 2005). For other analyses, see Scott M. Manetsch, "Holy Terror or Pastoral Care: Church Discipline in Calvin's Geneva, 1542–1596," *Calvin: Saint or Sinner?* (ed. Herman Selderhuis; Tübingen: Mohr Siebeck, 2010), 283–306; William G. Naphy, "Calvin's Church in Geneva: Constructed or Gathered? Local or Foreign? French or Swiss?," *Calvin and His Influence, 1509–2009* (ed. Irena Backus and Philip Benedict; New York: Oxford University Press, 2011), 102–118; E. William Monter, "The Consistory of Geneva, 1559–1569," in *Renaissance, Reformation, Resurgence* (ed. Peter De Klerk; Grand Rapids: Calvin Theological Seminary, 1976), 63–84; Diane C. Margolf, "Calvin and Church Discipline: Penance, Apology, and Reconciliation," *John Calvin, Myth and Reality: Images and Impact of Geneva's Reformer* (ed. Amy Nelson Burnett; Eugene: Cascade Books, 2011), 53–66.

[42] Witte and Kingdon have shown that matters pertaining to sex and marriage encompassed nearly 60 percent of the Consistory's caseload. Witte and Kingdon, *Sex, Marriage, and Family in John Calvin's Geneva*, 74 (Cf. 71–77). These cases included conflicts among betrothed and married couples such as breach of promise, desertion, or unfaithfulness. The pastors and elders spent much of their time seeking reconciliation among those in conflict. Roughly half of the cases resulted in some sort of deferral to the Council because they involved a severe violation of the civil laws. Such deferrals reflected the conviction that marriage was not a sacrament but a covenant designed to secure the temporal ends of love, chastity, and procreation. As Witte and Kingdon put it, Calvin viewed marriage and sexuality as matters of the "earthly kingdom" rather than the "heavenly kingdom." It was the Consistory's responsibility to guide and discipline Christians according to the law of Christ, but when the civil laws were violated, the case properly fell to the civil jurisdiction (39; Cf. 27–40). The Consistory therefore cooperated with the Council, each case being assigned to the respective spiritual and temporal authority as was necessary, an excellent example of the distinction and cooperation of the two governments with respect to an institution that was temporal, but to which scripture was seen to speak with moral clarity. Witte and Kingdon correlate the process to Calvin's distinction between the civil and spiritual uses of the law (78–79).

godparents, and they were often (though not always) subject to social ostracism. Those few individuals who refused to repent after being banned from the Supper were turned over to the civil government, as were those guilty of civil crimes, and in the latter cases the Consistory offered an assessment of the evidence and a recommendation regarding appropriate punishment.

But such civil penalties were carefully distinguished from church discipline itself. The Consistory truly was a pastoral body, its officers serving as counselors, arbiters, and instructors to ordinary Genevan Christians. The records show pastors and elders exhibiting genuine concern for people and their problems, while emphasizing the importance of spiritual transformation expressed in outward repentance and communal solidarity. The elders regularly intervened on behalf of the poor or other vulnerable persons, rebuked fathers who abused their wives or children, and confronted sons who refused to provide for their aging parents. They disciplined landlords who took advantage of their tenants, doctors who were incompetent or took advantage of the sick, merchants who were guilty of price gouging or preventing economic competition, and employers who mistreated or failed to pay their workers. And they consistently tried to reconcile neighbors and family members involved in bitter disputes.[43] By all accounts, they had a salutary effect on Genevan society.[44]

But the pastors and elders of the Genevan church, especially Calvin, were involved in civil affairs to a greater extent than is implied by their particular spiritual functions. For instance, Calvin wrote a Marriage Ordinance for Geneva in 1545–1546, one that was eventually enacted as law in 1561. The ordinance rejected canon law provisions relative to nearly every dimension of marriage (not to mention the ideal of celibacy) from betrothal and formation to the possibility of divorce, turning to biblical and Roman sources to reform the institution and place it under the decisive authority of the civil magistracy.[45] In 1541–1542 Calvin was a member of the committee that revised Geneva's civil code, though Monter observes that "his

---

[43] Manetsch, "Holy Terror or Pastoral Care?" 300–305. Offering a judgment shared by most recent scholars of the institution, Scott Manetsch notes that the records "portray Geneva's ministers as conscientious pastors, concerned to protect their spiritual flock in a variety of important ways" (300). Valeri observes that about 5 percent of the 50–200 cases dealt with by the Consistory each year from 1542–1564 dealt with "commercial practices such as fraud, usury, price gouging, or hoarding" (128). Mark Valeri, "Religion, Discipline, and the Economy in Calvin's Geneva," *Sixteenth Century Journal* 28 (1997): 123–142. Cf. Jane Dempsey Douglass, "Calvin's Relation to Social and Economic Change," *Church and Society* 74 (1984): 75–81; W. Fred Graham, *The Constructive Revolutionary: John Calvin and His Socio-Economic Impact* (Richmond, VA: John Knox Press, 1971), 62–63; Jeffrey R. Watt, "Women and the Consistory in Calvin's Geneva," *Sixteenth Century Journal* 24 (1983): 429–439; Robert M. Kingdon, "Calvin and the Family: The Work of the Consistory in Geneva," *Pacific Theological Review* 17 (1984): 5–18. See also Calvin's Sermon on Deuteronomy 20:19–20; CO 27: 639–640; Sermon on Deuteronomy 22:1–4; CO 28:5–27; Sermon on Deuteronomy 24:14–18; CO 28: 196–197.

[44] See Kingdon, "Calvin's Socio-Political Legacy," 121.

[45] Witte and Kingdon, *Sex, Marriage, and Family in John Calvin's Geneva*, 38–48.

role was passive and really little more than clerical."[46] In addition, Calvin and the Consistory sometimes recommended particular policies or laws to Geneva's civil government.[47] But everyone agreed that neither the pastors nor the Consistory held legal or civil authority, and that it was the Council's responsibility to draft and enforce appropriate laws. What *was* part of the responsibility of the pastors was to call the civil authorities to make just laws in accord with the moral law of God, and what *was* part of the authority of the Consistory was to hold Christians accountable to that high standard, above and beyond what the civil law could enforce.

CONFRONTATION, CRISIS, AND TRIUMPH (1546–1555)

Despite the solidarity of Geneva's ecclesiastical government after 1546, Calvin continued to receive opposition from prominent citizens and skeptical civil magistrates. Because of the ambiguity of the *Ecclesiastical Ordinances* regarding the final authority over excommunication, many of the magistrates viewed the Consistory simply as a committee of the state, a judgment echoed by some recent historians but vigorously rejected by Calvin and his supporters.[48] In 1546 a series of high profile disputes fueled the opposition to Calvin and the Consistory.[49] The most important

[46] "The finished product, Geneva's 1543 edicts on offices and officials, was essentially a codification of current practices. The best political historians concur in the judgment that Geneva's fundamental political dispositions were in no way modified by them." Monter, *Calvin's Geneva*, 72.

[47] As Graham puts it, "Nothing seems to have been beneath his notice, and no duty too trivial for the Council to ask his advice." Graham, *The Constructive Revolutionary*, 157 (Cf. 110–144). Witte and Kingdon, *Sex, Marriage, and Family in John Calvin's Geneva*, 69–70.

[48] Naphy insists, "one cannot consider the struggle about excommunication purely as a clash between the church and its ministers, on the one hand, and the state and its magistrates, on the other. Instead, as I said, it is a question of jurisdiction in the institutional structure of the state between one magisterial body, the Consistory, and another, the Petit Conseil." Naphy, "Calvin's Church in Geneva," 108–109. "[T]he Consistory was as much an expression of state and magisterial power as it was of religious and ministerial authority" (111). Cf. Kingdon, "Calvin's Socio-Political Legacy," 120. Naphy's assessment reflects the way Calvin's opponents saw the situation, and it accurately describes the situation as it existed in the early years. The problem with Naphy's statement is that it prejudges what was an ongoing conflict between sharply divergent perspectives. Calvin and his supporters interpreted the conflict as a struggle for the integrity of Christ's spiritual government of his church, distinct from the civil government of the political kingdom. Naphy's argument ignores this dogmatic theological conception, articulated in Calvin's *Institutes*, commentaries, and sermons, and it ignores Calvin's belief that, during the later years, this conception *was* established in Geneva, if imperfectly. As Naphy himself puts it, "Calvin had little or no intention of adhering to the Swiss model; his vision of the correct relationship between the Church and State in Geneva differed radically from that of the magistrates who recalled him." Naphy, *Calvin and the Consolidation of the Genevan Reformation*, 222. Cf. Graham, *The Constructive Revolutionary*, 59–61; J. Wayne Baker, "Christian Discipline and the Early Reformed Tradition: Bullinger and Calvin," *Calviniana: Ideas and Influence of Jean Calvin* (ed. Robert V. Schnucker; Kirksville, MO: Sixteenth Century Journal, 1988), 107–119.

[49] These include the case of Pierre Ameaux, who publicly criticized Calvin's teaching and was required to undergo a public display of penance. Another was that of Jacques Gruet, who was found guilty of blasphemy and treason and was executed. Broader clashes revolved around a pastor's preaching against a theatrical play and an attempt by the magistrates, in response to the urging of the pastors, to replace the city's taverns with "abbayes" for Bible reading and other spiritual activities. Monter, *Calvin's*

of these was a set of clashes over moral offenses (fornication, dancing, playing games during the Eucharist) between the Consistory and the prominent Favre family. The Favres despised and frequently defied the authority of the Consistory, insisting that they were only accountable to citizens of Geneva who were duly elected as magistrates. In the short run, these challenges to the Consistory's authority failed, but they contributed to the rise of a faction of opposition to Calvin that would eventually be led by the son-in-law of Francois Favre, Ami Perrin.[50] The most divisive clash between the pastors and Genevan society took place when the pastors persuaded the city government to prohibit names associated with Catholic superstition, including some prominent family names associated with local saints. Because the pastors enforced the prohibition by refusing to baptize certain children or by applying Christian names without warning to infants presented for baptism, they repeatedly provoked disorder and rioting. The Consistory tried to use excommunication against the disorderly, but it was rebuked by the Council in 1547.[51]

The assertiveness of the unified Company and Consistory after 1546 seems to have surprised the magistrates. On at least two occasions, in 1548 and 1552, the Petit Conseil rebuked Calvin for specific comments he made in his sermons against the civil government.[52] For his part Calvin complained that the magistrates were insufficiently supportive of the Consistory's discipline, blaming their reluctance on pervasive libertinism.[53] But the real issue was whether the pastors and elders held the spiritual authority of discipline distinct from the civil authority of the magistrates.

That issue was increasingly tied up with the foreign identity of the pastors and the international character of the faction that supported them. The city was being

---

Geneva, 74–77; Naphy, *Calvin and the Consolidation of the Genevan Reformation*, 93–100; Kingdon, *Adultery and Divorce in John Calvin's Geneva*, 31–70.

[50] Kingdon, "Anticlericalism in the Registers of the Geneva Consistory," 617–623.

[51] Nevertheless, the Council continued to stand by the pastors when it came to the prohibition of certain names. Naphy, *Calvin and the Consolidation of the Genevan Reformation*, 146–148. As a rule, Geneva's pastors did not push the city in legal directions different from those of other European cities. Geneva's sumptuary laws had secular purposes and were typical of laws across Europe. What made Geneva unique, for the most part, was the level of enforcement. See Graham, *The Constructive Revolutionary*, 73–75, 110–112, 127–128, 133–141. Höpfl, *The Christian Polity of John Calvin*, 138, 188, 197–201; Monter, *Calvin's Geneva*, 152.

[52] The reformer sometimes criticized the government or leading individuals in terms that made it obvious to all what he was talking about. Naphy, *Calvin and the Consolidation of the Genevan Reformation*, 160. But such statements were rare. Even in his sermons on Deuteronomy, "Calvin was exceedingly sparing in direct comment on the domestic issues of the day, and his allusions to his own times are somewhat general and not very revealing." Höpfl, *The Christian Polity of John Calvin*, 145.

[53] Naphy lists examples from Calvin's letters. Naphy, *Calvin and the Consolidation of the Genevan Reformation*, 120 (footnote 183). In fact, the magistrates were not much more tolerant of immorality than was Calvin. Rather, "the overwhelming number of cases ... involved problems related to interpersonal disputes, not immorality as such. These cases put the Consistory in the position of being very intrusive in the private lives of many Genevans in an extremely public manner" (111). Cf. Commentary on the Psalms, Preface [1557]; CO 31:27.

inundated with refugees, a major source of discontentment among native Genevans.[54] While poorer refugees required greater aid, straining the city's budget, the more affluent refugees who began to arrive after 1549 provoked economic, social, religious, and eventually political competition.[55] In the late 1540s, the *Bourse Francaise* was established as an independent diaconate responsible for the material needs of French refugees. Unlike the General Hospital, it was operated solely by the deacons under the oversight of Calvin and the other pastors without any involvement from the civil magistrates, and its deacons were popularly regarded as deacons and ministers of the church. In that sense, as Jeannine Olson observes, while Calvin's attempt to sacralize the work of the General Hospital in certain respects failed, the *Bourse* "fit much more closely the ideal of an organization headed by officers of the church."[56] Indeed, in part because the refugee-oriented *Bourse* established international ties with Protestant refugees throughout western Europe, it was the *Bourse*, not the General Hospital, that most influenced the nature of the diaconate in Reformed churches outside of Geneva.[57]

By the early 1550s, the influx of refugees, many of whom were receiving bourgeois status in Geneva, threatened the balance of power. Sufficiently devoted to the faith to flee home and country in order to practice it, these refugees were accustomed to membership in a church that was not supported by the state, and they overwhelmingly supported Calvin's vision of the church and church discipline. They also tended to avoid full integration with Genevan society.[58]

In 1553 the faction of Genevans opposed to Calvin's influence, led by Ami Perrin, won control of the city government. The Perrinist government sought to weaken the Consistory by replacing some of its longstanding elders with men less sympathetic to Calvin's approach to discipline, ultimately replacing two-thirds of them. They also attempted to reduce admissions to bourgeois status.[59] It was at this tumultuous time that the famous heretic Michael Servetus arrived in Geneva. Servetus was notorious

[54] Naphy, *Calvin and the Consolidation of the Genevan Reformation*, 121.

[55] Already in the late 1530s, Geneva was providing considerable hospitality to thousands of foreigners passing through the city. After 1546 many refugees began to stay in Geneva. Naphy, *Calvin and the Consolidation of the Genevan Reformation*, 121–127. In 1535–1554, around 250 people were awarded bourgeois status, a relatively small number but a significant total when considered cumulatively in a city of only 10,000 inhabitants (127–138).

[56] Jeannine E. Olson, *Calvin and Social Welfare: Deacons and the Bourse Francaise* (London and Toronto: Associated University Presses, 1989), 32. This book is the authoritative study of the *Bourse Francaise*.

[57] Olson, *Calvin and Social Welfare*, 28; Jeannine E. Olson, *One Ministry Many Roles: Deacons and Deaconesses Through the Centuries* (St. Louis: Concordia, 1992). Cf. Tuininga, "Good News for the Poor," 221–247.

[58] In 1551 the Petit Conseil recommended that bourgeois residents be denied the vote for twenty-five years. The controversial proposal failed, but the magistrates did succeed in banning bourgeois pastors from the General Council. Naphy, *Calvin and the Consolidation of the Genevan Reformation*, 127–138.

[59] Naphy, *Calvin and the Consolidation of the Genevan Reformation*, 176–178.

throughout Christendom for his vigorous public rejection of the orthodox doctrine of the Trinity. When he was recognized at a sermon in Geneva, Calvin did not hesitate to accuse him before the Council and personally led the effort to secure his conviction and subsequent capital punishment. But the trial was entirely a civil affair. Servetus never appeared before the Consistory.[60]

When Geneva executed Servetus, it did what many cities in Europe would have done, Protestant and Catholic alike. Protestant leaders were eager to demonstrate that Protestantism was orthodox and had an answer to the dangerous proliferation of theological anarchy and heresy.[61] But Servetus was the only person ever executed for heresy in Reformation Geneva.[62] Like Strasbourg, but in sharp contrast to Basel, Zurich, and Berne, Geneva refused to subject Anabaptists and other less radical dissenters to capital punishment, preferring to banish them instead.[63] As a humanist-trained lawyer, Calvin was no doubt surprised that his support for the execution of Servetus came under such heavy criticism. That heresy should be punished by death was embedded in the Justinian Code, which was the basis for European civil law for a thousand years and was commonly seen as a reliable reflection of natural law.[64]

Calvin's sharpest critics came from the circle of humanist writers gathered in Basel, many of whom were Italian refugees like Servetus and sympathetic to his theology. The most important was Sebastien Castellio.[65] Calvin responded to these critics in his *Defense of the Orthodox Faith against the Errors of Michel Servetus* in 1554.[66] While the emphasis of the work was on Servetus's theological errors, it began with a passionate defense of the obligation of civil government to suppress open heresy. Calvin acknowledged that this obligation was commonly abused, but he

[60] Calvin had made his intentions quite clear to Farel in advance. "[I]f he shall come, I shall never permit him to depart alive, provided my authority [*mea autoritas*] be of any avail." Letter 154, to Farel, February 13, 1546; CO 12:282–284. Cf. Letter to Sulzer, September 8, 1553; CO 14:614–616.

[61] Calvin sought to spare Servetus from being burned at the stake, but his appeal was rejected. Monter, *Calvin's Geneva*, 82–83; Baker, "Christian Discipline, Church and State, and Toleration," 44–48. Cf. Marian Hillar and Claire S. Allen, *Michael Servetus: Intellectual Giant, Humanist, and Martyr* (Lanham, MD: University Press of America, 2002); Eric Kayayan, "The Case of Michael Servetus," *Mid-America Journal of Theology* 8 (1992): 117–146; Jerome Friedman, *Michael Servetus: A Case Study in Total Heresy* (Geneva: Droz, 1978).

[62] In 1542–1564, 139 felons were executed in Geneva; only Servetus was executed for heresy. See William E. Monter, "Crime and Punishment in Calvin's Geneva, 1562," *Archive for Reformation History* 64 (1973): 281–287, 281.

[63] That was not because there were no other heresy trials. On the contrary, a number of Anabaptists were arrested and tried for their theological teachings. Balke, *Calvin and the Anabaptist Radicals*, 37, 80–93, 195. Several pastors and teachers, the most famous of whom was Sebastien Castellio, were exiled from the city. Geneva was criticized by the Swiss cities for being too harsh in the case of Jerome Bolsec, who in 1551 challenged Calvin's teaching on predestination. The Geneva council banished Bolsec, and he found refuge in Berne. Gordon, *Calvin*, 205–210; Naphy, *Calvin and the Consolidation of the Genevan Reformation*, 171–172; Baker, "Christian Discipline, Church and State, and Toleration," 38–40.

[64] Mark J. Larson, *Calvin's Doctrine of the State: A Reformed Doctrine and Its American Trajectory, The Revolutionary War, and the Founding of the Republic* (Eugene, OR: Wipf and Stock, 2009), 85.

[65] Baker, "Christian Discipline, Church and State, and Toleration," 44–48.

[66] See Hillar, *Michael Servetus*, 190–201, as well as Chapter 8.

insisted that when truth is widely and publicly recognized as being beyond dispute, it must be defended by civil magistrates, especially when a matter of such fundamental importance as religion is at stake.[67] "How will the religion persist, how will one be able to recognize the true Church, what will indeed Christ himself be, if the doctrine of piety becomes uncertain and doubtful?"[68] He would revisit the issue vigorously in his sermons on Deuteronomy, which he began to preach in March 1555, and again in his 1563 commentary on the books of Moses.[69]

Just as important for Calvin's legacy in Geneva was the growing number of individuals willing to challenge the authority of the Consistory in 1553. The decisive case became that of Philibert Berthelier. Berthelier struck the Consistory at its most vulnerable point: the ambiguity of the *Ecclesiastical Ordinances* regarding the ultimate authority over excommunication. Accused of sin, Berthelier appeared penitently before the Petit Conseil and asked that his excommunication be lifted. The Petit Conseil, without consulting with the Consistory, declared him eligible for communion. Calvin and the pastors were furious. In an echo of the confrontation of 1538, they declared that they could not tolerate this usurpation of the Consistory's spiritual power, and that they would accept death rather than serve Berthelier communion. The Council, stunned, sought to avoid confrontation by advising Berthelier to refrain voluntarily from the Supper. The Petit Conseil and the Deux Cents then declared that the Petit Conseil had concurrent jurisdiction over church discipline with the Consistory and could overturn sentences of excommunication.[70]

This left an impasse, with Calvin and the Consistory refusing to administer communion to excommunicants and the civil government maintaining its claims but unwilling to force the collective resignation of the pastors. In early 1555 the various councils agreed to deliberate once again, asking Calvin to make his case

---

[67] Gordon, *Calvin*, 224–228; Christoph Strohm, "Calvin and Religious Tolerance," *John Calvin's Impact on Church and Society* (ed. Martin Ernst Hirzel and Martin Smallmann; Grand Rapids: Eerdmans, 2009), 184–186.

[68] Cited in Strohm, "Calvin and Religious Tolerance," 185. CO 8:464. Soon after Castellio published his *Concerning Heretics and Whether They Are to Be Persecuted*, a systematic refutation of the use of force against heresy. See Hans R. Guggisberg, *Sebastian Castellio, 1515–1563: Humanist and Defender of Religious Toleration in a Confessional Age* (trans. Bruce Gordon; Burlington, VT: Ashgate, 2003). This time Calvin entrusted his French protegé Theodore Beza with writing a response, and Beza's *Antibellius* appeared in September 1554. Gordon, *Calvin*, 228–231.

[69] See analysis in Chapter 8.

[70] The Council sent letters requesting advice to the magistrates of Berne, Zurich, Basel, and Schaffhausen, while Calvin sent his own pleading letters to the pastors of those cities. The response was mixed, generally reflecting the Swiss cities' commitment to magisterial control over discipline, but hardly favorable to a purge of the pastors. Bullinger's influence in leading Zurich to support the status quo (without committing itself theologically) was pivotal. It was also ironic, given his fundamental rejection of Calvin's position. Kingdon, "Social Control and Political Control in Calvin's Geneva," 523–526; Naphy, *Calvin and the Consolidation of the Genevan Reformation*, 184–185; Baker, "Christian Discipline and the Early Reformed Tradition," 115–118; Baker, "Christian Discipline, Church and State, and Toleration," 40–44.

from scripture for autonomous church discipline. The result was a decisive victory for Calvin, as the Soixante (Council of Sixty) and Deux Cents overruled the Petit Conseil in favor of Calvin. The councils reaffirmed the order of discipline found in the *Ecclesiastical Ordinances*, but they now clarified for the first time that the Consistory's authority over church discipline was supreme. Excommunicants had no right of appeal to civil authority. Calvin thus won the autonomy of the church in what he believed was a fundamental expression of Christ's spiritual kingdom, the exercise of spiritual discipline by elders and pastors.[71]

The elections of 1555 produced a decisive shift in power toward Calvin's political supporters. The new government immediately admitted a large number of French refugees to bourgeois status. It took political and legal action against more than fifty Perrinists, several of whom were executed as a result of an allegedly treasonous riot on May 16.[72] They were charged with conspiring "to propose the abolition of the Consistory by the general assembly" and seeking to "destroy the ecclesiastical discipline and the Reformation, principally the ordinances of 1541."[73]

Although it was not evident at the time, the events of 1555 permanently secured Calvin's position in Geneva. From this point on, there was a marked stability in Genevan politics, with no major changes in leadership through the rest of Calvin's life. Many of the new magistrates were former elders who were devoted to Calvin's vision of the church.[74] In 1560 the magistrates legislated an important symbolic shift in the makeup of the Consistory, declaring that from now on elders could be chosen from among the foreign born and that when the syndic presided over the Consistory, he was no longer to carry his official baton, the sign of his magisterial office.[75] Both changes served to clarify the distinction between spiritual and temporal government in Calvin's Geneva. A similar, if less pronounced, shift took place with respect to Geneva's diaconate. Although the pastors were supposed to have the same role in the selection of procurators and hospitallers as they did of elders, they were rarely as involved.[76] Indeed, Calvin repeatedly criticized Genevans' tendency to view the

---

[71] Kingdon, "Social Control and Political Control in Calvin's Geneva," 527.

[72] By this time popular resentment toward the pro-Bernese Perrinist faction was growing. In 1554 a series of high profile displays of immorality shocked the city, and on January 27, 1555, three days after the councils affirmed his position on church discipline, Calvin preached sharply against moral and civil laxity. Naphy, *Calvin and the Consolidation of the Genevan Reformation*, 187–194.

[73] Monter, *Calvin's Geneva*, 88. The harsh suppression of the Perrinists did not please the Swiss cities. But as Gordon writes, "The Bernese church, for Calvin, was the anti-model of the Reformation, an object lesson in the consequences of permitting civil rulers, untrained in exposition of scripture, to interfere in spiritual matters." Gordon, *Calvin*, 216. Cf. Naphy, *Calvin and the Consolidation of the Genevan Reformation*, 197.

[74] Naphy, *Calvin and the Consolidation of the Genevan Reformation*, 212, 217, 221, 228.

[75] Monter, *Calvin's Geneva*, 139; Höpfl, *The Christian Polity of John Calvin*, 152. Cf. Baker, "Christian Discipline and the Early Reformed Tradition," 119; Manetsch, "Holy Terror or Pastoral Care?" 290–297.

[76] Kingdon argues that the diaconate was "a kind of standing committee or department of the city government." Kingdon, "Social Welfare in Calvin's Geneva," 56–57. Cf. Kingdon, "The Deacons of the Reformed Church in Calvin's Geneva," 84.

deacons as secular or political officials rather than as spiritual ministers of the church. But around 1561–1562, the Council finally began to select nominees for the office of deacon, like that of elder, in close consultation with the pastors.[77]

Years of preaching, discipline, catechesis, and immigration had had their effect. Geneva's reformation was solidifying along distinctly Calvinist lines, according to Calvin's two kingdoms theology, in sharp contrast to the other Swiss Reformed cities. Calvin had implemented his model of a genuinely Reformed, autonomous church, albeit it one fostered by a supportive state, and he was increasingly absorbed in seeing that model embraced abroad. His heart was especially set on a land where there was no religious uniformity and no supportive state: his native land of France.

GENEVA AND THE FRENCH REFORMED CHURCHES

The struggle to establish church discipline in Geneva was paralleled by a less successful struggle in the lands north of Geneva that had been conquered by Berne in 1536, the Pays de Vaud. Here Berne was sovereign, but the inhabitants were French-speaking and therefore culturally closer to Geneva. In 1537 the Lausanne Academy was established in the Pays de Vaud as the only French-speaking institution for the training of pastors in Europe. The school eventually trained hundreds of students, including key figures like Pierre Viret, Theodore Beza, Marthrin Courdier, Francois Hotman and Conrad Gessner, who stood solidly with Calvin in favor of church discipline. Although Berne had established consistories charged with the discipline of morals in the Pays de Vaud, these courts were not viewed as ecclesiastical bodies, and they could not administer excommunication. Viret was lobbying in Berne for church discipline but to no effect.[78]

By 1547 the Vaud pastors were dividing into two factions, with a Calvinist faction led by Viret and a pro-Berne faction led by Andre Zebedee.[79] In 1549 the Bernese city council abolished the weekly colloquies of pastors and professors that met in Lausanne. Viret and the pastors continued to press for church discipline, but when the pastors postponed the sacrament of the Lord's Supper without permission from Berne, claiming that its authorized visitation of the population was incomplete, the city cracked down. It expelled Viret and at least fourteen other pastors and

---

[77] Kingdon, "The Deacons of the Reformed Church in Calvin's Geneva," 85–87; Kingdon, "Social Welfare in Calvin's Geneva," 62–63; Monter, *Calvin's Geneva*, 139.

[78] Calvin complained to Viret that the Bernese opposed "the very things – excommunication, more frequent celebration of the Supper, and many other things – that we want and desire to be restored." Bruening, *Calvinism's First Battleground*, 180. For a thorough analysis of Viret's political thought see Robert Dean Linder, *The Political Ideas of Pierre Viret* (Geneva: Librairie Droz, 1964).

[79] That year Viret published *De la vertu et usage du ministere de la Parolle de Dieu et des sacraments*, in which he defended church discipline and the Calvinist view of the Lord's Supper while arguing that the civil government's role in ecclesiastical affairs should be limited. Bruening, *Calvinism's First Battleground*, 184–185.

closed the Lausanne Academy, driving several of its professors and many of its
students to Geneva, where the Academy of Geneva had been established under
Theodore Beza.[80]

Michael Bruening argues that it was in the struggle over the Pays de Vaud that
Calvin emerged as a regional leader beyond the walls of Geneva and that Calvinism
emerged as a theological and ecclesiological identity distinct from that of Zwingli,
Bullinger, and the Swiss Reformed.[81] At the same time, defeat in the Pays de Vaud
turned Calvin's eyes westward toward France, redirecting his energies from what
magistrates could enact to what could be accomplished under conditions of persecution. Echoing Heiko Oberman, Bruening writes, "If the French nation was to be
reformed, it would have to take place through the movement of refugees and the
illegal establishment of churches in the realm. In 1550, political Calvinism had
failed. The Reformation of the Refugees had just begun."[82]

During its first few decades, French Protestantism was subject to a variety
of influences including French humanism, Lutheranism, and Martin Bucer.
The churches were variously organized and were not unified. After the Placards
Affair of October 1534, they were subject to persecution by the French crown.
Persecution reached a high point toward the end of Francis II's reign in the mid-
1540s, but it would continue during the reign of Henri II (1547–1559). Approximately
500 individuals were put to death for heresy in France between 1523 and 1560.[83]

By the 1540s Calvin's writings were spreading throughout France, and around two-
thirds of the books censured by the Sorbonne were from Geneva. Geneva soon
emerged as the major printing center for the Reformation in France.[84] By the time
Strasbourg became Lutheran in 1547, when French refugees began to pour into
Geneva, Geneva's influence over French Protestantism was unrivaled. In addition

---

[80] Bruening, *Calvinism's First Battleground*, 211–255. In 1558 Viret and the pastors sent a new proposal to
Berne that included a discussion of the difference between civil magistrates and ecclesiastical order.
They rejected the Zwinglian argument that excommunication was appropriate for the early church
but not for Christians living under Christian rulers (247). Cf. Robert M. Kingdon, *Geneva and the
Coming of the Wars of Religion in France 1555–1563* (Geneva: Librairie Droz, 2007 [1956]), 15, 20–22;
Karin Maag, *Seminary or University?: The Genevan Academy and Reformed Higher Education,
1560–1620* (Brookfield, VT: Ashgate, 1995).

[81] Bruening, *Calvinism's First Battleground*, 2. Bruening agrees with Heiko Oberman's provocative thesis
regarding Calvin's focus on a "Reformation of the Refugees," but suggests that it was only after the
reformation in Vaud failed that Calvin focused his attention on France. *Calvinism's First Battleground*,
6.

[82] Bruening, *Calvinism's First Battleground*, 209 (Cf. 207–209).

[83] Gordon, *Calvin*, 308; Benedict, *Christ's Churches Purely Reformed*, 133.

[84] Sunshine, *Reforming French Protestantism*, 20. As Gordon has noted, "Calvin's was the voice of French
reform." Gordon, *Calvin*, 304. Genevan publishing reached a peak during the last few years of Calvin's
life in the early 1560s. Most of the master printers were French and much of the funding for the work
came from Frenchmen. Monter, *Calvin's Geneva*, 179–181. Geneva's magistrates worked closely with
the pastors to oversee the work of the printing presses. Kingdon, *Geneva and the Coming of the Wars of
Religion in France*, 93–103.

to the massive flow of literature, Genevan records show that at least 220 pastors were trained in Geneva and sent to France. Some 1,240 churches were organized in the kingdom during 1555–1570, most of them in 1559–1562. It has been estimated that approximately 1.5 to 2 million people became Reformed Protestants, about 10 percent of the population of France, with disproportionately high numbers coming from the nobility and literate classes.[85]

Pastors trained in Lausanne and Geneva and devoted to Calvin's understanding of the church began to flood into France in 1557, playing leading roles in the development of French Reformed ecclesiology and discipline. The Company of Pastors directed the whole process, often acting secretively so as to avoid implicating the city government in actions sure to upset the French monarchy.[86] In 1557 Calvin appeared before the Petit Conseil, requesting permission to send pastors to the church in Paris and "begging them to grant this request without inquiring further since these things if very secret would be less dangerous."[87] It was shrewd advice. In 1561 the King complained to the city about its actions, requesting that the pastors sent from Geneva and causing trouble in France be recalled. The Council replied that it had not sent any pastors to France, which was, strictly speaking, correct, as it was the Company that sent the pastors. However, by 1562 the Council was openly authorizing pastors to go to France.[88] Geneva did not control the French churches, but, especially early on, the Genevan church did serve as a court of appeals for theological and disciplinary disputes in France. Genevan pastors were in constant contact with the French churches, and even after the establishment of the French National Synod, churches and synods continued to ask Geneva for advice on matters pertaining to discipline, the Consistory, and the diaconate.[89]

---

[85] Benedict, *Christ's Churches Purely Reformed*, 134–137. The chief source on Geneva's role in training these pastors and sending them to France is the classic by Kingdon, *Geneva and the Coming of the Wars of Religion in France 1555–1563*. For the best analysis of the effect of Geneva's printing presses in France, see Andrew Pettegree, *The French Book and the European World* (Leiden: Brill, 2007), 89–106. In 1559, Genevan texts made up 78 percent of the Protestant texts printed in the French language (99–100).

[86] Geneva paid the professors' salaries and provided for the families of some of the student-pastors who were dispatched temporarily to France. The students were also provided apprenticeships in Geneva, which exposed them to Calvinist ecclesiology and church discipline. Kingdon, *Geneva and the Coming of the Wars of Religion in France*, 14–22. Cf. Peter Wilcox, "'The Progress of the Kingdom of Christ' in Calvin's Exposition of the Prophets," in *Calvinus Sincerioris Religionis Vindex* (Kirksville: Sixteenth Century Journal, 1997), 315–322; David Willis-Watkins, "Calvin's Prophetic Reinterpretation of Kingship," *Probing the Reformed Tradition* (ed. Elsie Anne McKee and Brian Armstrong; Louisville: Westminster/John Knox, 1989), 116–134, 127–128.

[87] Kingdon, *Geneva and the Coming of the Wars of Religion in France*, 34. The pastors were usually dispatched to specific congregations after having been examined by the Company of Pastors in Geneva (25–29).

[88] Kingdon, *Geneva and the Coming of the Wars of Religion in France*, 31–35.

[89] Kingdon, *Geneva and the Coming of the Wars of Religion in France*, 43–47. Kingdon now admits that *Geneva and the Coming of the Wars of Religion in France*, while accurate in its presentation of the evidence, exaggerates the level of control that Geneva held over the French churches.

Although Calvin's theology in general had a profound influence on French Protestantism, it was his political theology, so uniquely applicable to a context in which state and church were separated, that distinctly shaped the French church. In contrast to Melanchthon or Bullinger, Calvin stressed the distinction between the church and the political order, and he provided a model for a range of autonomous church government functions through the offices of pastor, elder, and deacon. Protestants among the nobility often embraced Calvin's theology in abstraction from his ecclesiology, seeking to maintain social and political authority within the church, but for those churches that did not meet under noble leadership (probably around half of the total), Calvin's model of church government was a godsend. In addition to the features already described, it offered a basis for national cohesion by assuming parity among congregations and pastors. The first national synod of the French Reformed Church, meeting in Paris in 1559, operated under decisive Calvinist influence. Its president, Francois Morel, and its leading figure, Antoine de la Roche Chandieu, had both been trained in Geneva.[90]

The Synod adopted the French *Confession of Faith*, which follows Calvin's theology closely.[91] Implicitly invoking Calvin's two kingdoms distinction, the preface declares to the King that Christ, "having given you power over our property, our bodies, and even our lives, demands that the control and dominion of our souls and consciences, which he purchased with his own blood, be reserved to him." Insisting that the Reformed church had in it "no rebellion or heresy whatsoever," the delegates maintained, "For nothing will be seen but what is decent and well-ordered, and nothing will be heard but the praise of God, exhortations to his service, and prayers for the preservation of your Majesty and your kingdom." In this way "we may thus be permitted, in serving your Majesty, to serve him who has raised you to your power and dignity."[92]

[90] Sunshine, *Reforming French Protestantism*, 21–26.

[91] The confession may have been influenced by one written by Calvin in 1557. Kingdon, *Geneva and the Coming of the Wars of Religion in France*, 46; Sunshine, *Reforming French Protestantism*, 27; Brian G. Armstrong, *Calvin and the Amyraut Heresy: Protestant Scholasticism and Humanism in Seventeenth-Century France* (Madison: University of Wisconsin Press, 1969), 25–30. On substance, it followed Calvin closely. With respect to the government of the church, the confession declares, "we believe that the order of the Church, established by his authority, ought to be sacred and inviolable" (Article 25). It emphasizes that all Christians are responsible to join themselves to the ministry and discipline of the true church "even if the magistrates and edicts are contrary to it"(Article 26). See "The French Confession of Faith. AD 1559," in *Reformed Confessions of the 16th Century* (ed. Arthur C. Cochrane; Philadelphia: The Westminster Press, 1966), 137–158.

[92] "French Confession of Faith," 141–143. The confession declares that God has given magistrates the sword "to suppress crimes against the first as well as against the second table of the Commandments of God." Magisterial authority is inviolable "even if they are unbelievers, provided that the sovereign empire of God remain intact." The confession opposes "all those who would like to reject authority, to establish community and confusion of property, and overthrow the order of justice" (Article 40). The 1559 Synod actually affirmed that heretics should be put to death by the civil magistrates. Kingdon, *Geneva and the Coming of the Wars of Religion in France*, 46.

The confession goes on to identify the preaching of the word and the administration of the sacraments as the two marks of the true church (Article 28), but like Calvin it also stresses the vital significance of discipline and poor relief as expressions of Christ's rule:

> As to the true Church, we believe that it should be governed according to the order established by our Lord Jesus Christ. That there should be pastors, overseers, and deacons, so that true doctrine may have its course, that errors may be corrected and suppressed, and the poor and all who are in affliction may be helped in their necessities (Article 29).

Church order may not bind the conscience, must always promote concord and obedience, and may never contradict scripture. The confession declares excommunication, appointed by Christ, to be "necessary" (Article 33), and it adheres closely to the Calvinist view of the Lord's Supper as a manifestation of the union of believers in Christ (Article 36). It rejects episcopacy, following Calvin in declaring all pastors to "have the same authority and equal power under one head, one only sovereign and universal bishop, Jesus Christ" (Article 31).[93]

The French confession thus owed much to Calvin, but the distinctive legacy of the French Reformed Church was to work out Calvin's ecclesiological principles in a national context where the church was separated from the state. This application was codified in the *Discipline Ecclésiastique* of 1559. Adapted and revised over the years, it eventually called for four distinct levels of church government: the local congregation, the colloquy, the provincial synod, and the national synod. The synodical or presbyterian system established by the French, built on the rejection of centralized control by magistrates or bishops, may have been the first thoroughly non-hierarchical system of church government in history.[94]

There were differences between church government as it functioned in the French Reformed Church and in Geneva, not the least of which pertained to the nature of the consistory. On the one hand, given the lack of magisterial control over the church, elders were neither magistrates nor chosen by the magistrates. On the other hand, for the same reason consistories became responsible for much more than just discipline,

[93] Sunshine, *Reforming French Protestantism*, 28, notes that Calvin did not reject episcopacy as long as it was not too hierarchical. The French church, however, would take equality between ministers and the autonomy of local congregations to a whole new level. Cf. Sunshine, "Reformed Theology and the Origins of Synodical Polity," 141–148.

[94] Sunshine notes, "Perhaps the greatest challenge in the Discipline was to develop a system of collective church government that would unite the disparate Protestant churches in the kingdom without the support of the magistrate and in the totally unprecedented absence of any form of hierarchical relationships between the churches." Sunshine, *Reforming French Protestantism*, 31 (Cf. 32–39). On Jean Morély's defence of a congregationalist model of church government see Gordon, *Calvin*, 326; Robert M. Kingdon, *Geneva and the Consolidation of the French Protestant Movement 1564–1572* (Madison, WI: University of Wisconsin Press, 1967), 43–137; Sunshine, *Reforming French Protestantism*, 83–90.

taking up some of the administrative tasks that in Geneva were performed by the Council, though in theory, such administrative matters were supposed to be dealt with at different meetings from those that handled discipline.[95] But the French church remained committed to the Calvinist understanding of church discipline. When the French learned in 1572 that Thomas Erastus was vigorously advocating magisterial control over the church and rejecting church discipline at Heidelberg, the national synod declared that it "rejects the error of the said Doctor [Erastus] and of all others who wish to abolish the Discipline of the Church, confusing it with the civil and political government of the Magistrates."[96]

In areas where the lesser magistrates were Protestants, the churches tried to clarify the proper relationship between the two kingdoms. In some places there were even localized magisterial reformations similar to that of Geneva.[97] More common was the situation of churches under Catholic magistrates. In these territories, churches sought to maintain their autonomy while securing legal status as corporations.[98] In the interests of churches seeking to maintain such status, the national synod sought to avoid addressing matters that were civil rather than ecclesiastical. The Synod of Lyons in 1563 carefully distinguished the authority of magistrates over pastors relative to civil matters from the authority of classes and synods in spiritual matters.[99]

[95] Sunshine, *Reforming French Protestantism*, 120–142. This distinction of tasks reflects the implicit distinction between spiritual government and the administration of mundane ecclesiastical affairs. The French churches also expanded the role of the diaconate. Deacons served on consistories, were delegates to synods, carried out liturgical functions, taught, catechized, and exercised discipline. Elders often supervised or assisted the deacons' charitable functions. Despite the efforts of synods to prevent it, over time the two offices essentially collapsed into one (94–119, 138–142). Cf. Glenn S. Sunshine, "Geneva Meets Rome: The Development of the French Reformed Diaconate," *Sixteenth Century Journal* 26 (1995): 329–346; Raymond A. Mentzer, "Acting on Calvin's Ideas: The Church in France," *Calvin and the Church* (ed. David Foxgrover; Grand Rapids: CRC, 2002), 29–41.

[96] Brian G. Armstrong, "*Semper Reformanda*: The Case of the French Reformed Church, 1559–1620," *Later Calvinism: International Perspectives* (ed. Fred Graham; Kirksville, MO: Sixteenth Century Journal, 1994), 119–140, 126–127. Up to half of the Protestant churches in France did not participate in the synodical structure but operated under the authority of the nobility. The political and military party known as the Huguenots was led by these nobility and not the pastors, elders and deacons of the Reformed church. Sunshine, *Reforming French Protestantism*, 31, 46.

[97] Kingdon, *Geneva and the Coming of the Wars of Religion in France*, 86–87; Benedict, *Christ's Churches Purely Reformed*, 143–145; Sunshine, *Reforming French Protestantism*, 149, 157–158.

[98] "The *droit des corps* gave corporations the right to regulate their own affairs within the bounds of the legitimate interests of the *corps*. In other words, by assuming the *droit des corps* applied to them, the churches could freely regulate internal matters of faith and discipline. On the other hand, the *droit des corps* also gave royal officers the right to oversee the corporation (in this case, the church and specifically the consistory) to make sure it did not regulate matters which were beyond its rightful interests." Sunshine, *Reforming French Protestantism*, 150.

[99] Sunshine, *Reforming French Protestantism*, 151–155. Sunshine quotes the Synod of Lyons: "[T]he office of ministers is to govern their flock according to the Word of God and the *Discipline ecclésiastique*, and it is the magistrate's task to see that all estates, even the ministers, walk roundly and rightly in their callings. And in those areas where the ministers fail, they are to have them admonished according to the order of the *Discipline ecclésiastique* by *classes* and synods, not intending this in any way to include faults punishable by the laws which are the jurisdiction of the magistrate" (152)

Philip Benedict argues that the French Reformed movement "epitomized more unmistakably than any other a Reformed church that regulated its internal affairs and carried out its disciplinary tasks independently of the secular authorities." The wars of religion taught them to rely on their own resources, operate autonomously, and distance themselves from civil government.[100] Circumstances made much of this innovation necessary, but there is little question that it was the ecclesiology that arose from Calvin's two kingdoms paradigm that offered the model French Protestants so desperately needed. The establishment of a vibrant French Reformed church, with its autonomous system of government separate from the state, demonstrates how appropriate Calvin's political theology was for conditions where competition between multiple religious groups made the existence of a *corpus Christianum* impossible. It suggests the particular usefulness of Calvin's two kingdoms theology for circumstances of religious pluralism.

The impact and limits of Calvin's political theology can also be discerned in the way the French Reformed churches responded to persecution and war in the 1550s and 1560s. Before 1562 Calvin and the other Genevan pastors urged the French Protestants to act with circumspection and subtlety, preserving the gospel from the slander that would accompany its association with disorder. Calvin worked hard at building relationships with leading French men and women, and the effort was remarkably successful. By the late 1550s a substantial portion of the nobility (ranging from 10–40 percent, depending on the area) supported the Reformation, including such high profile figures as Jeanne d'Albret, the Queen of Navarre (a niece of Francis I and the wife of Antoine of Bourbon, the First Prince of the Blood); Louis, the Prince of Condé (as Antoine's brother, also a prince of the blood); and Gaspard de Coligny, the Admiral of France.[101]

Nevertheless, inspired in part by Calvin's justification of resistance to tyranny by lower magistrates, some of the lesser nobles became involved in a series of plots, the most significant of which was the disastrous Conspiracy of Amboise of 1560. The alleged justification for this conspiracy had to do with the informal regency that was established during the teenage years of Francis II. The Bourbon family, led by Antoine of Navarre, was closest to the throne by blood and was therefore widely regarded as having the right to a leading role in the regency. But the regency was instead dominated by the Catholic House of Guise, who used their power to reinvigorate the persecution of Protestants.[102] The plot was the brainchild of

---

[100] Benedict, *Christ's Churches Purely Reformed*, 148.

[101] Kingdon, *Geneva and the Coming of the Wars of Religion in France*, 54–64; R.J. Knecht, *The French Wars of Religion 1559–1598* (2nd ed; New York: Longman, 1996 [1989]), 6–15; Benedict, *Christ's Churches Purely Reformed*, 137–139.

[102] Knecht, *The French Wars of Religion*, 20–23. On Calvin and the Amboise Conspiracy see N. M. Sutherland, "Calvinism and the Conspiracy of Amboise," *History* 47:160 (1962): 111–138.

a lesser nobleman, Jean du Barry, Sieur de La Renaudie. La Renaudie requested the support of Geneva's pastors, and while a number of figures claimed that Calvin did support it, the reformer consistently denied this, insisting that he had warned that the conspiracy would be disastrous. Calvin admitted that he had told the conspirators he would not oppose their campaign if it was led by Antoine de Bourbon, the first Prince of the Blood, "who ought to be chief of the Council of the King according to the laws of France."[103] But the campaign never attracted such high level leadership. Although some of Geneva's pastors seem to have supported the plot, including François Hotman and Theodore Beza,[104] most of the Reformed churches in France followed Calvin and refused to support anything smacking of sedition.[105]

When Francis II died it became necessary to establish an official regency for his ten-year old heir, Charles IX. By custom this regency should have belonged to Antoine de Bourbon, but this was deemed impossible because his family was Protestant. The result was that the Queen mother, Catherine de Médici, assumed the official regency. Catherine persuaded Antoine to sign a private agreement waiving his right to the regency and demonstrated leniency to his Protestant family. She gradually relaxed enforcement of anti-Protestant legislation, even tolerating private religious assemblies. In the Edict of January (1562) she granted Protestants limited freedom of worship for the first time, permitting worship in the rural territories of the nobility but not in the towns and cities where most other Protestant churches were.[106] The new period of toleration induced a new boldness

---

[103] Calvin claimed he had warned that "from a single drop [of blood] would immediately flow streams that would inundate France." Letter to Peter Martyr Vermigli, May 5, 1560; CO 18:82. Cf. John T. McNeill, "John Calvin on Civil Government," *Calvinism and the Political Order* (ed. George L. Hunt; Philadelphia: Westminster, 1965), 27–29. Kingdon suggests that Calvin would have been satisfied had the Prince of Condé been more actively involved. When Condé did lead a revolt in 1562, Calvin supported his cause wholeheartedly. Kingdon, *Geneva and the Coming of the Wars of Religion in France*, 68–69; Knecht, *The French Wars of Religion*, 22–25.

[104] In his *On the Authority of the Magistrate in the Punishment of Heretics*, which Calvin warmly approved, Beza argued that lesser magistrates have the right to defy their superiors on religious matters. Hotman and Beza became leading theorists of the right to resistance. Kingdon, *Geneva and the Coming of the Wars of Religion in France*, 68–72; Knecht, *The French Wars of Religion*, 24. On Beza, see Tadataka Maruyama, *The Ecclesiology of Theodore Beza: The Reform of the True Church* (Geneva: Librairie Droz, 1978); Scott M. Manetsch, *Theodore Beza and the Quest for Peace in France, 1572–1598* (Leiden: Brill, 2000).

[105] To be sure, in March 1560 the National Synod of Poitiers drew up a memorandum questioning the right of the House of Guise to control the French government and insisting that the princes of the blood had the right to choose the councilors of state in cooperation with the Estates General. This was the basic secular rationale for the Huguenot cause, and it was supported by Calvin. But it was no defense of conspiracy. The conspiracy was aristocratic in leadership, even though the Guises blamed it on Reformed pastors. Knecht, *The French Wars of Religion*, 10, 24; Kingdon, *Geneva and the Coming of the Wars of Religion in France*, 74–75, 85.

[106] Philip Benedict, "Un roi, une loi, deux fois: Parameters for the History of Catholic-Reformed Coexistence in France 1555–1685," *Tolerance and Intolerance in the European Reformation* (ed. Ole Peter Grell and Bob Scribner; Cambridge: Cambridge University Press, 1996), 69–70. Impatient for a church-wide council, Catherine called Catholic and Protestant representatives together to a colloquy at Poissy to seek conciliation. It was a failure. Knecht, *The French Wars of Religion*,

on the part of the French Protestants. There were outbreaks of rioting and icono-
clasm, although pastors and consistories usually denounced this.[107] Concerned as
always about the charge of disorder, Calvin had defended the Protestant pastors in
a letter to the King in 1561:

> With regard to the charge of stirring up disturbances and seditions, they protest
> against ever having entertained any such intention, and declare, on the contrary,
> that they have employed all their influence to check and prevent them. Also, that
> they have never given advice to make any innovations, or attempted anything
> criminal with respect to the established order of the state, but have exhorted those
> who are disposed to listen to them to remain in peaceful subjection to their prince.
> And if any disturbances have arisen, it has been to their great regret, and certainly
> not by their having furnished any pretext for them. And so far have they been from
> countenancing any such enterprises, they would willingly have lent their aid to
> repress them.[108]

Calvin was unable to diffuse the tension, and an attack on a Protestant congregation
by the Duke of Guise precipitated the outbreak of war in 1562.[109]

The Huguenot Prince of Condé's call for mobilization was accompanied by
a Declaration of Protestation that articulated just the sort of political and legal
rationale that Calvin could accept. It clarified that the war was a struggle of loyalty
to the king rather than a rebellion against him.

> (1) Firstly therefore, he [Condé] protests that no selfish passion leads him, but that
> his sole consideration is of what he owes God, with the duty he has particularly to
> the crown of France, under the government of the Queen, and finally the affection
> he bears to this kingdom, constrain him to look for all methods legitimate according
> to God and men, and according to the rank and degree which he holds in this
> kingdom, to return to full liberty the person of the King, the Queen and messieurs
> her children, and to maintain the observation of the edicts and ordinances of his
> Majesty, and namely the last edict issued concerning religion.[110]

Unlike the Conspiracy of Amboise, Calvin and the Protestant churches supported
the Huguenot cause in 1562–1563 because it was led by Condé, a prince of the blood.

25–27, 30–32. Beza was sent to lead the Protestant delegation at Poissy, nine out of eleven of whom had
been trained in Geneva. Kingdon, *Geneva and the Coming of the Wars of Religion in France*, 75–76,
79–81.

[107] Benedict, *Christ's Churches Purely Reformed*, 143; Gordon, *Calvin*, 323–324.

[108] Letter to King of France, January 28, 1561; CO 18:343–345; Quoted in Gordon, *Calvin*, 325. Cf. Letter
to the preachers of Lyons, May 13, 1562; CO 19:409.

[109] The Huguenots had been preparing for war, and this was their catalyst for mobilization. But the
Guises got to Catherine first, and Catherine blamed the Huguenots for the crisis. Knecht, *The French
Wars of Religion*, 35–38.

[110] Quoted in Kingdon, *Geneva and the Coming of the Wars of Religion in France*, 107. The document
went on to describe matters of taxation, debt, and the intimidation of the King by his councilors (108).

Over the following months the war turned against the Huguenots. In March 1563 Condé agreed to the Peace of Amboise, which guaranteed freedom of worship on the estates of nobility with rights of high justice, the right of private worship in the homes of lesser nobility, and freedom of worship in towns held by Protestants as of March 7. But no liberty of worship was granted in key cities like Paris, provoking intense criticism from the churches and from Calvin. While the nobility was willing to sacrifice much for peace, most of the pastors insisted that there should be no peace that would sacrifice congregations or give up the right to worship.[111] Such intransigence did little to assure the authorities that Protestant pastors were the obedient and peaceable subjects they claimed to be. After 1562 their churches faced increasingly difficult circumstances, and the rapid growth of previous years ground to a halt.[112]

Even so, the pastors were not as politically involved as it might have seemed. When the National Synod met in April 1562 in Orléans, just after Condé occupied the city at the beginning of the war, it touched hardly at all on political matters. The delegates even warned churches not to pass ordinances "touching the things which belong to the Magistrates."[113] There was a clear distinction in many pastors' minds between the political/military affairs of the Huguenot leadership and the ecclesiastical affairs of the Synod, and as a rule, the general oversight of military matters was given to political bodies. On the other hand, the Huguenot leadership sometimes used the ecclesiastical organization of the Reformed churches for purposes of mobilization, a phenomenon to which many ministers acquiesced.[114]

Calvin strongly supported the Huguenots during the war of 1562–1563. Indeed, he and the pastors worked hard to raise financial, military, and political support among the Swiss cities and the German princes. He wrote letters to churches in France appealing for money to pay for German mercenaries and rebuking churches for their stinginess. Yet Calvin tried to walk a fine line. He sternly rebuked the ministers of

[111] Knecht, *The French Wars of Religion*, 35–38; Gordon, *Calvin*, 322; Kingdon, *Geneva and the Consolidation of the French Protestant Movement*, 149–156. Eventually Condé, angered at the lack of realism on the part of the pastors, declared that in matters of high policy he would no longer consult with them. Kingdon notes that while the nobility often provoked the fighting in opposition to the pastors, once the war was underway, they were also typically more interested in settling for peace (153). The pastors were less involved in the plotting and diplomatic efforts associated with the second war in 1567 (162–166, 176–177).

[112] Benedict, *Christ's Churches Purely Reformed*, 145.

[113] Kingdon, *Geneva and the Coming of the Wars of Religion in France*, 87. Cf. 108–113.

[114] The Huguenots sent letters to the churches requesting soldiers and support, requests that were often answered favorably. In 1560 the Guyenne Synod of Clairac ordered its churches to organize military units, and many pastors used their pulpits to lobby for the cause or served as chaplains. Hotman and Beza were vigorously involved in the diplomatic campaign to secure foreign aid for the Huguenots. Kingdon, *Geneva and the Coming of the Wars of Religion in France*, 108–113. Sunshine argues that the "militarization and politicization" of French Protestantism provoked tension and division within the church. The wars "made the nobility the effective leaders within Protestantism instead of the pastors, though some pastors became involved in military activities as well, much to the chagrin of Calvin." Sunshine, *Reforming French Protestantism*, 145. Cf. 59, 143–166.

Lyons for carrying weapons and acting violently. He rejected riots and popular disorder, even when it was channeled in favor of the war effort.[115] Calvin's conduct in these very last years of his life confirmed his openness to a war of resistance that was duly led by appropriate magistrates and fought in the name of law and the king, even as he rejected, at least in theory, inappropriate involvement on the part of pastors and churches. Though his ultimate goal was the establishment of the Reformed church by the French monarchy, Calvin never claimed that religion justified violent rebellion. It was in defense of the French King, according to the law of his realm, and under the authority of a prince of the blood that the Huguenots had just cause to fight.

---

[115] Gordon, *Calvin*, 321; Kingdon, *Geneva and the Coming of the Wars of Religion in France*, 111–112. Geneva sought to maintain neutrality, refusing to send troops but encouraging its citizens and pastors to support the war in various ways (115–124).

3

The Kingdom of Christ

In Calvin's theology, the kingdom of Christ is the consummation of God's purposes for creation and for human beings. Calvin wrote in his commentary on the Psalms that "the world was originally created for this end, that every part of it should tend to the happiness of man as its great object."[1] Human beings were made in the image of God, endowed with immortal souls that impel them upward and forward, in body and in soul, to seek happiness in communion with God. When Adam and Eve fell into sin, however, the order of creation was disrupted and subjected to futility and chaos. Though humans retain the natural gifts of God, they, along with creation itself, can only be restored to their purpose in the spiritual kingdom of Christ. That kingdom has been inaugurated in the life and work of Jesus Christ. It transcends this temporal age in quality and time, but even now it is beginning to restore all things through the regeneration of human beings in union with Christ.

In this chapter I describe the bedrock doctrines that form the foundation of Calvin's two kingdoms theology. These are the doctrines of creation, humanity, sin, preservation, natural law, the restoration of the world, the Spirit, the kingdom of Christ, and hope. Without these concepts, Calvin's concept of the two kingdoms makes little sense. With them, it becomes a powerful way to describe the implications of the gospel for Christian social engagement in a fallen world.

Various scholars have claimed that Calvin's two kingdoms–related distinctions (of body and soul, earth and heaven, temporal and spiritual, outward and inward) are dualisms that owe more to Neoplatonism than to the Bible. To some of these scholars, Calvin's theology amounts to a negative rejection of the material world in favor of the ascent of individual souls to God.[2] More influential, perhaps, is the suggestion that Calvin's Neoplatonic philosophical inclinations lie in sharp tension

---

[1] Commentary on Psalm 8:6 [1557]; CO 31:94.
[2] See, for example, R.W. Battenhouse, "The Doctrine of Man in Calvin and in Renaissance Platonism," *Journal of the History of Ideas* 9 (1948): 447–471.

with his fidelity to Christian scripture, and that while the latter finally proves decisive in Calvin's conclusions, his theology as a whole remains somewhat tainted. For instance, in his classic *Calvin's Doctrine of the Last Things*, Heinrich Quistorp argues that Calvin has a "humanistic tendency to confine and spiritualize the hope [of world restoration] in the direction of the salvation of the individual." This leads Calvin to view the kingdom of God "preeminently as a heavenly and spiritual life which definitely begins at death with the liberation of the immortal soul, and which is completed in the immediate vision of God without the mediation of the humanity of Christ." This "spiritualizing tendency" is moderated by Calvin's fidelity to scripture, especially its teaching regarding the resurrection of the body, which preserves his theology's biblical character, but "that character is seriously threatened by the other aspect of his thought."[3]

Recent scholars challenge these claims. They point out that while Calvin – like the New Testament and the Christian tradition – used Greek philosophical concepts and terms when discussing human nature or society, he consistently subjected such resources to his biblical framework. Statements that sound Neoplatonic at first glance usually turn out to be biblical when interpreted in context. As Charles Partee observes, "Calvin was aware of the possibility of a Christian Platonism and rejected it in the strongest terms."[4]

The key to properly interpreting Calvin's kingdom theology – and hence his theology of the two kingdoms – is recognizing its fundamentally eschatological character,[5] for underlying much of the terminology that allegedly betrays Neoplatonic influence is

[3] Heinrich Quistorp, *Calvin's Doctrine of the Last Things* (trans. Harold Knight; London: Lutterworth Press, 1955), 192–193. See also J. H. Van Wyk, "John Calvin on the Kingdom of God and Eschatology," *In die Skriflig* 35.2 (2001): 191–205, 193, 197, 200–202; David E. Holwerda, "Eschatology and History: A Look at Calvin's Eschatological Vision," in *Readings in Calvin's Theology* (ed. Donald K. McKim; Grand Rapids: Baker, 1984), 311–342, 314–318; Gordon J. Spykman, "Sphere-Sovereignty in Calvin and the Calvinist Tradition," *Exploring the Heritage of John Calvin* (ed. David E. Holwerda; Grand Rapids: Baker, 1976), 163–208, 189–192.

[4] Partee notes that Calvin called Augustine "an 'extreme Platonist'" and "criticized Melanchthon for speaking as a philosopher and having no better authority to rest upon than Plato . . . The lens of Calvin's spectacles may have been tinted by Platonism, but the source of Calvin's view of soul and body was not Plato's *Dialogues*, nor the *Theologia Platonica*, but the Scripture." Charles Partee, "The Soul in Plato, Platonism, and Calvin," *Scottish Journal of Theology* 22 (1969): 278–295, 295. Cf. Charles Partee, *Calvin and Classical Philosophy* (Leiden: Brill, 1977); Irena Backus, *Historical Method and Confessional Identity in the Era of the Reformation (1378–1615)* (Leiden: Brill, 2003), 63–117; Thomas F. Torrance, *Kingdom and Church: Study in the Theology of the Reformation* (Edinburgh: Oliver & Boyd, 1956), 92–93; P. F. Theron, "The Kingdom of God and the Theology of Calvin: Response to the Paper by Prof. J. H. Van Wyk," *In die Skriflig* 35.2 (2001): 207–213; Harro Höpfl, *The Christian Polity of John Calvin* (Cambridge: Cambridge University Press, 1982), 9–11.

[5] For an argument on how this emphasis distinguishes Calvin's kingdom theology from Bucer, see Willem Van't Spijker, "The Kingdom of Christ According to Bucer and Calvin," *Calvin and the State* (ed. Peter De Klerk; Grand Rapids: Calvin Studies Society, 1993), 109–132, 118, 121–122. Tonkin argues that its eschatology distinguishes Calvin's two kingdoms theology from that of Luther. John Tonkin,

Calvin's Pauline commitment to the eschatological distinction between creation corrupted and creation restored, the present age and the age to come. Although in Christ the kingdom has already been established, it has not yet been consummated, and it is the resulting eschatological tension between the "already" and the "not-yet" that characterizes the kingdom in the present age.[6]

CREATION AND ANTHROPOLOGY

For Calvin the ultimate objective of human knowledge is the transcendent and future purpose for which humans were created: communion with God.[7] To put it in Calvin's terms, human beings are called to "meditation upon divine worship and the future life." Calvin writes in the *Institutes*,

> We cannot think upon either our first condition or to what purpose we were formed without being prompted to meditate upon immortality and to yearn for the Kingdom of God ... For what is that origin? It is that from which we have fallen. What is that end of our creation? It is that from which we have been completely estranged, so that sick of our miserable lot we groan, and in groaning we sigh for that lost worthiness (2.1.3).

Even before the fall into sin, Calvin believed (following the Christian tradition before him), human beings were expected to attain to this eschatological purpose, transcending their temporal and potentially corruptible state. "[T]he state of man was not perfected in the person of Adam" but was "only earthly, seeing it had no firm and settled constancy." Human beings possessed a "living soul" in the image of Adam, but they had not yet received the "quickening spirit" they inherit from Christ.[8] They were happy as well as righteous, their bodies not subject to mortality. But even if Adam had not sinned, "his earthly life truly would have been temporal," and once he had fulfilled his calling from God, "he would have passed into heaven

---

The Church and the Secular Order in Reformation Thought (New York: Columbia University Press, 1971), 112–116. Cf. Torrance, *Kingdom and Church*, 91, 155–163.

[6] Because Jesus Christ is the one in whom creation is restored and the future age inaugurated, T. F. Torrance is correct to observe that for Calvin "eschatology is the application of Christology to the work of the church in history. It is the understanding of the church and all creation – in terms of the *Regnum Christi* ... On the one hand, union with Christ means that we are already in the new creation, and are so joined to the new humanity that our whole life reaches upward and forward in eager hope and joy to the renewal of creation; but on the other hand, union with Christ and participation in His new humanity means that we must live out that humanity from day to day in the midst of history." Torrance, "Foreword," in Quistorp, *Calvin's Doctrine of the Last Things*, 8.

[7] On Calvin and the knowledge of God, see Paul Helm, *Calvin at the Centre* (Oxford: Oxford University Press, 2010), 4–39. Cf. Edward A. Dowey, *The Knowledge of God in Calvin's Theology* (New York: Columbia University Press, 1952); T. H. L. Parker, *Calvin's Doctrine of the Knowledge of God* (2nd ed.; Edinburgh: Oliver and Boyd, 1969).

[8] Commentary on Genesis 2:7 [1554]; CO 23:36.

without death and without injury."[9] Humans would have been elevated, body and soul, into the heavenly kingdom of God. "Truly the first man would have passed to a better life, had he remained upright, but there would have been no separation of the soul from the body, no corruption, no kind of destruction, and, in short, no violent change."[10] Human beings were created such that in response to the "magnificent theater of heaven and earth" they would naturally look upward and forward to the knowledge of God and to fellowship with him in his kingdom. "The natural order was that the frame of the universe should be the school in which we were to learn piety, and from it pass over to eternal life and perfect felicity" (2.6.1).

At the heart of Calvin's assessment of the nature and purpose of human life was his view of the immortal soul.[11] Typical of his ordinary approach to matters of natural revelation, the reformer articulated his understanding of the soul in conversation with leading pagan philosophers, including Plato, Aristotle, Themistius, and the Stoics. But his conclusions were governed at every key point by Christian conceptions of sin and redemption, and ultimately by his insistence on the decisive importance of the embodied nature of human life and the resurrection of the body.[12]

For Calvin, the existence of the soul is an important object of natural human knowledge.[13] Its primary evidence is the conscience. "Surely the conscience, which,

---

[9] Commentary on Genesis 2:17 [1554]; CO 23:45.

[10] Commentary on Genesis 3:19 [1554]; CO 23:77. Cf. Commentary on Matthew 16:26 [1555]; CO 45:482. This point is fundamental to understanding the coherence of Calvin's thought, as is clear from a consideration of Richard Prins, "The Image of God in Adam and the Restoration of Man in Jesus Christ: A Study in John Calvin," *Scottish Theological Journal* 25 (1972): 32–44. Prins thinks Calvin contradicts himself insofar as he makes Adam both earthly and potentially spiritual at the same time. He charges Calvin with conflating "two seemingly contradictory trains of thought" (40). On the one hand, human beings will be restored to Adam's original state; On the other hand, they will be transformed into the image of Christ. But there is nothing contradictory about such references to the restoration of Adam's original state. They reflect Calvin's understanding of Adam's original eschatological teleology. Adam was always intended to attain to what Christ actually accomplished.

[11] Even before he wrote the first edition of the *Institutes*, Calvin wrote his *Psychopannychia*, a tract whose purpose was to prove the immortality of the soul. Willem Balke, *Calvin and the Anabaptist Radicals* (trans. Willem Heyner. Grand Rapids: Eerdmans, 1981), 31 (Cf. 33). For the text of the *Psychopannychia* see *John Calvin's Tracts and Treatises* (3 vols; ed. Henry Beveridge; Edinburgh, 1844), 3:377–451; CO 5: 165–232.

[12] While most scholars have focused on the influence of Plato, Backus shows that Plato made up only one part of the synthesis. Calvin abandoned Augustine's view of the soul as being too speculative. In its place, he wove together elements from Plato, Themistius, Aristotle, and the Stoics "so as to arrive at a sort of simple syncretic model firmly anchored in the pagan doctrines of the soul but incorporating the doctrine of the original sin." Backus, *Historical Method*, 86. Calvin "reinterprets and simplifies" these sources "without paying any heed to tradition, so as to make them compatible with his own theological doctrine of Creation and Fall" (89). See also Susan E. Schreiner, *The Theater of His Glory: Nature and the Natural Order in the Thought of John Calvin* (Grand Rapids: Baker Academic, 1995), 55–63.

[13] Quistorp rightly observes that for Calvin "the immortality of the soul is not properly speaking a truth of revelation and faith." This is in contrast to "the specifically Biblical message of the resurrection of the

discerning between good and evil, responds to God's judgment, is an undoubted sign of the immortal spirit. For how could a motion without essence penetrate to God's judgment seat, and inflict itself with dread at its own guilt?" The knowledge and fear of the soul proves the transcendent and immortal purpose of human beings. "Now the very knowledge of God sufficiently proves that souls, which transcend the world, are immortal, for no transient energy could penetrate to the fountain of life" (1.15.2).[14] Calvin praises Plato as the philosopher who succeeded in recognizing the immortality of the soul (1.15.6).[15] He agrees with Plato that the soul is a substance separate from the body and immortal, gifted with reason and perception, and that as the nobler part of human beings, it differentiates them from animals.[16] He likewise agrees that "although properly it is not spatially limited, still, set in the body, it dwells there as in a house, not only that it may animate all its parts and render its organs fit and useful for their actions, but also that it may hold the first place in ruling man's life" (1.15.6). Calvin sounds nothing if not Platonic when he writes in the *Psychopannichia* that unlike animals, "the soul of man is not of the earth. It was made by the mouth of the Lord, i.e., by his secret power."[17] Thus there is the same "difference between a celestial soul and an earthly body that there is between heaven and earth."[18]

On the other hand, Calvin's commendation of pagan philosophical accounts of the soul is "severely qualified."[19] He points out that the philosophers could come to no agreement on the nature or origin of the soul because they lacked the wisdom of scripture.[20] After noting the philosophers' complex accounts of the various faculties of the soul, therefore, Calvin ends up presenting the soul simply in terms of two faculties, the understanding and the will (1.15.6).[21] He rejects Plato's speculation

---

dead which he here characterizes in the most emphatic terms as the content of the Christian hope." Quistorp, *Calvin's Doctrine of the Last Things*, 128.

[14] Likewise "the many preeminent gifts with which the human mind is endowed" demonstrate both that "something divine" is in human beings and that they have an "immortal essence." Animals, after all, do not sense anything beyond what is material, but human beings can investigate "heaven and earth and the secrets of nature," ordering and arranging their knowledge, and making use of the memory of the past while inferring what may happen in the future (1.15.2).

[15] "Calvin shares Plato's fundamental conviction that the essential person is the soul and that the soul is a spiritual substance orientated towards God." Backus, *Historical Method*, 94. Cf. Irena Backus, "Calvin's Knowledge of Greek Language and Philosophy," in *Calvinus Praeceptor Ecclesiae: Papers of the International Congress on Calvin Research, Princeton, August 20–24, 2002* (ed. Herman J. Selderhuis; Geneva: Droz, 2004), 343–350, 346; Quistorp, *Calvin's Doctrine of the Last Things*, 62–63.

[16] Calvin defines the soul as "an immortal yet created essence, which is his [man's] nobler part" (1.15.2).

[17] Calvin, *Psychopannychia*, 3:387; CO 5:181.   [18] Calvin, *Psychopannychia*, 3:407; CO 5:197.

[19] Partee, "The Soul in Plato, Platonism, and Calvin," 291.

[20] Calvin, *Psychopannychia*, 3:383–384; CO 5:178.

[21] See Schreiner, *The Theater of His Glory*, 64–65.

about the future life and insists that the immortality of the soul is inseparable from the hope of the resurrection.

> I readily acknowledge that the philosophers, who were ignorant of the resurrection of the body, have many discussions about the immortal essence of the soul, but they talk so foolishly about the state of the future life that their opinions have no weight. But since the scriptures inform us that the spiritual life depends on the hope of the resurrection, and that souls, when separated from the bodies, look forward to it, whoever destroys the resurrection deprives souls also of their immortality.[22]

The soul for Calvin, in contrast to Plato, does not have life in and of itself, but only as a gift from God. It can be distinguished from the body, but it cannot, in the final analysis, be forever separated from it.[23]

It is fair to say, as Margaret Miles does, that for Calvin "the soul *does* everything."[24] But Quistorp goes too far when he claims that "the soul is for Calvin the real man."[25] To be sure, in the *Psychopannychia* Calvin argued that in the human body the "image nowhere shines forth."[26] But Calvin later clarified that while the soul is the "proper seat" of the image of God (1.15.4), even in the body the image is "seen or glows in … outward marks." While the image cannot be "indiscriminately" extended to both the body and the soul, because to view it as such "mingles heaven and earth," nevertheless "the likeness of God extends to the whole excellence by which man's nature towers over all the kinds of living creatures." Thus the "primary seat" of the image is "the mind and heart, or in the soul and its powers, yet there was no part of man, not even the body itself, in which some sparks did not glow" (1.15.3).[27]

---

[22] Thus "the life of the soul, apart from the hope of the resurrection, will be a mere dream, for God does not declare that immediately after the death of the body souls live – as if their glory and happiness were already enjoyed by them in perfections – but delays the expectation of them till the last day." Commentary on Matthew 22:23 [1555]; CO 45:604–605. Cf. *Institutes*, 3.6.3; Commentary on 1 Peter 1:9 [1555]; CO 55:215; Holwerda, "Eschatology and History," 322.

[23] Partee, "The Soul in Plato, Platonism, and Calvin," 292.

[24] The soul does everything, but "the condition of the body accurately and intimately reflects the state of the soul." Margaret R. Miles, "Theology, Anthropology, and the Human Body in Calvin's *Institutes of the Christian Religion*," *Harvard Theological Review* 74 (1981): 303–323, 310. Miles criticizes Calvin for failing to grasp the whole significance of the human body. "For Calvin the capacity of the soul to affect the body is not matched by any capacity of the body to affect the soul." Calvin tends to assume that "the real significance of the human body is its capacity to reflect the dynamics of the soul" (318). Still, Miles recognizes that for Calvin the body is "not adventitious to human being, but an integral and permanent aspect" (319).

[25] Quistorp, *Calvin's Doctrine of the Last Things*, 64.   [26] Calvin, *Psychopannychia*, 3:386; CO 5:180.

[27] Schreiner writes, "Calvin defined the image as the original order in the soul and the relationship whereby Adam 'truly referred his excellence to the exceptional gifts bestowed on him by his Maker.' Because the soul was rightly ordered, the will was free to follow reason, the affections were kept within bounds, and the reason was capable of knowing and loving God." Schreiner, *The Theater of His Glory*, 65.

It is important to stress that for Calvin, it is not the human soul per se that qualifies a human being for the kingdom of God. It is, rather, the faculties of the soul that render the human being capable of being fit it for this purpose by the Spirit of God. Calvin does not tend to conflate that which pertains to the Spirit with the human soul or spirit, as Quistorp claims.[28] On the contrary, he distinguishes between 1) animal life, which consists in "motion and the bodily senses," 2) human life, which consists in the soul and the gifts associated with the image of God, and 3) the spiritual life, which is attained by those who participate in the heavenly kingdom.[29] The natural man is "any man that is endowed with nothing more than the faculties of nature," while the spiritual man "denotes the man whose understanding is regulated by the illumination of the Spirit of God." The natural man possesses the soul with its faculties in a "purely natural condition." The spiritual man, on the other hand, possesses the soul formed by the gifts of the Spirit. "For the soul belongs to nature, but the Spirit is of supernatural communication."[30] In the final analysis it is the soul that renders the human person capable of being directed upward and forward to her ultimate purpose by the Spirit of God, but it is the whole person, body and soul, that reflects God's glory and is destined for the kingdom of God.[31]

Susan Schreiner has shown that Calvin believed God designed creation as a theater through which humans could perceive God's glory and come to know him. "Human judgment, reason, and prudence sufficed, Calvin said, for the direction of earthly life and would have enabled the human being to rise up to God and eternal bliss."[32] God has inscribed a "sense of divinity [*divinitatis sensum*]" on every heart such that no person lives without a basic awareness and accountability to her creator, which explains why "from the beginning of the world there has been no region, no city, in short, no household, that could do without religion" (1.3.1).[33] The skill with which the mind studies life and attributes to it meaning, the manner

---

[28] Quistorp, *Calvin's Doctrine of the Last Things*, 65–66.

[29] Commentary on Ephesians 4:18 [1548]; CO 51:205. This contradicts Prins's claim that Calvin identifies "the body entirely with man's earthly nature, the image entirely with his spiritual nature," with the soul playing a mediating role. Prins, "The Image of God in Adam and the Restoration of Man in Jesus Christ," 34.

[30] Commentary on 1 Corinthians 2:14 [1546]; CO 49:343.

[31] Cf. Benjamin Milner, Jr., *Calvin's Doctrine of the Church* (Leiden: Brill, 1970), 20–23. "There is, then, an 'integrity' of man corresponding to the 'integrity' (or, order) of the world, the proper functioning of which would have 'led to eternal life and perfect felicity.' Calvin identifies this capacity for self-transcendence with the soul, and it is primarily the soul, as distinct from the body, to which this 'integrity' is ascribed" (20).

[32] Schreiner, *The Theater of His Glory*, 65. Thus it is not God's sheer power that was to direct humans to the service of God, as Hancock claims, but the contemplation of the order, providential governance and excellence of nature. See Ralph C. Hancock, *Calvin and the Foundations of Modern Politics* (Ithaca: Cornell University Press, 1989), 148–153.

[33] The complexity and mystery of life is such that "even the most stupid tribe" cannot escape the sense that there is a God or gods before whom they live (1.5.1). Anyone who has "a single spark of sound

in which it detects the significance of time, and its impressive capacities of memory, imagination, and dreaming are all "unfailing signs of divinity" in human beings. Just as telling is the conscience. "Shall we, indeed, distinguish between right and wrong by that judgment which has been imparted to us, yet will there be no judge in heaven? Will there remain for us even in sleep some remnant of intelligence, yet will no God keep watch in governing the world?" (1.5.5)[34] Likewise the cosmos, that "'mirror,' 'theater,' 'open volume,' or 'book,'" was created that humans might know and praise God through the "contemplation of nature."[35] Through God's artwork "the whole of mankind is invited and attracted to recognition of him, and from this to true and complete happiness." Men and women long for the life that only the knowledge of God can bring. "Knowledge of this sort, then, ought not only to arouse us to the worship of God but also to awaken and encourage us to the hope of the future life" (1.5.10).

SIN, NATURAL LAW, AND THE NEED FOR REDEMPTION

The fall of human beings into sin prevented them from attaining to their eschatological purpose and cast the entire creation into disorder. As Schreiner puts it, "The act of unbelief was, then, an act of disorder among the creatures, which unleashed disorder into God's fragile but ordered world."[36] The material world as well as human life and society gave way to disorder and confusion. For "so long as ungodliness has possession of the minds of men, the world, plunged as it is in darkness, must be considered as thrown into a state of confusion and of horrible disorder and misrule, for there can be no stability apart from God." Indeed, "no order can be said to prevail in the world until God erects his throne and reigns among men."[37]

---

judgment" should be able to see it. Commentary on 1 Corinthians 1:21 [1546]; CO 49:326–327; Cf. Commentary on Romans 1:19–23 [1556]; CO 49:23–26.

[34] "Why is it that the soul not only vaguely roves about but conceives many useful things, ponders . . . even divines the future – all while man sleeps? What ought we to say here except that the signs of immortality which have been implanted in man cannot be effaced? Now what reason would there be to believe that man is divine and not to recognize his Creator?" (1.5.5) Cf. Commentary on Psalm 8:5 [1557]; CO 31:92.

[35] Schreiner, *The Theater of His Glory*, 65. Cf. *Institutes*, 1.5.11.

[36] Schreiner, *The Theater of His Glory*, 28. On the rich theme of order and disorder in Calvin, see also Milner, *Calvin's Doctrine of the Church*, 7–70; David Little, *Religion, Order, and Law* (New York: Harper and Row, 1969), 33–79; Tonkin, *The Church and the Secular Order in Reformation Thought*, 119–130; Susan E. Schreiner, "Creation and Providence" *The Calvin Handbook* (ed. Herman J. Selderhuis; Grand Rapids: Eerdmans, 2009), 267–275; Derek S. Jeffreys, " 'It's a Miracle of God That There Is Any Common Weal Among Us': Unfaithfulness and Disorder in John Calvin's Political Thought," *The Review of Politics* (2000): 107–129.

[37] Commentary on Psalm 96:10 [1557]; CO 32:41–42. Cf. Commentary on Jeremiah 5:25 [1563]; CO 37:635.

Because of sin, humans turn away from the seed of religion that is within them, groveling like animals in what is earthly and transient. "There is, indeed, nothing more difficult than to keep our thoughts fixed on things in heaven, when the whole power of our [sinful] nature inclines downwards, and when Satan by numberless devices draws us back to the earth."[38] Because it is impossible for humans to lose their religious sense entirely, they do not abandon religion. Instead, they develop conceptions of God measured according to "the yardstick of their own carnal stupidity." Human religions are speculative and self-serving, ultimately forging an understanding of God that is idolatrous, "a figment and a dream of their own heart" (1.4.1). Indeed, "scarcely a single person has ever been found who did not fashion for himself an idol or specter in place of God" (1.5.12). In this context, the testimony of creation to the glory of God becomes vain. Because every people and tradition calls for allegiance to its own religion, even the pious find themselves unable to determine the right way to worship God. Because neither civic custom nor tradition are reliable guides, "it remains for God himself to give witness of himself from heaven" (1.5.13).

Calvin's evaluation of the destructive and distortive consequences of human sin is thoroughly Augustinian. Whatever abilities and potential Adam and Eve once had to attain eternal life through the right use of their free will, the fall into sin virtually destroyed the image of God and corrupted the blessings associated with it (1.15.8).[39] It is not the body that is to blame for this fall but the will, that faculty of the soul that has turned against God. But the result is the corruption of the whole human being. "God's image is the perfect excellence of human nature which shone in Adam before his defection but was subsequently so vitiated and almost blotted out that nothing remains after the ruin except what is confused, mutilated, and disease-ridden" (1.15.4).[40]

For Calvin, as for Augustine, the preeminent problem with human beings, in addition to unbelief, is pride, or self-love. "For since blind self-love is innate in all mortals, they are most freely persuaded that nothing inheres in themselves that deserves to be considered hateful. Thus even with no outside support the utterly vain opinion generally obtains credence that man is abundantly sufficient of himself to lead a good and blessed life" (2.1.2). Even "those of the philosophers who at any time most strongly contended that virtue should be pursued for its own sake were

---

[38] Commentary on Hebrews 6:11 [1549]; CO 55:76. For "if all men are born and live to the end that they may know God . . . it is clear that all those who do not direct every thought and action in their lives to this goal degenerate from the law of their creation" (1.3.3).

[39] See Schreiner, *The Theater of His Glory*, 65–70.

[40] Miles notes that for Calvin "the soul . . . [is the] the location of the crippling effects of the corruption of the image through the sin of the first human beings." "The body plays no role, for Calvin, either in the corruption of the soul or in its own corruption, but is the helpless victim, along with the soul, of the destructive hegemony of 'flesh.'" Miles, "Theology, Anthropology, and the Human Body in Calvin's *Institutes of the Christian Religion*," 309, 314. Cf. Schreiner, *The Theater of His Glory*, 99.

puffed up with such great arrogance as to show they sought after virtue for no other reason than to have occasion for pride" (3.7.2).[41] Unbelief and the prideful rejection of God's rule result in injustice and social chaos: "deceit, craft, treachery, cruelty, violence, and extortion, reign in the world, in short, . . . all things are thrown into disorder and darkness by injustice and wickedness."[42]

But Calvin did not believe human beings are wholly corrupted by sin, nor did he think the creation has been entirely abandoned to chaos. On the contrary, by his providence, God graciously restrains the effects of sin through his care for the material creation and his preservation of a modicum of human morality and society.[43] In the 1559 edition of the *Institutes*, Calvin explains the extent of God's preservation of human society by appealing to the Augustinian distinction between supernatural gifts, which are entirely lost to sinful humanity, and natural gifts, which are corrupted but not lost.

> Therefore, withdrawing from the kingdom of God, he is at the same time deprived of spiritual gifts, with which he had been furnished for the hope of eternal salvation. From this it follows that he is so banished from the Kingdom of God that all qualities belonging to the blessed life of the soul have been extinguished in him until he recovers them through the grace of regeneration. Among these are faith, love of God, charity toward neighbor, zeal for holiness and for righteousness. All

---

[41] Cf. *Institutes* 2.1.1; Commentary on Isaiah 11:9 [1559]; CO 36:243–244.

[42] Commentary on Psalm 11:4 [1557]; CO 31:123. The "present disorderly [*ataxian*] state of matters" anticipates a full judgment at which point "those things that are now confused must, of necessity, be restored to order [*restitui oportet*]." God will one day "remedy the state of matters in the world [*statum huius mundi corrigat*], so as to bring them into a better condition." Commentary on 2 Thessalonians 1:5 [1550]; CO 52:189 (Cf. 1:7; 52:191).

[43] Schreiner, *The Theater of His Glory*, 28–30, 79–82, 87, 94–95. Cf. Commentary on Hosea 2:18 [1557]; CO 42:248. Schreiner, following Bavinck and Kuiper, identifies this as Calvin's doctrine of common grace. See Herman Bavinck, "Common Grace," (trans. Raymond C. Van Leeuwen) *Calvin Theological Journal* 24:1 (1989): 35–65. Bavinck defines common grace in Calvin as "a grace that, while it does not inwardly renew, nevertheless restrains and compels" (51). However, for criticism of Bavinck's interpretation of Calvin's concept of common grace see Helm, *Calvin at the Centre*, 308–339. See also Herman Kuiper, *Calvin on Common Grace* (Grand Rapids: Smutter, 1928). Jeon closely identifies the distinction between special and common grace with the distinction between the two kingdoms. Jeong Koo Jeon, "Calvin and the Two Kingdoms: Calvin's Political Philosophy in Light of Contemporary Discussion," *Westminster Theological Journal* 72.2 (Fall, 2010): 301–305. VanDrunen makes the same conceptual link but presents common grace as a concept worked out within Neo-Calvinism. David VanDrunen, *Natural Law and the Two Kingdoms: A Study in the Development of Reformed Social Thought* (Grand Rapids: Eerdmans, 2010), 277–278, 294–313, 354–384. On the complementary relationship between common grace and natural law see Paul Helm, "Calvin and Natural Law," *Scottish Bulletin of Evangelical Theology* 2 (1984): 5–22, 18. While Schreiner rejects the notion that providence is a central doctrine for Calvin in the theological sense, she argues that it is nevertheless a "*Stammlehre* or, rather, a 'proscenium arch.'" Significantly, however, Schreiner views providence as a "foundational doctrine not in terms of predestination or the work of Christ, but in terms of creation" (7).

these, since Christ restores them in us, are considered adventitious and beyond nature, and for this reason we infer that they were taken away (2.2.12).

On the other hand, though the natural gifts possessed by human beings are corrupted, "some sparks still gleam." Such sparks include a measure of moral discernment, the ability to distinguish between good and evil. Human beings likewise maintain some freedom of the will, although that will is now bound to "wicked desires" such that it "cannot strive after the right." Even the longing for truth remains, though it now labors vainly, obsessed with "empty and worthless things" rather than with the things that matter (2.2.12). What is more, to a certain extent human beings continue to "taste something of things above" (2.2.13).[44]

Calvin further distinguishes between natural things and supernatural things, or between earthly things and heavenly things, in a passage that he added to the *Institutes* in 1539.

> I call "earthly things" those which do not pertain to God or his Kingdom, to true justice, or to the blessedness of the future life, but which have their significance and relationship with regard to the present life and are, in a sense, confined within its bounds. I call "heavenly things" the pure knowledge of God, the nature of true righteousness, and the mysteries of the Heavenly Kingdom. The first class includes government, household management, all mechanical skills, and the liberal arts. In the second are the knowledge of God and of his will, and the rule by which we conform our lives to it (2.2.13).

The key to the distinction is Calvin's eschatological understanding of the kingdom of God. Heavenly things are those things which pertain to "God or his Kingdom," to what is "true" and "pure" and participates in the "blessedness of the future life." The "Heavenly Kingdom" is the consummation of the blessed life in the age to come, the age characterized by true justice and righteousness. Earthly things, in contrast, pertain only to the "present life." What makes them earthly is not their materiality but their temporality. Earthly things are secular in the classic sense of the term: their significance is limited to the present age, "confined within its bounds" such that they will not survive into the kingdom of God. The distinction clearly reflects Calvin's two kingdoms paradigm, articulated in 1536, with "government, household management, all mechanical skills, and the liberal arts" all lying within the bounds of the political kingdom.

---

[44] Calvin contrasts the "natural gifts of God" with gifts "above the common order of nature." "That we are born men, that we are endued with reason and knowledge, that our life is supplied with necessary support, all this is indeed from God." Yet these are gifts of nature, distinct from "the peculiar endowments of the new and spiritual life, which derive their origin from the kingdom of Christ." Commentary on 2 Peter 1:3 [1551]; CO 55:445.

Calvin goes on to devote four sections to describing the impressive achievements (and limits) of natural human activity in political government, the liberal and manual arts, and science. He explains his remarkably positive evaluation as evidence for the continuing effect of natural law.

[S]ince man is by nature a social animal, he tends through natural instinct to foster and preserve society. Consequently, we observe that there exists in all men's minds universal impressions of a certain civic fair dealing and order. Hence no man is to be found who does not understand that every sort of human organization must be regulated by laws, and who does not comprehend the principles of those laws. Hence arises that unvarying consent of all nations and of individual mortals with regard to laws. For their seeds have, without teacher or lawgiver, been implanted in all men (2.2.13).

Natural law, for Calvin, is "that inward law [*lex ... interior*] ... written, even engraved, upon the hearts of all," that "in a sense asserts the very same things that are to be learned from the two Tables [of the Ten Commandments]" (2.8.1). It is nothing less than "the law of God which we call the moral law" (4.10.16).

Some scholars have insisted, following August Lang, that for Calvin natural law has "almost no importance at all."[45] They argue that for Calvin natural law plays only the negative role of convicting human beings of sin, and that where it does seem to play a positive role it rests uneasily in the context of Calvin's broader thought. They therefore place Calvin in sharp discontinuity with the medieval natural law tradition.[46] However, in recent years numerous scholars have demonstrated that while there are important points of discontinuity between Calvin and the medieval scholastics with respect to natural law, the points of continuity between them are greater, and that while Calvin did reject natural theology as a means of salvation

---

[45] August Lang, "The Reformation and Natural Law," *Calvin and the Reformation: Four Studies* (trans. J. Gresham Machen; New York: Fleming H. Revell, 1909), 56–98, 72.

[46] For Barth's influential argument see Karl Barth, "No!," in Emil Brunner, *Natural Theology* (trans. Peter Fraenkel; London: Geoffrey Bles: Centenary, 1946), 67–128. See also Wilhelm Niesel, *The Theology of Calvin* (trans. Harold Knight; London: Methuen, 1956), 102–103; François Wendel, *Calvin: The Origins and Development of his Religious Thought* (trans. Philip Mairet; London: Collins, 1963 [1950]), 206–208; Arthur C. Cochrane, "Natural Law in Calvin," in *Church-State Relations in Ecumenical Perspective* (ed. Elwyn A. Smith; Louvain: Duquesne University Press, 1966), 176–217; Höpfl, *The Christian Polity of John Calvin*, 180–187; William R. Stevenson, Jr., *Sovereign Grace: The Place and Significance of Christian Freedom in John Calvin's Political Thought* (New York: Oxford University Press, 1999), 44–49. Cf. Parker, *Calvin's Doctrine of the Knowledge of God*. Cf. I. John. Hesselink, *Calvin's Concept of the Law* (Allison Park, PA: Pickwick Publications, 1992), 69–70. A recent essay in this vein is Gene Haas, "Calvin, Natural Law, and the Two Kingdoms," *Kingdoms Apart: Engaging the Two Kingdoms Perspective* (ed. Ryan G. McIlhenny; Phillipsburg, NJ: Presbyterian and Reformed Publishing, 2012), 33–63. Cf. Guenther Haas, "Calvin's Ethics," *The Cambridge Companion to John Calvin* (ed. Donald K. McKim; Cambridge: Cambridge University Press, 2004), 93–105, 93–94.

(or of knowledge of *spiritual* things), he saw natural law as playing a fundamental and positive role in matters pertaining to the *present* life.[47] Schreiner shows that Calvin understood natural law as a vital expression of God's providential and gracious preservation of order in the world. Because of natural law the restraint of sinful human beings in this age need not be purely external and coercive. Calvin "assumed that ordered, civilized life in society could flourish because of the remaining natural instincts, perceptions, and abilities present in man's soul. The ability of human beings to recognize the truths of natural law was a means whereby people could still participate in the formation of government and a stable civic life."[48]

It is true that, unlike Aquinas, Calvin never attempted to articulate a systematic natural law theory.[49] And while Aquinas defined natural law as the rational creature's participation in eternal law through the use of reason, Calvin rejected what he viewed as the scholastics' overconfidence in reason, understanding natural law primarily (though not exclusively) in terms of the testimony of *conscience*. Here he followed Romans 2:14–15, Paul's declaration that the Gentiles "show that the work of

---

[47] Some of the best recent analyses include Stephen J. Grabill, *Rediscovering the Natural Law in Reformed Theological Ethics* (Grand Rapids: Eerdmans, 2006), 70–97; Irena Backus, "Calvin's Concept of Natural and Roman Law," *Calvin Theological Journal* 38 (2003): 7–26; Schreiner, *The Theater of His Glory*, 73–95; VanDrunen, *Natural Law and the Two Kingdoms*, 93–115; C. Scott Pryor, "God's Bridle: John Calvin's Application of Natural Law," *Journal of Law and Religion* 22.1 (2006–2007): 225–254. Cf. Susan Schreiner, "Calvin's Use of Natural Law," *A Preserving Grace: Protestants, Catholics and Natural Law* (ed. Michael Cromartie; Grand Rapids: Eerdmans, 1997), 51–76; Helm, "Calvin and Natural Law," 5–22; David Little, "Calvin and the Prospects for a Christian Theory of Natural Law," *Norm and Context in Christian Ethics* (ed. Gene H. Outka and Paul Ramsey; New York: Scribner's, 1968), 175–197; Dowey, *The Knowledge of God in Calvin's Theology*; John T. McNeill, "Natural Law in the Teaching of the Reformers," *Journal of Religion* 26 (1946): 168–182. For a summary of the natural law debate, see William Kempa, "Calvin on Natural Law," *John Calvin and the Church: A Prism of Reform* (ed. Timothy George; Louisville: Westminster John Knox Press, 2001), 73–76.

[48] Schreiner, "Calvin's Use of Natural Law," 68. Backus argues that Calvin sought "to establish a direct link between pagan consciences – the seat of natural moral law – and the civil laws they produced." Backus, "Calvin's Concept of Natural and Roman Law," 13. This enabled him to "view pagan legislative and moral thought as partly acceptable to Christians insofar as it issues from the same God-given natural law" (14). "Calvin separates natural moral law from biblical precepts and makes it stand for innate knowledge of right and wrong … Therefore by removing natural law in all its expressions from the purview of the church, Calvin automatically puts it in the purview of rulers and magistrates, in other words in chief *civil* legislators" (10). Cf. Backus, *Historical Method*, 63–129.

[49] Grabill, *Rediscovering the Natural Law in Reformed Theological Ethics*, 91; Schreiner, *The Theater of His Glory*, 77–79, 94; Backus, Calvin's Concept of Natural and Roman Law," 11–12; Haas, "Calvin's Ethics," 93–94; Little, *Religion, Order, and Law*, 51. Grabill and Backus each reflect extensively on the key differences between Calvin's and Aquinas's views of natural law. Cf. David VanDrunen, "Medieval Natural Law and the Reformation: A Comparison of Aquinas and Calvin," *American Catholic Philosophical Quarterly* 80 (2006): 77–98; David VanDrunen, "Natural Law, Custom, and Common Law in the Theology of Aquinas and Calvin," *University of British Columbia Law Review* 33 (2000): 699–717; Allen Verhey, "Natural Law in Aquinas and Calvin," *God and the Good: Essays in Honor of Henry Stob* (ed. Clifton Orlebeke and Lewis Smedes; Grand Rapids: Eerdmans, 1975), 80–92.

the law is written on their hearts, while their conscience also bears witness, and their thoughts accuse them among themselves or excuse them before God's judgment." The basic principles of morality, for Calvin, are not primarily conclusions drawn from rational inquiry, but inclinations and commitments deeply embedded in the human conscience. It is this conviction that enables Calvin to maintain a relevant concept of natural law while insisting that humans are predisposed to suppress the truth.

> [Paul] means not that it was so engraven on their will that they sought and diligently pursued it, but that they were so mastered by the power of truth that they could not disapprove of it. For why did they institute religious rites except that they were convinced that God ought to be worshiped? Why were they ashamed of adultery and theft except that they deemed them evils?[50]

On the other hand, as Stephen Grabill cautions, "Calvin never intended to sever the connection between reason and conscience."[51] The use of reason, for Calvin as for Aquinas, leads to genuine and useful knowledge. As human beings wrestle with the convictions of conscience, "which is equal to a thousand witnesses," they reason profitably concerning morality and justice. "There is then a certain knowledge of the law by nature which says, 'this is good and worthy of being desired; that ought to be abhorred." At the prompting of such knowledge, grounded in the conscience, "reasons come to our minds by which we defend what is rightly done."[52]

Like Aquinas, Calvin believed natural law reveals only general moral and social principles. Once particular interests and circumstances are in view, humans have no difficulty deceiving themselves as to right and wrong.[53] As a result, in particular matters there is all manner of disagreement and dispute, and the laws and customs of nations cannot naively be embraced as a moral authority without reflection.[54] Still, "while men dispute among themselves about individual sections of the law, they agree on the general conception of equity." Although they limp and stagger along, it is nevertheless clear that "some seed of political order has been implanted in all men" (2.2.13). Calvin could even say that "There is nothing more common than for

---

[50] Commentary on Romans 2:15 [1556]; CO 49:38. Calvin writes that "as some principles of equity and justice remain in the hearts of men, the consent of all nations is as it were the voice of nature." Commentary on Habakkuk 2:6 [1559]; CO 43:540–541. Cf. Commentary on Romans 1:26–29 [1556]; CO 49:28–29.

[51] Grabill, *Rediscovering the Natural Law in Reformed Theological Ethics*, 93.

[52] Commentary on Romans 2:15 [1556]; CO 49:38–39.

[53] Grabill, *Rediscovering the Natural Law in Reformed Theological Ethics*, 96; Guenther Haas, *The Concept of Equity in Calvin's Ethics* (Waterloo, Ontario: Wilfrid Laurier University Press, 1997), 69–70. See *Institutes* 2.2.24; Commentary on Matthew 7:12 [1555]; CO 45:220.

[54] See Commentary on Micah 7:7 [1559]; CO 43:409; Commentary on Genesis 50:3 [1554]; CO 23: 613–614; Commentary on Acts 19:27 [1554]; CO 48:452; Commentary on Daniel 6:24 [1561]; CO 41:29.

a man to be sufficiently instructed in a right standard of conduct by natural law"
(2.2.22).

> [T]here is no nation so lost to everything human that it does not keep within the
> limits of some laws ... they have some notions of justice and rectitude, which the
> Greeks call preconceptions, and which are implanted by nature in the hearts of
> men. They have then a law, though they are without law. For though they have not
> a written law, they are yet by no means wholly destitute of the knowledge of what is
> right and just, as they could not otherwise distinguish between vice and virtue, the
> first of which they restrain by punishment and the latter they commend, and
> manifest their approbation of it by honoring it with rewards.[55]

Calvin's confidence in what is known morally through the natural law is impressive.
Among those moral principles he believed are generally received among the nations
are: God ought to be worshiped; adultery, theft, and murder ought to be punished;
good faith must be kept in bargains and contracts; honesty is commendable;[56] the
unjust accumulation of great wealth will overcome a person;[57] the poor have a right to
sufficient food;[58] incest is shameful and abominable;[59] trials must be conducted with
evidence and just process;[60] a man should marry his deceased family member's wife in
order to preserve his family line;[61] nations are to show hospitality toward their international kin and pity for the distressed, even their enemies;[62] nations are to be kind to
international fugitives and exiles, especially those persecuted for their faithfulness to
God;[63] military captives should not be treated cruelly;[64] wars may be waged only for
just and necessary reasons, and with a solemn and public proclamation;[65] a man
should not have sex with a woman during her period;[66] children must obey and honor
their parents, people should obey their rulers, and slaves should obey their masters;[67]

---

[55] Commentary on Romans 2:14 [1556]; CO 49:37–38. Cf. *Harmony of the Law*, "End and Use of the
Law," [1563]; CO 24:725.

[56] Commentary on Romans 2:15 [1556]; CO 49:38. "All the Gentiles alike instituted religious rites, they
made laws to punish adultery, and theft, and murder, they commanded good faith in bargains and
contracts. They have thus indeed proved that God ought to be worshiped, that adultery and theft and
murder are evils, that honesty is commendable."

[57] Commentary on Habakkuk 2:6 [1559]; CO 43:540–541.

[58] Commentary on Isaiah 21:14 [1559]; CO 36:362.

[59] Commentary on Romans 5:1 [1556]; CO 49:377–378. Cf. Commentary on Leviticus 20:11–24 [1563];
CO 24:666.

[60] Commentary on John 18:31 [1553]; CO 47:401–402.

[61] Commentary on Genesis 38:8 [1554]; CO 23:495.

[62] Commentary on Obadiah 1:12–14 [1559]; CO 43:191.

[63] Commentary on Isaiah 16:4 [1559]; CO 36:302–303.

[64] Commentary on Isaiah 47:6 [1559]; CO 37:166.

[65] Commentary on Jeremiah 6:4–5 [1563]; CO 37:645.

[66] Commentary on Ezekiel 18:5–9 [1565]; CO 40:425–432. Cf. Commentary on Leviticus 18:19.

[67] Commentary on Exodus 20:12 [1563]; CO 24:602–606. Cf. Commentary on 1 Corinthians 7:37 [1546];
CO 49:425–426; Commentary on Ephesians 6:1 [1548]; CO 51:228.

the elderly should be honored;[68] human beings look upward during prayer;[69] and God will avenge those who cry out to hm for justice.[70] Calvin was sufficiently impressed with pagan morality to have speculated that there was greater integrity among the pagans of Abraham's day than there was among the Christians of Calvin's time.[71]

Calvin spoke even more positively about human abilities in the liberal and manual arts. Virtually everyone, he observed, has a certain aptitude or talent in one area or another (2.2.14).

> Shall we deny that the truth shone upon the ancient jurists who established civic order and discipline with such great equity? Shall we say that the philosophers were blind in their fine observation and artful description of nature? Shall we say that those men were devoid of understanding who conceived the art of disputation and taught us to speak reasonably? Shall we say that they are insane who developed medicine, devoting their labor to our benefit? What shall we say of all the mathematical sciences? Shall we consider them the ravings of madmen? No, we cannot read the writings of the ancients on these subjects without great admiration. We marvel at them because we are compelled to recognize how preeminent they are (2.2.15).

Calvin waxes just as eloquently in his commentary on 1 Corinthians:

> For what is more noble than man's reason, in which man excels the other animals? How richly deserving of honor are the liberal sciences, which polish man so as to give him the dignity of true humanity! … Who would not extol with the highest commendations civil prudence (not to speak of other things) by which governments, principalities, and kingdoms are maintained?[72]

---

[68] Commentary on Leviticus 19:32 [1563]; CO 24:610.

[69] Commentary on 1 Timothy 2:8 [1548]; CO 52:274.

[70] " When any one disturbs the whole world by his ambition and avarice, or everywhere commits plunders, or oppresses miserable nations, when he distresses the innocent, all cry out, How long? And this cry, proceeding as it does from the feeling of nature and the dictate of justice, is at length heard by the Lord. For how comes it that all, being touched with weariness, cry out, How long? except that they know that this confusion of order and justice is not to be endured? And this feeling, is it not implanted in us by the Lord? It is then the same as though God heard himself, when he hears the cries and greenings of those who cannot bear injustice." Commentary on Habakkuk 2:6 [1559]; CO 43: 540–541. For a provocative analysis of the significance of this and similar passages for Calvin's theology of injustice, see Nicholas Wolterstorff, "The Wounds of God: Calvin's Theology of Social Injustice," *Reformed Journal* 37.6 (June 1987): 14–22.

[71] Commentary on Genesis 12:15 [1554]; CO 23:186. Commentary on Genesis 20:4 [1554]; CO 23:289. For other lists, see Höpfl, *The Christian Polity of John Calvin*, 180; Schreiner, *The Theater of His Glory*, 87–90. Given all of this evidence, Stevenson's comment that "the idea of an independent or independently reachable set of moral provisions apart from Scripture [i.e., natural law] was for Calvin unthinkable" is unwarranted. Stevenson, *Sovereign Grace*, 44.

[72] Commentary on 1 Corinthians 1:20 [1546]; CO 49:325. Cf. Commentary on Isaiah 3:4 [1559]; CO 36:83; 28:29; CO 36:483–484.

Calvin did not hesitate to judge pagan societies superior in the liberal arts to the Christian society of his own day.[73] To such preeminence in earthly affairs, Christians could only respond with deference and admiration.

The basis for Calvin's approval of much of pagan culture was his belief that "the knowledge of all that is most excellent in human life is ... communicated to us through the Spirit of God." The Spirit's general work is pervasive as "he fills, moves, and quickens all things" according to "the law of creation." Christians are thus obligated to learn from and depend upon the contributions of unbelievers. For "if the Lord has willed that we be helped in physics, dialectic, mathematics, and other like disciplines by the work and ministry of the ungodly, let us use this assistance. For if we neglect God's gift freely offered in these arts, we ought to suffer just punishment for our sloths" (2.2.16). Christians "shall neither reject the truth itself, nor despise it wherever it shall appear, unless we wish to dishonor the Spirit of God" (2.2.15).[74]

On the other hand, Calvin was equally adamant about the limitations of natural law. He warns that it should not be concluded from Romans 2:14–15 "that there is in men a full knowledge of the law, but that there are only some seeds of what is right implanted in their nature."[75] Only with scripture as a set of spectacles can human beings see the world rightly (1.6.2). In its ultimate aim, the intent of the natural law is spiritual, and fallen human beings can neither fully understand it nor keep it. "Let us consider, however, for what purpose men have been endowed with this knowledge of the law. How far it can lead them toward the goal of reason and truth will then immediately appear." It is from the perspective of its spiritual purpose, then, that Calvin defines natural law negatively, as "that apprehension of the conscience which distinguishes sufficiently between just and unjust, and which deprives men of the excuse of ignorance, while it proves them guilty by their own testimony" (2.2.22).[76]

Calvin believed human inability is particularly obvious with reference to matters pertaining to the first table of the law, matters of piety and worship, and for this reason some scholars have suggested that Calvin conceived of natural law's positive role simply with respect to the second table.[77] But this assessment is simplistic.

---

[73] Commentary on Daniel 1:4 [1561]; 40:537–540.

[74] Those who "do not venture to borrow anything from heathen authors" are guilty of superstition. "All truth is from God, and consequently, if wicked men have said anything that is true and just, we ought not to reject it, for it has come from God." Commentary on Titus 1:12 [1550]; CO 52:414–415. Cf. Milner, *Calvin's Doctrine of the Church*, 16–19. Cf. Commentary on 1 Corinthians 8:1–2 [1546]; CO 49: 428–429; 15:33; CO 49:554.

[75] Commentary on Romans 2:15 [1556]; CO 49:38. Cf. 4:23; CO 49:86.

[76] Cf. Commentary on the Harmony of the Law [1563]; CO 24:725.

[77] Haas puts it too strongly when he writes, "The insight that sinful humans have into the moral law of God is restricted to the second table of the Decalogue, the final six commandments," though he is

On the one hand, Calvin praised Plato and other pagan writers for recognizing the importance of the soul and of piety. On the other hand, he warned that even with respect to justice and civil affairs, human achievements are but a pale imitation of true righteousness. Humans focus on outward actions while ignoring sins like concupiscence and lust (2.2.24). They understand and desire to practice a particular virtue, but fail (2.2.26). With respect to the second table of the law also, therefore, the power of natural law is limited.

> In the writings of heathen authors there are no doubt to be found true and useful sentences scattered here and there, and it is also true that God has put into the minds of men some knowledge of justice and uprightness, but in consequence of the corruption of our nature, the true light of truth is not to be found among men where revelation is not enjoyed, but only certain mutilated principles which are involved in much obscurity and doubt.[78]

Human wisdom can never seem to get the affairs of society and politics quite right: "Matters are never so well regulated in this world but that many things are involved in darkness, and that there is never so much light, but that many things remain in obscurity."[79]

The key to making sense of Calvin's variously positive and negative statements regarding the usefulness of natural law, therefore, is not interpreting them with respect to the two tables per se, but with respect to the difference between the law's *temporal* purpose and its *spiritual* purpose, between *earthly* things and *heavenly* things. Human reason cannot attain to "God's kingdom and to spiritual insight," for in both of these areas "the greatest geniuses are blinder than moles" (2.2.18; Cf. 2.2.20). The problem is not that the philosophers know *nothing* of God or of the good life, but that they do not know how to attain to their eschatological purpose. "For whatever the philosophers may have ever said of the chief good, it was nothing but cold and vain, for they confined man to himself, while it is necessary for us to go out of ourselves to find happiness. The chief good of man is nothing else but union with God."[80] They understand that God must be worshiped, but they fail to understand

---

correct to emphasize that they have a much better understanding of the second table. Haas, "Calvin's Ethics," 94. Cf. Haas, *The Concept of Equity in Calvin's Ethics*, 68, 72; Backus, "Calvin's Concept of Natural and Roman Law," 13–14. For a fuller picture see Potter, "'The Whole Office of the Law' in the Theology of John Calvin," 123–128.

[78] Commentary on Psalm 19:7 [1557]; CO 31:199–200.

[79] Commentary on 1 Corinthians 4:5 [1546]; CO 49:365–366.

[80] Commentary on Hebrews 4:10 [1549]; CO 55:48. Even the best philosophers and statesmen of antiquity, "even Plato himself," turned their natural knowledge of God into an image that corresponded to their own corrupt reason. Commentary on Romans 1:23 [1556]; CO 49:26. "Whoever then wishes to be truly wise, he must begin with the fear of God and with reverence to his word; for where there is no religion, men cannot certainly understand any thing aright." Commentary on Hosea 14:9

what true piety is. They recognize that it is wrong to commit adultery or murder, but fail to recognize the gravity of lust or malice.[81]

This is why Calvin distinguishes civil virtue from true spiritual righteousness, the righteousness of man from the righteousness of God. The righteousness of God is "that which is approved before his tribunal," in contrast to the righteousness of men, "which is by men counted and supposed to be righteousness, though it be only vapor."[82] The former is inward while the latter is merely outward. But God "will not heed outward appearances, nor be satisfied with any outward work, except what has proceeded from real sincerity of heart." He cares not only for "disguised righteousness," but also for "secret motives and feelings."[83] Though there are "remarkable instances of gentleness, integrity, temperance, and generosity" in the unregenerate, these are in the final analysis "specious disguises" that are impressive "only in the sight of men and as members of civil society."[84] Even in its best works, the world is guided by "mere ambition or by self-love, or some other perverse motive" (3.14.3). Thus, such

[1557]; CO 42:511. Cf. *Institutes* 3.6.1; Commentary on Hebrews 6:11 [1549]; CO 55:76; Commentary on Colossians 2:8 [1548]; CO 52:103; Commentary on Romans 12:1 [1556]; CO 49:232–233; Commentary on 1 Corinthians 1:21 [1546]; CO 49:326–327. David VanDrunen writes, "Natural law, therefore, has a positive function to play in the life of the earthly, civil kingdom, according to Calvin. But . . . natural law has only a negative function to play in regard to spiritual things and the heavenly kingdom of Christ." VanDrunen, *Natural Law and the Two Kingdoms*, 112. Grabill, like VanDrunen, rightly roots the distinction in Calvin's *duplex cognitio*, that is, the distinction between the knowledge of God as creator and the knowledge of God as redeemer. For Calvin, he argues, "the nonsaving, natural knowledge of God still functions competently in the earthly spheres of law, society, politics, economics, and ethics." Grabill, *Rediscovering the Natural Law*, 84. Emphasis added. Cf. Milner, *Calvin's Doctrine of the Church*, 29–31; VanDrunen, *Natural Law and the Two Kingdoms*, 99. I. John Hesselink likewise concludes, "The clue to distinguishing Calvin's meaning as he speaks first positively of the knowledge and convictions of all people concerning God and his law and then negatively of their ignorance, errors, and complete failure, is this: the knowledge which humanity by nature possesses of the law, and their observance to a certain extent of what the second table of the law declares, though not unimportant, is nevertheless external, superficial, and thus finally worthless as far as in any way gaining God's approval." Because "the law is spiritual and its requirements are spiritual," fallen human beings cannot keep it, even though they are "capable of a certain civil virtue." Hesselink, *Calvin's Concept of the Law*, 64 (Cf. 58–59). Cf. Schreiner, *The Theater of His Glory*, 87–94. Schreiner writes, "Like Luther and Melanchthon, Calvin distinguished carefully between the issue of justification and the role of reason within the natural created order. Their belief in human depravity did not imply the annihilation or the uselessness of the natural. The Reformers were well aware that just as divine providence preserved the cosmos, so God left to the human being the ability to foster political and social life. Calvin carefully reminded his readers that the human intellect and will did not simply disappear in the Fall; they were condemned with reference only to justification and salvation but continued to function in the formation of civilized life" (91).

[81] Commentary on Romans 2:15 [1556]; CO 49:38. Cf. Commentary on Romans 7:7 [1556]; CO 49:124.

[82] Commentary on Romans 1:17 [1556]; CO 49:20–21. Cf. Commentary on Isaiah 11:3 [1559]; CO 36:237.

[83] Commentary on Romans 2:2 [1556]; CO 49:31. Cf. 2:11, 16; CO 49:36, 39; *Institutes*, 3.14.1.

[84] Commentary on Galatians 5:22 [1548]; CO 50:255.

acts of civility, which are customary among men, are no proof whatever of charity. To perform any act in the hope of a reward to rich men, from whom we expect a similar return, is not generosity but a system of commercial exchange, and, in like manner, kind offices rendered from mercenary views are of no account in the sight of God and do not deserve to be ascribed to charity.[85]

This doesn't mean civil virtue is without value. On the contrary, unbelievers receive "notable endowments" as gifts from God, and many conduct themselves with a degree of justice, moderation, equity, continence, and respect for the law. Reason requires that Christians acknowledge and honor such persons. Civic virtue is not to be taken for granted, for "if we confuse these things, what order will remain in the world?" (3.14.2)[86] All virtues, even those that fall short of perfection, are gifts of God and worthy of praise, and God uses them "for the preservation of human society in righteousness, continence, friendship, temperance, fortitude, and prudence" (3.14.3). Christians must embrace such natural and political blessings for what they are while directing them toward their higher spiritual purpose.[87] This involves replacing pride with humility and turning all human endeavors toward the ends of piety and love. "We must therefore lay it down as a settled principle that knowledge is good in itself, but as piety is its only foundation, it becomes empty and useless in wicked men. As love is its true seasoning, where that is wanting it is tasteless."[88]

Thus it is impossible on the basis of natural human knowledge to experience a true restoration of order or to attain to the spiritual kingdom of Christ. Humans are not simply alienated from God in body or the "inferior part of the soul," as the philosophers assume. They need a "renovation [*innovatio*]" that is "of the mind, which is the most excellent part of us, and to which philosophers ascribe the supremacy."[89] The world cannot attain to true happiness "when men foolishly and

---

[85] Commentary on Luke 14:12 [1555]; CO 45:396. Cf. Commentary on Hebrews 4:17 [1549]; CO 55:205; 11:31; CO 55:165; Commentary on 1 Timothy 1:15 [1548]; CO 55:260; *Institutes*, 3.14.3.

[86] "For there is such a great difference between the righteous and the unrighteous that it appears even in the dead image thereof" (*Institutes* 3.14.2). "[H]istory shows that there have been great men, endued with heroic virtues, who yet were wholly unacquainted with Christ, and it seems unreasonable that men of so great eminence had no honor." Commentary on 1 John 5:12 [1551]; CO 55:368. God even blesses such virtues (*Institutes*, 3.14.2).

[87] The Christian calling is not to "renounce the wisdom that is implanted in us by nature, or acquired by long practice, but simply that we subject it to the service of God." Commentary on 1 Corinthians 3:18 [1546]; CO 49:359. Cf. Commentary on 1 Corinthians 3:19 [1546]; CO 49:359–360.

[88] Commentary on 1 Corinthians 8:1 [1546]; CO 49:428–429.

[89] Commentary on Romans 12:2 [1556]; CO 49:235. The old man refers not simply to the "inferior appetites or desires" but also to "that part of the soul which is reckoned most noble and excellent." Commentary on Hebrews 4:23 [1549]; CO 55:208. It is true that "the mind holds the highest rank in the human condition, is the seat of reason, presides over the will, and restrains sinful desires." But all this is vanity, for "with respect to the kingdom of God [*regnum Dei*] and all that relates to the spiritual life, the light of human

without the fear of the Lord exult in vanity, that is, in the world, and intoxicated with a transient felicity, look no higher than the earth.⁹⁰ The world remains characterized by disorder, because as long as humans are "outside Christ's kingdom [*extra Christi regnum*]," they remain under the "dominion" and "kingdom of Satan [*Satanae regno*]."⁹¹

THE RESTORATION OF THE WORLD

The scope and purpose of the kingdom of Christ in Calvin's theology is nothing less than the restoration of all things. For human beings, this includes a restoration to their eternal spiritual purpose. "The kingdom of God among men," Calvin writes, "is nothing else than a restoration to a happy life [*restitutio ad beatam vitam*], or in other words, it is true and everlasting happiness [*felicitas*]."⁹² The hope of the resurrection entails "that we ought to expect from him the full restoration of all things and perfect happiness, and in short, that he was sent to erect and prepare the true and perfect state of the kingdom of God."⁹³ The reference to "all things" extends to justice and reconciliation among the nations.⁹⁴ It includes the material creation as well. Calvin argues that the miracles that Jesus performed were in part "intended to inform us that he came to bestow upon us every blessing, to rescue us from the tyranny of Satan and of death, to heal our diseases and sins, and to relieve us from all our miseries."⁹⁵ When Jesus spoke of the peace intended for Israel, Calvin points out, he included, "according to the meaning of the Hebrew phrase, all that is essential to happiness."⁹⁶ The world was created good, designed for the purpose of human happiness, and despite all the worst that the Devil, sin, and humans have done, the creation's destiny remains fixed in God's purposes.

reason differs little from darkness." Commentary on Ephesians 4:17 [1548]; CO 51:204. Cf. Commentary on John 1:5 [1553]; CO 47:6–7. Commentary on 1 Corinthians 3:19 [1546]; CO 49:359–360; 1:20–21; CO 49:324–325; Commentary on Acts 1:7 [1552]; CO 48:9; 20:21, 27; CO 48:463, 28:23; CO 48:569; Commentary on Hebrews 13:8 [1549]; CO 55:189; Commentary on Jeremiah 10:7 [1563]; CO 38:67.

⁹⁰ Commentary on 2 Corinthians 7:10 [1548]; CO 50:89. Cf. Commentary on 1 Peter 2:25 [1551]; CO 55:253.

⁹¹ Commentary on Ephesians 2:2 [1548]; CO 51:161. Cf. Commentary on Romans, Preface [1556]; CO 49:4; Commentary on 1 Timothy 5:15 [1548]; CO 52:314.

⁹² Commentary on Matthew 3:2 [1555]; CO 45:111. Cf. Commentary on Matthew 9:35 [1555]; CO 45:262; Commentary on Psalm 85:10 [1557]; CO 31:789–790.

⁹³ Commentary on John 11:27 [1553]; CO 47:263.

⁹⁴ Commentary on Acts 17:21 [1554]; CO 48:387; Commentary on Ephesians 3:9 [1548]; CO 51:182; Commentary on James 5:7 [1550]; CO 55:425; Commentary on Romans 3:6 [1556]; CO 49:50.

⁹⁵ Commentary on Matthew 10:8 [1555]; CO 45:275. Cf. Commentary on Matthew 14:16 [1555]; CO 45:438; Commentary on John 6:11 [1553]; CO 47:133.

⁹⁶ Commentary on Luke 19:42 [1555]; CO 45:576. Cf. Commentary on Romans 8:6 [1556]; CO 49:142.

While numerous scholars have drawn attention to Calvin's emphasis on the restoration of creation, some have suggested that Calvin minimized the theme.[97] This is in part a reflection of Calvin's reluctance to speculate about the nature of the new creation, given scripture's relative silence on the matter.[98] It also reflects the reformer's emphasis on the eschatological nature of the kingdom of Christ and his consistent tendency to identify it with the church.[99] Finally, as David Holwerda points out, most of the attention Calvin gives the theme appears in his commentaries, which receive much less scholarly attention than does Calvin's *Institutes*.[100]

These caveats aside, Calvin presents his understanding of the kingdom of Christ as the restoration of the world in clear and decisive terms. The sorts of words he typically uses are *instauro*, *restituo*, and *renovatio*, words often translated interchangeably as "renewal," "restoration," and "renovation." Calvin frequently alludes to Acts 3:21 in connection with "the day of renovation and restoration" that will take

---

[97] Quistorp recognizes that Calvin taught "a perfecting of the world or cosmos as a whole," but he criticizes Calvin for failing to develop the point. Quistorp, *Calvin's Doctrine of the Last Things*, 12–13, 181–186. Quistorp complains that Luther and Calvin "fail to do justice to the ideas of the perfection of the new humanity as a whole, of the church in the coming kingdom of God and of the new creation in a new heaven and earth" (12–13). Hesselink suggests that "there are places – granted, not so many – where Calvin speaks of the kingdom of Christ in terms of the renewal and restoration of the *world*." Even where Calvin does speak in this way, "he does not explain precisely what the term 'reform' or the renovation of the world involves" (156–157). I. John Hesselink, "Calvin on the Kingdom of Christ," *Religion Without Ulterior Motive* (ed. E. A. J. G. Van Der Borght. Leiden: Brill, 2006), 139–158. He notes "at least one place" where it "may, in fact, have to do with the renewal of society" (148). VanDrunen gives little attention to the restoration of creation in his work on Calvin's two kingdoms doctrine, despite his interest in Calvin's distinction between creation and redemption. VanDrunen, *Natural Law and the Two Kingdoms*, 69–93. Cf. Cornel Venema, "The Restoration of All Things to Proper Order: An Assessment of the 'Two Kingdoms/Natural Law' Interpretation of Calvin's Public Theology," *Kingdoms Apart: Engaging the Two Kingdoms Perspective* (ed. Ryan G. McIlhenny; Phillipsburg, NJ: Presbyterian and Reformed, 2012), 26–31. Venema, however, wants to press the continuity between creation and redemption much farther than Calvin does (26–27), as does Paul Helm, *Calvin: A Guide for the Perplexed* (London: T&T Clar, 2008), 134–135.

[98] Calvin warns that too many people spend too much time philosophizing about the state of the life to come, but they forget entirely to make sure they will attain to that kingdom. Commentary on Acts 1:8 [1552]; CO 48:10.

[99] Hesselink writes that while for Calvin the kingdom and the church are not coterminous, Calvin "usually simply identifies the kingdom with the church." "Calvin occasionally acknowledges the wider dimension, the 'more,' of the kingdom in relation to the church, but it is a muted motif. Generally, for him kingdom and church are interchangeable." Hesselink, "Calvin on the Kingdom of Christ," 145 (Cf. 145–148). Torrance notes that for Calvin, considered from a certain perspective, "the Church and the Kingdom are essentially correlative." Torrance, *Kingdom and Church*, 133–134. VanDrunen argues that Calvin made a "basic identification" of the kingdom with the church. The church is the "institutional manifestation of the spiritual kingdom in the present life" and it is the "only" such institutional manifestation, "notwithstanding the perpetuation of claims to the contrary." VanDrunen, *Natural Law and the Two Kingdoms*, 79, 81.

[100] Holwerda, "Eschatology and History," 339.

place at Jesus' return. It is a restoration of "all things" [*omnia*], or of the "order" [*ordo*] or "state" [*status*] of creation.[101] When Christ returns he will "establish perfect order in heaven and earth."[102]

The *locus classicus* for Calvin's discussion of the restoration of creation is his commentary on Romans 8:19–21. Taking quite seriously Paul's declaration that the whole creation groans for its redemption, Calvin writes, "I understand the passage to have this meaning – that there is no element and no part of the world which, being touched as it were with a sense of its present misery, does not intensely hope for a resurrection." God has "implanted inwardly the hope of renovation [*renovationis*]" to all things.[103] All creatures shall be renewed, not in the particular sense that individual human beings are, but in the sense that "they, according to their nature, shall be participators of a better condition, for God will restore [*restituet*] to a perfect state [*modo melioris status*] the world, now fallen, together with mankind."[104] Calvin admits that it is not entirely clear just what this sort of restoration will entail, and he warns against speculation. But nevertheless, he specifies two of its most important features. First, the material creation will be liberated from corruption, decay, and death.[105] Second, what it yearns *for* is "eternal" or "celestial glory."[106] In some sense, then, creation will undergo a qualitative transformation that will render it glorious and permanent. But Calvin does not speak of the *progressive* transformation of the material creation prior to Christ's return, for creatures, "being now subject to corruption, cannot be restored [*instaurari*] until the sons of God shall be wholly restored [*restituantur*].[107] The order and flourishing of creation is tied up with the

---

[101] In addition to the references engaged in the following pages, see Commentary on Colossians 1:22 [1548]; CO 52:91; Commentary on Acts 5:31 [1552]; CO 48:111; Commentary on Isaiah 35:1 [1559]; CO 36:590–591; Commentary on Isaiah 42:10 [1559]; CO 37:67; Commentary on Amos 9:11 [1559]; CO 43: 170–171; Commentary on Zechariah 14:8 [1559]; CO 44:371; Commentary on Haggai 2:20–23 [1559]; CO 44:120–121.

[102] Commentary on Matthew 25:31 [1555]; CO 45:686.

[103] Commentary on Romans 8:19 [1556]; CO 49:152. Cf. Schreiner, *The Theater of His Glory*, 97–98.

[104] Commentary on Romans 8:21 [1556]; CO 49:153. Elsewhere Calvin writes that "things created are subject to decay, but Christ's kingdom is eternal; then all creatures must needs be brought into a better state." Commentary on Hebrews 12:28 [1549]; CO 55:186.

[105] What matters is "that such will be the constitution and the complete order of things that nothing will be deformed [*deforme*] or fading [*fluxum*]." "But what that perfection will be, as to beasts as well as plants and metals, it is not meet nor right in us to inquire more curiously, for the chief effect of corruption is decay." Commentary on Romans 8:21 [1556]; CO 49:153.

[106] Commentary on Romans 8:19 [1556]; CO 49:152. Cf. Commentary on Romans 8:17 [1556]; CO 49: 150–151.

[107] Hence they, longing for their renewal [*instaurationem*], look forward to the manifestation of the celestial kingdom [*regni coelestis*]." Commentary on Romans 8:19 [1556]; CO 49:152. Insofar as Calvin thinks of the kingdom and its history in terms of progress, it is progress defined by the preaching of the gospel and the gathering of the church. See Peter Wilcox, "'The Progress of the Kingdom of Christ' in Calvin's Exposition of the Prophets," in *Calvinus Sincerioris Religionis Vindex* (Kirksville: Sixteenth Century Journal, 1997), 315–322, 319.

order and flourishing of human beings. The creation longs for the restoration to which it will attain when humans have themselves been restored.[108]

In the commentary on Romans 8:19–21 Calvin cross-references related passages in 2 Peter 3 and Isaiah 65.[109] When Peter says that the earth will be consumed, Calvin argues in his commentary on 2 Peter, he did not mean that it would literally be destroyed. "Of the elements of the world I shall only say this one thing, that they are to be consumed only that they may be renovated, their substance still remaining the same, as it may be easily gathered from Romans 8:21 and from other passages."[110] Calvin warns against speculation, but his argument here presupposes the Aristotelian distinction between an object's substance and accidents. In its substance, creation will be restored and continue into the kingdom of Christ, but speculation as to what that will mean in practical terms (i.e., the accidents of creation) must be avoided.

Calvin offers a similar interpretation of God's proclamation in Isaiah 65, "Behold, I create new heavens and a new earth." He suggests that the proclamation is "exaggerated" but that such hyperbole is an appropriate representation of the radical changes that accompany the coming of Christ. Thus "when we shall be perfectly renewed, heaven and earth shall also be fully renewed, and shall regain their former state."[111] Here again Calvin notes that the renovation of creation awaits the more particular renovation of human beings, and it is therefore human renewal that is the focus of Isaiah's prophecy. For humans "hold the first rank, and it is through our sin that 'the creatures groan and are subject to vanity,' as Paul shows (Romans 8:20)."[112] In that respect Calvin warns against taking Isaiah 65 too literally with reference to the particulars of creation, "that none may think that this relates to trees, or beasts, or the order of the stars, for it must be referred to the inward renewal of man."[113] When the prophet predicts that "everything shall be fully restored when Christ shall reign," therefore, he is primarily concerned with the order of *human* affairs.

> But since it is the office of Christ to bring back everything to its condition and order, that is the reason why he declares that the confusion or ruin that now exists in

---

[108] See Holwerda, "Eschatology and History," 338; Millner, *Calvin's Doctrine of the Church*, 20, 37–38, 46–47; Schreiner, *The Theater of His Glory*, 99–100.

[109] Commentary on Romans 8:21 [1556]; CO 49:153.

[110] Commentary on 2 Peter 3:10 [1551]; CO 55:476. Cf. 2:5; CO 55:462; Commentary on 1 Peter 4:7 [1555]; CO 55:274; Schreiner, *The Theater of His Glory*, 98–99; Venema, "The Restoration of All Things to Proper Order," 30.

[111] Commentary on Isaiah 65:17 [1559]; CO 37:428–429.

[112] Commentary on Isaiah 65:17 [1559]; CO 37:429. "[T]hese things take place in us so far as we are renewed. But we are only in part renewed, and therefore we do not yet see a new heaven and a new earth."

[113] Commentary on Isaiah 66:22 [1559]; CO 37:453.

human affairs shall be removed by the coming of Christ, because at that time, corruptions having been taken away, the world shall return to its first origin."[114]

Two of the passages on which Calvin makes some of his most poignant remarks about Jesus' restoration of the world are John 12:31 and John 16:11. When Jesus spoke of his "judgment" of the world and the Devil, Calvin writes that Jesus meant

> that the world must be restored to a proper order, for the Hebrew word *mishpat*, which is translated judgment, means a well-ordered state. Now we know that out of Christ there is nothing but confusion in the world, and though Christ had already begun to erect the kingdom of God, yet his death was the commencement of a well-regulated condition and the full restoration of the world."[115]

Christ has won the decisive victory over the Devil through his death and resurrection, commencing the restoration of all things and the inauguration of his kingdom.

> Judgment, therefore, is contrasted with what is confused and disordered, or to express it briefly, it is the opposite of confusion, or we might call it righteousness, a sense which it often bears in scripture. The meaning therefore is that Satan, so long as he retains the government, perplexes and disturbs all things, so that there is an unseemly and disgraceful confusion in the works of God, but when he is stripped of his tyranny by Christ, then the world is restored and good order is seen to reign."[116]

The means by which the order of human affairs is renewed is through the regeneration of human beings, for "it is in a manner a renovation of the world when men suffer themselves to be ruled by God."[117] In a typical statement Calvin drives that point home:

> Christ was sent in order to bring the whole world under the authority of God and obedience to him, and this shows that without him everything is confused and disordered ... Now, we ought to judge of this government from the nature of his kingdom, which is not external but belongs to the inner man, for it consists of a good conscience and uprightness of life, not what is so reckoned before men, but what is so reckoned before God."[118]

It is important to stress, though, that Calvin clearly avoids reducing the kingdom to a narrow salvation of individuals, or even of the church, despite concerns to the

---

[114] Commentary on Isaiah 65:25 [1559]; CO 37:433–434. What does it mean that God will "restore everything to its proper order?" Calvin answers, "'in Christ,' as Paul says, 'are collected all things that are either in heaven or in earth' (Ephesians 1:10)." Commentary on Isaiah 51:16 [1559]; CO 37:237.

[115] Commentary on John 12:31 [1553]; CO 47:293–294. Cf. Commentary on John 12:32 [1553]; CO 47:294.

[116] Commentary on John 16:11 [1553]; CO 47:360–361.

[117] Commentary on Jeremiah 31:33 [1563]; CO 38:691–692. Cf. Commentary on 1 Thessalonians 5:23 [1550]; CO 52:178; Commentary on Acts 8:5 [1552]; CO 48:177.

[118] Commentary on Isaiah 42:1 [1559]; CO 37:59–60.

contrary.[119] For while he certainly has an anthropocentric emphasis, it is consistently moderated by his insistence that renewed human beings are the first fruits of a restoration of the entire physical creation.[120] Calvin exalts in the rhetoric of a passage like Psalm 96:11, "Let the heavens be glad, and let the earth rejoice; let the sea roar, and all that fills it; let the field exult, and everything in it!" Although the psalmist makes use of literary hyperbole, Calvin admits, "the hyperbole here employed does not want a certain foundation of a more literal kind. As all elements in the creation groan and travail together with us, according to Paul's declaration (Romans 8), they may reasonably rejoice in the restoration of all things according to their earnest desire."[121] As Isaiah's prophecy of a wolf lying down with a lamb suggested, Christ will not only defeat all evil, but he will "restore to its former beauty the world which lay under the curse."[122]

The point is not simply abstract for Calvin. In various places the reformer carefully describes redemption in terms of the restoration of humans' right relation to the material world. For instance, in his commentary on 1 Timothy 4 he explains,

> God has appointed to his children alone the whole world and all that is in the world. For this reason they are also called the heirs of the world, for at the beginning Adam was appointed to be lord of all on this condition, that he should continue in obedience to God. Accordingly, his rebellion against God deprived of the right, which had been bestowed on him, not only himself but his posterity. And since all things are subject to Christ, we are fully restored by his mediation, and that through

---

[119] See Quistorp, *Calvin's Doctrine of the Last Things*, 161, 180, 192–193; Hesselink, "Calvin on the Kingdom of Christ," 156. To the contrary, Douglass argues, for Calvin, "restored humanity is not individual but social. To be redeemed by Christ and made a member of his body is to be incorporated into the church, the household of faith. The church represents the inbreaking of the kingdom of God; it already shows forth the new creation to some degree, though never fully in this fallen world" (75). Jane Dempsey Douglass, "Calvin's Relation to Social and Economic Change," *Church and Society* 74 (1984): 75–81.

[120] For example, Calvin typically insists in his commentary on Colossians 1:15–20 that when the Apostle Paul describes Christ as having created and reconciled "all things," he likely has angels and humans primarily in view. But he admits that the statement is *true* if interpreted in a broader sense. It is of "no great importance" whether "all things" be taken as a reference to all creatures or to everything absolutely. The phrase can be taken either way, and "the simple meaning is that all things are subjected to his sway." His work of both creation and redemption extend to "the whole world [*toto quoque mundo*]." Commentary on Colossians 1:17 [1548]; CO 52:86 (Cf. 1:18; 52:87). Cf. Commentary on Micah 5:1–2 [1559]; CO 43:368. Holwerda thus correctly summarizes Calvin's thought: "The history of salvation which becomes visible in the church contains within it the meaning of the history of the world. And the renewal manifesting itself in the body of Christ is the renewal that embraces the whole creation." Holwerda, "Eschatology and History," 337. Cf. Tonkin, *The Church and the Secular Order in the Theology of the Reformers*, 116; Schreiner, *The Theater of His Glory*, 97–114.

[121] Commentary on Psalm 96:11 [1557]; CO 32:42.

[122] Commentary on Isaiah 11:6 [1559]; CO 36:241–242.

faith, and therefore all that unbelievers enjoy may be regarded as the property of others, which they rob or steal.[123]

While no human being has any right to the good gifts of creation, Christ has taken it upon himself to restore all these good gifts to those who follow him by faith.[124] "If the fullness of the earth is the Lord's there is nothing in the world that is not sacred [*sanctum*] and pure."[125]

In his commentary on Romans 4:13, Calvin confesses that it is at first glance surprising that the Apostle Paul described Abraham as the "heir of the world" given that the great patriarch was famous for having looked beyond this world to a salvation that was spiritual and eternal. But, Calvin writes, the apostle "calls Christ the heir of all the good things of God [in Hebrews 1:2], for the adoption which we obtain through his favor restores to us the possession of the inheritance which we lost in Adam." Lest the material significance of the point be lost, Calvin drives it home. When believers "enter on the full possession of their inheritance, . . . all creatures shall be made subservient to their glory. For both heaven and earth shall be renewed for this end, that according to their measure they may contribute to render glorious the kingdom of God."[126] The meek, Jesus said, will inherit the earth.[127]

---

[123] Commentary on 1 Timothy 4:3 [1548]; CO 52:296. "For God had at the beginning constituted man as his son, the heir of all good things, but through sin the first man became alienated from God and deprived himself and his posterity of all good things, as well as of the favor of God. We hence only then begin to enjoy by right the good things of God when Christ, the universal heir, admits us into an union with himself, for he is an heir that he may endow us with his riches." Commentary on Hebrews 1:2 [1549]; CO 55:11. Cf. Commentary on Daniel 7:17–18 [1561]; CO 41:66–67; Commentary on Romans 4:13 [1556]; CO 49:77; Commentary on 1 Corinthians 15:27 [1546]; CO 49:548. Calvin did not invent this argument. Medieval theologians like Giles of Rome had gone so far as to suggest that unbelievers derive rights to property and rule only from the pope. See Oliver O'Donovan and Joan Lockwood O'Donovan, *From Irenaeus to Grotius: A Sourcebook in Christian Political Thought* (Grand Rapids: Eerdmans, 1999), 231–236. But Calvin never suggested that believers could claim special prerogative over the material of this world. In his commentary on Hebrews 2:5 he specified that a distinction must be made between right and legitimate use by virtue of God's grace. Adam was denied the good things of creation, "not that he was denied the use of them, but that he could have had no right to them," and futility, suffering, and death were to be constant reminders "of this loss of right." Commentary on Hebrews 2:5 [1549]; CO 55:24. The full realization of Christ's lordship awaits Jesus' second coming. Commentary on Hebrews 2:8 [1549]; CO 55:25.

[124] Christ's lordship extends "not only [to] things needful for eternal blessedness, but also such inferior things as serve to supply the wants of the body." Commentary on Hebrews 2:8 [1549]; CO 55:26. "Here it ought to be observed, that we cannot possess our wealth and have the peaceful and lawful enjoyment of it in any other way than by dwelling in the kingdom of Christ, who is the only heir of the world, and without being engrafted into his body." Commentary on Isaiah 65:21–22 [1559]; CO 37:431. Cf. Commentary on 1 Timothy 4:5 [1548]; CO 52:297. Cf. Haas, "Calvin's Ethics," 96; Tonkin, *The Church and the Secular Order in Reformation Thought*, 118.

[125] Commentary on 1 Corinthians 10:26 [1546]; CO 49:469. Cf. 10:31; CO 49:471.

[126] Commentary on Romans 4:13 [1556]; CO 49:77. The godly acknowledge the earth as their own possession already in the present life, enjoying created things "as pledges and earnests of eternal life."

[127] Commentary on Matthew 5:5 [1555]; CO 45:162–163.

Thus the renovation of the world is presented in scripture as an event in chronological relation to time (albeit beyond ordinary history) rather than as a form of hierarchical transcendence as understood in Neoplatonic terms. The "world to come, or the future world," is the "renovated [*renovato*] world. To make the thing clearer, let us suppose two worlds [*duplicem mundum*] – the first the old, corrupted by Adam's sin, the other later in time, as renewed by Christ."[128] It is within this context of the renovation of the world that Calvin's insistence on the importance of the resurrection must be interpreted. For Calvin the resurrection is "that by which we are translated from the kingdom of death [*regno mortis*] to the kingdom of life [*regnum vitae*]."[129] Not even the souls of the faithful in heaven have the fullness of life without the resurrection of their *material* bodies. Rather "the whole of their felicity and consolation depends exclusively on the resurrection, because it is well with them on this account and no other, that they wait for that day on which they shall be called to the possession of the kingdom of God."[130] Christians, Calvin maintains, do not long for a day in which their immortal souls, having been liberated from the material creation, will inhabit an eternal afterlife in the "Elysian fields," let alone dream of any other such ethereal fantasy. Rather, they look forward to the day when, along with the entire creation, they will be restored to perfect life, order, and happiness in communion with God.[131] As Calvin writes in his commentary on Isaiah 32:20,

> since Christ has restored to believers the inheritance of the world, with good reason do the prophets assert that he would renew the earth, so as to remove its filthiness and restore that beauty which it had lost. They who complain that it is not yet fulfilled ought to consider whether or not they themselves are purified from every stain of sin. And if they are still at a great distance from spiritual righteousness, let them be satisfied with enjoying the blessing of God according to the measure of regeneration, the full enjoyment of which we must not expect to obtain until, freed from the pollution of the flesh, we shall bear the perfect image of God.[132]

THE SPIRITUALITY OF THE KINGDOM

Calvin introduces his understanding of the kingdom in his *Institutes* with the declaration, "It would be pointless to speak of this without first warning my readers

---

[128] Commentary on Hebrews 2:5 [1549]; CO 55:24.

[129] Commentary on Romans 11:15 [1556]; CO 49:220. Cf. Quistorp, *Calvin's Doctrine of the Last Things*, 108.

[130] Commentary on 1 Corinthians 15:18 [1546]; CO 49:543.

[131] Commentary on 1 Corinthians 15:19 [1546]; CO 49:544–545. Cf. Commentary on Luke 23:43 [1555]; CO 45:776.

[132] Commentary on Isaiah 32:20 [1559]; CO 36:555. Cf. Commentary on Romans 10:19 [1556]; CO 49:209; Holwerda, "Eschatology and History," 326–327.

that it is spiritual in nature" (2.15.3).[133] By saying that it is "spiritual," Calvin does not mean that the kingdom is immaterial or ethereal in some way. Rather, the term spiritual means that 1) the power of the kingdom is that of the Holy Spirit, 2) the kingdom completes creation's eschatological purpose, and 3) the kingdom will be consummated only at Christ's return. Put simply, the kingdom is 1) from the Spirit of God, 2) leads human beings upward to God, and 3) leads them forward to eternity. Although its full manifestation is future, the kingdom breaks into the present age by means of the hidden work of the Holy Spirit, which is why Jesus describes the kingdom as inward. As he told the Pharisees in Luke 17, "because the Kingdom of God is within us, it will not come with observation." Jesus' hearers may have taunted him for outward signs, but "he enjoined them to enter into their own consciences, because 'the Kingdom of God ... is righteousness and peace and joy in the Holy Spirit'" (2.15.4).[134]

Calvin was convinced that it was a cardinal Jewish error to assume that the messiah's kingdom would be just like David's kingdom of old. His writings are scattered with criticisms of the Jewish expectation of an earthly kingdom, a false hope, he warned, that blinded them from seeing the kingdom of Christ.[135] He believed the same error plagued Christendom. In a typical statement he warns, "because we are more than we ought set upon the seeking of the peace of the flesh, whereby it comes to pass that many tie the grace of Christ to the present life, it is expedient for us to be accustomed to think otherwise, that we may know that the kingdom of Christ is spiritual [*spirituale esse Christi regnum*]."[136] The problem is that "nothing is more contrary to our natural judgment than to seek life in death, riches in poverty and want, glory in shame and disgrace – to be wanderers in this world, and at the same time its heirs!"[137]

The disciples themselves falsely imagined that Christ would obtain "an earthly kingdom" immediately characterized by "the highest prosperity and wealth."[138]

---

[133] Cf. Commentary on Hebrews 12:1 [1549]; CO 55:171; Commentary on Luke 1:33 [1555]; CO 45:29.

[134] Cf. Commentary on Isaiah 59:21 [1559]; CO 37:352. Cf. Hesselink, "Calvin on the Kingdom of Christ," 143–145, 152–155; Quistorp, *Calvin's Doctrine of the Last Things*, 111.

[135] Commentary on Matthew 22:4 [1555]; CO 45:399.

[136] Commentary on Acts 2:20 [1552]; CO 48:35. Cf. 28:23; CO 48:568. "[T]he kingdom of Christ is spiritual [*Christi regnum est spirituale*]." Commentary on Ephesians 1:3 [1548]; CO 51:146. Cf. Commentary on Hebrews 13:13 [1549]; CO 55:192; Commentary on 1 Corinthians, [1546] Dedication; CO 12:258–260.

[137] Rabbi Abarbinel, Calvin writes, "rejects our idea of the spiritual reign of Christ as a foolish imagination. For the kingdom of God, he says, is established under the whole heavens and is given to the people of the saints. If it is established under heaven, says he, it is earthly, and if earthly, therefore not spiritual." Calvin responds that while it is true that Jesus' kingdom exists *in* this world, it is not *of* it. "God ... exercises his heavenly reign in the world because he dwells in the hearts of his people by his Spirit." Commentary on Daniel 7:27 [1561]; CO 41:81–86.

[138] Commentary on Matthew 18:1 [1555]; CO 45:499. The disciples' error simply reflected "the common error of their nation." Commentary on Acts 1:8 [1552]; CO 48:10. Cf. Commentary on Matthew 17:22

Calvin identified the disciples as making two errors, one corresponding to the nature or quality of Christ's kingdom, the other to the time of its completion. First, the disciples conceived of the kingdom according to their carnal senses, rather than looking to heaven to understand its nature. Second, they expected the kingdom to be established immediately, failing to grasp that they had first to go the way of the cross.[139] In his commentary on Acts 1, Calvin writes, "They ask him concerning a kingdom, but they dream of an earthly kingdom which should flow with riches, with dainties, with external peace, and with such like good things, and while they assign the present time to the restoring of the same, they desire to triumph before the battle."[140] The two errors were closely related. The disciples expected a *merely* earthly kingdom, and they expected it right away. In Calvin's view Jesus' kingdom will restore all things, but because full restoration awaits his return, in the present age this restoration is only experienced in the work of the Holy Spirit.

Yet Calvin concedes that the disciples' confusion was understandable. "Now we know what splendid promises of peace, righteousness, joy, and abundance of all blessings are to be found everywhere in scripture."[141] The prophets tended to describe the kingdom of Christ with breathtaking imagery, portraying his first and second coming and everything in between as one decisive event. Given this prophetic tradition, it was no wonder that the Jews expected that at the messiah's coming they would be delivered from war, injustice, and suffering. But they failed to understand that all of this would not take place at one time. "Not that those prophecies which I have just mentioned will fail to be accomplished, but because the full accomplishment of them does not immediately appear in one day. For it is enough that believers now obtain a taste of those blessings, so as to cherish the hope of the full enjoyment of them at a future period."[142]

[1555]; CO 45:495; 20:21–22; CO 45:553; 24:29; CO 45:666–667; Commentary on 2 Peter 2:1 [1551]; CO 55:459.

[139] Commentary on Matthew 24:4 [1555]; CO 45:650; Commentary on Luke 19:11 [1555]; CO 45:567; Commentary on Acts 1:8 [1552]; CO 48:10. In his commentary on Isaiah 9:7 Calvin explains that when Isaiah prophesied that the government of the messiah would be perpetual, he was referring "both to time and to quality." "Though the kingdom of Christ is in such a condition that it appears as if it were about to perish at every moment, yet God not only protects and defends it, but also extends its boundaries far and wide, and then preserves and carries it forward in uninterrupted progression to eternity." Believers should not expect outward glory, but rather "an unseen extension of the kingdom." CO 36:198–199. In his Commentary on Matthew 10:7, Calvin notes that the gospel writers use the phrases "kingdom of God" and "kingdom of heaven" interchangeably. Why? "It was to inform the Jews, first, that they owed their restoration to divine agency, and not to the kindness of men; secondly, that under the reign of God their condition would be prosperous; and, thirdly, that the happiness which had been promised to them was not earthly and fading, but heavenly and eternal." CO 45:275.

[140] Commentary on Acts 1:6 [1552]; CO 48:8 (Cf. 1:8; 48:10).

[141] Commentary on Matt 24:4 [1555]; CO 45:650.

[142] Commentary on Matt 24:4 [1555]; CO 45:650. The ordinary mode of the prophets is to to speak of "the whole kingdom of Christ, from the beginning to the end." Sometimes they refer to its

Calvin believed this same confusion plagued the church of his own day. "Now, though our condition is different because we have not been educated among the shadows of the law so as to be infatuated by that superstition of an earthly kingdom of Christ, yet scarcely one person in a hundred is to be found who does not labor under a very similar disease."[143] Christians often assumed they knew just what form the progress of the kingdom would take, "but when we think that the kingdom of God can, nay, must, be advanced in this particular manner or in that ... we are often mistaken in our opinion."[144] The papists were guilty of exploiting the prophets' declarations that the church will one day reign with Christ, claiming temporal dominion and magisterial authority over souls. "The papists seize upon such testimonies to clothe themselves in the spoils of God, as if God had resigned his right to them! But they are immersed in the same error with the Jews."[145]

The chiliasts, for their part, erroneously imagined that Christ would establish a temporal kingdom as part of an age of prosperity before his return at the end of the age.[146] Calvin agreed that the gospel will, in the course of history, "put to flight the darkness in which Antichrist will reign." But why would Christ establish such a temporal kingdom only to see it pass away before "that final day of the restoration [*instaurationis*] of all things"?[147] Referring to Isaiah's prophecy that one day every person will bow in submission to Jesus, Calvin cautions, "if we examine it more closely it will be evident that its complete fulfillment is not now taking place, nor has it ever taken place, nor is it to be hoped for in future ages." Only when Jesus returns at the end of the ages can Christians expect to see this prophecy fulfilled.[148]

commencement, and at other times to its termination, but often they simply "mark out by one delineation the whole course of the kingdom of Christ, from its beginning to its end." Commentary on Joel 2:30–31 [1559]; CO 42:573–574. Cf. Commentary on Isaiah 45:23 [1559]; CO 37:149–150; 60:21; CO 37:368; 43:8; CO 37:86; 43:18; CO 37:94; 40:1; CO 37:3–4; 42:1; CO 37:58; 65:17; CO 37:428–429; Commentary on Zechariah 14:21 1559); CO 44:390; Commentary on Daniel 7:27 [1561]; CO 41:81–86. Wilcox writes that for Calvin prophecy has a triple reference, "first to an imminent historical event ... second, to Christ (by which he can mean the 'incarnation,' 'the ascension,' or even 'the apostolic era and the preaching of the Gospel'; and third, to the whole course of history up until the Last Day (on which grounds he applies them to the sixteenth century church)." Peter Wilcox, "The Progress of the Kingdom of Christ," 317. Cf. Richard A. Muller, "The Hermeneutic of Promise and Fulfillment in Calvin's Exegesis of the Old Testament Prophecies of the Kingdom," *The Bible in the Sixteenth Century* (ed. by David C. Steinmetz; Durham and London: Duke University Press, 1990), 58–82.

[143] Commentary on Matthew 24:3 [1555]; CO 45:649.

[144] Commentary on 1 Corinthians 12:8 [154]; CO 49:140–141.

[145] Commentary on Daniel 7:27 [1561]; CO 41:81–86.

[146] Commentary on Acts 1:8 [1552]; CO 48:11.

[147] Commentary on 2 Thessalonians 2:8 [1550]; CO 48:201. Cf. Commentary on 1 Timothy 3:1–2 [1548]; CO 52:376. On Calvin's critique of millennialism, see Quistorp, *Calvin's Doctrine of the Last Things*, 158–160; Bolt, 257–260. Balke notes that Calvin viewed chiliasm as a "*horrendum dictu delirium* and a secularization of the *regnum Christi*." Balke, *Calvin and the Radical Anabaptists*, 297 (Cf. 295–299).

[148] Commentary on Romans 14:11 [1556]; CO 49:263. Cf. 2:16; CO 49:39; Commentary on Acts 4:25 [1552]; CO 48:91.

Christians should have had no trouble recognizing the spiritual nature of the kingdom in light of the poverty and weakness that characterized Jesus' life. The announcement of Jesus' birth, Calvin marvels, was made to lowly shepherds, the first people to recognize the new child as the Christ.[149] Matthew's account of the birth adds to the paradox:

> A beautiful instance of real harmony amidst apparent contradiction is here exhibited. A star from heaven announces that he is a king, to whom a manger intended for cattle serves for a throne because he is refused admittance among the lowest of the people. His majesty shines in the East, while in Judea it is so far from being acknowledged that it is visited by many marks of dishonor. Why is this? The heavenly Father chose to appoint the star and the Magi as our guides to lead directly to his Son, while he stripped him of all earthly splendor for the purpose of informing us that his kingdom is spiritual.[150]

The same paradox was communicated through his triumphal entry. "In order to lay claim to the honors of royalty, he enters Jerusalem riding an ass. A magnificent display, truly! More especially when the ass was borrowed from some person, and when the want of a saddle and of accouterments compelled the disciples to throw their garments on it, which was a mark of mean and disgraceful poverty."[151] While neither the Jews nor Jesus' own disciples grasped what their messiah was doing, Calvin beams with admiration for the thief on the cross because he discovered Jesus' glory at the moment it was most shrouded in humiliation: "He adores Christ as a king while on the gallows, celebrates his kingdom in the midst of shocking and worse than revolting abasement, and declares him when dying to be the Author of life."[152]

Given the temptation to interpret Calvin's rhetoric in Neoplatonic terms, it is necessary to emphasize that Calvin did not view the kingdom of Christ as some sort of ethereal realm beyond the material creation. To be sure, like the broader Christian tradition, Calvin did often use otherworldly rhetoric. For example, in his commentary on John 6:32, he writes that Jesus "shows that the heavenly life ought to be preferred to this earthly life because the godly have no other reason for living here

---

[149] Commentary on Luke 2:8 [1555]; CO 45:73. [150] Commentary on Matthew 2:1 [1555]; CO 45:81.

[151] "[T]he meaning is that his kingdom ... is spiritual." Commentary on John 12:14 [1553]; CO 47:285. Cf. 12:12; 47:281–282; Commentary on Matthew 21:1 [1555]; CO 45:572.

[152] Commentary on Luke 23:42 [1555]; CO 45:774. Cf. Commentary on John 1:45 [1553]; CO 47:33; Commentary on Matthew 16:27 [1555]; CO 45:483. Calvin concedes that Jesus exhibited astonishing power during the course of his ministry, but he points out that the gospel writers take pains to show that he worked only by the power of the Spirit and that the intent of his ministry was therefore spiritual. Commentary on Matthew 8:17 [1555]; CO 45:155–156. Cf. 14:34; CO 45:444; 4:12; CO 45:138; Commentary on 1 Timothy 3:16 [1548]; CO 52:290.

than that, being sojourners in the world, they may travel rapidly towards their heavenly country."[153] Other similar examples could also be cited.[154]

The question is, did Calvin use such terminology to denote a literal place beyond this world that could be identified as heaven (or as the kingdom of Christ)? In his commentary on Acts 1:11, Calvin notes that the word "heaven" can have several meanings. "I grant that this word heaven is interpreted diverse ways, sometimes for the air, sometimes for the whole system of the spheres, sometimes for the glorious kingdom of God, where the majesty of God has its proper seat, even though it fills the whole world."[155] Notably, while observing this flexibility of interpretation, Calvin explicitly rejected Neoplatonic speculation about heaven as an ethereal place hierarchically superior to the material world.[156] He likewise spurned speculation about a created place to which Christ has ascended. "[Some,] cavilling, facetiously ask, 'In what region of the empyreal heaven does Christ sit?' Let them indeed enjoy these fine speculations. I am taught by the Holy Spirit that he is *above all heavens* [*supra omnes coelos*]."[157] In his commentary on John 3, Calvin criticized the conflation of the kingdom of God with a place called heaven: "they are mistaken who suppose that the kingdom of God means heaven, for it rather means the spiritual life which is begun by faith in this world and gradually increases every day according to the continued progress of faith."[158] Indeed, when Paul wrote in Galatians 4 of the Jerusalem that is above, Calvin observes, he was not referring to a place at all.

> The Jerusalem which he calls above, or heavenly, is not contained in heaven, nor are we to seek for it out of this world [*extra mundum*], for the church is spread over the whole world and is a "stranger and pilgrim on the earth." Why then is it said to be from heaven? Because it originates in heavenly grace, for the sons of God are "born not of blood, nor of the will of the flesh, nor of the will of man," but by the power of the Holy Spirit.[159]

---

[153] Commentary on John 6:27 [1553]; CO 47:139–140.

[154] Commenting on 2 Peter 1:11 he writes, "He calls it the kingdom of Christ because we cannot ascend to heaven except under his banner and guidance." Commentary on 2 Peter 1:11 [1551]; CO 55:451. Cf. Commentary on John 12:25 [1553]; CO 47:289; Commentary on Philippians 3:21 [1546]; CO 52:56.

[155] Commentary on Acts 1:11 [1552]; CO 48:13.

[156] From such speculation, he writes, "has sprung up a great part of scholastic theology and everything which that trifler Dionysius has been so daring as to contrive in reference to the heavenly hierarchies." Commentary on 2 Corinthians 12:4 [1548]; CO 50:138. Cf. Schreiner, *The Theater of His Glory*, 22.

[157] "According to the common mode of speaking in Scripture, I call *whatever is beyond the world* [*extra mundum*] heaven." Dedication to Commentary on Jeremiah [1563]; CO 20:75. Emphasis added.

[158] Commentary on John 3:3 [1553]; CO 47:54. Some might ask, "Will his throne be in heaven or also on earth?" Calvin answers, "Christ reigns not only among angels but also among men, lest we should think that in order to seek him we must enter into heaven." Commentary on Isaiah 16:5 [1559]; CO 36: 304–305.

[159] Commentary on Galatians 4:26 [1548]; CO 50:239.

If the heavenly kingdom is not a place, what is it? Because Calvin used the word "heaven" flexibly, any given instance has to be interpreted contextually. But as these few quotations suggest, he often used the word to denote the governing power of God that is qualitatively superior to any created power. Thus he could write in his commentary on 2 Corinthians 12, "the term heaven, taken by itself, denotes here the blessed and glorious kingdom of God which is above all the spheres and the firmament itself, and even the entire framework of the world."[160] That Christ ascended to heaven likewise means not that he has arrived at a particular location but that he possesses all power in heaven and on earth.[161] In his commentary on Ephesians 1:20–22 Calvin argues that Christ's session at God's right hand is simply a metaphor taken "from earthly princes who confer the honor of sitting alone with themselves on those whom they have clothed with the highest authority." Its purpose is to demonstrate that Christ has received absolute power from the Father, "that he may administer in his name the government of heaven and earth." Its implication is not that Christ's kingdom exists in a place called heaven, but that it is universal. "As the right hand of God fills heaven and earth, it follows that the kingdom and power of Christ [*regnum Christi*] are equally extensive."[162] The kingdom of Christ is heavenly or spiritual, therefore, not because it constitutes a celestial realm above the material world, but because it exists wherever people submit themselves wholeheartedly to Christ's government through his Holy Spirit.[163]

The primary purpose and effect of Christ's ascension was that Christ might commence his rule on earth through the Holy Spirit, a reality that the disciples came to understand at Pentecost.[164] "As his body was raised above all the heavens, so his power and energy were diffused and spread beyond all the bounds of heaven and earth" (2.16.14).

> He therefore sits on high, transfusing us with his power, that he may quicken us to spiritual life, sanctify us by his Spirit, adorn his church with divers gifts of his grace,

---

[160] Commentary on 2 Corinthians 12:2–3 [1548]; CO 50:137.

[161] Commentary on John 20:17 [1553]; CO 47:33. Cf. 6:51, 58; CO 47:152, 157; Commentary on Philippians 3:20 [1548]; CO 52:56.

[162] Commentary on Ephesians 1:20 [1548]; CO 51:158. "For where shall we erect him a throne, that he may sit at the right hand of God the Father, seeing God fills all things in such sort, that we ought to imagine no place for his right hand?" He goes on, "Therefore, the whole text is a metaphor." Commentary on Acts 7:56 [1552]; CO 48:168. Cf. Commentary on Matthew 22:44 [1555]; CO 45:619; Commentary on Hebrews 1:13 [1549]; CO 55:19; Commentary on Romans 8:34 [1556]; CO 40:164; Commentary on John 20:18 [1553]; CO 47:435; Commentary on Mark 16:19 [1555]; CO 45:828; Commentary on 1 Peter 3:22 [1551]; CO 55:269; Commentary on Colossians 3:1 [1548]; CO 52:117–118.

[163] See Tonkin, *The Church and the Secular Order in the Theology of the Reformers*, 127; Torrance, *Kingdom and Church*, 123; Hesselink, "Calvin on the Kingdom of Christ," 155.

[164] Commentary on Matthew 16:28 [1555]; CO 45:483. The Spirit's "office" is now to "establish the kingdom of Christ." Commentary on John 16:14 [1553]; CO 47:363. Cf. 16:11; 47:360–361; *Institutes* 3.3.2; Commentary on John 7:39 [1553]; CO 47:182; 14:18; CO 47:330.

keep it safe from all harm by his protection, restrain the raging enemies of his cross and of our salvation by the strength of his hand, and finally hold all power in heaven and on earth. All this he does until he shall lay low all his enemies (who are our enemies too) and complete the building of his church. This is the true state of his Kingdom; this is the power that the Father has conferred upon him, until, in coming to judge the living and the dead, he accomplishes his final act (2.16.16).

Calvin notes that the prophet Isaiah declared the messiah would be different from earthly kings in the way that the Spirit "rested upon him" (2.15.5). The Spirit gave Christ the power and virtues associated with his kingship in order that he might communicate these blessings to human beings.[165] "Christ's Kingdom lies in the Spirit, not in earthly pleasures or pomp . . . For the Spirit has chosen Christ as his seat, that from him might abundantly flow the heavenly riches of which we are in such need" (2.15.5).

UPWARD TO GOD

The Spirit leads fallen humans to rediscover the meaning of life, drawing them through the word to the "upward" calling for which they were created.[166] When Calvin uses vertical images of believers' looking upward or ascending to heaven, he is not echoing Neoplatonic philosophy but referring to a spiritual reorientation toward God. This is the case, for instance, when he writes that God blesses human beings with material things "that we may ascend, as it were by steps, from earth to heaven."[167] As fallen beings, humans are too enamored by the immediate enjoyment of this world and pay little attention to their spiritual purpose. "[H]e who does not aspire to the kingdom of God, but rests satisfied with the conveniences of the present life, seeks nothing else than to fill his belly . . . In seeking Christ, therefore, the chief point is to despise the world and seek the kingdom of God and his righteousness."[168] After all, "in what do the children of God differ from asses and dogs except they aspire after spiritual life?"[169]

---

[165] Commentary on Matthew 3:16 [1555]; CO 45:126; Commentary on John 1:16, 32 [1553]; CO 47:17–18, 27; 3:34; CO 47:74–75; 7:38; CO 47:181–182; Commentary on Isaiah 11:2 [1559]; CO 36:235.

[166] The "word" is itself "spiritual because it calls us upwards to seek Christ in his heavenly glory through the guidance of the Spirit, by faith, and not by our carnal perception." Commentary on John 6:63 [1553]; CO 47:160. When humans are absorbed with the present life without reference to God it becomes "the world" in the Johannine sense, characterized by corruption and rebellion. Commentary on 1 John 2:15 [1551]; CO 55:318–319. Cf. Commentary on Hebrews 6:19 [1549]; CO 55:81; Commentary on Isaiah 36:17 [1559]; CO 36:610.

[167] Commentary on Matthew 6:11 [1555]; CO 45:199. Cf. Commentary on Luke 2:12 [1555]; CO 45:75–76; Commentary on 1 Timothy 4:8 [1548]; CO 52:300.

[168] Commentary on John 6:26 [1553]; CO 47:138–139. Cf. Commentary on Matthew 6:33 [1555]; CO 45:212–213.

[169] Commentary on Joel 2:28 [1559]; CO 42:564–569.

That the kingdom of Christ is spiritual therefore means that it is oriented toward the sincere worship of God. God is uncreated spirit and therefore desires, as Jesus declares in John 4:23, that human beings "worship the Father in spirit and truth." The worship of God consists in the spirit "because it is nothing else than that inward faith of the heart which produces prayer, and next, purity of conscience and self-denial, that we may be dedicated to obedience to God as holy sacrifices."[170] In the time of the Old Testament, the spirituality of worship was obscured by outward types and shadows, but after the coming of Christ, worship cannot "consist in things outward and frail which have no connection with the spiritual kingdom of God."[171] The "spiritual kingdom of Christ" does not consist in "drink and food and clothing, which are things that are transient and liable to corruption and perish by abuse," but in simple obedience to God's commands and the loving service of believers.[172]

That does not mean that the kingdom of Christ does not extend to material things such as the body. The spiritual kingdom of Christ does not abandon the body or creation but directs them to their spiritual purpose. Even now, Calvin insists, "the spiritual connection which we have with Christ belongs not merely to the soul, but also to the body, so that we are flesh of his flesh." The union is "that of nature – full and complete."[173] Thus "religion is strictly spiritual," but "the outward acknowledgment of it relates to the body."[174] Salvation "ought yet to be viewed as properly belonging to our souls," but it also "extends to our bodies."[175] For this reason worship includes the sacrifice of material wealth to God in service to the needs of the poor.[176] The kingdom of Christ is characterized by devotion to God that is expressed in service to one's neighbor in every area of life. Christians are to "lead a heavenly life in this world," using and enjoying its resources while being "conversant with heaven in mind and affection."[177]

[170] Commentary on John 4:23 [1553]; CO 47:88–90.
[171] Commentary on Colossians 2:22 [1548]; CO 52:114.
[172] Commentary on Colossians 2:22–23 [1548]; CO 52:115–116.
[173] Commentary on 1 Corinthians 6:15 [1546]; CO 49:398. Quistorp is utterly wrong to assume that "spiritual always implies for Calvin non-corporeal." Quistorp, *Calvin's Doctrine of the Last Things*, 171. Cf. Miles, "Theology, Anthropology, and the Human Body in Calvin's *Institutes of the Christian Religion*," 316.
[174] Commentary on Matthew 4:10 [1555]; CO 45:136.
[175] Commentary on Jeremiah 23:5–6 [1563]; CO 38:411. Cf. Commentary on Matthew 12:29 [1555]; CO 45:338.
[176] In his interpretation of the Sermon on the Mount, Calvin synthesizes Matthew's reference to the blessing of the "poor in spirit" with Luke's reference to the "poor" so that it includes the dimension of material poverty Commentary on Matthew 5:3 and Luke 6:20 [1555]; CO 45:161–162. Cf. Luke 4:18; CO 45:141–142.
[177] Commentary on Philippians 3:20 [1548]; CO 52:55. Cf. Commentary on Joel 3:18–19 [1559]; CO 42:598.

In his commentary on the Psalms, Calvin specifically refutes the assumption that bodily flourishing is unrelated to the purpose of the kingdom of God:

> If it is objected that these two subjects – the spiritual kingdom of Christ and the fruitfulness of the earth – are improperly intermingled, it may be easily observed in reply that there is nothing at all incongruous in this when we consider that God, while he bestows upon his people spiritual blessings, gives them in addition to these some taste of his fatherly love in the outward benefits which relate to the life of the body.[178]

God created the world for the purpose of human happiness, and while human beings have fallen hard from this "happy condition," God continues to show them "liberality." The faithful therefore "enjoy so much of the fragments of the good things which they lost in Adam as may furnish them with abundant matter of wonder at the singularly gracious manner in which God deals with them." Such wonder enables them to rise above merely temporal blessings "to contemplate the invaluable treasures of the kingdom of heaven which he has unfolded in Christ and all the gifts which belong to the spiritual life."[179]

FORWARD TO ETERNITY

The kingdom of Christ also leads humans forward to the hope of the future life. "In short, when any one of us hears that Christ's kingship is spiritual, aroused by this word let him attain to the hope of a better life; and since it is now protected by Christ's hand, let him await the full fruit of this grace in the age to come" (2.15.3). The kingdom awaits its full manifestation and consummation even as its power is already displayed in temporal life. Calvin thus speaks interchangeably of the "future life [*futurae vitae*]" and the "heavenly life [*coelestis vitae*]," the "beginnings of which" are evident in the gospel, but the final completion of which will take place at "the coming of Christ."[180]

In his discussion of the disciples' twofold mistake about the coming kingdom, Calvin explains why Jesus' kingdom would not "commence immediately a course of prosperity." While Christ "sits at the right hand of the Father and holds the government of heaven and earth," he "has not yet subdued his enemies – has not yet appeared as judge of the world, or revealed his majesty." As long as he is bodily absent, he will not be "clothed with his new sovereignty." At the same time, Christ's kingdom is not entirely absent, for he rules by the Spirit.

---

[178] Commentary on Psalm 85:12 [1557]; CO 31:790.
[179] Commentary on Psalm 8:7 [1557]; CO 31:95. Cf. Commentary on Romans 2:4 [1556]; CO 40:32–33.
[180] Commentary on Romans 13:12 [1556]; CO 49:255–256.

It is true indeed that he now reigns while he regenerates his people to the heavenly life, forms them anew to the image of God, and associates them with angels; while he governs the church by his word, guards it by his protection, enriches it with the gifts of the Spirit, nourishes it by his grace, and maintains it by his power, and in short, supplies it with all that is necessary for salvation; while he restrains the fury of Satan and of all the ungodly and defeats all their schemes. But as this way of reigning is concealed from the flesh, his manifestation is properly said to be delayed till the last day.[181]

T. F. Torrance is therefore correct to point out that Calvin characterizes the kingdom of God in terms of "two great eschatological moments" corresponding to "the present condition of the Kingdom and its future glory."[182] The disciples' error was to "associate the coming of Christ and the end of the world as things inseparable from each other."[183] But Christ taught his disciples that the kingdom consisted of two distinct phases or conditions, the first having been inaugurated by Christ at his incarnation and the second awaiting Christ's return at the end of the age, "'the day of renovation and restoration' (Acts 3:21)."[184]

Because of the kingdom's various eschatological conditions, Calvin could declare that it has already been established, is being established, and is yet to be established. In a definitive sense, "God, restoring the world by the hand of his Son, has completely established his kingdom."[185] The decisive event in history in which Jesus established his kingdom and in which all things "have been restored to order," according to Calvin, was his resurrection and ascent into heaven to sit at God's right hand.[186] In that event was inaugurated "the celestial government of Christ and the power of the Spirit in defending his own, in establishing justice and equity, in restoring order, in abolishing the tyranny of sin, and in putting to flight all the enemies of the church."[187]

On the other hand, the kingdom still awaits its perfect consummation. "As Christ carries on war continually with various enemies, it is doubtless evident that he has no

---

[181] Commentary on Matthew 20:12 [1555]; CO 45:567–568.
[182] Torrance, *Kingdom and Church*, 113, 115, 122, citing Calvin's Commentary on Matthew 24:30. Hesselink accurately shows that Calvin uses the terms "kingdom of Christ" and "kingdom of God" interchangeably. Hesselink, "Calvin on the Kingdom of Christ," 142.
[183] Commentary on Matthew 24:3 [1555]; CO 45:649.
[184] Commentary on Isaiah 35:1 [1559]; CO 36:590–591. Cf. Commentary on Matthew 24:32 [1555]; CO 45:670; Commentary on Daniel 2:27–28 [1561]; CO 40:585; Commentary on Isaiah 11:13 [1559]; CO 36:247.
[185] Commentary on Matthew 5:19 [1555]; CO 45:173. Cf. Commentary on Matthew 19:28 [1555]; CO 45:545.
[186] Commentary on Ephesians 1:10 [1548]; CO 51:151.
[187] Commentary on Acts 1:21 [1552]; CO 48:21. Cf. *Institutes* 2.16.15–16; Commentary on Luke 24:31 [1555]; CO 45:809; Commentary on 1 Corinthians 15:27 [1546]; CO 49:548.

quiet possession of his kingdom."[188] The kingdom "lies hidden in the earth, so to speak, under the lowness of the flesh" (2.16.17). Christ is the heir of heaven and earth, but "he has not as yet actually entered upon the full possession of his empire and dominion."[189] Because "many still oppose and boldly despise him,"[190] his kingdom will continue to be opposed in the world.[191] Thus the kingdom remains in a constant state of eschatological tension between the "already" and the "not yet."

> [T]he kingdom of Christ is on such a footing that it is every day growing and making improvement, while at the same time perfection is not yet attained, nor will be until the final day of reckoning. Thus both things hold true – that all things are now subject to Christ and that this subjection will, nevertheless, not be complete until the day of the resurrection, because that which is now only begun will then be completed.[192]

Calvin believed that at Christ's return both creation and the human body will undergo a process of qualitative transformation.[193] The *substance* of that which participates in Christ through the regeneration of the Spirit will enter the kingdom of God, but all other things will pass away. Thus in order to enter the kingdom of Christ a person must become a new creature in the same way that the world must become a "new heavens and a new earth." Because "Christ's kingdom is spiritual, this change must take place chiefly in the Spirit." All things that are not "formed anew by the Spirit of God" will pass away.[194]

The way in which Calvin uses the word "spiritual" to describe the transformation of the body tells us much about how he uses the word "spiritual" in general. It demonstrates clearly that, for Calvin, spirituality does not denote immateriality, nor does it imply a relativization or marginalization of the physical creation. In his commentary on 1 Corinthians 15, Calvin describes the soul as the *animating* principle of the body in this passing mortal life, in contrast to that which is "more excellent," the Spirit, who will be the *inspiring* principle of the body in the future

---

[188] Commentary on Hebrews 2:8 [1549]; CO 55:26.

[189] Commentary on Psalm 8:6 [1557]; CO 31:94. Cf. Commentary on 1 Corinthians 15:25 [1546]; CO 49:547. Commentary on Hebrews 10:11 [1549]; CO 55:126; Commentary on Galatians 1:4 [1548]; CO 50:170–171.

[190] Commentary on Isaiah 45:23 [1559]; CO 37:149–150.

[191] Commentary on Matthew 24:9 [1555]; CO 45:653.

[192] Commentary on Philippians 2:10 [1548]; CO 52:29. Cf. Commentary on Hebrews 10:1 [1549]; CO 55:121; 2:5, 8; CO 55:24–25; Calvin thinks that while Jews tended to identify the kingdom with the messiah's first coming, Christians often reduce it to Christ's return. Commentary on Isaiah 26:19 [1559]; CO 36:441–442.

[193] Quistorp, *Calvin's Doctrine of the Last Things*, 137–140, 183–184.

[194] Commentary on 2 Corinthians 5:17 [1548]; CO 50:69. When Paul declared that all things are of God he was therefore referring to "all things that belong to Christ's kingdom," everything else passing away (5:18; 50:70).

life. "Now that is called animal which is quickened by the soul; that is spiritual which is quickened by the Spirit."[195] At his return, Jesus will not restore the body to its original state, as experienced by the first human beings, but will "raise it up to a better condition than ever."[196] Christ "brought us from heaven a life-giving Spirit that he might regenerate us into a better life, and elevated above the earth." The contrast, stated in terms of earth and heaven, is between the corruptibility of the present world and the incorruptibility of the new. "[W]e have it from Adam that we live in this world . . . Christ, on the other hand, is the beginning and author of the heavenly life."[197]

Calvin uses the same Aristotelian logic to describe the body's transformation as he does to describe the transformation of creation in 2 Peter 3. "Let us, however, always bear in mind what we have seen previously – that the substance [*substantiam*] of the body is the same and that it is the quality [*qualitate*] only that is here treated of. Let the present quality of the body be called . . . animation; let the future receive the name of inspiration."[198] The transformation that believers experience during this life is spiritual, but it does not extend to the full transformation of body and soul that, like the creation, they will experience at Jesus' return.

> For we now begin to bear the image of Christ, and are every day more and more transformed into it, but that image still consists in spiritual regeneration. But then it will be fully restored both in body and in soul, and what is now begun will be perfected, and accordingly we will obtain in reality what we as yet only hope for.[199]

Calvin explains that when the Apostle Paul writes that "flesh and blood cannot inherit the kingdom of God," he is referring to the human being corrupted by sin.

> Mark how we shall live in the kingdom of God both in body and in soul, while at the same time flesh and blood cannot inherit the kingdom of God – for they shall previously be delivered from corruption. Our nature then, as being now corruptible and mortal, is not admissible into the kingdom of God, but when it shall have put off corruption, and shall have been beautified with incorruption, it will then make its way into it.[200]

---

[195] Commentary on 1 Corinthians 15:44 [1546]; CO 49:557–558.
[196] Commentary on 1 Corinthians 15:45 [1546]; CO 49:558–559.
[197] Commentary on 1 Corinthians 15:47 [1546]; CO 49:559. Quistorp thinks that "obviously Calvin is here contradicting his statements in the *Institutio*." But Quistorp's analysis is confused by his assumption that for Calvin the spiritual pertains to the soul and is immaterial. See Quistorp, *Calvin's Doctrine of the Last Things*, 68.
[198] Commentary on 1 Corinthians 15:44 [1546]; CO 49:557–558. Cf. 15:47; CO 49:559.
[199] Commentary on 1 Corinthians 15:49 [1546]; CO 49:560.
[200] Commentary on 1 Corinthians 15:53 [1546]; CO 49:562–563. Cf. *Institutes* 3.14.12.

How will this bodily transformation affect life in the coming kingdom? Calvin's tendency was to emphasize discontinuity between the affairs of the present age and those of the age to come.[201] Despite his warnings against speculation, he himself speculates that humans will no longer need drink, food, clothing, or sleep, having been freed from mortality.[202] The Jews "committed the error of estimating the glory of the heavenly life according to the present state," but Calvin argues that the institutions of the present age will not be maintained in the kingdom. For instance, he explains Jesus' declaration that in the age to come there will not be marriage as being due to the fact that where there is no mortality, there is no need for procreation.[203] Sexuality, gender, and marriage are temporal and will not be part of the kingdom of God.

Calvin makes a similar argument about the intellectual accomplishments of human culture. The Apostle Paul's famous comparison of love, which is eternal, with various virtues and gifts that will "pass away" raises a "question of no small importance – whether those who in this world excel either in learning or in other gifts will be on a level with idiots in the kingdom of God?" Calvin warns against speculation here as well, but he goes on to suggest that the gifts of knowledge and learning are indeed temporal. "So far as I can conjecture and am able even to gather in part from this passage, inasmuch as learning, knowledge of languages, and similar gifts are subservient to the necessity of this life, I do not think that there will be any of them remaining."[204] All of these cultural accomplishments (and the inequalities between humans that flow from them) will be transcended as humans attain to the maturity and perfection for which they were created.[205] The kingdom of God will remain in substantive continuity with the original creation, but all things will be transformed as that creation is brought to perfection.

---

[201] Commentary on Matthew 21:29 [1555]; CO 45:606. The Jews assumed that in the kingdom, God would "restore whatever he had given to them in the world." Commentary on Matthew 21:24 [1555]; CO 45:605.

[202] Commentary on 1 Corinthians 15:44 [1546]; CO 49:557–558. Cf. Commentary on 1 Thessalonians 4:16 [1550]; CO 52:167; Commentary on Philippians 3:21 [1546]; CO 52:56. An obvious counterpoint to Calvin's claim here is that the resurrected Jesus ate food. Calvin has difficulty with this, and he proceeds to explain that the resurrected Jesus would not have had to pass waste! Commentary on Luke 24:41 [1555]; CO 45:814–815.

[203] Commentary on Matthew 21:30 [1555]; CO 45:606. See Quistorp, *Calvin's Doctrine of the Last Things*, 175.

[204] Commentary on 1 Corinthians 13:8 [1546]; CO 49:512–513. Even the gifts of prophecy and of the outward ministry of the gospel will pass away, being intended only to lead human beings to the future kingdom (13:12; CO 49:514–515). The resurrected will be able to see God even apart from Jesus' mediation. Commentary on 1 John 3:2 [1551]; CO 55:331–332.

[205] Commentary on 1 Corinthians 13:11 [1546]; CO 49:513–514. See Quistorp, *Calvin's Doctrine of the Last Things*, 162–165.

THE RIGHTEOUSNESS OF THE KINGDOM

The kingdom of Christ breaks into the present age by "the secret energy of the Spirit, by which we come to enjoy Christ and all his benefits" (3.1.1). Humans do not merely require the outward reformation of the body or its actions. Corruption extends to the human soul, the primary seat of the image of God which was to direct humans to their spiritual purpose. The whole person, body and soul, must be regenerated by the Holy Spirit and united with Christ. Spiritual regeneration enables believers to put off the "old man," which refers to the corrupt nature humans inherit from Adam, and to put on the "new man," Christ, in whom the sinful nature is transformed and the image of God is restored.[206] It should therefore be evident "how much is the difference between the children of Adam who are born only into the world, and the children of God who are renewed into a heavenly life."[207]

Calvin discusses this process of salvation in Book 3 of the *Institutes* before he proceeds to his analysis of the church in Book 4. It is important to remember, however, that for Calvin, the renewal of the creation does not consist merely in the regeneration of individuals, but in the regeneration of a new humanity, the church.[208] I turn to Calvin's understanding of the church as Christ's kingdom in Chapter 5. Here it is important to clarify his understanding of the gospel and the way in which it renews the world by establishing righteousness.[209]

Calvin describes the extent of Christ's reconciliation in universal terms. God "shows himself to be reconciled to the whole world when he invites all men without exception to the faith of Christ, which is nothing else than an entrance into life."[210] Faith is essential, in Calvin's view, because it is the means through which the Holy

---

[206] Commentary on Colossians 3:9 [1548]; CO 52:121; Commentary on Romans 6:6 [1556]; CO 49: 107–108; 6:10; 109–110; 5:12; 95. See Miles, "Theology, Anthropology, and the Human Body in Calvin's *Institutes of the Christian Religion*," 305–309, 314–315. Cf. Ronald S. Wallace, *Calvin's Doctrine of the Christian Life* (Grand Rapids: Eerdmans, 1959), 106–107; Lucien Richard, *The Spirituality of John Calvin* (Atlanta: John Knox Press, 1974), 111–116; Schreiner, *The Theater of His Glory*, 101.

[207] Commentary on 1 Peter 1:23 [1551]; CO 55:229–230 (Cf. 1:13–16; 220).

[208] Torrance writes that "by substantial union with Christ the Church actually and continuously participates in the new humanity of the resurrection and in the *Regnum Christi*." Torrance, *Kingdom and Church*, 116 (Cf. 95, 131–133). Merwin S. Johnson argues that participation with Christ is the core feature of Calvin's ethic. Merwin S. Johnson, "Calvin's Ethical Legacy," *The Legacy of John Calvin* (ed. David Foxgrover; Grand Rapids: CRC, 2000), 63–83. "The church is not so much an institution in history in which the restoration of order has been accomplished," Milner clarifies, "as it is itself the history of that restoration." Milner, *Calvin's Doctrine of the Church*, 47. Cf. Haas, *The Concept of Equity in Calvin's Ethics*, 49; Tonkin, *The Church and the Secular Order in the Theology of the Reformers*, 106–111. Tonkin carefully refutes the claim that Calvin's soteriology is individualist. Cf. Emil Brunner, *The Misunderstanding of the Church* (Philadelphia: Westminster, 1953), 9.

[209] Cf. Wendel, *Calvin*, 242–254; Niesel, *The Theology of Calvin*, 120–139; Haas, "Calvin's Ethics," 94–96.

[210] Commentary on John 3:16 [1553]; CO 47:65.

Spirit unites human beings to Christ, and only through union with Christ can women and men enter into his kingdom. Only in Jesus do believers discover what they cannot find in themselves:

> We still lie under the power of death, but he, raised from the dead by heavenly power, has the dominion of life. We labor under the bondage of sin, and surrounded by endless vexations, are engaged in a hard warfare, but he, sitting at the right hand of the Father, exercises the highest government in heaven and earth [*summam in coelo et terra gubernationem*], and triumphs gloriously over the enemies whom he has subdued and vanquished.[211]

Christ has conquered sin and death, entering into the glory of the kingdom. "Yet, in consequence of the secret union [of the head with the body]," this glory "belongs truly to the members."[212] While believers continue in this "bodily life," which is subject to corruption, by their union with Jesus they are shaped increasingly by the "heavenly life of Christ." Thus "while we live in the world, we are at the same time in heaven, not only because our head is there, but because in virtue of union we enjoy a life in common with him."[213]

But while Christ is the source of all blessings, "Christ himself . . . is communicated to us by the Spirit."[214] Apart from the Spirit, women and men are under corruption and sin, and they "ought to be reckoned dead, whatever may be the pretended life of which they boast."[215] It is therefore the Spirit's "principal work" to lead human beings into the kingdom (3.1.4). The Spirit is the "root and seed of heavenly life" in human beings (3.1.2) in a manner distinct from his general work in maintaining and enlivening creation. Thus he "may rightly be called the key that unlocks for us the treasures of the Kingdom of Heaven" (3.1.4).[216] Only through the Spirit's work can humans develop the sort of faith that is not mere intellectual assent but love and trust, a complete reorientation of the whole person toward God (3.2.1).[217]

---

[211] Commentary on Ephesians 1:20 [1548]; CO 51:157–158. Cf. *Institutes* 2.16.19; 3.2.24; Quistorp, *Calvin's Doctrine of the Last Things*, 20–22; Tonkin, *The Church and the Secular Order in the Theology of the Reformers*, 103, 113.

[212] Commentary on Ephesians 2:6 [1548]; CO 51:164. Cf. Commentary on John 14:2 [1553]; CO 47:322; 8:52; CO 47:212.

[213] Commentary on Galatians 2:20 [1548]; CO 50:199.

[214] Commentary on 1 Corinthians 6:11 [1546]; CO 49:395. Cf. 15:27; CO 49:548; Commentary on Galatians 6:15 [1548]; CO 50:266.

[215] Commentary on John 7:39 [1553]; CO 47:182.

[216] Cf. Commentary on Acts 2:17 [1552]; CO 48:32; Commentary on 1 Peter 1:10 [1551]; CO 55:217; Commentary on 1 Corinthians 2:10 [1546]; CO 49:340–341.

[217] It is "more of the heart than of the brain," Calvin writes, "more of the disposition than of the understanding" (3.2.8), and "consists in assurance rather than in comprehension" (3.2.14). The "mysteries of Christ's kingdom" are not so much difficult to grasp intellectually as they are "obscure" and "hidden . . . to the perception of the flesh." Commentary on 2 Peter 3:16 [1551]; CO 55:478. Cf. *Institutes* 3.6.4. For Calvin's definition of faith see *Institutes*, 3.2.7. Cf. 3.2.41. See Miles,

The mark of the Spirit's work in a believer is the righteousness of the kingdom. Calvin typically summarized this in terms of the "twofold righteousness" of the forgiveness of sins and active righteousness.[218] Most foundational is the forgiveness of sins, the doctrine of justification by faith that Calvin considered "the main hinge on which religion turns." Without the knowledge of justification "the conscience can have no rest at all, no peace with God, no assurance or security" (3.4.2). Christians grasp that "their only ground of hope for the inheritance of a heavenly kingdom lies in the fact that, being engrafted in the body of Christ, they are freely accounted righteous" (3.13.5). Such a hope cannot be the result of outward exercises that comes between the individual and God (3.4.24). Peace of conscience must be preserved at all costs.[219]

In addition to the passive righteousness of the forgiveness of sins, proclaimed in the ministry of the church, Calvin emphasizes the active righteousness that characterizes the church as the society of believers progressing in the Christian life.[220] Calvin highlights this sort of righteousness in his explanation of the Lord's Prayer. He argues that the third petition of the prayer, "Your will be done," is an extension of the second, "Your kingdom come," an "explanation that God will be king in the world when all submit to his will" (3.20.43). God's kingdom is present when people "voluntarily devote and submit themselves to be governed by him."[221] Calvin thus emphasizes that the primary focus of the second petition of the Lord's Prayer is on the establishment of the kingdom through the voluntary submission of human

---

"Theology, Anthropology, and the Human Body in Calvin's *Institutes of the Christian Religion*," 306–309, 314.

[218] Commentary on Acts 19:8 [1554]; CO 48:443; 28:30; CO 48:573–574.

[219] Commentary on Romans 5:1 [1556]; CO 49:88–89. Cf. Commentary on Luke 2:14 [1555]; CO 45:77; *Institutes* 3.11.10, 20. The one who is justified is the one who, "excluded from the righteousness of works, grasps the righteousness of Christ through faith, and clothed in it, appears in God's sight not as a sinner but as a righteous man" (3.11.2).

[220] Torrance, *Kingdom and Church*, 96, 115. "When we speak of the kingdom of Christ, we must respect two things; the doctrine of the gospel, by which Christ gathers to himself a church, and by which he governs the same, being gathered together; secondly, the society of the godly, who being coupled together by the sincere faith of the gospel, are truly accounted the people of God." Calvin's Dedication to the Commentary on Acts [1552]; CO 14:293. Cf. *Institutes*, 3.3.19; Commentary on Acts 1:3 [1552]; CO 48:4; Hesselink, "Calvin on the Kingdom of Christ," 155–156; Milner, *Calvin's Doctrine of the Church*, 179–188.

[221] Commentary on Matthew 6:10 [1555]; CO 45:197–198. In short, "the kingdom of God consists in righteousness" (6:33; CO 45:212–213). Cf. 6:12; CO 45:200–201; 12:29; CO 45:339; *Institutes* 3.20.42. When anyone is reconciled to God "the kingdom of God [*regnum Dei*] fully prevails and flourishes in him." The result is that such a person "with a quiet and peaceful conscience serves Christ in righteousness [*iustitiam*]." This means that wherever there is "righteousness and peace and spiritual joy [*iustitia et pax et gaudium spirituale*], there the kingdom of God is complete in all its parts [*regnum Dei suis omnibus numeris est absolutum*]." Commentary on Romans 14:18 [1556]; CO 49:266. Cf. *Institutes*, 3.2.33; Commentary on 1 Timothy 3:16 [1548]; CO 52:291; Commentary on 1 John 3:8 [1551]; CO 55:335; Commentary on Acts 1:3 [1552]; CO 48:4–5.

beings to God's righteousness. The intent is that God "would enlighten the world by the light of his word – would form the hearts of men by the influences of his Spirit to obey his justice – and would restore to order, by the gracious exercise of his power, all the disorder that exists in the world." The kingdom is present insofar as order has been restored and justice is practiced, and in that sense the kingdom is "continually growing and advancing to the end of the world" even as we must yet pray that "it may come."[222] It is in this regeneration of human beings that the restoration of the world is beginning to take place in fulfillment of the Old Testament prophecies of true righteousness and peace among the nations.[223]

And yet, Calvin spurned any sort of triumphalism about the earthly establishment of the kingdom or the righteousness of Christians. Even those regenerated by the Spirit, he insists, never attain to the full blessings of the kingdom in the present life. "We have not a single work going forth from the saints that if it be judged in itself deserves not shame as its just reward" (3.14.9).[224] That is why Christians must also pray daily, "forgive us our debts, as we forgive our debtors." Augustine was right when he said, "The righteousness of the saints in this world consists more in the forgiveness of sins than in perfection of virtues" (3.11.22).

HOPE

For Calvin, hope is the virtue by which Christians navigate the tension between the two conditions of the kingdom and the two kinds of righteousness. The problem is that so much of Christian experience contradicts the promises associated with the kingdom. In terms brutally accurate regarding life in sixteenth-century Europe, Calvin writes,

> Various diseases repeatedly trouble us: now plague rages; now we are cruelly beset by the calamities of war; now ice and hail, consuming the year's expectation, lead to

---

[222] Commentary on Matthew 6:10 [1555]; CO 45:197–198. Cf. Commentary on 2 Thessalonians 3:1 [1550]; CO 52:209; Commentary on Romans 8:31 [1556]; CO 49:162–163; Commentary on 1 John 3:5 [1551]; CO 55:333.

[223] In his Commentary on Isaiah 2:4, Calvin connects Isaiah's prophecy of peace among the nations with the regeneration that takes place among human beings. "[A]s the gospel is the doctrine of reconciliation, which removes the enmity between us and God, so it brings men into peace and harmony with each other." "But this [progress in brotherly love] cannot be done before the consciences have been brought into a state of peace with God; for we must begin there, in order that we may also be at peace with men." Commentary on Isaiah 2:4 [1559]; CO 36:65–66. In that sense the kingdom is a kingdom of peace in the full Hebrew sense of a "prosperous and happy state." Commentary on Hebrews 7:1 [1549]; CO 55:83. Cf. Holwerda, "Eschatology and History," 339; Hesselink, "Calvin on the Kingdom of Christ," 158.

[224] Cf. Commentary on Matthew 6:12 [1555]; CO 45:200–201; Commentary on John 7:38 [1553]; CO 47: 181–182; Institutes 3.20.45; Tonkin, The Church and the Secular Order in the Theology of the Reformers, 112, 116.

barrenness, which reduces us to poverty; wife, parents, children, neighbors, are snatched away by death; our house is burned by fire. It is on account of these occurrences that men curse their life, loathe the day of their birth, abominate heaven and the light of day, rail against God, and as they are eloquent in blasphemy, accuse him of injustice and cruelty (3.7.10).

During this life "death is always before our eyes. We are also subject to a thousand miseries and the soul is exposed to innumerable evils, so that we find always a hell within us."[225]

It is into this tension that hope enters as the Christian's anchor.

Promised to us is eternal life, but it is promised to the dead; we are assured of a happy resurrection, but we are as yet involved in corruption; we are pronounced just, as yet sin dwells in us; we hear that we are happy, but we are as yet in the midst of many miseries; an abundance of all good things is promised to us, but still we often hunger and thirst; God proclaims that he will come quickly, but he seems deaf when we cry to him. What would become of us were we not supported by hope?[226]

Salvation, in short, "lies hidden under hope."[227] The basis for Calvin's theology of hope is the completed work of Christ. Through the hope that they "already" have by virtue of their union with Christ, believers are able to look beyond the limitations of the "not yet."[228] By looking beyond the "present aspect of things" toward the future life, they are able "in the depth of despair to exercise nevertheless a feeling of hope."[229]

The Christian life is therefore characterized by meditation on the future life (*meditatio vitae futurae*) that already exists in the absent Christ. Thus the focus of hope is not primarily on what might happen during the present age but on the certainty of what will occur at Christ's return. "For if our life is shut up in Christ, it must be hid until he shall appear."[230] Yet this hope in Christ is so certain that it "may

---

[225] Commentary on 1 John 3:2 [1551]; CO 55:330.

[226] Commentary on Hebrews 11:1 [1549]; CO 55:143–144. Cf. Commentary on Matthew 25:20, 34 [1555]; CO 45:569, 687; *Institutes*, 3.8.10.

[227] This phrase appears repeatedly in Calvin's writings. Commentary on John 16:21 [1553]; CO 47:36; Commentary on Matthew 13:44–52 [1555]; CO 45:375 (Cf. 371–376); Commentary on Philippians 1:6 [1548]; CO 51:9–10; Commentary on Isaiah 42:9 [1559]; CO 37:66.

[228] In his classic *Kingdom and Church*, T. F. Torrance justifiably characterizes Calvin's theology as a theology of hope. Moltmann traces his own theology of hope in part to that of Calvin. See Jürgen Moltmann, *Theology of Hope: On the Ground and the Implications of a Christian Eschatology* (New York: Harper & Row, 1967), 18–20. Cf. Quistorp, *Calvin's Doctrine of the Last Things*, 15.

[229] Commentary on Philippians 4:7 [1548]; CO 52:62. Cf. 1:23; CO 52:19; *Institutes* 3.2.21, 28; Commentary on Romans 8:24 [1556]; CO 49:155.

[230] Commentary on Colossians 3:4 [1548]; CO 52:119. Cf. Commentary on 1 Peter 1:3–7 [1551]; CO 55: 210–213; Commentary on 1 Thessalonians 1:9 [1550]; CO 52:144–145; Commentary on Romans 8:25 [1556]; CO 49:156; 12:12; CO 49:242; Commentary on 2 Timothy 4:8 [1548]; CO 52:390; Commentary on Philippians 1:6 [1548]; CO 51:9–10. See Quistorp, *Calvin's Doctrine of the Last Things*, 40–49.

be justly compared to a present possession."[231] By faith, believers "already sit in the heavenly glory with Christ by hope, and they have the kingdom of God already established within them."[232] In short, through hope Christians can be said already to possess what they do not possess in point of fact. Having been united with Christ, "we have already entered the kingdom of God, and . . . we already, in hope, sit in heavenly places," even though "we nevertheless have it not as yet in possession" but enjoy it only "in hope."[233]

For Calvin, hope is not merely a passive attitude. On the contrary, it involves what Quistorp calls "a waiting and a hastening."[234] Christians demonstrate their hope by "hastening toward the heavenly kingdom" (3.10.1), applying themselves to the practices of justice and piety. Through virtues and good works they are trained "to hasten . . . to seek the blessed hope held out to us in heaven" (3.18.3). With meditation on the future life, therefore, the desire for love and service is stirred up.

> For the hope of eternal life will never be inactive in us so as not to produce love in us. For it is of necessity that the man who is fully persuaded that a treasure of life is laid up for him in heaven will aspire thither, looking down upon this world. Meditation, however, upon the heavenly life stirs up our affections both to the worship of God, and to exercises of love.[235]

And yet, those scholars who see in Calvin an optimism regarding the progressive socio-political transformation of society as an expression of the kingdom of God take the reformer's understanding of progressive righteousness out of context. Calvin emphasizes the limited degree to which the kingdom will be perfected during the present age. People naturally shrink back from suffering and the cross, he points out, and this leads them to strive "without moderation" for the perfection of the kingdom on earth. But such impatience actually demonstrates itself to be "without hope" because it seeks "to rush forward unseasonably to the fruit of hope." Those who fall into this error "confound the perfection of Christ's reign with the commencement of it, and wish to enjoy on earth what they ought to seek for in heaven."[236] Christ will indeed restore the creation, but

> the full accomplishment of this promise ought not to be expected in the present life, for as it is through hope that we are blessed, so our happiness, which is now in some

---

[231] Commentary on Romans 8:30 [1556]; CO 49:161. Christians are pilgrims on earth, but "they yet by hope scale the heavens, so that they quietly enjoy in their own bosoms their future inheritance" (5:2; CO 49:89).

[232] Commentary on John 5:24 [1553]; CO 47:116.

[233] Commentary on Philippians 3:12 [1548]; CO 52:51. Cf. Commentary on Titus 3:7 [1550]; CO 52:432.

[234] Quistorp, *Calvin's Doctrine of the Last Things*, 26.

[235] Commentary on Colossians 1:5 [1548]; CO 52:79. Cf. Commentary on Titus 1:2, 12 [1550]; CO 52: 405–406, 423.

[236] Commentary on Matthew 24:3 [1555]; CO 45:649.

respects concealed, must be an object of hope till the last day, and it is enough that some taste of it be enjoyed in this world, that we may more ardently long for that perfect happiness.[237]

CONCLUSION

Calvin's doctrines of creation, humanity, sin, preservation, natural law, the restoration of the world, the Spirit, the kingdom of Christ, and hope provide the fundamental premises for the reformer's two kingdoms theology. Calvin believed God had created the world and human beings for a purpose: communion with him and with one another. Had humans been obedient, they, along with the whole creation, would have been elevated into that state of eternal glory that is the spiritual kingdom of Christ. But human beings sinned, and the creation fell into corruption. Only God's common grace – working through means such as providence, natural law, and civil government – preserves the order that makes human life possible.

In addition to this work of preservation, God is restoring the world and human beings through the kingdom of Christ. Having been established in Christ's death, resurrection, and ascension, the kingdom now breaks into the present age by regenerating human beings through Christ's word and Spirit. But it is spiritual. This does not mean that it is immaterial or ethereal in some way, but that it does not immediately take the form of wealth and power. On the contrary, the spiritual kingdom of Christ is expressed in the regeneration that establishes true righteousness and peace among believers. Human beings can live in hope that these are but the beginnings of a restoration that will one day encompass all things. In the meantime, believers are caught between the tension of the "already" and the "not yet," and it is this tension that provides the foundation for Calvin's two kingdoms theology.

[237] Commentary on Isaiah 35:7 [1559]; CO 36:594–595. Cf. Commentary on Acts 3:21 [1552]; CO 48: 72–73; Commentary on Isaiah 60:17–18 [1559]; CO 37:366–367; Commentary on 2 Thessalonians 1:10 [1550]; CO 52:192; Commentary on Matthew 5:2 [1555]; CO 45:161.

4

Two Kingdoms

Calvin's two kingdoms theology arises logically from his interpretation of creation, the fall, and the restoration of the world. All of life falls under the lordship of the ascended Christ and is subject to his law, but Christ exercises his lordship in two different ways, one preservative (the political order), and the other restorative (the spiritual kingdom). In the latter kingdom, which Calvin identifies with the church, human beings are regenerated by the word and Spirit such that they voluntarily submit themselves to the love and justice of God. In hope, they begin to experience the perfect liberty, equality, and peace that characterize Christ's kingdom.[1] At the same time, they continue to serve God in a fallen, temporal world, whose institutions and cultural phenomena, though governed by Christ's providence and law, are destined to pass away. Thus, in the spirit of self-sacrificial service that characterizes the love of Christ, Christians continue to submit themselves where necessary to temporal institutions, even where these institutions seem to contradict the kingdom's liberty, equality, and peace. Some institutions are the expressions of the natural, created order, such as gender and marriage, while others are the products of the fall into sin, such as slavery and coercive civil government. Yet God uses all of these institutions as means of preserving outward or civil righteousness for the welfare of human society. Civil government in particular acts coercively according to the civil use of the law to preserve a modicum of piety, justice, and peace. But only the kingdom of Christ restores humans to the spiritual use of the law so as to create inward, spiritual righteousness, the true forms of piety, justice, and peace.

In this chapter I describe the various layers or dimensions of Calvin's two kingdoms doctrine. It is important to excavate Calvin's political theology in this way because many discussions of Calvin's two kingdoms doctrine focus on it primarily as

[1] See John Tonkin, *The Church and the Secular Order in Reformation Thought* (New York: Columbia University Press, 1971), 99, 113, 120; Thomas F. Torrance, *Kingdom and Church: Study in the Theology of the Reformation* (Edinburgh: Oliver & Boyd, 1956), 90–164; Benjamin Milner, Jr., *Calvin's Doctrine of the Church* (Leiden: Brill, 1970), 164–188.

a theology of institutions or differentiated spheres, without carefully taking into account the eschatological and theological concerns that provide its *raison d'être*.[2]

Before outlining the various dimensions of Calvin's two kingdoms theology, it is useful briefly to identify the meaning of some of the reformer's key terms. It must be remembered, however, that Calvin uses all of these terms fluidly and sometimes interchangeably. Here I describe his *typical* use of concepts and terms.

The foundational dimension of Calvin's two kingdoms theology, the eschatological distinction between the present age and the eternal kingdom of Christ, has already been described in Chapter 3. When referring to this dimension, Calvin tends to speak of the contrast between the "earthly" and the "heavenly," or between the "temporal" and the "spiritual." A second dimension is anthropological, distinguishing between human beings as they participate in the present, mortal life and as they participate in the coming kingdom. Here Calvin typically speaks of a contrast between the "outward" and the "inward," "body" and "soul," "flesh and Spirit." A third dimension refers to the twofold way in which Christ governs human beings: one by political institutions, the other by his word and Spirit. Here Calvin tends to speak of the "two kingdoms (or reigns)" or the "twofold government (or regiment)." The contrast intended is between the "political," "temporal," "secular," or "universal," on the one hand, and the "spiritual" or "peculiar" on the other. Finally, a fourth dimension denotes the specific institutions that correspond to the two kingdoms or governments, which Calvin follows medieval usage in speaking of as two "jurisdictions," but which he also typically describes simply as two "governments." These are various "civil" and "political" institutions, the most prominent of which is coercive civil government, on the one hand, and the church with its "ecclesiastical" government, which is spiritual insofar as it expresses the rule of Christ's word, sacraments, and discipline, on the other. It is in correspondence to these institutions and their functions that Calvin tends to distinguish between "civil" and "spiritual" righteousness, or between the "civil" and "spiritual" uses of the law.

---

[2] Calvin understood the two kingdoms fundamentally in eschatological terms, as Milner rightly notes, not as "two externally divided and recognizable spheres." Milner, *Calvin's Doctrine of the Church*, 171. Scholars sometimes claim that Calvin's eschatology diminishes the significance of the two kingdoms concept in his thought. For instance, Torrance claims that "for Calvin the operative eschatological distinction is not so much that between the two kingdoms in Luther's sense, as between the two conditions of the Church." Torrance, *Kingdom and Church*, 159. In my view it is clearer to say that for Calvin the eschatological nature of the kingdom (i.e., its two conditions) decisively shapes the two kingdoms distinction. Tonkin mistakenly places Calvin's eschatology in contrast to his two kingdoms concept. "In Calvin, this kind of [two kingdoms] distinction enters only in relation to politics and ethics, and his thought is dominated rather by the eschatological tension between the present and future states of the one kingdom of Christ" (115). It does not seem to occur to Tonkin that Calvin understands the two kingdoms distinction eschatologically, which is why it remains relevant for politics and ethics. Tonkin, *The Church and the Secular Order in the Theology of the Reformers*, 115 (Cf. 99, 116).

In what follows, I begin by describing the theological context in which Calvin introduces his classic statement of the two kingdoms doctrine, his discussion of Christian liberty. I then turn to his distinction between Christ's universal and spiritual government, which sets the stage for a discussion of the meaning and significance of the anthropological terms that Calvin uses to describe the difference between the temporal and the spiritual: outward/inward, body/soul, flesh/spirit, temporal/eternal. From here I turn to Calvin's conception of the nature of Christian service in the institutions of the political order, focusing specifically on gender and slavery. Finally, I set the stage for the second part of this book by focusing on Calvin's understanding of the difference between civil and spiritual government, with the related distinctions between the two kinds of righteousness and the two (constructive) uses of the law.[3]

THE TWO KINGDOMS IN THEOLOGICAL CONTEXT

The immediate context for Calvin's classic statement on the two kingdoms is his discussion of Christian liberty. The doctrine of Christian liberty was the decisive (and potentially revolutionary) implication of the Reformation doctrine of justification by faith alone.[4] The reformers insisted that human beings participate in the restoration of order in the world through the forgiveness of sins by faith. They likewise maintained that the freedom that arises from this forgiveness must be protected at all costs. Even the practice of righteousness that necessarily arises from the Christian's justification must be understood only in light of the "prime necessity" of Christian liberty, for without it, "consciences dare undertake almost nothing without doubting" (3.19.1).[5] The driving concern of the reformers was that the papal church had burdened Christians with a host of ceremonies, laws, and works, thus destroying the liberty of the gospel. Anything that would place the soul of a Christian under the rule of another person was an assault on the kingdom of Christ.

And yet, Calvin feared the *abuse* of Christian liberty. "Some, on the pretext of this freedom, shake off all obedience toward God and break out into unbridled license.

---

[3] There are, of course, three uses of the law for Calvin, but in this chapter I focus on the critical distinction between the civil and spiritual uses.

[4] On the revolutionary implications of Christian liberty, see especially William R. Stevenson, Jr., *Sovereign Grace: The Place and Significance of Christian Freedom in John Calvin's Political Thought* (New York: Oxford University Press, 1999); John Witte, Jr., *The Reformation of Rights: Law, Religion, and Human Rights in Early Modern Calvinism* (Cambridge: Cambridge University Press, 2007); Roland Boer, *Political Grace: The Revolutionary Theology of John Calvin* (Louisville: Westminster John Knox Press, 2009).

[5] Harro Höpfl is therefore unwarranted in suggesting that Calvin saw the doctrine of Christian liberty as anything other than pivotal for the Christian life. Harro Höpfl, *The Christian Polity of John Calvin* (Cambridge: Cambridge University Press, 1982), 35, 69.

Others disdain it, thinking that it takes away all moderation, order, and choice of things" (3.19.1). One of Calvin's primary reasons for writing the *Institutes* was that faithful evangelicals were being persecuted on the pretext that they held such radical views and were "overthrowing not only religion but also all civil order."[6] He regarded the charge of rebellion as one of the oldest and most dangerous threats to the kingdom of Christ. "Kings too are, for the most part, so fiercely haughty, that they reckon it impossible for Christ to reign without some diminution of their own power, and, therefore, they always listen favorably to such an accusation as that which was once brought unjustly against Christ."[7]

Clearly, then, the doctrine had to be addressed: "We must take care that so necessary a part of doctrine be not suppressed, yet at the same time that those absurd objections which are wont to arise be met" (3.19.1). It was to meet this great need, to defend the doctrine of Christian liberty, and to clarify the relation of the kingdom of Christ to political order that Calvin introduced the two kingdoms doctrine.

Calvin explains Christian liberty as having three basic dimensions. First, it refers to the liberty of conscience that believers have before the judgment seat of God by virtue of the doctrine of justification. When justification is being discussed Christians need to lay aside all talk of law, works, or human power, and consider God's mercy in Jesus alone (3.19.2).

The second dimension of Christian liberty is freedom from the coercion and rigor of the law. Calvin argues that "consciences observe the law, not as if constrained by the necessity of the law, but that freed from the law's yoke they willingly obey God's will." Christians must be freed from the binding legal authority of the law if they are to escape a state of "perpetual dread" (3.19.4). They know that they are "emancipated from the law by grace, so that their works are not to be measured according to its rules." They are able to love and serve God as children serve a father who they trust is graciously disposed toward them (3.19.5). To be sure, the law, properly interpreted in light of the work, example, and teaching of Christ, continues to be the only perfect revelation of God's moral will.[8] Conscience, reason, and philosophy may provide

---

[6] Preface to Psalms, July 22, 1557; CO 31:23. Cf. Höpfl, *The Christian Polity of John Calvin*, 21.

[7] Commentary on Matthew 27:11 [1555]; CO 45:751.

[8] While the law is a perfect statement of righteousness, it is on Christ that God has "stamped for us the likeness to which he would have us conform." Christ "has been set before us as an example, whose pattern we ought to express in our life. What more effective thing can you require than this one thing? Nay, what can you require beyond this one thing? For we have been adopted as sons by the Lord with this one condition: that our life express Christ, the bond of our adoption" (3.6.3). Calvin argues that the gospel is worth more reverence than the law to the degree that Christ is greater than the angels through whom the law was mediated. Commentary on Hebrews 2:1 [1549]; CO 55:21. Cf. Commentary on 1 Corinthians 11:1 [1546]; CO 49:472. Johnson observes that for Calvin, the law's force becomes "descriptive rather than prescriptive." Merwin S. Johnson, "Calvin's Ethical Legacy," *The Legacy of John Calvin* (ed. David Foxgrover; Grand Rapids: CRC, 2000), 63–83, 68 (Cf. 67–70). Cf. Guenther Haas, *The Concept of Equity in Calvin's Ethics* (Waterloo, Ontario: Wilfrid Laurier

humans with some knowledge of God's will, but in the context of sin they utterly fail to communicate the law's spiritual objective. But while the law is "the finest and best-disposed method of ordering a man's life" the "more explicit plan" by which believers are conformed to that law is the call of Romans 12:1–2 to "present their bodies to God as a living sacrifice, holy and acceptable to him" (3.7.1).[9] "God wills to be freely worshiped, freely loved" (3.26.2).

The third implication of Christian freedom is the liberty from "outward things that are themselves 'indifferent.'" Whether Christians perform or do not perform these outward and indifferent activities is ultimately irrelevant from God's perspective, though love or scripture may dictate one activity or another at any particular time (3.19.7). For "the kingdom of God, which is spiritual [*regnum Dei, quod spirituale est*], does not consist in these outward observances [*externis observationibus*]," and "things indifferent are in themselves of no importance in the sight of God."[10] Calvin explains that "here are included all ceremonies whose observance is optional, that our consciences may not be constrained by any necessity to observe them but may remember that by God's beneficence their use is for edification made subject to him." In outward matters, Christians are free to do what is loving or edifying within the bounds of scripture (3.19.8). "Paul would exempt the consciences of the pious from all decrees, laws, and censures of men."[11]

Scholars sometimes present Calvin's concept of *adiaphora*, or indifferent matters, as if it refers to areas in which Christians have complete liberty of action. Where Calvin claims that scripture regulates certain indifferent matters, therefore, or where he calls Christians to submit to one another or to the church, they see a contradiction. "Calvin seems constantly to be giving with one hand and taking away with the other," Höpfl complains.[12] But as John Thompson shows, the fundamental characteristic of indifferent matters (or matters of polity), for Calvin, is not

University Press, 1997), 58–60; Mary Lane Potter, "The 'Whole Office of the Law' in the Theology of John Calvin," *Journal of Law and Religion* 3 (1985): 132; I. John. Hesselink, *Calvin's Concept of the Law* (Allison Park, PA: Pickwick Publications, 1992), 278–281; Eric Fuchs, "Calvin's Ethics," *John Calvin's Impact on Church and Society* (ed. Martin Ernst Hirzel and Martin Smallmann; Grand Rapids: Eerdmans, 2009), 145–158.

9 The gospel creates in believers not a "servile fear" but a "voluntary and cheerful love of righteousness" that results from God's astonishing favor. Commentary on Romans 12:1 [1556]; CO 49:233.

10 Commentary on 1 Corinthians 8:8 [1546]; CO 49:434.

11 Commentary on 1 Corinthians 2:15 [1546]; CO 49:345. The one who judges a fellow Christian usurps Christ of his dominion as Lord, for within the kingdom of God "an equality ought to be preserved." Commentary on Romans 14:10 [1556]; CO 49:262. Cf. Commentary on James 4:11 [1551]; CO 55:419; 4:12; CO 55:420.

12 Höpfl, *The Christian Polity of John Calvin*, 37. Cf. Oliver O'Donovan and Joan Lockwood O'Donovan, *From Irenaeus to Grotius: A Sourcebook in Christian Political Thought* (Grand Rapids: Eerdmans, 1999), 663; Jane Dempsey Douglass, "Christian Freedom: What Calvin Learned at the School of Women," *Church History* 53 (June 1984): 155–173.

that action with respect to them is unrestrained, but that it has no spiritual or eternal significance in and of itself.[13] Indifferent matters are of merely temporal concern, pertaining simply to decorum and polity, or to decency and harmony among people, but they are still subject to the rule of love and are sometimes even regulated by scripture.

It is to clarify the difference between indifferent matters and spiritual matters that Calvin introduces the two kingdoms concept. After outlining the three dimensions of Christian liberty, he cautions his readers that Christian liberty should not be mistaken for license. Christians are to use their liberty to serve God and edify their neighbors according to the governing principle of love. For while it is true that "Christ's death is nullified if we put our souls under men's subjection," this hardly means that "all human obedience were at the same time removed and cast down" (3.19.14). Calvin thus declares,

> Therefore, in order that none of us may stumble on that stone, let us first consider that there is a twofold government in man [*duplex esse in homine regimen*]: one aspect is spiritual [*spirituale*], whereby the conscience is instructed in piety and in reverencing God; the second is political [*politicum*], whereby man is educated for the duties of humanity and citizenship that must be maintained among men. These are usually called the 'spiritual' and the 'temporal' jurisdiction [*iurisdictio spiritualis et temporalis*] (not improper terms) by which is meant that the former sort of government pertains to the life of the soul, while the latter has to do with the concerns of the present life – not only with food and clothing but with laying down laws whereby a man may live his life among other men holily, honorably, and temperately. For the former resides in the inner mind, while the latter regulates only outward behavior. The one we may call the spiritual kingdom [*regnum spirituale*], the other, the political kingdom [*regnum politicum*]. Now these two, as we have divided them, must always be examined separately; and while one is being considered, we must call away and turn aside the mind from thinking about the other. There are in man, so to speak, two worlds [*mundi duo*], over which different kings and different laws [*varii reges et variae leges*] have authority (3.19.15).

Calvin's explicit reference to the medieval distinction between spiritual and temporal jurisdiction make it clear that he views the two kingdoms distinction as a revised version of the old medieval two swords doctrine. In the 1543 *Institutes*, Calvin added a further statement:

---

[13] "Calvin has used *police* not to designate a realm in which externals are subject to human or ecclesial discretion, but to distinguish the external orders of this present life from the spiritual concerns of the life to come. In this latter sense, *police* is by no means left to human discretion." See John Lee Thompson, *John Calvin and the Daughters of Sarah: Women in Regular and Exceptional Roles in the Exegesis of John Calvin, His Predecessors and His Contemporaries* (Geneva: Droz, 1992), 262 (Cf. 246–264).

Through this distinction it comes about that we are not to misapply to the political order [*politicum ordinem*] the gospel teaching on spiritual freedom, as if Christians were less subject, as concerns outward government [*externum regimen*], to human laws, because their consciences have been set free in God's sight; as if they were released from all bodily servitude because they are free according to the spirit.

The time to address "civil government [*civili regimine*]," as well as those "church laws [*legibus ... ecclesiasticis*]" that "seem to apply to the spiritual kingdom [*spirituale regnum*]," Calvin writes, will be Book 4 (3.19.15).

Like so much of the terminology Calvin uses to describe eschatological realities, this basic statement of the two kingdoms doctrine is readily subject to misinterpretation if read too rigidly. Spiritual government, spiritual jurisdiction, the spiritual kingdom, the conscience, the soul, piety, and the inner mind line up on one side. Political government, the political kingdom, the temporal jurisdiction, the present life, the duties of humanity and citizenship, and outward behavior characterize the other. Interpreted too rigidly, the statement has been read to correspond to the difference between forgiveness and active righteousness, or even between piety and justice.[14] Yet such readings place it in blatant contradiction to Calvin's understanding of the kingdom of Christ as extending to the restoration of the entire creation, including the human body and affairs among human beings. Calvin's description of the spiritual kingdom in terms of piety and the soul should not be interpreted in an exclusive sense any more than should his numerous other statements that declare salvation to be an affair of the soul or that describe the conscience as only pertaining to human interaction with God. Calvin's point is not sharply and precisely to delineate two hermetically sealed realms or spheres into which life can neatly be divided, but to distinguish the spiritual kingdom of Christ from temporal affairs with respect to each kingdom's most prominent and defining characteristics. The point is not that Christ's spiritual kingdom has nothing to do with politics, humanity, citizenship, or outward behavior, but that its power penetrates further than these phenomena, toward spiritual matters, the conscience, the soul, piety, and the inner mind. On the other hand, Calvin's meaning is not that civil government should have no concern for spiritual realities, the conscience, the soul, piety, and the inner mind, but that the political order is properly limited in its powers to matters of polity, humanity, citizenship, and outward behavior.

Read in the context of Calvin's broader theology and exegesis, the two kingdoms distinction arises from the eschatological distinction between the present age and

---

[14] Torrance Kirby, "A Reformed Culture of Persuasion: John Calvin's 'Two Kingdoms' and the Theological Origins of the Public Sphere," *Calvin@500:Theology, History, and Practice* (ed. Richard R. Topping and John A. Vissers; Eugene, OR: Wipf and Stock, 2011), 52–66, 62; Stevenson, *Sovereign Grace*, 52.

the age to come, from which Calvin draws a distinction between Christ's universal government and his spiritual kingdom.

UNIVERSAL AND SPIRITUAL GOVERNMENT

At various places in his writings, Calvin distinguishes Christ's rule over all things as creator from his renewal and regeneration of all things as savior. In his commentary on John 1:5 he explains,

> For there are two distinct powers which belong to the Son of God: the first, which is manifested in the structure of the world and the order of nature, and the second, by which he renews and restores fallen nature. As he is the eternal Speech of God, by him the world was made; by his power all things continue to possess the life which they once received; man especially was endued with an extraordinary gift of understanding; and though by his revolt he lost the light of understanding, yet he still sees and understands, so that what he naturally possesses from the grace of the Son of God is not entirely destroyed. But since by his stupidity and perverseness he darkens the light which still dwells in him, it remains that a new office be undertaken by the Son of God, the office of mediator, to renew by the Spirit of regeneration man who had been ruined.[15]

The fundamental distinction here is between Christ's sovereignty over all things as the Son of God, by whom all things were created, and his sovereignty over all things as the human messiah, who has ascended in triumph to God's right hand. "As the eternal Word of God, Christ, it is true, has always had in his hands by right sovereign authority and majesty, and as such can receive no accessions thereto. But still, he is exalted in human nature, in which he took upon himself the form of a servant."[16] Carefully distinguishing between Christ "as to his divine essence" and Christ "as a partaker of our flesh,"[17] Calvin argues that "the word heir is ascribed to Christ as manifested in the flesh, for being made man, he put on our nature and, as such, received this heirship, and that for this purpose, that he might restore us to what we had lost in Adam."[18]

---

[15] Commentary on John 1:5 [1553]; CO 47:6–7. [16] Commentary on Psalm 2:8 [1557]; CO 31:47–48.

[17] Commentary on Hebrews 1:3 [1549]; CO 55:11.

[18] Commentary on Hebrews 1:2 [1549]; CO 55:11. Cf. Commentary on Matthew 28:18 [1555]; CO 45: 820–821; Commentary on Acts, Dedication to Second Edition [1560]; CO 18:157; Commentary on Psalm 66:7 [1557]; CO 31:612; Commentary on Galatians, Argument [1548]; CO 50:163; Commentary on the Harmony of the Gospels, Dedicatory [1555]; CO 15:710–712. This dynamic leads some scholars to interpret Calvin's two kingdoms doctrine within the context of what became known in sixteenth-century polemics as the *extra Calvinisticum*. This doctrine taught that the Son of God's existence and power is not restricted to the embodied person of Jesus. David Willis writes, "The confession that the *Logos* is united to the flesh but exists *etiam extra carnem* corresponds to the relation between Christ's Lordship over the Church and his Lordship *etiam extra ecclesiam* . . . Christ reigns particularly over the

The purpose of Christ's ascension, then, was that he might receive all power as a human messiah in order to direct the world to its final restoration and to preserve his church in the process. "Christ left the world and ascended to the Father, first, to subdue all powers to himself and to render angels obedient; next, to restrain the devil and to protect and preserve the church by his help, as well as all the elect of God the Father."[19] In his ascension to God's right hand, therefore, Jesus was given both the universal and spiritual governments, both "the government of heaven and earth and the perpetual government of the church."[20] The Father has given Christ "full power over all things in heaven and in the earth"[21] so that by his authority and judgment he might bring about "the full restoration of all things."[22] This means that there can be

---

Church and generally over all mankind. His reign over the Church involves voluntary obedience from the faithful through the exercise of his gifts of grace and the secret operation of the Spirit where the Gospel is communicated. His reign over all men compels them, even against their will, to serve his purposes now and will finally drag them before his seat of righteous judgment." E. David. Willis, *Calvin's Catholic Christology: The Function of the So-Called Extra Calvinisticum in Calvin's Theology* (Leiden: Brill, 1966), 135–136. If the gospel is the means by which Christ rules his kingdom proper, Willis argues, Calvin "gives special attention to the order of nature as the instrument of Christ's reign *etiam extra ecclesiam.*" Thus "The theme of Christ's rulership over the world is surely present in Calvin's thought, but it never becomes synonymous with the primary meaning he gives to the kingdom of Christ: the spiritual reign over the Church." "He never allows the specificity of the Church's task to preach the Gospel to be substituted with a general ethic which would blur the distinction between Church and world, and which would define the Church in terms of a works righteousness in social ethics rather than in terms of an open confession of Christ by his elected ones." "Order and justice beyond the Church are not for salvation but are for the preservation and maintenance of society. Through them, God protects his creation from chaos so that it remains the milieu of redemption and sanctification." Willis, *Calvin's Catholic Christology*, 145. Cf. Heiko A. Oberman, "The 'Extra' Dimension in the Theology of Calvin," *Journal of Ecclesiastical History* 21 (1970): 43–64.

[19] To be sure, "the events which the Prophet here narrates are not yet complete; but this ought to be familiar to all the pious, for whenever the kingdom of Christ is treated of, his glory is magnificently extolled as if it were now absolutely complete in all its parts." Commentary on Daniel 7:14 [1561]; CO 41:62–63.

[20] Commentary on Acts 10:42 [1552]; CO 48:248.   [21] Commentary on John 5:27 [1553]; CO 47:118.

[22] Commentary on John 5:28 [1553]; CO 47:119 (Cf. 5:23; CO 47:114). Cf. Commentary on 1 Corinthians 8:6 [1546]; CO 49:432; Dedication to Commentary on Jeremiah and Lamentations [1563]; CO 20: 74–75. On Calvin's understanding of the ultimate relationship of Christ's deity to his humanity see his Commentary on 1 Corinthians 15:27 [1546]; CO 49:549. Cf. Commentary on John 14:28 [1553]; CO 47:336; Commentary on Romans 5:2 [1556]; CO 49:89–90; Commentary on Hebrews 1:13 [1549]; CO 55:19. Moltmann, following Quistorp, argues that Calvin sees Christ's human nature in purely functional and even temporary terms. Jürgen Moltmann, *The Crucified God: The Cross of Christ as the Foundation and Criticism of Christian Theology* (New York: Harper and Row, 1974 [1973]), 258–259. Heinrich Quistorp, *Calvin's Doctrine of the Last Things* (trans. Harold Knight; London: Lutterworth Press, 1955), 166–171. Richard Muller shows, however, that in contrast to Moltmann's and Quistorp's assumptions, Calvin rejects the notion that Christ will ever set aside his humanity. For Calvin, Muller points out, the spirituality of the future body does not imply its incorporeality (36). See Richard A. Muller, "Christ in the Eschaton: Calvin and Moltmann on the Duration of the *Munus Regium*," *Harvard Theological Review* 74.1 (1981): 31–59. Cf. Torrance, *Kingdom and Church*, 138.

no authority or power that is not subject to his reign, whether in this age or the age to come.[23]

But while Christ has been given all power in heaven and earth in order to bring about the restoration of all things, that restoration is not yet complete. For as was seen in Chapter 3, where there is not voluntary submission to Christ, the kingdom has not yet been established. Those who have not been regenerated by the Spirit remain exiles from Christ's kingdom and are under the dominion and government of the Devil, for "there is no middle condition."[24] Calvin therefore consistently distinguishes between Christ's "spiritual government of the church [*spirituali ecclesiae gubernatione*]" and "the universal government of the world [*universali mundi gubernatione*],"[25] between "that government of God which is general in its nature," and "that special and spiritual jurisdiction which he exercises over the Church."[26] Both governments are of Christ, though one is more properly Christ's kingdom than is the other.[27] Jesus is lord of heaven and earth but "he is in a peculiar manner the Lord of believers, who yield willingly and cheerfully to his authority, for it is only of 'his body' that he is 'the head' (Ephesians 1:22–23)."[28] Usually Calvin limits the term "kingdom of Christ" to the spiritual kingdom, and where he uses the term in a broader sense, he ordinarily qualifies it. As he puts it in his commentary on John, "the kingdom of Christ [*regnum Christi*] extends, no doubt, to all men, but it brings salvation to none but the elect, who with voluntary obedience follow the voice of the Shepherd; for the others are compelled by violence to obey him, till at length he utterly bruise them with his iron scepter."[29]

[23] Calvin observes of Paul's words in Ephesians 1, "The age that is to come is expressly mentioned, to point out that the exalted rank of Christ is not temporal, but eternal [*non temporalem sed aeternam*], and that it is not limited to this world, but shines illustriously in the kingdom of God." Commentary on Ephesians 1:21 [1548]; CO 51:159. It includes "the administration [*dispensatio*] of all things," and "the entire command and government [*potestas et administratio*] of the universe" (1:22; CO 51:159).

[24] Commentary on 1 John 3:8 [1551]; CO 55:334. For this reason the whole world "is regarded as nothing but darkness in the sight of God, because apart from the kingdom of Christ there is no light." Commentary on Colossians 1:13 [1548]; CO 52:84. Cf. Commentary on Romans 11:22–23 [1556]; CO 49: 224–225; Commentary on Hebrews 2:5 [1549]; CO 55:24; Commentary on Ephesians 1:12 [1548]; CO 52:83; Commentary on 1 John 5:19 [1551]; CO 55:374.

[25] Commentary on Ephesians 1:23 [1548]; CO 51:160. He admits that the statement that Christ has been set over all things can refer to either of these governments but suggests that in this case it should be interpreted in terms of the spiritual government.

[26] Commentary on Psalm 67:3 [1557]; CO 31:618.

[27] Both governments are also expressions of God's providence, but that providence is "especially acknowledged in the government of his own church." Commentary on 1 Peter 4:17 [1551]; CO 55:281. Cf. 2:7; CO 55:238; Commentary on Isaiah 52:10 [1559]; CO 37:249.

[28] Commentary on Luke 1:43 [1555]; CO 45:35.

[29] Commentary on John 17:2 [1553]; CO 47:376. Calvin occasionally uses the term "kingdom of Christ" in the broader sense. In his commentary on Genesis, he writes that in creation "the invisible kingdom of Christ [*invisibile Christi regnum*] fills all things, and his spiritual grace is diffused through all." Commentary on Genesis, Argument [1554]; CO 23:10. As David Willis puts it, "The kingdom of

Calvin often distinguishes Christ's spiritual and universal governments by virtue of the fact that the former pertains to believers while the latter extends to unbelievers. In his commentary on the Lord's Prayer, for example, specifically the petition "Thy kingdom come," Calvin carefully explains as the primary meaning of the petition that God would, by his Spirit, bring all people to voluntary allegiance to Christ. But he then goes on to distinguish this rule from the form of Christ's rule over his enemies. "There is still another way in which God reigns, and that is when he overthrows his enemies and compels them, with Satan their head, to yield a reluctant subjection to his authority."[30] Although the petition focuses on God's reign through his word and Spirit, Calvin notes in the *Institutes* that it extends in a different way to those who refuse to submit to that reign. Christians should pray that God will "cast down all enemies of pure teaching and religion; that he scatter their counsels and crush their efforts" (3.20.42). In his commentary on Psalm 2, Calvin offers the same distinction with reference to the subjection of the world to the Son's authority. The "beauty and glory of the kingdom … are more illustriously displayed when a willing people run to Christ in the day of his power, to show themselves his obedient subjects." But in his exaltation Jesus is "furnished with power by which to reign even over those who are averse to his authority, and refuse to obey him." These "he shall subdue by force, and compel to submit to him."[31]

Christ's universal government manifests his justice and care for human beings. It is God's responsibility "to govern the world and to exercise care over mankind, and also to make a difference between good and evil, to help the miserable, to punish all wickedness, to check injustice and violence." That some people deny God's governance of the world is evident in the fact that they "seek to extinguish the distinction between right and wrong in their consciences." They imagine that "God concerns not himself with human affairs."[32] But the rise and fall of nations testifies that God rules, graciously yet justly, over human affairs.[33] His providential rule is displayed in that he maintains complete control over kings, regardless of whether or not they

---

Christ is, above all, for Calvin, that spiritual and heavenly reign exercised by Christ over his people through the Gospel." Willis, *Calvin's Catholic Christology*, 136. Oberman agrees, but rightly adds, "Yet, from the fall of Adam onwards, the eternal Son of God manipulates the kingdom of Satan as part of his hidden and incomprehensible reign … Calvin wants it to be clearly understood that in this sense the rule of Christ obtains *etiam extra ecclesiam*." Oberman, "The 'Extra' Dimension in the Theology of Calvin," 47. Oberman also notes the priority of Christ's rule within the church (62).

[30] Commentary on Matthew 6:10 [1555]; CO 45:197–198. Cf. Commentary on Daniel 7:25 [1561]; CO 41: 76–80.

[31] Commentary on Psalm 2:9 [1557]; CO 31:48–49. Cf. Commentary on Jeremiah 49:38 [1563]; CO 39:389.

[32] Commentary on Zephaniah 1:12 [1559]; CO 44:22.

[33] Commentary on Daniel 2:21 [1561]; CO 40:576–578. Cf. Commentary on Luke 1:52 [1555]; CO 45:41.

serve him.[34] Civil magistrates, parents, masters, and all those in authority have been placed in power "not by chance, but by God's providence."[35]

OUTWARD AND INWARD, BODY AND SOUL, FLESH AND SPIRIT, TEMPORAL AND ETERNAL

The fundamental distinction underlying Calvin's two kingdoms doctrine is the contrast between the present age, marked by corruption and temporality, and the future eternal kingdom of Christ. "For we see that whatever is earthly is of the world and of time, and is indeed fleeting. Therefore Christ, to lift our hope to heaven, declares that his 'kingship is not of this world'" (2.15.3). In his commentary on 1 Timothy, Calvin writes, "All that is in the world [*saeculo*] has the taste of its nature, so that it is fading and quickly passes away."[36]

This distinction is still in view when Calvin describes the political kingdom as that which pertains to "food and clothing," "outward behavior," and "life among other men," in contrast to the spiritual kingdom which pertains to the "soul," to the "conscience," and to the "inner mind" (3.19.15). Although such language might seem to be merely a reflection of the anthropological distinction between the body and the soul,[37] Calvin actually uses it to refer to the eschatological difference between what is "earthly" and what is "heavenly," or between the affairs of the "present life," and those of the life to come. Those things that pertain to the outward person are earthly things, things that will pass away. Those things that pertain to the inward person are heavenly things, things that will endure as part of the kingdom of Christ. In his commentary on 2 Corinthians 4:17, Calvin articulates this connection explicitly. When the Apostle Paul refers to the "outward man," he argues, the term denotes

> everything that relates to the present life. As he here sets before us two men, so you must place before your view two kinds of life – the earthly and the heavenly [*terrenam et coelestem*]. The outward man is the maintenance of the earthly life, which consists not merely in the flower of one's age, and in good health, but also in riches, honors, friendships, and other resources.[38]

To be sure, often Calvin presents the outward/inward distinction using the language of body and soul. "By the inner man Paul means the soul, and whatever

---

[34] Commentary on Daniel 5:18–20 [1561]; CO 40:711–713.
[35] Commentary on 1 Peter 2:13 [1551]; CO 55:244.
[36] Commentary on 1 Timothy 6:17 [1548]; CO 52:333. Indeed, "nothing on earth is solidly founded, but everything may be said to be in a floating condition" (6:18; CO 52:334).
[37] Cf. David VanDrunen, *Natural Law and the Two Kingdoms: A Study in the Development of Reformed Social Thought* (Grand Rapids: Eerdmans, 2010), 91.
[38] Commentary on 2 Corinthians 4:16 [1548]; CO 50:58.

relates to the spiritual life of the soul, as the outward man denotes the body, with everything that belongs to it, health, honors, riches, vigor, beauty, and everything of that nature."[39] But Calvin emphasizes that the contrast between the body and soul, like that between the flesh and the spirit, is not to be interpreted as a narrow anthropological distinction but as an eschatological distinction. For instance, in his commentary on 2 Corinthians 5:16, he notes that when the Apostle Paul says Christians should no longer view a person according to the "flesh," the term "flesh" does not denote physical human embodiment. After all, Christians are called to fix their hopes on Jesus, who "does now as certainly lead a glorious life in our flesh as he once suffered in it," and it is by his body that Christ "has opened up for our nature the kingdom of God."[40] Christians should therefore regard Christ in the flesh, but "not in a fleshly manner." Jesus "is spiritual to us, not as if he laid aside the body and became a spirit, but because he regenerates and governs his own people by the influence of his Spirit."[41]

Calvin thus uses the terms "body," "flesh," and "outward" to denote the *whole human being as a participant in the present passing age*, corrupted and marred by sin. In his commentary on 1 Corinthians 3, he stresses, "the term flesh is not restricted to the lower appetites merely, as the Sophists pretend, the seat of which they call sensuality, but is employed to describe man's whole nature."[42] Likewise when Paul refers to the mind, he does not mean the rational part of the soul as described by the philosophers, but the part of the soul illuminated by the Spirit of God.[43] The soul is no more virtuous than the body, and it is the whole person, body and soul, that Paul describes as "corporeal." Thus "the nature of man is said to be corporeal because he is destitute of celestial grace and is only a sort of empty shadow or image. We may add that the body ... is said by Paul to be mortal ... to teach us that the whole nature of man tends to death and ruin."[44] In short, Calvin's language of body and soul, like the Pauline language of flesh and spirit, constitutes an analogy. The relationship between the soul and the body, or the spirit and the flesh, represents the relationship between the regenerate human being and the corrupt human

---

[39] Commentary on Ephesians 3:16 [1548]; CO 51:186.

[40] Commentary on 2 Corinthians 5:16 [1548]; CO 50:68. Confusion on this point leads Quistorp erroneously to claim, "for Calvin this mortal body is to be equated with the sinful flesh. Again and again he identifies the anthropological difference of the soul and body with the theological opposition of *sarx* and *pneuma* (in the Biblical-Pauline sense) although as an exegete he is well aware that these two antitheses are not the same." Quistorp, *Calvin's Doctrine of the Last Things*, 57.

[41] Commentary on 2 Corinthians 5:16 [1548]; CO 50:69.

[42] Commentary on 1 Corinthians 3:3 [1546]; CO 49:348. Cf. Margaret R. Miles, "Theology, Anthropology, and the Human Body in Calvin's *Institutes of the Christian Religion*," *Harvard Theological Review* 74 (1981): 311–314.

[43] Commentary on Romans 7:25 [1556]; CO 49:135–136.

[44] Commentary on Romans 6:12 [1556]; CO 49:111.

being.[45] But the analogy should not be taken too literally. "[B]oth terms, flesh as well as spirit, belong to the soul, but the latter to that part which is renewed, and the former to that which still retains its natural character . . . . The inner man then is not simply the soul, but that spiritual part which has been regenerated by God, and the members signify the other remaining part."[46] Similarly, "the word body means the same as the external man and members," the person insofar as she remains "carnal and earthly."[47] The terms of the analogy are anthropological, but its meaning is eschatological.

Why use such an anthropological analogy at all? The primary reason, for Calvin, is that the analogy comes from scripture. But why does the Apostle Paul use it? According to Calvin, the apostle wanted to "clearly show that the hidden renovation is concealed from and escapes our observation, except it be apprehended by faith."[48] The kingdom of Christ is future, and Christians should not expect to experience complete renewal apart from the transformation of their bodies at the end of the age.[49] By distancing themselves from outward matters, they train themselves to seek first the kingdom of God. Indeed, "it is necessary that the condition of the present life should decay in order that the inward man may be in a flourishing state, because in proportion as the earthly life declines the heavenly life advances, at least in believers."[50]

The distinction between the outward person, characterized by bodily suffering, and the inward person, characterized by renewal, thus enables believers to make sense of the cruciform character of the Christian life.[51] As Paul explains in Romans 8: 25–31, in his decree of election, God ordained that Christians must be conformed to the image of Jesus through suffering, so "connecting, as by a kind of necessary chain, our salvation with the bearing of the cross."[52] Christ is the pattern: "He will have all

[45] Commentary on Romans 7:22 [1556]; CO 49:133–134.
[46] Commentary on Romans 7:18 [1556]; CO 49:132.
[47] Commentary on Romans 7:24 [1556]; CO 49:135.
[48] Commentary on Romans 7:22 [1556]; CO 49:133–134.
[49] Commentary on Romans 7:15 [1556]; CO 49:130; Commentary on Matthew 13:43 [1555]; CO 45:371.
[50] Commentary on 2 Corinthians 4:16 [1548]; CO 50:58. Christians must be taught the "connection between the death of our present life and spiritual renovation." Commentary on Romans 6:5 [1556]; CO 49:107. Cf. Commentary on Ephesians 3:16 [1548]; CO 51:186.
[51] Christians should expect life "under the cross." "[W]e ought to know that the happiness promised us in Christ does not consist in outward advantages – such as leading a joyous and peaceful life, having rich possessions, being safe from all harm, and abounding with delights such as the flesh commonly longs after. No, our happiness belongs to the heavenly life!" (2.15.4) Christians are called to endure the "ignominy of the cross [*crucis ignominiam*]," the "abasement of the cross [*humilitate crucis*]," and those "marks of Christ" emblematic of suffering. Commentary on 1 Corinthians 4:10–12, 14 [1546]; CO 49: 369–370, 371. Cf. *Institutes* 3.8.1; 3.9.6; Commentary on Matthew 5:10 [1555]; CO 45:164; 7:15; CO 45: 224–225; Commentary on Colossians 1:11 [1548]; CO 52:82; Commentary on Hebrews 1:13 [1549]; CO 55:19.
[52] Commentary on Romans 8:28 [1556]; CO 49:158–159. The decree of adoption "is inseparable from the other decree which determines that we are to bear the cross, for no one can be an heir of heaven

those whom he adopts to be the heirs of his kingdom to be conformed to his example."[53] Those who resent the call to suffering show that they place a much higher value on the "fleeting and vanishing shadow of the present life" than on the future life to come.[54] Yet they should meditate on what Christ's suffering reveals about the love of God for humanity and consider themselves blessed to be able to share in Christ's suffering, that they might also "enjoy along with him immortal glory."[55]

Calvin explains that a person's participation in Christ's suffering and death involves her in a process of mortification that is twofold (3.20.42). "The one is inward – what the Scripture is wont to term the mortification of the flesh, or the crucifixion of the old man, of which Paul treats in the sixth chapter of the Romans. The other is outward – what is termed the mortification of the outward man. It is the endurance of the cross, of which he treats in the eighth chapter of the same epistle."[56] Inward mortification is the experience of regeneration and sanctification, the gradual conformity of the believer to Christ's piety and justice. Through suffering believers learn humility (3.8.2–3), patience, and obedience (3.8.4–5), and are sometimes graciously corrected by God (3.8.6). They experience joy not because, like the Stoics, they think suffering does not harm them, but because the harm that they experience works toward their ultimate salvation (3.8.11).

Equally central to the Christian life is the experience of outward mortification, a primary purpose of which is to prevent humans from inadvertently setting their hearts on the present life. In his commentary on 1 Timothy 4:8, Calvin notes that it is crucial for believers to "distinguish between the good things of the present and of the future life" in order that they might not make an idol of the former. For this reason God intentionally mingles the present life with "very many afflictions."[57] He allows

---

without being conformed to the image of the only begotten son of God" (8:29; CO 49:159–160). Cf. Commentary on Hebrews 5:8 [1549]; CO 55:63–64. Cf. 2:10; CO 55:27; Commentary on Acts 8:33 [1552]; CO 48:194.

[53] Commentary on Romans 8:29 [1556]; CO 49:160. Cf. 8:30; CO 49:161; Commentary on Colossians 1:24 [1548]; CO 52:93–95; Commentary on Philippians 1:29 [1548]; CO 52: 22; Commentary on Hebrews 12:3, 5 [1549]; CO 55:172–173.

[54] Commentary on Matthew 10:28 [1555]; CO 45:288. "If we are branded with disgrace and ignominy, we but have a fuller place in the Kingdom of God." *Institutes* 3.8.7. Cf. Commentary on Luke 14:28 [1555]; CO 45:295–296.

[55] Commentary on Isaiah 53:12 [1559]; CO 37:267. Cf. Commentary on Colossians 2:3 [1548]; CO 52:100; Commentary on Matthew 16:20–28 [1555]; CO 45:479; 27:33; CO 45:764–765; Commentary on 1 Corinthians 4:16 [1546]; CO 49:374; Commentary on 2 Corinthians 13:4 [1548]; CO 50:149–150; Commentary on Philippians 3:15 [1548]; CO 52:53; Commentary on 2 Timothy 2:11 [1548]; CO 52: 364–365; Commentary on 1 Peter 4:12 [1551]; CO 55:278–279.

[56] Commentary on Philippians 3:11 [1548]; CO 52:50. Cf. Commentary on 2 Corinthians 4:17 [1548]; CO 50:58–59; 4:10; CO 49:54–55; Quistorp, *Calvin's Doctrine of the Last Things*, 37–40.

[57] Commentary on 1 Timothy 4:8 [1548]; CO 52:299–300.

Christian nations to fall into war, Christian homes to be robbed or burned, Christian marriages to fall apart, and Christian children to abandon the faith.

> Then only do we rightly advance by the discipline of the cross, when we learn that this life, judged in itself, is troubled, turbulent, unhappy in countless ways, and in no respect clearly happy; that all those things which are judged to be its goods are uncertain, fleeting, vain, and vitiated by many intermingled evils. From this, at the same time, we conclude that in this life we are to seek and hope for nothing but struggle. When we think of our crown, we are to raise our eyes to heaven. For this we must believe: that the mind is never seriously aroused to desire and ponder the life to come unless it be previously imbued with contempt for the present life (3.9.1).

Christians are "enclosed as slaves in the prison of our flesh,"[58] bound within "the earthly prison of the body" (3.6.5). For as the kingdom of Christ "lies beyond this world, . . . we must, by contempt of this present life and mortification of the outward man, set ourselves with the whole bent of our mind to meditation on a blessed immortality."[59]

Interpreted out of context, these kinds of comments resemble a form of Neoplatonic dualism. But again, Calvin's comments about the body must be interpreted in eschatological rather than anthropological terms.[60] His disparaging comments about the body refer to the body that is corrupted by sin and destined for death, and his exhortation to Christians to hold the world in contempt refers specifically to the world corrupted by sin and destined for judgment. They do *not* refer to the body or to the world as created by God and destined for restoration in the kingdom of Christ. Proper contempt for the mortal body and the fallen world is simply the recognition that these gifts are corrupted and destined for death until they are

---

[58] Commentary on 1 John 3:2 [1551]; CO 55:330. Cf. Commentary on 1 Thessalonians 4:5 [1551]; CO 52:161.

[59] Commentary on 2 Corinthians, Argument [1548]; CO 50:7. In his comments on 2 Corinthians 5, Calvin writes that Christians are to display a healthy "contempt of the world" in order to replace their "misplaced attachment to this life" with the hope of the "felicity and glory of the future life." The Apostle Paul can speak of the mortal body as a tent from which believers depart willingly (5:1–2; CO 50:60–61). All that human beings experience during the present life is like smoke, destined rapidly to pass away. It is for this reason that believers, "holding the world in contempt . . . strive with all our heart to meditate upon the life to come" (3.9.2). Cf. Commentary on 1 John 2:17 [1551]; CO 55:320; Commentary on 1 Timothy 6:16 [1548]; CO 52:331; Commentary on 2 Thessalonians 1:5 [1551]; CO 55:188–190; Commentary on Colossians 3:5 [1548]; CO 52:119; Commentary on 1 Peter, argument [1551]; CO 55:205; 1:13–16; CO 55:220; Commentary on James 1:10 [1550]; CO 55:388.

[60] Lucien Richard, *The Spirituality of John Calvin* (Atlanta: John Knox Press, 1974); David E. Holwerda, "Eschatology and History: A Look at Calvin's Eschatological Vision," in *Readings in Calvin's Theology* (ed. Donald K. McKim; Grand Rapids: Baker, 1984), 318–321; Torrance, *Kingdom and Church*, 92–93. Quistorp, *Calvin's Doctrine of the Last Things*, 44–47, 56–57. Quistorp fails to take seriously the extent to which Calvin's contempt for the present life is a longing for the resurrection rather than death (89; Cf. 171).

restored in the kingdom of Christ. Calvin warns, "let believers accustom themselves to a contempt of the present life that engenders no hatred of it or ingratitude against God. Indeed, this life, however crammed with infinite miseries it may be, is still rightly to be counted among those blessings of God which are not to be spurned" (3.9.3). It is not *creation* that believers are to hold in contempt, nor is it *life*, both of which are good gifts of God. It is the *corruption* and *mortality* of this life that Christians despise. "Of course it is never to be hated except in so far as it holds us subject to sin; although not even hatred of that condition may ever properly be turned against life itself" (3.9.4).[61]

What is "perverse" for Calvin is infatuation with a world of sin and death:

> When it comes to a comparison with the life to come, the present life ... must be utterly despised and loathed. For, if heaven is our homeland, what else is the earth but our place of exile? If departure from the world is entry into life, what else is the world but a sepulcher? And what else is it for us to remain in life but to be immersed in death? If to be freed from the body is to be released into perfect freedom, what else is the body but a prison? (3.9.4)

Likewise, "if we deem this unstable, defective, corruptible, fleeting, wasting, rotting tabernacle of our body to be so dissolved that it is soon renewed unto a firm, perfect, incorruptible, and finally, heavenly glory, will not faith compel us ardently to seek what nature dreads?" It is not death for which the Christian yearns but the life beyond death. "But, someone will object, there is nothing that does not crave to endure. To be sure, I agree; and so I maintain that we must have regard for the immortality to come, where a firm condition will be ours which nowhere appears on earth. For Paul very well teaches that believers eagerly hasten to death not because they want to be unclothed but because they long to be more fully clothed." If mere animals, trees, and even stones "long for the final day of resurrection," the end of their corruption, should not humans do the same?" (3.9.5).[62]

On the other hand, Christians should desire to remain in this world as long as they can be useful to their neighbors, maintaining their post like soldiers in battle (3.9.4). They need not renounce temporal goods or seek suffering for its own sake. On the

---

[61] Cf. *Institutes*, 3.9.3; Commentary on Galatians 6:14 [1548]; CO 50:265; Miles, "Theology, Anthropology, and the Human Body in Calvin's *Institutes of the Christian Religion*," 311–319.

[62] "For death of itself will never be desired, because such a desire is at variance with natural feeling, but is desired for some particular reason, or with a view to some other end. Persons in despair have recourse to it from having become weary of life. Believers, on the other hand, willingly hasten forward to it because it is a deliverance from the bondage of sin and an introduction into the kingdom of heaven ... believers do not cease to regard death with horror, but when they turn their eyes to that life which follows death, they easily overcome all dread by means of that consolation." Commentary on Philippians 1:23 [1548]; CO 52:18. Cf. Commentary on Philippians 2:27 [1548]; CO 52:40; Commentary on John 21:18 [1553]; CO 47:455. Cf. Commentary on 1 Corinthians 5:6 [1546]; CO 49:381–382; Commentary on 2 Corinthians 5:4, 6 [1548]; CO 50:61–62, 63.

contrary, they "wish well to others, and study so much as lies in them to ease them of all trouble."[63] They "use this world [*praesenti saeculo*] without abusing it,"[64] directing all of God's good gifts toward the good end for which he created them (3.10.2).

Calvin's two kingdoms distinction thus clarifies that the kingdom of Christ is only partially realized in the present age. It does not consist in "external things [*rebus externis*]" like meat and drink, according to Romans 14:17, a text Calvin repeatedly quotes with this theme in view, but of "spiritual things [*rebus spiritualibus*]" such as "righteousness and peace and joy in the Holy Spirit."[65] Its establishment is always qualified, always conditioned by the cross. Believers thus live modestly, "having their minds always intent upon the future manifestation of Christ's kingdom."[66] And the transient political and social circumstances in which they find themselves must be distinguished from the spiritual kingdom of Christ, which is eternal. Such "outward things [*rebus externis*]" are to be used for the "necessity of the present life [*praesentis vitae*], which passes away quickly as a shadow [*instar umbrae subito praeterfluit*]."[67]

CHRISTIAN SERVICE IN THE POLITICAL ORDER

Among those temporary things that will pass away and be abolished when Christ presents his kingdom to the Father, Calvin includes "all powers that are lawful [*potestates legitimae*] and ordained by God." For "we know that all earthly principalities and honors are connected exclusively with the keeping up of the present life [*vitae praesentis*] and consequently are a part of the world [*mundi*]. Hence it follows that they are temporary." All political and social relationships are and will be transcended within the kingdom of Christ. "Hence as the world will have an end, so also will government and magistracy and laws and distinctions of ranks and different orders of dignities and everything of that nature. There will be no more any distinction between servant and master, between king and peasant, between magistrate and private citizen." Indeed, even angelic principalities and "ministries and superiorities in the church" will end, that "God may exercise his power and dominion by himself alone, and not by the hands of men or angels."[68]

---

[63] Commentary on Acts 27:30 [1554]; CO 48:549. Cf. Commentary on Philippians 3:8 [1548]; CO 52: 47–48; Commentary on Hebrews 12:1 [1549]; CO 55:171.

[64] Commentary on Romans 13:14 [1556]; CO 49:256. Cf. *Institutes*, 3.10.3.

[65] Commentary on Romans 14:17 [1556]; CO 49:265–266. Cf. Commentary on Psalm 85:10 [1557]; CO 31: 789–790.

[66] Commentary on 2 Thessalonians 1:10 [1550]; CO 52:192. Cf. *Institutes*, 3.18.6.

[67] Commentary on 1 Corinthians 6:13 [1546]; CO 49:397.

[68] Commentary on 1 Corinthians 15:24 [1546]; CO 49:546–547.

From the perspective of the spiritual kingdom of Christ, Calvin argues, the various relations associated with wealth, class, labor, gender, and government are entirely transcended. In Christ humans are free from every temporal power that might possibly lay a claim on them. Our "liberty," he declares in his comments on Colossians 2:15, the classic *Christus victor* text, "is the spoil which Christ has rescued from the devil ... For there is no tribunal so magnificent, no throne so stately, no show of triumph so distinguished, no chariot so elevated, as is the gibbet on which Christ has subdued death and the devil, the prince of death, nay more, has utterly trodden them under his feet."[69] Paul's statement in Galatians 3:28 should therefore be taken at face value: "There is neither Jew nor Greek, there is neither slave nor free, there is neither male nor female, for you are all one in Christ Jesus." The reformer concludes, "it is of no consequence to what nation or condition any one may belong, nor is circumcision any more regarded than sex or civil rank."[70] As he puts it earlier in the same commentary, "in the government of the world distinctions of rank are admitted, but in the spiritual kingdom of Christ [*spirituali ... Christi regno*] they can have no place."[71]

Such a perspective is potentially revolutionary, but only when the other side of Calvin's two kingdoms theology is forgotten.[72] For while Calvin uses the two kingdoms distinction to demonstrate the ultimate liberty of Christians from all orders, ranks, and governments, he uses the same doctrine to insist that Christians are nevertheless bound to submit to such manifestations of God's providence as the context for service. Christ has been given all authority in heaven and on earth, but

---

[69] Commentary on Colossians 2:15 [1548]; CO 52:109.

[70] Commentary on Galatians 3:28 [1548]; CO 50:222–223.

[71] Commentary on Galatians 2:6 [1548]; CO 50:186–187. It is worth noting that Calvin was unwilling to say that there will be absolute equality in the future kingdom of God. His point was that the inequalities and vocations of the present age would not endure into that kingdom. As he puts it in his Commentary on Matthew 20:23, "It is also worthy of our notice, that these words do not imply that there will be equality among the children of God, after they have been admitted to the heavenly glory, but rather that to each is promised that degree of honor to which he has been set apart by the eternal purpose of God." Commentary on Matthew 20:23 [1555]; CO 45:555.

[72] Stevenson plausibly identifies in Calvin's concept of Christian liberty a "new appreciation of human individuality" that has the potential of enhancing the individual's "moral and political status." Stevenson, *Sovereign Grace*, 11. There can be little doubt that Calvin's view of humanity contributes to an "egalitarian impulse" (27). It even "calls into question all institutional inequalities" (28). But for Calvin conscience "confirms the individual's place in a larger order of creation, judgment, and redemption," establishing humility and self-denial as fundamental Christian virtues, and directing believers toward their neighbors in "mutual subjection and mutual service" (42). Christian liberty is therefore qualified by "communal responsibility" (55). In the final analysis, "The last thing Calvin wished to propose was an individual fully sufficient and fully independent. Individual *insufficiency* and individual *dependence* worked themselves out clearly in the world. Believers found their strength and progress with*in* their membership in institutional society" (56).

this is not to be taken as meaning that worldly distinctions [*mundi ordines*] are abolished. For Paul speaks here of spiritual dominion [*spirituali dominio*], while the governments of the world are political [*dominia ... politica*] ... While, therefore, our religion acknowledges but one Lord, this is no hindrance in the way of civil governments having many lords, to whom honor and respect are due in that one Lord [*in illo unico Domino*].[73]

Likewise, while Christians are not to judge one another with regard to outward matters, "let us remember that the subject here is not civil government [*externa politia*], in which the edicts and laws of magistrates have place, but the spiritual government of the soul [*spirituali animae regimine*], in which the word of God alone ought to bear rule."[74]

How does Calvin justify such a practical limitation of Christian liberty in social and political affairs, while at the same time insisting on its radical implications with respect to the kingdom of God? Liberty characterizes the relation between a human being and God, he argues, but it does not always have to be exercised before others in order to be meaningful.[75] Calvin's rhetoric is reminiscent of Luther in this respect. First, Christians "are constituted lords of all things in such a way that we are not to bring ourselves under bondage to anything." Christian liberty should not be used as a pretext for injustice and vice, in other words, because such yielding to lust actually places Christians in "subjection to outward things, which ought to be under subjection to us."[76] Second, Christian liberty with respect to "outward things" does not justify disobedience to God, for the Apostle Paul "shows that the body is subject to God no less than the soul" as both are temples of the Holy Spirit. God rules by his word "even the outward actions of our life."[77]

Third, "everyone has liberty inwardly in the sight of God on this condition, that all must restrict the use of their liberty with a view to mutual edification."[78] Liberty is always regulated by the obligation to love one's neighbor, and "it is contrary to love to occasion grief to anyone."[79] Christians should serve their neighbors winsomely with the goal of winning them to Christ.[80] Thus an important distinction must be maintained. "Liberty lies in the conscience and looks to God," but "the use of it

---

[73] Commentary on 1 Corinthians 8:6 [1546]; CO 49:432. Cf. W. Fred Graham, *The Constructive Revolutionary: John Calvin and His Socio-Economic Impact* (Richmond, VA: John Knox Press, 1971), 57–59.

[74] Commentary on James 4:12 [1551]; CO 55:420.

[75] Commentary on Romans 15:22 [1556]; CO 49:267–268.

[76] Commentary on 1 Corinthians 6:12 [1546]; CO 49:396.

[77] Commentary on 1 Corinthians 6:20 [1546]; CO 49:400.

[78] Commentary on 1 Corinthians 6:12 [1546]; CO 49:396.

[79] Commentary on Romans 14:15 [1556]; CO 49:265. Cf. Stevenson, *Sovereign Grace*, 71–72.

[80] They are "debtors to all, even strangers that we may, if possible, gain them." Commentary on 1 Corinthians 10:32 [1546]; CO 49:471.

lies in outward matters and deals not with God only but with men."[81] Finally, Christian freedom is always to be exercised in obedience to what Calvin describes as "the law of Christian freedom," the call to be content whatever one's outward state. "They say that these are things indifferent. I admit it, provided they are used indifferently. But when they are coveted too greedily, when they are proudly boasted of, when they are lavishly squandered, things that were of themselves otherwise lawful are certainly defiled by these vices" (3.19.9).[82]

Calvin further explains the paradox of Christian liberty by considering two dimensions to the human conscience. On the one hand, he defines conscience proper as a human "awareness of divine judgment," an internal "witness which does not let them hide their sins but arraigns them as guilty before the judgment seat" (4.10.3).[83] The conscience judges the actions that a person exercises toward others, of course, but it does so before God, who sees the heart, not before other human beings, who only regard outward actions. This is what Calvin means when he says that "a law is said to bind the conscience when it simply binds man, without regard to other men, or without having any consideration for them" (4.10.4).[84] In this strict sense the conscience only binds a person before God.

On the other hand, Calvin explains that the conscience can be understood in a broader sense as well, which binds a person to serve and submit to his fellow human beings even where he is free before God. For instance, Romans 13:5 calls Christians to submit to the governing authorities for conscience' sake.[85] While divine laws bind human consciences in and of themselves (or in each *species*), the laws of magistrates simply bind human consciences in general (or as a *genus*). "For even though individual [civil] laws may not apply to the conscience as it binds, we are still held by God's general command, which commends to us the authority of magistrates" (4.10.5). In other words, there is a distinction between the general command to obey the magistrate, which binds the conscience, and the particular laws framed by the magistrate, which do not bind the conscience directly (in and of themselves, or before God), but indirectly (because they come from the magistrate). It is this dynamic that obligates believers to submit to magistrates even on matters regarding which they would otherwise be free before God. Calvin suggests that it is

---

[81] Commentary on Galatians 5:13 [1548]; CO 50:250.

[82] Cf. Commentary on 1 Peter 3:3 [1551]; CO 55:254.

[83] The conscience is the inner testimony of a person's mind, "imprinted on their hearts" by natural law, enabling a process of discrimination and judgment through which they "distinguish between what is just and unjust." Commentary on Romans 2:15 [1556]; CO 49:38–39. Cf. Commentary on 1 Peter 3:21 [1551]; CO 55:269.

[84] Cf. Commentary on Acts 24:16 [1554]; CO 48:523–524.

[85] Commentary on 1 Corinthians 10:29 [1546]; CO 49:470. "For there is a certain inward sense or feeling which has respect to God alone, and from this arises faithfulness and integrity which we exercise towards men." Commentary on Acts 24:16 [1554]; CO 48:524.

in the same indirect sense that believers are often obligated to yield their liberty to serve their neighbors. Christians are to "accommodate ourselves to weak brethren" in matters where they are otherwise free "because we are to this extent subject to them in the sight of God."[86] For instance, a person is free regarding the "indifferent" matter of eating meat offered to idols. But the pious person is obligated to love and serve his neighbor. Thus if eating the meat would offend a sister it is a sin to do so, even though it is not a sin before God.[87] The person is not bound in conscience directly, or before God. He is still free to eat meat in and of itself (liberty with respect to the *species*, or specific command), but he is not free to offend his fellow believer (liberty with respect to the *genus*, or general obligation of loving service). One can be free before God while being bound before human beings (4.10.4).[88]

This obligation of conscience – to serve one's neighbors – underlies the whole range of human relationships, from the casual to the institutional. Calvin makes this point clear in his introduction to the household codes in the epistle to the Ephesians, observing that the Apostle Paul presents mutual submission as the foundation of the entire discourse.

> God has bound us so strongly to each other that no man ought to endeavor to avoid subjection, and where love reigns, mutual services will be rendered. I do not except even kings and governors, whose very authority is held for the service of the community. It is highly proper that all should be exhorted to be subject to each other in their turn.[89]

Vocation is thus the primary means through which human beings share the "sacred bond" of society.[90] Specific vocations, the "various conditions [*gradus*] of life," are simply particularized expressions of the broader obligation of human service, "for besides the universal bond of subjection, some are more closely bound to each other according to their respective callings [*vocatio*]."[91] Thus, "let every one serve his

---

[86] Commentary on 1 Corinthians 10:29 [1546]; CO 49:470.

[87] Calvin distinguishes between genuinely weak Christians and pharisaical Christians, between offense received and offense taken. See, for instance, *Institutes* 3.19.11–13; Commentary on 1 Corinthians 8:9, 13 [1546]; CO 49:434, 435–436; Commentary on Galatians 2:3–5, 11–14 [1548]; CO 50:184–185, 192–193.

[88] Höpfl complains that this distinction, with reference to the constitutions of the church, is a "hair-splitting distinction, an *argutia* of the sort he abominated in the scholastics" (38), a "distinction without a difference" (39). Höpfl, *The Christian Polity of John Calvin*, 38–39, 115. Yet if the distinction makes sense with respect to political laws, matters of vocation, and the principle of charity, it is hard to see why it becomes so problematic with respect to the general order of ecclesiastical affairs.

[89] Commentary on Ephesians 5:21 [1548]; CO 51:221–222.

[90] Commentary on Genesis 37:25 [1554]; CO 23:488

[91] Commentary on Ephesians 5:22 [1548]; CO 51:222. Aristotle was wrong to suggest that the good life is the life of contemplation. Commentary on Luke 10:38 [1555]; CO 45:382. But the Greeks were right to say that the human person is a social animal (10:30; CO 45:613–614). Cf. Commentary on Colossians 3:20 [1548]; CO 52:126; Commentary on Psalm 55:12 [1557]; CO 31:540; Commentary on Matthew 25:24

nearest neighbors as far as charity will allow and as custom demands."[92] God will surely bless a society, in both its public and private dimensions, in which each person submits himself to providence by following his vocation and serving the general advantage.[93]

Consistent with his belief that God's providence preserves order in a fallen world, Calvin believed a person's vocation is dictated by the circumstances of providence. Living as he did in a time of limited vocational mobility, he feared that those who became too anxious about their circumstances were likely to disrupt the social order. God "has appointed duties for every man in his particular way of life," in part in order that people will not "heedlessly wander about throughout life" (3.10.6).[94] Injustice most often takes place, Calvin suggests, when each person is "too tenacious of his own rights" without regard to the rights of others.[95] When it comes to outward matters, the Christian is called to the love, service, and edification of his neighbors before all private advantage.

Calvin places the obligations of service and vocation in close counterpoint to Christian liberty in his commentary on 1 Peter. Because the gospel proclaims that Christians are heirs of the world, he observes, many in the early church "thought the gospel was a proclamation of such liberty that everyone might deem himself as free from servitude."[96] Yet Peter shows that all Christian liberty is to be directed to the good of our neighbors. "In short, it is a free servitude and a serving freedom [*In summa, est libera servitus, et serva libertas*]." To be sure, "our consciences become free, but this does not prevent us from serving God, who requires us also to be subject to men."[97] Christians "ought to cultivate, as far as we can, peace and friendship with all."[98] This emphasis is the context for Peter's discussion of the relations between masters and slaves, husbands and wives, and magistrates and subjects. Faithfulness to "the duties of humanity and kindness" helps to ensure that unbelievers will allow Christians to live in peace.[99] It increases the likelihood that "the unbelieving, led by our good works, would become obedient to God."[100] Calvin quickly dismisses the objection that "the unbelieving are by no means worthy

[1555]; CO 45:570; Commentary on Lamentations 5:14 [1563]; CO 39:639; David Little, *Religion, Order, and Law* (New York: Harper and Row, 1969), 58–60.

[92] Commentary on Daniel 6:17 [1561]; CO 41:20.

[93] Commentary on Psalm 127:1 [1557]; CO 32:321–322.

[94] Commentary on 1 Thessalonians 4:11 [1550]; CO 52:163–164. Cf. Miles, "Theology, Anthropology, and the Human Body in Calvin's *Institutes of the Christian Religion*," 305.

[95] Commentary on Matthew 5:25 [1555]; CO 45:177.

[96] Commentary on 1 Peter 2:13 [1551]; CO 55:243 (Cf. 2:11; CO 55:242).

[97] Commentary on 1 Peter 2:16 [1551]; CO 55:246.

[98] Commentary on 1 Peter 2:17 [1551]; CO 55:247.

[99] Christians "will do more towards obtaining a quiet life by kindness than by violence and promptitude in taking revenge." Commentary on 1 Peter 3:14 [1551]; CO 55:260–261.

[100] Commentary on 1 Peter 2:12 [1551]; CO 55:243 (Cf. 2:13; CO 55:243).

of so much regard that God's children should form their life to please them."
Such an objection ignores the clear command of God.[101] *In summa, est libera
servitus, et serva libertas.*

Calvin's two kingdoms paradigm shaped his understanding of temporal institutions that he viewed as evils, such as slavery. Slavery, unlike civil government,
is a curse on the human race rather than a blessing. God desires human beings
to be free, and in the kingdom of Christ, slavery will be abolished.[102] The Apostle
Paul urged that slaves should seek their freedom if possible because "liberty is
not merely good but also more advantageous than servitude."[103] Calvin thus
applauds the abolition of slavery in Christendom. It is "by no means to be
wished that there should be slaves among us as there were formerly among all
nations, and as there are now among barbarians."[104] In this respect he is
sympathetic toward the sort of logic that led many in the early church to believe
the gospel freed them from slavery. For "the name of brother may be thought to
constitute equality [*aequalitatem*], and consequently to take away dominion
[*dominium*]."[105] Similarly, those who were slaves of unbelieving masters judged
it "unreasonable that they who serve the devil should have dominion over the
children of God."[106]

On the other hand, sensitive to the witness of scripture, Calvin insists that in
God's providence, slavery sometimes "forms a part of civil or social subjection"
within which Christians find themselves.[107] While slavery is alien to the kingdom
of Christ, "it is owing to the providence of God that there are different ranks and
stations [*gradus et ordines*] in the world."[108] Calvin therefore ponders,
"Is perpetual servitude so displeasing to God that it ought not to be deemed
lawful?" The answer, he thinks, is obvious: the example of the patriarchs and
the writings of the apostles demonstrate that slavery is sometimes lawful.[109]
Although Christians possess "the liberty of the spirit [*libertas spiritus*]," they are

---

[101] Commentary on 1 Peter 2:15 [1551]; CO 55:246.

[102] Commentary on Jeremiah 34:8–17 [1563]; CO 39:87–91. Cf. Commentary on Lamentations 5:8 [1563];
CO 39:635–636.

[103] Commentary on 1 Corinthians 7:21 [1546]; CO 49:416 (Cf. 7:22; CO 49:416).

[104] Commentary on Jeremiah 34:8–17 [1563]; CO 39:87–91. Cf. Commentary on Genesis 16:8 [1554]; CO
23:227–228).

[105] Commentary on 1 Timothy 6:2 [1548]; CO 52:323.

[106] Commentary on 1 Timothy 6:1 [1548]; CO 52:322.

[107] Commentary on 1 Peter 2:18 [1551]; CO 55:247. Cf. Commentary on Philemon 1:20 [1550]; CO
52:448.

[108] Commentary on 1 Corinthians 7:21 [1546]; CO 49:416. Slaves should "not suppose that by the
judgment of men" they have been "thrown into slavery." Commentary on Ephesians 6:5 [1548]; CO
51:230–231.

[109] "If, then, servitude were unlawful, the apostles would have never tolerated it." Commentary on
Jeremiah 34:8–17 [1563]; CO 39:87–91.

not to reason from this that they will necessarily be blessed in this life with the "the liberty of the flesh [*carnis libertati*]."[110]

Calvin's two kingdoms perspective therefore leads him to critique slavery by emphasizing the liberty of the Christian and the equality of master and slave, while at the same time calling Christian masters to treat their slaves justly and Christian slaves freely to serve their masters. On the one hand, the New Testament affirms a startling equality between master and slave. "It is no small honor that God has made them [slaves] equal [*aequavit*] to earthly lords in that which is of the highest importance, for they have the same adoption in common with them."[111] Thus the Apostle Paul prescribes "mutual equity [*mutuamque aequabilitatem*]" between master and slave, that is, an "analogical or distributive right [*iure analogo, aut distributivo*]."[112] For Aristotle the concept of analogical right implied that true justice does not exist between master and slave. For Calvin, in contrast, spiritual equality required true justice.[113]

Still, Calvin argues that Christian slaves are called to serve their masters, not as if their masters have any fundamental right to their service, but as a voluntary expression of the love of Christ. In other words, obedience on the part of the slave is a duty of conscience only in the sense that it is the slave's means of serving his neighbor as called by God.[114] Christians are called to the imitation of Christ, remembering that those who would serve God "must necessarily endeavor to overcome evil with good."[115] But the Christian's "service is done to men in such a way that Christ at the same time holds supremacy of dominion and is the supreme master." At the same time, they look in hopeful expectation for the "judgment of God" that will make their freedom complete.[116] They are only obligated to obey their masters in "external things [*rebus externis*],"[117] and they are under no circumstances "to subject themselves to the wicked or depraved inclinations of their masters."[118]

---

[110] Commentary on 1 Corinthians 7:22 [1546]; CO 49:416. Cf. Commentary on Ephesians 6:5 [1548]; CO 51:230.

[111] Commentary on 1 Timothy 6:2 [1548]; CO 52:323. Cf. Commentary on Genesis 17:12 [1554]; CO 23:242.

[112] Commentary on Colossians 4:1 [1548]; CO 52:127.

[113] Slavery must be "consistent with the law of love." Commentary on Ephesians 6:9 [1548]; CO 51: 231–232.

[114] While an unjust master "does not for the present lose his right," that right is merely political. The Christian slave "performs his duty not from a regard to men but to God." Commentary on 1 Peter 2:18 [1551]; CO 55:247–248.

[115] Commentary on 1 Peter 2:19 [1551]; CO 55:248–249. Cf. Commentary on 1 Timothy 6:1–2 [1548]; CO 52:322–323.

[116] Commentary on Colossians 3:22 [1548]; CO 52:126–127. Cf. Commentary on Philemon 1:16 [1550]; CO 52:447.

[117] Commentary on 1 Corinthians 7:18 [1546]; CO 49:414. Cf. Commentary on Ephesians 6:5 [1548]; CO 51:230–231.

[118] Commentary on 1 Corinthians 7:23 [1546]; CO 49:416–417.

The two kingdoms framework also guided Calvin's analysis of institutions that he regarded as creational, yet temporal and corrupted, such as gender. In the spiritual kingdom there is equality between men and women, he argues, while in the civil order, men and women have distinct roles, women being in subjection to men.[119] Thus Calvin acknowledges a tension between Paul's declaration in Galatians 3:28 that in Christ there is neither male nor female and his statement in 1 Corinthians 11:3 that while a man's head is Christ, a woman's head is her husband.

When he says that there is no difference between the man and woman, he is treating of Christ's spiritual kingdom [*de spirituali Christi regno*], in which individual distinctions are not regarded or made any account of, for it has nothing to do with the body and has nothing to do with the outward relationships of mankind [*externam hominum societatem*], but has to do solely with the soul – on which account he declares that there is no difference, even between bond and free. In the meantime, however, he does not disturb civil order or honorary distinctions, which cannot be dispensed with in ordinary life. Here, on the other hand, he reasons respecting outward propriety and decorum – which is a part of ecclesiastical polity [*politiae ecclesiasticae*]. Hence, as regards spiritual connection [*spiritualem coniunctionem*] in the sight of God, and inwardly in the conscience, Christ is the head of the man and of the woman without any distinction, because as to that there is no regard paid to male or female, but as regards external arrangement and political decorum [*externam compositionem et decorum politicum*], the man follows Christ and the woman the man, so that they are not upon the same footing [*gradus*], but on the contrary, this inequality [*inaequalitas*] exists.[120]

In his sermon on Galatians 3:28, Calvin puts the distinction in eschatological terms, noting of the various relationships of civil order, including that of man and woman, that "when we come to the heavenly life, let us assure ourselves that all worldly things pass and vanish away, as the world and its fashion passes."[121] In the kingdom of God, as Douglass summarizes Calvin's position, "all differences of sex and social status will be destroyed and spiritual equality made manifest."[122]

On the other hand, Calvin regards gender and patriarchy as being rooted in creation. The woman is a kind of "appendage to the man" and is joined to him on the condition that she obeys him. Since "God did not create two chiefs of equal

---

[119] The subjection is not simply within marriage "but also in celibacy, for I do not speak of cohabitation merely, but also of civil offices [*civilibus officiis*]." Commentary on 1 Corinthians 11:11 [1546]; CO 49: 477–478. Paul has in view "God's perpetual law [*perpetuam Dei legem*], which has made the female sex subject to the authority [*imperio*] of men. On this account all women are born, that they may acknowledge themselves inferior in consequence of the superiority [*praestantiae*] of the male sex" (11:10; CO 49:477).

[120] Commentary on 1 Corinthians 11:3 [1546]; CO 49:474. Cf. 11:7; CO 49:476; Commentary on Genesis 1:26 [1554]; CO 23:27).

[121] Sermon on Galatians 3:28 (23rd Sermon); CO 50:568.   [122] Douglass, "Christian Freedom," 161.

power [*aequa potestate*] ... the Apostle justly reminds us of that order of creation in which the eternal and inviolable [*aeterna et inviolabilis*] appointment of God is strikingly displayed."[123] A woman "by nature (that is, by the ordinary law of God) is formed to obey, for *gunaikokratia* (the government of women) has always been regarded by all wise persons as a monstrous thing."[124] Calvin believed this principle was revealed in nature by "universal consent and custom" as well as "common sense."[125]

Yet because marriage and gender are temporal, matters of "external polity [*externa politia*]," Christians must remember that Paul's instructions about gender in the church "are intermediate and indifferent [*medias et indifferentes*], in which there is nothing unlawful [*illicitum*] but what is at variance with propriety [*decoro*] and edification."[126] Gender distinctions are not matters of conscience. They are transcended in the kingdom of Christ and can occasionally be suspended without injustice. God gave Paul "wisdom that he might recommend this order in external things at Corinth and in other places, not that it might be an inviolable law [*lex inviolabilis*], like those that relate to the spiritual worship of God, but that it might be a useful directory [*forma utilis*] to all the sons of God, and not by any means to be ignored."[127] For instance, "it was an extraordinary thing when God gave authority to a woman, as was the case with [the prophetess] Deborah, that no one may consider this singular precedent as a common rule."[128] Similar are the biblical examples of Miriam, Huldah, the women appointed to proclaim the gospel of the resurrection to the eleven disciples, and Priscilla. "We know that the gift of prophecy is sometimes though rarely allowed to women."[129] Calvin thus defended the

---

[123] Commentary on 1 Timothy 2:13 [1548]; CO 52:277. Calvin uses the words "eternal" and "inviolable" with reference to the permanence of the general temporal order rather than to its particular expressions or to the kingdom of Christ. For, as will be seen, he ordinarily insists that this order is neither eternal, nor are its particular expressions inviolable. Cf. Commentary on 1 Corinthians 11:7–8 [1546]; CO 49:476; Sermon on Galatians 3:28 (23rd Sermon); CO 50:568; Thompson, *Calvin and the Daughters of Sarah*, 256.

[124] Commentary on 1 Timothy 2:11 [1548]; CO 52:276. Cf. 5:14; CO 52:314.

[125] "Unquestionably, wherever even natural propriety has been maintained, women have in all ages been excluded from the public management of affairs [*publica administratione exclusae*]. It is the dictate of common sense that female government [*gynaecocratian*] is improper and unseemly." Commentary on 1 Corinthians 14:34 [1546]; CO 49:533. The Apostle "sets forth nature as the mistress of decorum, and what was at that time in common use by universal consent and custom – even among the Greeks – he speaks of as being natural" (11:12; CO 49:478). Cf. Cf. 11:4; CO 49:475.

[126] Commentary on 1 Corinthians 14:35 [1546]; CO 49:533.

[127] Commentary on 1 Corinthians 14:37 [1546]; CO 49:534–535.

[128] Commentary on Micah 6:4 [1559]; CO 43:388.

[129] Commentary on Ezekiel 13:17–18 [1565]; CO 40:288. Cf. Commentary on Matthew 28:1–7 [1555]; CO 45:792–793; Commentary on Acts 18:26 [1554]; CO 48:437–438; Commentary on Exodus 15:20 [1565]; CO 24:162.

legitimacy of Queen Elizabeth's rule over England.[130] He not only affirmed that women should hold the ecclesiastical office of deacon, but, rare for his time, that in emergencies they might teach and administer the sacraments.[131]

Calvin also recognized the ways in which the kingdom of Christ relativizes the universality and importance of marriage.[132] Because "the anxieties and distresses in which married persons are involved arise from the affairs of the world" (or of the "outward man" that is passing away), marriage can distract a Christian woman from the kingdom of Christ.[133] Women freed from such hindrances, on the other hand, are able to "devote ourselves wholly to meditation on heavenly things."[134] Although married persons can also seek first the kingdom of God, and most people will continue to be called into marriage, it remains the case that "celibacy is better than marriage because it has more liberty so that persons can serve God with greater freedom."[135]

What complicated the matter further for Calvin is that marriage and gender relations are corrupted by sin. The place of women is now "less voluntary and agreeable" than it was before the fall, being "deprived of all liberty and placed under the yoke."[136] Their temporal subjection is in part, therefore, a punishment. "She had, indeed, previously been subject to her husband, but that was a liberal and gentle subjection. Now, however, she is cast into servitude."[137] One consequence was the widespread male attitude that women are a "necessary evil," valuable only for sex, procreation, and the raising of children. Like the subjects of an unjust government, women often have to submit themselves to this "temporal punishment"

---

[130] Letter to William Cecil, 1559; CO 17:490–491; Cf. Letter to Bullinger, April 28, 1554; CO 15:125.

[131] Cf. Thompson, *Calvin and the Daughters of Sarah*, 260; Douglass, "Christian Freedom," 169–172. Douglass wrongly assumes that because Calvin viewed matters relating to gender as indifferent, to be transcended in the future kingdom, he therefore viewed them as subject to change during the present age. Douglass, "Christian Freedom," 155–173. Cf. Thompson, *Calvin and the Daughters of Sarah*, 265–266. But Calvin was no feminist. Throughout his writings he betrayed numerous patriarchal stereotypes about women, and his biases sometimes muddied his exegetical judgments. He insisted that cases of female leadership are exceptions that do not alter the general rule, speculating that God occasionally gives women authority over men to shame the latter. "Extraordinary acts done by God do not overturn the ordinary rules of government [*communem politiam*]." Commentary on 1 Timothy 2:11 [1548]; CO 52:276. In one of his weaker exegetical moments, Calvin insists that when the apostle condemns the practice of a woman prophesying "with her head uncovered" in 1 Corinthians 11:6, he does not intend to commend the practice of a woman prophesying with her head covered. Commentary on 1 Corinthians 11:6 [1546]; CO 49:475–476. Cf. Commentary on Isaiah 3:16–17 [1559]; CO 36:90–92; Commentary on Matthew 28:1–7 [1555]; CO 45:792–793 (Cf. 27:55; CO 45:785–786).

[132] Commentary on 1 Corinthians 7:25 [1546]; CO 49:417–418.

[133] Commentary on 1 Corinthians 7:28 [1546]; CO 49:419. Cf. 7:32–33; CO 49:421–422; 7:1; CO 49:401.

[134] Commentary on 1 Corinthians 7:1 [1546]; CO 49:401.

[135] Commentary on 1 Corinthians 7:38 [1546]; CO 49:426.

[136] Commentary on 1 Timothy 2:14 [1548]; CO 52:277.

[137] Commentary on Genesis 3:16 [1554]; CO 23:72. Cf. Commentary on Leviticus 12:4 [1563]; CO 24:314.

for the sake of the political order.[138] But this was not God's intent from creation. On the contrary, God gave Adam a wife that she might be the inseparable associate of his life."[139] Because of the fundamental equality of women and men in Christ, Calvin follows Paul in insisting on a measure of equality in the marriage relationship.[140] For instance, "though in other matters the husband holds the superiority, as to the marriage bed the wife has an equal right," which means that she has equal right to divorce in cases of adultery.[141] With respect to sexual intercourse, the Apostle Paul "puts them on an equality [*pares*], instead of requiring from the wife obedience and subjection." In this respect "the condition of both is equal [*aequalis*]."[142] Finally, both husbands and wives are called to direct their temporal union toward the heavenly life, where it will be transcended in the kingdom of Christ.[143]

Numerous writers correctly identify Calvin's emphasis on the authority of providence and scripture as underlying the reformer's conservatism with respect to political matters otherwise indifferent.[144] Calvin believed that although the gospel of the kingdom promises believers perfect justice, peace, liberty, and equality,

---

[138] Commentary on 1 Timothy 2:15 [1548]; CO 52:278. Cf. Commentary on 1 Corinthians 7:14 [1546]; CO 49:411–412; Commentary on Ephesians 5:23 [1548]; CO 51:222; Commentary on Titus 2:4 [1550]; CO 52:420; Commentary on Genesis 34:1, 5 [1554]; CO 23:456, 457.

[139] Commentary on Genesis 2:18 [1554[; CO 23:46–48. Cf. 2:24; CO 23:50); 1:27; CO 23:28; Commentary on 1 Corinthians 7:1, 11 [1546]; CO 49:401–402, 410; 11:11; CO 49:477–478; Commentary on 1 Timothy 5:14 [1548]; CO 52:313–314; Commentary on Ephesians 5:31 [1548]; CO 51:226.

[140] "For since the Lord is pleased to bestow in common on husbands and wives the same graces, he invites them to seek an equality in them." Commentary on 1 Peter 3:7 [1551]; CO 55:256. Christian marriages, though under the "common law of marriage," are to reflect the "spiritual union between Christ and his church." Commentary on Ephesians 5:31 [1548]; CO 51:226. Cf. Commentary on Matthew 12:48 [1555]; CO 45:350–351.

[141] Commentary on Matthew 19:9 [1555]; CO 45:531. Cf. Commentary on 1 Corinthians 7:40 [1546]; CO 49:427.

[142] On this basis polygamy is unjust, because unequal. Commentary on 1 Corinthians 7:4 [1546]; CO 49:403. Sex is not the prerogative [*liberam deliberationem*] of a husband but a matter of mutual consent (7:5; CO 49:403).

[143] Commentary on 1 Corinthians 7:29 [1546]; CO 49:420.

[144] Stevenson writes, "there is in Calvin's teaching a stern warning that believers not casually assume that their present circumstances are offensive to God. Their call is as much to seek God's will *in* their present surroundings as to follow his call to renew and restore those surroundings. God seeks their attentiveness, their patience, and their perseverance as much as he seeks their hope, their zeal for progressive change" (107). Cf. Boer, *Political Grace*; Ernst Troeltsch, *The Social Teaching of the Christian Churches* (trans. Olive Wyon; 2 vols.; Louisville: Westminster/John Knox Press, 1992 [1912]), 2:620; Brandt B Boeke, "Calvin's Doctrine of Civil Government," *Studia Biblica et Theologica* 11 (1981): 57–79; Graham, *The Constructive Revolutionary*, 71; Mark J. Larson, *Calvin's Doctrine of the State: A Reformed Doctrine and Its American Trajectory, The Revolutionary War, and the Founding of the Republic* (Eugene, OR: Wipf and Stock, 2009), xv; Little, *Religion, Order, and Law*, 56. But Miles exaggerates Calvin's conservatism when she claims that "in external things, he counsels only a status quo" or that "Calvin effectively blocks every impulse to social or political reform." Miles, "Theology, Anthropology, and the Human Body in Calvin's *Institutes of the Christian Religion*," 305.

during this life they are called to serve in vocations that fall far short of these realities. Like Christ, they are called to set aside their own interests in favor of serving others to the point of self-sacrifice, permitting God to guide their lives by his providence and by the clear prescriptions of scripture. To be sure, God does not sanction all that takes place by his providence, and unrighteousness must always be resisted. The church (and, of course, Calvin!) can interpret scripture incorrectly. But the authority of scripture, properly interpreted, remains inviolable, as does that of the powers providentially ordained by God. In that respect, as disappointing as it may be to those seeking the foundations of modern liberalism in Calvin's radical concept of the kingdom of God, the reformer of Geneva was no revolutionary. As Douglass puts it, "Though in the kingdom of God all persons will be equal, and indeed already are in the spiritual kingdom of Christ, male and female, kings, shepherds, and mechanics, Frenchmen and Germans, pastors and laypeople, till this world passes away, the order of creation remains the pattern according to which governing in external things is organized."[145]

CIVIL AND SPIRITUAL GOVERNMENT

I offer a full analysis of Calvin's understanding of spiritual and civil government in the second half of this book, but for now it is important to show how Calvin understood the basic distinction. It is crucial to stress that Calvin considered civil government to be under the universal lordship of Christ, even though he did not consider it to be part of Christ's spiritual kingdom.[146] In his commentary on Jesus' classic statement, "Render to Caesar the things that are Caesar's, and to God the things that are God's," Calvin provides one of his fullest presentations of the two kingdoms distinction. The Jewish leaders sought to trap Jesus, he observes, by forcing him to choose between speaking against Rome and so winning the people's approval, or affirming Rome's authority and so forfeiting his popular influence. Yet,

> Christ's reply ... lays down a clear distinction between spiritual and civil government [*spirituale et politicum regimen*], in order to inform us that outward subjection does not prevent us from having within us a conscience free in the sight of God. For Christ intended to refute the error of those who did not think that they would be the people of God unless they were free from every yoke of human authority ... In short, Christ declares that it is no violation of the authority of

---

[145] Jane Dempsey Douglass, "Calvin's Relation to Social and Economic Change," *Church and Society* 74 (1984): 75. Stevenson's *Sovereign Grace* provocatively explores the revolutionary yet conservative implications of Calvin's concept of Christian freedom.

[146] See Gordon J. Keddie, "Calvin on Civil Government," *Scottish Bulletin of Evangelical Theology* 32 (1981): 23–35.

God or any injury done to his service if, in respect of outward polity, the Jews obey the Romans.[147]

To be sure, political authority is under God, and its authority comes from God. But that does not take away from the relevance of the distinction. Calvin's comments are worth quoting at length:

> We might be apt to think, no doubt, that the distinction does not apply, for, strictly speaking, when we perform our duty towards men we thereby render obedience to God. But Christ, accommodating his discourse to the common people, reckoned it enough to draw a distinction between the spiritual kingdom of God [*spirituale Dei regnum*], on the one hand, and political order and the condition of the present life [*ordine politico et praesentis vitae statu*], on the other. We must therefore attend to this distinction, that, while the Lord wishes to be the only lawgiver for governing souls, the rule for worshiping him must not be sought from any other source than from his own word, and that we ought to abide by the only and pure worship which is there enjoined; but that the power of the sword, the laws, and the decisions of tribunals do not hinder the worship of God from remaining entire among us. But this doctrine extends still farther, that every man, according to his calling, ought to perform the duty which he owes to men; that children ought willingly to submit to their parents and servants to their masters; that they ought to be courteous and obliging towards each other according to the law of charity, provided that God always retain the highest authority, to which every thing that can be due to men is, as we say, subordinate. The amount of it therefore is that those who destroy political order [*politicum ordinem*] are rebellious against God, and therefore that obedience to princes and magistrates is always joined to the worship and fear of God; but that, on the other hand, if princes claim any part of the authority of God we ought not to obey them any farther than can be done without offending God.[148]

The primary context in which Calvin insists on the distinction of civil government from the spiritual kingdom of Christ is when he is engaging the perspectives he associates with the Anabaptists. By arguing that Christians cannot serve as civil magistrates, swear public oaths, or hold private property, as Calvin saw it, the Anabaptists were overthrowing the political order.[149] Calvin agreed that God

---

[147] Commentary on Matthew 21:21 [1555]; CO 45:601–602.

[148] Commentary on Matthew 21:21 [1555]; CO 45:602. The Anabaptists, according to Calvin, argue that Christians are not bound by earthly kingdoms, but like Jesus, they voluntarily cooperate with them. Calvin will have none of it. Jesus' situation is unique: "For, though his kingdom be spiritual, still we must maintain that as he is the only Son of God he is also the heir of the whole world, so that all things ought to be subject to him and to acknowledge his authority." Christ chose freely to submit to political authority; believers are subjected to it by God. Commentary on Matthew 17:24 [1555]; 45:522–523. Cf. 26:62–64; CO 45:738–739; 27:12; CO 45:752.

[149] Calvin describes the Anabaptists as "fanatical spirits, who feign a commonality or participation together of goods by which all policy or civil government is taken away." Commentary on Acts 2:44

"approves no other distribution of good things than one joined with love" (3.10.5), and "love made that common to the poor and needy which was proper to every man," but he insisted that such a principle should not be used to undermine the political order providentially established by God.[150] It was necessary that the civil order permit the ownership of property in order to preserve peace among human beings (4.1.3).

The Anabaptists' fundamental mistake, in Calvin's view, was to misapply what Christ taught about the spiritual kingdom to the political order. For example, the Anabaptists argued that just as Jesus refused to mediate in a property dispute (Luke 12:13), so Christians are to avoid involvement in the magistracy. Not so, Calvin retorts. Jesus refused to mediate the dispute because it was not a part of his calling to take up the office of judge and because he wanted to prevent against any misunderstanding that his kingdom would be earthly or carnal, or that "he was effecting a revolution in the state." While the Jews expected a "carnal redemption," Jesus was teaching that "the kingdom of Christ is spiritual." Furthermore, "our Lord intended to draw a distinction between the political kingdoms of this world and the government of his church." The government of Christ's kingdom is not a magisterial government, despite the fact that the Roman clergy "have dared to usurp an earthly and secular jurisdiction."[151]

Calvin makes the same point in his interpretation of Jesus' warning to the disciples not to be like the rulers of this world. The Anabaptists mistakenly interpreted this passage as drawing a distinction between Christians and unbelievers, so prohibiting Christians from serving in political office. But they failed to take into consideration the distinction between the two kingdoms. "[T]he design of Christ was, as I have said, to distinguish between the spiritual government of his church and the empires of the world." Whereas political government requires pomp, splendor, wealth, a crown, and a scepter, the spiritual government of the church is defined by self-sacrificial service, humility, and the way of the cross. "Christ appoints pastors of his church, not to rule, but to serve." Yes, kings and magistrates are also obligated to perform their vocations in service, but whereas the service of civil governments requires pomp and power, ministers of the church are to have none of that.[152] That

---

[1552]; CO 48:59–60. Cf. Commentary on 1 Corinthians 1:26–27 [1546]; CO 49:330; Commentary on Luke 6:24 [1555]; CO 45:166; 16:25; CO 45:411; Commentary on Matthew 13:37 [1555]; CO 45:369; Paul Mundey, "John Calvin and Anabaptists on War," *Brethren Life and Thought* 23 (1978): 239–247; Willem Balke, *Calvin and the Anabaptist Radicals* (trans. Willem Heyner. Grand Rapids: Eerdmans, 1981), 34, 39–46, 62, 70, 253–260. In fact, most Anabaptists did not think all things should be held in common in the way that Calvin claimed (270–275).

[150] Commentary on Acts 4:34 [1552]; CO 48:96. Cf. Commentary on James 5:2 [1550]; CO 55:423; 2:1–5; CO 397–399.

[151] Commentary on Luke 12:13 [1555]; CO 45:383–384.

[152] Commentary on Matthew 20:25 [1555]; CO 45:556–558.

Christ did not take up a magisterial role was not because Christians are forbidden from doing so but because his calling was not to be a judge but to be a savior who "offers salvation to all without reserve and stretches out his arms to embrace all, that all may be the more encouraged to repent."[153] It was Christ's role to proclaim mercy, not judgment, and the same is true for his ministers.[154]

Calvin believed that by questioning the Christian's place in government the Anabaptists were undermining a gift of God's providence that is not only essential to human life, but "pleasant and agreeable."[155] Whereas anarchy "would end in prey and plunder, and in the mere license of fraud and murder," government provides the order and security that is essential for life. Commenting on imagery from the book of Daniel, Calvin writes, "God appointed the existence of governments in the world for this purpose – to be like trees on whose fruits all men feed, and under whose shadow they rest." Indeed, "pasture and food and shelter signify the various forms of usefulness which political order provides for us." In his gracious providence God uses even corrupt and tyrannical regimes. "Tyrants endeavor to extinguish the whole light of equity and justice and to mingle all things, but the Lord meanwhile restrains them in a secret and wonderful manner, and thus they are compelled to act usefully to the human race, whether they will or not." Thus "men of every rank feel no small utility in the protection of princes."[156] Indeed, as was seen in Chapter 3, Calvin believed that the Spirit uses civil government to preserve a modicum of justice and order in the world. For "there never was any portion whatever of righteousness in the world that did not proceed from the Spirit of God and that was not maintained by his heavenly power, as none of the kings of the earth can frame or defend good order except so far as he shall be assisted by the same Spirit."[157] God has given civil authorities a "sacred character and title," a stamp of divine authority.[158]

At the same time, civil government should never be confused with the spiritual kingdom of Christ because the power of civil government is rooted in coercion. In contrast, Christ's kingdom is characterized by mercy and liberality,[159] and the obedience of its subjects is voluntary.[160] Christ has been appointed "not to rule after the manner of princes, by the force of arms and by surrounding himself with other external defenses to make himself an object of terror to his people, but his whole

---

[153] Commentary on John 12:47 [1553]; CO 47:303.
[154] Commentary on Matthew 20:26 [1555]; CO 45:558. Cf. 20:28; CO 45:558
[155] Commentary on Deuteronomy 16:18 [1563]; CO 24:610–611.
[156] Commentary on Daniel 4:10–16 [1561]; CO 40:657–658.
[157] Commentary on Matthew 12:18 [1555]; CO 45:332.
[158] Commentary on Psalm 82:6 [1557]; CO 31:771. Psalm 82 goes so far as to refer to magistrates as "gods" and the civil order as the "assembly of God." Commentary on Psalm 82:1 [1557]; CO 31:768–769.
[159] Unlike most human kings, Christ is "humane and merciful, as to be ready to afford succor to the most despised." Commentary on Psalm 72:12 [1557]; CO 31:669 (Cf. 45:3; CO 31:450–451).
[160] Commentary on Hebrews 2:11 [1549]; CO 55:29.

authority consists in doctrine, in the preaching of which he wishes to be sought and acknowledged, for nowhere else will he be found."[161] He is the lord of nations not because they are "forced by arms to undertake his yoke," but because, "being subdued by his doctrine, they spontaneously obey him."[162] In contrast to "earthly princes," who use "arms and forces," who "fill their enemies with fear, who fortify their borders, prepare an army, and set up every defense to ward off assaults," Christ's kingdom is providentially preserved by God in the midst of weakness and suffering.[163] It "speak[s] peace . . . to the nations."[164]

Calvin thus emphasizes that as a coercive force established by providence for the preservation of order, civil government is temporal and has no power to restore true spiritual order, righteousness, or piety.[165] And while the prophets sometimes compare Christ to earthly kings, accommodating the weakness of their hearers, "yet there is no equality."

> Hence, the difference between the righteousness of Christ and the righteousness of kings ought to be here noticed. They who rule well can in no other way administer righteousness and judgment than by being careful to render to every one his own, and that by checking the audacity of the wicked and by defending the good and the innocent. This only is what can be expected from earthly kings. But Christ is far different, for he is not only wise so as to know what is right and best, but he also endues his own people with wisdom and knowledge. He executes judgment and righteousness, not only because he defends the innocent, aids them who are oppressed, gives help to the miserable, and restrains the wicked, but he does righteousness because he regenerates us by his Spirit, and he also does judgment because he bridles, as it were, the devil.[166]

For Calvin, only Christ's kingdom accomplishes spiritual ends; it alone regenerates and sanctifies. Political leaders may sometimes be called "kings of righteousness," but "though this honor is ascribed to kings who rule with moderation and in equity, yet this belongs really to Christ alone, who not only exercises authority justly as others do, but also communicates to us the righteousness of God . . . He is then

---

[161] Commentary on Isaiah 49:2 [1559]; CO 37:191. Cf. 9:7; CO 36:200; 53:2; CO 37:256.

[162] Commentary on Hebrews 2:13 [1549]; CO 55:30.

[163] Commentary on Zechariah 9:9 [1559]; CO 44:271–272.

[164] "Christ and his people would not be kept safe and secure by human defenses, by means of many soldiers and of similar helps being at hand; but that God would restrain, and even compose and allay all warlike commotions, so that there would be no need of such aids." Commentary on Zechariah 9:10 [1559]; CO 44:273–274. Cf. Commentary on Matthew 12:18 [1555]; CO 45:332.

[165] Commentary on Zechariah 9:9 [1559]; CO 44:271–272; Commentary on 1 Corinthians 2:6 [1546]; CO 49:337. Cf. Commentary on Psalm 72:17 [1557]; CO 31:671; Commentary on Isaiah 16:5 [1559]; CO 36:304–305.

[166] "[W]e ought to mark the transcendency of Christ over earthly kings and also the analogy; for there is some likeness and some difference." Commentary on Jeremiah 23:5–6 [1563]; CO 38:410.

called the king of righteousness because of what he effects in diffusing righteousness on all his people."[167] Political authorities can maintain a degree of outward justice, but they have no spiritual power. They cannot actually make people just.

At the center of Calvin's understanding of the difference between the two kingdoms, then, lies his distinction between true (spiritual) righteousness and civil righteousness, which in turn gives rise to the distinction between the spiritual and civil uses of the law.[168] Calvin distinguishes between

> two righteousnesses of the law. The one is spiritual – perfect love to God and our neighbors. It is contained in doctrine and had never an existence in the life of any [sinful] man. The other is literal, such as appears in the view of men, while in the meantime hypocrisy reigns in the heart, and there is in the sight of God nothing but iniquity.[169]

In both cases God's natural moral law, summarized in the Ten Commandments, is the perfect rule of righteousness. Indeed, "whenever holiness is made to consist in any thing else than in observing the law of God, men are led to believe that the law may be violated without danger."[170] But God's law functions in different ways that correspond directly to the fundamental difference between the two kingdoms and the two kinds of righteousness.

Calvin explains the difference between the spiritual and civil uses of the law in his discussion of the threefold use of the law in the *Institutes*.[171] The spiritual and "principal use" of the law constitutes the "proper purpose of the law" because it "finds its place among believers in whose hearts the Spirit of God already lives and reigns" (2.7.12). Because it presupposes the liberty from the law that comes through justification of by faith, it is entirely free of the law's rigor and threats. "For the law is

---

[167] Commentary on Hebrews 7:1 [1549]; CO 55:82. In contrast to secular kingdoms, "righteousness in the kingdom of Christ has a wider meaning, for he by his gospel, which is his spiritual scepter, renews us after the righteousness of God" (1:8; CO 55:17–18). Cf. Commentary on Romans 8:5 [1556]; CO 49:141; Commentary on Isaiah 11:5 [1559]; CO 36:241.

[168] See Haas, *The Concept of Equity in Calvin's Ethics*, 65–67.

[169] Commentary on Philippians 3:6 [1548]; CO 52:46.

[170] Commentary on Matthew 15:3 [1555]; CO 45:449. Cf. Commentary on Romans 8:7 [1556]; CO 49: 142–143; 9:21; CO 49:447–448; 3:31; CO 49:68; Commentary on 2 Timothy 3:16 [1548]; CO 52:382–384; Commentary on Titus 2:12 [1550]; CO 52:423; Commentary on Psalm 19:8 [1557]; CO 31:200–201; Commentary on 2 Thessalonians 3:6–10 [1550]; CO 52:211; Commentary on James 2:12 [1550]; CO 55:402.

[171] These are the second and third uses of the law. The first use of the law, which corresponds to the law in its narrow sense, pertains to the "natural man," who is entirely unable to attain to the purpose and end for which God created the world and human beings. It achieves nothing but condemnation. "[S]ince our carnal and corrupted nature contends violently against God's spiritual law and is in no way corrected by its discipline, it follows that the law which had been given for salvation, provided it met with suitable hearers, turns into an occasion for sin and death" (2.7.7). See Hesselink, *Calvin's Concept of the Law*, 217–276.

not now acting toward us as a rigorous enforcement officer who is not satisfied unless the requirements are met. But in this perfection to which it exhorts us, the law points out the goal toward which throughout life we are to strive" (2.7.13). As was seen in Chapter 3, for Calvin the law was always fundamentally spiritual in purpose. "[T]hrough the law man's life is molded not only to outward honesty but to inward and spiritual righteousness." Quoting Paul's declaration in Romans 7:14 that the law is spiritual, Calvin comments, "By this he means that it not only demands obedience of soul, mind, and will, but requires an angelic purity which, cleansed of every pollution of the flesh, savors nothing but the spirit" (2.8.6). It points to "renewed nature, which God forms anew after his own image."[172] People considering the prohibitions against killing, committing adultery, or stealing might assume that the law's demands are merely outward, but the Tenth Commandment, "You shall not covet," demonstrates that God demands the "sincere affection of the heart."[173]

In essence, the spiritual use of the law consists in education and exhortation.[174] As an educational instrument the law teaches those who want to love and know God how they can go about fulfilling their desire. This "daily instruction of the law" is necessary in addition to the guidance of the Spirit if believers are to know God's will (2.7.12). As a means of exhortation, the law arouses the regenerate to obey God's will, "for, however eagerly they may in accordance with the Spirit strive toward God's righteousness, the listless flesh always so burdens them that they do not proceed with due readiness." Ready with a vivid analogy, Calvin proposes, "The law is to the flesh like a whip to an idle and bulky ass, to arouse it to work. Even for a spiritual man not yet free of the weight of the flesh the law remains a constant sting that will not let him stand still" (2.7.12).

The civil use of the law applies to all human beings, not simply those who are sanctified by the Spirit.[175] Its purpose is neither to sanctify nor to condemn human beings, but to give order to temporal society, through coercion if necessary. It is merely outward in scope, extending to human actions; it cannot touch or transform

---

[172] Commentary on Romans 7:14 [1556]; CO 49:128. Calvin argues that "perfect righteousness is prescribed in the law," and that the inward virtues of "piety, justice, judgment and truth . . . are the chief matters of the law." Commentary on Romans 2:13, 27 [1556]; CO 49:37, 45. "The sum of the law is this, that we may worship God with true faith and a pure conscience, and that we may love one another." Commentary on 1 Timothy 1:5 [1548]; CO 52:252.

[173] Commentary on Exodus 20:17 [1563]; CO 24:719 (Cf. 20:13; CO 24:611–613). The Pharisees "had changed the doctrine of the law into a political order, and had made obedience to it to consist entirely in the performance of outward duties . . . This was an intolerable profanation of the law: for it is certain that Moses everywhere demands the spiritual worship of God . . . Christ charges them with turning into a political scheme the law of God, which had been given for the government of the heart." Commentary on Matthew 5:21 [1555]; CO 45:174–175. Cf. Commentary on Leviticus 19:17–18 [1563]; CO 613–614.

[174] See Haas, *The Concept of Equity in Calvin's Ethics*, 66.

[175] Cf. Commentary on 1 Timothy 1:9 [1548]; CO 52:255.

the inward person, nor can it drive her upward and forward to the spiritual kingdom of Christ. The "mortal lawgiver's jurisdiction extends only to the outward political order." Insofar as it is concerned with purposes or intentions, it is only concerned with them when they "come forth into the open," and it can do nothing unless "actual crimes are committed" (2.8.6).[176] The civil use of the law cannot create true righteousness but only civil righteousness. Still, Calvin insists, "this constrained and forced righteousness is necessary for the public community of men." Even believers need this external enforcement of the law because their sanctification is incomplete (2.7.10).

Initially Calvin limited his discussion of the civil use of the law to a purely secular purpose, but in the 1543 *Institutes*, he suggested that the civil law also plays a role as a "tutor unto Christ," as described by the Apostle Paul in Galatians 3:24. But he is clear that it does so not by any sort of spiritual influence but as a preservative, preventing those who might one day be subject to the Spirit's power from being destroyed by their own sin. Many people, Calvin writes,

> have need of a bridle to restrain them from so slackening the reins on the lust of the flesh as to fall clean away from all pursuit of righteousness. For where the Spirit of God does not yet rule, lusts sometimes so boil that there is danger lest they plunge the soul bound over to them into forgetfulness and contempt of God. And such would happen if God did not oppose it with this remedy. Therefore, if he does not immediately regenerate those whom he has destined to inherit his Kingdom, until the time of his visitation, he keeps them safe through the works of the law under fear. This is not that chaste and pure fear such as ought to be in his sons, but a fear useful in teaching them true godliness according to their capacity.

In short, the coercive use of the law by civil government works to preserve unbelievers from the worst effects of sin in hope of future salvation. Calvin does not offer any scriptural support for this argument. He merely appeals to experience.

> We have so many proofs of this matter that no example is needed. For all who have at any time groped about in ignorance of God will admit that it happened to them in

---

[176] In a sermon on Deuteronomy 5:17 Calvin declared, "It is true that when magistrates create laws, their manner is different from God's. But then their purpose has to do only with the way we govern ourselves with respect to the external civil order to the end that no one might be violated, and that each might have his rights and have peace and concord among men. That is their intention when they create laws. And why? [Because] they are mortal men; they cannot reform inner and hidden affections. That belongs to God." CO 26:328. Cited in Witte, *The Reformation of Rights*, 64. As Marc Chenevière observes, even though Calvin believed civil magistrates are to enforce both tables of the Ten Commandments, "in obliging men to respect the Decalogue the magistrate does not claim to effect an inward change, but merely to cause them to observe outwardly a relative morality sufficient to secure for them, in spite of themselves, or even contrary to themselves, an existence worthy of the name." Marc Chenevière, "Did Calvin Advocate Theocracy?" *Evangelical Quarterly* 9 (1937): 160–168, 166.

such a way that the bridle of the law restrained them in some fear and reverence toward God until, regenerated by the Spirit, they began wholeheartedly to love him" (2.7.11).

As this last statement makes clear, Calvin's point is not that the civil law sanctifies believers or promotes spiritual righteousness. He is merely saying that it can preserve them for the later influence of the gospel. While civil government is established by God and is therefore an expression of the lordship of Christ, Calvin never leverages this point so as to collapse the fundamental distinction between the two kingdoms. It is true that he gave civil government the responsibility to promote and defend the kingdom of Christ and that he believed civil government should enforce both tables of the Ten Commandments, securing both outward piety and outward justice. I consider these points at length in the second part of this book. But for now it is important to keep in mind two fundamental points. First, Calvin always distinguishes the spiritual use of the law, through which believers grow in sanctification and true righteousness, and the civil use of the law, through which people are coerced into performing outward acts of piety and righteousness. Second, as I show in Chapter 8, Calvin distinguishes between the *direct* establishment and protection of the kingdom of Christ, which takes place through the providence of God and the ministry of the gospel, and the *indirect* establishment and protection of the spiritual kingdom, in which civil government plays a role.[177]

What is important to stress here is that although Calvin believed the righteousness of the kingdom of Christ is expressed in every area of life, he insisted that the affairs of the political order remain temporal. Thus the righteousness of believers expresses the restoration of the world and witnesses to its future completion, but it does not serve as an instrument for the gradual transformation of the social and political order into the kingdom of Christ, a key distinction sometimes overlooked by scholars.[178] Calvin never made the church or Christians an agency of progressive socio-political transformation. As Höpfl observes, Calvin "explicitly

---

[177] David Little writes, "In terms of Calvin's pattern of order, nothing is surer than that the Kingdom of God, toward which all things move, includes overcoming the engines of coercion in favor of voluntary obedience to the will of God." Little, *Religion, Order, and Law*, 53. The church is the community in which obedience becomes voluntary. "Because Christ reigns in Word, sacrament, and Spirit in the Church, the old order is decisively broken there and the new is beginning. Therefore, the hallmark of the old order, coercion, is by definition excluded from it." Little, *Religion, Order, and Law*, 72. Civil government can only contribute indirectly to this process. As Torrance puts it, while civil government also serves the glory of God by promoting *humanitas*, it only does so indirectly, being "given authority to make room for the Church and to bring about *the conditions of humanity* on earth." Torrance, *Kingdom and Church*, 158–159. Emphasis in original.

[178] For instance, Susan E. Schreiner, *The Theater of His Glory: Nature and the Natural Order in the Thought of John Calvin* (Grand Rapids: Baker Academic, 1995), 107, 109–110, 114; Tonkin, *The Church and the Secular Order in the Theology of the Reformers*, 114.

disassociated" the sanctification of Christians from "institutional changes in society." Temporal vocations and institutions remain temporal for him, even as spiritual righteousness transforms the way in which believers inhabit them.[179] When it came to institutions, Calvin identified the spiritual kingdom of Christ with the church, not with the socio-political order. It is to the church as Christ's spiritual kingdom that I turn in Chapter 5.

APPENDIX: BEATING THEIR SWORDS INTO PLOWSHARES

An excellent example of Calvin's two kingdoms paradigm at work appears in his commentaries on the well-known prophecy of Isaiah and Micah that in the kingdom of God, the nations will beat their swords into plowshares and their spears into pruning hooks, and they shall not learn war anymore. It is worth considering these commentaries in detail because they show how Calvin's two kingdoms theology functions in a specific exegetical context.

Calvin understands the prophecy as a clear indication that the kingdom of Christ will subdue the nations through voluntary obedience to the proclamation of the word rather than through coercion or the power of the sword. The whole prophecy, he argues, is about "God's spiritual kingdom." The means by which Christ rules, his scepter, is the gospel. "We hence see that an earthly empire is not what is here predicted, but what exists through the word and celestial doctrine."[180] That the kingdom is spiritual, however, does not mean that it holds no relevance for life in the present age. When the prophets declare that the nations will be reconciled to one another, they mean that those who formerly lived in hatred and lust will devote themselves to kindness. This reconciliation is a manifestation of God's spiritual kingdom, distinct from his broader government of the world.

---

[179] "The changes in the relations between men that the Gospel brings about, therefore, are not principally new laws or new institutions, but an actual conformity to laws mostly already in existence." Höpfl, *The Christian Polity of John Calvin*, 195. "There is no doubt ... that Calvin attributed a transformative power to the Gospel, and more particularly to its agents, and that he expected such transformation to bear visible fruit in the lives of men. What is in doubt is the propriety of calling this 'the regeneration of society' or 'the creation of a new order' and of seeing it as a cumulative process building up to a climax in the last days. For the latter implies an open-endedness in the transformations and a progressive triumph of righteousness in the world, and this is not at all what Calvin imagined. There is nothing whatever in his works to suggest that the church would not always be a beleaguered and persecuted minority until a dramatic and sudden termination of its sufferings in the last days. What is more, the most proximate and perhaps the only vocabulary available in the sixteenth century for anything akin to the later doctrine of progress was millennialism, which was so badly compromised by its Anabaptist associations that Calvin would have no truck with it whatever" (194). Cf. Wilhelm Niesel, *The Theology of Calvin* (trans. Harold Knight; London: Methuen, 1956), 229.

[180] Commentary on Micah 4:1–2 [1559]; CO 43:341.

God has indeed ever governed the world by his hidden providence, as he does still govern it ... But the scripture speaks of God's kingdom in two respects. God does indeed govern the devil and all the wicked, but not by his word, nor by the sanctifying power of his Spirit. It is so done that they obey God, not willingly, but against their will. The peculiar government of God is that of his church only [*peculiare Dei imperium pertinet ad solam ecclesiam*], where by his word and Spirit he bends the hearts of men to obedience so that they follow him voluntarily and willingly, being taught inwardly and outwardly – inwardly by the influence of the Spirit – outwardly by the preaching of the word [*intus, spiritus instinctu: foris, verbi praedicatione*] ... This, then, is the beginning of the kingdom of Christ [*regni Christi*].[181]

What is unique here about the peculiar government of God, or the kingdom of Christ, is that it operates by the word and Spirit, it establishes obedience that is voluntary, and the place where this happens is in the church. The definitive mark of the kingdom is that it empowers voluntary and genuine righteousness: "that strong men, when thus reproved, shall offer themselves, without any resistance, to be ruled by God. Correction is indeed necessary, but God employs no external force nor any armed power when he makes the church subject to himself, and yet he collects strong nations."[182] The result is genuine peace and justice. While the world apart from the gospel is marked by tyranny, oppression, dissension, and fighting, the gospel restores the world to the "cultivation of peace and concord."[183]

Calvin views Micah's prophecy as an indictment of Christendom for its lack of "progress ... in brotherly love." Christians claim the reconciliation of Christ, "but in the meantime we tear one another, we sharpen our teeth, our dispositions are cruel." Indeed, "when the gospel was at first preached the whole world boiled with wars more than ever," and even now "discords and contentions do not cease."[184] How can the church, then, be the genuine fulfillment of this prophecy?

Calvin addresses the problem by appealing to the eschatological nature of the church's existence under the cross:

My answer to this is that as the kingdom of Christ was only begun in the world when God commanded the gospel to be everywhere proclaimed, and as at this day its course is not as yet completed, so that which the prophet says here has not hitherto taken place. But inasmuch as the number of the faithful is small, and the greater part despise and reject the gospel, so it happens that plunders and hostilities continue in the world. How so? Because the prophet speaks here only of the

[181] Commentary on Micah 4:3 [1559]; CO 43:344–345.
[182] Commentary on Micah 4:3 [1559]; CO 43:345.
[183] Commentary on Micah 4:3 [1559]; CO 43:346.
[184] Commentary on Micah 4:3 [1559]; CO 43:347.

disciples of Christ. He shows the fruit of his doctrine, that wherever it strikes a living root it brings forth fruit, but the doctrine of the gospel strikes roots hardly in one out of a hundred.[185]

In other words, the kingdom is limited in extent; very few walk as true disciples of Christ. What is more, even those who are true disciples continue to struggle with sin.[186]

Calvin takes this as an opportunity to emphasize the continuing importance of civil government subject to the rule of Christ.

> It is also easy hence to see how foolish is the conceit of those who seek to take away the use of the sword on account of the gospel. The Anabaptists, we know, have been turbulent, as though all political order [*ordo politicus*] were inconsistent with the kingdom of Christ [*Christi regno*], as though the kingdom of Christ [*regnum Christi*] was made up of doctrine only, and that doctrine without any influence.[187]

Calvin's point is not that the sword is an expression of the spiritual kingdom of Christ, or of the church, but that where the kingdom of Christ is established, it calls forth obedience and righteousness that is compatible with, and finds expression in, the political order. In other words, Christians may, and sometimes must, take up the sword when called to serve in civil government.

But the distinction between the kingdoms remains. Indeed, the fundamental premise of Calvin's argument is that because the political order is distinct from the spiritual kingdom of Christ, the prophecy of Micah and Isaiah must not be understood in terms of a literal end to the sword, but in terms of reconciliation and peace among believers in all nations. "[T]his was not fulfilled, we are certain, at the coming of Christ, in a manner visible to men ... [T]his kingdom is spiritual [*regnum hoc spirituale esse*], for he did not ascribe to Christ a golden scepter, but a doctrine."[188] Thus

> peace exists among us only as far as the kingdom of Christ [*Christi regnum*] flourishes ... Would that Christ reigned [*regnaret Christus*] entirely in us! for then would peace also have its perfect influence. But since we are still widely

---

[185] Commentary on Micah 4:3 [1559]; CO 43:348.

[186] "[T]he good have not yet reached the goal, and are widely distant from that perfection which is required from them." Commentary on Isaiah 2:4 [1559]; CO 36:65–66.

[187] Commentary on Micah 4:3 [1559]; CO 43:348. In his commentary on the parallel passage, Calvin uses the word "church" to make the same point, charging that "madman torture this passage to promote anarchy, as if it took away from the church [*ecclesiae*] entirely the right to use the sword, and bring it forward for condemning with great severity every kind of wars." Commentary on Isaiah 2:4 [1559]; CO 36:66.

[188] Commentary on Micah 4:8 [1559]; CO 43:356–357. Cf. 4:11–13; CO 43:362–363.

distant from the perfection of that peaceful kingdom [*perfectione pacifici istius regni*], we must always think of making progress, and it is excessive folly not to consider that the kingdom of Christ [*regnum Christi*] here is only beginning.

The ultimate fulfillment of Isaiah's prophecy, therefore, could only take place after Jesus' return. "It is enough if we experience the beginning, and if, being reconciled to God through Christ, we cultivate mutual friendship and abstain from doing harm to any one."[189]

---

[189] Commentary on Isaiah 2:4 [1559]; CO 36:66.

5

Christ's Spiritual Government

One of Calvin's most emphatic claims throughout his works is that the church is Christ's kingdom. Calvin does not entirely equate the two concepts, for the scope of Christ's kingdom will ultimately be the restoration of the entire creation, and the progress of the kingdom through the rule of the Holy Spirit expresses itself in the outward conduct of believers.[1] Still, during the present age, the kingdom is established only where the gospel is proclaimed and humans respond in faith and obedience, which is to say, in the true visible church.[2] Calvin writes, "When we speak of the kingdom of Christ [*Christi regno*] we must respect two things: the doctrine of the gospel, by which Christ gathers to himself a church, and by which he governs [*gubernat*] it ... and secondly, the society of the godly, who being coupled

---

[1] See Benjamin Milner, Jr., *Calvin's Doctrine of the Church* (Leiden: Brill, 1970), 169–170; John Witte, Jr., *The Reformation of Rights: Law, Religion, and Human Rights in Early Modern Calvinism* (Cambridge: Cambridge University Press, 2007), 61; Susan E. Schreiner, *The Theater of His Glory: Nature and the Natural Order in the Thought of John Calvin* (Grand Rapids: Baker Academic, 1995), 107–110; Thomas F. Torrance, *Kingdom and Church: Study in the Theology of the Reformation* (Edinburgh: Oliver & Boyd, 1956), 91, 134. Calvin sometimes refers to the kingdom in distinction from the church. Commentary on Ephesians 1:14 [1548]; CO 51:154. On the other hand, he so equates the church with Christ's kingdom that he can say that there are false teachers in Christ's kingdom. Commentary on Deuteronomy 13:1 [1563]; CO 24:275.

[2] Calvin often uses the terms kingdom and church interchangeably: "... in the kingdom of Christ, or in the Christian church ..." Commentary on Galatians 5:6 [1548]; CO 50:246; "... the church, that is, the kingdom of Christ ..." Commentary on Isaiah 45:18 [1559]; CO 37:143. He consistently identifies the kingdom with the preaching of the gospel. Commentary on Mark 1:14 [1555]; CO 45:138–139; 15:43; CO 45:788–789; Commentary on Matthew 4:23 [1555]; CO 45:151; 5:19; CO 45:172; 9:35; CO 45:262; 11:11; CO 45:303; 17:11; CO 45:491; 25:1; CO 45:682; 28:18; CO 45:820–821; Commentary on Acts, Argument [1552]; CO 48:vii; 19:9; CO 48:444; Commentary on Colossians 4:11 [1548]; CO 52:131; Commentary on 2 Corinthians 6:2 [1548]; CO 50:75–76; Commentary on 2 Thessalonians 2:9 [1550]; CO 52:202; Commentary on 1 John 1:2 [1551]; CO 55:301; Commentary on Isaiah 2:4 [1559]; CO 36:64; 11:9; 36: 243–244; 52:7; CO 37:247; 54:2; CO 37:270; Commentary on Romans 5:2 [1556]; CO 49:89; 15:21; CO 49:279; 16:21–27; 49:292; Commentary on a Harmony of the Gospels, Argument [1555]; CO 45:2; Commentary on 1 Thessalonians 5:10 [1550]; CO 52:170–171; Commentary on Genesis 28:17 [1554]; CO 23:394.

together by the sincere faith of the gospel, are truly accounted the people of God."[3] Each individual church is an outpost of the spiritual kingdom, for "Christ, by his ministers, has subdued to his dominion the whole world, and has erected as many principalities under his authority as there have been churches gathered to him in diverse nations by their preaching."[4] Calvin describes the church as Christ's kingdom because he defines the two according to the same mark, the preaching of Christ's word (4.1.5).[5] "To sum up, since the church is Christ's Kingdom, and he reigns by his word alone, will it not be clear to any man that those are lying words by which the Kingdom of Christ is imagined to exist apart from his scepter (that is, his most holy word)?" (4.2.4)

In this chapter I show that Calvin's identification of the church as Christ's spiritual kingdom, identifiable by the mark of the word, is the foundation for the reformer's whole ecclesiology. Despite the tendency of other reformers, such as Zwingli, Bullinger, and later Hooker, to identify the visible church with the political order, Calvin does just the opposite, identifying the ministry of the church, including discipline, with Christ's spiritual kingdom. But I also demonstrate that Calvin vigorously rejects the tendency of the papal church to claim magisterial authority over spiritual matters and spiritual authority over political matters. He decisively limits pastors' authority in preaching, teaching, and discipline to the ministerial authority of the word. Only where various regulations are necessary for order and decorum in church affairs does he permit a sort of political rule in the church, whether on the part of magistrates or pastors.

THE CHURCH AS CHRIST'S SPIRITUAL KINGDOM

A few scholars have alleged that, like the Zurich reformers and Hooker, Calvin identified the visible church with the political order, limiting the spiritual kingdom

---

[3] Commentary on Acts, Dedication to Second Edition [1560]; CO 18:157. Cf. 20:1 [1554]; CO 48:455.

[4] Commentary on Psalm 45:16 [1557]; CO 31:458–459. This means that the history of the church, as Milner observes, is "the history of restoration of order in the world." Milner, *Calvin's Doctrine of the Church*, 194. Cf. Wilhelm Niesel, *The Theology of Calvin* (trans. Harold Knight; London: Methuen, 1956), 183–185; Willem Van't Spijker, "The Kingdom of Christ According to Bucer and Calvin," *Calvin and the State* (ed. Peter De Klerk; Grand Rapids: Calvin Studies Society, 1993), 109–132, 120; Peter Wilcox, "'The Progress of the Kingdom of Christ' in Calvin's Exposition of the Prophets," in *Calvinus Sincerioris Religionis Vindex* (Kirksville: Sixteenth Century Journal, 1997), 315–322, 321; Frederik A.V. Harms, *In God's Custody: The Church, A History of Divine Protection: A Study of John Calvin's Ecclesiology Based on His Commentary on the Minor Prophets* (Gottingen: Vandenhoeck & Ruprecht, 2010), 109, 112–114, 118, 130–131.

[5] "Isaiah had long before distinguished Christ's Kingdom by this mark: 'My spirit which is upon you, and my words which I have put in your mouth, shall never depart out of your mouth'" (4.1.5). It is the same mark, along with the administration of Christ's sacraments, that make the true church "visible to our eyes" (4.1.9). Cf. Commentary on John 10:16 [1553]; CO 47:244–245; Commentary on 1 Thessalonians 1:1 [1550]; CO 52:139. Commentary on Isaiah 33:22 [1559]; CO 36:576. Commentary on Obadiah 1:21 [1559]; CO 43:200. Cf. Torrance, *Kingdom and Church*, 98, 123.

to the invisible church.[6] Torrance Kirby thus claims that Calvin's two kingdoms correspond not to the chapters in Book 4 on church (1–19) and civil government (20) respectively, but to the distinction between the inward work of the Spirit (Book 3) and the outward means of grace (Book 4). Preaching, the sacraments, and discipline, along with civil government, thus make up the outward or political realm. Calvin, he argues, engaged in the "profanizing disenchantment of ecclesiastical functions."[7]

These arguments miss the fact that for Calvin the fundamental difference between the two kingdoms is not that one is inward and the other is outward, but that one is spiritual and eternal, and the other is temporal and political.[8] The visible church, in Calvin's paradigm, truly administers the spiritual government of Christ.[9] Calvin repeatedly and explicitly identifies the core elements of church government with Christ's spiritual government of the church, which is to say, the spiritual kingdom. "As the Lord governs [*gubernat*] the church by his word, as with a scepter, the administration of the gospel [*evangelii administratio*] is often called the kingdom of God [*regnum Dei*]."[10] Calvin notes that when Paul refers to those who preside in the Lord,

---

[6] Edward A. Dowey claims that Calvin used the two kingdoms doctrine as a lens through which to view the church from a double perspective, one kingdom encompassing the invisible church, the realm of faith, election, and grace, and the other kingdom encompassing the visible church, the realm of sanctification and church polity. "Calvin's massive fourth book in his *Institutes* is not about the Church as 'invisible' but as 'visible' ... The 'External Means' of book four (Church, Sacraments, and State) are not themselves the eschaton, but specially accommodated *instruments* or *means* for supporting the faith by which believers now participate in Christ's Kingdom." Edward A. Dowey, "Calvin on Church and State," *Reformed and Presbyterian World* 24 (1957): 244–252, 247–248. "Thus, if one pole of Calvin's doctrine of the Church concerns faith and election, the realm where all is done freely by God's grace, the other pole is expressed in sanctification with visible churchly judicatories as guides, goads, and admonishers to holiness of life" (249). Cf. John T. McNeill, "John Calvin on Civil Government," *Calvinism and the Political Order* (ed. George L. Hunt; Philadelphia: Westminster, 1965), 23–45, 41.

[7] Torrance Kirby, "A Reformed Culture of Persuasion: John Calvin's 'Two Kingdoms' and the Theological Origins of the Public Sphere," *Calvin@500:Theology, History, and Practice* (ed. Richard R. Topping and John A. Vissers; Eugene, OR: Wipf and Stock, 2011), 52–66, 61. Kirby argues that Calvin shoved church government and the means of grace out of the forum of conscience and into the political forum, so clearing the way for the doctrine of justification by faith alone. He oddly reduces the spiritual/temporal distinction to the canon law distinction between "the outward forum of an external jurisdiction exercised in the ecclesiastical courts and the internal forum of spiritual jurisdiction in the practice of penance," rather than relating it to the broader medieval two swords distinction (55). Cf. W. J. Torrance Kirby, *Richard Hooker's Doctrine of the Royal Supremacy* (Leiden: Brill, 1997).

[8] On Calvin's identification of the visible church as the true church, see Niesel, *The Theology of Calvin*, 191–193. Cf. John Tonkin, *The Church and the Secular Order in Reformation Thought* (New York: Columbia University Press, 1971), 129–130.

[9] As Peter Wilcox observes, "Calvin identifies the Kingdom of Christ with the Church ... Furthermore, this identification is of the Kingdom of Christ not with 'the elect' (the invisible Church), but with the institutional (or visible) Church." Wilcox, "'The Progress of the Kingdom of Christ' in Calvin's Exposition of the Prophets," 320.

[10] Commentary on 1 Corinthians 4:20 [1546]; CO 49:376.

This seems to be added to denote spiritual government [*spirituale regimen*]. For although kings and magistrates also preside by the appointment of God, yet as the Lord would have the government of the church [*ecclesiae gubernationem*] to be specially recognized as his, those that govern the church [*ecclesiam gubernant*] in the name and by the commandment of Christ are for this reason spoken of particularly as presiding [*praesse*] in the Lord."

To be sure, with the specter of the Roman Church constantly in his mind, Calvin agreed that not every element of ecclesiastical government is an expression of Christ's spiritual government. But he clearly identified the core elements of faithful ecclesiastical government, including preaching and discipline, with the spiritual kingdom.[12]

In fact, it is Calvin's emphasis on the visible expression of the kingdom of Christ in the outward ministry of the church that most practically distinguishes his two kingdoms theology from that of Luther.[13] The key is the Genevan reformer's eschatology. For Calvin the heavenly kingdom is already being actualized in the life of the church. Through the word and sacraments the visible church enjoys union with Christ, and his kingdom is genuinely established. "The new creation has ontological reality here and now in the Church."[14] In fact, for Calvin the order of the church, including its discipline, initiates among believers the restoration of the world that will fully take place when Christ returns.[15] It is true that Calvin believed the ministry of the word and sacraments will pass away at Christ's return and are in

---

[11] Commentary on 1 Thessalonians 5:12 [1550]; CO 52:172. See also Commentary on John 21:15 [1553]; CO 47:45; Commentary on Acts 4:19 [1552]; CO 48:88; 10:25; CO 48:237.

[12] See Niesel, *The Theology of Calvin*, 199–200, 206–208); François Wendel, *Calvin: The Origins and Development of his Religious Thought* (trans. Philip Mairet; London: Collins, 1963 [1950]), 302–303, 307.

[13] As T. F. Torrance puts it, "In contrast to Luther, Calvin laid greater emphasis upon the *ecclesia externa sive visibilis*. The Kingdom of Christ consists not only in the Gospel, not only in a hidden community of believers, but in the historical communication of the Gospel, and the building up of the Church on earth by human agency (*humanitus*)." Torrance, *Kingdom and Church*, 148 (Cf. 91, 150). Cf. Tonkin, *The Church and the Secular Order in Reformation Thought*, 119, 122, 124, 128; Wendel, *Calvin*, 302, 360.

[14] Torrance, *Kingdom and Church*, 150.

[15] Torrance writes, "The order of the Church is therefore the *rectitude* or *spiritual jurisdiction* of the *Regnum Christi* in actual operation ... That is why the establishment of *order* in the Church was for Calvin a promotion of the Kingdom of Christ ... Therefore the Church can be spoken of as the Kingdom, or the Kingdom as the renovation of the Church." Torrance, *Kingdom and Church*, 153. Cf. 133, 154. See also Milner, *Calvin's Doctrine of the Church*, 169–179. Milner points out, "In the conception of discipline, then, we have the heart of Calvin's doctrine of the kingdom of Christ (and thus of his doctrine of sanctification)" (178–179). Yet Milner is guilty of oversimplification when he claims that the correlation between Spirit and word underlies all of the dualisms and distinctions that Calvin explains by the formula *distinctio, sed non separatio*, including law and gospel, sign and substance, visible and invisible, outward means and spiritual power, civil and spiritual government (191). Cf. 173–179.

that sense temporary.[16] But what makes the government of the church spiritual is not that its functions or offices are eternal but that the *power it administers* is spiritual and eternal. The faithful government of the church is a ministry of the Spirit and word of Christ.

PAPAL CHURCH GOVERNMENT

Calvin's primary foil for his understanding of the church was Rome, and understanding the reformer's criticism of Rome helps to explain the sense in which he identified the church with Christ's spiritual kingdom and the sense in which he did not. Like Luther, Calvin saw Rome as a false church[17] that confused its own magisterial political claims with the ministry of Christ's spiritual government. Although critics of Calvinist ecclesiology accused him of reestablishing the same sort of tyranny that characterized the papal church, Calvin presented his understanding of church government in stark contrast to papal claims to the plenipotentiality of power.[18] Calvin claims Rome made essentially the same mistake as the "fanatics" and "libertines" when it claimed that "the church is ruled by the Holy Spirit immediately, and therefore that it cannot err."[19] While Christ promises his Spirit to the church, he admits, what is received is "only the first fruits and some taste of his Spirit" (4.8.11). Thus "the riches of the church are always far from that supreme perfection of which our adversaries boast" (4.8.12).

Calvin devotes two entire chapters of the *Institutes* to a critique of the papacy, that "capstone of the whole structure" of Roman government. The pope claimed to be the vicar of Christ, Calvin writes, and that he "presides over the whole church in Christ's place; and the church cannot otherwise be well constituted unless that see hold primacy over all others" (4.6.1). What is more, by virtue of the two swords doctrine the papacy claimed that this primacy included "earthly dominion" and "civil power," as well as "supreme jurisdiction" in all ecclesiastical matters, including "adjudicating and defining doctrines, or in laying down laws, or in

[16] The present "order in the Kingdom of Christ [*Christi regno ordinem*]" is appropriate for "our present weakness" but "in that perfect glory the administration of the Kingdom [*regni administrationem*] will not be as it now is" (2.15.5). Cf. Commentary on 1 Corinthians 13:12 [1546]; CO 49:514–515; Heinrich Quistorp, *Calvin's Doctrine of the Last Things* (trans. Harold Knight; London: Lutterworth Press, 1955), 162–165; Torrance, *Kingdom and Church*, 126, 134–137.

[17] Calvin conceded that God had preserved certain outward means such as baptism, which ensured the survival of the gospel and of a true church within Rome. Thus "when we categorically deny to the papists the title of *the* church, we do not for this reason impugn the existence of churches among them" (4.2.4). Yet in the churches under the papacy, "Christ lies hidden, half buried, the gospel overthrown, piety scattered, the worship of God nearly wiped out" (4.2.12). Cf. Commentary on Isaiah 33:22 [1559]; CO 37:576.

[18] Niesel, *The Theology of Calvin*, 186–187; Wendel, *Calvin*, 305–306.

[19] Commentary on Ezekiel 3:16–17 [1565]; CO 40:90–91.

establishing discipline, or in rendering judgments" (4.7.19).[20] Calvin retorts that it was sheer "madness" for the canon lawyers to imagine that Jesus gave the disciples, and through them bishops, a "double jurisdiction [*duplici iurisdictione*]" of spiritual and political power.[21]

Calvin argues that although Bernard of Clairveaux was the source for the two swords analogy, Bernard had clearly distinguished the "earthly things" governed by political rulers from the "keys to the Kingdom of Heaven," and "lordship" from "ministry." The popes, however, claimed "the supreme right to both swords ... by divine right" (4.11.11). From this came

> the tyranny of the pope, whom they wish to possess supreme power over kings and princes. They speak impudent falsehood when they say that he is Christ's deputy, for Christ's kingdom is not of this world. The pope rules barbarously and tyrannically and claims the power of changing and disposing of kingdoms. But kings submit to Christ in such a manner that they do not cease to be kings, but exercise all their power for preserving the worship of God and administering righteous government.[22]

The Roman church was infatuated with "secular power" and "lust for dominion" (4.11.14).

Rome confused the two kingdoms by conflating temporal and spiritual glory. "They say that the dignity of the church is decently sustained by this magnificence. And they have certain ones of their sect so shameless as to dare openly to boast that only thus are those prophecies fulfilled with which the ancient prophets describe the splendor of Christ's Kingdom, when that kingly magnificence is beheld in the priestly order" (4.5.17). Under such pretenses those who "ought to have been a singular example of frugality, modesty, continence, and humility" came to "rival the magnificence of princes in number of retainers, splendor of buildings, elegance of apparel, and banquets." They "lay hands on villages and castles," and "carry off vast provinces, ... seize whole kingdoms!" (4.5.19)

The prelates of the church, imagining that catholicity and orthodoxy flowed from the episcopal succession, showed themselves to be more interested in exercising magisterial power than in fulfilling their spiritual functions as ministers of Christ (4.2.10). "Here there is no preaching, no care for discipline, no zeal toward the

---

[20] By claiming the plenitude of power in both spiritual and temporal affairs, "they leave no jurisdiction on earth to control or restrain their lust if they abuse such boundless power." The pope can be judged "neither by emperor, nor by kings, nor by all the clergy, nor by the people," even if "he scatter and lay waste Christ's Kingdom" (4.7.19).

[21] Commentary on Luke 22:38 [1555]; CO 45:717. Cf. Commentary on Matthew 26:51 [1555]; CO 45:732.

[22] Commentary on Isaiah 60:10 [1559]; CO 37:361–362. Cf. 60:11–14; CO 37:362–364. "Kings and nations are said ... to 'serve the Church,' not that she exercises any dominion over them, but because God has committed to her the scepter of his word by which he rules" (363).

churches, no spiritual activity – in short, nothing but the world" (4.7.22). "As if a horned mitre, a ring richly set in jewels, or a silver cross and other trifles, accompanied by idle display, constituted the spiritual government of a church [*spirituale ecclesiae regimen*], which can no more be separated from doctrine than any one of us can be separated from his own soul."[23] The pope deceived the masses by mere "masks [*larvae*]" (4.5.5), while establishing "unbounded dominion [*dominationem*]."[24]

The problem had filtered through the entire clergy. When the papists chose a bishop "they choose a lawyer who knows how to plead in a court rather than how to preach in a church" (4.5.1), and the bishops simply immersed themselves in the political interests of their benefices (4.5.6). Whereas the task of a presbyter is "to feed the church, and administer the spiritual Kingdom of Christ" (4.5.9), the Roman clergy "have cast off as burdens too troublesome the preaching of the word, the care of discipline, and the administering of the sacraments." Instead, they were consumed with a myriad of titles and innovations that had nothing to do with the "spiritual government [*regiminis spiritualis*]" appointed by Christ (4.5.10).[25] As for the deacons, "There is nothing of alms, nothing of the care of the poor, nothing of that whole function which they once performed" (4.5.15).[26] Calvin rejected wholesale the distinction between monks and secular clergy, arguing that there should be no clergy who do not fulfill an office of ministry as appointed by Christ (4.5.8).

The problem was not simply the politicization of ecclesiastical authority, but the exercise of magisterial power *over* religion, as if Christ had placed his authority at the discretion of the church.[27] The greatest sin was the tyrannizing of consciences. While the church refused to hold its clergy accountable to divine standards of justice and piety, it enforced human laws ruthlessly, such as the law requiring clerical celibacy (4.12.23) or the "cruel tyranny" of burdensome vows (4.13.1).[28] As for the laity, "ecclesiastical constitutions" were "thrust upon men as true and necessary worship of God" (4.10.6). A prime example was the practice of auricular confession.

---

[23] Commentary on 1 Timothy 3:2 [1548]; CO 52:283. Cf. *Institutes*, 4.7.30; Commentary on 2 Corinthians 7:15 [1548]; CO 50:94.

[24] Commentary on 2 Corinthians 13:8 [1548]; CO 50:152. Cf. 11:14; CO 50:129; Commentary on 1 John 4:1 [1551]; CO 55:347–348

[25] "Today the courts resound with more lawsuits over priestly offices than almost anything else" (*Institutes*, 4.5.6). Cf. *Institutes*, 4.5.4; Commentary on Acts 20:28 [1554]; CO 48:469.

[26] "Therefore, they mock the church with a false diaconate" (4.5.15; Cf. 4.5.4). Calvin appealed to the canon laws that suggested that "at least one half" of the church's wealth should be devoted to the poor (4.5.16).

[27] Thus the pope "does not hesitate to change the whole of religion at his own pleasure." Commentary on 2 Thessalonians 2:4 [1550]; CO 52:198–199. Cf. Commentary on 1 Corinthians 4:15 [1546]; CO 49:372.

[28] Calvin rejected the whole concept of monasticism (4.13.12), arguing that God calls human beings to serve him through some "definite calling" among the "duties of society" (4.13.16).

The papal clergy acted as if they had some sort of "magical power" over the absolution of sins.[29] They piled up requirements regarding honor to images, specific prayers, and pilgrimages. There were the prohibitions of meat on Fridays, work on holy days, and marriage by priests. In all of this "they punish even the slightest infraction of their decree with no lighter penalty than prison, exile, fire, or sword" (4.10.10). All of this amounted to a reversion to Judaism warned against by the Apostle Paul (4.10.11). "For they have partly taken their pattern from the ravings of the Gentiles, partly, like apes, have rashly imitated the ancient rites of the Mosaic law, which apply to us no more than do animal sacrifices and other like things" (4.10.12).

Often lodging his charges against the scholars at the Sorbonne in Paris, Calvin accused them of claiming a "magisterial [*magistralis*] freedom" to force doctrinal speculations and practical contrivances on Christians.[30] Devoting their energies to endless speculation, developing "vast labyrinths about the hierarchies of heaven, relationships, and similar contrivances," they then imposed their conclusions on consciences in "authoritative decisions" that found no support in scripture.[31] As a result, papal theology was no better than the carnal philosophy of the pagans.[32] They failed to grasp that "the spiritual kingdom of Christ [*regnum Christi spirituale*]" does not consist in outward exercises, but in "yield[ing] obedience simply to his commands."[33]

Calvin concedes that the bishops claimed to be exercising Christ's government in imposing such laws. "Our false bishops, therefore, burden our consciences with new laws on the pretext that they have been appointed by the Lord spiritual lawgivers [*spirituales legislatores*], as a consequence of which the government of the church [*ecclesiae gubernatio*] has been entrusted to them" (4.10.6). But the clergy falsely imagined that the authority of God was attached to their very office, as if bound to their control and discretion.[34] It was "as though they had said, 'We possess an ordinary jurisdiction [*iurisdictione ordinaria*], for God has set us over his church. Whatever then proceeds from us ought to be deemed inviolable.'" While the clergy

---

[29] Commentary on Matthew 23:13 [1555]; CO 45:627–628. Cf. Commentary on John 20:23 [1553]; CO 47: 440–442; Commentary on 2 Corinthians 5:19 [1548]; CO 50:72.

[30] Commentary on Colossians 2:18 [1548]; CO 52:112.

[31] Commentary on 1 Timothy 1:7 [1548]; CO 52:254. Cf. Commentary on Titus 1:10 [1550]; CO 52:413; Commentary on Mark 1:22 [1555]; CO 45:153.

[32] Commentary on Colossians 1:9 [1548]; CO 52:81. Cf. 2:19; CO 52:113–114; Commentary on Acts 20:21, 27 [1554]; CO 48:463, 466–467; 28:23; CO 48:569.

[33] Commentary on Colossians 2:23 [1548]. CO 52:115–116. The papists "make religion consist in things outward and frail, which have no connection with the spiritual kingdom of God [*spirituale Dei regnum*]" (2:22; CO 52:114–115). Cf. Commentary on 1 Timothy 4:2 [1548]; CO 52:294; *Institutes*, 3.4.1.

[34] Commentary on Malachi 2:4 [1559]; CO 44:431–433; Commentary on 1 Corinthians 4:2 [1546]; CO 49:362; Commentary on Matthew 3:9 [1555]; CO 45:118.

held legitimate office within the church, Calvin admitted, "it does not yet hence follow that they are true ministers of God."[35]

What made such misuses of power so destructive was Rome's effort to enforce them by means of excommunication as well as civil coercion. Calvin complains of the "barbarous tyranny which the pretended bishops have exercised in enslaving the people, . . . and now we see with what cruelty they throw this dart of excommunication against all who worship God."[36] The church enforced its decrees ruthlessly, even "by fire and sword."[37] To be sure, the church has the right to expel those who do not keep its teachings, Calvin admits, but only if those teachings come from the word. "Men must listen to the church, they say. Who denies this? The reason is that the church makes no pronouncement except from the Lord's word. If they require anything more, let them know that these words of Christ afford them no support" (4.8.15).

Calvin gathers evidence from church history and scripture to prove that the papacy's claims were unwarranted.[38] Rome argued that the papacy fulfilled a role in continuity with that of the Old Testament high priest, with its associated powers and privileges. In response, Calvin appeals to the New Testament's identification of Christ as the true high priest, who alone possesses all priestly functions (4.6.2): "Since now one sole priest, who is also our master, even Christ, is set over us, woe to us if we do not simply submit ourselves to his word."[39] Calvin is equally dismissive of papal appeals to Jesus' various promises and exhortations to Peter in passages like Matthew 16:18–19 and John 21:15. These passages say nothing, he argues, about possessing "power over all churches" or the right to "rule the whole world" (4.6.3).

---

[35] Commentary on Jeremiah 18:18 [1563]; CO 38:310 (Cf. 29:24–27; CO 38:608). "[E]ven though they might justly claim ordinary jurisdiction, yet, if they overturn the sacred house of God, it is only in name that they must be reckoned builders." Commentary on Matthew 21:42 [1555]; CO 45:596. Cf. Commentary on Ezekiel 13:9 [1565]; CO 40:280–281; Commentary on 1 Corinthians 1:1 [1546]; CO 49:305–306; Commentary on 1 Peter 2:7 [1551]; CO 55:238; Commentary on 2 Corinthians 5:20 [1548]; CO 50:72–73; *Institutes*, 4.9.4.

[36] Commentary on John 9:22 [1553]; CO 47:227–228. Cf. 12:42; CO 47:300.

[37] Commentary on 1 Corinthians 11:25 [1546]; CO 49:490; Cf. 14:17; CO 49:523. Cf. *Institutes*, 4.11.9–10.

[38] Calvin's arguments, positive and negative, involve figures as diverse as Cyprian, Pope Gregory I, Pope Leo I, Pepin the Short of Gaul, and Bernard of Clairvaux, in whose day ecclesiastical order hit its nadir. *Institutes*, 4.7.11, 13, 17, 18. Cf. Commentary on Philippians 1:1–2 [1548]; CO 52:7. Cf. *Institutes*, 4.4.2, 4.

[39] In any case, Calvin maintains, Israelite priests were never given the authority indiscriminately to judge "civil causes and earthly affairs." Rather, the priests were to rule only on "matters of the Lord," those things revealed in the law, speaking nothing but what they received "as from the mouth of God," and so serving as the teachers of the church. Commentary on Deuteronomy 17:8 [1563]; CO 24:470–471. Cf. Commentary on Zechariah 3:6–7 [1559]; CO 44:172–176; Commentary on Malachi 2:9 [1559]; CO 44:440–442. To be sure, even within the church "the political distinction of ranks is not to be repudiated, for natural reason itself dictates this in order to take away confusion," but such is entirely distinct from the spiritual government of the church. Commentary on Numbers 3:5 [1563]; CO 24:444–445. Cf. Commentary on Hebrews 7:12 [1549]; CO 55:89–90.

Even if Peter was raised to a prominence above the other apostles, "Rank is a different thing from power, and to be elevated to the highest place of honor among a few persons is a different thing from embracing the whole world under his dominion." The apostles were indeed given the keys to the kingdom, but "power to bind and to loose can no more be separated from the office of teaching and the apostleship than light or heat can be separated from the sun."[40] Only Christ has "lordship [*dominium; dominatione*]" in the church[41] and he does not bestow the "spiritual government of the church [*spirituali ecclesiae gubernatione*]" on any man such that he might exercise it "according to his own pleasure."[42]

For Calvin the doctrine of Christ's spiritual government by the word was the decisive difference between the Reformed churches and the papacy. "This, then, is the difference. Our opponents locate the authority of the church outside God's word; but we insist that it be attached to the word, and do not allow it to be separated from it" (4.8.13). Rome was a false church because it lacked the fundamental mark of Christ's kingdom, the ministry of the word:

> Where in their church is there a ministry such as Christ's institution requires? . . . I should like to know what one episcopal quality the pontiff himself has. The first task of the bishop's office is to teach the people from God's word. The second and next is to administer the sacraments. The third is to admonish and exhort, also to correct those who sin and to keep the people under holy discipline. What of these offices does he perform? Indeed, what does he even pretend to do? Let them say, therefore, in what way they would have him regarded a bishop, who does not even in pretense touch any part of this office with his little finger (4.7.23).[43]

THE SPIRITUAL GOVERNMENT OF THE CHURCH

The grounding assumption of Calvin's doctrine of the spiritual government of the church is that Jesus Christ is the *sole* head of the church, despite competing papal and magisterial claims to that title. As its only "lord and master [*dominus ac magister*]," "Christ alone must reign [*regnare*] in the church," he has "exclusive authority [*magisterium*] in the church," and he has sole "dominion [*dominium*]." Thus it is intolerable "to rob Christ of the honor of being the sole head of the church,

[40] Commentary on Matthew 16:18 [1555]; CO 45:473–474. Cf. Commentary on 1 Corinthians 9:5 [1546]; CO 49:440.

[41] Commentary on 1 Corinthians 9:5 [1546]; CO 49:440.

[42] Commentary on John 21:15 [1553]; CO 47:452. Cf. 10:10; CO 47:240.

[43] Calvin did not hesitate to charge that the papacy had become the Antichrist itself because it placed itself in opposition to the kingdom of Christ (4.7.26). But Calvin identified the antichrist with a movement rather than a particular person, and he also viewed Nero, Islam, and "all the sects by which the church has been lessened from the beginning" as expressions of it. Commentary on 2 Thessalonians 2:3 [1550]; CO 52:196–197. Cf. 2:4; CO 52:198–199; 2:9; CO 52:202.

the sole teacher, the sole master [*solus sit caput ecclesiae, solus doctor, solus magister*], or to draw away from him any part of that honor, with the view of transferring it to men." To be sure, "There is, it is true, a certain degree of honor that is due to Christ's ministers [*Christi ministris*], and they are also themselves masters [*magistri*] in their own place, but this exception must always be kept in view, that Christ must have without any infringement what belongs to him – that he shall nevertheless be the sole Master [*magister*], and looked upon as such." All faithful ministers "claim for him exclusively power, authority, and glory [*imperium, autoritatem, gloriam*], fight under his banner, obey him alone, and bring others in subjection to his sway [*imperio*]."[44] While Calvin was willing to tolerate the analogous application of terms like "lord" and "father" to human beings, and even to pastors, he would not accept the title of head [*caput*] of the church for anyone but Christ. "I am also well aware of the cavil by which they attempt to escape – that the pope is a ministerial [*ministeriale*] head. The name, however, of head is too august to be rightfully transferred to any mortal man, under any pretext, especially without the command of Christ." For "it is Christ that alone has authority to govern the church [*potestatem habeat regendae ecclesiae*]."[45]

On the other hand, Christ does not govern his church without means. Having taken his place at God's right hand, he now establishes, governs, and grows his kingdom through the ministry of human beings. Calvin's *locus classicus* for this argument – the passage he repeatedly invokes in its defense – is Ephesians 4.[46] The text declares that "There is one body and one Spirit . . . one Lord, one faith, one baptism, one God and Father of all, who is over all and through all and in all" (Ephesians 4:3–6). It then paraphrases Psalm 68's celebration of the messianic king's victory over his enemies, "When he ascended on high he led a host of captives, and he gave gifts to men" (Ephesians 4:8). The writer declares this psalm to have been fulfilled in Christ. Having ascended to heaven, Christ now gives the church a multitude of gifts, the most important of which are "the apostles, the prophets, the evangelists, the pastors and teachers, to equip the saints for the work of ministry,

[44] Commentary on 1 Corinthians 1:12 [1546]; CO 49:316–317. Cf. Commentary on Matthew 23:6–11 [1555]; CO 45:624–626; Commentary on Acts 1:13 [1552]; CO 48:15; 15:16; CO 48:357; *Institutes*, 4.6.9; Harro Höpfl, *The Christian Polity of John Calvin* (Cambridge: Cambridge University Press, 1982), 113.

[45] Commentary on Colossians 1:18 [1548]; CO 52:86–87. Any "supremacy of man [*primatum hominis*] . . . involves sacrilege [*sacrilegum*]." Commentary on 1 Corinthians 3:21 [1546]; CO 49:360. Cf. 4:15; CO 49:373; Commentary on Ephesians 4:15 [1548]; CO 51:202; Commentary on 1 Thessalonians 1:2 [1550]; CO 52:250; Commentary on Titus 1:4 [1550]; CO 52:407; Brian Tierney, *Origins of Papal Infallibility 1150–1350: A Study on the Concepts of Infallibility, Sovereignty and Tradition in the Middle Ages* (Leiden: E. J. Brill, 1972), 146.

[46] See Commentary on John 20:21 [1553]; CO 47:438; Commentary on 1 Timothy 4:15 [1548]; CO 52:303; Commentary on Acts 1:2 [1552]; CO 48:3. Cf. Wilcox, "The Progress of the Kingdom of Christ' in Calvin's Exposition of the Prophets," 318.

for building up the body of Christ, until we all attain to the unity of the faith and of the knowledge of the Son of God, to mature manhood, to the measure of the stature of the fullness of Christ" (Ephesian 4:11–13).

Calvin interprets Ephesians 4 as a description of the way in which God "governs and protects his church, which is by the gospel preached by men,"[47] and he argues that its description of the "government of the church [*ecclesiae regmine*]" was written for the express purpose of "maintaining unity among Christians."[48] Significantly, in his commentary on the passage, Calvin commences his discussion of Christ's spiritual government of the church only after first distinguishing the "universal government [*universali gubernatione*]" of God, by which he "upholds, and maintains, and rules, all things," from that "spiritual one, which belongs to the church [*spirituali tantum, quae ad ecclesiam pertinet*]," by which God graciously draws human beings to himself.[49] He returns to this distinction when he considers the effect of Christ's ascension to God's right hand. He explains, "by his ascension into heaven, Christ entered into the possession of the authority given to him by the Father, that he might rule and govern [*regat . . . moderetur*] all things." Indeed, he now "fills all thing by the power of his Spirit."[50] Still, Christ has not yet brought that rule over all things to the sort of fulfillment that would turn his enemies into voluntary subjects. He therefore rules in two distinct ways. Where his kingdom has not been fully established he binds his enemies with "chains of iron" and restrains them from "exerting their fury beyond the limits which he shall assign."[51] Where voluntary obedience has been rendered, on the other hand, Christ has established his "glorious reign over the church [*glorioso imperio ecclesiam*]." It is this government that is administered through the gifts described in Ephesians 4. This "government of the church [*regimen ecclesiae*], by the ministry of the word, is not a contrivance of men, but an appointment made by the Son of God."[52]

In contrast to Rome, which insisted that Christ is present in the church through the Mass, and in contrast to Luther, who claimed that Christ is physically omnipresent, Calvin argued that by virtue of his ascension Christ is physically absent

---

[47] Commentary on Ephesians, Introduction [1548]; CO 51:143.

[48] Commentary on Ephesians 4:1 [1548]; CO 51:189. Cf. 4:4; CO 51:190–191.

[49] Calvin admits that when Ephesians declares the one God to be over all and through all and in all it is true "in a general sense, not only of all men but of all creatures," but he stresses that in context Paul is clearly talking about the body of believers. "To this relation we must limit what is said about God's government [*imperio*] and presence." Commentary on Ephesians 4:6 [1548]; CO 51:192. Cf. 1:23; CO 51:160).

[50] Commentary on Ephesians 4:10 [1548]; CO 51:195–196. Cf. Torrance, *Kingdom and Church*, 162.

[51] Commentary on Ephesians 4:8 [1548]; CO 51:193–194. Cf. Commentary on Galatians 1:1 [1548]; CO 50:169.

[52] Commentary on Ephesians 4:11 [1548]; CO 51:196–197.

from believers. How then could he promise to be with his church until the end of the age? Calvin answers that Christ is present by his word and Spirit, that is, through the ministry of the church.

> Christ, he says, is present with us. How? By the ministry of men, whom he has set over the governing of the church. Why not, rather, through the ministerial head, to whom he has entrusted his functions? Paul mentions unity, but in God and in faith in Christ. To men he assigns nothing but the common ministry, and a particular mode to each. Why did he, in that commendation of unity, after he had mentioned "one body, one Spirit, . . . one hope of calling, one God, one faith, one baptism", not immediately also add, one supreme pontiff, to keep the church in unity? For nothing more appropriate could have been said, if indeed it had been an actual fact. Let that passage be diligently pondered. No doubt Paul deeply meant to represent here the sacred and spiritual government of the church [*sacrum et spirituale ecclesiae regimen*], which his successors have called "hierarchy." He not only lays down no monarchy among the ministers but also points out that there is none. No doubt Paul meant to express the manner of connection, by which believers cleave to Christ, the Head. There he not only mentions no ministerial head, but assigns particular functions to each member, according to the measure of grace bestowed upon each (4.6.10).[53]

Although Christ has ascended to heaven in order that he might fill all things, this process is only fulfilled when "through the ministers to whom he has entrusted this office and has conferred the grace to carry it out, he dispenses and distributes his gifts to the church; and he shows himself as though present by manifesting the power of his Spirit in this his institution" (4.3.2). The ministry, then, is not only the "mode of governing and keeping the church." It is nothing less than "the administration of the Spirit and of righteousness and of eternal life" (4.3.3). When Jesus said that the Spirit would come to judge the world, "he notes no other kind of authority than that which he exercises by the ministry of the church."[54] The word has been committed to the church "like a scepter," and it can be said that "by the word the pastors of the church exercise the jurisdiction of the Holy Spirit [*iurisdictionem spiritus*]."[55]

In his discussion of the five offices mentioned in Ephesians 4, Calvin makes two crucial points. First, he argues that the offices of apostle, prophet, and evangelist were temporary offices designed for the unique circumstances of the apostolic

---

[53] Cf. Commentary on Ephesians 4:11 [1548]; CO 51:198; 4:13; CO 51:199–200; Commentary on Matthew 18:20 [1555]; CO 45:517; Commentary on Acts 1:2 [1552]; CO 48:3.

[54] Commentary on Acts 5:9 [1552]; CO 48:102. Cf. Commentary on John 12:48 [1553]; CO 47:303–304.

[55] Commentary on Psalm 47:3 [1557]; CO 31:467–468. Calvin writes, "how Christ designs to rule in his Church, we know, for the scepter of his kingdom is the gospel." For "when we believe the gospel we choose Christ for our king, as it were, by a voluntary consent." Commentary on Hosea 1:11 [1557]; CO 42:221. Cf. Commentary on Micah 2:7 [1559]; CO 43:307–308; Commentary on Ezekiel 17:24 [1565]; CO 40:420–421.

age (4.3.4). The offices of pastor and teacher, on the other hand, are permanent. Second, he argues that "pastors ... have the same charge as the apostles" (4.3.5). That charge is to "raise up" and "establish his Kingdom everywhere by the preaching of the gospel," or to put it another way, "as the first builders of the church, to lay its foundations in all the world" (4.3.4).[56] At first glance it is hard to see what substantive exegetical basis might justify these concrete conclusions. But as McKee observes, Calvin's method is not to determine the specific offices that Christ has appointed for the church and then to determine from scripture the nature and function of those offices.[57] Rather, his method is to identify specific functions that Christ has appointed, by virtue of the gifts he has given, and then to identify offices responsible for performing those functions. What the five offices have in common is that they pertain to the "external ministry [*externum verbi ministerium*] of the word." "This is the arrangement by which the Lord is pleased to govern his church [*ecclesiam ... gubernare*], to maintain its existence, and ultimately to secure its highest perfection."[58] The point is not that Christ governs his church through particular offices, but that Christ governs his church through the function of the proclamation of his word, which is carried out by pastors.

The work of pastors, therefore, is nothing less than "the edification of the church, the everlasting salvation of souls, the restoration [*reparatio*] of the world, and, in fine, the kingdom of God and Christ."[59] Through preaching and teaching, faithful pastors "renovate the world, as if God formed heaven and earth anew by their hand."[60]

Christ could expand and govern his kingdom immediately through the Holy Spirit if he chose to do so; in this case, only the "invisible church," the body of the elect (4.1.2–3), could truly be identified with Christ's spiritual kingdom. But Christ has determined to govern through the "instrumentality" of men, by "the external ministry of the word [*externo verbi ministerio*]," through "outward preaching [*externam praedicationem*]." As a result, "We must allow ourselves to be ruled [*regi*] and taught by men." Calvin's emphasis on the importance of the visible church can sound Catholic to some Protestant ears. The reformer approvingly affirms the

---

[56] Cf. Commentary on Ephesians 4:11 [1548]; CO 51:197.
[57] Elsie Anne McKee, *Elders and the Plural Ministry: The Role of Exegetical History in Illuminating John Calvin's Theology* (Geneva: Librairie Droz, 1988), 155–165. McKee offers an excellent analysis of Calvin's interpretation of Ephesians 4 in the context of the historical exegesis of the passage. See also Niesel, *The Theology of Calvin*, 201–203; Wendel, *Calvin*, 305.
[58] Commentary on Ephesians 4:11 [1548]; CO 51:196.
[59] Commentary on 1 Thessalonians 5:12 [1550]; CO 52:172 (Cf. 2:19; CO 52:155). Cf. Commentary on 1 Corinthians 4:8 [1546]; CO 49:368; 3:8; CO 49:351–352; 4:3, 15; CO 49:363, 373.
[60] Commentary on Isaiah 51:16 [1559]; CO 37:237. Women should take no offense that they are prohibited from occupying the pastoral office because most men are prohibited as well. Commentary on 1 Timothy 3:1 [1548]; CO 52:280.

fathers' tendency to refer to the visible church as our "mother." "The church is the common mother of all the godly, which bears, nourishes, and brings up children to God, kings and peasants alike, and this is done by the ministry."[61] In the *Institutes*, he goes so far as to insist that "there is no other way to enter into life unless this mother conceive us in her womb, give us birth, nourish us at her breast . . . [A]way from her bosom one cannot hope for any forgiveness of sins or any salvation" (4.1.4). Only in the visible church do those people gather who have voluntarily subjected themselves to Christ's lordship. "For the Lord esteems the communion of his church so highly that he counts as a traitor and apostate from Christianity anyone who arrogantly leaves any Christian society, provided it cherishes the true ministry of word and sacraments" (4.1.10).[62]

It is important to note, however, that for Calvin the ministry of the word does not consist in preaching alone. The ministry of the word involves three major tasks: "to instruct the people to true godliness, to administer the sacred mysteries and to keep and exercise upright discipline." Calvin identified only the preaching of the word and the administration of the sacraments as the marks of a true church, but he viewed discipline as an extension of the ministry of the word, essential to the church's health, if not its existence (4.3.6).[63]

Nor are the offices of pastor and teacher the only permanent ecclesiastical offices. In *Institutes* 4.3, Calvin introduces the office of elder, with the function of church discipline, and the office of deacon, with the function of care for the poor, and when he refers to the ministers of the church, he often has these offices in mind as well. In his discussion of ordination, he points out that the early church used the rite of the laying on of hands "whenever they called anyone to the ministry of the church. In this way they consecrated the pastors and teachers, and the deacons" (4.3.16).[64] In 4.4 Calvin describes the elders and deacons (including an order of women) as ministers of the church according to the "order of church government" established

---

[61] Commentary on Ephesians 4:12 [1548]; CO 51:199. Calvin discussion of the invisible church is remarkably brief, and he quickly calls his readers to focus their attention on the visible church (4.1.1–3).

[62] Calvin lambasts the "apostates who have a passion for splitting churches" (4.1.5). Cf. Commentary on 1 Timothy 3:15 [1548]; CO 52:288–289.

[63] The pastoral office includes "discipline, or administering the sacraments, or warnings and exhortations" (4.3.4). In his commentary on 1 Corinthians 4:1, which declares the apostles to be "stewards of the mysteries of God," Calvin argues that "the sacraments are connected with these mysteries as appendages." Commentary on 1 Corinthians 4:1 [1546]; CO 49:68. Cf. Commentary on Titus 1:5 [1550]; CO 52:408; Sermon on Deuteronomy 17:14–18; CO 27:466. Cited in Van't Spijker, "The Kingdom of Christ According to Bucer and Calvin," 120.

[64] Calvin seems to have thought that the appointment of elders does not require the laying on of hands. See McKee, *Elders and the Plural Ministry*, 29. When noting the qualifications for bishops in Titus 1:7 and 1 Timothy 3:1–7, he notes that "the very same requirements apply to deacons and presbyters" (4.3.12).

by Christ in his word. "We have stated that Scripture sets before us three kinds of ministers ... For from the order of presbyters (1) part were chosen pastors and teachers; (2) the remaining part were charged with the censure and correction of morals; (3) the care of the poor and the distribution of alms were committed to the deacons" (4.4.1).[65]

In 4.8, furthermore, Calvin describes teaching as only one of the three main parts of the "power of the church [*ecclesiae potestate*]," the other two being the church's powers of discipline and of making laws. In introducing these other types of power he makes it clear that he is still discussing Christ's spiritual government of his church: "I speak only of the spiritual power [*spirituali ... potestate*], which is proper to the church [*propria est ecclesiae*]." Calvin then divides this power, as he did in 4.1, into the three parts of "doctrine," "jurisdiction [*iurisdictione*]" (discipline), and "making laws [*legibus ferendis*]" (concerning worship). He divides the church's power over doctrine into two parts, "authority [*autoritatem*] to lay down articles of faith, and authority to explain them" (4.8.1). I will discuss each of these three types of spiritual power in turn, addressing the offices of elder and deacon under the categories of discipline and making laws respectively.[66]

DOCTRINE

In the *Institutes*, Calvin summarizes the nature of the ministry of the word as follows:

> Now we must speak of the order by which the Lord willed his church to be governed. He alone should rule and reign in the church as well as have authority or pre-eminence in it, and this authority should be exercised and administered by his word alone. Nevertheless, because he does not dwell among us in visible presence, we have said that he uses the ministry of men to declare openly his will to us by mouth, as a sort of delegated work, not by transferring to them his right and honor, but only that through their mouths he may do his own work – just as a workman uses a tool to do his work (4.3.1).[67]

---

[65] All four offices share the purpose of "proclaiming Christ and His reign." Niesel, *The Theology of Calvin*, 200.

[66] Calvin did not place the diaconate in this category, but since the diaconate raises many of the same questions as arise under the power to make laws, it makes sense to discuss it in the same context.

[67] On Calvin's concept of the pastorate see Scott M. Manetsch, *Calvin's Company of Pastors: Pastoral Care and the Emerging Reformed Church, 1536–1609* (New York: Oxford University Press, 2013). Cf. Elsie Anne McKee, "Calvin and His Colleagues as Pastors: Some New Insights into the Collegial Ministry of Word and Sacraments," *Calvinus Praeceptor Ecclesiae: Papers of the International Congress on Calvin Research, Princeton, August 20–24, 2002* (ed. Herman J. Selderhuis; Geneva: Droz, 2004), 9–42, as well as the essays in *Calvin and the Company of Pastors: Papers Presented at the 14th Colloquium of the Calvin Studies Society May 22–24, 2003* (ed. David Foxgrover; Grand Rapids: CRC Product Services, 2004.

Throughout his commentary on Isaiah Calvin describes the preaching of the gospel as "the spiritual scepter of Christ." Thus "no man can bow down submissively before Christ without also obeying the church," even as "Christ their Head alone reigns, and alone exercises his authority."[68] Of faithful ministers he writes, "Christ acts by them in such a manner that he wishes their mouth to be reckoned as his mouth, and their lips as his lips; that is, when they speak from his mouth and faithfully declare his word."

> Here we must again call to remembrance what is the nature of Christ's kingdom. As he does not wear a golden crown or employ earthly armor, so he does not rule over the world by the power of arms, or gain authority by gaudy and ostentatious display, or constrain his people by terror and dread, but the doctrine of the gospel is his royal banner, which assembles believers under his dominion. Wherever, therefore, the doctrine of the Gospel is preached in purity, there we are certain that Christ reigns, and where it is rejected, his government is also set aside.[69]

The implications for the doctrine of church government are significant.

Like Rome, Calvin took seriously the passages in which Christ promises his disciples the keys of the kingdom, identifying pastors as "porters, so to speak, of the kingdom of heaven, because they carry its keys."[70] When the people hear the pastor proclaim the forgiveness of sins, they "may not less highly value the reconciliation which is offered by the voice of men than if God himself stretched out his hand from heaven."[71] Pastors are therefore to be received and heard as speaking with the voice and authority of Christ himself. "[H]e wishes that God should be heard speaking by them."[72] Even if a pastor has come from the "lowest dregs of the people," nevertheless, Christians must "hear him ... in the same manner as if he were descending from heaven or making known his will to us by angels."[73]

On the other hand, Calvin insists that the church may not teach anything beyond what is found in the word of God. Only if pastors restrain themselves to teaching Christ's word can their government be said to be his government. Thus "teachers are his ministers in such a manner that he ought to be heard in them," and "they are

---

[68] Commentary on Isaiah 45:14 [1559]; CO 37:140–141. Cf. Commentary on Obadiah 1:21 [1559]; CO 43:200.

[69] Commentary on Isaiah 11:4 [1559]; CO 36:240. Cf. 51:4; CO 37:229; Commentary on 1 Corinthians 1:18 [1546]; CO 49:321; Commentary on John 7:48 [1553]; CO 47:185–186.

[70] Commentary on Matthew 16:19 [1555]; CO 45:474–475. Cf. Commentary on Matthew 23:13 [1555]; CO 45:627–628.

[71] Commentary on John 20:23 [1553]; CO 47:440–442. Cf. Commentary on Exodus 14:31 [1563]; CO 24:156.

[72] Commentary on John 10:4 [1553]; CO 47:237. Cf. Commentary on Psalm 2:7 [1557]; CO 31:46; Commentary on Haggai 1:12 [1559]; CO 44:93–95.

[73] Commentary on Luke 10:16 [1555]; CO 45:314.

masters under him [only] so far as they represent his person." His authority remains supreme. "Thus he is the only Pastor; but yet he admits many pastors under him, provided that he hold the preeminence over them all, and that by them he alone govern the Church."[74]

One of Calvin's favorite analogies for the function of a pastor is that of the "ambassador" of reconciliation. When a minister proclaims the gospel "he is to be listened to just as an ambassador of God [*Dei legatus*]." He sustains "a public [*publicam*] character" and is furnished with "rightful authority [*autoritate*]."[75] But his task is simply to "enforce by arguments what he brings forward in the name of his prince."[76] Thus Christ "alone is endowed with authority [*autoritate*] to rule [*regendos*] us by his word." Ministers are appointed with the sole mission of communicating that word, and "not that they should exercise dominion [*dominationem*] over our consciences."[77] Ministers may not rule in an "authoritative manner in the church [*imperio ecclesiae regimini*], but are subject to Christ's authority [*Christi imperio subesse*]." They are "servants, not masters [*ministros, non dominos*]."[78] Thus the church's authority is *ministerial* rather than *magisterial*, spiritual, rather than political. Pastors "have no external power, and exercise no civil government."[79] Pastors do not possess a "worldly stewardship [*profana villicatione*]" but are "faithfully to deliver to others, as from hand to hand, the doctrine received from God."[80] Indeed, they have no personal authority at all, nor does their office, in and of itself. Power is given "not to the men personally, but to the ministry to which they have been appointed; or (to speak more briefly) to the word" (4.8.2). "The power of the church, therefore, is not infinite but subject to the Lord's word and, as it were, enclosed within it" (4.8.4).[81]

---

[74] Commentary on Matthew 23:6 [1555]; CO 45:624.

[75] Commentary on 2 Corinthians 5:18 [1548]; CO 50:70–71.

[76] Commentary on 2 Corinthians 6:1 [1548]; CO 50:75. Cf. Commentary on 2 Timothy 1:11 [1548]; CO 52:354; Commentary on John 20:21 [1553]; CO 47:438; Commentary on Matthew 16:19 [1555]; CO 45:476.

[77] Commentary on 1 Corinthians 3:22 [1546]; CO 49:361.

[78] Commentary on 1 Corinthians 4:1 [1546]; CO 49:362. "[T]here is no spiritual dominion [*dominium spirituale*] except that of God only." "[P]astors have no peculiar dominion [*imperium*; French: *jurisdiction*] over men's consciences inasmuch as they are ministers, not lords." Commentary on 2 Corinthians 1:24 [1548]; CO 50:25–26. Cf. 2:14; CO 50:33; 4:5; CO 50:52; Commentary on 1 Peter 5:1–4 [1551]; CO 55:284.

[79] Commentary on Isaiah 11:6 [1559]; CO 36:242. Cf. Torrance, *Kingdom and Church*, 154.

[80] Commentary on 1 Peter 4:11 [1551]; CO 55:276–277. Cf. Commentary on Jeremiah 14:14 [1563]; CO 38:193.

[81] "[T]he whole power [*potestas*] of ministers is included in the word – but in such a way, nevertheless, that Christ may always remain lord and master [*dominus . . . magister*]." Commentary on 2 Corinthians 10:8 [1548]; CO 50:118. Cf. Commentary on Titus 1:9 [1550]; CO 52:412; Commentary on 1 Thessalonians 5:12 [1550]; CO 52:172; Commentary on 1 Peter 2:7 [1551]; CO 55:238; Commentary on 1 Corinthians 3:17 [1546]; CO 49:358.

One of the crucial implications of this point for Calvin is that pastors have no right to use the pulpit or pastoral office to promulgate their own agenda. "The power of the church is . . . to be kept within definite limits, that it may not be drawn hither and thither according to men's whim" (4.8.1). Ministers "may not mix any of their own fictions with his pure doctrine."[82] The upshot is that the church is constantly called to make judgments regarding whether or not what a pastor teaches comes from the word. Christians "are at liberty to withhold our assent to their doctrine until they show that it is from Christ."[83] No teacher is beyond scrutiny. Calvin was aware that this caveat might threaten to undermine the teaching authority of pastors: "If everyone has the right and the liberty to judge, nothing can be settled as certain, but on the contrary the whole of religion will be uncertain." He therefore identifies two levels at which such judgment must take place, the first at the level of the individual hearer, a "private trial," the second at the level of the church as a whole, a "public trial." Both an individual conscience and a church council might err, but the Spirit will not abandon the church as long as it genuinely seeks to submit to the teaching of the word, which always remains the final authority.[84]

In addition to the distinction between the pastor and the word of God, Calvin insists on an equally important distinction between the word and the Spirit. For, as the Genevan reformer recognized, to say that the human proclamation of the word is *always* effective through the work of the Holy Spirit is to place the Spirit under human control. In 1559 Calvin added a section to the *Institutes* acknowledging that "there has been great controversy over the efficacy of the ministry. Some exaggerate its dignity beyond measure. Others contend that what belongs to the Holy Spirit is wrongly transferred to mortal men – if we suppose that ministers and teachers penetrate into minds and hearts and so correct both blindness of mind and hardness of heart" (4.1.6).

---

[82] Commentary on Jeremiah 1:9 [1563]; CO 37:479–483. "If . . . a prophet mingles anything of his own, he is proved to be false and is not worthy of any credit" (14:14; CO 38:193. Cf. Commentary on Matthew 28:20 [1555]; CO 45:825–826; Commentary on Ezekiel 3:16–17 [1565]; CO 40:90; Commentary on John 3:29 [1553]; CO 47:71.

[83] Commentary on 1 Corinthians 3:22 [1546]; CO 49:361. Cf. 4:3; CO 49:363.

[84] Commentary on 1 John 4:1 [1551]; CO 55:347–348. Calvin chronicles example after example from scripture of cases in which church councils erred (4.9.8). Calvin even questions the distinction between the clergy and the laity. "It was, indeed, an ancient way of speaking to call the whole order of ministers clergy, but I wish that it had never occurred to the fathers to speak thus, for what Scripture ascribes in common to the whole church it was by no means right to confine to a few men." Commentary on 1 Peter 5:3 [1551]; CO 55:286. Cf. *Institutes*, 4.10.7; Wendel, *Calvin*, 304; Höpfl, *The Christian Polity of John Calvin*, 97–98. Calvin agreed, at least in principle, that the liberty of the Spirit is not limited to those ordained to the pastoral office, for "the one Spirit [must] be listened to by whatever mouth he speaks." Commentary on 1 Corinthians 14:30 [1546]; CO 49:529–530. Cf. 14:32; CO 49:531. Of course, Calvin insisted that pastors must be called and ordained by the church. Willem Balke, *Calvin and the Anabaptist Radicals* (trans. Willem Heyner. Grand Rapids: Eerdmans, 1981), 160–165.

To address this controversy, Calvin suggests that scripture describes the phenomena in two different ways that reflect opposite sides of the same coin. "God sometimes connects himself with his servants and sometimes separates himself from them. When he connects himself with them he transfers to them what never ceases to dwell in him, for he never resigns to them his own office, but makes them partakers of it only ... But when God separates himself from his ministers nothing remains in them."[85] In the first set of passages scripture "furnishes him ... with the efficacy of the Holy Spirit" for "raising up the kingdom of Christ."[86] God is described as working through pastors as instruments or "organs of the Holy Spirit [*spiritus sancti organa*]."[87] In another set of passages, God is described as accomplishing this work as if the means of preaching was entirely irrelevant. Here the pastor is described as "a servant, not a master – an instrument, not the hand, and in short as man, not God. Viewed in that aspect he leaves him nothing but his labor, and that too, dead and powerless, if the Lord does not make it efficacious by the Spirit."[88]

Both perspectives, Calvin maintains, are important. It is by the word and Spirit joined together that the kingdom is established.[89] "God has therefore two ways of teaching, for first he sounds in our ears by the mouth of men, and secondly he addresses us inwardly by his Spirit, and he does this either at the same moment or at different times, as he thinks fit."[90] Divine and human agency, the "inward calling" of the Spirit and the "outward voice" of men, are two parts of one act.[91] God is the "efficient cause" while human preaching is the "instrument."[92] The preaching of the word can therefore be compared to the sacraments. God promises to work through them, but the power that operates in them must be distinguished from the outward

[85] Commentary on Malachi 4:6 [1559]; CO 44:497.

[86] Commentary on 1 Corinthians 3:7 [1546]; CO 49:350–351. Pastors "are rightly called the vicars of God who purely and faithfully teach from his mouth." Commentary on Zechariah 3:6–7 [1559]; CO 44: 172–176. Cf. Commentary on 2 Corinthians 4:6 [1548]; CO 50:53; Commentary on Joel 1:1–4 [1559]; CO 42:517–518.

[87] Commentary on Micah 2:7 [1559]; CO 43:307–308. Teaching is the "organ [*organum*]" of the Holy Spirit." God uses pastors as "instruments [*instrumenta*]." CO 49:349. Commentary on 1 Corinthians 3:5 [1546]; CO 49:349. Cf. 3:9; CO 49:352; 9:1; CO 49:437–438; Commentary on John 15:16 [1553]; CO 47:348; Commentary on 1 John 4:1 [1551]; CO 55:347–348; Commentary on Deuteronomy 18:17 [1563]; CO 24:274.

[88] Commentary on 1 Corinthians 3:7 [1546]; CO 49:350–351. Cf. 2:5; CO 49:335–336; Commentary on Hebrews 3:3 [1549]; CO 52:37; Commentary on John 20:22 [1553]; CO 47:438; Commentary on Romans 10:17 [1556]; CO 49:206; Commentary on Acts 20:28 [1554]; CO 48:468.

[89] The "bare voice" must be joined with the "inward power of the Spirit ... in order that the kingdom of God may be established." Commentary on Matthew 6:10 [1555]; CO 45:197–198. Cf. *Institutes*, 3.20.42.

[90] Commentary on John 14:26 [1553]; CO 47:334–335. Cf. *Institutes*, 4.1.6.

[91] Commentary on Romans 10:16 [1556]; CO 49:206. God renders "outward doctrine" an "efficacious instrument" only when it is united with the "secret influence of his Spirit." Commentary on Luke 1:16 [1555]; CO 45:16. Cf. Commentary on John 12:13 [1553]; 47:282–284.

[92] Commentary on 1 Corinthians 9:1 [1546]; CO 49:437–438. Cf. 2:5; CO 49:335–336; 1:17; CO 49:319–322.

means.[93] Calvin clarifies the spiritual nature of the ministry in a comment on 2 Corinthians 3:6.

> When Paul ... calls himself a minister of the Spirit, he does not mean by this that the grace of the Holy Spirit and his influence were tied to his preaching, so that he could, whenever he pleased, breath forth the Spirit along with the utterance of the voice. He simply means that Christ blessed his ministry and thus accomplished what was predicted respecting the gospel. It is one thing for Christ to connect his influence with a man's doctrine and quite another for the man's doctrine to have such efficacy of itself. We are, then, ministers of the Spirit, not as if we held him enclosed within us, or as it were captive – not as if we could at our pleasure confer his grace upon all or upon whom we pleased – but because Christ, through our instrumentality, illuminates the minds of men, renews their hearts, and in short, regenerates them wholly. It is in consequence of their being such a connection and bond of union between Christ's grace and man's effort that in many cases that is ascribed to the minister which belongs exclusively to the Lord.[94]

The presence of the Spirit in the faithful ministry of the word means that the ministry is itself spiritual. Calvin does not view the word and sacraments as mere masks (*"larva dei"*) of *inward* means of grace, but as effective means of grace (*"vera facies"*).[95] Calvin makes this point explicitly in his commentary on 1 Corinthians 4:20. Contrasting outward tools of eloquence and rhetoric, which he compares to a "body," and the inward power of faithful preaching, which is like a "soul," he points out that God "would not have us rest in outward masks [*externis larvis*], but depend solely on the internal power of the Holy Spirit [*internae ... spiritus sancti virtuti*]." The contrast intended here is not between the outward means of preaching and the inward work of the Spirit, but between the inefficacy of mere outward rhetoric and the spiritual power of faithful inwardly empowered preaching. "We have already seen that *the preaching of the gospel* is of such a nature, that it *is inwardly replete with a kind of solid majesty.* This majesty shows itself when *a minister strives by means of power rather than of speech,* that is, when he does not place confidence in his own intellect or eloquence, but, furnished with spiritual armor, ... he applies himself diligently to the Lord's work."[96] Calvin warns against those "fanatics," "libertines, and other furies of that stamp," who dismiss preaching as merely an outward work.[97]

---

[93] Commentary on 1 Corinthians 3:7 [1546]; CO 49:350–351. Cf. Milner, *Calvin's Doctrine of the Church*, 190.

[94] Commentary on 2 Corinthians 3:6 [1548]; CO 50:40.

[95] Torrance, *Kingdom and Church*, 149–150.

[96] Commentary on 1 Corinthians 4:20 [1546]; CO 49:376. Emphasis added.

[97] Commentary on 1 Thessalonians 5:20 [1550]; CO 52:176. Cf. Commentary on Isaiah 59:21 [1559]; CO 37:352.

[D]elirious and even dangerous are those notions that though the internal word is efficacious, yet that which proceeds from the mouth of man is lifeless and destitute of all power. I indeed admit that the power does not proceed from the tongue of man, nor exists in mere sound, but that the whole power is to be ascribed altogether to the Holy Spirit. There is, however, nothing in this to hinder the Spirit from putting forth his power in the word preached.[98]

The power of God consists in "vocal preaching."[99]

Understood in these terms, the faithful preaching of the word possesses authority superior to that of any political government.

Here, then, is the sovereign power with which the pastors of the church, by whatever name they be called, ought to be endowed. That is that they may dare boldly to do all things by God's word; may compel all worldly power, glory, wisdom, and exaltation to yield to and obey his majesty; supported by his power, may command all from the highest even to the last ... but do all things [only] in God's word (4.8.9).

Pastors are in the same position as the prophets of old, whom God set "over nations and kingdoms, to pluck up and to root out, to destroy and to overthrow, to build and to plant" (Jeremiah 1:9–10) (4.8.3). Their task is to "reduce the world to order," and "even kings are not excepted" from their authority.[100] When Jeremiah "had to exercise his spiritual jurisdiction [*spiritualis jurisdictio*] in God's name, he spared not the king nor his counselors, for he knew that his doctrine was above all kings."[101] The temptation for most teachers, Calvin believed, is to flatter kings and princes.[102] Yet God's commission to Jeremiah should give them courage. "Whatever ... is precious and excellent in the world must come to nothing if it derogates even in the least degree from the glory of God or from the authority of his truth."[103] Thus "all who are chosen to the office of teaching cannot faithfully discharge their duty except

---

[98] Commentary on Hebrews 4:12 [1549]; CO 55:51.

[99] Commentary on Romans 1:16 [1556]; CO 49:19–20. God regenerates by "human means" (10:17; CO 49:206).

[100] Commentary on Jeremiah 1:9 [1563]; CO 37:479–483. Cf. William R. Stevenson, Jr., *Sovereign Grace: The Place and Significance of Christian Freedom in John Calvin's Political Thought* (New York: Oxford University Press, 1999), 91–92.

[101] Commentary on Jeremiah 27:12 [1563]; CO 38:552. Cf. Commentary on 2 Corinthians 4:5 [1548]; CO 50:52; Commentary on Micah 3:9–10 [1559]; 43:332; Commentary on Haggai 1:1 [1559]; CO 44:83; 1:13–14; CO 44:96; Commentary on Isaiah 39:5 [1559]; CO 36:668–669.

[102] Some preachers are content to leave politics alone "provided such liberality towards their order be ever continued." Commentary on Micah 3:5 [1559]; CO 43:324. But they are "not to wink at the faults of princes, so as to purchase their favor at this price, however advantageous that favor might appear to be to the public interests." Commentary on Matthew 14:5 [1555]; CO 45:432. Cf. Commentary on Jeremiah 15:19 [1563]; CO 38:234–235; 36:16, 20–21; CO 39:125–126, 127.

[103] Commentary on Jeremiah 13:12–14 [1563]; CO 38:160–161.

they boldly and with intrepid spirit dare to reprove both kings and queens; for the word of God is not to be restricted to the common people or men in humble life, but it subjects to itself all, from the least to the greatest."[104]

Although Calvin thus gives pastors authority over magistrates, he is quick to remind his readers that the authority of teachers is spiritual, not political, and therefore does not diminish in the slightest the political authority of magistrates. Every single proclamation, warning, and exhortation must be derived from the word.[105] Jeremiah held a public office as God's prophet, "but as to the government of the city he was a private individual, one of the people."[106] Where pastors claim authority beyond the word in civil matters princes need not take them seriously.

> [W]hosoever claims such a power must necessarily bring forth the word of God, and really prove that he is a prophet and that he introduces no fictions of his own. And hence we see how fatuitous is the boasting of the pope and of his filthy clergy, when they wickedly dare to appropriate to themselves what is here said. "We are," they say, "above both kings and nations." . . . Now let the pope show that he is furnished with the word of God, that he claims for himself nothing that is his own, or apart from God, in a word, that he introduces nothing of his own devices, and we shall willingly allow that he is preeminent above the whole world. For God is not to be separated from his word.[107]

No heed need be paid to pastors whose preaching reflects their own private or political agenda rather than the clear teaching of scripture. The pastoral office must be free of politicization for the sake of its own credibility.

> [I]f they quarrel with this or that man about worldly things, then it cannot be but that the word of God will be evil spoken of through their fault. Hence great care ought to be taken that those who sustain the office of public teaching should not engage in worldly business and be thus exposed to the necessity of contending about worldly things. They have enough to do, and more than enough, in the warfare in which the Lord has engaged them.[108]

Thus pastors should avoid using their authority to address specific details of policy. For instance, although magistrates are to be called to collect and use revenues justly and in accord with the welfare of the whole people (4.20.13), "it does not belong to us

---

[104] Commentary on Jeremiah 13:18 [1563]; CO 38:167. Cf. 34:21; CO 39:98.
[105] Cf. Commentary on Jeremiah 36:29–30 [1563]; CO 39:134. Cf. Balke, *Calvin and the Anabaptist Radicals*, 259.
[106] Commentary on Jeremiah 38:1–4 [1563]; CO 39:156–160.
[107] Commentary on Jeremiah 1:9 [1563]; CO 37:479–483. Cf. 27:12; CO 38:552.
[108] Commentary on Jeremiah 15:10 [1563]; CO 38:219.

[ministers or subjects] either to prescribe to princes how much they ought to expend in every affair or to call them to account."[109] As he put it in a sermon on 1 Samuel,

> The gospel is not to change the administration [*polices*] of the world and to make laws which pertain to the temporal state. It is very true that kings, princes, and magistrates ought always to consult the mouth of God and to conform themselves to his word, but our Lord has given them liberty to make the laws which they know to be proper and useful by the rule which is committed to them.[110]

It is true, as Graham points out, that in Geneva the pastors did try to "influence the making and enforcing of good laws." It is also true that today Christians might disagree with Calvin and his contemporaries regarding the way in which scriptural principles of piety, charity, or justice should be applied to particular political or economic matters.[111] Still, Calvin believed that what pastors preach must come from scripture as properly interpreted in light of the work of Christ and the analogy of faith. What was appropriate for Jeremiah to say to the leaders of his time may not be what is appropriate for pastors to say in another time, for "the present order differs very much from what existed in former times" (4.8.5). Even the prophet Daniel, when he addressed the Babylonian King Nebuchadnezzar, "treats the profane king more indulgently than if he had addressed his own nation." Daniel spoke prophetically, but "because he knew the king did not hold the first rudiments of piety, he here undertakes only the office of a counselor, since he was not an ordinary teacher." Daniel tempered his words with the awareness that the king was being gracious in giving him an opportunity to speak.[112] As I show in Chapters 6 and 9, Calvin rejected the notion that the Old Testament civil law is normative for modern nations, and he likewise rejected the claim that civil government should enforce the full rigor of the moral law. Such limitations on the way in which scripture can be applied to politics

---

[109] Commentary on Romans 13:6 [1556]; CO 49:252. Cf. Commentary on 1 Timothy 2:9 [1549]; CO 52:275. Chenevière rightly extends the point to the church's political engagement. For Calvin, "The Church should not even occupy itself actively with accessory questions, social or otherwise, which belong to the domain of the State, and which can only hinder the accomplishment of its Divine mission." Marc Chenevière, "Did Calvin Advocate Theocracy?" *Evangelical Quarterly* 9 (1937): 160–168, 163. This is in sharp contrast to the view of Biéler, who claims that Calvin called the church "to receive constantly afresh the enduring teaching of the Word of God, to examine repeatedly afresh the real nature of economic, political and social institutions in which it exists, and to invent freshly produced responses in order to adapt the teaching to that reality and so to display its moral faithfulness and its obedience through practical activities." André Biéler, *Calvin's Economic and Social Thought* (ed. Edward Dommen; trans. James Greig; Geneva: World Alliance of Reformed Churches, 2005 [1961]), 456.

[110] Sermon on 1 Samuel 42; CO 51:797. Cited in W. Fred Graham, *The Constructive Revolutionary: John Calvin and His Socio-Economic Impact* (Richmond, VA: John Knox Press, 1971), 158–159.

[111] Graham, *The Constructive Revolutionary*, 161. Yet Graham exaggerates the degree to which Calvin thought that the church and its pastors should involve themselves politically.

[112] Commentary on Daniel 4:27 [1561]; CO 40:672–675.

must necessarily limit what pastors should proclaim as the authoritative will of God for policy. They must apply scripture with sensitivity to its context, taking seriously the distinction between the two kingdoms and the complexities of politics.

DISCIPLINE

It is often pointed out that in contrast to much of the Reformed tradition, Calvin did not make church discipline a mark of the church.[113] Calvin argued that where the word is faithfully preached and the sacraments administered, there a true church exists, "even if it otherwise swarms with many faults." Even doctrine and the sacraments may be somewhat corrupted, but as long as what is essential is maintained, there is no justification for schism over "nonessential matters [*rebus istis non ita necessariis*]" (4.1.12). Calvin identified the refusal to see a true church where discipline is lacking with the Anabaptists, whom he in turn associated with the Donatists.[114] "When they do not see a quality of life corresponding to the doctrine of the gospel among those to whom it is announced, they immediately judge that no church exists in that place" (4.1.13). Calvin approvingly quotes Augustine's invocation of Ephesians 4 to emphasize that unity must be an objective of church discipline. "All pious method and measure of ecclesiastical discipline ought ever to look to 'the unity of the Spirit in the bond of peace,' and when such unity is not preserved, the medicine of punishment begins to be not only superfluous but also harmful, and so ceases to be medicine" (4.12.11).

The Anabaptists were guilty of forgetting that there is only one kingdom of Christ, and that kingdom is embodied in one true visible church. To separate from the visible church as a means of addressing its moral problems is to destroy its unity and is "on that account no remedy at all." Christians must practice mercy and patience,

> lest, while they seem strenuous and courageous vindicators of righteousness they depart from the Kingdom of Heaven, which is the only kingdom of righteousness. For because God willed that the communion of his church be maintained in this outward society, he who out of hatred of the wicked breaks the token of that society treads a path that slopes to a fall from the communion of saints (4.1.16).

That path led to sectarianism, which Calvin abhorred. The kingdom of Christ was not to be played off against the true church.[115]

---

[113] See Glenn S. Sunshine, "Discipline as a Third Mark of the Chruch: Three Views," *Calvin Theological Journal* 33:2 (1998): 469–480; R. N. Caswell, "Calvin's View of Ecclesiastical Discipline," *John Calvin: A Collection of Essays* (ed. G. E. Duffield; Grand Rapids: Eerdmans, 1966), 210–226; Milner, *Calvin's Doctrine of the Church*, 175; Niesel, *The Theology of Calvin*, 198–199; Wendel, *Calvin*, 301; Höpfl, *The Christian Polity of John Calvin*, 86–88.

[114] Commentary on Psalm 15:1 [1557]; CO 31:143.

[115] Commentary on 1 Corinthians 1:2 [1546]; CO 49:307.

The problem was that the Anabaptists expected the church to attain to the perfection of the consummated kingdom of Christ.[116] Although the church is the kingdom of righteousness, for Calvin, in the present age, it labors under the cross. Calvin points his readers to Jesus' parables of the net (Matthew 13:47–58), of the tares (Matthew 13:24–30), and of the threshing floor (Matthew 3:12) to defend his claim that on this side of Christ's return, the church will always be a blemished mixture of believers and hypocrites (4.1.13): The church must resign itself to a "mixture of the good and the bad" until "the end of the world, because till that time a true and perfect restoration of the Church will not take place." Caught in the tension between the two ages, the faithful must avoid both slackness and overzealousness.[117] Pastors will "labor strenuously to purify the church," but they must also recognize that "when all shall have devoted their united exertions to the general advantage they will not succeed in such a manner as to purify the church entirely from every defilement."[118]

In the present age, therefore, the kingdom is manifested primarily through the church's ministry of the forgiveness of sins. Even the fruit of sanctification takes place in a context of confession and mercy. "Not only does the Lord through forgiveness of sins receive and adopt us once for all into the church, but through the same means he preserves and protects us there" (4.1.21). This is why Christians are instructed daily to pray, "Forgive us our debts," and it is why Jesus commanded believers continually to forgive their brothers and sisters (4.1.23). It also explains why the essence of church government is the church's use of the keys of the kingdom in the proclamation of the forgiveness of sins. "Therefore, in the communion of saints, our sins are continually forgiven us by the ministry of the church itself when the presbyters or bishops to whom this office has been committed strengthen godly consciences by the gospel promises in the hope of pardon and forgiveness." But apart from participation in the visible church this ministry of the keys cannot be received (4.1.22). The credal statement regarding the forgiveness of sins follows that regarding the church because God has "promised his mercy solely in the communion of saints." To separate from that communion in the name of purity, therefore, is to gut the church of its chief mark, the proclamation of the forgiveness of sins (4.1.20).[119]

---

[116] Cf. *Institutes*, 4.12.12; Commentary on 1 Timothy 3:1–2 [1548]; CO 52:376–377.

[117] "Our God is the God of order, and not of confusion, and therefore recommends to us discipline, but he permits hypocrites to remain for a time among believers, till the last day, when he will bring his kingdom to a state of perfection." Commentary on Matthew 13:47 [1555]; CO 45:376. Cf. 13:24–43; CO 45:367–368).

[118] Commentary on Matthew 13:39 [1555]; CO 45:369–370. "[T]here is nothing that distresses more the faithful ministers of the church than to see no way of correcting evils, and to be compelled to endure hypocrites." Commentary on 1 Timothy 5:24 [1548]; CO 52:320.

[119] Cf. Commentary on Isaiah 33:24 [1559]; CO 36:578; *Institutes* 4.1.3.

All that said, Calvin agreed with the Anabaptists that discipline is essential to the church's health and survival. Troeltsch was correct to claim that Calvin synthesized the idea of the (state) church with that of the sect.[120] As Calvin puts it in *Institutes* 4.12, "Accordingly, as the saving doctrine of Christ is the soul of the church, so does discipline serve as its sinews, through which the members of the body hold together, each in its own place." To eliminate discipline is therefore is to bring about the "dissolution of the church" (4.12.1). A few sections later he warns, "Those who trust that without this bond of discipline the church can long stand are, I say, mistaken; unless, perhaps, we can with impunity go without that aid which the Lord foresaw would be necessary for us" (4.12.4). Calvin thought a church might exist for a time without church discipline, but he didn't think it would last very long. Discipline is necessary "like a bridle to restrain and tame those who rage against the doctrine of Christ; or like a spur to arouse those of little inclination; and also sometimes like a father's rod to chastise mildly and with the gentleness of Christ's Spirit those who have more seriously lapsed" (4.12.1).

Calvin suggests that discipline has three chief purposes, all of them spiritual. First, it preserves the honor of God and of the Lord's Supper. Second, it protects the members of the body from corruption by those who do evil. Third, it enables "those overcome by shame for their baseness . . . to repent" (4.12.5).[121] Underlying all of these purposes is the reality that in the visible society of the church God has begun to restore the order of piety, love, and justice among human beings. The Lord's Supper is not simply individual believers' celebration of their union with Christ, but a communion of brothers and sisters in "love, peace, and concord." Thus

> None of the brethren can be injured, despised, rejected, abused, or in any way offended by us, without at the same time, injuring, despising, and abusing Christ by the wrongs we do; that we cannot disagree with our brethren without at the same time disagreeing with Christ; that we cannot love Christ without loving him in the brethren; that we ought to take the same care of our brethren's bodies as we take of our own; for they are members of our body; and that, as no part of our body is touched by any feeling of pain which is not spread among all the rest, so we ought not to allow a brother to be affected by any evil, without being touched with

[120] Ernst Troeltsch, *The Social Teaching of the Christian Churches* (trans. Olive Wyon; 2 vols.; Louisville: Westminster/John Knox Press, 1992 [1912]), 2:579, 593–598, 602, 623, 627. Cf. Balke, *Calvin and the Anabaptist Radicals*, 76–77. Cf. Milner, *Calvin's Doctrine of the Church*, 194; David Little, *Religion, Order, and Law* (New York: Harper and Row, 1969), 76.

[121] Elsewhere he lists as various reasons "that contagion may spread no farther, that the personal wickedness of one individual may not tend to the common disgrace of the church, and that the example of severity may induce others to fear," but he observes that Paul's primary focus is on encouraging repentance through shame. Commentary on 2 Thessalonians 3:14 [1550]; CO 52: 215–216.

compassion for him. Accordingly, Augustine with good reason frequently calls this Sacrament "the bond of love" (4.17.38).

Where discipline does not promote such love, the Supper is a mere exercise in hypocrisy.[122]

Calvin begins his analysis of "ecclesiastical jurisdiction [*ecclesiae iurisdictio*]," or the "discipline of morals," in *Institutes* 4.11, identifying it as "the most important [part of ecclesiastical power] in a well-ordered state [*statu bene composito*]." He introduces the discussion by comparing the church to a city, but he immediately clarifies that the two are in fact quite different.

> For as no city or township can function without magistrate and polity [*magistratu et politia*], so the church of God (as I have already taught, but am now compelled to repeat) needs a spiritual polity [*spirituali politia*]. This is, however, quite distinct from the civil polity, yet does not hinder or threaten it but rather greatly helps and furthers it (4.11.1).[123]

Despite the view of some scholars that Genevan church discipline was a political enterprise, Calvin makes it eminently clear that this power is an expression of the spiritual government of Christ's church, not of civil government. First, he identifies the jurisdiction of which he is speaking with "the exercise of the office of the keys," that is, the keys of the spiritual kingdom of Christ. Second, he invokes 1 Corinthians 12:28 and Romans 12:8 as evidence for the office of elder, declaring explicitly that the Apostle Paul, "is not addressing the magistrates ... but those who were joined with the pastors in the spiritual government of the church [*spirituale ecclesiae regimen*]." He adds a reference to 1 Timothy 5:17 as evidence that some presbyters were responsible not for preaching but "to supervise morals and to use the whole power of the keys" (4.11.1). Finally, at the beginning of 4.12 he writes, "Discipline depends for the most part upon the power of the keys and upon spiritual jurisdiction [*spirituali iurisdictione*]" (4.12.1).

Calvin was aware that his teaching on discipline contradicted the assumption of virtually all Protestant leaders that the discipline of morals was a magisterial prerogative. The Swiss reformers Zwingli and Bullinger, whose opinions prevailed in every Reformed city until Calvin established ecclesiastical discipline in Geneva, argued that the elders or governors mentioned in the New Testament

---

[122] See Robert White, "Oil and Vinegar: Calvin on Church Discipline," *Scottish Journal of Theology* 38 (1985): 25–40, 26 (Cf. 25–40). Cf. Graham, *The Constructive Revolutionary*, 54–55; Mark Valeri, "Religion, Discipline, and the Economy in Calvin's Geneva," *Sixteenth Century Journal* 28 (1997): 123–142, 141–142.

[123] Cf. 4.12.1; John Lee Thompson, *John Calvin and the Daughters of Sarah: Women in Regular and Exceptional Roles in the Exegesis of John Calvin, His Predecessors and His Contemporaries* (Geneva: Droz, 1992), 251–252.

occupied a temporary office whose function was now better served by Christian magistrates.[124] Because they made no substantive distinction between the city and the church, they viewed the magisterial office as an office of the church. "Christ," they say, "entrusted these functions to the church, since there was no magistrate to carry them out." Calvin responds by explaining why church discipline cannot be performed by civil government.

> Some imagine that all those things were temporary, lasting while the magistrates were still strangers to the profession of our religion. In this they are mistaken, because they do not notice how great a difference and unlikeness there is between ecclesiastical and civil power [*ecclesiasticae et civilis potestatis*]. For the church does not have the right of the sword to punish or compel, not the authority to force; not imprisonment, nor the other punishments which the magistrate commonly inflicts. Then [in the church], it is not a question of punishing the sinner against his will, but of the sinner professing his repentance in a voluntary chastisement. The two conceptions are very different. The church does not assume what is proper to the magistrate; nor can the magistrate execute what is carried out by the church (4.11.3).

In other words, government by the sword cannot be an office of the church because it relies on coercion. To eliminate church discipline because of the existence of magistrates is to confuse the two kingdoms, conflating civil righteousness with spiritual righteousness and the civil use of the law with its spiritual use. For Calvin, discipline was first and foremost a means of grace, not a means of civil punishment or social control.[125]

Reducing his opponents' position to the absurd, Calvin points out that the assumption that the function of church discipline is taken up by Christian magistrates, taken to its logical conclusion, could be made about "the whole ministry of the word."

> Today, then, according to our opponents, let pastors stop rebuking manifest misdeeds; let them cease to chide, to accuse, to rebuke. For there are Christian magistrates who ought to correct these things by laws and sword. And as the magistrate ought by punishment and physical restraint to cleanse the church of

---

[124] See Chapter 1. Cf. J. Wayne Baker, "Christian Discipline and the Early Reformed Tradition: Bullinger and Calvin," *Calviniana: Ideas and Influence of Jean Calvin* (ed. Robert V. Schnucker; Kirksville, MO: Sixteenth Century Journal, 1988), 107–119.

[125] As White puts it, "Discipline is, in the final analysis, a means of grace." White, "Oil and Vinegar," 40. Wendel rightly concludes, "The theory of the relations between Church and State that Calvin elaborated is therefore as remote from the teaching of Zwingli, which led to confusion between Church and State, as it is incompatible with that submission of the Churches to the State to which things had come in Germany." Wendel, *Calvin*, 310 (Cf. 300, 308–309). Cf. Little, *Religion, Order, and Law*, 78.

offenses, so the minister of the word ought to help the magistrate in order that not so many may sin. Their functions ought so to be joined that each serves to help, not hinder, the other (4.11.3).

Calvin clearly finds this conclusion to be absurd. Confusing church discipline with the work of civil government confuses the function of ministers with that of the civil magistrate. In Matthew 18, he argues, Christ established a "set and permanent order of the church, not a temporary one" (4.11.4). As Calvin puts it later in the chapter, "If we seek the authority of Christ in this matter, there is no doubt that he wished to bar the ministers of his word from civil rule and earthly authority when he said, 'The rulers of the Gentiles lord it over them, . . . but you do not do so.' He means not only that the office of pastor is distinct from that of prince but also that the things are so different that they cannot come together in one man" (4.11.8).[126]

Calvin bolsters these arguments with several others. He points out that if civil government is to take the role of administering discipline, then Christians must do precisely what Paul criticized the Corinthians for doing: accuse one another before magistrates. He further notes that when magistrates began to convert to Christianity in the early church, they did not abolish the "spiritual jurisdiction [*spiritualis iurisdictio*]" or confuse it with the "civil" jurisdiction. On the contrary, "the magistrate, if he is godly, will not want to exempt himself from the common subjection of God's children. It is by no means the least significant part of this for him to subject himself to the church, which judges according to God's word – so far ought he to be from setting that judgment aside!" As Calvin quotes Ambrose, "a good emperor is within the church, not over the church" (4.11.4).[127] What is more, the bishops of the early church recognized that "this spiritual power [*spiritualis potestas*]" must be "completely separated from the right of the sword." They "did not exercise their power through fines or prisons or other civil penalties but used the Lord's word alone." Thus "the jurisdiction of the ancient church [*veteris ecclesiae iurisdictio*]" reflected what the Apostle Paul instructed concerning the "spiritual power of pastors [*spirituali pastorum potestate*]" (4.11.5). Finally, Calvin argues that unlike political laws excommunication is part of the "jurisdiction [*iurisdictione*] that belongs peculiarly to the church." This means that its scope is "confined to the church [*intra ecclesiam continetur*] and does not extend to strangers."[128] However much the church and the citizenry of Geneva might have been coterminous in practice, in principle they were sharply distinguished.

---

[126] McKee notes that Calvin's argument here assumes that "the church is a distinct, though (ideally) not separate society from the earthly community." McKee, *Plural Ministry*, 43.

[127] Cf. *Institutes*, 4.12.7.

[128] Commentary on 1 Corinthians 5:12 [1546]; CO 49:386. Cf. 5:13; CO 49:387.

The lynchpin of Calvin's argument is his insistence that church discipline is an exercise of the keys of the kingdom and an extension of the ministry of the word.[129] To be sure, Calvin does not conflate preaching and discipline. He argues that while in Matthew 16:19 and John 20:23 Jesus' reference to the binding and loosing of the keys refers to the church's "doctrinal authority," Matthew 18:15–18 uses the same language to describe discipline. In the former passages "the power of the keys is simply the preaching of the gospel." Because it is contained entirely in the word "it is not so much power [*potestatem*] as ministry" (4.11.1). Matthew 18 is different from these, but not "so different as not to possess considerable connection between them." The passages describe the "same power [*potestas*] of binding and loosing (that is, through God's word), the same command, the same promise." The only difference is that "the first passage is particularly concerned with the preaching which the ministers of the word execute; the latter applies to the discipline of excommunication which is entrusted to the [whole] church" (4.11.2).

The similarity between discipline and the teaching of the word owes to the fact that faithful discipline is nothing less than an extension of the word. Calvin is emphatic on this point:

> Therefore, that no one may stubbornly despise the judgment of the church, or think it immaterial that he has been condemned by the vote of the believers, the Lord testifies that such judgment by believers is nothing but the proclamation of his own sentence, and that whatever they have done on earth is ratified in heaven. For they have the word of God with which to condemn the perverse; they have the word with which to receive the repentant into grace. They cannot err or disagree with God's judgment, for they judge solely according to God's law, which is no uncertain or earthly opinion but God's holy will and heavenly oracle (4.11.2).

Calvin repeats this assertion about ecclesiastical discipline throughout his commentaries. Discipline is an appendage to doctrine, an exercise of the keys of the kingdom. This is true especially of the church's proclamation of forgiveness to a repentant sinner, but it is also true of excommunication. In either case, the voice of the church is ratified in heaven by the one who has "the whole claim to the government of the church, so that he approves and ratifies the decisions of which he is himself the author."[130] As Calvin puts it elsewhere, "For although God does not thunder forth immediately on the minister's pronouncing the sentence, yet the decision is ratified [*ratum*] and will be accomplished in its own time."[131]

---

[129] "[E]xcommunication is part and parcel of the church's stewardship of the Word." White, "Oil and Vinegar," 27.

[130] Commentary on Matthew 18:19 [1555]; CO 45:516–517.

[131] Commentary on 2 Corinthians 10:6 [1548]; CO 50:116. Cf. Commentary on 1 Corinthians 6:2 [1546]; CO 49:389.

Like the preaching of the gospel, therefore, ecclesiastical jurisdiction actually opens and closes the kingdom of Christ to human beings. Paul describes excommunication in terms of handing a person over to Satan in 1 Corinthians 5:5, Calvin points out, because the church is Christ's kingdom: "as Christ reigns in the church, so Satan reigns out of the church [*in ecclesia regnat Christus, ita Satan extra ecclesiam*]." Thus the one who is "cast out of the church [*eiicitur extra ecclesiam*] is in a manner delivered over to the power of Satan, for he becomes an alien and is cast out of Christ's kingdom [*extraneus fit et alienatur a Christi regno*]."[132] Calvin makes the same point repeatedly. Excommunication holds spiritual force, "for since in the church Christ holds the seat of his kingdom [*in ecclesia sedem regni*], outside there is nothing but the dominion of Satan. Accordingly, he who is cast out of the church must be placed for a time under the tyranny of Satan until, being reconciled to the church, he returns to Christ."[133]

But is not such a power – to expel a person from the kingdom of Christ – precisely what made Rome so tyrannical? Calvin offers several responses to this objection. The first is the same response that he offers to those who challenged the authority of the ministry of the word.

> If it be objected that in this way God is made a sort of petty judge, who concurs in the sentence of mortal men, the reply is at hand. For when Christ maintains the authority of his church, he does not diminish his own power or that of his Father, but on the contrary supports the majesty of his word. As in the former case he did not intend to confirm indiscriminately every kind of doctrine, but only that which had proceeded out of his mouth, so neither does he say in this place that every kind of decision will be approved and ratified, but only that in which he presides, and that too not only by his Spirit, but by his word . . . For though Christ alone is the Judge of the world, yet he chooses to have ministers to proclaim his word. Besides, he wishes that his own decision should be pronounced by the church, and thus he takes nothing from his own authority by employing the ministry of men, but it is himself alone that looses and binds.[134]

In other words, like the ministry of the word, the power of church discipline is neither magisterial nor discretionary, but ministerial. It is bound up entirely with the word. There is no spiritual power of excommunication attached to the church itself, or to any ecclesiastical office. "For it is certain that the power [*potentiam*] of Christ is not tied to the inclination or opinions of mankind." Only when the church's actions are those of the word and Spirit is it the case that "excommunication is an ordinance of God and not of men."[135]

[132] Commentary on 1 Corinthians 5:5 [1546]; CO 49:381.
[133] Commentary on 1 Timothy 1:20 [1548]; CO 52:264–265. Cf. Commentary on 2 Corinthians 13:2 [1548]; CO 50:148; Commentary on John 9:35 [1553]; CO 47:232.
[134] Commentary on Matthew 18:18 [1555]; CO 45:515–516.
[135] Commentary on 1 Corinthians 5:4 [1546]; CO 49:380.

Calvin's second response is to refuse the power of discipline to the pastors alone. It was because the power of discipline was given to only a few officers of the church, he argues, that it had fallen into tyrannical misuse. "For it was a very wicked misdeed that one man, transferring the common power to himself, both opened the way to tyrannous license and seized from the church what had belonged to it, and suppressed and dissolved the assembly ordained by Christ's Spirit" (4.11.6). Things had regressed to the point that the bishops delegated discipline to lesser officials who "do not differ from secular judges" (4.11.7). In contrast, Christ gave the power of discipline to the church as a whole, the people being represented by elders appointed with the specific function of exercising church discipline (4.11.5). Thus the early church made use of an "assembly of the elders, which was to the church what the Senate is to the city" (4.11.6).[136]

Not even the Apostle Paul had the authority to excommunicate a person on his own because it is to be carried out by "common authority [*communi autoritate*]."

> [T]his authority [*potestatem*] does not belong to any one individual. As, however, a multitude never accomplishes anything with moderation or seriousness if not governed by a counsel [*consilio regatur*], there was appointed in the ancient church a presbytery [*ordinatum presbyterium*], that is, an assembly of elders [*collegium seniorum*] who, by the consent of all, had the first judgment in the case.

The matter was then to be brought to the people for ratification. Excommunication was thus to be "exercised by the common counsel of the elders [*communi seniorum consilio*] and with the consent of the people."[137] Calvin stipulates that in cases of public sins the assembly of elders is to provide an immediate public rebuke (4.12.3), but in the case of private sins, the procedure outlined in Matthew 18 is to be followed. Individual Christians must first admonish one another. If this fails, witnesses should be enlisted, and only if that fails does the matter properly come before the "public authority" of the church (4.12.2). Properly ordered, the whole process "ought to have that gravity which bespeaks the presence of Christ in order that there may be no doubt that he himself presides at his own tribunal" (4.12.7).

Unlike in many Reformed churches since the Reformation, therefore, Calvin did not view elders as those responsible for church government in general. Rather, he identified them as those representatives of the church responsible for the function of church discipline in particular. With respect to elders, as with pastors and deacons,

---

[136] Cf. Commentary on Matthew 18:18 [1555]; CO 45:515–516.

[137] Commentary on 1 Corinthians 5:4 [1546]; CO 49:379–380. Cf. 5:11; CO 49:386. Calvin did not expect the people to play any more than a ratifying role. The elders must act with the consent of the "knowledge and approval of the church," such that the people do not decide the action "but observe as witness and guardian so that nothing may be done according to the whim of a few" (4.12.7). Cf. White, "Oil and Vinegar," 31, 35–36.

he identifies in scripture a function, then identifies the office responsible for that function. "Governors were, I believe, elders chosen from the people, who were charged with the censure of morals and the exercise of discipline along with the bishops ... Each church, therefore, had from its beginning a senate ... which had jurisdiction over the correcting of faults" (4.3.8).[138]

Third, Calvin emphasizes that the purpose of excommunication is not vengeance but salvation (4.12.5). Its sentence is not permanent but conditional. Christians are not "to erase from the number of the elect those who have been expelled from the church, or to despair as if they were already lost. It is lawful to regard them as estranged from the church, and thus from Christ – but only for such time as they remain separated." The church's discipline is the verdict of Christ, but it is not his final verdict. Ultimate and final judgment is left to God alone, and the excommunicant is handed over to "the Lord's judgment" in hope for better things to come. "While we follow this rule, we rather take our stand upon the divine judgment than put forward our own." In doing so, the church is careful not to "confine [God's] mercy by law" (4.12.9). The process of church discipline is akin to the work of a physician. "[E]xcommunication does not tend to drive men from the Lord's flock but rather to bring them back when wandering and going astray."[139] It is a punishment, but one designed to restore rather than to condemn.[140]

Calvin adamantly distinguished the provisional judgment that is excommunication from the papal practice of declaring a person anathema: "the latter, taking away all pardon, condemns and consigns a man to eternal destruction; the former, rather, avenges and chastens his moral conduct" (4.12.10). The person anathematized by Rome was "utterly cast away, as if they were cut off from all hope of salvation," but salvation is always held out to the excommunicant.[141] To be sure, Calvin agreed that if a person is excommunicated, "no believer ought to receive him into terms of intimacy [*familiaritatem*] with him. Otherwise the authority of the church [*ecclesiae autoritas*] would be brought into contempt, if each individual were at liberty to admit to his table those who have been excluded from the table of the Lord."

[138] "We may learn from this that there were at that time two kinds of elders, for all were not ordained to teach." Those who did not teach were "united with the pastors in a common council and authority, administered the discipline of the church and were a kind of censors for the correction of morals." Commentary on 1 Timothy 5:17 [1548]; CO 52:315. In addition to 1 Timothy 5:17, Calvin draws on two other texts as his primary evidence for an office of elder responsible for church discipline. See Commentary on Romans 12:8 [1556]; CO 49:239–240; Commentary on 1 Corinthians 12:28 [1546]; CO 49:507. Cf. Commentary on James 5:15 [1551]; CO 55:431; Commentary on Acts 14:23 [1554]; CO 48:332.

[139] Commentary on 2 Thessalonians 3:15 [1550]; CO 52:216. Cf. Commentary on Isaiah 42:3 [1559]; CO 37:61.

[140] See Commentary on 1 Corinthians 5:5 [1546]; CO 49:381. (Cf. 5:2; CO 49:379; 7:11; CO 50:91; Commentary on Galatians 2:14 [1548]; CO 50:193.

[141] Commentary on 2 Thessalonians 3:15 [1550]; CO 52:216.

He maintains that "insofar as it is in our power [*liberum*] we are to shun [*fugiendam*] the society [*consuetudinem*] of those whom the church has cast off [*resecuit*] from her communion." But he distinguishes intimacy in the form of "living together or familiar association in means," which is to be avoided, from association in the form of eating at inns or public places, from which we do not have "authority [*potestas*] to exclude them." Calvin condemned the papal interdicts for "prohibiting anyone from helping one that has been excommunicated to food or fuel or drink, or any other of the supports of life," declaring them to be a "tyrannical and barbarous cruelty." The apostle means "not that he [the excommunicant] should be counted as an enemy but as a brother," and the "public mark of disgrace [*publica ignominiae nota*]" is not a civil penalty but a call to repentance. While civil punishment might be appropriate in some cases, "this kind of interdict is altogether unsuitable to an ecclesiastical court [*foro ecclesiastico*]."[142]

Calvin also rejected the early church practice of penance that was defended by reformers such as Martin Bucer. In fact, he shows a marked reluctance to use the word punishment to refer to any part of discipline except the ultimate step of excommunication. If the sinner repents, he insists, there is no need for further action. "Therefore, when a sinner gives testimony of his repentance to the church, and by this testimony wipes out the offense as far as he can, he is not to be urged any further" (4.12.8). The Apostle Paul provided the church with an example of mildness, kindness, and even indulgence, demonstrating "with what equity and clemency the discipline of the church ought to be regulated" in order to prevent a disciplined person from becoming "dispirited" and so tempting that person to leave the church or become a hypocrite.[143] Calvin warns that "zeal for discipline" frequently gives rise to "pharisaical rigor" that "hurries on the miserable offender to ruin, instead of curing him."[144] Discipline motivated by malevolence has nothing in common with Christ's spiritual government.[145]

Finally, Calvin insists that excommunication should be exercised only as a last resort and only in cases of intentional, unrepentant, and blatant violations of God's law. "For such great severity is not to be used in lighter sins, but verbal chastisement is enough (and that mild and fatherly)" (4.12.6). The only one who should be punished with excommunication is one "whose sin has become a matter of notoriety." Discipline could not extend to "inward impiety, and anything that is secret," for these do "not fall within the judgment of the church

---

[142] Commentary on 1 Corinthians 5:11 [1546]; CO 49:386. Cf. Commentary on 2 Thessalonians 3:14 [1550]; CO 52:215–216; Höpfl, *The Christian Polity of John Calvin*, 119.
[143] Commentary on 2 Corinthians 2:6 [1548]; CO 50:29. Cf. 2:7; CO 50:29; 7:12; CO 50:92–93.
[144] Commentary on 2 Corinthians 2:11 [1548]; CO 50:30.
[145] Commentary on Matthew 18:21 [1555]; CO 45:519–520.

[*ecclesia non iudicantur*]."[146] The point here is not to question the inward nature of Christ's spiritual government but to ensure – by focusing on actions specifically prohibited in scripture and readily identified – that the church's judgment is actually that of God's word.[147]

> For, properly speaking, we do not assume anything to ourselves when we recite what has proceeded from the mouth of God. God condemns adulterers, thieves, drunkards, murderers, enviers, slanderers, oppressors: if one inveigh against an adulterer, another a thief, a third a drunkard, shall we say that they take upon themselves more than they ought? By no means, because they do not pronounce of themselves as we have said, but God has said it, and they are but witnesses and messengers of his sentence.[148]

Only when the church condemns "crimes or shameful acts" that are clearly contrary to Christ's will is its discipline the "spiritual jurisdiction of the church [*spiritualis ecclesiae iurisdictio*]." Because the person's guilt is beyond a shadow of a doubt, "the Lord has testified that this is nothing but the publication of his own sentence, and what they have done on earth is ratified in heaven" (4.12.4).

When excommunication is exercised tyrannically and beyond the authority of the word, on the other hand, believers need not take it seriously.

> But we ought to believe that excommunication, when it is violently applied to a different purpose by the passions of men, may safely be treated with contempt. For when God committed to his Church the power of excommunicating he did not arm tyrants or executioners to strangle souls, but laid down a rule for governing his people, and that on the condition that he should hold the supreme government and that he should have men for his ministers.[149]

Discipline, like teaching, is only Christ's spiritual government insofar as it is a ministry of the word.

LAWS

The third part of the spiritual power represented in the government of the church is the power of the church to make laws, specifically laws concerning worship. Here again, Calvin specifies that he is concerned with the spiritual kingdom, not with the political order.

[146] Commentary on 1 Corinthians 5:11 [1546]; CO 49:385.
[147] Milner, *Calvin's Doctrine of the Church*, 176–178.
[148] Commentary on Ezekiel 3:18 [1565]; CO 40:92.
[149] Commentary on John 9:22 [1553]; CO 47:227–228. Calvin observes that John 9 teaches "how trivial and how little to be dreaded are the excommunications of the enemies of Christ" (9:35; CO 47:232). Cf. 16:2; CO 47:356.

This is the power now to be discussed, whether the church may lawfully bind consciences by its laws. In this discussion we are not dealing with the political order [*ordo politicus*], but are only concerned with how God is to be duly worshiped according to the rule laid down by him, and how the spiritual freedom [*spiritualis libertas*] which looks to God may remain unimpaired for us (4.10.1).

In fact, a cursory glance through *Institutes* 4.10 demonstrates that Calvin does discuss ecclesiastical laws that fall outside of the spiritual order. Indeed, the major burden of the chapter is to distinguish between the spiritual laws a church may enact, binding consciences, and the ecclesiastical laws necessary to preserve order and decorum in the church's worship. Calvin believed that many of the laws of the papal church represented a third category that confused this distinction, imposing unnecessary measures (or, at best, matters necessary only to order and decorum) as spiritual laws binding Christian consciences. He distinguishes between "holy and useful church institutions which provide for the preservation of discipline or honesty or peace" and "decrees concerning the worship of God put forward by men apart from his word," that is, "human traditions." He affirms the importance of the former but declares that the latter sort of decrees amount to an invasion of Christ's kingdom. When the clergy invent laws and declare them to be "spiritual [*spirituales*]" laws, binding on the soul and necessary for eternal life, "the Kingdom of Christ . . . is invaded; thus the freedom given by him to the consciences of believers is utterly oppressed and cast down." Where Christ has given believers liberty, Calvin insists, no one has the right to bind them. Believers "should acknowledge one King, their deliverer Christ, and should be governed by one law of freedom, the holy word of the gospel . . . They must be held in no bondage, and bound by no bonds" (4.10.1). Yet the Lord is "deprived of his Kingdom . . . whenever he is worshiped by laws of human devising" (4.10.23).[150]

Calvin therefore explores the problem of ecclesiastical laws in the context of his two kingdoms distinction. He admits that the problem "embarrasses most men," but he suggests that it does so only because "they do not distinguish subtly enough between the outward forum (as they call it) and the forum of conscience [*externum . . . et conscientiae forum*]."[151] They are, in part, confused by the fact that in Romans 13, Paul commands believers to submit to magistrates' political laws "because of conscience" (4.10.3), and "it seems to follow from this that the rulers' laws also have dominion over the conscience. Now if this is true, the same also will have to be said of church laws" (4.10.4). In fact, if this is true, Calvin admits, all that

---

[150] Human traditions are inappropriate when promulgated as if "consciences are bound to keep [them]" (4.10.8). Bishops were not appointed as "spiritual lawgivers [*spirituales legislatores*]" who can "force their ordinances upon the people committed to them" (4.10.6). Cf. Commentary on Matthew 15:2 [1555]; CO 45:447–448.

[151] Later he refers to it as the "earthly forum [*terrenum . . . forum*]" (4.10.5).

he said in 3.19 "and what I am now going to say about spiritual government [*spirituali regimine*] would fall" (4.10.3).[152] If civil government does exercise dominion over consciences, what is left of Christian liberty? At stake, in other words, is the fundamental distinction between "civil government, in which the edicts and laws of magistrates have place," and "the spiritual government of the soul [*spirituali animae regimine*], in which the word of God alone ought to bear rule."[153]

In Chapter 4, I explored Calvin's explanation of the difference between spiritual laws, which inherently bind the conscience (in each *species*), and political laws, which only indirectly bind the conscience (as a *genus*) by way of the law of charity. To quote Calvin once again, "even though individual [political] laws may not apply to the conscience as it binds, we are still held by God's general command, which commends to us the authority of magistrates" (4.10.5). For instance, the magistrate could require its subjects to attend public services on Sunday, as did the civil government of Geneva. If I were a subject of Geneva, I would be bound by conscience to obey the command, but my conscience would not be bound in the particular matter itself (as if Sunday is a holy day in God's eyes) because the time and day of worship is simply a matter of "polity [*politae*]" and "external order [*ordinis externi*]."[154] Should the magistrate require me to attend church on Tuesday, I would then be bound to attend church on Tuesday. I obey the magistrate because of her office, not because the particular time of worship is essential to my relationship with God. The laws of the magistrate do not "apply to the inward governing of the soul" (4.10.5).

In the last section of 4.10, Calvin observes that some Christians reject all laws regulating the "order of the church [*ecclesiae ordo*]" on the pretext of Christian liberty. Calvin's response is to point out that *all* societies require some sort of political organization:

> "[S]ome form of organization [*politiam*] is necessary in all human society to foster the common peace and maintain concord. We further see that in human transactions some procedure is always in effect, which is to be respected in the interests of public decency, and even of humanity itself. This ought especially to be observed in churches, which are best sustained when all things are under a well-ordered constitution, and which without concord become no churches at all (4.10.27).

---

[152] Calvin writes in his Commentary on Romans 13:5 that God has given civil government wide ranging discretionary power over those placed under it, but such civil government may not "exercise dominion over consciences [*dominatum in conscientias*]." Commentary on Romans 13:5 [1556]. CO 49:251–252.

[153] Commentary on James 4:11–12 [1551]; CO 55:420.

[154] Paul forbids Christians to distinguish between days "with a view to religion [i.e., conscience] and not with a view to polity or external order." Commentary on Romans 16:2 [1556]; CO 49:566–567. Cf. Commentary on Galatians 4:10 [1548]; CO 50:230; Commentary on Colossians 2:16 [1548]; CO 52:110.

Insofar as it is similar to all political societies, then, the institutional church possesses a political dimension.[155] Ecclesiastical laws pertaining to this dimension are similar to political laws that help Christians accommodate and serve their neighbors in indifferent matters. In this limited sense, the institutional church straddles the distinction between the two kingdoms, which is why it can be ordered to a certain extent by civil government.

It is important to note that unlike the later Reformed and Presbyterian tradition, Calvin did not suggest that the task of general ecclesiastical oversight should be given to the elders. Rather, the elders' sole function was church discipline.[156] In Geneva the political regulation of church life was shared between the civil government and the Company of Pastors. Calvin clearly wanted to reduce the role of civil government in this area, but in the *Institutes*, he takes both authorities into account. Thus "human laws, whether made by magistrate or by church, even though they have to be observed (I speak of good and just laws), still do not of themselves bind the conscience. For all obligation to observe laws looks to the general purpose, but does not consist in the things enjoined." Calvin therefore agreed that bishops have some legislative authority, "as much as is required duly to maintain the government of the church" (4.10.6). When churches lack civil laws "their very sinews disintegrate and they are wholly deformed and scattered." But such laws do not bind the conscience and are not part of (or "associated with") the worship of God or the spiritual government of Christ's church (4.10.27).[157]

Calvin was confident that he had articulated a "most excellent and dependable mark" to distinguish "impious constitutions" from "legitimate church observances" (although many of his critics have felt otherwise). The church needs some ceremonies, of course, but "the means used ought to show Christ, not to hide him" (4.10.14). Legitimate laws are those that ensure that all things are done "decently and with becoming dignity" and that "humanity and moderation" are maintained. They ensure that "love be fostered among us by common effort" and

---

[155] Wendel, *Calvin*, 307; Cf. Milner, *Calvin's Doctrine of the Church*, 173–174.

[156] In arguing that Calvin laid the foundation for Presbyterianism, Larson fails to acknowledge that Calvin's elders *only* conducted church discipline. They were not the church's governors *in general*. Mark J. Larson, *Calvin's Doctrine of the State: A Reformed Doctrine and Its American Trajectory, The Revolutionary War, and the Founding of the Republic* (Eugene, OR: Wipf and Stock, 2009), 12–13; Mark J. Larson, "John Calvin and Genevan Presbyterianism," *Westminster Theological Journal* 60 (1998): 43–69. Cf. Thomas F. Torrance, "The Eldership in the Reformed Church," *Scottish Journal of Theology* 37 (1984): 509; Robert M. Kingdon, "Calvin and 'Presbytery': the Geneva Company of Pastors," *Pacific Theological Review* 18 (1985): 43–55.

[157] "We must then distinguish between civil laws, such as are introduced to preserve order, or for some other end, and spiritual laws, such as are introduced into God's worship, and by which religion is enjoined, and necessity is laid on consciences." Commentary on Jeremiah 35:1–7 [1563]; CO 39:105. Cf. *Institutes* 4.10.5, 16, 20; Chenevière, "Did Calvin Advocate Theocracy?" 163.

they promote "reverence," "piety," "modesty," and "gravity" (4.10.28).[158] They fall into two general types. First there are those which provide "appropriate adornment" for acts of worship, such as Paul's requirements that believers practice moderation in drinking at the Lord's Supper, that women wear head coverings, and that men keep their heads bare and kneel in prayer. Second are those that ensure an "arrangement which takes away all confusion, barbarity, obstinacy, turbulence, and dissension." This requires the setting of times for worship, moments of silence within a liturgy, the selection of times for the observance of the Lord's Supper, and the prohibition of women teachers. This second type also gives procedural order to "those things which maintain discipline, such as catechizing, church censures, excommunication, fasting, and whatever can be referred to the same list" (4.10.29).[159]

Calvin seeks to clarify the way in which scripture regulates ecclesiastical laws. There will always be those who use ecclesiastical laws as a means of tyranny, he observes, while on the other hand others will be "overscrupulous and ... leave no place whatever for church laws." So Calvin produces a new principle: "I approve only those human constitutions which are founded upon God's authority, drawn from Scripture, and, therefore, wholly divine" (4.10.30). That seems to put the point quite strongly. Calvin does believe some particulars of polity are "divinely established [*divinitus institutis*],"[160] but he goes on to indicate that ordinarily things are not so cut and dried. Because God "did not will in outward discipline and ceremonies to prescribe in detail what we ought to do (because he foresaw that this depended upon the state of the times, and he did not deem one form suitable for all ages), here we must take refuge in those general rules which he has given, that whatever the necessity of the church will require for order and decorum should be tested against these." What is useful "for the upbuilding of the church" should be "variously accommodated to the customs of each nation and age," and may therefore be altered where profitable. In short, human constitutions must be *consistent* with scripture, as well as with the rule of love and edification (4.10.30).[161]

---

[158] Such are not to be confused with "theatrical props" of "useless elegance and fruitless extravagance" (4.10.29).

[159] It is evident that Calvin is referring to the proper ordering of things like excommunication here (rather than excommunication itself), because in 4.11–12, he presents the discipline of morals and excommunication as part of the church's spiritual government, or the exercise of the keys. Calvin discusses some of the legitimate exercises and ceremonies in 4.12, including "fasting" or "solemn supplications, ... of which the time, the manner, and the form are not prescribed by God's word, but left to the judgment of the church" (4.12.14).

[160] Commentary on 1 Corinthians 11:3 [1546]; CO 49:474. For instance, much of 1 Corinthians concerns matters of "decorum [*decorum*]," "public order [*publicum ordinem*]," or "polity [*politiam*]" (11:2; CO 472–473). Cf. Thompson, *John Calvin and the Daughters of Sarah*, 244–264; Wendel, *Calvin*, 302–303.

[161] Cf. Commentary on 1 Corinthians 14:40 [1546]; CO 49:535–536.

But there should be no legalism or dogmatism in matters of polity (4.10.32). In some cases, such as head coverings, it is sufficient if biblical prescriptions are observed symbolically,[162] while in other cases, such as the prohibition against women speaking in church, they are to be observed as general rules that might sometimes be suspended.[163] As matters of "external polity [*externam politiam*]," they do not bind consciences "as if they were in themselves necessary," but are simply important for "propriety and peace [*decoro pacique*]."[164] "Although not all of us need them, we all use them, for we are mutually bound, one to another, to nourish mutual love." Circumstances may vary and emergencies may arise, but "the established custom of the region, or humanity itself and the rule of modesty, dictate what is to be done or avoided in these matters" (4.10.31).[165] Such wise regulations, like those specifically laid down in scripture, "have a manifest approval, as it were, from the mouth of Christ itself."[166]

Calvin repeatedly invokes Isaiah 29:13, used by Jesus to condemn the legalism of the Pharisees in Matthew 15:7–9, to argue that God hates all worship based on human law. The papists "worship God by useless ringing of bells, mumbling, wax candles, incense, splendid dresses, and a thousand trifles of the same sort," but in so doing, they make traditions of men into the commandments of God.[167] Not only does God care more about obedience than sacrifice, he also wants human beings to realize that God is the "sole ruler of souls [*animarum regem*]" (4.10.7). Calvin was aware of the argument that since many Christians were illiterate and untutored, they needed the assistance of an "elementary discipline" similar to that of the Jews in the Old Testament. But he argues that an excess of ceremonies actually obscures the simplicity of the gospel in the New Testament age. "It was not in vain that God set this difference between us and the ancient folk, that he willed to teach them as children by signs and figures but to teach us more simply, without such outward trappings." Christ buried the Jewish symbols on which so much of the Roman worship was based, and he had freed Christians from their tutelage under the law.

> Paul [in Galatians 4] does not merely say that the yoke which had been laid upon the Jews is removed from us, but expressly lays down a distinction in the government [*regiminis*] which God has commanded to be observed. I acknowledge that we are now at liberty as to all outward matters, but only on the condition that the church

---

[162] Commentary on 1 Corinthians 11:4 [1546]; CO 49:475.
[163] Commentary on 1 Corinthians 14:34 [1546]; CO 49:532–533.
[164] Commentary on 1 Corinthians 14:40 [1546]; CO 49:535.
[165] Practices should not be altered unnecessarily nor should regulations be piled up beyond usefulness. Churches should err on the side of simplicity (4.10.32). Cf. Commentary on 1 Corinthians 11:16 [1546]; CO 49:478–479.
[166] Commentary on 1 Corinthians 14:40 [1546]; CO 49:536.
[167] Commentary on Isaiah 29:13 [1559]; CO 36:493–494.

shall not be burdened with a multitude of ceremonies, nor Christianity confounded with Judaism.[168]

Although Calvin's focus with respect to ecclesiastical laws is on matters pertaining to worship, it is important to note that he extends the principle of distinguishing between spiritual and political laws to general matters of church government. The church is to be characterized by a "just and orderly arrangement" according to the "regular administration of law."[169] Yet this administration is not to be confused with the spiritual government of Christ's church, even as it is to be carried out consistently with principles of love, edification, peace, and unity. For this reason, no individual or group of individuals, whether clergy or magistrates, can be permitted to dominate the affairs of the church to the prejudice of the common good. Calvin looks to the Jerusalem Council described in Acts 15 as the perfect example of a council in which the apostles and pastors of the church, working with the participation of the people and under the guidance of the Holy Spirit, developed helpful precepts for the edification of the church.[170] The apostles claimed no binding authority for their judgments apart from what was revealed by the Spirit. Their precepts only touched on what was necessary for the maintenance of unity, and even that necessity was "accidental or external," as appears from the fact that the decrees were later abolished. "[T]he last thing they meant was to set down a perpetual law, whereby they might bind the faithful." They merely established a "political [*politicam*] law which could not ensnare the conscience," and which conformed to the "rule of charity."[171]

Calvin sees the same principles of government at work in the election of ministers. On the one hand, "no government is to be set up in the church by the will of men," but Christ is to govern by his Holy Spirit. On the other hand, as with matters of polity, scripture does not reveal which leaders should be chosen or how, but merely provides general principles. Such principles include the fact that the individuals being chosen must be called by God, and they must be appointed to a function prescribed by God.[172] The ministers should not be chosen and appointed by one person but prayerfully by the whole church under the guidance of its leaders and the leading of the Spirit (4.4.10).[173] The early church followed the customary mode of

---

[168] Commentary on Galatians 4:2 [1548]; CO 50:226. Cf. Commentary on John 4:23 [1553]; CO 47:88–90.

[169] Commentary on Ephesians 4:12 [1548]; CO 198–199.

[170] These precepts pertained to "indifferent" matters, and they merely bound the church as a matter of "brotherly concord." Commentary on Acts 15:19 [1554]; CO 48:358. Cf. 15:22; CO 48:360; 21:18; CO 48:481.

[171] Commentary on Acts 15:28–29 [1554]; CO 48:362–363.

[172] Commentary on Hebrews 5:4 [1549]; CO 55:59. Cf. Commentary on Acts 13:2 [1554]; CO 48:279–281.

[173] Cf. Commentary on Acts 14:23 [1554]; CO 48:333; Commentary on 1 Titus 1:5 [1550]; CO 52:409; Commentary on 2 Timothy 1:6 [1548]; CO 52:349–350.

elections among the Greeks according to which "the leaders [*praeibant*] took the precedence by authority and counsel and regulated the whole proceeding, while the common people intimated their approval."[174] In the medieval period magistrates took a greater role, and Calvin was willing to yield to a magistrate the honor of "confirm[ing] a lawful election by his own authority" as long as the right of the church to choose its own ministers was not usurped (4.4.13). When it came to Rome's claim over the appointment of bishops, however, Calvin was unflinching. He argues that by removing the power to elect bishops from the people and by giving it to the canons, the papists "despoiled the church of its right" (4.5.2). Indeed, clerical abuses merely provided the princes with an excuse to intervene in the presentation of bishops, for the princes "preferred it to be their own gift, rather than to belong to persons who had no more right to it than they, and who abused it just as wickedly" (4.5.3).

Calvin's willingness to allow magisterial involvement in the selection of the ministers arose from his view that such procedural matters are matters of polity rather than of spiritual governance. For the same reason, he believed that pastors must be subject to "common courts and laws." When a spiritual matter was at stake, it should be tried in an ecclesiastical court, not a civil court, as the church father Ambrose insisted (4.11.15), but Calvin points out that Ambrose refused to resist princes when they regulated the indifferent matters of the church. Indeed, he even permitted them to ensure the proper ordering of its spiritual affairs as long as they did not usurp its spiritual functions. By 1543, Calvin was arguing that the church needs such care from civil government because it does not have the authority or power to enforce its own laws.

> They did not ... disapprove of princes interposing their authority in ecclesiastical matters, provided it was done to preserve the order of the church, not to disrupt it; and to establish discipline, not to dissolve it. For since the church does not have the power to coerce, and ought not to seek it (I am speaking of civil coercion), it is the duty of godly kings and princes to sustain religion by laws, edicts, and judgments (4.11.16).[175]

This argument about coercion and the duty of civil government to sustain religion takes Calvin well beyond simply recognizing the need for civil laws in the church. I turn to Calvin's understanding of civil government's responsibilities toward religion in Chapters 6 and 8. For now it is sufficient to emphasize that Calvin sharply distinguished a magisterial role in the governance of the church from the

---

[174] Commentary on 2 Corinthians 8:18 [1548]; CO 50:103–104. See Calvin's comments on the method approved by the Council of Laodicea (*Institutes*, 4.4.12).

[175] See Höpfl, *The Christian Polity of John Calvin*, 123–124.

spiritual government of the church. Civil government could sustain religion outwardly, but it could not usurp its spiritual functions.

APPENDIX: THE DIACONATE

The diaconate is somewhat of an ambiguous element in Calvin's view of church government.[176] On the one hand, the ordinary work of the deacons – "the care of the poor" – seems quite different from that of teaching and discipline in that it cannot be identified in any obvious sense with the ministry of the word. On the other hand, Calvin was explicit and adamant that the diaconate is part of Christ's spiritual government of his church, and that, in contrast to civil government, it is spiritual, not secular. In the *Institutes*, Calvin introduces the diaconate in connection with several key texts. From Acts 6 he draws that the deacons are to focus on caring for the poor, enabling the pastors to focus on teaching and prayer. In Romans 12:8, he identifies two types of deacons, those who "distribute the alms," and those who "devoted themselves to the care of the poor and sick." The latter group, he argues from 1 Timothy 5:9–10, once included an order of women who also occupied an office and ministry of the church (4.3.9).[177]

As with the offices of presbyter and bishop, Calvin argues that over the centuries, the church gradually lost sight of the true purpose of the diaconate. Originally the deacons "received the daily offerings of believers and the yearly income of the church. These they were to devote to proper uses, that is, to distribute some to feed the ministers, [and] some to feed the poor." It was the specific task of the deacons to serve as the "stewards of the poor," but, significantly, they conducted their work "under the bishop" and in that sense as an extension of the pastoral office (4.4.5).[178] The diaconate, for Calvin, reflects the ancient

---

[176] For a fuller analysis of the relationship between Calvin's view of the diaconate and the two kingdoms doctrine, see Matthew J. Tuininga, "Good News for the Poor: An Analysis of Calvin's Concept of Poor Relief and the Diaconate in Light of His Two Kingdoms Paradigm," *Calvin Theological Journal* 49:2 (November, 2014): 221–247.

[177] Calvin describes the women as widows above sixty years who served as "deaconesses" in the "public ministry of the church toward the poor." *Institutes*, 4.13.18–19. They occupied an "office [*officiis*]" and "ministry of the church [*ministerium ecclesiae*]." Commentary on 1 Timothy 5:9–10 [1548]; CO 52:310. Cf. 5:3; CO 52:305. They could occupy such "public offices [*publico officio*]" if they were unencumbered by children or other domestic concerns. Commentary on Romans 16:1 [1556]; CO 284–285. Cf. Elsie Anne McKee, *John Calvin on the Diaconate and Liturgical Almsgiving* (Geneva: Librairie Droz, 1984); Jeannine E. Olson, *Calvin and Social Welfare: Deacons and the Bourse française* (London and Toronto: Associated University Presses, 1989); Bonnie L. Pattison, *Poverty in the Theology of John Calvin* (Eugene, OR: Wipf and Stock Publishers, 2006).

[178] Cf. Commentary on Acts 11:30 [1552]; CO 48:265–266.

principle that "all that the church possesses, either in lands or in money, is the patrimony of the poor" (4.4.6).[179]

Although, in Geneva, the diaconate functioned in many respects like a civil institution, Calvin worked hard to dispel confusion when the diaconate came up in the course of his exegetical preaching through Acts and 1 Timothy. He acknowledged that some people assumed that the diaconate is an office of little importance but insisted that it is "not a profane or mundane office, but a spiritual charge."[180] Poor relief, likewise, is not simply something that Christians should do. It is a *sine qua non*, part of the fundamental order of the church itself. "God declares what kind of government, what kind of order and regulations he wants to prescribe for our use. If we wish to be respected and esteemed as his church, we must practice what he declares to us here." If Christ is "to rule and have order in the church," then "[t]he poor must be cared for. And for that, we need deacons."[181] Acts 6 teaches that although the preaching of the gospel is of the utmost importance, the cause of the poor is sufficiently important that it requires a perpetual office in Christ's spiritual government.[182]

Preaching on 1 Timothy 3:8–13, Calvin distinguished the office of civil magistrate from that of deacon and identified the latter with Christ's spiritual government. "It is true that those who are in the office of justice also do God service ... But these deacons appertain to the spiritual government which God has established."[183] This is why God "wills that they who are ordained, whether to preach the gospel or to care for the poor, be of unblameable life."[184] Calvin then turned to a striking criticism of the Reformed churches for their attitude toward the diaconate.

> Well then, shall we show that there is a reformation among us? We must begin at the end, that is to say, there must be ministers to preach the doctrine of salvation purely, there must be deacons to have care of the poor. *Truth it is that we have some: but it is taken as a profane office. Those that men call hospitallers and procurators of hospitals, do we think that they have an ecclesiastical office? Nay, do they themselves know it?* For if they thought, "see, God has called us to an office and to a holy state, it is joined with the office of the ministers and preachers and those that have charge to govern the church of God," it is certain that men would walk otherwise in it than they do, with a great deal more reverence than we see.[185]

---

[179] Calvin endorses the canon law provisions that divided the possessions of the church into four parts: for the clergy, the poor, church buildings, and the bishop's hospitality to travelers, prisoners, and to the poor (4.4.7).

[180] Sermon on Acts 6:1–3; SC 8:200.   [181] Sermon on Acts 6:1–3; SC 8:202.

[182] Cf. Commentary on Acts 6:2 [1552]; CO 48:119–120.

[183] Sermon on 1 Timothy 3:6–7; CO 53:291.   [184] Sermon on 1 Timothy 3:6–7; CO 53:289.

[185] Sermon on 1 Timothy 3:6–7; CO 53: 290. Emphasis added.

In his next sermon, Calvin went so far as to say that if the church did not have a well-run diaconate, "it is certain that we cannot brag that we have a church well-ordered and after the doctrine of the gospel."[186] Clearly Calvin was not satisfied to see civil government administer poor relief. He wanted it to be administered by the church as well, and he wanted it to be recognized as a spiritual work. The diaconate is "not only an earthly office, but a spiritual charge, which serves the church of God," and therefore the deacons "must be near the ministers of the word."[187] Where such a diaconate does not exist, we "have no regard, either to God's honor, or to the necessity of the poor, or to the government that God will have among us."[188]

Calvin viewed the diaconate as a part of the spiritual government of the church because he interpreted communion among believers as an expression of the kingdom of Christ that will restore all things, including both body and soul. Christians are called to render "every kind of assistance to each other," he argues in his commentary on Ephesians 4. The same unity that is grounded in the ministry of the word is reflected in the diaconate. Both express Christ's spiritual government of his kingdom.[189]

CONCLUSION

Calvin identified the church as Christ's kingdom because it is the church that administers Christ's spiritual government through the ministry of the word. In contrast to the Swiss reformers, Calvin insisted that the ministry of the visible church, including its discipline, is Christ's spiritual government. Against Rome he denied that the church has magisterial power in spiritual matters or spiritual authority over political matters. The entire spiritual authority of the church, he insisted, is contained within the word. When the church teaches and disciplines faithfully according to the word, its authority is that of Christ himself. Where, on the other hand, it is necessary for the church to regulate matters of polity or decorum – or to become involved in political affairs – the church must take care not to claim authority over consciences. Through the church, Christ has begun to establish his kingdom and restore the world, but the manifestation of the kingdom in the church is eschatological and spiritual. It should never be confused with the political order over which Christ also rules.

---

[186] Sermon on 1 Timothy 3:8–10; CO 53:293. [187] Sermon on 1 Timothy 3:6–7; CO 53:291.
[188] Sermon on 1 Timothy 3:8–10; CO 53:295, 301.
[189] Commentary on Ephesians 4:4 [1548]; CO 51:190–191.

6

Christ's Political Government

Early Formulations

Unlike the chapters on Christ's spiritual government, the chapter of the *Institutes* on civil government changed relatively little between 1536 and 1559. From the first to the last edition of the *Institutes*, Calvin described the role and nature of civil government in the same basic terms and with the same general arguments, always against the backdrop of the two kingdoms doctrine. He doggedly defended coercive political authority as having been established by God to preserve order and civil righteousness in a world corrupted by sin. He maintained that civil government has a responsibility to protect the true religion against public offenses, enforcing outward obedience to the moral law summarized in both tables of the Ten Commandments. He rejected the claim that Old Testament civil law binds contemporary political societies, insisting instead on the governing authority of natural law, equity, and the rule of love. He distinguished biblical teaching from the practical questions of political philosophy, calling Christians to be open to a wide range of types of political institutions. And he insisted that although Christians must submit to civil magistrates in all political matters, they may never submit to commands to act impiously or unjustly, and those with public authority must resist tyranny and oppression. Calvin never abandoned these early principles of his political theology.

But Calvin's emphases did change over the years. In his 1536 *Institutes* and in his 1540 commentary on Romans, Calvin's emphasis was on the secular purposes of government and the limited relevance of Old Testament law. In 1539 he had begun to work out a sophisticated biblical covenant theology, one that would profoundly shape his understanding of the relevance of Israel and its law for the politics of Christendom. But only after his return to Geneva in 1541 (after his interaction with Anabaptists in Strasbourg) did he begin to focus on the religious obligations of magistrates and the enduring political relevance of the Old Testament. His letters to foreign dignitaries and kings show that by 1548 he had worked out his mature theory of the responsibilities of magistrates relative to piety, worship, and doctrine.

In this chapter, I trace these early developments in Calvin's work, setting the stage for a consideration of Calvin's interpretation of the Old Testament in Chapter 7, followed by an examination of his mature political theology in Chapters 8 and 9.

It is important to note that Calvin's focus was almost always on the politics of a *Christian* commonwealth.[1] Most of what he said about government presupposes the context of Christendom. But while Calvin believed in the ideal of Christendom, he maintained that a pagan government is no less ordained by God, and no less legitimate, than is a Christian one. His respect for pagan philosophy and Roman law is evident in his first published book, his commentary on Seneca's *De Clementia* (1532), which Calvin wrote before his conversion to the Reformation.[2] Here the young humanist displayed the thorough knowledge of classical philosophy and Roman law, as well as of the general problems and questions associated with political theory, that would inform his political reflection throughout his career. Indeed, the book testifies to the rich humanist education that underlay Calvin's claim, discussed in Chapter 3, that by virtue of natural law, even pagans are capable of impressive political and ethical achievements.[3]

In the prefatory address to the *Institutes*, which Calvin wrote to Francis I, "Most Christian King of the French, His Sovereign," in 1535, Calvin declares that although he initially wrote the *Institutes* as a theological guide for Christians, he now also intends it to serve as a "confession" and "defense" against the false accusations that had led to the persecution of Protestants. The evangelical faith had been subject to lying and slander, "as if this doctrine looked to no other end than to subvert all orders and civil governments, to disrupt the peace, to abolish all laws, to scatter all lordships and possessions – in short, to turn everything upside down!" If this were actually true, Calvin admits, "the whole world would rightly judge this doctrine and its authors worthy of a thousand fires and crosses." But evangelical theology had not been granted a fair trial. With what right, then, was the new faith condemned?[4]

[1] John T. McNeill, "Calvin and Civil Government," *Readings in Calvin's Theology* (ed. Donald McKim; Grand Rapids: Baker, 1984), 260–274, 265; John T. McNeill, "The Democratic Element in Calvin's Thought," *Church History* 18 (September 1949): 153–171, 157; W. Robert Godfrey, "Calvin and Theonomy," *Theonomy: A Reformed Critique* (ed. William S. Barker, et al.; Grand Rapids: Zondervan, 1990), 298–312, 300.

[2] See Ford Lewis Battles and André Malan Hugo, *Calvin's Commentary on Seneca's 'De Clementia'* (Leiden: Brill, 1969); CO 5:1–162.

[3] While it is true that traces of Calvin's later views on the nature and forms of civil government can be found in this early writing, it is equally true that as a commentary, it avoids constructive engagement with such matters. For a good analysis of the significance of *De Clementia* and its place within Calvin's broader thought, see Harro Höpfl, *The Christian Polity of John Calvin* (Cambridge: Cambridge University Press, 1982), 5–18.

[4] John Calvin, *Institutes of the Christian Religion* [1536] (trans. Ford Lewis Battles; Grand Rapids: Eerdmans, 1975), Preface, 1.

Calvin affirms the right and responsibility of King Francis "to undertake a full inquiry into this case" with the "judicial gravity" befitting a subject of the true King of kings:

> Worthy indeed is this matter of your hearing, worthy of your cognizance, worthy of your royal throne! Indeed, this consideration makes a true king: to recognize himself a minister of God in governing his kingdom. Now that king who in ruling over his realm does not serve God's glory exercises not kingly rule but brigandage. Furthermore, he is deceived who looks for enduring prosperity in his kingdom when it is not ruled by God's scepter, that is, his Holy Word.[5]

If Francis was to be faithful to God, he could not evaluate the new faith based on the judgment of the pope or his bishops, let alone the opinions of the easily manipulated masses, but he must measure it according to scripture and the "analogy of faith."[6] For the reformers were not teaching something that was "doubtful and uncertain," nor were they "forging some new gospel."[7] What is more, "not one seditious word was ever heard" from faithful evangelicals. Indeed, "we ... do not cease to pray for the full prosperity of yourself and your kingdom." Calvin heartily concedes that if anyone uses the gospel as a pretext for rebellion "there are laws and legal penalties by which they may be severely restrained according to their deserts."[8]

THE INSTITUTES OF THE CHRISTIAN RELIGION (1536)

When Calvin introduces his analysis of civil government in the last part of the *Institutes*, he announces that, having considered Christ's spiritual kingdom, he is now turning to the political order.

> Now, since we have established above that man is under a twofold government, and since we have discussed already at sufficient length the kind that resides in the soul or inner man and pertains to eternal life, this is the place to say something also about the other kind, which pertains only to the establishment of civil justice and outward morality.[9]

In this first edition of the *Institutes*, civil and ecclesiastical government are both discussed in the same chapter on Christian freedom in which Calvin introduces the two kingdoms concept. Calvin presents these governments as the institutional correlates of the two kingdoms.

In fact, Calvin stresses up front that, as with the spiritual government of the church, so with civil government, the distinction between the two kingdoms must be kept constantly in mind. "But whoever knows how to distinguish between body

---

[5] *Institutes* [1536], Preface, 2.   [6] *Institutes* [1536], Preface, 2, 5.   [7] *Institutes* [1536], Preface, 3.
[8] *Institutes* [1536], Preface, 8.   [9] *Institutes* [1536], VI.C.35.

and soul, between this present fleeting life and that future eternal life, will without difficulty know that Christ's spiritual Kingdom [*spirituale Christi regnum*] and the civil jurisdiction [*civilem ordinationem*] are things completely distinct."[10] Civil government is necessary because of the eschatological nature of the kingdom of Christ. This point is so essential for Calvin that it is worth quoting at length:

> But as we have just now pointed out that this kind of government is distinct from that spiritual and inward Kingdom of Christ [*spirituali . . . et interno Christi regno*], so we must know that they are not at variance. For spiritual government, indeed, is already initiating in us upon earth certain beginnings of the Heavenly Kingdom [*coelestis regni*], and in this mortal and fleeting life affords a certain forecast of an immortal and incorruptible blessedness. Yet civil government has as its appointed end, so long as we live among men, to adjust our life to the society of men, to form our social behavior to civil righteousness, to reconcile us with one another, and to promote and foster general peace and tranquility. All of this I admit to be superfluous, if God's Kingdom, such as it is now among us, wipes out the present life . . .
>
> 37. Our adversaries claim that there ought to be such great perfection in the church of God that its government should suffice for law. But they stupidly imagine such a perfection as can never be found in a community of men. For since the insolence of evil men is so great, their wickedness so stubborn, that it can scarcely be restrained by extremely severe laws, what do we expect them to do if they see that their depravity can go scot-free – when no power can force them to cease from doing evil?[11]

It is important to pay attention to the sorts of words Calvin uses to describe the task of civil government. Its purposes relate to the "society of men," to "civil righteousness," and to the "present life." Civil government would not be necessary if the kingdom of Christ was fully established and human beings were perfect, but during the present age its coercion is needed to restrain the worst expressions of human depravity.[12]

Calvin wrote these words with the Anabaptists and their perfectionism at the forefront of his mind,[13] but he also had an even more radical group in view –

[10] *Institutes* [1536], VI.C.35.

[11] *Institutes* [1536], VI.C.36–37. Cf. Commentary on Isaiah 3:5 [1559]; CO 36:83–84.

[12] Chenevière writes that for Calvin, "Human society is natural; the State in itself is not." Marc Chenevière, "Did Calvin Advocate Theocracy?" *Evangelical Quarterly* 9 (1937): 160–168, 164. Cf. Susan E. Schreiner, *The Theater of His Glory: Nature and the Natural Order in the Thought of John Calvin* (Grand Rapids: Baker Academic, 1995), 82–83; McNeill, "The Democratic Element in Calvin's Thought," 156.

[13] Balke observes that while Calvin understood the difference between the Anabaptists and the Libertines, and between various stripes of Anabaptists, he tended to lump the latter together without paying much attention to the diversity within the movement. Calvin rarely engaged specific Anabaptists or specific Anabaptist writings. He operated within the polemical rules of his day, which allowed him to attribute anything one Anabaptist said to the group as a whole. Willem Balke, *Calvin*

probably the Libertines. He accuses "certain men" of teaching that Christian free-dom "acknowledges no king and no magistrate among men, but looks to Christ alone." Such men "think that nothing will be safe unless the whole world is reshaped to a new form, where there are neither courts, nor laws, nor magistrates, nor anything similar which in their opinion restricts their freedom."[14] They argue that once believers have entered Christ's kingdom, "it is a thing unworthy of us and set far beneath our excellence to be occupied with those vile and worldly cares which have to do with business foreign to a Christian man."[15]

The problem, for Calvin, is that the Libertines' and Anabaptists' over-realized eschatology led them to confuse the two kingdoms. Falling prey to "Jewish vanity," insofar as they "seek and enclose Christ's Kingdom within the elements of this world," they confused Christian freedom with political freedom. "For why is it that the same apostle who bids us stand and not submit to the 'yoke of bondage' elsewhere forbids slaves to be anxious about their state, unless it be that spiritual freedom can perfectly well exist along with civil bondage?" It is true that in Christ "there is neither Jew nor Greek, neither male nor female, neither slave nor free," but temporal distinctions remain as a fundamental part of the political order. "[I]t makes no difference what your condition among men may be or under what nation's laws you live, since the Kingdom of Christ does not at all consist in these things."[16]

As long as the world remains plagued by sin and disorder, the restraining role of civil government remains "no less than that of bread, water, sun, and air." For not only does government seek to ensure that people "breathe, eat, drink, and are kept warm," which it does when it "provides for their living together," but it ensures that the moral law is publicly obeyed.[17] Like the other magisterial reformers, Calvin could see no reason why civil government should punish crimes against justice but not crimes against the truth or against God.[18] Relative to the first table, or what Calvin calls "a public manifestation of religion . . . among Christians," government "prevents idolatry, sacrilege against God's name, blasphemies against his truth, and other public offenses against religion from arising and spreading among the people."

and the Anabaptist Radicals (trans. Willem Heyner. Grand Rapids: Eerdmans, 1981), 9–12, 20, 30–34, 60–65, 330–331; Cf. Höpfl, The Christian Polity of John Calvin, 46–48.

[14] Institutes [1536], VI.C.35. On Calvin's interaction with the Libertines, see John Calvin, Treatises against the Anabaptists and against the Libertines (trans. Benjamin Wirt Farley; Grand Rapids: Baker, 1982), 159–326, especially Farley's Commentary on pp. 161–186.

[15] Institutes [1536], VI.C.36. Cf. Commentary on Jude 9 [1551]; CO 55:494.

[16] Institutes [1536], VI.C.35. Cf. Commentary on Galatians 3:28 [1548]; CO 50:222–223; Commentary on Colossians 3:11 [1548]; CO 52:121–122.

[17] Institutes [1536], VI.C.37. Cf. W. Fred Graham, The Constructive Revolutionary: John Calvin and His Socio-Economic Impact (Richmond, VA: John Knox Press, 1971), 73; Wilhelm Niesel, The Theology of Calvin (trans. Harold Knight; London: Methuen, 1956), 232.

[18] Cf. Nicholas Wolterstorff, The Mighty and the Almighty: An Essay in Political Theology (Cambridge: Cambridge University Press, 2012), 144; Höpfl, The Christian Polity of John Calvin, 18.

Relative to the second table, which Calvin refers to as "humanity . . . among men," it "prevents the public peace from being disturbed; it provides that each man may keep his property safe and intact; that men may carry on blameless intercourse among themselves."[19]

Calvin realized that readers who tracked with him on the two kingdoms distinction might be "disturbed that I now commit to civil government the duty of rightly establishing religion, which I seem above to have put outside of human decision." But Calvin argues that there is a difference between the government's responsibility to ensure that the true religion is not "openly and with public sacrilege violated and defiled with impunity," and allowing that same government "to make laws according to their own decision concerning religion and the worship of God."[20] In other words, government is obligated to protect religion by preserving civil piety and defending the truth, but that does not mean it has a role in Christ's spiritual government. The emphasis here is on prohibiting *outward* and *public* offenses against religion rather than on promoting inward piety. Government's role is with respect to the civil use of the law rather than its spiritual use. And even with respect to that limited role, Calvin's comments in the 1536 edition are brief and passing. The rest of the chapter focuses entirely on matters pertaining to justice and the second table of the law. His only other substantive reference to the matter in the 1536 *Institutes* is an insistence that "Turks and Saracens, and other enemies of religion" should *not* be persecuted by the sword of the civil magistrate. "Far be it from us to approve those methods by which many until now have tried to force them to our faith, when they forbid them the use of fire and water and the common elements, when they deny to them all offices of humanity, when they pursue them with sword and arms."[21]

Calvin's substantive discussion of the responsibilities of government in the 1536 *Institutes* focuses entirely on matters of justice and peace. Invoking Jeremiah 22:3, he

---

[19] *Institutes* [1536], VI.C.37. Calvin divides the Ten Commandments into two tables, the first pertaining "to those duties of religion which particularly concern the worship of his [God's] majesty; the second, to the duties of love that have to do with "human society." The first is the foundation for the second. "[A]part from the fear of God men do not preserve equity and love among themselves. Therefore we call the worship of God the beginning and foundation of righteousness" (*Institutes*, 2.8.11). Cf. Commentary on Matthew 23:23–28 [1555]; CO 45:631–633.

[20] *Institutes* [1536], VI.C.37.

[21] *Institutes* [1536], II.28; CO 1:77. Calvin omitted this comment from subsequent editions, but as R. White demonstrates, the omission is best explained by literary and pastoral considerations rather than a change in views (or, as Castellio charged, in Calvin's opportunism). In his tract against Servetus and his Commentary on the Torah, Calvin maintained the view that only heretics and apostates, not pagans, should be punished by the sword. See R. White, "Castellio Against Calvin: The Turk in the Toleration Controversy of the Sixteenth Century," *Bibliothèque d'Humanisme et Renaissance* 46.3 (1984): 573–586. Cf. Christoph Strohm, "Calvin and Religious Tolerance," *John Calvin's Impact on Church and Society* (ed. Martin Ernst Hirzel and Martin Smallmann; Grand Rapids: Eerdmans, 2009), 183–184.

argues that government is to "'do justice and righteousness,' to 'deliver him who has been oppressed by force from the hand of the malicious prosecutor,' not to 'grieve or wrong the alien, the widow, and the fatherless' or 'shed innocent blood.'" He cites several passages from Deuteronomy to demonstrate that magistrates are to judge impartially and not to take bribes, and he cites the "law of the king" in Deuteronomy 17, but he says not a word about government's responsibility toward religion. He summarizes the basic task of magistrates in essentially secular terms: "We see, therefore, that they are ordained protectors and vindicators of public innocence, modesty, decency, and tranquility, and that their sole endeavor should be to provide for the common safety and peace of all." The primary way that government provides for such safety and peace is by promoting respect for virtue and restraining acts of injustice. "For the care of equity and justice grows cold in the minds of many, unless due honor has been prepared for virtue; and the lust of wicked men cannot be restrained except by severity and the infliction of penalties." Governments are both to execute justice – "to receive into safekeeping, to embrace, to protect, vindicate, and free the innocent," – and judgment – "to withstand the boldness of the impious, to repress their violence, to punish their misdeeds." In stark contrast to the emphases of his later career, Calvin says nothing here about any responsibilities of government relative to worship, doctrine, or ecclesiastical discipline.[22]

Nevertheless, the magistrate is a minister of God and governs with divine authority. As "God's representatives" and "vicegerents," magistrates are even referred to in Psalm 82 and John 10:35 as "gods."[23] From Deuteronomy 1 and Proverbs 8, Calvin insists that they exercise judgment on God's behalf, not on behalf of human beings. "[I]t has not come about by human perversity that the authority over all things on earth is in the hands of kings and other rulers, but by divine providence and holy ordinance."[24] Calvin relies most decisively on Romans 13, noting Paul's description

---

[22] *Institutes* [1536], VI.C.43.

[23] *Institutes* [1536], VI.C.39. We should not read too much into Calvin's application of the term "minister" to magistrates, as Calvin writes that "Satan himself ... is so far [God's] minister that he acts not but by his command." Commentary on Romans 9:18 [1556]; CO 49:184. Cf. 1:24; 27; Commentary on Psalm 82:1 [1557]; CO 31:768–769; 82:6; CO 31:771; Commentary on 1 Timothy 6:15 [1548]; CO 52:331. Commentary on Ephesians 2:2 [1548]; CO 51:161; Commentary on Isaiah 10:5 [1559]; CO 36:213–215.

[24] *Institutes* [1536], VI.C.39. Elsewhere Calvin writes that pagan philosophers "acutely point out the means of erecting a commonwealth, and on the other hand the vices by which a well-regulated state is commonly corrupted; in short, they discourse with consummate skill upon everything that is necessary to be known on this subject, except that they omit the principal point," which is that they can accomplish nothing unless God "makes use of them as his instruments." Commentary on Psalm 127:1 [1557]; CO 32:321–322. In the first edition of the *Institutes*, Calvin listed Romans 12:8 as evidence that magistrates rule on behalf of God. In 1539, however, he added a qualification that the text primarily denotes elders who are to preside over church discipline. See Elsie Anne McKee, *Elders and the Plural Ministry: The Role of Exegetical History in Illuminating John Calvin's Theology* (Geneva: Librairie Droz, 1988), 40–41.

of government as "an ordinance of God," and princes as "ministers of God, for those doing good unto praise; for those doing evil, avengers unto wrath." But he also notes the examples of numerous Old Testament leaders such as David, Josiah, Hezekiah, Joseph, Daniel, Moses, Joshua, and the judges. In light of God's approval of these men, he writes, it is evident not only that civil government is a "holy and lawful" vocation, but that it is "the most sacred and by far the most honorable of all callings in the whole life of mortal men."[25] It extends not to "profane affairs or those alien to a servant of God," but is "a most holy office, since they are serving as God's deputies."[26] It is not enough to view government as a "necessary evil," or even to recognize that it is conducive of the public welfare. Rather, magistrates are to be honored with "full veneration and dignity," and they are to be obeyed as a matter of conscience rather than out of fear of coercion.[27] Although such statements are often cited as evidence that Calvin viewed magistrates as even more important than ministers of the church, in the context of Calvin's reference to "callings" and the life of "mortal men" it is more likely that he is simply comparing the magistracy to other secular callings.[28] But the statement is no less provocative for that. Calvin viewed civil government as absolutely crucial to human life.

Does such a lofty view of magistrates encourage arrogance, or even tyranny? Calvin thinks, on the contrary, that it is lack of accountability to God that spawns tyranny, while accountability to God inspires princes to "great zeal for uprightness, for prudence, gentleness, self-control, and for innocence." As vicars of God, princes are called "to present in themselves . . . some image of divine providence, protection, goodness, benevolence, and justice." Their judgments are to be those of God, and must therefore be in accord with the law of God.

> How will they have the brazenness to admit injustice to their judgment seat which they are told is the throne of the living God? How will they have the boldness to pronounce an unjust sentence by the mouth they know has been appointed an instrument of divine truth? With what conscience will they sign wicked decrees by their hand which they know has been appointed to record the acts of God?

As deputies of God, magistrates know that they will have to "render account" for all they do.[29]

---

[25] *Institutes* [1536], VI.C.39. Cf. Commentary on 2 Peter 2:10 [1551]; CO 55:465.

[26] *Institutes* [1536], VI.C.40.   [27] *Institutes* [1536], VI.C.52.

[28] Calvin also writes, "there is nothing in which we can better serve God than when we help his servants who labor for the truth of the gospel." Commentary on Philippians 2:30 [1548]; CO 52:42. Cf. Gordon J. Keddie, "Calvin on Civil Government," *Scottish Bulletin of Evangelical Theology* 32 (1981): 65–67; Reprinted in *Calvin's Thought on Economic and Social Issues and the Relationship of Church and State* (ed. Richard C. Gamble; New York: Garland, 1992), 27.

[29] *Institutes* [1536], VI.C.40. Cf. Commentary on Jeremiah 48:10 [1563]; CO 39:320–321; Commentary on Isaiah 3:14–15 [1559]; CO 36:89–90; Commentary on John 19:11 [1553]; CO 47:411.

The primary purpose of Calvin's emphasis on the dignity of magistrates is to serve as an apologetic against the Anabaptists, those who think "this holy ministry" is incompatible with "Christian religion and piety."[30] Subjects owe not only obedience, he argues, but are responsible for "undertaking public offices and burdens which pertain to the common defense." They are to support their governments, as Paul teaches in 1 Timothy 2, with "supplications, prayers, intercessions, and thanksgivings."[31]

The Anabaptists liked to quote Luke 22:25–26, in which Jesus told his disciples that they were not to lord it over one another like the nations. Calvin's response is to invoke the two kingdoms distinction. "To silence this vain ambition [of the disciples who aspired to lordship], the Lord taught them that their ministry is not like kingdoms, in which one is pre-eminent above the rest." The "kingly office is not the ministry of an apostle."[32] The distinction between the two kingdoms underlies Calvin's arguments throughout the next few sections. In response to the Anabaptist argument that killing is incompatible with the life of a Christian, he appeals to the distinction between a person and that person's political office, between personal violence and the just public use of the sword. A Christian magistrate "does nothing by himself, but carries out the very judgments of God." Vengeance on the part of the ministers of God against those who do harm "is not to hurt or to afflict" in the sense forbidden by scripture because it is done on the authority of God and in defense of the innocent. Given the purpose of civil government as God's means of restraining injustice, Christian magistrates are complicit in injustice if, refusing to take up the sword due to private scruples, they stand by "while abandoned men wickedly range about with slaughter and massacre."[33]

The same logic drives Calvin's version of just war theory.[34] War is just when the appropriate authority exercises an act of "public vengeance" against unjust violence. "For it makes no difference whether it be a king or the lowest of the common folk who invades a foreign country in which he has no right, and harries it as an enemy. All such must, equally, be considered as robbers and punished accordingly." As an act of just punishment, however, war is limited by the same principles of love and clemency that are to characterize all acts of public justice. Thus "if they have to punish, let them not be carried away with headlong anger, or be seized with hatred,

---

[30] Institutes [1536], VI.C.41. Cf. Balke, Calvin and the Anabaptist Radicals, 278–282, 289–295.
[31] Institutes [1536], VI.C.52.   [32] Institutes [1536], VI.C.41.
[33] Institutes [1536], VI.C.44. "Unless perhaps restraint is laid upon God's justice, that it may not punish misdeeds." Elsewhere he writes, "But without the sword laws are dead, and legal judgments have no forth or authority." Commentary on Luke 3:12 [1555]; CO 45:120–121.
[34] On Calvin's just war theory, see Mark J. Larson, Calvin's Doctrine of the State: A Reformed Doctrine and Its American Trajectory, The Revolutionary War, and the Founding of the Republic (Eugene, OR: Wipf and Stock, 2009); William K. Smith, Calvin's Ethics of War: A Documentary Study (Annapolis: Academic Fellowship, 1972).

or burn with implacable severity." Soldiers and princes are to recognize their enemies as human beings made in the image of God, having pity, as Augustine argues, "on the common nature in the one whose special fault they are punishing." War should be a last resort and it must always have peace as its objective.[35]

The distinction between the two kingdoms also characterizes Calvin's discussion of Christian involvement in litigation. Citing Romans 13, he observes that the magistrate has been appointed so that Christians, among others, might be protected from injustice, therefore living "a quiet and serene life."[36] How could it be that the magistrate would be appointed for their defense, and yet Christians are not "allowed to enjoy such benefit" by appealing to it for protection? On the other hand, Calvin concedes that many people "carry on their lawsuits with bitter and deadly hatred, and an insane passion to revenge and hurt" on the "pretense of legal procedure."[37] Calvin therefore articulates a theory of just litigation analogous to his theory of just war. Litigation must be pursued in a spirit of love, compassion, and a desire to do good to an offender. Litigation could be of benefit to both the accuser and the accused "if the defendant ... defends himself without bitterness, but only with this intent, to defend what is his by right," and if the plaintiff "puts himself in the care of the magistrate ... and seeks what is fair and good." But each side should be "prepared to yield his own and suffer anything" rather than yield to hatred or the desire to harm. For no matter how just the claim, the lawsuit is immoral "unless he treat his adversary with the same love and good will as if the business under controversy were already amicably settled and composed." Calvin concedes that this requires little short of a "miracle," and that "an example of an upright litigant is rare."[38] As with war, therefore, Christians should go to court only as a last resort. "To sum up ... love will give every man the best counsel. Everything undertaken apart from love and all disputes that go beyond it, we regard as incontrovertibly unjust and impious."[39] The reformer observes that Paul's prohibition of revenge in Romans 12 is accompanied by the command to wait on the Lord to avenge injustice, while Romans 13:4 declares that "the magistrate's revenge is not man's but God's." Thus Christians appropriately make the same distinction: between the spiritual

---

[35] *Institutes* [1536], VI.C.45.   [36] *Institutes* [1536], VI.C.50.   [37] *Institutes* [1536], VI.C.51.

[38] *Institutes* [1536], VI.C.51. Cf. Commentary on 1 Corinthians 6:1–7 [1546]; CO 49:387–392. Calvin observes that Christians do not exceed pagans in legal expertise, though they have a refined sense of "equity and conscientiousness" (6:2; CO 49:388). Where legal expertise is necessary, it is preferable for Christians to turn to secular authorities, lest the pastors of the church claim "jurisdiction [*iurisdictio*] ... in money matters" (6:4; 390). Cf. Commentary on 1 Peter 2:21–23 [1551]; CO 55: 249–251; Commentary on Matthew 5:40 [1555]; CO 45:185.

[39] *Institutes* [1536], VI.C.51. A Christian may not exercise revenge "either by himself, or by means of the magistrate, nor even desire it." Commentary on 1 Corinthians 6:7 [1546]; CO 49:391. The goal of appealing to a judge is simply "to learn ... what is right and just." Commentary on Exodus 18:15 [1563]; CO 24:187.

righteousness they are always called to practice and the civil righteousness that government must always defend.[40]

Calvin makes the same distinction with respect to Christ's command in the Sermon on the Mount not to resist evil but to turn the other cheek. Jesus "indeed wills that the hearts of his people so utterly recoil from any desire to retaliate that they should rather allow double injury to be done them than to increase their intention to pay it back." Christians should get used to bearing slander, injury, hatred, deception, and mockery, "promising themselves throughout life nothing but the bearing of a perpetual cross," even as they continue to "do good to those who do them harm, and bless those who curse them." Thus "they will so suffer their body to be maimed, and their possessions to be maliciously seized, that they will forgive and voluntarily pardon those wrongs as soon as they have been inflicted upon them." Still, a Christian can legitimately seek the aid of a magistrate "to prevent the efforts of a destructive man from doing harm to society."[41] Christians are to be conformed to the image of Christ in submission to his spiritual kingdom, but that does not detract from the necessity of civil justice in the political order.[42]

Calvin's two kingdoms doctrine further informs the reformer's flexible approach toward the laws and form of government appropriate for a "common society of Christians."[43] He reminds his readers that it is not his task as a theologian "to instruct the magistrates themselves." Rather, his purpose is "to teach others what magistrates are and to what end God has appointed them."[44] Although laws form the soul and sinews of a commonwealth, "without which the magistracy cannot stand," it is not within Calvin's purpose to craft a philosophical treatise on "the best kind of laws." There is a need for that sort of work, but despite his training as a lawyer, Calvin indicates his willingness to defer to others on such points. His task is simply to communicate the clear teaching of scripture.[45]

In fact, Calvin declares, he would have preferred not to discuss civil government at all. The only reason why he addresses the question of "with what laws a Christian state ought to be governed"[46] is to refute those "who deny that a commonwealth is duly framed which neglects the political system of Moses, and is ruled [instead] by the common laws of nations." For Calvin this claim is arguably "perilous and seditious," and his goal is to prove it to be "false and foolish."[47] His primary concern

---

[40] *Institutes* [1536], VI.C.51. [41] *Institutes* [1536], VI.C.51.

[42] In 1543 Calvin invoked Augustine's argument that Christ's commandments pertain more to "the preparation of the heart which is within than to the work which is done in the open" (*Institutes*, 4.20.20), though elsewhere he indicates some discomfort with it (Commentary on Matthew 5:39 [1555]; CO 45:184). Cf. Commentary on John 18:23 [1553]; 47:399; Commentary on Acts 23:5 [1554]; CO 48:505.

[43] *Institutes* [1536], VI.C.50. [44] *Institutes* [1536], VI.C.43. [45] *Institutes* [1536], VI.C.47.

[46] *Institutes* [1536], VI.C.47.

[47] *Institutes* [1536], VI.C.48. See Godfrey, "Calvin and Theonomy," 298–312.

in discussing political laws is not to call the magistrate to enforce the laws of scripture or promote Christian virtue but to nullify dogmatic attempts to impose biblical laws on Christian governments. To be sure, Calvin identified the Old Testament as a legitimate source of insight regarding the will of God for civil law. But he viewed it as one source among others – albeit the best – from which to infer the nature of natural law. For a particular claim of jurisprudence or political theory derived from the Old Testament to be normative, one had to demonstrate that it was a precept of natural law, consistent with reason and experience, and appropriate to one's particular circumstances.

Calvin begins his argument by reminding his readers of the classic Christian division of the law of Moses into moral, ceremonial, and judicial laws. He points out that the basic purpose of this distinction is to separate the timeless principles of morality from the particular laws that can be changed or abrogated in various times and places. He defines the moral law as "the true and eternal rule of righteousness, prescribed for men of all nations and times, who wish to conform their lives to God's will." He defines the ceremonial law as "the tutelage of the Jews, with which it seemed good to the Lord to train this people, as it were, in their childhood, until the fullness of time [i.e., Christ] should come." The judicial law is the law of civil government that "imparted definite formulas of equity and justice, by which they [the Jews] might live together blamelessly and peaceably."[48]

Calvin admits that in a sense the ceremonial and judicial laws "pertain also to morals." But while the ceremonial laws pertain to piety and worship, they "yet could be distinguished from piety itself," which is regulated by the moral law. Similarly the judicial law, "although it had no other intent than how best to preserve that very love which is enjoined by God's eternal law, had something distinct from that precept of love." Thus the ceremonial and judicial laws can be abrogated without violating the eternal laws of piety and love.[49] This leads to a fundamental political theological principle: "If this is true, surely every nation is left free to make such laws, as it foresees to be profitable for itself. Yet these must be in conformity to that perpetual rule of love, so that they indeed vary in form but have the same purpose." Like Aquinas, Calvin argues that although there is wide latitude in the laws that nations can make for their own welfare, laws that *contradict* the moral law are to be regarded as no laws at all.[50]

Calvin describes the distinction between the rule of love, or natural law, and the Mosaic judicial law in terms of the distinction between equity and the particulars of

---

[48] *Institutes* [1536], VI.C.48. This threefold distinction is carefully articulated by Aquinas, but its origins appear already in the church fathers. See C. Douais, "Saint Augustin et la Bible," *Révue Biblique* 3 (1894):420ff, cited in Battles, *Institutes of the Christian Religion*, 333.

[49] *Institutes* [1536], VI.C.48.

[50] *Institutes* [1536], VI.C.49. Cf. McNeill, "The Democratic Element in Calvin's Thought," 159.

a constitution. While the former is binding in all times and places, constitutions may legitimately vary "provided all equally press toward the same goal of equity."

> It should be clear that the law of God which we call the moral law is nothing else than a testimony of natural law and of that conscience which God has engraved upon men's hearts. Consequently, the entire scheme of this equity of which we are now speaking has been recorded in it. Hence, this equity alone must be the goal and rule and limit of all laws. Whatever laws shall be framed to that rule, directed to that goal, bound by that limit, there is no reason why we should disapprove of them, howsoever they may differ from the Jewish law or among themselves.[51]

As an example, Calvin offers the law forbidding theft. The Torah prescribes certain penalties for theft that differ from the laws of other nations. They are similar in what they forbid, but for various reasons they vary in the nature or rigor of enforcement. Still, "we see how, with such diversity, all laws tend to the same end. For, together with one voice, they pronounce punishment against those crimes which God's eternal law has condemned, namely, murder, theft, adultery, and false witness." To oppose such variety in the laws of nations is to be "malicious and hateful toward public welfare." The law of Moses "had never been enacted for us," and it is not dishonored when set aside or abrogated in favor of another law. "For the Lord through the hand of Moses did not give that law to be proclaimed among all nations." Rather, it was designed for the Jewish nation with whom God had established a special relationship.[52] Calvin maintained this position throughout his life.

Calvin's flexible attitude toward civil laws is mirrored in his discussion of forms of government. Here he stresses that it is not his task to philosophize about the best form of government, nor should "men in private life, who are disqualified from deliberating on the organization of any commonwealth," trouble themselves by idly disputing over the "best kind of government." As a lawyer and humanist, Calvin was familiar with the classic philosophical discussions. Following Aristotle, he argues that at the level of abstract theory, it is virtually impossible to say that one form is superior to another, whether monarchy, aristocracy, or democracy. Political judgments about the best form of government depend "especially upon the circumstances." Each community consists of different elements in different proportions and is "best held together according to their own particular inequality." Those for whom

---

[51] *Institutes* [1536], VI.C.49. On equity see Commentary on 2 Corinthians 11:31 [1548]: CO 50:135; Commentary on Acts 9:25 [1552]; CO 48:212. The best study on Calvin's understanding of equity is Guenther Haas, *The Concept of Equity in Calvin's Ethics* (Waterloo, Ontario: Wilfrid Laurier University Press, 1997). Haas emphasizes that equity for Calvin "provides the guideline for the implementation of love in our dealings with others" (50). "It does so by appealing to the intention of the law and to the motives of the people involved" (71).

[52] *Institutes* [1536], VI.C.49. Cf. Höpfl, *The Christian Polity of John Calvin*, 183.

"the will of the Lord is enough" can therefore resign themselves to the fact that "divine providence has wisely arranged that various countries should be administered by various kinds of government." As far as Christians are concerned, "it is our duty to show ourselves compliant and obedient to whomever he sets over the places where we live."[53] That government fulfills its role justly is more important than the form that it takes.

Calvin admits that most magistrates do not deserve this sort of honor or obedience. A good magistrate is one thing, but many princes are careless, lazy, corrupt, immoral, and tyrannical, some even "exercis[ing] sheer robbery, plundering houses, raping virgins and matrons, and slaughtering the guiltless." Are even such tyrants as these to be honored and obeyed? Calvin maintains that scripture calls Christians to be subject even to tyrants that "perform not a whit of the princes' office." Even when the persons occupying it do not fulfill their purpose or serve the welfare of their people, the magisterial office maintains its authority and dignity. Even tyrants possess "that noble and divine power" that God has given "the ministers of his justice and judgment," and they are to be held in the same honor as is "the best of kings."[54] The office bears an "inviolable majesty."[55]

At the foundation of Calvin's insistence that Christians owe obedience even to tyrannical regimes is his conviction that whatever governments exist have been ordained through the providence of God. Indeed, in many cases, "they who rule unjustly and incompetently have been raised by him to punish the wickedness of the people." Calvin provides a litany of scriptural evidence to prove this conclusion, devoting more exegetical energy to this argument than to any other in his discussion of civil government. To be sure, God's providence is not to be confused with his moral will. For instance, the tyrant described by the prophet Samuel would "not do this by . . . right [*iure*], since the law trained them to all restraint." Nevertheless, from the perspective of the people the king's actions should be viewed as within his "right [*ius*]" because "they had to obey it and were not allowed to resist."[56] That the Israelites had to obey the very Babylonian king who destroyed Jerusalem and took them into exile is compelling for Calvin. Like Augustine before him, he invokes the prophet Jeremiah's instructions to the exiles to seek the peace of Babylon. Christians

---

[53] *Institutes* [1536], VI.C.42.

[54] *Institutes* [1536], VI.C.54. Calvin observes in the 1559 edition that such reverence is not due to "the men themselves" but to the office (4.20.22).

[55] *Institutes* [1536], VI.C.55. Honor is owed even to tyrants because there has never been a tyranny "in which some portion of equity has not appeared, and further, some kind of government, however deformed and corrupt it may be, is still better and more beneficial than anarchy." Commentary on 1 Peter 2:14 [1551]; CO 55:245.

[56] *Institutes* [1536], VI.C.54. Calvin's explanation of 1 Samuel 8 illustrates that he understood the difference between legal right and moral right, or that a person can have legal authority without necessarily *being* right.

are to pray for their magistrate, not as they would for an enemy, but "that his kingdom may be preserved safe and peaceful, that under him they too may prosper."[57]

In the last four sections of the *Institutes*, however, Calvin shifts gears to consider what options are available to people who seek redress from tyranny. Here again the two kingdoms distinction controls the reformer's thought, as he struggles to balance Christians' spiritual obligations of piety and justice with their political obligations of obedience, the duties of Christians as private persons with the duties of those who hold political office. For Christians as individuals, conformity to Christ and his spiritual kingdom is determinative. "For, if the correction of unbridled despotism is the Lord's to avenge, let us not at once think that it is entrusted to us, to whom no command has been given except to obey and suffer."[58] Ordinarily "private citizens" should exercise public restraint, "that they may not deliberately intrude in public affairs, or pointlessly invade the magistrate's office, or undertake anything at all politically." They should not "raise a tumult" or seek by themselves to change public ordinances but should "commit the matter to the judgment of the magistrate."[59] Calvin acknowledges the objection that "rulers owe responsibilities in turn to their subjects," but he denies that a ruler's failure to keep his side of the bargain relieves his subjects from their obligation of obedience. Each person should focus on his own duties rather than on the duties of those who have been set over him. The fact is, it is not for subjects to restrain their kings. Rather, they should "implore the Lord's help," trusting that he will judge all tyrants as he has promised to do.[60]

Calvin observes that "sometimes he [God] raises up open avengers from among his servants, and arms them with his command to punish the wicked government and deliver his people." In such rare cases of divine intervention – Calvin only identifies examples of men who had a "lawful calling to carry out such acts" from the Old Testament – the avengers act on behalf of God, so upholding the majesty of kings by "subdu[ing] the lesser power with the greater." On other occasions, however, God "directs to this end the rage of men who intend one thing and undertake another." In such cases the avengers act unjustly, but they are nevertheless used by God. Here, Calvin thinks, is a sober warning: "Let the princes hear and be afraid."[61]

In addition to divine or providential intervention Calvin describes two sorts of resistance to tyranny, one appropriate to individual Christians by virtue of their spiritual duties, the other appropriate to certain civil magistrates by virtue of their political duties. In the first case, he argues, a Christian is obligated as a matter of conscience to disobey a law that forces her to commit impiety or

---

[57] *Institutes* [1536], VI.C.54.   [58] *Institutes* [1536], VI.C.55.   [59] *Institutes* [1536], VI.C.53.
[60] *Institutes* [1536], VI.C.55.   [61] *Institutes* [1536], VI.C.55.

injustice. Obedience to God is always preeminent. "If they command anything against him, let it go unesteemed." A magistrate's dignity is not undermined in such circumstances because that dignity itself is derivative of God's authority. Under no circumstances may Christians give up their allegiance to the spiritual kingdom – the realm of conscience. When political authorities attempt to invade that spiritual kingdom, Christians should "suffer anything rather than turn aside from piety." "[W]e have been redeemed by Christ at so great a price … so that we should not enslave ourselves to the wicked desires of men."[62]

The second form of resistance is appropriate to some who hold public office in the political order. All of the preceding comments about submission, Calvin observes, are to be understood as referring to "private individuals." As for the "magistrates of the people," not only may they resist tyranny against the people; they *must*.

> For if there are now any magistrates of the people [*populares magistratus*], appointed to restrain [*oppositi*] the willfulness of kings (as in ancient times the ephors were set against the Spartan kings, or the tribunes of the people against the Roman consuls, or the demarchs against the senate of the Athenians; and perhaps, as things now are, such power as the three estates exercise in every realm when they hold their chief assemblies), I am so far from forbidding them to withstand, in accordance with their duty [*pro officio intercedere*], the fierce licentiousness of kings, that, if they wink at kings who violently fall upon and assault the lowly common folk, I declare that their dissimulation involves nefarious perfidy, for by it they dishonestly betray the freedom of the people [*populi libertatem*], of which they know that they have been appointed protectors [*tutores*] by God's ordinance.[63]

Here the place for justified resistance is not simply at the point at which the tyrant has commanded impiety or injustice. It extends to the tyrant's oppression and violation of the people's liberty, of which the popular magistrates are appointed to be protectors. Calvin's argument here is pregnant with ambiguity, as suggestive as it is definitive. He does not specify just who might qualify as popular magistrates, or whether the term might include various degrees of nobility. The three estates had some form of power in virtually every kingdom of Europe, but they had not met for thirty years when Calvin first published the *Institutes*. Still, Calvin's principle is clear. There *is* a place for resistance to tyranny on the part of some lower magistrates. These officials can even legally empower citizens to take up the sword. "For when the ruler gives his command, private citizens receive public authority."[64] Ordinarily Christians must be subject to magistrates in all areas not contrary God's will, but within the political kingdom there is public authority to resist tyranny.

[62] *Institutes* [1536], VI.C.56.   [63] *Institutes* [1536], VI.C.55.   [64] *Institutes* [1536], VI.C.53.

COMMENTARY ON ROMANS (1540)

Calvin's commentary on Romans 13, the classic Christian text regarding civil government, bears some of the same characteristics as his discussion of civil government in the 1536 *Institutes*. Most striking is its overwhelmingly secular emphasis. Calvin's discussion of Romans 13 does not contain even a hint that magistrates should be concerned about piety or religion. The role of the magistrate is presented entirely in terms of justice toward human beings and the obligations of Christian love.[65]

Calvin's opening remarks indicate that he remained concerned with the problems that informed the *Institutes*. Some "tumultuous spirits" insisted that the establishment of the kingdom of Christ frees Christians from every form of human subjection, including civil government. In doing so they committed the same mistake as the Jews, who assumed that the kingdom of Christ would be political like that of King David. For the early church, the temptation was somewhat different. Early Christians found it difficult to imagine that political authorities openly hostile to Jesus' kingdom could hold any claim to their allegiance. But the temptation to question by what right (*quo iure*) governments derive their power is one that Christians must resist. It is enough that they exist and have therefore been established by the providence of God.[66] It is true that magistrates are not ordained by God in the same sense as is a natural disaster. The foundation of their power is not brute force but the legitimate authority that has been delegated to them by God. Though a product of the fall, it is good in its essence. Thus even if a legitimate government is too weak to enforce its commands, believers must still submit to it. On the other hand, this does not mean that whatever magistrates do is approved by God. In that sense tyranny is indeed an evil on the same level as a natural disaster. It must be accepted as a matter of providence, but it has no moral legitimacy.[67]

Calvin's discussion is guided by his emphasis on human welfare. Government is established because of its usefulness [*utilitate*] in preserving human life. Those who oppose it are "public enemies of the human race." Even tyrannical regimes,

---

[65] See David C. Steinmetz, *Calvin in Context* (2nd ed.; Oxford: Oxford University Press, 2010), 197–206; Richard A. Muller, "Calvin, Beza, and the Exegetical History of Romans 13:1–7," *The Identity of Geneva: The Christian Commonwealth, 1564–1864* (ed. John B. Roney and Martin I. Klauber; Westport, CT: Greenwood Press, 1998), 39–56.

[66] "[T]o despise his providence is to carry on war with him." Commentary on Romans 13:1 [1540]; T. H. L. Parker's *Iohannis Calvini Commentarius in Epistolam Pauli ad Romanos* (Leiden: Brill: 1981), 282. Cf. CO 49:248–249. Cf. Commentary on Titus 3:1 [1550]: CO 52:425–426.

[67] Commentary on Romans 13:1 [1540]; Calvin, *Iohannis Calvini Commentarius in Epistolam Pauli ad Romanos*, 282; Cf. CO 49:248–249. In later editions he adds, "though tyrannies and unjust exercise of power ... are not an ordained government [*ordinata gubernatione*], yet the right of government [*ius imperii*] is ordained [*ordinatem*] by God." Calvin, *Iohannis Calvini Commentarius in Epistolam Pauli ad Romanos*, 282.

providentially ordained by God, preserve at least a modicum of social order, for anarchy is worse than tyranny.[68] But magistrates are accountable for their use of power, both to God and to their subjects.

> Magistrates . . . are not to rule for their own interest, but for the public good [*publico bono*]. Nor are they endued with unbridled power [*effraeni potentia*], but what is restricted to the wellbeing of their subjects [*subditorum saluti*]. In short, they are responsible to God and to men in the exercise of their power. For as they are deputed [*legati*] by God and do his business, they must give an account to him. And then the ministration [*ministerium*] which God has committed to them has a regard to the subjects [*subditos*], so they are therefore debtors [*debitores*] also to them.[69]

While Calvin emphasizes that it is God's judgment that magistrates exercise when they punish offenders, he also stresses that civil judgment is temporal and limited to matters of temporal concern. The whole discussion, he reminds his readers, pertains to civil government, not to a government over consciences. The operative virtue in Romans 13 is love, not piety.[70] The passage presents love for one's neighbor (Romans 13:8–10) as the foundation for submission to civil government (Romans 13:1–7), and Calvin explicitly connects the two, observing that love is the basis for the civil order. "[F]or if you wish well to the good (and not to wish this is inhuman), you ought to strive that the laws and judgments may prevail, and that the administrators of the laws may have an obedient people, so that through them peace may be secured to all. He then who introduces anarchy violates love, for what immediately follows anarchy is the confusion of all things."[71] Love demands that a person secure his neighbor's rights.[72]

To be sure, the first table of the law is not entirely absent. Genuine love for one's neighbor, Calvin argues, is possible only when one has genuine love for God. But he

---

[68] Commentary on Romans 13:3 [1540]; Calvin, *Iohannis Calvini Commentarius in Epistolam Pauli ad Romanos*, 283; Cf. CO 49:250.

[69] At the same time, magistrates must "inflict such punishment on their [subjects'] offenses as God's judgment requires." Commentary on Romans 13:4 [1540]; Calvin, *Iohannis Calvini Commentarius in Epistolam Pauli ad Romanos*, 284; Cf. CO 49:251.

[70] Commentary on Romans 13:5 [1540]; Calvin, *Iohannis Calvini Commentarius in Epistolam Pauli ad Romanos*, 284–285; Cf. CO 49:251–252.

[71] Commentary on Romans 13:8 [1540]; Calvin, *Iohannis Calvini Commentarius in Epistolam Pauli ad Romanos*, 286; Cf. CO 49:252–253. In the preface he writes that some persons thought "Christian liberty [*libertatem christianam*]" required the end of civil government. "But that Paul might not appear to impose on the Church any duties but those of love, he declares that this obedience is included in what love requires" (Calvin, *Iohannis Calvini Commentarius in Epistolam Pauli ad Romanos*, 9–10; Cf. CO 49:6).

[72] Commentary on Romans 13:10 [1540]; Calvin, *Iohannis Calvini Commentarius in Epistolam Pauli ad Romanos*, 287; Cf. CO 49:254. In the 1551 edition he added, "he who desires that his own right [*ius*] should be secured to everyone . . . ought to defend, as far as he can, the power of magistrates [*ordinem magistraruum*]." Calvin, *Iohannis Calvini Commentarius in Epistolam Pauli ad Romanos*, 287.

says nothing about a magistrate's responsibilities concerning piety, worship, or doctrine. His only explicit reference to the first table of the law is to declare that "the first table of the law, which contains what we owe to God, is not here referred to at all."[73] The omission of even a mention of such responsibilities in a lengthy discussion of this classic text of Protestant political theology is telling. Calvin's early attitude toward civil government was remarkably secular in emphasis.

In sharp contrast to this characterization of civil government in the Romans commentary is Calvin's definition of the kingdom of Christ. "Wherever then there is justice and peace and spiritual joy, there the kingdom of God [*regnum Dei*] is complete in all its parts. It does not then consist of material things [*rebus ...corporeis*]."[74] Jesus' kingdom is spiritual, and "God does not now rule [*regnat*] otherwise in the world than by his gospel."[75] Christ prohibits Christians from desiring revenge even through legal procedures, and he calls them to pray for their enemies and overcome evil with good. Magistrates are also his subjects, but they serve a political vocation distinct from that of Christ's spiritual government. They must carefully distinguish their judicial functions from any personal desires or claims. Christian virtue should shape their conduct, but their work of judgment is sharply distinguished from that of Christ's kingdom.[76]

THE TREATISE AGAINST THE ANABAPTISTS (1544)

During the years after 1536, Calvin began to develop a sophisticated biblical theology, in part due to a desire to distinguish evangelical theology from that of the Anabaptists. Like Bullinger before him, he devoted careful attention to the relation between the old and new covenants. This work began to bear fruit in 1539, when two new chapters comparing the Old and New Testaments appeared in the second edition of the *Institutes*.[77] It took years of commentaries, sermons, lectures, and successive editions of the *Institutes* to work out the implications of this biblical theology, but over time it profoundly shaped the reformer's political theology. Some of these developments made their way into successive editions of the *Institutes*. Others did not.

---

[73] Commentary on Romans 13:10 [1540]; Calvin, *Iohannis Calvini Commentarius in Epistolam Pauli ad Romanos*, 287; Cf. CO 49:254.

[74] Commentary on Romans 14:18 [1540]; Calvin, *Iohannis Calvini Commentarius in Epistolam Pauli ad Romanos*, 301; Cf. CO 49:266.

[75] Commentary on Romans 14:11 [1540]; Calvin, *Iohannis Calvini Commentarius in Epistolam Pauli ad Romanos*, 298; Cf. CO 49:263.

[76] Commentary on Romans 12:8, 19 [1540]; Calvin, *Iohannis Calvini Commentarius in Epistolam Pauli ad Romanos*, 272, 279; Cf. CO 49:239–240, 247.

[77] Balke argues that Calvin's controversies with the Anabaptists "occasioned much of the overall expansion of the *Institutes*" in 1539. Balke, *Calvin and the Anabaptist Radicals*, 121.

That Calvin recognized the insufficiency of his refutation of the Anabaptists in the 1536 *Institutes* is evident from slight changes he made to the chapter on civil government in 1543. Most significantly, in a new paragraph Calvin addresses the objection that while war may have been lawful for Old Testament Israel, the New Testament provides no evidence that it is lawful for Christians. He offers three arguments in response. First, he notes that whatever the differences between the old and new covenants, the obligation of magistrates to protect the innocent and punish the unjust remains. The third argument he offers is drawn from Augustine, and simply notes that when soldiers desiring to repent approached John the Baptist he did not tell them to give up their vocation.[78] But the second is most important because it lays down what, for Calvin, became a fundamental biblical theological principle. "Secondly, I say that an express declaration of this matter is not to be sought in the writings of the apostles, for their purpose is not to fashion a civil government, but to establish the spiritual kingdom of Christ" (4.20.12). For the Anabaptists the shift from Old Testament to New Testament signified a radical change in the form of life God demands of his people. For Calvin the discontinuity implies fulfillment, but the need for civil government remains fundamentally the same.

These changes presaged Calvin's 1544 treatise against the Anabaptists, the *Brief Instruction for Arming All the Good Faithful Against the Errors of the Common Sect of the Anabaptists*, which he wrote as a response to the Schleitheim Confession.[79] This treatise is broadly consistent with Calvin's earlier work, but its defense of traditional Christian views of civil government is freshly articulated in terms of Calvin's developing biblical theology. The fresh approach appears in four ways. First, Calvin produces a new set of texts designed to show that scripture explicitly teaches the divine authorization of civil magistrates even in the time of the kingdom of Christ. These texts, which found their way into the *Institutes* in 1559, became the foundational texts invoked by Calvin over and over throughout his career to prove the sanctity of Christian magistrates. Second, Calvin engages a myriad of Anabaptist proof-texts with a growing awareness of his opponents' nuance and sophistication. Third, although in the 1536 *Institutes* Calvin offered a powerful polemical argument against the position that the Mosaic law should be the law for Christian governments, beginning in 1544 it was evident that he was far more concerned with those who deny the relevance of the law's proscriptions and

---

[78] Cf. Commentary on Luke 3:12 [1555]; CO45:120–121.

[79] John Calvin, "Brief Instruction for Arming All the Good Faithful Against the Errors of the Common Sect of the Anabaptists," in Farley, *Treatises Against the Anabaptists and Against the Libertines*; CO 7: 45–142. Cf. Balke, *Calvin and the Anabaptist Radicals*, 177; Akira Demura, "From Zwingli to Calvin: A Comparative Study of Zwingli's *Elenchus* and Calvin's *Brière Instruction*," *Zürcher Beiträge zur Reformationsgeschichte* (ed. Alfred Schindler and Hans Stickelberger; Bern: Peter Lang, 2001), 87–99.

penalties for contemporary politics. Calvin never retracted his early arguments, but he did shift his emphasis. Finally, whereas in the 1536 *Institutes* and the 1540 commentary on Romans, Calvin primarily describes the role of government in secular terms, the 1544 *Brief Instruction* suggests a distinctly Christian priority for government: the maintenance of the glory and honor of God.

The shift in attitude toward the Mosaic law is more a matter of emphasis than of principle. Calvin always insisted that in the Sermon on the Mount, Jesus did not introduce a new law for Christians but merely clarified and restored the "true meaning of the law." With regard to "true spiritual justice [*la vraye iustice spirituelle*]" and righteousness "before God," in other words, "there exists a plain and complete guideline for it in the law of Moses, to which we need simply cling if we want to follow the right path."[80] If the vocation of civil magistrate was honorable in the Mosaic law, how could it become immoral after the coming of Christ?

Calvin was aware that there was an obvious rejoinder to this claim. "They will reply, possibly, that the civil government [*gouvernement civil*] of the people of Israel was a figure of the spiritual kingdom of Jesus Christ [*regne spirituel de Iesus Christ*] and lasted only until his coming." Calvin's response is illustrative of the way in which he approaches the Old Testament. He affirms that the Israelite nation was a figure of Christ's spiritual kingdom but denies that it can be reduced to that. The New Testament clearly teaches that the Levitical priesthood has come to an end, he agrees, but nowhere does it say that this is true of Israel's "external order [*police externe*]," that is to say, of "political government [*gouvernement politique*], which is a requirement among all people." Calvin's point here is not to advocate the particularities of Israel's government but the fact of it. He marshals a set of passages from the prophetic writings to prove that civil government is a permanent order established by God, one that did not expire with the abrogation of the law. "For when the prophets speak of the kingdom of Jesus Christ [*regne de Iesus Christ*], it is written that kings will come to worship and pay homage to him. It is not said that they will abdicate their positions in order to become Christians, but rather, being appointed with royal dignity, they will be subject to Jesus Christ [*subiectz à Iesus Christ*] as to their sovereign Lord [*leur Seigneur souverain*]."[81]

The first key text is Psalm 2, in which David calls the kings of the earth to cease their rebellion and to "kiss the Son." It is certain, Calvin argues, that David speaks here of "the kingdom of our Lord Jesus [*regne de nostre Seigneur Iesus*]." In the second text, Isaiah 49:23, the prophet predicts that "kings will become the foster fathers of the Christian church and that queens will nurse it with their breasts." Calvin observes that not only does this text reveal the legitimacy of magistrates in

---

[80] Calvin, "Brief Instruction," 78; CO 7:81.   [81] Calvin, "Brief Instruction," 78–79; CO 7:81–82.

the kingdom, but it ordains them "protectors of his church [*protecteurs de son Eglise*]."[82] Later he builds on this argument, rejecting the claim that "all the anxieties of princes are those of this world" and invoking Isaiah's promise that "earthly kings will serve in the heavenly and spiritual kingdom of Jesus Christ [*les Roys terriens serviront à maintenir le Royaume celeste et spirituel de Iesus Christ*]"[83]

The third foundational text, 1 Timothy 2:2, is perhaps most important, because it is found in the New Testament. Here Paul urges Christians to pray for all people, including those in positions of authority, "that we may lead a peaceful and quiet life, godly and dignified in every way." The reason for Paul's command to Christians to pray for magistrates, Calvin argues, is that it was tempting for the early church to reject the legitimacy of rulers so openly hostile to the gospel. In his first reference to this text in his *Brief Instruction*, Calvin emphasizes Paul's reference to the universality of the gospel call and the lack of any indication that its universality requires magistrates to resign their political office.[84] Later he returns to the same text, introducing the argument that Paul's intent is not to describe "the principal end [*la principale fin*]" of magistrates as being to "maintain the peace of their subjects according to the flesh [*paix selon la chair*]" (in granting them the freedom to live a peaceful, quiet, and godly life), but that they might "ensure that God is served and honored in their countries and that each person leads a good and honest life." Thus not only are political rulers legitimate authorities, but they are called "to take pain to see that the name of God is exalted."[85] Over the years Calvin gave this text increasing weight as the one New Testament text that, in his view, affirms the continuing responsibility of magistrates to defend and promote piety, worship, and doctrine.

In addition to his new set of texts, in the *Brief Instruction*, Calvin also displays a new sensitivity to the nuances in Anabaptist claims that magistrates are alien to the new covenant. Most important is his argument concerning John 8, the story of the woman caught in adultery. Calvin breaks with the influential interpretation of Augustine, who argued that in freeing the woman from judgment, Jesus proclaimed the supersession of the Torah's law of capital punishment by the grace of the new covenant.[86] The reason why Jesus did not call for the woman to be put to death in accordance with the Mosaic law was not that this law no longer binds Christians, Calvin argues, but that it was not Jesus' vocation to execute the sentence.

> Now it is certain that our Lord did not want to change anything about the government or the civil order [*la police, ou de l'ordre civil*], but without reviling it in any way, he made his office, for which he came into the world, that of forgiving

---

[82] Calvin, "Brief Instruction," 79; CO 7:82.   [83] Calvin, "Brief Instruction," 91; CO 7:92.
[84] Calvin, "Brief Instruction," 81–82; CO 7:84–85.   [85] Calvin, "Brief Instruction," 91; CO 7:92.
[86] Calvin, "Brief Instruction," 193; CO 7:85. The Anabaptists claimed that in the church Christ had replaced the sword with excommunication, an argument Calvin dismissed on the basis that Jesus did not excommunicate this woman. Balke, *Calvin and the Anabaptist Radicals*, 193.

sins. For he was not sent by God his father in order to perform the office of an earthly judge [*iuge terrien*], but to ransom the world by his death and to testify, by the preaching of the gospel, to the grace of this redemption and similarly to all the benefits which we receive through him.[87]

Calvin uses similar logic to explain other scenarios in the gospel narratives. Jesus refused to arbitrate in a property dispute (Luke 12:14) because it was not in line with his vocation, but the world continues to need arbitration "in order to settle quarrels regarding possessions, inheritance, and other matters."[88] The Jews wanted Jesus to assume a magisterial office, but Jesus refused (John 6:15) because "his kingdom is not carnal, nor of this world, but spiritual [*son Royaume n'est pas charnel, ny de ce monde: mais spirituel*]."[89] Jesus is lord of all kings, but his rule is expressed in terms of two kingdoms. When he forbade the disciples to lord it over one another, therefore, he did not mean that Christians may not become magistrates. Rather, distinguishing between political ministers and spiritual ministers, he taught that because "his kingdom is spiritual and ... does not consist in worldly pride, pomp, or lordly power, ... all the preeminence that his [spiritual] ministers and officers have is to serve."[90]

The 1544 *Brief Instruction* represents a new level of sophistication in Calvin's political theology. It illustrates his determination to be sensitive to the differences between the Old and New Testaments, even as he sought substantive guidance from the Old Testament. Calvin rejected the Anabaptist tendency to conflate the two kingdoms doctrine with the distinction between Old Testament Israel and the New Testament church. Yet like the 1536 *Institutes*, the *Brief Instruction* leaves undeveloped the precise relation between temporal Christian magistrates and Israelite kings. It affirms that magistrates should be concerned about piety and the honor of God, but it leaves considerable ambiguity as to what this means in practice.

EXHORTATIONS TO CIVIL MAGISTRATES (1541–1552)

Other writings by Calvin from the 1540s confirm his expanding vision about the sort of care that magistrates are to provide for true religion. In a letter to the Geneva Council in 1541 Calvin urged the governing body to use all its means to ensure that the church was constituted and ruled according to the "order of our Lord [*l'ordre de nostre seigneur*]."[91] Calvin's attempt to have a confession of faith imposed by oath on

---

[87] Calvin, "Brief Instruction," 83; CO 7:85–86.   [88] Calvin, "Brief Instruction," 85; CO 7:87.
[89] Calvin, "Brief Instruction," 86; CO 7:88.   [90] Calvin, "Brief Instruction," 87; CO 7:88–89.
[91] See Letter to the Geneva Seigneury, February 19, 1541; CO 11:158–159. Cf. Letter to the Geneva Seigneury, July 18, 1543; CO 11:587–589. Later Calvin told the Geneva Council that it was its task to restrain slander against him. Dedication of the Commentary on John to the Council of Geneva [1553]; CO 47:vi.

all Genevans indicates that he conceived of the well-ordered Christian city as *ideally* being coterminous with the church. It is clear from a letter Calvin wrote to Farel concerning Servetus that by 1546 he supported the death penalty for individuals guilty of notorious heresy.[92]

By the late 1540s Calvin had a nuanced theory of just how magistrates are to care for the true religion, and he was enthusiastically exhorting foreign magistrates to carry it out. Some of the most prominent examples of such exhortation are the various letters and dedications he wrote to the Duke of Somerset, who was the Protector of England during the childhood of King Edward VI, and to the king himself.[93] In 1548 Calvin dedicated his commentary on Paul's epistles to Timothy to Somerset. He praised Somerset for

> making the restoration of religion your principal object [*instaurandae religionis curam inprimis susciperes*] ... for then do kingdoms enjoy solid prosperity and faithful guardianship, when he on whom they were founded and by whom they are preserved – the Son of God himself – rules over them [*praesideat*]. Thus you could not have established more firmly that of England than by banishing idols and setting up there the pure worship of God.[94]

Calvin tried to persuade Somerset that the health of an earthly kingdom is insepar- able from the cause of Christ's spiritual kingdom within its bounds, a theme to which he would return over and over in his letters to the English leaders. By establishing the true religion within England's bounds, he would turn away the chastising hand of God. The result, "were all the nobility and those who administer justice to submit themselves in uprightness and all humility to this great king Jesus Christ [*la subiec- tion de ce grand Roy Jesus Christ*]," would be the blessing of the whole kingdom.[95] By restoring the church King Edward would "unquestionably" receive the blessing of God and England would derive "inestimable advantage."[96]

Such encouragement marked a shift in emphasis from his earlier years, but in Calvin's mind it did not involve a change in principle. An important function – and what Calvin increasingly saw as *the* most important function – of civil government was to establish, protect, and promote Christ's spiritual kingdom. True doctrine had to be restored, "and what is that but to place Christ on his throne?" Rulers needed to

[92] Letter to Farel, February 13, 1546; CO 12:282–284; Cf. Letter to Viret, July 2, 1547; CO 12:545–548; Letter to the Seigneury of Geneva, May, 1550; CO 13:568–570; Letter to Farel, September, 1538; CO 10:247.

[93] See Brandt B. Boeke, "Calvin's Doctrine of Civil Government." *Studia Biblica et Theologica* 11 (1981): 61–67.

[94] Dedication of the Commentary on 1 and 2 Timothy to Edward, Duke of Somerset, July 25, 1548; CO 13: 16–18 (16–17).

[95] Letter to the Protector Somerset, October 22, 1548; CO 13:64–77 (69).

[96] Dedication of the First Commentary on Isaiah to Edward VI, December 25, 1550; CO 13:669–674 (673).

"own the subjection of their high rank to the spiritual scepter of Christ."[97] Calvin urged Somerset to advance God's cause "until you have established his kingdom [*estably son regne*] in as great perfection as is to be looked for in the world." This involved "setting up the purity and right order [*droicte reigle*] of his worship" and "establishing the doctrine of salvation [*faire que la doctrine de salut*], that it may there be faithfully proclaimed to all those who shall consent to hear it." The government should oversee the enactment of a confession binding on the clergy, the drafting of a catechism for the instruction of the young, and the establishment of public liturgy.[98]

To be sure, Calvin made it quite clear that neither Somerset nor the king could do the spiritual work of building Christ's kingdom. Christ governs his kingdom through the ministry of the gospel, Calvin explains, and "herein you may also perceive why the gospel is called the kingdom of God [*lEvangile est appelle le Regne de Dieu*]." Although "the edicts and statutes of princes are good helps for advancing and upholding the state of Christianity [*bonnes aydes pour advancer et maintenir lestat de la chrestienté*], yet God is pleased to declare his sovereign power by this spiritual sword of his word [*sa vertu souveraine en ce glayve spirituel de sa parolle*], when it is made known by the pastors."[99] Thus earthly princes were called to govern as subjects of Jesus Christ by "taking order that he may have his own sovereign authority over all, both small and great."[100] The king was to display for his people an example of submission to the "spiritual scepter" of Christ, "to be a Christian king, to serve as his lieutenant in maintaining the kingdom of Jesus Christ in England [*pour maintenir le Royaume de Iesus Christ en Angleterre*]."[101]

While the kingdom of Christ consists in doctrine rather than in the power of the temporal sword, the sword had its role in defending the gospel against assailants like Rome and the Anabaptists. Both groups had to be "repressed by the sword which is committed to you, since they not only attack the king, but strive with God, who has placed him upon a royal throne, and has committed to you the protection as well of his person as of his majesty."[102] In a dedication to Edward VI, written in 1551, Calvin reminded the young king, "you must bear in mind that it is a duty which belongs to your majesty to vindicate from unworthy calumnies the true and genuine interpretation of Scripture, so that pure religion may flourish."[103]

---

[97] Dedication of the Commentary on 1 and 2 Timothy; CO 13:17.
[98] Letter to the Protector Somerset, October 22, 1548; CO 13:65.
[99] Letter to the Protector Somerset, October 22, 1548; CO 13:72.
[100] Letter to the Protector Somerset, October 22, 1548; CO 13:69. Cf. Letter 281, July 25, 1551; CO 14: 155–157.
[101] Letter to Edward VI, July 4, 1552; CO 14:342.
[102] Letter to the Protector Somerset, October 22, 1548; CO 13:68–69.
[103] Dedication of Commentary on James, 1 and 2 Peter, 1 John, and Jude; January 24, 1551; CO 14:30–37 (37).

At the same time, the people were to be called to obedience and social responsibility, and Calvin urged Somerset to punish crimes some people thought were of little significance: "whoredom and adultery, drunkenness, and blaspheming of the name of God." Scripture teaches that blasphemy defiles a whole country, he argued, and even the pagans exercised more rigor in punishing adultery than did most Christian nations. "Be it remembered also, that whoremongers and drunkards are banished from the kingdom of God [*banniz du royaume de Dieu*] on such terms that we are forbidden to converse with them, whence it clearly follows that they ought not to be endured in the church." True, civil government is not to usurp the place of the bishops and curates responsible for exercising spiritual discipline in the church, but "the chief responsibility returns upon you, who have a special charge given you to set the others in motion . . . that the order which shall have been established may be duly observed."[104]

Already in these early years, Calvin consistently presented faithful Israelite kings as models for contemporary Christian magistrates. In a letter to Somerset in 1548, he acknowledged that the social upheaval that accompanied religious changes was significant, but he urged him to continue the struggle in accord with the example of "good King Hezekiah," who was constantly opposed in his efforts to reform the church. No doubt God provided the example of Hezekiah to warn all princes that "however earnest they may be in banishing idolatry and in promoting the true worship of God," the road to peace and public tranquility would not be smooth.[105] There would always be those who opposed change, but there could be no compromise with regard to establishing "the spiritual governance of the church [*regime spirituel de lEglise*]," whether to "modify or curtail, advance or retreat." Scripture does not praise those Israelite kings who stopped short of removing all idolatry.[106]

In his dedication of the first commentary on Isaiah, Calvin set Hezekiah before Edward as a model of the right attitude of a king toward a faithful pastor. Hezekiah "not only treated the holy man [Isaiah] with reverence, but modestly submitted to his doctrine like one of the common people, and, what is still more, endured patiently severe reproof when it was found necessary." Likewise, in Christendom, kings ought to assist and protect pastors while submitting to the word faithfully proclaimed.[107] Calvin invoked Isaiah 49:23, one of the key passages set forward in his *Brief Instruction*, which proclaimed kings to be "nursing-fathers of the church." The text "pronounces a woe on all kings and nations who refuse to give her [the church] their support," obligating magistrates "to restore her to her former

---

[104] Letter to the Protector Somerset, October 22, 1548; CO 13:76.
[105] Letter to the Protector Somerset, October 22, 1548; CO 13:66.
[106] Letter to the Protector Somerset, October 22, 1548; CO 13:74–75. Cf. Letter to the King of England, January, 1551; CO 14:38–41.
[107] Dedication of the First Commentary on Isaiah to Edward VI, December 25, 1550; CO 13:669–670.

condition."[108] Just as Moses commanded the king to study and keep the Torah, so "kings have themselves need of this remarkable doctrine and are especially enjoined to defend and maintain it."[109]

CONCLUSION

In his early writings, Calvin worked out the implications of the two kingdoms doctrine for civil government, articulating the principles that would be definitive for his political theology. He argued that God has granted civil government the sword for the purpose of restraining evil during this temporal age. He defended Christian participation in civil government, while rejecting the claim that the Mosaic law is normative for Christian politics. He consistently used two kingdoms logic when discussing an array of practical moral, legal and political matters. At the same time, Calvin's emphases shifted. In the 1536 *Institutes* and the 1540 commentary on Romans, he emphasized government's secular responsibilities. Later, however, he began to emphasize government's obligation to promote and defend the true religion, and he increasingly turned to the Old Testament as a norm for politics. In coming years his two kingdoms theology would shape the ways in which he continued to develop these lines of thought.

[108] Dedication of the First Commentary on Isaiah to Edward VI, December 25, 1550; CO 13:672–673.
[109] Dedication of the Commentary on James, 1 and 2 Peter, 1 John, and Jude; January 24, 1551; CO 14:37. Calvin praised King Sigismund Augustus of Poland for being "already engaged in the work of restoring the kingdom of Christ [*instaurandum Christi regnum*]." The happiness of the Polish kingdom would "only be solid, when it adopts Christ as its chief ruler and governor, so that it may be defended by his safeguard and protection, for to submit your scepter to him is not inconsistent with that elevation in which you are placed." Dedication of the Commentary on Hebrews [1549], May 23, 1549; CO 13: 281–286 (282). The king was to ensure that religion be reformed according to scripture that "Christ may take an entire possession of his own kingdom" (283).

7

Covenant and Law

In 1539 Calvin introduced into the *Institutes* a lengthy discussion of the relationship between the Old and New Testaments (or covenants), or between the law and the gospel (2.11). This covenant theology forms a crucial part of Calvin's political theology because it dictates his understanding of the relationship between Old Testament Israel and the New Testament kingdom of Christ. That understanding, in turn, informs Calvin's view of the relevance of the nation of Israel and the Mosaic law for the politics of Christendom. For Calvin the Mosaic law, including the Ten Commandments, was first and foremost a covenantal document. Its commands, promises, and threats, and the sense in which they do or do not bind Christians, could not be understood apart from their covenantal context.

Like Zwingli and Bullinger, Calvin approached covenant theology as a means of refuting the Anabaptist tendency to reject the direct relevance of the Old Testament for Christians. Like Bullinger, Calvin insisted that all of the major covenants of scripture ultimately represent one eternal gracious covenant between God and human beings. This one covenant includes the authoritative revelation of the natural moral law in the Ten Commandments. But Calvin agreed with the Anabaptists that there are important differences between the Old and New Testaments, and he explained many of these differences by means of the Aristotelian distinction between substance and accidents. The substance of the covenant always remains the same, he argued, but it varies throughout salvation history in its administration and forms. "[T]he difference between us and the ancient fathers lies in accidents [*accidentibus*], not in substance [*substantia*]. In all the leading characters of the testament or covenant we agree: the ceremonies and form of government [*regimen*], in which we differ, are mere additions."[1]

The differences Calvin identified between the covenants, especially between the law (the Mosaic covenant) and the gospel (the new covenant), correspond to

---

[1] Commentary on Galatians 4:1 [1548]; CO 50:224–225.

a certain extent to his two kingdoms distinction. For instance, Calvin observes that Israelite worship and polity was outward and typological, while in the new covenant era the church's worship and government are inward and spiritual. In addition, the Mosaic covenant contained a narrowly legal dimension of judgment that is distinct from the eternal gracious covenant and contrary in principle to the gracious character of the gospel. Both of these differences led Calvin to reject the claim that Israel and its civil law could be embraced as inviolable norms for Christian politics. Insofar as Israel's government and law reflected the timeless principles of natural law, it was an institution of the *political* kingdom and could serve as an example for temporal Christian polities, but insofar as Israel was a type of the spiritual kingdom of Christ, it was unique and could not serve as such a model.[2]

In this chapter I focus on Calvin's covenant theology as it informs his understanding of the significance of Israel and the Mosaic law for politics.[3] After briefly outlining Calvin's understanding of the substantive unity among the covenants, I focus primarily on the various differences between the covenants. I conclude by reflecting on some of the implications of Calvin's covenant theology for his two kingdoms doctrine, though I leave most of my analysis of Calvin's wrestling with practical political questions for Chapters 8 and 9.

THE COVENANT: ONE IN SUBSTANCE

Calvin's teaching on the unity of the covenant was targeted at "certain madmen of the Anabaptist sect" who denied the spiritual significance of Old Testament Israel. Calvin charged Servetus in particular with believing that the Israelites had no "hope of heavenly immortality" (2.10.1).[4] Such views flew in the face of

---

[2] In this respect Calvin's view was similar to that of Luther, who also insisted that the Mosaic law only binds Christians insofar as it testifies to natural law. See Johannes Heckel, *Lex Charitatis: A Juristic Disquisition on Law in the Theology of Martin Luther* (trans. Gottfried G. Krodel; Grand Rapids: Eerdmans, 2010 [1973]).

[3] Much of the work on Calvin's covenant theology focuses on its relation to that of Zwingli and Bullinger, to later Reformed covenant theology, and to the doctrine of predestination. For a clear demonstration that Calvin's covenant theology is not substantially different from that of Zwingli and Bullinger, see Lyle D. Bierma, "Federal Theology in the Sixteenth Century: Two Traditions?," *Westminster Theological Journal* 45 (1983): 304–321. Cf. Peter Alan Lillback, *The Binding of God: Calvin's Role in the Development of Covenant Theology* (Grand Rapids: Baker, 2001). On the connection to predestination, see Anthony Hoekema, "The Covenant of Grace in Calvin's Teaching," *Calvin Theological Journal* 2 (1967): 133–161; M. Eugene Osterhaven, "Calvin on the Covenant," *Readings in Calvin's Theology* (ed. Donald McKim; Grand Rapids: Baker, 1984), 89–106.

[4] Calvin complains about fanatics who "regard the promises of the Old Testament as temporal [*carne*]" and confine them to the present world [*praesentem mundum*]." Commentary on Romans 15:8 [1556]; CO 49:273.

Calvin's understanding of God's eternal purpose for human beings: fellowship with God in his eternal kingdom. All that was "external" in the Old Testament, Calvin argues, whether pertaining to worship or to Israel's civil affairs, must be distinguished from Israel's spiritual purpose: "Surely the gospel does not confine men's hearts to delight in the present life, but lifts them to the hope of immortality." Given that they also heard the promises of the gospel, Old Testament saints must also have looked upward and forward to the consummation of creation in the "future life" (2.10.3). Faithful Israelites "entered into God's immortal kingdom," for "theirs was a real participation in God, which cannot be without the blessing of eternal life" (2.10.7). By faithfulness in the midst of earthly misery, the patriarchs "testified that they hoped to receive the fruit of the promise only after death" (2.10.13).

Though he skips over it in the *Institutes*, in his commentaries Calvin stresses that the Mosaic covenant (or Sinai covenant) was also an administration of the one eternal covenant. "[T]he law was nothing more than a renewal of the covenant, and more fully sanctioned the remembrance of it."[5] The Sinai covenant was "the covenant of gratuitous adoption." Its ceremonial confirmation in blood was "the blood of Christ in type and shadow."[6] When the people confidently declared, "All the words that the LORD has spoken we will do," Calvin insists, the "faithful among them" made the oath based on the promise of God's gracious reconciliation, as they looked beyond the law to Christ. "[T]he office of the law was to lead men step by step to Christ, that they might seek of him pardon and the Spirit of regeneration."[7]

The same was true of David, Job, Samuel, and the prophets. Throughout the Old Testament, God progressively revealed the truth that one day Christ's kingdom would be consummated in the whole earth. The prophets represented the blessings of the kingdom "under the lineaments, so to speak, of temporal benefits. But they painted a portrait such as to lift up the minds of the people above the earth, above the elements of the world and the perishing age ... to the happiness of the spiritual life to come" (2.10.20). For Calvin this is a fundamental principle of Old Testament interpretation. The old covenant "had not been limited to earthly things, but contained a promise of spiritual and eternal life." Now that Christ has come, to cling to earthly pomp and power resembles "the obtuseness of the whole Jewish nation today in awaiting the Messiah's earthly kingdom" (2.11.23).[8]

---

[5] Commentary on Romans 9:4 [1556]; CO 49:173.   [6] Commentary on Exodus 24:5 [1563]; CO 25:75.

[7] Commentary on Exodus 24:5 [1563]; CO 25:76.

[8] But Calvin refused to *reduce* the prophecies' meaning entirely to the spiritual kingdom. See Commentary on Isaiah 52:10 (1559); CO 37:249–250; Commentary on Jeremiah 23:7–8 (1563); CO 38: 414–415.

THE OLD AND NEW COVENANTS: DIFFERENCES OF FORM

Calvin's account of the differences between the Old and New Testaments can be categorized into two different types: 1) differences of *form* between the Mosaic and new administrations of the one eternal covenant, both of them expressions of the gospel, and 2) differences in principle between the Mosaic law in its peculiar office of judgment and the eternal covenant of grace.[9] Before considering these two types of differences, however, it is important to recognize that the exegetically sensitive Calvin used the word "law" in a range of different ways, as does scripture itself. Most prominently, in Calvin's writings, law can refer 1) to the old covenant in general (i.e., the doctrine of the Old Testament, or the Torah, the "broad" law), especially in contrast to the new covenant, then designated as the "gospel"; 2) more narrowly to the Mosaic covenant as ratified at Sinai (i.e., what is peculiar to Moses), with all its commandments, ceremonies, and threats; and 3) to God's timeless moral will represented in the Ten Commandments, or natural law (i.e., the moral law). With respect to the second category (i.e., what is peculiar to Moses), he sometimes includes the ceremonies and sacrifices that are types of Christ (2a), whereas other times he focuses more narrowly on the principle of works as the basis for reward and punishment (i.e., the narrow law) (2b). When he describes the Mosaic covenant as a distinctive covenant with respect to the ceremonies and sacrifices (#2a), he is speaking of a distinction of form between administrations of the covenant of grace, whereas when he does so with respect to the narrow law (#2b), he is speaking of a distinction of principle between the legal covenant and the one covenant of grace. Identifying which of these meanings Calvin is using is sometimes difficult, but it is essential to understanding his meaning.[10]

[9] In his excellent book *Calvin's Concept of the Law*, I. John Hesselink categorizes the differences that Calvin draws between the Old and New Testaments in *Institutes* 2.11 into two types. The first involves differences of form, degree, or measure of fulfillment. The second involves an essentially antithetical contrast. I. John Hesselink, *Calvin's Concept of the Law* (Allison Park, PA: Pickwick Publications, 1992), 170–171. Peter Lillback writes, "Calvin speaks of the covenant of the law as both part of the covenant of grace and distinct from it. This seeming contradiction is solved when one considers that the covenant of the law in both the broad and narrow senses is the same in administration (i.e., under Moses) yet different in substance (i.e., human merit vs. the righteousness of Christ)." In his Commentary on Galatians, Calvin is comparing "the covenant of the law in the narrow sense and the covenant of grace in the broad sense." Lillback, *The Binding of God*, 160. "Calvin employs a twofold use of the covenant of the 'law.' It can be used to describe the Mosaic economy either in the strict Pauline sense of self-congratulatory works of merit, or in the broad sense of the rule of living well which is coupled with God's gracious enablement and the Messiah's forgiveness" (158). Cf. 154, 161. Cf. Frederik A.V. Harms, *In God's Custody: The Church, A History of Divine Protection: A Study of John Calvin's Ecclesiology Based on his Commentary on the Minor Prophets* (Gottingen: Vandenhoeck & Ruprecht, 2010), 105, 112–114.

[10] Calvin also uses the words for "covenant" in different ways. Typically he uses the words *foedus* or *pactum* to refer to the one eternal covenant. He does not like using these words with reference to the Mosaic administration more narrowly considered, but recognizing that scripture often does so, he follows its lead on numerous occasions, usually using the word *pactum*.

The basic difference between the form of the old covenant (the law) and the form of the new covenant (the gospel) is that the former was designed to lead the people of Israel through outward types and shadows, "as by steps," to Christ, whereas in the latter Christ himself is clearly present. Perhaps the *locus classicus* for this distinction is Calvin's commentary on Jeremiah 31:31–34. Calvin grounds the discussion with a reminder that the law in general (#1) is "a rule of the most perfect doctrine."[11] He then argues that the Sinai covenant was not a new covenant between God and Israel, but simply a ratification of the covenant God had made with Abraham some 400 years before. God, he writes, "had already made his covenant with Abraham, and the law [#2] was a confirmation of that covenant. As then the law depended on that covenant which God made with his servant Abraham, it follows that God could never have made a new, that is, a contrary or a different covenant."[12]

Why then does Jeremiah call it the "*new* covenant"? The reason, Calvin declares, is because of the change in the covenant's *form*. "But the substance remains the same. By substance I understand the doctrine; for God in the gospel brings forward nothing but what the law [#1] contains . . . For he has included in the law the rule of a perfect life and has also shown what is the way of salvation, and by types and figures led the people to Christ."[13] Thus "the newness . . . was not so as to the substance, but as to the form only, for God does not say here, 'I will give you another law,' but I will write my law, that is, the same law, which had formerly been delivered to the fathers."[14] The substance of the law (#1) continues, but its form (#2) does not.

Why was a new covenant necessary? Because a remedy had to be found for the sin that had led to the breakdown of the old covenant. This remedy is the forgiveness of sins and the writing of the law on human hearts. To be sure, these blessings were not alien to Israel, a point Calvin never tires of emphasizing. But they were obscured by types and shadows, and they were experienced as promises rather than as realities. What is more, the blessings to which faithful Israelites looked forward were alien to the form of the law (#2). "Therefore, if the law is regarded in itself [#2], the promise

---

[11] Commentary on Jeremiah 31:31–32 [1563]; CO 38:686–687.

[12] Here Calvin is not saying that the law, as a new covenant, could not annul or replace the earlier Abrahamic covenant. Rather, he is saying that the law is not a new covenant at all. "These things no doubt sufficiently show that God has never made any other covenant than that which he made formerly with Abraham, and at length confirmed by the hand of Moses." "God is never inconsistent with himself." Commentary on Jeremiah 31:31–32 [1563]; CO 38:688.

[13] Commentary on Jeremiah 31:31–32 [1563]; CO 38:688. Calvin admits that when Jeremiah says that the new covenant will not be like the one made with their fathers, he is contrasting the new covenant with the law (#2). For the Jews, he says, it was inconceivable that anything could be better than the Mosaic law. Commentary on Jeremiah 31:31–32 [1563]; CO 38:689–690. In his Commentary on Ezekiel 16:61, he explains that "a contrast must be understood between the people's covenant and God's." The people had broken the covenant and therefore rendered it vain. Yet God remained faithful "and so he again erected his own covenant towards them." Commentary on Ezekiel 16:61 [1565]; CO 40:395.

[14] Commentary on Jeremiah 31:33 [1563]; CO 38:691.

in the new covenant will not be found in it . . . We see then that the difference which Jeremiah points out was really true, and yet the new covenant so flowed from the old that it was almost the same in substance [#1], while distinguished in form [#2]."[15]

It is under this general rubric of substance and form that in *Institutes* 2.11 Calvin outlines five differences between the old and new covenants. The first difference is that through *earthly* promises and blessings, the Old Testament saints were pointed to *spiritual* or *eternal* realities. The contrast here is not between material and immaterial realities. Rather, it is between temporal blessings and those of the coming kingdom. Old Testament believers participated in the spiritual kingdom of Christ through earthly types, including the land of Canaan, looking beyond their earthly inheritance to a future heavenly one. Their "future and eternal happiness" was "signified and figured under earthly benefits, [and] the gravity of spiritual death under physical punishments" (2.11.3). In contrast, "now that the gospel has more plainly and clearly revealed the grace of the future life, the Lord leads our minds to meditate upon it directly, laying aside the lower mode of training that he used with the Israelites" (2.11.1).[16]

Israelite hopes were tied up with the Davidic kingdom, Calvin points out, but David's sins against Bathsheba and Uriah should have taught them that David's was a temporal kingdom,[17] "a sort of prelude of the everlasting kingdom which was to be manifested at the proper time."[18] Likewise, the psalms speak of David winning an inheritance over the heathen, and while David did win some battles over Israel's enemies, "how little was this in comparison with the amplitude of Christ's kingdom, which extends from the east to the west?"[19] Yet the Jews often missed this truth, focusing on the earthly realities in a way that left them deprived of the "spiritual Jerusalem."[20] Indeed, that was the error of the Jews all the way to Calvin's day. "For the Jews, in consequence of having imagined to themselves a king who had been suggested to them by their own senses, rejected Christ crucified . . . while we regard it as the best and highest reason for believing that he voluntarily subjected himself on our account to the ignominy of the cross."[21] The point is not to emphasize the

[15] Commentary on Ezekiel 16:61 [1565]; CO 40:396.
[16] Indeed "the land of Canaan was not otherwise so much valued except for this reason, because it was an image and a symbol of the spiritual inheritance." Commentary on Hebrews 4:8 [1549]; CO 55:47. Cf. Commentary on 1 Corinthians 10:1 [1546]; CO 49:451–453. Commentary on Genesis 27:27 [1554]; CO 23:378; 17:20; CO 23:246–247; 49:10; CO 23:598–599.
[17] Commentary on Matthew 1:6 [1555]; CO 45:60; Commentary on Luke 1:32 [1555]; CO 45:28.
[18] Commentary on John 12:13 [1553]; CO 47:282. Cf. Commentary on Genesis 49:10 [1554]; CO 23: 598–599; Commentary on Isaiah 9:7 [1559]; CO 36:198–199.
[19] Commentary on Hebrews 1:5 [1549]; CO 55:14. Cf. Commentary on Romans 3:18 [1556]; CO 49:54; Commentary on Acts 2:34 [1552]; CO 48:48–49.
[20] Commentary on Galatians 4:27 [1548]; CO 49:240.
[21] Commentary on Matthew 27:42 [1555]; CO 45:771.

immateriality of the kingdom, but its *futurity*. Calvin makes this point explicitly: "It must be observed, however, that Christ speaks only of the beginnings of the kingdom of God, for we now begin to be formed anew by the Spirit after the image of God in order that our entire renovation, and that of the whole world, may afterwards follow in due time."[22]

Calvin stresses the importance of reading the prophets through this exegetical lens. The prophets intentionally described Christ's kingdom in metaphorical, typological, and analogical terms, accommodating themselves to the people's weakness by using images they could understand to communicate spiritual truths. "[W]e must grasp this analogy in the prophets: when they discuss Christ's Kingdom, they set forth God's outward blessings as figures of spiritual goods" (3.13.4). This principle is one of the most important elements of Calvin's exegetical method. The prophets, he writes,

> describe the kingdom of Christ in a way suitable to the comprehension of a rude people, and hence they set before them external images; for when Christ's kingdom is the subject, mention is made of gold, of silver, of every kind of wealth, and also of great splendor and of great power, for we know that what is beyond and above the world cannot be immediately comprehended by the human mind ... As, then, the kingdom of Christ is spiritual and celestial, it cannot be comprehended by human minds, except he raises up our thoughts, as he does, by degrees. This, then, is the reason why the prophets have set forth the kingdom of Christ by comparing it to earthly kingdoms.[23]

Calvin often draws lessons for Christians from the comparison between Israel and the kingdom of Christ. "Unbelievers differ from the children of God in this respect, that while they enjoy in common with them the bounties of providence, they devour them like cattle and look no higher. The children of God, on the other hand, knowing that all their blessings have been sanctified by the promises ... are often directed in this way to the hope of eternal life."[24]

The second difference is that the Old Testament used images and ceremonies to teach the people about spiritual realities that, in the New Testament, believers enjoy

---

[22] Commentary on Luke 17:20 [1555]; CO 45:424–425. Cf. Commentary on Isaiah 11:14 [1559]; CO 36:248.

[23] Commentary on Jeremiah 31:12 [1563]; CO 38:660. The prophets "adopt metaphorical expressions ... for they accommodated their mode of speaking to the notions of that ancient people." Commentary on Hosea 9:13 [1557]; CO 42:172–173. Cf. 9:15; CO 42:175–17; Commentary on Psalm 45:6 [1557]; CO 31:453; 45:10; CO 31:456; 72:15; CO 31:670; Commentary on Haggai 2:6–9 [1559]; CO 44:106–108; Commentary on Joel 2:30–31 [1559]; CO 42:569–573; Commentary on Isaiah 2:2 [1559]; CO 36:59–60; 9:6; CO 36:198; 11:2; CO 36:235; 25:8–9; CO 36:419, 421; 30:25; CO 36:524–525; 42:7; CO 37:65; 55:13; CO 37:292–293; 60:2; CO 37:355; 61:5; CO 37:375; 62:8; CO 37:388; Commentary on Daniel 7:27 [1561]; CO 41:81–86; Arnold Huijgen, *Divine Accommodation in John Calvin's Theology: Analysis and Assessment* (Göttingen: Vandenhoeck & Ruprecht, 2011).

[24] Commentary on Galatians 3:6 [1548]; CO 49:206. Cf. Commentary on Colossians 3:1 [1548]; CO 52: 117–118; Commentary on Hebrews 11:10–16, 35 [1549]; CO 55:153–156, 168–169; 6:4; CO 55:71.

directly in Christ. In this sense "the Old Testament of the Lord was that covenant wrapped up in the shadowy and ineffectual observance of ceremonies and delivered to the Jews; it was temporary because it remained, as it were, in suspense until it might rest upon a firm and substantial confirmation" (2.11.4). To be sure, "there was a real spiritual meaning in these things."[25] But that meaning was packaged in symbols and practices designed for children. Christians, on the other hand, have the substance of Christ, and focus on him with simplicity.[26]

Separated from faith in Christ and from the power of Christ's work, Calvin argues, the ceremonies of the law were worse than meaningless. Yet even when viewed in light of Christ, the Old Testament rites constituted a burden insofar as they were designed to highlight the ongoing guilt of sin and the constant threat of judgment. "Whatever was done at that time showed in itself nothing but obligation. Grace was in a manner suspended until the advent of Christ."[27] The Old Testament sacrifices were earthly and "did not reach the soul."[28] "[F]or what end did sacrifices and washings serve but to keep the mind continually fixed on pollution and condemnation?" Only once the law had established conviction of sin by an "immense variety of exercises," did it lead the people "by the hand to Christ."[29] Sins were remitted under the fathers, but only in anticipation of Christ's work, not because of the sacrifices.[30]

Calvin argues that when Hebrews speaks of the abrogation of the old covenant, it is the abolition of these ceremonies (#2a) that is in view. Just as the priesthood of Aaron was "annulled" at the coming of Christ, so too was the "ministry of Moses." But only that which "peculiarly belonged to Moses" was abolished. Insofar as the Mosaic covenant encompassed the "gratuitous covenant of life" (#1) it was not abolished:

> For Christ is here compared with Moses. Whatever then they had in common is not here to be taken to the account, but only the things in which they differ. They in common offer God's mercy to us, prescribe the rule of a holy and godly life, teach us

---

[25] Commentary on Hebrews 8:5 [1549]; CO 55:99.

[26] Commentary on Colossians 2:8 [1548]; CO 52:103–104. Cf. 3:1; CO 52:117; Commentary on Jeremiah 31:34 [1563]; CO 38:693. The Israelites were "governed [*gubernabantur*] by an economy that outwardly appeared as slavery, even though inwardly they were free in God's sight." The gospel governs believers in a more "liberal" manner. Commentary on Galatians 4:24 [1548]; CO 50:238. See Harms, *In God's Custody*, 92–94.

[27] All the Mosaic ceremonies involved "acknowledgment of guilt, which bound those that observed them with a firmer tie, as it were, in the view of God's judgment." Commentary on Colossians 2:14 [1548]; CO 52:108.

[28] Commentary on Hebrews 9:9 [1549]; CO 55:108–109.

[29] Commentary on Galatians 3:24 [1548]; CO 50:220–221.

[30] Commentary on Hebrews 9:15 [1549]; CO 55:112. Cf. 8:2, 4; CO 55:97, 98; 10:22; CO 55:129; 12:18; CO 55:182; Commentary on Colossians 2:14 [1548]; CO 52:108.

the true worship of God, and exhort us to exercise faith and patience and all the duties of godliness. But Moses was different from Christ in this respect, that while the love of the gospel was not as yet made known, he kept the people under veils, set forth the knowledge of Christ by types and shadows, and, in short, accommodated himself to the capacity of ignorant people and did not rise higher than to puerile elements. We must then remember that the law is that part of the ministration which Moses had as peculiarly his own, and different from that of Christ. That law, as it was subordinate to the ancient priesthood, was abolished when the priesthood was abolished.[31]

Here Calvin identifies the ministry of Moses as its own covenant due to its differences of form from the new covenant (i.e., #2a). Thus he goes on to write that "the covenant which God has made by Christ with us is far more excellent than the old covenant of which Moses was the interpreter."[32] The Mosaic covenant is the "covenant of the law [that] was neither valid nor permanent,"[33] even though in substance it was the same eternal covenant of grace. Calvin thus stresses that the fathers had all of the spiritual blessings that Christians have; they simply did not realize them to the same extent, or with the same clarity, and "whatever spiritual gifts the fathers obtained, they were accidental ... to their age, for it was necessary for them to direct their eyes to Christ in order to become possessed of them."[34]

In contrast to the saints of the old covenant, believers cling simply to Christ, and attempts to bind their consciences to forms or ceremonies is an invasion of Christ's spiritual kingdom. "The apostles invented no new worship of God, they had erected no new spiritual government"; they do not reign as lords over souls, but merely minister the spiritual government of Christ.[35] Paul "expressly lays down a distinction in the government [*discrimen regiminis*] which God has commanded to be observed." Whereas the Israelites were bound like children, "God has broken those chains, governs [*regit*] his church in a more indulgent manner, and lays not upon us such severe restraint."[36]

---

[31] Commentary on Hebrews 7:12 [1549]; CO 55:89.

[32] Commentary on Hebrews 7:20 [1549]; CO 55:93. Later he adds that "it was but right that Moses and Aaron should give way to Christ as to one more excellent, because the gospel is a more excellent covenant than the law ... But the comparison made by the Apostle refers to the form rather than to the substance" (8:6; CO 55:100).

[33] Commentary on Hebrews 8:7 [1549]; CO 55:100–101. Cf. 8:8; CO 55:101.

[34] Commentary on Hebrews 7:15 [1549]; CO 55:90–91. Cf. 7:17; CO 55:91; 8:10; CO 55:103; 9:23; CO 55:117; Commentary on 1 Corinthians 10:4 [1546]; CO 49:455–456.

[35] Commentary on Acts 16:4 [1554]; CO 48:372. "Paul did so order external things that he was principally careful for the kingdom of God, which consists in the doctrine of the gospel, and far surpasses and surmounts external order." Commentary on Acts 16:5 [1554]; CO 48:372–373.

[36] Christians "are now at liberty as to all outward matters, but only on the condition that the church shall not be burdened with a multitude of ceremonies." Commentary on Galatians 4:1 [1548]; CO 50: 225–226. Cf. 3:23; CO 50:219. This includes the Sabbath. Christians don't observe days as if there were

The third difference is the Pauline contrast of "letter" and "spirit." Calvin summarizes the contrast by observing that the Old Testament, when viewed in light of what is proper to it, represents the letter that has no real power, while the New Testament, when viewed in light of what is proper to it, contains life itself (2.11.7).[37] He introduces the letter/spirit contrast with reference to 2 Corinthians 3:6–11, where Paul correlates the Old and New Testaments with death and life, condemnation and mercy. Calvin explains, "The Old Testament is of the letter, for it was published without the working of the Spirit. The New is spiritual because the Lord has engraved it spiritually upon men's hearts" (2.11.8). In his commentary Calvin explains that Christ is the "spirit" of the law, for "it will be living and life-giving only if it is breathed into by Christ." Just as the body dies when its soul is removed, so the law brings death when Christ is separated from it. Calvin suggests that this is one of the keys to reconciling the "encomiums" David heaps upon the law with Paul's statements that seem so critical of it. "For when it is animated by Christ, those things that David makes mention of are justly applicable to it. If Christ is taken away, it is altogether such as Paul describes."[38]

But again, Calvin is quick to stress that this does not mean the Old Testament saints did not have the Spirit. The contrast between letter and Spirit applies not to the whole of the old covenant or the whole of the new, but to what is proper to, or derived from, each source respectively. "[T]he fathers who were formerly regenerated obtained this favor through Christ, so that we may say that it was, as it were, transferred to them from another source. The power then to penetrate into the heart was not inherent in the law, but it was a benefit transferred to the law from the gospel." Thus "the main thing is to consider what the *law of itself* is, and what is *peculiar to the gospel* … [T]he prophet speaks of the law in itself, as apart from

any "sacredness in holidays [*in feriis aliqua sit religio*], or as though it were not lawful to labor upon them." To the extent that Christians set aside days for worship or rest, "respect is paid to government and order [*politiae et ordinis*], not to days." Commentary on Colossians 2:16 [1548]; CO 52:110. Cf. Commentary on Exodus 31:13 [1563]; CO 24:583–584.

37　This difference is arguably the most difficult to categorize according to Hesselink's schema because it involves dimensions of "degree" as well as dimensions that are "antithetical." In addition, Calvin applies it with considerable flexibility in his commentaries, using it to explain meaning and form with respect to the Old Testament ceremonies (Commentary on Philippians 3:3 [1548]; CO 52:44), the New Testament sacraments (Commentary on John 10:3 [1553]; CO47:453–455), and the commands of God (Commentary on Romans 2:28 [1556]; CO 49:45), in addition to the general distinction between the two covenants.

38　Commentary on 2 Corinthians 3:17 [1548]; CO 50:45–46. Calvin offers the same interpretation of John 1:17, "The law came through Moses; grace and truth came through Jesus Christ." He explains, "By the word grace I understand the spiritual fulfillment of those things, the bare letter of which was contained in the Law." "Christ is the soul which gives life to that which would otherwise have been dead under the law." Commentary on John 1:17 [1553]; CO 47:18.

the gospel, for the law then is dead and destitute of the Spirit of regeneration."[39] The law promised salvation and was a sufficient guide to faith, but it did not provide salvation itself, for such benefits were "adventitious, and . . . do not properly belong to the law." When Moses is rightly regarded as pointing to Christ [#1], the law contains the gospel. "But if Moses be set in opposition to Christ, he becomes the minister of death, and his doctrine leads to destruction, for the letter, as Paul in 2 Corinthians 3:6 calls it, kills."[40]

The fourth difference Calvin identifies between the Old and New Testaments is that the former was accompanied by the experience of fear and bondage whereas the latter is one of freedom, trust, and assurance. "The Old held consciences bound by the yoke of bondage; the New by its spirit of liberality emancipates them into freedom." This difference is arguably the most antithetical, and it overlaps closely with what was peculiar to the narrow law as described below (though it is not precisely the same thing). Old Testament believers could attain freedom of conscience insofar as they saw Christ, Calvin argues, but they still experienced the burden of ceremonial requirements and legal stipulations accompanied by the threatened judgment of God. They therefore enjoyed peace of conscience in an anticipatory way insofar as they lived "in hope of spiritual, heavenly, and eternal benefits" (2.11.10).

The fifth difference is that in the Old Testament God set aside one nation to himself, allowing the other nations to walk in "vanity," whereas in the New Testament God has broken down the wall that divides the nations (2.11.11). "The calling of the Gentiles, therefore, is a notable mark of the excellence of the New Testament over the Old" (2.11.12). The obvious proof-text for this principle is Ephesians 2:11–15, which declares, as Calvin summarizes it, that while the Gentiles were once "aliens from Christ, from the hope of salvation, and from the church and kingdom of God [*ecclesia et regno Dei*],"[41] now in Christ Jews and Gentiles have been incorporated into "one holy body [*sancti corporis unitatem*]."[42] What has made

---

[39] Commentary on Jeremiah 31:33 [1563]; CO 38:691. Cf. Commentary on 2 Timothy 1:7 [1548]; CO 52:351.

[40] Commentary on Jeremiah 31:34 [1563]; CO 38:697. At times Calvin presents the letter/Spirit contrast in terms of a sharp antithesis. In his Commentary on Romans Calvin writes, "Paul compares here the hidden power of the Spirit with the external letter of the law, as though he had said, 'Christ inwardly forms our souls in a better way than when the law constrains them by threatening and terrifying us." Commentary on Romans 6:17 [1556]; CO 49:115. "What the law does, in the absence of the inward teacher, the Spirit, is increasingly to inflame our hearts so that they boil up with lusts." The only solution is emancipation. "It hence follows that the kingdom of righteousness [*iustitiae regnum*] is not established except when Christ emancipates us from the law" (7:5; CO 49:122) and grants us his Spirit (7:6; CO 49:123; Cf. 8:3; CO 49:140; 8:9; CO 49:144).

[41] Commentary on Ephesians 2:11 [1548]; CO 51:168.

[42] Commentary on Ephesians 2:12 [1548]; CO 51:169.

this possible is the abolition of the "law of commandments and ordinances."[43] This expansion of Christ's kingdom to all nations was predicted throughout the Old Testament. For instance, Psalm 47 declared that the kingdom of Christ would be "the common privilege of all nations."[44] Unlike in the "time of the law, when God confined his empire, or kingdom, within the boundaries of Judea," Christ's kingdom would be extended "far and wide, so as to occupy the whole world from one end to the other."[45]

THE LAW AND THE GOSPEL: DIFFERENCES OF PRINCIPLE

While in the *Institutes* Calvin pays substantial attention to the differences of form between the Old and New Testaments, scholars have paid less attention to the sharp antithesis between the gospel and the principle of the law understood in a narrow sense that he articulates in his commentaries.[46] Calvin typically gets to the matter by comparing the rhetoric of King David to that of the Apostle Paul, which seem "wholly contradictory" to one another.

> Paul makes the law the minister of death, declares that it effects nothing but to bring on us the wrath of God, that it was given to increase sin, that it lives in order to kill us. David, on the other hand, says that it is sweeter than honey and more desirable than gold, and among other recommendations he mentions the following – that it cheers hearts, converts to the Lord, and quickens.[47]

Calvin offers various explanations for this seeming discrepancy. In his commentary on 1 John, he explains that Paul considered the law in light of human corruption,

---

[43] Here Calvin breaks with his typical interpretation of Paul's use of the word "law," in which he insists that the covenant of the law (#2) is in view, suggesting that here Paul simply has in view the ceremonial law. Commentary on Ephesians 2:14 [1548]; CO 51:171. For his more typical interpretation, see Commentary on Romans 3:20 [1556]; CO 49:57; Commentary on Galatians 2:15 [1548]; CO 50: 193–196; 3:17; CO 50:213.

[44] Commentary on Psalm 47:3 [1557]; CO 31:467–468. Cf. 67:1; CO 31:617; Commentary on Hebrews 12:26 [1549]; CO 55:185; Commentary on Ephesians 3:4 [1548]; CO 51:179.

[45] Commentary on Psalm 47:8 [1557]; CO 31:470.

[46] I. John Hesselink writes, "What is not always recognized – particularly by the critics of Calvin's view of law and gospel – is that there is not only a difference of form between the law and the gospel (or the two covenants) but also an antithesis between them in so far as the law in a narrower sense is opposed to the gospel." Hesselink, *Calvin's Concept of the Law*, 157. This law "is not the whole law, the *tota lex*, but the bare law, the *nuda lex*. It is the law abstracted from its real setting which is the covenant" (158).

[47] Commentary on 1 John 5:3 [1551]; CO 55:363. David takes "such sweet delight in God's law, which, according to the testimony of Paul, does nothing else but strike fear into men." Commentary on Psalm 119:103 [1557]; CO 32:258. "The design of Paul is to show what the law can do for us taken by itself, that is to say, what it can do for us when, without the promise of grace, it strictly and rigorously exacts from us the duty which we owe to God. But David, in praising it as he here does, speaks of the whole doctrine of the law, which includes also the gospel, and, therefore, under the law he comprehends Christ." Commentary on Psalm 19:8 [1557]; CO 31:199–200.

whereas David praised it as experienced by those regenerated by the Spirit.[48] In his commentary on Psalm 119, he explains that Paul viewed the law simply in terms of its "commandments and threatenings," whereas David "comprehends the whole doctrine of the law, the chief part of which is the free covenant of salvation."[49] Calvin also suggests that Paul's rhetoric about the law was shaped by his polemic with the Judaizers. "Paul, who had to deal with persons who perverted and abused the law and separated it from the grace and the Spirit of Christ, refers to the ministry of Moses viewed merely by itself, and according to the letter."[50] In order to paint a stark contrast between the "literal disciples of the law" and the "faithful whom Christ . . . teaches inwardly and effectually by his Spirit," Paul had to take the perspective that "regards nothing but what was peculiar to the law itself, as it commands and forbids, and restrains transgressors by the denunciation of death." In this sense, Calvin admits, the law is properly understood as a covenant of works: "He sets forth the law only, as that by which God covenants [*paciscitur*] with us on the ground of works."[51]

But is Calvin saying that Paul merely granted this function of the law for the sake of argument? Is Peter Lillback correct that for Paul this is not the law's "normative use"?[52] On the contrary, Calvin is quite clear that the works principle[53] was a genuine function of the law, part of its purpose as covenanted by God.[54] The law thus stands in "apparent contradiction" with the covenant of grace in the sense that they propose alternative modes of justification, even though they are not in actual contradiction in the sense that one only condemns, while the other saves.[55]

---

[48] Commentary on 1 John 5:3 [1551]; CO 55:363.

[49] Commentary on Psalm 119:103 [1557]; CO 32:258. David is praising "the whole doctrine of Moses." Only when viewed through the lens of the gospel is law worthy of such encomium (19:7; CO 31:199).

[50] Commentary on Psalm 19:8 [1557]; CO 31:199–200.

[51] "And then, if the law be viewed in itself, it can do nothing but restrain those, devoted to its miserable bondage, by the horror of death; for it promises no good except under condition [*conditione*], and denounces death on all transgressors." Commentary on Romans 8:15 [1556]; CO 49:148–149. Cf. Commentary on 2 Corinthians 3:12–13 [1548]; CO 50:44; Commentary on Galatians 3:27 [1548]; CO 50:222.

[52] "It is the law severed from Christ, and so is not its normative use." Lillback, *The Binding of God*, 223 (Cf. 155).

[53] By the phrase "works principle," I refer to the principle Calvin describes as follows: "It annexes to works a reward and a punishment; that is, it promises life to those who keep it, and curses all transgressors." Commentary on Galatians 3:25 [1548]; CO 50:221.

[54] "We admit that the doers of the law, if there were any such, are righteous, but since that is a conditional agreement, all are excluded from life because no man performs that righteousness which he ought." Commentary on Galatians 3:12 [1548]; CO 50:209.

[55] Commentary on Galatians 3:21 [1548]; CO 50:217. "The crucial distinction for Calvin is this: the antithesis lies in the special or peculiar office, function, and ministry of the law. Something intrinsic and inherent in the law, something characteristic of its very nature, sets it over against the gospel in the sharpest possible way. (The reference now is neither to the substance nor even the form of the law as such.) For what separates the law from the gospel like fire and water is the matter of justification. There are two kinds of promises and two kinds of righteousness: legal promises and evangelical promises, the

Paul's opponents were not wrong to identify the works principle within the law. Rather, they were wrong to identify it as a reliable means of attaining righteousness for fallen human beings, and so they failed to grasp that even the works principle was intended as a means "to lead us as by the hand to another righteousness." By failing to understand the narrow law (#2b) in the context of the broad law (#1), the Jews "rejected its soul, and seized on the dead body of the letter. For though the law promises reward to those who observe its righteousness, it yet substitutes, after having proved all guilty, another righteousness in Christ, which is not attained by works, but is received by faith as a free gift."[56] The covenant of the law was never intended to stand in isolation, but in subservience to one eternal covenant.

How does this square with viewing the Mosaic covenant as an administration of the covenant of grace? Calvin distinguishes between Moses' role as an administrator of the eternal covenant from his more peculiar or proper role as an administrator of the law understood narrowly.[57] Calvin's fullest explanation of this distinction appears in his discussion of Exodus 19:1–2 in his commentary on the law. Here Calvin presents the Sinai covenant, including the Ten Commandments, as a renewal of the covenant made with Abraham. God had made an "eternal, and inviolable covenant" with Abraham, "but because it had grown into disregard … it became needful that it should be again renewed. To this end, then, it was engraved upon the tables of stone and written in a book, that the marvelous grace which God had conferred on the race of Abraham should never sink into oblivion."[58] In other words, the Sinai covenant *is*, in its essence, the Abrahamic covenant, the one covenant that endures for all time.

On the other hand, the matter is more complicated. For Calvin quickly explains that the Sinai covenant is actually quite different from the Abrahamic covenant, holding its own peculiarly legal and conditional character.

> But in the first place we must observe that although the law is a testimony of God's gratuitous adoption and teaches that salvation is based upon His mercy and invites men to call upon God with sure confidence, yet it has this peculiar property, that it covenants conditionally [*sub conditione paciscitur*]. Therefore it is worthwhile to distinguish between the general doctrine which was delivered by Moses and the special command which he received.[59]

righteousness of works and the righteousness of faith. Here there is no more or less, no gradation. These are two opposing systems which are totally irreconcilable." Hesselink, *Calvin's Concept of the Law*, 195–196. Thus Hesselink rightly concludes that for Calvin "the origin of this concept of the law is not to be traced to a mere misunderstanding or misuse of the law; nor can these strong words of Paul be dismissed simply as a polemic against an abuse of the law" (193–194).

[56] Commentary on Romans 10:4 [1556]; CO 49:196–197.
[57] See Hesselink, *Calvin's Concept of the Law*, 196.
[58] Commentary on Exodus 19:1 [1563]; CO 24:192.
[59] Commentary on Exodus 19:1 [1563]; CO 24:192–193.

Here again is that distinction between the law considered broadly (#1) and the law considered narrowly (#2), but the emphasis is on the law considered *very* narrowly (i.e., #2b). The "general doctrine," or broad law, is represented by Moses' proclamation of pardon and reconciliation. As for the "special command," or narrow law, "this office was separately imposed upon him, to demand perfect righteousness of the people and to promise them a reward, as if by compact [*ex compacto*], upon no other condition than that they should fulfill whatever was enjoined them, but to threaten and to denounce vengeance against them if ever they wandered from the way." This leads Calvin to a discussion of various Pauline passages in which the apostle characterizes the law in terms of its "peculiar office," distinct from the promises of grace. "But we must not pass over what I lately asserted to be peculiar to the law, viz., to fill men's minds with fear, and by setting forth its terrible curse, to cut off the hope of salvation."[60] It was always the distinct function of the law to drive the people "by fear to implore God's mercy."[61]

In his commentaries on the Pauline epistles, Calvin makes the same distinction. "The law has a twofold meaning; it sometimes includes the whole of what has been taught by Moses and sometimes that part only which was peculiar [*propria*] to his ministration, which consisted of precepts, rewards, and punishments." The faith taught by Moses involves promises of mercy and grace, and in this sense he was a preacher of the gospel. Yet he also had a more distinctive responsibility, which was to reduce the people to humility by means of the condition of works.

> It was now the duty of the people to consider in how many ways they drew curses on themselves and how far they were from deserving anything at God's hands by their works, that being thus led to despair as to their own righteousness, they might flee to the haven of divine goodness and so to Christ himself. This was the end or design of the Mosaic dispensation.[62]

Calvin thus stresses that when Paul is discussing the law, he typically has in view this narrow sense of the law as a covenant binding human beings to obedience as a condition for blessing and threatening punishment for disobedience. As he puts it in one place, "Paul is not reasoning here as to mere ceremonies." Rather, he has in view the "whole of the Old Testament, *insofar as it is opposed to the gospel.*" Or to put it another way, it is "the ministry of Moses, which was peculiar to him and is distinguished from the gospel," that is "abolished."[63]

---

[60] Commentary on Exodus 19:1 [1563]; CO 24:193. Cf. Commentary on 2 Corinthians 3:6–7 [1548]; CO 50:40–41.

[61] Commentary on Exodus 19:1 [1563]; CO 24:194.

[62] Commentary on Romans 10:5 [1556]; CO 49:197–198.

[63] Commentary on 2 Corinthians 3:7 [1548]; CO 50:42. Emphasis added. Calvin distinguishes between the "whole of that administration [*totam illiam administrationem temporalem*]," that is, the narrow law, which was "temporal," and "the whole law [*totam legem*]," that is, the law in its broad sense, which is

Let it be observed that Paul does not speak of the moral law only, but of everything connected with the office held by Moses. That office, which was peculiar [*proprium*] to Moses, consisted in laying down a rule of life and ceremonies to be observed in the worship of God and in afterwards adding promises and threatenings. Many promises, no doubt, relating to the free mercy of God and to Christ are to be found in his writings, and these promises belong to faith. But this must be viewed as accidental and altogether foreign [*accidentale et aliunde accersitum*] to the inquiry so far as a comparison is made between the law and the doctrine of grace.[64]

Calvin argues that in the writings of Moses, like those of Paul, this narrow sense is predominant.

But as the evangelical promises are only found scattered in the writings of Moses, and these also somewhat obscure, and as the precepts and rewards allotted to the observers of the law frequently occur, it rightly appertained to Moses as his own and peculiar [*proprie ac peculiariter*] office to teach what is the real righteousness of works and then to show what remuneration awaits the observance of it and what punishment awaits those who come short of it.[65]

In Calvin's view, at Sinai the people of Israel were placed in a covenantal relationship distinct from the covenant made with Abraham, though embedded within that broader covenant. Thus in his commentary on Galatians Calvin follows Paul in identifying the narrow and broad law with distinct covenants. He presents the doctrine that is "legal" and that which is "evangelical" as corresponding to these "two covenants [*duorum testamentorum/duplex . . . pactum*]."[66] The law was a renewal of the covenant made with Abraham, but it also functioned as a distinct covenant. To be under the law [*sub lege*], then, is to be under "the covenant of the law [*legis pactum*]," by which is meant the "law with its appendages [*appendicibus*]," which is different from the sense in which all believers are under the law [*sub lege*]."[67]

---

not abolished. Calvin is saying that considered from one perspective, the law, or the Mosaic office, is simply an administration of the covenant of grace, its forms being accidental to that covenant. But within the peculiar Mosaic office, the works principle is central and definitive. Commentary on Galatians 3:19 [1548]; CO 50:216. When Paul says that Christians are no longer under a guardian, he "embraces the whole economy by which the Lord governed his people under the Old Testament [*totam oeconomiam . . . gubernauit*]" (3:23; CO 50:219).

[64] Commentary on Galatians 3:19–22 [1548]; CO 50:215.

[65] Commentary on Romans 10:5 [1556]; CO 49:197–198.

[66] Commentary on Galatians 4:22–24 [1548]; CO 50:236–238. Cf. Commentary on Galatians 3:17 [1548]; CO 214.

[67] Commentary on Galatians 4:21 [1548]; CO 50:236. For "all who remain bound to the dominion of the law are subject to a curse; it is then certain that they are excluded from the participation of grace." Commentary on Romans 4:16 [1556]; CO 49:80.

Interestingly, Calvin invokes the medieval scholastics to clarify that had God not made such a legal covenant, he would have had no obligation to reward the obedient. "Nor was this unknown to the schoolmen, who held it as an approved and common maxim that works have no intrinsic worthiness but become meritorious by covenant [*ex pacto*]." The scholastics underestimated human depravity, "yet this principle is still true, that the reward for works depends on the free promise of the law."[68] There is no principle of merit inherent to the moral law. A works principle only arises from a covenant.

> Paul took into account what was certainly true, that except by a covenant with God [*Dei pacto*] no reward is due to works. Admitting, then, that the law justifies, yet before the law [was enacted] men could not merit salvation by works because there was no covenant [*pactum*]. All that I am now affirming is granted by the scholastic theologians, for they maintain that works are meritorious of salvation not by their intrinsic worth, but by the acceptance of God (to use their own phrase) and on the ground of a covenant [*pacti*]. Consequently, where no divine covenant [*Dei pactum*], no declaration of acceptance is found, no works will be available for justification.

But is there such a covenant? Absolutely. "He tells us that God made two covenants [*duplex ... pactum*] with men; one through Abraham, and another through Moses."[69] The latter covenant is the covenant of law, and it carries within it the principle of reward for good works.

Calvin stresses that this reward promised by the covenant of law was not limited to blessing in "this earthly and transitory life." Those who limit it in this way do so because they want to preserve the doctrine of justification by faith, and they wrongly assume that in order to defend justification by faith they need to rule out the possibility that the law promises justification by works. In Calvin's view, by contrast, the reason the law does not bring justification is not that it does not promise justification for good works, but because human depravity makes such good works impossible.

> Scripture does not therefore deny that men are justified by works because the law itself is imperfect or does not give instructions for perfect righteousness, but because the promise is made of no effect by our corruption and sin ... Foolishly, then, do some reject as an absurdity the statement that if a man fulfills the law he attains to

---

[68] Paul speaks of the "works of the law" because works take their conditional character only because of the law. Commentary on Romans 3:20 [1556]; CO 49:56. Cf. 3:28; CO 49:65–66. "And this has been pointed out even by the common theologians, that the reward of good works does not depend upon their dignity or merit, but upon his covenant [*ex pacto*]." Commentary on Leviticus 18:5 [1563]; CO 25:6.

[69] Commentary on Galatians 3:17 [1548]; CO 50:213–214.

righteousness, for the defect does not arise from the doctrine of the law, but from the infirmity of men.[70]

Calvin therefore insists that "the original covenant [*prima pactio*] [of law] only avails to man's condemnation."[71] Only by turning from that covenant to the promise of mercy can human beings attain to its blessing. "For the law, as respects its doctrine, contains in it life and death. For the reward of eternal life is not promised in it in vain, but since no one is found worthy of the promised reward, Paul justly teaches that the law ministers death. Still this is accidental, and proceeds not from any fault in the doctrine, but from the corruption of men."[72]

Calvin's covenant theology undergirds his theology of the uses of the law to a degree insufficiently appreciated by scholars.[73] It is this covenant of the law that gives rise to the theological use of the law, which only serves to condemn human beings, and it is the eternal covenant of grace that gives rise to the spiritual use of the

---

[70] Commentary on Leviticus 18:5 [1563]; CO 25:7. The law "was given in order that we by keeping the law of the Lord might obtain eternal life, except our corruption stood in the way." Commentary on Romans 7:10 [1556]; CO 49:126.

[71] Commentary on Deuteronomy 7:12 [1563]; CO 25:20–21.

[72] The works principle was part of Moses' distinct "legation," "the office peculiarly entrusted to him" and distinct from that of Christ. Commentary on Deuteronomy 30:19 [1563]; CO 25:56–58. Cf. 30:11; CO 24:258. It is with respect to that office that it is the unique and proper function of the law to condemn. Calvin admits that in 2 Corinthians 2:16, Paul refers to the gospel as the "odor of death" to unbelievers, suggesting the possibility that the condemning attribute is by no means unique to the law. But whereas this effect is *accidental* to the gospel, it is *proper* to the law. "We must always therefore distinguish between the proper [*proprium*] office of the gospel and the accidental [*accidentali*] one (so to speak) which must be imputed to the depravity of mankind." Commentary on 2 Corinthians 2:15 [1548]; CO 50:34. But has Calvin not said that it is also accidental, i.e., a result of human sin, that the law condemns? Yes, Calvin admits, but there is a difference between the law and the gospel that is even more basic: *only* the gospel brings regeneration and reconciliation with God. "The law, on the other hand, as it simply prescribes the rule of a good life, does not renew men's hearts to the obedience of righteousness, and denounces everlasting death upon transgressors, can do nothing but condemn. Or if you prefer it in another way, the office of the law is to show us the disease, in such a way as to show us at the same time no hope of cure; the office of the gospel is to bring a remedy to those that were past hope" (3:7; CO 50:42). In other words, the law *necessarily and always* brings death to sinners (the effect is perpetual and inseparable), while the gospel has the power to bring life. Cf. Commentary on Isaiah 11:4 [1559]; CO 36:239.

[73] Thus while some scholars have legitimately explained the relationship between Calvin's positive and negative statements about the law by correlating them to the difference between justification and sanctification, they have not adequately discerned its relation to Calvin's *covenant* theology, which arises out of his reading of the biblical text. They have not recognized that Calvin's distinction between justification and sanctification is reflected in his understanding of the distinction between the (narrow) covenant of the law and the eternal covenant of grace. For instance, see Mary Lane Potter, "The 'Whole Office of the Law' in the Theology of John Calvin," *Journal of Law and Religion* 3 (1985): 117–139; Anthony Hoekema, "Calvin's Doctrine of the Covenant of Grace." *Reformed Review* 15 (1962): 1–12; See James B. Torrance, "The Concept of Federal Theology – Was Calvin a Federal Theologian?," *Calvinus Sacrae Scripturae Professor: Calvin as Confessor of Holy Scripture* (ed. Wilhelm H. Neuser; Grand Rapids: Eerdmans, 1994), 15–40.

law, which educates and exhorts the regenerate to true righteousness. Christians are no longer under the law in its narrow covenantal sense (i.e., the first, or theological use of the law), but they remain under the law in its broader covenantal sense, as a school for teaching and exhortation (i.e., the third, or spiritual use of the law). In the former sense the law not only has a "subordinate rank [*subservire*]" to Christ, but it is "abolished [*abrogatum*]."[74] Where the Spirit reigns the law has no dominion, "so that our intercourse with him is not regulated by its covenant [*pacto*], nor our consciences bound by its sentence of condemnation."[75] In the latter sense, however, Calvin views the moral content of the Ten Commandments as "the covenantal law of God as a rule for his life."[76]

Thus for Calvin the spiritual use of the law is necessarily separated from its distinctive role within the Sinai covenant. When Paul declared in Romans 6:14 that Christians are "not under law but under grace," he was making just this point. As Calvin puts it, "we are freed from the strictness of the law, so that God no more deals with us according to the high demands of justice. There is then no doubt but that he meant here to indicate some freedom from the very law of God." The result is that Christians' works "are not now tested by the strict rule of the law" or subject to its "rigorous requirements." They are "no longer subject to the law as requiring perfect righteousness and pronouncing death on all who deviate from it in any part."[77] On the other hand, the "righteousness which God approves of in his law" is not abolished, because that righteousness is inherent to the one eternal covenant.[78]

Calvin makes the same argument regarding the "great question respecting the use of the law."[79] Paul's description of the believer's relation to the law as being like a widow's relation to her former husband demonstrates "that we are so loosed from the law that it does not any longer, properly and by its own right, retain over us any authority."[80] To be sure, this refers

> only to that office of the law which was peculiar [*propria*] to the dispensation of Moses. For as far as God has in the Ten Commandments taught us what is just and right and given directions for guiding our life, no abrogation of the law is to be dreamt of, for the will of God must stand the same forever. We ought carefully to

---

[74] Commentary on Galatians 3:19 [1548]; CO 50:215–216.
[75] Commentary on Galatians 5:23 [1548]; CO 50:256. Cf. Commentary on Hebrews 6:4 [1549]; CO 55:71; 12:19; CO 55:182–183; Commentary on John 16:10 [1553]; CO 47:360; Commentary on Acts 15:10–11 [1554]; CO 48:347–352.
[76] Lillback, *The Binding of God*, 265.   [77] Commentary on Romans 6:14 [1556]; CO 49:112–113.
[78] Commentary on Romans 6:15 [1556]; CO 49:113–114. Cf. Commentary on Matthew 5:17 [1555]; CO 45: 171–172.
[79] Commentary on Romans 7:1 [1556]; CO 49:119.
[80] Commentary on Romans 7:2 [1556]; CO 49:120.

remember that this is not a release from the righteousness which is taught in the law but from its rigid requirements and from the curse which thence follows.[81]

Under the "kingdom of Christ ... the law has resigned its office," but it is not "so abolished that we have nothing to do with it." Rather, "the law, so far as it is a rule of life, a bridle to keep us in the fear of the Lord, a spur to correct the sluggishness of our flesh – so far, in short, as it is 'profitable for doctrine, for reproof, for correction, of instruction in righteousness, that believers may be instructed in every good work' (2 Timothy 3:16) – is as much in force as ever."[82]

ISRAEL AND THE POLITICS OF CHRISTENDOM

Calvin's covenant theology informed his answer to the question of how the law and politics of Israel should serve as a model for contemporary politics. His exegesis of Psalm 2 illustrates his nuanced and paradoxical understanding of the Israelite kingdom. On the one hand, the Davidic kingdom was a uniquely "sacred kingdom," a type of Christ's kingdom to come. On the other hand, it was temporal, "merely a shadow" of that kingdom. Calvin thus articulates a fundamental exegetical principle:

> [I]n order to learn to apply to Christ whatever David, in times past, sang concerning himself, we must hold this principle, which we meet with everywhere in all the prophets: that he, with his posterity, was made king, not so much for his own sake, as to be a type of the Redeemer ... David's temporal kingdom was a kind of earnest to God's ancient people of the eternal kingdom, which at length was truly established in the person of Christ.[83]

The distinction between Israel and Christ's spiritual kingdom thus bears a close relationship to the two kingdoms distinction. On the one hand, Christ's kingdom is spiritual, while Israel, being a temporal kingdom, was political. On the other hand, compared to other temporal kingdoms, Israel was typological and therefore spiritual. Israel's law and polity will seem more or less relevant to contemporary politics depending on which of these perspectives one takes when considering any particular instance of it. Insofar as Calvin viewed Israel as a type of the spiritual kingdom of Christ, he no longer deemed it a model for Christian polities. However, insofar as he considered Israel to be a temporal kingdom, he considered it to be a divinely inspired

---

[81] Commentary on Romans 7:2–3 [1556]; CO 49:120–121. As he puts it in his Commentary on Romans 8:3, the law contains the "perfect rule of righteousness." Commentary on Romans 8:3 [1556]; CO 49:138.

[82] Commentary on Galatians 3:25 [1548]; CO 50:221; Cf. 4:4; CO 50:227.

[83] Commentary on Psalm 2:1 [1557]; CO 31:42–43. Cf. 45:1; CO 31:449; 110:1–4; CO 32:160–164; 89:19; CO 31:818; David Willis-Watkins, "Calvin's Prophetic Reinterpretation of Kingship," in *Probing the Reformed Tradition* (ed. Elsie Anne McKee and Brian Armstrong; Louisville: Westminster/John Knox, 1989), 116–134.

(though imperfect) model of a civil government ruling in broad conformity to natural law.

Calvin believed that although all kingdoms are established by God, God governed Judah (the faithful southern part of Israel) "in a peculiar manner . . . because under this figure of a kingdom he held up Christ to their view."[84] Thus although God is "the rightful proprietor of the whole earth, it is declared that he chose one people over whom he might reign."[85] In Jerusalem alone was God's spiritual government established.[86] Indeed, "when David was constituted king the foundation of that everlasting kingdom, which was eventually manifested in the advent of Christ, was then laid."[87]

The distinction between Israel and the nations extended to the unique character of Israelite kings. Calvin distinguished between mere "earthly kings" and the sacerdotal kings of Israel. The kings of the earth also obtained their authority "by God's decree," but "the king from David's posterity was first-begotten among them all. In short, it was a sacerdotal, and even a sacred kingdom, because God had peculiarly dedicated that throne to himself."[88] Whereas ordinary kings come to rule by ordinary providential means, the Davidic monarchy was specifically appointed by God through prophetic intervention and is "not to be estimated according to the common order of nature."[89] The kingdom of David "was a priestly kingdom and a type of that celestial kingdom which was afterwards fully revealed in Christ."[90] Christian commonwealths are fundamentally different from Israel. In Israel, the king was considered to be "the soul of the community," but for Christians, political office is much more mundane. "We have not now an earthly king who is Christ's image, but it is Christ alone who vivifies the church."[91]

---

[84] Commentary on Isaiah 10:27 [1559]; CO 36:230. Cf. Commentary on Psalm 18:43 [1557]; CO 31:190; 20; CO 31:207; 21:3; CO 31:214; 21:7; 216; Commentary on Jeremiah 33:17–18 [1563]; CO 39:69–70; Commentary on Isaiah 2:4 [1559]; CO 36:64; 32:1, 15; CO 36:542, 552; 33:20; CO 36:575.

[85] Commentary on Psalm 105:6 [1557]; CO 32:100.

[86] Commentary on Psalm 87:1 [1557]; CO 31:800–801. Cf. 66:7; CO 31:612.

[87] Commentary on Psalm 118:25 [1557]; CO 32:210. Cf. Commentary on Jeremiah 41:9 [1563]; CO 39:422; Commentary on Hosea 8:4 [1557]; CO 42:365; Hesselink, "Calvin on the Kingdom of Christ," 150.

[88] Commentary on Lamentations 4:20; CO 39:624–625. Cf. 2:2; CO 39:536.

[89] Commentary on Psalm 89:36 [1557]; CO 31:825.Cf. 89:19, 26; CO 31:818, 820. "God indeed invests kings with authority, but they are not consecrated as David was, that like him, in consequence of the holy anointing oil, they might be elevated to the rank of Christ's vicegerents." David "is not to be classed with the ordinary kings of the earth," because "he reigned by a divine right." Earthly kings often claim to rule "by the grace of God," but in practice they "imagine that they reign either by their own policy, by hereditary right, or by the kindness of fortune" (110:1; CO 32:160–161).

[90] Commentary on Jeremiah 22:1–3 [1563]; CO 38:371–374.

[91] Commentary on Jeremiah 30:21 [1563]; CO 38:635. Thus it was appropriate for Israelites to pray for salvation through their civil government. In contrast, while Christians should pray for their rulers, they must "renounce all hope of salvation from any other quarter" but Christ. Commentary on Psalm 20:9 [1557]; CO 31:211–212.

That the Israelite kingdom was sacerdotal meant that the monarchy was integrated with the worship and the priesthood. In Israel God had "joined the kingdom and priesthood together."[92] They were not unified in one person, but they were institutionally fused in a way that pointed forward to their more perfect union in the person of Christ.[93] "God decreed nothing in relation to the kingdom but what had a certain connection with the sanctuary, the more perfectly to prefigure the mediator who was to come, and who was both priest and king after the order of Melchizedek. The kingdom and tabernacle were, therefore, closely allied."[94]

From this perspective, Calvin makes it clear that the typological nature of Israel prohibits the simplistic drawing of lessons for Christian polities. For instance, the psalms describe the king's triumph over Israel's enemies, but whereas Israelite kings forced the nations into slavish obedience by means of the sword, this is not something that Christian governments should imitate. The true fulfillment of such psalms is Christ's subjugation of the nations to a willing obedience by means of his word and Spirit. Thus in David's victories "God exhibited a type of the conquest which Christ would make of the Gentiles, who, by the preaching of the gospel alone, were subdued and brought voluntarily to submit to his dominion."[95] The fulfillment of such psalms is not in "that government of God which is general in its nature," which manifests itself in civil government, but in that "spiritual jurisdiction which he exercises over the church."[96]

Likewise when the prophets speak in terms of the material blessing of Israel, such prophecies are to be interpreted as fulfilled in Christ. They should be applied to the church only when interpreted in light of the church's spiritual union with Christ, and not to temporal polities at all. The prophets describe the nations coming to Jerusalem with tribute for Israel, and the papists used such prophecies as a pretext for "their luxuries, wealth, and magnificence."[97] In contrast, Calvin warns, "We must not understand the enjoyment of the wealth of others to mean that they who are converted to Christ shall seize on the wealth, or glory, or rank of others, which is most inconsistent with true religion," but that "all things shall be brought under the dominion of Christ, so that he alone shall hold authority and rule."[98]

---

[92] Commentary on Psalm 20:2 [1557]; CO 31:208.

[93] Commentary on Zechariah 3:5 [1559]; 44:171–172; 6:12–13; CO 44:215. Cf. Commentary on Psalm 78:70 [1557]; CO 31:745–746; Harms, *In God's Custody*, 115–116.

[94] Commentary on Psalm 132:13 [1557]; CO 32:349–350. Cf. Commentary on Hosea 11:12 [1557]; CO 42:448; Commentary on Lamentations 2:6; CO 39:541.

[95] Commentary on Psalm 18:44 [1557]; CO 31:190–191. Cf. 22:28; CO 31:234–235; 47:2–3; CO 31:466–468.

[96] Commentary on Psalm 67:3 [1557]; CO 31:618.

[97] Commentary on Isaiah 60:6 (1559); CO 37:357–358.

[98] Because of the connection between the head and the members, however, "they are called ours, because Christ possesses nothing separate from his Church." Commentary on Isaiah 61:6 [1559]; CO 37:375–376.

By the same argument, the church should not use prophecies of the kingdom's political power to claim authority over civil governments, as did the papacy, for it is Christ whom the nations will serve, not the church.

> In this sense also government is ascribed to the church, not so as to obscure by haughty rule the glory of her head, or even to claim the authority which belongs to him, or, in a word, so as to have anything separate from her head, but because the preaching of the gospel, which is committed to her, is the spiritual scepter of Christ, by which he displays his power. In this respect no man can bow down submissively before Christ without also obeying the church so far as the obedience of faith is joined to the ministry of doctrine, yet so that Christ their head alone reigns and alone exercises his authority.[99]

Because of the relation between the head and the members, "where Christ shines, there the church, which is his body, is said to reign, for Christ's will is that he should have nothing apart from his members."[100]

Thus when the prophets declare that the coming king will establish good government, the just administration of law, the protection of the good, and the restraint of the wicked, such prophecies must be interpreted spiritually rather than politically.

> It is ... necessary to bear in mind the character of Christ's kingdom. It is, we know, spiritual, but it is set forth under the image or form of an earthly and civil government. For whenever the prophets speak of Christ's kingdom they set before us an earthly form, because spiritual truth, without any metaphor, could not have been sufficiently understood by a rude people in their childhood. There is no wonder, then, that the prophets, wishing to accommodate their words to the capacity of the Jews, should so speak of Christ's kingdom as to portray it before them as an earthly and civil government.[101]

The primary significance of such prophecies is therefore for Christ's spiritual kingdom, not for Christian politics, and the location of Christ's spiritual kingdom and priesthood in the present age is the church.[102] When it comes to politics, the

---

[99] Commentary on Isaiah 45:14 [1559]; CO 37:140–141.
[100] Commentary on Zechariah 2:9 [1559]; CO 44:161.
[101] Commentary on Jeremiah 33:15 [1563]; CO 39:66–67.
[102] "As then it is spiritual, the justice and judgment of which the Prophet speaks do not belong only to civil and external order, but rather to that rectitude by which it comes that men are reformed according to God's image, which is in righteousness and truth. Christ then is said to reign over us in justice and judgment not only because he keeps us by laws within the range of our duty, defends the good and the innocent, and represses the audacity of the wicked, but because he rules us by his Spirit ... [through his] spiritual jurisdiction." Commentary on Jeremiah 33:15 [1563]; CO 39:66–67. "For where the kingdom and priesthood of Christ are found, there, no doubt, is the church." "Let us then learn to begin with the kingdom and the priesthood, when we speak of the state and government of the

prophetic text must be applied in a manner qualified by the difference between the two kingdoms. The messianic hope of justice and righteousness is not to be sought in the affairs of this world but in "the spiritual and celestial kingdom of Christ."[103] In the meantime, not only is it unhelpful for Christians to seek a political manifestation of the kingdom of Christ, but it is actually

> injurious, as it would draw us back from the enjoyment of heavenly things. For we ought to distinguish between our state and that of the ancient people. Paul reminds us that they were children under a schoolmaster, being under the law, but that we are grown up, and that, therefore, the bondage under which the fathers lived has come to an end through the coming of Christ (Galatians 3:23–25).[104]

On the other hand, for Calvin, the very temporality of Israel's politics meant that it could still be a useful example for contemporary societies if interpreted properly. For instance, Calvin observes that the kingdom and priesthood were never combined in one person before Christ, not even in Israel. The offices were to remain sharply separated, their occupants even coming from different families (the priesthood belonged to that of Aaron, the kingship to that of David).[105] In this respect, Israelite kings served as a critical example for pagan kings, who tended improperly to appropriate for themselves priestly and sacerdotal tasks.[106] Israelite kings served as a vocational model for contemporary Christian magistrates insofar as they were forbidden to claim for themselves spiritual powers of word, sacrament, or ecclesiastical discipline. Yet this very point enabled Calvin to claim, on the other hand, that as temporal rulers responsible for the care of true religion, Israelite kings were also models for their secular counterparts. While he therefore emphasized discontinuity between sacerdotal Israel and contemporary Christian societies, Calvin emphasized continuity between temporal Israel and contemporary polities. It was his covenant theology, with its careful articulation of the similarities and differences between the covenants, that enabled him to conceptualize this difference.

---

church" (33:17–18; CO 39:69–70). Cf. 30:10; CO 38:622; Commentary on Zechariah 10:2 [1559]; CO 44:287; 14:8; CO 44:372; Commentary on Psalm 72:2, 7 [1557]; CO 31:665, 667; Commentary on 1 Peter 2:9 [1551]; CO 55:240; Thomas F. Torrance, *Kingdom and Church: Study in the Theology of the Reformation* (Edinburgh: Oliver & Boyd, 1956), 156–157.

[103] Commentary on Jeremiah 33:16 [1563]; CO 39:68. Though later Reformed thinkers developed the idea, I see no evidence for Haas's claim that Calvin's political theology is rooted in his concept of the covenant. Guenther Haas, *The Concept of Equity in Calvin's Ethics* (Waterloo, Ontario: Wilfrid Laurier University Press, 1997), 108.

[104] Commentary on Jeremiah 31:12 [1563]; CO 38:660.

[105] Commentary of Zechariah 6:9–11 [1559]; 44:211.

[106] Commentary on Psalm 110:4 [1557]; CO 32:164.

CONCLUSION

Calvin's nuanced interpretation of Old Testament law arose directly out of his sophisticated covenant theology. On the one hand, Calvin stressed that both the old and new covenants are administrations of the one eternal covenant of grace. For this reason, he could emphasize that the moral law as revealed in the Old Testament remains binding on all persons, in all times and places. On the other hand, Calvin stressed the differences of form that characterized the old covenant, rendering it earthly, outward, and temporal, in contrast to the new covenant, which is heavenly, inward, and spiritual. He likewise argued that the Mosaic covenant contained a peculiar dimension, a works principle that only condemns sinners. These differences informed Calvin's nuanced understanding of the ways in which the Old Testament is and is not useful as a norm for Christian polities as they grapple with questions revolving around the magisterial care of religion, the nature of civil law, the best form of government, and resistance to tyranny.

8

The Magistrate's Care of Religion

Calvin's eschatological distinction between the spiritual kingdom of Christ and the political order (Chapter 4) and his covenantal distinction between Old Testament Israel and contemporary Christian commonwealths (Chapter 7) gave him theological reasons to support religious liberty and a sharp distinction between church and state. For Calvin, the two kingdoms doctrine had concrete implications for the church's autonomy and the nature of its authority with respect to teaching, worship, and discipline, as I demonstrated in Chapter 5, as well as for the nature and function of civil government, as I demonstrated in Chapter 6. On an institutional level, Calvin distinguished between church and civil government more sharply than any of the other magisterial reformers, as was seen in Chapters 1–2.

Nevertheless, Calvin's model of ecclesiastical/civil engagement was one of cooperation rather than separation. He affirmed the authority of civil government to establish, defend, regulate, and fund the church and its various ministries.[1] In fact, all of the magisterial reformers viewed these as basic elements of what they called the care of religion (*cura religionis*), and here Calvin was no different. After all, Christ is the lord of *both* kingdoms, and both kingdoms must serve his purposes.[2] Some

---

[1] Harro Höpfl, *The Christian Polity of John Calvin* (Cambridge: Cambridge University Press, 1982), 190–191. Cf. Harro Höpfl, *Luther and Calvin on Secular Authority* (Cambridge: Cambridge University Press, 1991), xxii.

[2] See Heiko A. Oberman, "The 'Extra' Dimension in the Theology of Calvin," *Journal of Ecclesiastical History* 21 (1970): 43–64, 48; Gordon J. Keddie, "Calvin on Civil Government," *Scottish Bulletin of Evangelical Theology* 32 (1981): 23–35; Brandt B. Boeke, "Calvin's Doctrine of Civil Government," *Studia Biblica et Theologica* 11 (1981): 57–79, 61. Witte and VanDrunen suggest that Calvin superimposed on the Lutheran two kingdoms doctrine a "Gelasius-like" model of ecclesiastical and civil cooperation. John Witte, Jr., *The Reformation of Rights: Law, Religion, and Human Rights in Early Modern Calvinism* (Cambridge: Cambridge University Press, 2007), 58. Cf. 76; David VanDrunen, *Natural Law and the Two Kingdoms: A Study in the Development of Reformed Social Thought* (Grand Rapids: Eerdmans, 2010), 93.

scholars have even gone as far as to claim that Calvin ultimately collapsed the distinction between the two kingdoms, or that he assigned spiritual functions such as sanctification or edification to civil government.[3]

But Calvin's understanding of the magistrate's obligation to care for religion was more nuanced than this assessment assumes.[4] First, consistent with his view of Israel and Israel's law described in Chapter 7, Calvin's fundamental argument concerning the care of religion was less the product of direct exegesis of the Old Testament than of what he saw as the universal consensus arising from natural law. His arguments from the Old Testament presupposed philosophical and political commitments that he shared with the majority of Christian theologians and pagan philosophers alike. Second, Calvin consistently argued that civil government can only care *indirectly* for religion. Magistrates cannot exercise spiritual functions nor can they enforce spiritual righteousness. Third, Calvin believed magistrates should only punish heresy or idolatry in contexts in which the people have embraced the true religion. Only if religious crimes constitute willful defiance of known truth should they be punished by law.

In this chapter, I outline Calvin's defense of the magisterial care of religion in light of these important nuances. I trace his arguments as they developed chronologically through his New Testament commentaries (1546–1555), his 1554 *Defense of the Orthodox Faith*, his 1559 *Institutes*, and his Old Testament commentaries (1551–1564). I conclude by describing what Calvin conceived of as the ideal Christian commonwealth and by considering the extent to which he conceived of the possibility of pluralism.

---

[3] Willem Van't Spijker, *Calvin: A Brief Guide to His Life and Thought* (trans. Lyle D. Bierma; Louisville: Westminster John Knox Press, 2009), 143; William R. Stevenson, Jr., *Sovereign Grace: The Place and Significance of Christian Freedom in John Calvin's Political Thought* (New York: Oxford University Press, 1999), 52; Thomas G. Sanders, *Protestant Concepts of Church and State* (New York: Holt, Rinehart and Winston, 1964), 225–227. Cf. Guenther Haas, *The Concept of Equity in Calvin's Ethics* (Waterloo, Ontario: Wilfrid Laurier University Press, 1997), 95, 107–108; Mary Lane Potter, "The 'Whole Office of the Law' in the Theology of John Calvin," *Journal of Law and Religion* 3 (1985): 117–139, 130; I. John Hesselink, *Calvin's Concept of the Law* (Allison Park, PA: Pickwick Publications, 1992), 247–249; Frederik A. V. Harms, *In God's Custody: The Church, A History of Divine Protection: A Study of John Calvin's Ecclesiology Based on His Commentary on the Minor Prophets* (Gottingen: Vandenhoeck & Ruprecht, 2010), 132; Oliver O'Donovan and Joan Lockwood O'Donovan, *From Irenaeus to Grotius: A Sourcebook in Christian Political Thought* (Grand Rapids: Eerdmans, 1999), 665.

[4] Ironically, Karl Barth argued that the tendency of Calvin's two kingdoms doctrine was to *undermine* Christian political engagement by obscuring the Christological foundation of the state. Karl Barth, *Community, State, and Church: Three Essays* (Eugene: Wipf and Stock, 1960), 102. Barth claimed that Calvin offered insufficient explanation of the degree to which civil government belongs to the external means by which God invites human beings and retains them within the society of Christ (104). Cf. I. W. C. Van Wyk, "The Political Responsibility of the Church: On the Necessity and Boundaries of the Theory of the Two Kingdoms," *Hervormde Teologiese Studies* 61.3 (September, 2005): 647–682, 665.

ARGUMENTS FROM THE NEW TESTAMENT

During the 1540s and early 1550s, Calvin offered little exegetical defense of his claims about the magistrate's role in protecting the true religion.[5] In large part this is because during these years he was devoting his exegetical energies to a series of commentaries on the New Testament, which is silent about such a magisterial role. But Calvin did not hesitate to exploit whatever arguments he could muster from the New Testament. The best example of this is his use of 1 Timothy 2:2, a passage that Calvin forced to bear almost the entire weight of his claim that the New Testament confirms the teaching of the Old with respect to the magisterial care of religion. In his commentary on the passage, Calvin insists that when Paul calls Christians to pray that magistrates will allow them to live in peace, godliness, and decency, he is not simply urging them to pray for religious toleration.[6] On the contrary, Paul is summarizing "the fruits which are yielded to us by a well regulated government [*principatu rite composito*]." This means that, along with peace and public decency, a magistrate is responsible to establish godliness, "to promote religion [*fovendam religionem*], to maintain the worship of God [*asserendum Dei cultum*], and to take care that sacred ordinances be preserved with due reverence [*sacrorum reverentiam exigendam*]."[7]

What about magistrates who fail to perform these functions? Christians should pray that such leaders would

> begin to impart to us those benefits of which they formerly deprived us. It is our duty, therefore, not only to pray for those who are already worthy, but we must pray to God that he may make bad men good. We must always hold by this principle that magistrates were appointed by God for the protection of religion [*religionis ... publicae custodiam*], as well as of the peace and decency of society, in exactly the same manner that the earth is appointed to produce food.[8]

As was seen in Chapter 6, Calvin had invoked 1 Timothy 2:2 before with respect to the nature of government, but this is the first time he used it to justify his position on the care of religion.

A second New Testament text in which Calvin found warrant for the magisterial establishment of religion was Luke 14:23, the text Augustine famously used to justify the coercion of the Donatists. The context is the parable of Jesus in which the host of a feast commands his servants not only to invite various social outcasts to attend, but to "compel them to come in." Calvin admits that the primary meaning of the phrase is simply that the preaching of the gospel should be accompanied by "fervent

---

[5] See Witte, *The Reformation of Rights*, 41, 56.   [6] Commentary on 1 Timothy 2:4 [1548]: CO 52:269.

[7] Commentary on 1 Timothy 2:2 [1548]: CO 52:267.

[8] Commentary on 1 Timothy 2:2 [1548]: CO 52:267.

exhortations," but he cannot resist insisting that Augustine rightly used the text "to prove that godly princes may lawfully issue edicts for compelling obstinate and rebellious persons to worship the true God and to maintain the unity of the faith. For though faith is voluntary, yet we see that such methods are useful for subduing the obstinacy of those who will not yield until they are compelled."[9]

If both of these arguments seem weak compared to the typical rigor of Calvin's exegesis, the precariousness of Calvin's position is equally evident from his attempts to refute arguments that used the New Testament *against* his position. Calvin didn't hesitate to argue with the church fathers, rejecting any suggestion that the gospel has implications for the severity of civil law.[10] The most striking of such examples is Calvin's rejection of Augustine's interpretation of John 8, the story of the woman caught in adultery. Whereas Augustine interpreted Jesus' refusal to judge the woman as testimony to the transcendence of grace over the Old Testament's capital laws, Calvin distinguishes himself from "the ingenuity of Augustine, who thinks that in this manner the distinction between the law and the gospel is pointed out."[11] Calvin uses his commentary as an opportunity to argue that adultery should be punished by death. We must remember, he insists, that Jesus did "not overturn political order or reverse the sentences and punishments appointed by the laws."[12] Elsewhere he appeals to Roman law to prove that adultery was punished with death "almost by the common law of nations."[13]

One of the most fascinating strands of Calvin's thinking that runs throughout his New Testament commentaries is his reflection on instances of government involvement – or lack of it – in various religious disputes. Strikingly, he consistently defends the various political powers that persecuted the early church as having the authority *in principle* to defend the true religion. The problem is simply that they misinterpreted what that true religion was. Even more ironic is that Calvin is resoundingly critical of the civil authorities that provided liberty and protection to the early church, criticizing them for their apathy toward religious truth. His evaluative comments in these instances say more about Calvin than they do about the biblical narratives themselves, revealing the precommitments that colored his reading of the texts.

In his commentaries on John and Acts, for instance, Calvin defends the Jews for their instincts in seeking the death penalty for Jesus and the evangelist Stephen.[14] As he puts it in the case of Jesus and the accusation of blasphemy:

---

[9] Commentary on Luke 14:23 [1555]; CO 45:401.
[10] For an argument with Chrysostom, see Commentary on 1 Corinthians 5:13 [1546] CO 49:387. Cf. Commentary on Titus 3:10 [1550]; CO 52:436; Commentary on Hebrews 10:29 [1549]; CO 55:136.
[11] Commentary on John 8:6 [1553]; CO 47:189.
[12] Commentary on John 8:11 [1553]; CO 47:190–191.
[13] Commentary on 1 Corinthians 7:10 [1546]; CO 49:410.
[14] Commentary on Acts 7:58 [1552]; CO 48:169.

Besides, this accusation was not altogether void of plausibility, but they erred grievously in the application of it. The general doctrine was undoubtedly true, that it was not lawful for men to assume any honor which is due to God and that they who claimed for themselves what is peculiar to God alone deserved to be put to death. But the source of their error related to the person of Christ, because they did not consider what are the titles given by scripture to the messiah, from which they might easily have learned that he was the Son of God, and did not even deign to inquire whether or not Jesus was the messiah whom God had formerly promised. We see then how they drew a false conclusion from a true principle, for they reason badly. This example warns us to distinguish carefully between a general doctrine and the application of it, for there are many ignorant and unsteady persons who reject the very principles of scripture if they have once been deceived by the semblance of truth.[15]

Calvin suggests that the papacy's error was much the same. The papists legitimately claimed divine sanction in defending the faith, but then they persecuted true doctrine and defended what was false.[16]

Calvin's concern to defend the religious responsibilities of magistrates led him to criticize the Pharisee Gamaliel's suggestion, recorded in Acts 5, that the Jewish leadership should refrain from persecuting the Christian movement in order to determine whether it was of God or not. Calvin finds Gamaliel's advice absurd, for by the same logic, civil magistrates should never punish anyone, nor should "any wicked fact . . . be corrected." Gamaliel's advice would be sound if it pertained to a "doubtful matter," Calvin concedes, but the word of God is not doubtful. To be sure, the word of God is able to flourish against any human power. But while Christ's kingdom does not need the protection of human authority per se, humans should still do their part, consistent with their vocation, to advance and protect it. God's promises are "no cause why the servants of Christ should be less diligent in maintaining the truth, . . . [or] why they should carelessly wink at their wickedness who endeavor to turn all things topsy-turvy."[17]

Calvin is equally critical of the various pagan authorities whose actions toward the Christian movement recorded in the book of Acts range from apathetic to tolerant. He sharply criticizes the city of Athens for the atmosphere of free speech and religious toleration that made it possible for Paul to speak freely on Mars Hill. Anywhere else, he notes, to speak in a public place and draw a crowd like this would have been "a crime worthy of death." In Athens, however, "because those who

---

[15] Commentary on John 19:7 [1553]; CO 47:408

[16] Commentary on John 19:7 [1553]; CO 47:408–409.

[17] Commentary on Acts 5:34 [1552]; CO 48:113–114. Calvin criticizes the Jews of Gamaliel's day and the papists of his own day for their lack of confidence in using scripture to refute those they deemed heretics. Commentary on Acts 9:22 [1552]; CO 48:211.

did carry about trifles had liberty granted them to prate by reason of the immoderate desire they had to hear news, Paul was permitted to entreat of the mysteries of faith." The policy promoted an infatuation with novelty and a predilection to idleness that rendered the Athenians unable to unite around a common philosophy or faith. "Wherefore, there could never be any certain government set down in that city, which was, notwithstanding, the mistress of sciences." Eventually, Calvin claims, this policy brought Greece to its ruin.[18]

Calvin also criticizes the Roman authorities for their reluctance to intervene in the controversy between Paul and the Jewish leaders. Convinced that religion was a matter in which there can be no certainty, the Romans mistakenly believed that religious pluralism should be tolerated. Yet this belief flew in the face of what all people understand by nature:

> Here we see what the ignorance of true godliness does in setting in order the state of every commonwealth and dominion. All men confess that this is the principal thing, that true religion be in force and flourish. Now, when the true God is known and the certain and sure rule of worshiping him is understood, there is nothing more equitable than that which God commands in his law, to wit, that those who bear rule with power (having abolished contrary superstitions) defend the pure worship of the true God ... But seeing that the Romans observed their rites only through pride and stubbornness, and seeing they had no certainty where there was no truth, they thought that this was the best way they could take if they should grant liberty to those who dwelt in the provinces to live as they desired. But nothing is more absurd than to leave the worship of God to men's choice.

It was precisely for this reason, Calvin argues, that the Torah stipulated that the king should possess and study his own copy of the law, "that being well instructed, and certain of his faith, he might with more courage take in hand to maintain that which he knew certainly was right."[19] Disputes about religion are not, as the Roman official Gallio mistakenly thought, mere "vain contentions," but "a matter of all others most serious."[20] It is important to notice the direction of Calvin's reasoning here. He begins by appealing to what "all men confess," and then declares that there is "nothing more equitable" than that the command in the law concerning the magisterial obligation toward true religion be carried out. Only then does he invoke the Torah.

Because the Romans disregarded the law of God, they cared nothing about the charge that Paul had apostatized from that law, let alone that he troubled the "church" with false opinions. But while profane persons might think religion is of

---

[18] Commentary on Acts 17:19 [1554]; CO 48:407.
[19] Commentary on Acts 18:12–14 [1554]; CO 48:431–432.
[20] Commentary on Acts 18:15 [1554]; CO 48:432.

little concern to political authorities, "among the people of God it is an offense worthy of no less punishment to corrupt the doctrine of godliness with wicked and false opinions than to do injury to or commit wickedness among men."[21] The Romans dismissed the Jewish law as mere superstition because they "had not learned that the rule of godliness must be sought from the mouth of God."[22] Calvin thus saw no virtue in the Romans' protection of Paul, nor did he believe Christians should put much faith in the toleration of their opponents. On the contrary, when "enemies of godliness" do not persecute Christians "let us know that we need not thank their moderation and clemency for this, but because, when the Lord spares his sheep, he does not suffer them [his enemies] to do so much hurt as they would."[23]

Calvin's comments evaluating the reaction of various political authorities to the emergence of early Christianity showcase the strength of his conviction that protecting and upholding religious truth is central to the magisterial vocation. He reasoned from the responsibilities of a patriarch or householder to those of a prince: "If this duty [of making one's household an image of the church] be required at the hands of the householder, much more of a prince, that as much as it lies in him he does not suffer the name of God to be profaned in his realm."[24] If earthly fathers are called to lead their households in religion, though their vocation "properly belongs to the civil world," it can be no contradiction to say that magistrates should establish true religion, even though their office is secular. Here, though, Calvin quickly qualifies the point: "[T]hough it belongs to magistrates to defend religion, yet we say that their office is confined to the limits of this life, for otherwise the civil and earthly government cannot be distinguished from the spiritual kingdom of Christ."[25] The magistracy has a responsibility toward the true religion but its power remains outward, coercive, and temporal.

Calvin seeks to explain this paradox in his comments on Jesus' declaration to Pontius Pilate in John 18, "My kingdom is not of this world."[26] While the Jews slanderously charged Jesus with seeking to overthrow the political order, Calvin interprets Jesus' statement as a clear declaration to the contrary: "There is no disagreement between his kingdom and political government or order." The reformer paraphrases Jesus to make the point. "I am falsely accused, as if I had attempted to produce a disturbance or to make a revolution in public affairs. I have preached about the kingdom of God, but that is spiritual, and therefore you have no right to suspect me of aspiring to kingly power." To be sure, the kingdom of Christ is *in* the world, "for we

---

[21] Commentary on Acts 23:29 [1554]; CO 48:516. Cf. Commentary on Acts 25:18–19 [1554]; CO 48: 533–534.

[22] Commentary on Acts 25:18–19 [1554]; CO 48:534.

[23] Commentary on Acts 12:2 [1552]; CO 48:267.   [24] Commentary on Acts 16:15 [1554]; CO 48:379.

[25] Commentary on Hebrews 12:10 [1549]; CO 55:176.

[26] Commentary on John 6:15 [1553]; CO 47:134.

know that it has its seat in our hearts, as also Christ says elsewhere, 'The kingdom of God is within you.' But strictly speaking, the kingdom of God, while it dwells in us, is a stranger to the world because its condition is totally different." What is the difference? Jesus answers the question when he says that his kingdom does not use the sword as earthly kingdoms do.[27]

This leads Calvin to what is arguably *the* great tension within his political theology.

> But here a question arises, is it not lawful to defend the kingdom of Christ by arms? For when kings and princes are commanded to kiss the Son of God, not only are they enjoined to submit to his authority in their private capacity, but also to employ all the power that they possess in defending the church and maintaining godliness.

Calvin responds that "they who draw this conclusion, that the doctrine of the gospel and the pure worship of God ought not to be defended by arms, are unskillful and ignorant reasoners." First, Jesus' point in differentiating his kingdom from those that bear the sword was not to prohibit the defense of his church but to refute the charges of the Jews that his intentions were political. The second reason Calvin offers is his most sophisticated argument to date on the magistrate's responsibility to the kingdom of Christ:

> [T]hough godly kings defend the kingdom of Christ by the sword, still it is done in a different manner from that in which worldly kingdoms are wont to be defended. For the kingdom of Christ, being spiritual, must be founded on the doctrine and power of the Spirit. In the same manner too its edification is promoted, for neither the laws and edicts of men nor the punishments inflicted by them enter into the consciences. Yet this does not hinder princes from *accidentally* defending the kingdom of Christ, partly by appointing external discipline and partly by lending their protection to the Church against wicked men. It results, however, from the depravity of the world that the kingdom of Christ is strengthened more by the blood of the martyrs than by the aid of arms.[28]

This is a remarkable passage. More than anything Calvin wrote up to this point, it clarifies just how and in what respect Calvin believed civil magistrates use temporal means to establish, promote, or defend Christ's kingdom. It is important to pay close attention to several crucial elements.

First, Calvin argues that when foundational passages like Psalm 2 call magistrates to submit to Christ's rule, they call them to do so as magistrates, not simply as private individuals. He assumes that it is self-evident what this means: Magistrates must defend the church and maintain godliness. But he does not defend that claim here.

---

[27] Commentary on John 18:36 [1553]; CO 47:403–404.
[28] Commentary on John 18:36 [1553]; CO 47:403–404. Emphasis added.

Second, Calvin's final sentence reflects an irony that potentially undermines his argument. He suggests that the "blood of the martyrs" contributes more to the strength of Christ's kingdom than does the "aid of arms." Perhaps he is simply using rhetorical exaggeration to bemoan the injustice of magistrates. But if so, why not draw the implication that magisterial involvement in religious matters causes more harm than good? If, on the other hand, Calvin means his statement quite literally, that is, that the efforts of magistrates contribute more to the strength of Christ's kingdom when they oppose it than when they defend it, why insist that magistrates use the sword to defend it?

Finally, Calvin recognizes that there is something counterintuitive about claiming that a political authority whose power is merely external could defend a kingdom whose power is spiritual and inward. His response is to acknowledge that magistrates defend the kingdom of Christ in a different sense than they defend their own realms. After all, in a direct sense they cannot defend the kingdom of Christ at all. They can only defend it *accidentally* or *indirectly*. Here he mentions two means by which they do so: establishing external discipline and providing physical protection. In both cases what the magistrate is really doing is establishing and protecting the ministry of the church, which is itself the means of Christ's spiritual government. Calvin explicitly declares that the civil government's laws cannot promote spiritual edification because they do not enter into the conscience. At no point does civil government become spiritual, use spiritual power, or accomplish directly spiritual ends.[29]

Calvin's distinction undermines Höpfl's claim that Calvin "worked out in very great detail . . . the character of a Christian polity designed precisely to serve as an aid to sanctification: a polity devoted to the honor and glory of God, to *pietas*, to *aequitas* and to *aedifcatio*."[30] His description of Calvin's polity fails adequately to account for the reformer's theological distinction between what magistrates can do directly – coerce outward action – and what they can do indirectly – create a context conducive of the work of spiritual government. Civil coercion may be an indirect aid to sanctification, according to Calvin, but by no means do magistrates actually

---

[29] See Marc Chenevière, "Did Calvin Advocate Theocracy?" *Evangelical Quarterly* 9 (1937): 167; Brandt B. Boeke, "Calvin's Doctrine of Civil Government," 60; John T. McNeill, "The Democratic Element in Calvin's Thought," *Church History* 18 (September 1949): 153–171, 156.

[30] Höpfl, *The Christian Polity of John Calvin*, 211. Höpfl claims that Calvin believed "the business of magistrates is to enforce virtue." To be sure, Höpfl recognizes that "[Calvin] did not think that true righteousness can be enforced" (189). Yet he claims that for Calvin the distinction between the spiritual and civil uses of the law did not lead to the conclusion that "neither virtue nor piety ought to be the concern of governors" because Calvin viewed civil coercion as an "aid to sanctification" (190), if "primarily in a ground-clearing capacity" (191), and as an "external support for the pursuit of sanctification" (212). He claims that for Calvin, the Christian polity is an "educational enterprise," but he immediately admits that "it does not appear that Calvin ever presented it in quite that light" (203).

participate in sanctification or *aedificatio*, nor is it the business of magistrates to enforce true virtue. For Calvin the church, not the civil order, is the school of virtue.[31]

Before turning to Calvin's later writings, it is worth emphasizing that while Calvin's New Testament commentaries feature a theoretically sophisticated account of the magisterial obligation to establish and defend true religion, in most cases that account is *defensive*. In only two cases, both of them tenuous, did he offer *constructive* arguments drawn from the text. This suggests that the real foundation for Calvin's position did not lay in the New Testament but in his other philosophical and theological commitments.[32]

DEFENSE OF THE ORTHODOX FAITH (1554)

Calvin's most sustained defense of the civil punishment of heresy appeared in his 1554 treatise in defense of Geneva's execution of Servetus.[33] While most of the work is a refutation of Servetus's antitrinitarian theology, Calvin devotes nearly fifty pages at the beginning of the work to a defense of the claim that just as magistrates punish temporal crimes, so they should punish those who blaspheme God and harm others by distorting the truth. Freedom of speech is not inherently good, for while people should be free to speak the truth, they should not be free to spew falsehood. "For what religion would remain any longer in the world? What

---

[31] Little argues that Calvin's theology required him either to separate church and state or to subordinate the state to the church, and that the reformer leaned toward the latter option. Still, Calvin always maintained a sharp distinction between the two, and the church "was always the primary focus of Calvin's considerable energies for organizational reform." David Little, *Religion, Order, and Law* (New York: Harper and Row, 1969), 74. Cf. Derek S. Jeffreys, "'It's a Miracle of God That There Is Any Common Weal Among Us': Unfaithfulness and Disorder in John Calvin's Political Thought," *The Review of Politics* (2000): 107–129, 124–125.

[32] Cf. Höpfl, *The Christian Polity of John Calvin*, 53.

[33] For background on this see Chapter 2. The work remains untranslated into English and has received little scholarly attention. The Latin title is *Defensio orthodoxae fidei de sacra Trinitate, contra prodigiosos errores Michaelis Serveti Hispani, ubi ostenditur haereticos iure gladii coercendos esse, et nominatim de homine hoc tam impio iuste et merito sumptum Genevae fuisse supplicium* (CO 8:453–644). The extended French title is: *Déclaration pour maintenir la vraye foy que tiennent tous chrestiens de la Trinité des personnes en un seul Dieu: Congre les erreurs détestables de Michel Servet Espaignol. Où il est aussi monstré qu'il est licite de punir les hérétiques, et qu'à bon droict ce meschant a esté executé par iustice en la ville de Genève* (Geneva: Jean Crespin, 1554; available at the Post-Reformation Digital Library, www.prdl.org/search.php?q=Déclaration+pour+maintenir+la+vraye+foy). The following citations are my translations from the French except where otherwise specified. Cf. Marian Hillar and Claire S. Allen, *Michael Servetus: Intellectual Giant, Humanist, and Martyr* (Lanham, MD: University Press of America, 2002), 193–201; Christoph Strohm, "Calvin and Religious Tolerance," *John Calvin's Impact on Church and Society* (ed. Martin Ernst Hirzel and Martin Smallmann; Grand Rapids: Eerdmans, 2009), 184–191.

mark would there be for discerning the true church? In brief, what would
be[come] of the things of God and of Jesus Christ if doctrine is uncertain and,
as it were, placed in suspension?"[34] Magistrates who fail to punish blatant heresy
are complicit in its guilt, "for in order to spare the wolves they make the poor
sheep to be prey."[35]

The premise of Calvin's argument is that with respect to religion the truth has
been established with certainty and is not in serious question. Where religion is in
legitimate question, he concedes, free debate should be permitted. Coercion should
never be used in defense of doctrines that are doubtful or that have been invented by
human beings. This was an important point for Calvin, because he was aware that
some orthodox Protestants opposed the punishment of heretics on the grounds that
the papists were using such methods to persecute the faithful.[36] Calvin addresses this
concern by arguing that Rome's use of force was rooted in ignorance rather than
reason. The papal abuse of coercion to defend falsehood hardly meant that it was
unjust for a magistrate to defend the "true faith of which he is certain."[37] The key is
that magistrates must only defend a cause that is known and established, always
being careful to investigate the cases that come before them and making sure that the
truth is publicly taught.[38]

Of course, there is a problem with Calvin's argument. If the truth is so certain, why
does it require magistrates to preserve its certainty? Calvin's answer is that while the
truth is certain to those with education and wisdom, the masses, who lack such gifts,
are easily manipulated by arguments that have the mere appearance of credibility.
These latter arguments need to be suppressed. But to argue that the teachings of
scripture are not certain is to call God a liar.[39]

In the first part of the section on the punishment of heretics, Calvin offers
a running critique of a litany of arguments his critics brought against his position.
Like Calvin's New Testament commentaries, this section is largely deconstruc-
tive. Much of it simply repeats arguments that Calvin had already articulated in
his commentaries. At the heart of Calvin's opponents' position, as he describes it,
was their claim that the punishment of religious crimes was abolished at the
coming of Christ[40] (which implied, as Servetus explicitly charged, that Calvin

---

[34] *Déclaration pour maintenir la vraye foy*, 17.   [35] *Déclaration pour maintenir la vraye foy*, 35.
[36] *Déclaration pour maintenir la vraye foy*, 17–19, 26.   [37] *Déclaration pour maintenir la vraye foy*, 23.
[38] *Déclaration pour maintenir la vraye foy*, 24–26. There should always be a careful combination of
teaching and force, because coercion without teaching makes hypocrites, while teaching without
coercion only hardens those who are stubborn (36).
[39] *Déclaration pour maintenir la vraye foy*, 17.
[40] They argued that Jesus desired to have his kingdom established by the spiritual sword of the gospel. He
called his followers to be prepared to suffer, but never to inflict suffering on others. *Déclaration pour
maintenir la vraye foy*, 27. They appealed to the parable of the wheat and the tares (36), to Jesus'

was guilty of the Judaizing error of insisting on obedience to the Old Testament law).[41]

Calvin responds to these arguments with his standard refutations. The logical extension of his opponents' arguments, he claims, would be to abolish all criminal punishment because Jesus never commanded his disciples to punish thieves, adulterers, or murderers either.[42] The only reason Jesus did not take up these tasks himself was because it was not his vocation. His mission was to establish his "spiritual rule" and to atone for the sin of the world.[43] Calvin concedes that the kingdom was initially established in a context of weakness and suffering in order that the disciples' truthfulness might be vindicated by their willingness to suffer for it and that the gospel's triumph might appear all the more miraculous.[44] But he observes that the apostles never claimed "that one should not maintain the service of God by the sword," and sometimes they even administered temporal (if miraculous) punishment.[45] In any case, conditions had changed. Jesus had since chosen other ministers, including magistrates, to serve his kingdom. Just as God gives pastors temporal gifts such as eloquence, so "the Christian religion and faith, even as it is sustained only by the hand of God and triumphs under the cross, is nevertheless aided by men and has some support from their authority when it so pleases God."[46]

Calvin's opponents raised another argument as well. They insisted that it is impossible to coerce a person to believe a religious doctrine. With this, significantly, Calvin agreed. He concedes that "it is not in the hand of princes to enter into the heart of men by their edicts and to touch them such that they subject themselves to God and agree to the truth." But Calvin invokes the logic of Augustine, reminding his readers that the purpose of punishment is not to create faith but to render the stubborn "benign and docile" so that they might be susceptible to teaching. In any case, civil punishments are appropriate for the sole reason that it is part of the

---

command to Peter to put his sword back in its sheath (40), and to his refusal to condemn the woman caught in adultery (13–14).

[41] *Déclaration pour maintenir la vraye foy*, 13–14.

[42] *Déclaration pour maintenir la vraye foy*, 17, 27. Cf. 15–16, 38–39.

[43] *Déclaration pour maintenir la vraye foy*, 33–34. Thus he remained silent when tried by Pilate, but that does not mean Christians are obligated to do the same when falsely accused in court. Thus he called Peter to avoid defending him with the sword, but that does not mean "that the hands of magistrates and of princes are bound from any longer exercising their ordained office." *Déclaration pour maintenir la vraye foy*, 40.

[44] *Déclaration pour maintenir la vraye foy*, 27–28.

[45] *Déclaration pour maintenir la vraye foy*, 19. If Peter proclaimed the death of Ananias and Sapphira, and Paul struck Elymas with blindness, while informing the Corinthian church that some of their number had died due to their disrespect for the Lord's Supper, how much more should civil magistrates punish religious sins? (15, 35).

[46] *Déclaration pour maintenir la vraye foy*, 30 (Cf. 31, 38–39).

magistrate's obligation to protect the name of God, his word, and his service from slander.[47]

In the second part of the section, Calvin turns to his constructive argument. His intent, he declares, is to show "that not only is it licit for magistrates to chastise those who attempt to corrupt the heavenly doctrine, but also that it is commanded to them to do so." Significantly, Calvin begins his constructive argument not with scripture but with an appeal to natural law. Pagan writers bore witness that "the natural sense teaches that religion must have the principal place in any well-regulated polity, and that it must be maintained by the laws. When one reads all the philosophers who have treated of this matter, there are none who do not begin with the service of God and who do not give the first degree to religion." Indeed, the pagan writers considered a legislator "barbarous" if "he did not care that the gods be served and honored."[48]

But some claimed that the pagans made these arguments because of superstition. Calvin responds by attempting to show that the arguments are reasonable. If it is just for a magistrate to punish crimes against human beings, why should he not punish crimes against the God? Indeed, it is in the interests of humanity for him to do so, for the glory of God is essential to human morality and well-being. Thus, "since the goal of a good polity and of right concerns a legitimate order between human beings, let us see, when the honor of God is held in contempt, if the principal order is not so dissipated that the life of men becomes brutal." The very enterprise of government is "imperfect without religion," and "magistrates are only shadows, or as little runts half-formed, when they only occupy themselves with their civil procedures, not taking care to maintain the service of God."[49]

Having established a case from natural law, Calvin then turns to scripture for confirmation. He bridges the two approaches by considering the example of the pagan king Nebuchadnezzar. As recorded in the book of Daniel, Nebuchadnezzar condemned to death anyone who blasphemed against the God of Israel. Calvin claims that the Spirit intended this action to be an example for all magistrates. How can Christian rulers not "take care to guarantee the glory of God" and "preserve it in its entirety, seeing that the king of Babylon makes himself its guardian and protector?"[50] The example of a pagan king makes Christian princes – who are "servants of the church, and to whom the truth of God is entirely clear" – "doubly culpable of villainous cowardice, if they do not demonstrate more courage in maintaining it."[51]

Only after having laid the foundation of an argument from natural law and having confirmed it from scripture does Calvin finally turn to the Old Testament, the

---

[47] *Déclaration pour maintenir la vraye foy*, 32–33.   [48] *Déclaration pour maintenir la vraye foy*, 41.
[49] *Déclaration pour maintenir la vraye foy*, 42.   [50] *Déclaration pour maintenir la vraye foy*, 43.
[51] *Déclaration pour maintenir la vraye foy*, 44. Cf. 22–23.

revealed law of God. The law confirms that it is not mere human authority that calls for the defense of true religion. Not only did God command Israel to put to death false prophets who sought to lead the people astray. He told the people to have no mercy on their own brothers, sons, daughters, wives, neighbors, and friends who committed the same offense. God's demand for such zeal, Calvin argues, makes mockery of the claim that crimes against religion should be tolerated.[52]

At this point Calvin makes two fundamental qualifications to his argument. First, he notes that God did not command that all religion should be maintained by magistrates, but only "that which he has ordained by his own mouth." The use of the sword to defend merely human religion is therefore unjust, and Calvin warns that those who shed innocent blood will be accountable for every drop. Second, pagans (i.e., adherents of foreign religions) are not to be punished, but only "those who, after having received the doctrine of the law, would become apostates."[53] "God does not command that one punish indifferently all those who have sown wicked doctrine, but only the apostates who are alienated and straying from the true religion and who work to seduce others." Thus, as he had claimed in the 1536 *Institutes*, so here again Calvin confirms that "the Jews, the Turks, and similar peoples" are not to be punished.[54]

Calvin draws from the Torah concrete implications for how these principles might be applied, distinguishing three levels of error and the degree of suppression appropriate to each:

> Thus there are to be differentiated three degrees of errors: [1] those we admit, that are to be tolerated, and [2] others that are to be punished by moderate means so that [3] only the obvious impiety may be punished by a capital penalty . . . Certainly this means that if there is a certain small superstition or ignorance occupying the minds of the simple people, one should be patient in trying to correct them rather than too hastily seek violent retribution. Thus people should be punished according to their errors. Even the moderate type of errors call for severity. However, though the errors producing damage to the Church and resulting from negligence and ambition deserve a punishment – nevertheless, when there is no contempt of God and rebellion combined with mutiny, the severity should not be excessive so that the indulgence may not nourish the audacity and defiance of those who would desire to

---

[52] *Déclaration pour maintenir la vraye foy*, 44–47. Calvin argues that though it may be a virtue to use clemency when it comes to sins against human beings, when it comes to sins against God judges must use all rigor (49–50).

[53] *Déclaration pour maintenir la vraye foy*, 45.

[54] *Déclaration pour maintenir la vraye foy*, 46. Only apostates and those who lure others to apostasy, so threatening the salvation of their souls and the peace and unity of the church, are to be punished (26). Cf. Strohm, "Calvin and Religious Tolerance," 183–184; R. White, "Castellio Against Calvin: The Turk in the Toleration Controversy of the Sixteenth Century," *Bibliothèque d'Humanisme et Renaissance* 46.3 (1984): 573–586.

tear apart the unity of faith. But since there are those who attempt to undermine religion at its foundations, and who profess execrable blasphemies against God and by impious and poisonous dogmas they drag the soul to ruin, in sum – those who attempt to revolt the public from the unique God and his doctrine, it is necessary to have a recourse to the extreme measure in order to prevent further spreading of the mortal poison. Such a rule which Moses received from the mouth of God he himself had followed faithfully.[55]

No doubt Calvin found the first degree of error rampant in Geneva, but he expected it to be corrected through teaching and church discipline. The second degree of error would land a person before the Council, facing penalties such as brief imprisonment, rebuke or banishment. The third degree of error resulted in a capital sentence. Such a sentence was only encountered once in Genevan history, in the case of Servetus. The purpose of *Defense of the Orthodox Faith* was to prove that Servetus did indeed "merit being exterminated from the world."[56]

Calvin concludes his defense of the punishment of heretics by returning to the objection that the punishment of heresy is "not suitable to the reign of Christ (which is spiritual) . . . seeing that in the church this is not commanded to judges."[57] He responds by formulating a fundamental exegetical principle arising from the two kingdoms distinction: "[T]he advent of Christ did not change that which pertains to political order and subtracted and retracted nothing from the right office of magistrates."[58] He then offers his standard litany of proof-texts, Psalm 2, Isaiah 49:23, and 1 Timothy 2:2, concluding that Christian magistrates have no right to abandon the responsibility of caring for religion. "Therefore there is no doubt that this charge is committed by God to all faithful magistrates: to maintain the kingdom of our Lord Jesus in its state and to apply to this the authority of their sword."[59]

INSTITUTES OF THE CHRISTIAN RELIGION (1559)

Some scholars argue that it is significant that, in the 1559 *Institutes*, Calvin entitled Book 4, which contains his chapter on civil government, "the external means or aims by which God invites us into the society of Christ and holds us therein." Just below that title, Calvin writes that God has provided outward helps "to beget and increase

---

[55] Quoted in Hillar, *Michael Servetus*, 201, a translation from the Latin text: *Defensio orthodoxae fidei*, CO 8:477. For the French, see *Déclaration pour maintenir la vraye foy*, 48–49.
[56] *Déclaration pour maintenir la vraye foy*, 57.   [57] *Déclaration pour maintenir la vraye foy*, 50.
[58] *Déclaration pour maintenir la vraye foy*, 50–51.
[59] *Déclaration pour maintenir la vraye foy*, 52. On 1 Timothy 2:2, he writes that Paul "does not limit their charge to rendering to men what belongs to them, and enabling one to live in peace and good equity, . . . but he specifically pronounces that they are established to maintain religion. Then it follows that the sword is placed in their hand for defending the truth of God when it is needed, punishing heretics who oppose it" (52–53).

faith within us, and advance it to its goal" (4.1.1). Some argue that Calvin intended these descriptions to apply to the work of civil government, the subject of the last of Book 4's twenty chapters.[60] For instance, Stevenson suggests that by making civil government one of the outward means of grace, Calvin associates the work of civil government with the spiritual use of the law. He observes that for Calvin, Christians have a "need for external aids or helps," and that God provides these helps in the institutions of church and civil government.[61] Thus "Sanctification [is] effectuated by the Holy Spirit through the instrumentalities of spiritual and political communities."[62] It "logically and inevitably" follows that "the institutions of church and state are simply two dimensions of one divine help."[63]

Yet Calvin himself is clear that this is not the case. Nowhere in his writings does he describe civil government as one of the "external means" or "outward helps" of spiritual grace. Here, when he writes that God has provided outward helps "to beget and increase faith within us, and advance it to its goal," he is simply informing his readers that as a whole, Book 4 is concerned with the ministry of the church as the means by which God brings about justification and sanctification. In fact, he immediately identifies the means he is talking about: the word, right order, and the sacraments, concluding that by these means God has accommodated himself to human beings to draw them to himself. In context there is no need to interpret right order as referring to civil government, because the church also has its right order. Significantly, it is only after this that Calvin declares what will be his outline in the book: "the church, its government, orders, and power; then the sacraments; and lastly, the civil order" (4.1.1).[64] None of this suggests that Calvin views the civil order as one of the means by which God justifies and sanctifies human beings. It simply indicates that Calvin left a relatively brief chapter on civil government at the end of a massive book on the church.

[60] See Balke, *Calvin and the Anabaptist Radicals*, 257; Höpfl, *The Christian Polity of John Calvin*, 191–192, 208; Wilhelm Niesel, *The Theology of Calvin* (trans. Harold Knight; London: Methuen, 1956), 229–237; Ralph C. Hancock, *Calvin and the Foundations of Modern Politics* (Ithaca: Cornell University Press, 1989), 64, 79; Paul (Sueng Hoon) Chung, *Spirituality and Social Ethics in John Calvin: A Pneumatological Perspective* (New York: University Press of America, 2000), 116–117. Cf. W. Robert Godfrey, "Calvin and Theonomy," *Theonomy: A Reformed Critique* (ed. William S. Barker, et al.; Grand Rapids: Zondervan, 1990), 298–312, 300–301.

[61] Stevenson, *Sovereign Grace*, 45. "Calvin finds the effort to distinguish sharply between sacred law and secular law to be, in many ways, an artificial endeavor" (50).

[62] Stevenson, *Sovereign Grace*, 53. He claims that for Calvin human exercises of power such as civil government are "legitimate only when they work toward the same goals of renewal and revivification" (61). The Consistory is an example of civil government's "spiritual' responsibilities" (98). Thus civil government "serves spiritual and pedagogical purposes." Stevenson, "Calvin and Political Issues," 174.

[63] Stevenson, *Sovereign Grace*, 52. In part, Stevenson bases his claim on a conflation of Calvin's two kingdoms doctrine and his concept of the two tables of the law (52).

[64] Roughly Calvin does follow this order. Chapters 1–13 discuss the church with its government, orders, and power, Chapters 14–19 discuss the sacraments, and Chapter 20 discusses civil government.

Significantly, Calvin admits that the chapter on civil government fits oddly with the rest of the book. He only turns to civil government after reminding his readers that "we have established above that man is under a twofold government," and that "we have elsewhere discussed at sufficient length the kind that resides in the soul or inner man and pertains to eternal life." Now, he says, he will turn to "the other kind, which pertains only to the establishment of civil justice and outward morality" (4.20.1). Clearly he is differentiating 4.1–19, which pertains to the spiritual government, from 4.20, which pertains to the political order. Lest the point be unclear, in a section he added in 1559, the same edition in which he added the title about the "external means," Calvin confesses that "this topic seems by nature alien to the spiritual doctrine of faith which I have undertaken to discuss." Still, he writes, "what follows will show that I am right in joining them, in fact, that necessity compels me to do so." In other words, civil government is not part of Book 4 because it is part of the spiritual doctrine of faith, but because for several reasons it is necessary to discuss them together. What are those reasons? Calvin gives three: First, because "insane and barbarous men furiously strive to overturn this divinely established order." Second, because "the flatterers of princes, immoderately praising their power, do not hesitate to set them against the rule of God himself." (These two threats need to be taken seriously by Christians because God uses civil government to protect and establish the ministry of his spiritual kingdom. Thus "Unless both these evils are checked, purity of faith will perish.") Third, because "it is of no slight importance to us to know how lovingly God has provided in this respect for mankind, that greater zeal for piety may flourish in us to attest our gratefulness" (4.20.1).

What is crucial is what Calvin does *not* say. He does not say – nor does he ever say it – that civil government is a means of grace by which God justifies or sanctifies human beings. On the contrary, he is consistently emphatic that spiritual and political government are quite distinct. Civil government defends and establishes the kingdom of Christ, but it does so indirectly, not directly. The two kingdoms always remain distinct.

It is true that, in the 1559 edition, Calvin made significant additions emphasizing civil government's responsibility to care for religion. For instance, to the list of purposes for which civil government was ordained he explicitly adds the care of religion: "to cherish and protect the outward worship of God, to defend sound doctrine of piety and the position of the church" (4.20.2). And where in the next paragraph he adds the clause "that honesty and modesty may be preserved among men" (4.20.3), it is difficult to doubt that by the preservation of honesty he means to include honesty about religious truth.[65] Likewise in an entirely new section targeted

---

[65] In addition, when he describes "the flatterers of princes [who], immoderately praising their power, do not hesitate to set them against the rule of God himself," he may have in mind those magistrates across

at the Anabaptists, Calvin incorporated the triumvirate of texts he liked to use to defend the magistrate's responsibility for religion: Psalm 2, Isaiah 49:23, and 1 Timothy 2:2 (4.20.5).

Even more telling than these additions was a significant expansion of Calvin's discussion of "the office of magistrates, how it is described in the word of God and the things in which it consists." Whereas in all previous editions Calvin's description of the task of government had focused entirely on the second table of the law, now he added a vigorous defense of magistrates' responsibilities to enforce the first table as well. It is of tremendous significance that, once again, he introduces this new argument with an appeal to natural law. He points out that even if scripture did not teach that government's task extends to the first table of the law,

> we could learn this from secular writers: for no one has discussed the office of magistrates, the making of laws, and public welfare, without beginning at religion and divine worship. And thus all have confessed that no government can be happily established unless piety is the first concern; and that those laws are preposterous which neglect God's right and provide only for men. Since, therefore, among all philosophers religion takes first place, and since this fact has always been observed by universal consent of all nations, let Christian princes and magistrates be ashamed of their negligence if they do not apply themselves to this concern (4.20.9).[66]

Calvin's foundational appeal is to a consensus of secular writers, philosophers, and the laws of nations regarding the natural law, and only from there does he turn to scripture.

In fact, Calvin's emphasis on "secular writers" so dominates his argument that he hardly supplements it with proof-texts from scripture. The closest he comes to offering a substantive biblical argument is to declare that "holy kings are greatly praised in scripture because they restored the worship of God when it was corrupted or destroyed, or took care of religion that under them it might flourish pure and unblemished." From that brief reference to the kings of Old Testament Israel, he immediately shifts to an argument from reason. It is absurd, he maintains, to think that God would have appointed magistrates for the purpose of deciding "earthly controversies" and "rendering justice among men," and yet would have refused them authority to address matters of "far greater importance – that he himself should

---

the Protestant world who refused to establish ecclesiastical church discipline, usurping that power for themselves, as well as those Catholic magistrates who actively persecuted the true faith (4.20.1).

[66] Keddie thus writes, "The conclusion seems inescapable that Calvin regards 'rightly establishing religion' as the prime duty of a civil government. 'Civil righteousness' is clearly secondary in his thinking, though necessary to the proper accomplishment of the establishment of religion." Keddie, "Calvin on Civil Government," 26. But while for Calvin the care of religion is the highest magisterial duty in a well-regulated Christian commonwealth, for civil government in general it is the preservation of basic justice that is its *sine qua non*.

be purely worshiped according to the prescription of his law." Aside from a general reference to Psalm 101, that is the extent of Calvin's exegetical argument in the *Institutes* that government must enforce the first table of the law (4.20.9).

THE ARGUMENT FROM THE OLD TESTAMENT

Throughout his Old Testament commentaries Calvin maintains the same approach to the magisterial care of religion as is found in the 1554 *Defense of the Orthodox Faith* and the 1559 *Institutes*. He consistently begins his arguments with appeals to natural law before turning to scripture for confirmation and then refuting arguments that the magisterial care of religion is no longer appropriate in the new covenant era.[67] The specific lesson Calvin drew from pagan testimony about natural law was that Israelite kings cared for religion as an obligation of their general vocation rather than of their unique typological function as types of Christ. To be sure, Calvin did not consider the kings of Israel to be equal to Christian kings. On the contrary, he emphasized that the Israelite kingdom was uniquely a type of the kingdom of Christ. This perspective gave him the theological option of dismissing the relevance of Israelite kings as models for their Christian counterparts. Just as Christians do not follow outward and earthly Old Testament prescriptions for worship, he could have argued, so there is no need for Christians to follow outward and earthly Old Testament prescriptions regarding polity. For unlike Israelite kings, Christian magistrates are not representatives of the kingdom of Christ.

On the other hand, the fact that Israel was also an outward, earthly kingdom, in sharp contrast to the spiritual kingdom of which it was a type, made it possible for Calvin to embrace it as a source of guidance for Christian politics. The key was to show that the relevant functions of Israelite kings arose out of their political vocation rather than their typological purpose. And to establish this point Calvin tended to rely on arguments from reason and natural law.

Nowhere is this tendency more evident than in Calvin's *Harmony of the Law*, which he published only one year before his death.[68] This commentary on the law, like his commentary on the synoptic gospels, does not follow the chronological method of his other commentaries. Rather, he approaches the text topically, organizing the various laws according to the outline of the Ten Commandments, which

---

[67] For instance, while admitting that scripture typically describes good government according to the simple phrase "righteousness and judgment," he maintains that "it is undoubtedly true that the duty of a good prince embraces a wider extent than 'righteousness and judgment,' for his great aim ought to be to defend the honor of God and religion." Commentary on Isaiah 32:1 [1559]; CO 36:542.

[68] Cf. Philip C. Holtrop, *The Bolsec Controversy on Predestination, from 1551–1555* (2 vols.; Lewiston, NY: Edwin Mellen, 1993), 2:212–229; Sermon on Deuteronomy 13:6–11 [1555]; CO 27:260; Sermon on Deuteronomy 13:12–18 [1555]; CO 27:265, 271.

Calvin treats as a representative summary of the law. Under each commandment he distinguishes between the moral law, which is always binding on human beings, and its political and ceremonial supplements, which are instances of the civil and ceremonial law unique to Israel. Calvin's discussion of the care of religion appears largely in his discussion of the first commandment, "You shall have no other gods before me."

Calvin begins with a general principle that blurs the line between the two kingdoms: "political laws [*leges politicae*] are not only enacted with reference to earthly affairs [*terrenis negotiis*], in order that men should maintain mutual equity with each other and should follow and observe what is right, but that they should exercise themselves in the veneration of God."[69] In other words, civil government should be concerned about both tables of the law. Later in the commentary, he articulates the principle more precisely: "[T]he worship of God should be by no means passed over in civil and earthly government [*civili et terrena gubernatione*], for although its direct object [*scopum dirigitur*] is to preserve mutual equity between men, yet religion always ought to hold the first place [*primum . . . gradum*]."[70] The distinction between the "direct object" of political government and the "first place" that religion ought to hold is significant. Civil government, like any other human endeavor, should give the first place to the worship of God, but as a political institution its role with respect to spiritual matters is indirect.

Here again Calvin begins with the argument from natural law. "For Plato also begins from hence when he lays down the legitimate constitution of a republic and calls the fear of God the preface of all laws; nor has any profane author ever existed who has not confessed that this is the principal part of a well-constituted state, that all with one consent should reverence and worship God."[71] This suggests that the care of religion is a requirement of natural law and equity rather than of the Mosaic law unique to Israel. Yet magistrates do not have the discretionary authority to *determine* the true religion, but merely the executive authority to *recognize* and establish it. This they can do only if they submit themselves to God's word. "It has been wisely forbidden by human legislators that men should make to themselves private gods, but all this is vain unless the knowledge of the true God enlightens and directs them."[72]

Thus as in his *Defense of the Orthodox Faith*, Calvin maintains that there are limits on what action Christian magistrates may take to defend religion. First, capital punishment is only to be applied if the error is so serious that it constitutes outright

[69] Commentary on Deuteronomy 18:19 [1563]; CO 24:354.
[70] Commentary on Deuteronomy 20:1 [1563]; CO 24:372.
[71] Commentary on Deuteronomy 18:19 [1563]; CO 24:354–355.
[72] Commentary on Deuteronomy 18:19 [1563]; CO 24:355. Cf. Commentary on 1 Corinthians 2:6 [1546]; CO 49:337.

apostasy.[73] Second, punishment is only to be applied in societies where the true religion has been publicly accepted and its certainty is beyond doubt. Thus "the season of this severity would not be until a positive religion should be established [*stabilita est certa religio*]."[74] God had revealed himself to Israel through a miraculous redemption that left no room for doubt. "It must then be remembered that the crime of impiety would not otherwise merit punishment unless the religion had not only been received by public consent and the suffrages of the people, but, being supported also by sure and indisputable proofs, should place its truth above the reach of doubt."[75] Heresy was unpardonable for the very reason that "its authors, being educated in the doctrines of the law, could not be deceived involuntarily, nor unless they had . . . set their hearts on the impostures of the devil."[76] Those guilty of false teaching must realize that they have willfully contradicted the truth, lest the act of punishment be dismissed as merely a human judgment. "[T]his severity must not be resorted to except when the religion is suffering which is not only received by public authority and general opinion, but which is proved on solid grounds to be true, so that it may clearly appear that we are the avengers of God against the wicked."[77]

Calvin used his comments on the law's call for destruction of entire cities to refute the growing chorus of those who claimed he was harsh for supporting a capital sentence for Servetus. "But if so many together are to be dragged to death in crowds, their impudence is more than detestable, and their pity cruelty itself, who would take no account of God's injured majesty so that one man may be spared."[78] These impudent critics simply "desire to be at liberty to make disturbances with impunity," openly defying God, who has clearly commanded false prophets to be put to death. Here the reformer of Geneva abandons his exegetical and political theological principles about natural law, equity, and love, writing as if the Torah's decree is argument enough. "But it is superfluous to contend by argument when God has once pronounced what is his will, for we must needs abide by his inviolable decree."[79]

---

[73] Commentary on Deuteronomy 13:5 [1563]; CO 24:355–357. Cf. 17:2; CO 24:557–558; Commentary on Exodus 22:18 [1563]; CO 24:365–366.

[74] Commentary on Deuteronomy 13:5 [1563]; CO 24:355–356. Cf. Paul Woolley, "Calvin and Toleration," *The Heritage of John Calvin* (ed. John H. Bratt; Grand Rapids: Eerdmans, 1973), 141–149.

[75] Commentary on Deuteronomy 13:5 [1563]; CO 24:356. Cf. 17:12–13; CO 24:358).

[76] Commentary on Deuteronomy 13:15 [1563]; CO 24:363.

[77] Commentary on Deuteronomy 13:12 [1563]; CO 24:362. Where such is clear, however, there is to be no mercy (13:6–7; CO 24:359–361). "Hence too we are admonished that zeal for God's glory is but cold among us unless true religion is held to be of more value than the preservation of a single city or people" (13:12; CO 24:362). Cf. Commentary on Exodus 32:27 [1563]; CO 25:94–95. Not even one's closest neighbors or family members should be spared. Cf. Commentary on Matthew 10:21 [1555]; CO 45:284; Commentary on Zechariah 13:3 [1559]; CO 44:346–347.

[78] Commentary on Deuteronomy 13:12 [1563]; CO 24:362.

[79] Commentary on Deuteronomy 13:5 [1563]; CO 24:356.

Having thus undermined the credibility of his opponents, Calvin turns to their arguments. When it comes to their most basic principle, he admits, he agrees with them. "As to their denial that the truth of God stands in need of such support, it is very true . . . God might, indeed, do without the assistance of the sword in defending religion." But then Calvin falls back on God's will. God could defend his kingdom without the use of magistrates, "but such is not his will," and those who say he should not use civil government are guilty of "imposing a law upon God." The reformer then launches a barrage of rhetorical arguments from analogy. If God demands that political rulers punish theft, fornication, and drunkenness, how much more the violation of worship and religion? If capital punishment is appropriate for adulterers, how much more for those who "adulterate the doctrines of salvation"? If those who murder the body are put to death, how much more those who lead souls to eternal destruction? If those guilty of treason, how much more those who reject the authority of God?[80]

For all of his polemical passion, however, Calvin was too conscious of his two kingdoms theology to imagine that a simple appeal to the law was sufficient to prove his point. After all, the very point in question was whether this command of the law is universal in application.

> But it is questioned whether the law pertains to the kingdom of Christ, which is spiritual and distinct from all earthly dominion [*Christi regnum, quod spirituale est ac remotum a terrenis imperiis*], and there are some men, not otherwise ill-disposed, to whom it appears that our condition under the gospel is different from that of the ancient people under the law, not only because the kingdom of Christ is not of this world, but because Christ was unwilling that the beginnings of his kingdom should be aided by the sword [*exordia regni sui Christus noluit gladio adiuvari*].

Here Calvin addresses head on those two distinctions so fundamental to his political theology: the distinction between the spiritual kingdom of Christ and civil government and the distinction between the spiritual kingdom of Christ and Old Testament Israel.[81]

He begins by denying that when magistrates use the sword in religious matters, they threaten the nature of Christ's kingdom. "But when earthly judges consecrate their work to the promotion of Christ's kingdom [*promovendo Christi regno consecrant suam operam terreni iudices*], I deny that on that account its nature is changed." To be sure, the work of building Christ's kingdom is entirely that of the word, and it was evidently Jesus' will that his disciples should preach the word "like sheep among wolves." But this does not mean that magistrates are to restrain themselves from protecting Christ's kingdom. "He did not impose on himself an

[80] Commentary on Deuteronomy 13:5 [1563]; CO 24:356.
[81] Commentary on Deuteronomy 13:5 [1563]; CO 24:356–357.

eternal law that he should never bring kings under his subjection [*reges ipsos in obsequium cogeret*], nor tame their violence, nor change them from being cruel persecutors into the patrons and guardians of his church [*ecclesiae suae patronos et custodes*]." Here again Calvin turns to his classic triumvirate of biblical citations: Psalm 2, Isaiah 49:23, and 1 Timothy 2:2. Magistrates who fail to punish false teachers are responsible when weak souls are led astray.[82]

But were not such arguments irresponsible in a time when Protestants were being savagely persecuted by the civil authorities in France? Calvin will have none of this objection.

> But if under this pretext the superstitious have dared to shed innocent blood, I reply that what God has once commanded must not be brought to naught on account of any abuse or corruption of men. For if the cause alone abundantly distinguishes the martyrs of Christ from malefactors, though their punishment may be identical, so the papal executioners will not bring it to pass by their unjust cruelty that the zeal of pious magistrates in punishing false and noxious teachers should be otherwise than pleasing to God.[83]

The pervasive abuse of authority does not render authority itself unjust.

Elsewhere Calvin goes to great lengths to show that the law requiring capital punishment for false teachers was not unique to typological Israel. Discussing the prophet Zechariah's allusion to the law of Deuteronomy 13:1, according to which fathers were to put their own family members to death rather than see the true religion corrupted, Calvin observes that "this zeal under the reign of Christ is approved by God, for Zechariah does not here confine what he teaches to the time of the law but shows what would take place when Christ came."[84] In other contexts Calvin is quick to remind his readers that the prophets regularly used metaphorical language appropriate to the circumstances of their hearers to describe future spiritual realities, but here he permits no such qualification. Those who "imagine" that the command was given only to the Jews are "fanatics" who desire license to "disturb the whole world."[85]

In fact, Calvin was clearly aware that it was not simply fanatics and libertines who questioned this interpretation of the prophetic idiom, because he turns again to the work of persuasion, offering an argument from reason. If those who commit temporal crimes are punished, how much more so are those who destroy souls, "who by their poison corrupt pure doctrine, which is spiritual food, who take away from God

---

[82] Commentary on Deuteronomy 13:5 [1563]; CO 24:357.
[83] Commentary on Deuteronomy 13:5 [1563]; CO 24:357.
[84] Commentary on Zechariah 13:3 [1559]; CO 44:347.
[85] Commentary on Zechariah 13:3 [1559]; CO 44:347. Cf. Commentary on Isaiah 2:4 [1559]; CO 36: 65–66.

his own honor, who confound the whole order of the church?"[86] Those who disagree fail to grasp what is at stake. To misrepresent God by speaking falsely in his name is to make him an "abettor of falsehood." Indeed, "is it not the same thing as though one substituted the devil in the place of God?" How can it be doubted that Christians "are to exterminate from the world such pests as deprive God of his own honor and attempt to extinguish the light of true and genuine religion."[87]

At the heart of Calvin's appeal to reason was his conviction that all people are called to do whatever they can within the limits of their vocation to defend true religion. The greater power associated with a particular vocation, the greater responsibility it carries to promote the honor and cause of God. "[T]he higher persons have risen and the nearer they have been brought to God, the more sacredly are they bound to proclaim his goodness. The more intolerable is the wickedness of kings and princes who claim exemption from the common rule, when they ought rather to inculcate it upon others and lead the way."[88] To say that the magisterial office exempts a person from having to promote true religion gets things exactly backwards, for it is precisely such persons who must "lead the way." As he puts it in his commentary on Jeremiah, "the truth is more necessary for them than even for the common people, for not only the duty of the head of a family lies on each of them, but the Lord has also set them over a whole people."[89] Persons in positions of political leadership "are, as it were, the eyes of the community; as the eyes direct the whole body, so also they ... show the right way to others."[90]

Old Testament stories about pagan rulers like Pharaoh of Egypt and Nebuchadnezzar of Babylon provided excellent opportunities for Calvin to demonstrate that even the pagans recognized the duty of magistrates to protect true religion.[91] As with his observations on New Testament narratives, Calvin's arguments often went beyond the clear intent of the text itself. For instance, although the text of Genesis describes the actions of Joseph and Pharaoh largely without evaluative comment, Calvin openly expresses his admiration for Pharaoh's attitude toward religion. The narrative describes how during a devastating seven-year famine, Joseph, governing in the name of Pharaoh, gradually enslaved the Egyptian population while sparing the property of the priests. For Calvin the significance was obvious. "Moses wished distinctly to testify ... that a heathen king paid particular attention to divine worship." Moses' intent was to provide a "mirror" in which it can be discerned that "a sentiment of piety which they cannot wholly efface is implanted

---

[86] Commentary on Zechariah 13:3 [1559]; CO 44:347.
[87] Commentary on Zechariah 13:3 [1559]; CO 44:348.
[88] Commentary on Psalm 148:11 [1557]; CO 32:435.
[89] Commentary on Jeremiah 26:10 [1563]; CO 38:522.
[90] Commentary on Micah 3:1–3 [1559]; CO 43:318–321.
[91] Cf. Commentary on Isaiah 22:21 [1559]; CO 36:382.

in the minds of men." Pharaoh's motives were informed by "wicked superstition," but his "inconsiderate devotion ... flowed from a right principle." What then "should be the conduct of our princes, who desire to be deemed Christians?"[92]

Calvin was similarly impressed with the story of Nineveh, in which a pagan king led his people to respond penitently to the prophet Jonah's warning of judgment. The story was a powerful confirmation that even heathen kings, "who understood not a syllable of true religion," recognized their responsibility to lead their people in repentance.

> Hence this edict of the king ought to fill us with more shame than if one adduced the same doctrine only from the word of God, for though the authority of that king is not the same with that of God, yet when that miserable and blind prince acknowledged through the dictates of nature that God is to be pacified by prayer, what excuse, as I have said, can remain for us?[93]

Indeed, Calvin has no difficulty with Nebuchadnezzar's decree that "any people, nation, or language that speaks anything against the God of Shadrach, Meshach, and Abednego shall be torn limb from limb, and their houses laid in ruins" (Daniel 3:29). "The edict is," he insists, "by itself pious and praiseworthy."[94] It was recorded in the "testimony of the Spirit" in order "to show the fruit of conversion" in the king. "Hence, without doubt, King Nebuchadnezzar bore witness to his repentance when he celebrated the God of Israel among all people and when he proclaimed a punishment to all who spoke reproachfully against God."[95] On other occasions, Calvin makes a point of clarifying that scripture often praises individuals for their faith and motives even if their particular actions are sinful.[96] Here, in contrast, he claims the silence of the text as evidence of the Spirit's approval. Similarly, Calvin usually stressed that idolatry should only be punished in a community where the true religion was acknowledged as certain. Here he conveniently ignores that principle.

Yet Calvin does take the opportunity to refute those who defended the fundamental Donatist principle that "No punishment ought to be inflicted on those who differ from others in religious doctrine,"[97] not the least of whom were "that dog Castellio and his companions." It is "clear enough," he declares, that such people are "impious despisers of God" who "wish to render everything uncertain in

---

92 Commentary on Genesis 47:22 [1554]; CO 23:574–575.
93 Commentary on Jonah 3:6–8 [1559]; CO 43:256–257.
94 Commentary on Daniel 3:29 [1561]; CO 40:645.
95 Commentary on Daniel 4:1–3 [1561]; CO 40:649.
96 Cf. Commentary on Exodus 1:18 [1563]; CO 24:18–19; Commentary on Joshua 2:7 [1564]; CO 25: 441–442.
97 Commentary on Daniel 4:1–3 [1561]; CO 40:649–651.

religion." With the desire of "vomiting forth their poison, they strive eagerly for freedom from punishment and deny the right of inflicting punishment on heretics and blasphemers." If

> King Nebuchadnezzar's edict was praised by the approval of the Holy Spirit ... it follows that kings are bound to defend the worship of God [*partes regum esse tueri Dei cultum*] and to execute vengeance [*vindictam sumere*] upon those who profanely despise it, and on those who endeavor to reduce it to nothing or to adulterate the true doctrine by their errors, and so dissipate the unity of the faith and disturb the church's peace.

Augustine showed "how ashamed Christian princes ought to be of their slothfulness if they are indulgent to heretics and blasphemers and do not vindicate God's glory by lawful punishments [*asserant legitimis poenis Dei gloriam*], since King Nebuchadnezzar, who was never truly converted, yet promulgated this decree by a kind of secret instinct."[98]

But Calvin realized that the text of Daniel raised a potential problem for this interpretation. The narrative describes how Nebuchadnezzar issued a decree that the Chaldeans were to be put to death for failing to interpret the king's dream. Under the right conditions this would be laudable: "they deserved to be exterminated from the world, and the pest must be removed if it could possibly be accomplished. If Nebuchadnezzar had been like David, or Hezekiah, or Josiah, he might most justly have destroyed them all and have purged the land from such defilements." The problem is that the text describes how Daniel *saved* the Chaldeans from the king's death sentence. Why would Daniel have defended such pagan charlatans if the king's decree was just? Calvin's solution is to suggest that Daniel was defending due process of law. The king was a hypocrite with no legal basis for his actions.[99] In cases such as this, "we ought to spare their persons, not through their worthiness, but through our own habitual sense of equity and rectitude."[100] Here Calvin recognizes, if only begrudgingly, that the magisterial defense of true religion is complicated where there is religious diversity under the rule of law.

Calvin's appeals to reason and the pagans as examples of what natural law requires are all the more striking in the context of his insistence that sometimes what the law commanded Israel to do should *not* be taken as an example of what natural law requires. For instance, Israel was commanded to destroy the Canaanites, but "God does not now command us to execute vengeance by putting all the wicked to death, nor is a certain country assigned to the church in which it

---

[98] Commentary on Daniel 4:1–3 [1561]; CO 40:649–650.
[99] Commentary on Daniel 2:13–15 [1561]; CO 40:570.
[100] Commentary on Daniel 2:24 [1561]; CO 40:582–583.

may dwell apart and have dominion."[101] In contrast to Israel, Christian nations are obligated to follow the principles of justice and equity "naturally implanted in all nations," abstaining from bloodshed as much as possible.[102] Calvin struggled to come to grips with the genocide of the Canaanites, admitting, "our reason struggles against this." Still, he insists, we must trust the command of God: "If it does not appear to us agreeable to reason that the whole race of evil-doers should be exterminated, let us understand that God is defrauded of his rights whenever we measure his infinite greatness ... by our own feelings."[103] On the other hand, Christians remain bound by what reason dictates according to natural law. Thus for Christians to practice such "indiscriminate and promiscuous slaughter" without the express command of God would be "barbarous and atrocious cruelty."[104] Christians are not to imitate Old Testament heroes like Moses and Phinehas, who at the inspiration of the Spirit avenged murderers and fornicators. It amounts to a

> confounding of times, when men, devoting their whole attention to the examples of the fathers, do not consider that the Lord has since enjoined a different rule of conduct which they ought to follow .... Now, since the coming of Christ, matters are entirely changed. We ought therefore to consider what he enjoins on us under the gospel, that we may not follow at random what the fathers observed under the law.[105]

Calvin recognized that even Israel's penal code had spiritual and typological significance. Writing on Zephaniah 1:7–9, he suggests that "the executions on the gallows, when the wicked suffer, may be said to be sacrifices to God."[106] When Israel was called to put a particular person to death by stoning, "the land was to be purged, as by a propitiation."[107] Calvin likewise differentiated between the

---

[101] Commentary on Exodus 34:11 [1563]; CO 24:548–549. Cf. Commentary on Joshua 23:12 [1564]; CO 25: 561–562; Commentary on Deuteronomy 7:20–25 [1563]; CO 24:553–554. Similarly while God used violence to deliver the Israelites from slavery in Egypt, Christians could not do the same under other circumstances. Commentary on Exodus 4:22 [1563]; CO 24:62–63. Cf. Commentary on Jeremiah 34: 8–17 [1563]; CO 39:87–91.

[102] Commentary on Deuteronomy 20:10 [1563]; CO 24:632. Cf. Commentary on Exodus 1:9 [1563]; CO 24:13–14.

[103] Commentary on Deuteronomy 13:15 [1563]; CO 24:363.

[104] Commentary on Joshua 6:20 [1564]; CO 25:469. "Had he proceeded of his own accord to commit an indiscriminate massacre of women and children, no excuse could have exculpated him from the guilt of detestable cruelty, cruelty surpassing anything of which we read as having been perpetrated by savage tribes scarcely raised above the level of the brutes" (10:40; CO 25:505–506). Cf. 7:25; CO 25: 480–481; Commentary on Deuteronomy 7:2 [1563]; 24:550–551. Calvin's view is not that God is above law, as Schreiner claims; God has his higher purposes, but they are always in accord with justice. See Susan E. Schreiner, *The Theater of His Glory: Nature and the Natural Order in the Thought of John Calvin* (Grand Rapids: Baker Academic, 1995), 78.

[105] Commentary on John 4:20 [1553]; CO 47:85–86.

[106] Commentary on Zephaniah 1:7–9 [1559]; CO 44:14–18.

[107] Commentary on Deuteronomy 17:7 [1563]; CO 24:558–559. Calvin also notes that the Apostle Paul identified the judicial curse of the law as having been fulfilled in Christ (21:22–23; CO 24:629). These

vengeance David was called to exercise as a typological spiritual king from what is appropriate for Christian kings. For instance, David governed the "posterity of Abraham" as brothers, but he treated foreigners as slaves because "it was allowable for him to exercise greater severities upon the profane and the uncircumcised." Yet modern rulers should not claim precedent from David's actions. "In this he affords no precedent to conquerors who would inflict lawless oppression upon nations taken in war, for they want the divine warrant and commission which David had, invested as he was not only with the authority of a king, but with the character of an avenger of the church."[108] David, like Israel, had a special typological calling. "Farther, let us remember that under this type there is shadowed forth the invincible character and condition of the kingdom of Christ, who, trusting to and sustained by the power of God, overthrows and destroys his enemies." Christian magistrates are authorized to "reign under Christ and acknowledge him as their head," but they are not to exercise this typological vengeance.[109] Psalm 149 declares that the godly will execute vengeance on the nations with the sword, but Calvin warns that the reference to the sword "applies more especially to the Jews and not properly to us." For Christians, "the sword now put into our hand is of another kind, that of the word and Spirit, that we may slay for a sacrifice to God those who formerly were enemies or again deliver them over to everlasting destruction unless they repent."[110]

On the other hand, even in these passages, Calvin sees a continuing relevance for those who bear the vocation of magistrate and "are vested by God with the sword to punish all manner of violence."[111] In his commentary on Psalm 106, he argues that while Christian magistrates may not wipe out whole nations, they should approach the calling to execute civil judgments with a similar zeal. "For if the Israelites are condemned for sparing some of these nations wholly, what are we to think of those judges who, from a timid and apathetic attention to the responsible duties of their office, exercise too much lenity to a few persons, thus weakening the restraints of the inlets to vice, to the great detriment of the public weal?"[112] Calvin draws similar lessons from the obligation of Old Testament kings to establish piety and justice. Drawing from Psalm 72, a description of the reign of God's anointed

---

observations gave Calvin clear warrant to distinguish the penalties appropriate to Israel's unique circumstances from those appropriate for Christendom, though he never explicitly used this argument.

[108] Commentary on Psalm 60:8 [1557]; CO 31:578. Cf. 45:6; CO 31:452–454. Calvin places Israelite kings in the category of earthly kings, but also adds that "the holy king of Israel, who was anointed to his office by divine appointment, is distinguished from other earthly kings" (72:1; CO 31:664–665).

[109] Commentary on Psalm 18:37 [1557]; CO 31:187–188.

[110] Commentary on Psalm 149:9 [1557]; CO 32:440.

[111] Commentary on Psalm 149:9 [1557]; CO 32:440. Cf. 18:47; CO 31:192–193.

[112] Commentary on Psalm 106:34 [1557]; CO 32:130.

one, he explains that the just kingdom will not only secure the rights of the poor and the vulnerable, but "will draw in its train true religion and the fear of God," for its ultimate goal is nothing less than "the advancement of the service and honor of God."[113] To be sure, temporal governments cannot establish true piety or justice directly.[114] Psalm 72 therefore finds its "highest fulfillment" in Christ's kingship, because only Christ actually transforms human character.[115] But the psalm maintains its relevance for temporal magistrates too. David intends to show us that a "holy and righteous government . . . will draw in its train true religion and the fear of God," for "there is no small danger, were civil government overthrown, of religion being destroyed and the worship of God annihilated."[116]

Calvin's method of distinguishing between what is typological and unique to Old Testament Israel and what is required by natural law and discernible even by reason and the pagans, thus, gives him a flexible method for appropriating the Old Testament's content regarding law and politics. Depending on his philosophical and political judgments regarding the particular matter in view, he could emphasize radical discontinuity between the politics of Israel and the politics of Christendom, or he could insist upon decisive continuity between the vocation of Old Testament kings and that of Christian magistrates.

THE POSSIBILITIES AND PITFALLS OF THE CARE OF RELIGION

Calvin's favorite text for describing the positive obligations of magistrates toward the true religion in the new covenant era was Isaiah 49:23. To Calvin, the passage proved that the advancement of the true religion is to be a magistrate's "chief care [*primam . . . curam*]."[117] The text describes magistrates as nurses raising and nurturing children, he argues, because they "shall supply everything that is necessary for nourishing the offspring of the church." This occurred when governments devoted their wealth "to raise up and maintain the church of Christ [*erigendam et fovendam Christi ecclesiam*] so as to be her guardians and defenders [*patronos ac tutores*]." The Lord has bestowed on magistrates "authority and power [*autoritas et potentia*] to defend the Church [*ecclesiam tueantur*] and to promote the glory of God [*gloriam Dei procurent*]."[118]

---

[113] Commentary on Psalm 72:5 [1557]; CO 31:666–667.

[114] Nor could David have done so. Commentary on Psalm 101:8 [1557]; CO 32:60.

[115] "It was, indeed, the duty of Solomon to maintain the righteous, but it is the proper office of Christ to make men righteous. He not only gives to every man his own, but also reforms their hearts through the agency of his Spirit." Commentary on Psalm 72:7 [1557]; CO 31:667. The ultimate reference of the psalm is to the "spiritual kingdom of Christ" (72:11; CO 31:669).

[116] Commentary on Psalm 72:5 [1557]; CO 31:666–667.

[117] Dedication of Commentary on Isaiah to Queen Elizabeth [1559]; CO 17:413–415 (414).

[118] "This is indeed the duty of all, but kings, in proportion as their power is greater, ought to devote themselves to it more earnestly, and to labor in it more diligently." Commentary on Isaiah 49:23 [1559];

Interestingly, Calvin admits that texts like Isaiah 49:23 were horribly abused, especially by the papists. "The papists have no other idea of kings being 'nursing-fathers' of the church," he charges, "than that they have left to their priests and monks very large revenues, rich possessions, and prebends on which they might fatten like hogs in a sty." Rome was also guilty of distorting Isaiah's prophecy in its insistence that secular rulers were to adore the pope. But Calvin maintains that such material extravagance contradicted the fact that Christ's kingdom is spiritual and exists in the present age under the cross. Magistrates serve the church by fulfilling their vocation in obedience to the word. Isaiah's prophecy is therefore about "removing superstitions and putting an end to all wicked idolatry, about advancing the kingdom of Christ [*promovendo Christi regno*] and maintaining purity of doctrine, about purging scandals and cleansing from the filth that corrupts piety and impairs the luster of the divine majesty."[119]

Still, Calvin couldn't resist finding justification here for magistrates to sponsor a whole panoply of church ministries. Political authorities are to

> supply the pastors and ministers of the word with all that is necessary for food and maintenance, provide for the poor and guard the Church against the disgrace of pauperism, erect schools and appoint salaries for the teachers and board for the students, build poor-houses and hospitals, and make every other arrangement that belongs to the protection and defense of the church.[120]

The magistracy's support for the church is not to be extravagant, but it is no less material for that. Calvin was in the difficult exegetical position of claiming that the church's calling to serve under the cross meant that it should not be characterized by wealth and honor, while insisting at the same time that magistrates are to sponsor the whole range of church ministries and enforce the church's monopoly on teaching and worship at the point of the sword.[121]

On the other hand, for all of his insistence that magistrates must promote and defend the true religion, Calvin was well aware of the pitfalls of magisterial interference. He conceded that the vast majority, even of Christian magistrates, had anything but the interests of the kingdom of Christ at heart. "If any one could enter into the hearts of kings, he would find scarcely one in a hundred who does not despise everything divine."[122] But magistrates loved to use religion for their own purposes.

CO 37:210. Those who fail to "enjoin what is good and right, and especially to defend the honor of God . . . ought to be reckoned impostors and not rulers, for they give rise to miserable confusion" (9:16; CO 36:205).

[119] Commentary on Isaiah 49:23 [1559]; CO 37:211.
[120] Commentary on Isaiah 49:23 [1559]; CO 37:211.
[121] Cf. Commentary on Isaiah 60:16 [1559]; CO 37:365–366.
[122] Commentary on Daniel 6:6–7 [1561]; CO 41:7. Cf. 3:13–15; CO 40:629; Commentary on Acts 16:22 [1554]; CO 48:384.

In these days monarchs, in their titles, always put forward themselves as kings, generals, and counts, 'by the grace of God,' but how many falsely pretend to apply God's name to themselves for the purpose of securing the supreme power! For what is the meaning of that title of kings and princes – 'by the grace of God' – except to avoid the acknowledgment of a superior? . . . It is mere pretense therefore to boast that they reign through God's favor.[123]

Most political leaders, Calvin wagers, "think that religion should yield to them, and so far as they imagine that it will be of service to them [they] follow it, or rather bend and change it for their own convenience."[124] They may "worship him by outward ceremonies," tolerating the sort of civil religion that advances their own agenda, but they "cannot bear to be subject to reason and laws."[125]

Quite often, then, the problem was not so much getting magistrates to take seriously their obligations toward religion as it was their claiming *too much* control over religion. Calvin believed the English King Henry VIII, whom he compared to the apostate Israelite King Jeroboam, was the prime example of this tendency. Kings like Henry justified their policies as being conducive of the peace of the community, but they falsely assumed that kings have the right to establish religion according to their own preferences. "They who at first extolled Henry, King of England, were certainly inconsiderate men. They gave him the supreme power in all things [*summam rerum omnium potestatem*], and this always vexed me grievously, for they were guilty of blasphemy when they called him the chief Head of the Church under Christ [*summum caput ecclesiae sub Christo*]." Henry's chancellor erroneously claimed

that it was in the power of the king to abrogate statutes and to institute new rites – that as to fasting the king could forbid or command the people to eat flesh on this or that days, that it was lawful for the king to prohibit priests from marrying, that it was lawful for the king to interdict to the people the use of the cup in the Supper, that it was lawful for the king to appoint this or that thing in his own kingdom. How so? Because supreme power is vested in the king [*Potestas enim summa est penes regem*].[126]

---

[123] Commentary on Daniel 4:25 [1561]; CO 40:670–671. Earlier in the commentary, Calvin launches into a discussion of three kinds of ancient gods: philosophical, political, and poetical. The religion of the philosophical gods, inspired by "natural reason," has Calvin's admiration. The poets, on the other hand, were guilty of pandering to human desires. The political gods were the gods received by common consent. As the foci for shared piety, they served to unite a commonwealth under a common civil religion (3:6–7; CO 40:620–625).

[124] Commentary on Isaiah 22:23 [1559]; CO 36:383.

[125] Commentary on Psalm 82:1 [1557]; CO 31:768–769. Cf. Commentary on Jeremiah 15:17 [1563]; CO 38:229.

[126] Commentary on Amos 7:10–13 [1559]; CO 43:134. Calvin describes Henry VIII as even worse than many Catholic princes, "for they who continue under that bondage retain at least some kind of religion." Henry was like Israel's King Jehu, who enthusiastically obeyed the call of a prophet to overthrow the dynasty of Ahab but refused to put an end to idolatry. Henry "pretended great zeal for

Calvin responds that when Isaiah called princes to "become patrons of religion and nursers of the church" he did not call them to rule *over* the church but to preserve its liberty.[127]

Too often, especially among the German princes and the Swiss cities, civil governments claimed spiritual power for themselves, so confusing the two kingdoms.

> But still they are inconsiderate men who make them too spiritual [*faciunt illos nimis spirituales*], and this evil is everywhere dominant in Germany. Even in these regions [the Swiss Confederation] it prevails too much. And we now find what fruit is produced by this root, which is this: that princes and those who are in power think themselves so spiritual that there is no longer any church government [*ecclesiasticum regimen*]. And this sacrilege greatly prevails among us, for they do not limit their office by fixed and legitimate boundaries but think that they cannot rule unless they abolish every authority in the church and become chief judges as well in doctrine as in all spiritual government [*in toto spirituali regimine*].

The primary evidence of such usurpation was the refusal of magistrates to permit church discipline. They acted as if the church was merely a department of civil government, to be administered in whatever way they deemed prudent, running roughshod over Christ's spiritual government of his church.[128]

Calvin was equally aware that where reformation was led by magistrates, it was often superficial. "[T]he common people are always blinded by prejudices so that they will not examine the matter itself . . . [T]here is nothing steady or fixed in the common people, for they are carried here and there like the wind, which blows now from this quarter and then from that."[129] In his commentary on Hosea, he describes the cycle he had no doubt observed in numerous cities and territories in Europe.

> When pious men have the government of a city and act prudently, then the whole people will give some hope that they will fear the Lord, and when any king, influenced by a desire of advancing the glory of God, endeavors to preserve all his subjects in the pure worship of God, then the same feeling of piety will be seen in all. But when an ungodly king succeeds him the greater part will immediately fall back again, and when a magistrate neglects his duty, the greater portion of the people will break out into open impiety. I wish there were no proofs of these things, but throughout the world the Lord has designed that there should exist examples of them.

a time: he afterwards raged cruelly against all the godly and duplicated the tyranny of the Roman Pontiff." Commentary on Hosea 1:3–4 [1557]; CO 42:208.

[127] Commentary on Amos 7:10–13 [1559]; CO 43:135.

[128] Princes "wish to change religion according to their will and fancy [*inflectere religionem pro suo arbitrio ac libidine*], and . . . for their own advantage." Commentary on Amos 7:10–13 [1559]; CO 43:135.

[129] Commentary on Jeremiah 26:16 [1563]; CO 38:528. Cf. Commentary on Acts 17:11 [1554]; CO 48:400.

Thus "when all readily embrace what a few introduce, it is quite evident that they have no living root of piety or of the fear of God."[130] Even the reformation of the great King Josiah, whom Calvin so often praises as an example for Christian magistrates, was largely superficial. The people "apparently pretended to worship God, and in order to please the king, embraced the worship divinely prescribed in their law. Yet the event proved that it was a mere act of dissimulation, yea, of perfidy"; for all of Josiah's exemplary diligence, "he did not yet gain his object."[131]

Such examples reminded Calvin that the kingdom of Christ advances by spiritual means alone. Godly magistrates can seek to establish and promote the kingdom of Christ, but they can only do so indirectly, and their work is vain apart from the word and Spirit. In his Commentary on Isaiah 62:6–7 Calvin specifies that the watchmen identified in the text, through whom God defends his kingdom, are pastors, not civil magistrates. "[W]e ought always to consider what is the nature of Christ's kingdom, for it is not defended by the weapons of war or by arms, but, being spiritual, is protected by spiritual arms and guards."[132]

> In vain will the magistrate employ the sword, which undoubtedly he must employ, to restrain wicked teachers and false prophets. In vain I say will he attempt all these things unless this sword of the word go before. This ought to be carefully observed in opposition to the papists who, when the word fails them, betake themselves to new weapons by the aid of which they think that they will gain the victory.[133]

Coercion is useless unless it is accompanied by the persuasion of the word of God.

As for the people, they needed to learn to follow true teaching rather than constantly defer to self-interested magistrates. "For we see how the common people think everything permitted to them which is approved by their kings and counselors. For in the common opinion of men, on what does the whole foundation of right and wrong rest except on the arbitrary will and lust of kings?" Calvin warns that the people need to learn to obey the prophets "even if a thousand kings should obstruct them."[134] Each person is charged to submit to the word of God for herself. Nevertheless, the refusal of magistrates to attest to that word was leading the masses astray. "Because the princes and preeminent ones of the world do not willingly submit to the yoke of Christ, now even the rude multitude reject what is salutary before they even taste it."[135]

---

[130] Commentary on Hosea 7:3 [1557]; CO 42:340–341.
[131] Commentary on Zephaniah 1:2–3 [1559]; CO 44:3–4.
[132] Commentary on Isaiah 62:6 [1559]; CO 37:386. Cf. Commentary on Psalm 118:25 [1557]; CO 32: 212–213.
[133] Commentary on Isaiah 11:4 [1559]; CO 36:240. Cf. 22:17; CO 36 379.
[134] Commentary on Daniel 9:5–7 [1561]; CO 41:135–140. Cf. Commentary on Jeremiah 44:17 [1563]; CO 39:262–263.
[135] Dedication of the Commentary on Daniel to the French Protestants [1561]; CO 18:618.

Calvin thus insisted that magistrates must make the care of religion their first priority, despite his realism about what magistrates could accomplish. If the masses were easily manipulated and if bad magistrates did so much damage, it was all the more essential that princes and governors act faithfully and use their power for good.[136] And for all of his skepticism, Calvin did believe God often uses political authorities to bring about the conversion of a population.[137] Calvin insisted that the story of the city of Nineveh was a case in point. Though the text describes the repentance of the population before it refers to the command of the king, he reasons that the people must have humbled themselves in response to the king's decree. For "it is by no means probable that a fast was proclaimed in the royal city by the mere consent of the people." It was therefore "not any movement among the people" that led to the repentance but the action of the king, even if popular movements do "sometimes" happen.[138]

The difficulty of securing a true reformation, even with the guidance of a pious king, simply made Calvin all the more sure that such political leadership was necessary. The futility of Josiah's efforts merely made him an example of persever-ance: "let us learn to look to Josiah, who in his own time left undone nothing which might serve to establish the true worship of God, and when he saw that he effected but little and next to nothing, he still persevered and with firm and invincible greatness of mind proceeded in his course."[139] Josiah was not able to cleanse the land, so Christian magistrates should not be discouraged if they have the same experience.[140] At the very least, they should continue to labor diligently "lest the state of the church should degenerate, for however vigilant they may be, they can yet hardly, even with the greatest care, keep things (as mankind are so full of vices) from becoming very soon worse."[141]

In the final analysis, regardless of questions of effectiveneess, Calvin fell back on his understanding of vocation. All of God's servants ought to oppose evil as much as they can, "each in his particular sphere and vocation," but magistrates in particular cannot shirk this task.[142] For "if those who hold a situation so honorable do not exert themselves to the utmost of their power to remove all defilements, they are charge-able with polluting as much as in them lies the sanctuary of God, and they not only act unfaithfully towards men by betraying their welfare, but also commit high

---

[136] The susceptibility of the people to manipulation means that "they may also be easily restored ... to a right mind." Commentary on Jeremiah 26:11 [1563]; CO 38:523.
[137] Commentary on Isaiah 1:26 [1559]; CO 36: 1:53.
[138] Commentary on Jonah 3:6–8 [1559]; CO 43:252–253.
[139] Commentary on Zephaniah 1:2–3 [1559]; CO 44:3–4.
[140] Commentary on Zephaniah 1:4 [1559]; CO 44:8.
[141] Commentary on Micah 3:11–12 [1559]; CO 43:337.
[142] Commentary on Zephaniah 1:4 [1559]; CO 44:8.

treason against God himself."[143] A magistrate inevitably sets the direction for the whole commonwealth. "For as no disease is more injurious than that which spreads from the head into the whole body, so no evil is more destructive in a commonwealth than a wicked and depraved prince who conveys his corruptions into the whole body both by his example and by the liberty which he allows."[144]

It is important to remember that in all of this, Calvin presupposed the context of a well-regulated state in which the word of God was embraced by public consensus (even if that society was in dire need of reformation). In his commentary on Isaiah he identifies what he considered the prophet's "comprehensive description of a well-regulated state [*status rite ordinati*]."[145] Such a commonwealth exists when its various orders, including "judges and senators, soldiers, captains, artificers, and teachers, aid each other by mutual intercourse and join in promoting the general safety of the whole people."[146] It is a unified Christian community under a twofold spiritual and temporal government.[147]

In his lectures on the prophets Calvin used a new metaphor to describe the functions of magistrates and pastors within such a Christian society, one that emphasizes organic unity and complementarity between church and political society. When the prophet speaks of the watchmen of the church in Isaiah 56, he declares, "He includes both kinds of government, that of princes and that of the ministers of the word, whom the Lord has placed as the two eyes in the body, to govern the established church [*regendam ecclesiam constituit*]."[148] Calvin had no difficulty synthesizing this organic metaphor with his two kingdoms doctrine. Within Israel, there was a twofold public government, he writes in 1563, the priests ruling the "church with regard to the law, so that their government was spiritual," and the elders managing "civil affairs." The two were sharply distinguished, but they cooperated closely, as "there were some things in which they ruled in common."[149]

THE POSSIBILITY AND PROBLEM OF PLURALISM

But what about a commonwealth in which the gospel is *not* publicly accepted or a country that does *not* have a well-regulated state? Calvin hardly addresses

---

[143] It is a "cruel kindness which gives loose reins to the wicked." Commentary on Psalm 101:8 [1557]; CO 32:60.

[144] Commentary on Isaiah 1:23 [1559]; CO 36:50. Cf. Commentary on Hosea 5:10 [1557]; CO 42:310.

[145] Commentary on Isaiah 3:2 [1559]; CO 36:81–82.

[146] Commentary on Isaiah 3:4 [1559]; CO 36:82–83.   [147] See Van't Spijker, *Calvin*, 142.

[148] Commentary on Isaiah 56:10 [1559]; CO 37:302. Cf. 3:2; CO 36:81; Commentary on Jeremiah 32:32 [1563]; CO 39:28; Commentary on Lamentations 4:13; CO 39:617.

[149] Commentary on Jeremiah 19:1–3 [1563]; CO 38:320. Cf. Commentary on Micah 3:1–3 [1559]; CO 43: 318–321; Commentary on Deuteronomy 17:8 [1563]; CO 24:470–471.

this question in his writings, nor are the answers he provides entirely consistent. As has been seen, Calvin emphasizes the magisterial care of religion especially when commenting on pagan governments. Yet he also insists that civil government has no discretionary authority over religion and that idolatry and false teaching should only be punished in societies where the true religion has been acknowledged by public consensus. He therefore finds himself repeatedly praising pagan magistrates for seeking to defend true religion, while at the same time criticizing them for defending the wrong religion and doing it for the wrong reasons. For "no law can be passed nor any edict promulgated concerning religion and the worship of God unless a real knowledge of God shines forth."[150] Sometimes the best that can be hoped for is for pagan magistrates to provide religious liberty. Calvin presents the Persian King Darius as an example to Christian kings in that, although he was a pagan, he gave freedom of worship to Daniel and his fellow Jews. But even Darius comes under sharp criticism for commanding the worship of God as just one religion among others.[151] Calvin does not explain why Darius should have punished false religion in a society where the true religion was not embraced by public consensus. But it seems clear that he regarded the toleration of idolatry in pagan contexts as, at best, a necessary evil.

On the other hand, Calvin offers greater concessions to something like pluralism when he thinks of the problems facing Christian magistrates serving in pagan countries. The story of Joseph involves just such a scenario, presenting Joseph, a faithful worshiper of God, as the governor who upheld Egypt's pagan religious establishment. Was it legitimate for Joseph to cooperate with policies that supported idolatry? Here Calvin was baffled. "I dare not absolutely condemn this act, nor can I, however, deny that he may have erred in not resisting these superstitions with sufficient boldness." Calvin's tentative solution, as with the case of Daniel noted above, is to take refuge in the rule of law. He explains that as a minister obligated to execute Pharaoh's laws, Joseph "was not altogether allowed to dispense the king's corn at his own pleasure. If the king wished that food should be gratuitously supplied to the priests, he was no more at liberty to deny it to them than to the nobles at court."[152] Here Calvin's two kingdoms distinction guides his logic: Joseph was a faithful servant of God, but he could not refuse to fulfill the duty imposed upon him by a lawful civil authority. A magistrate should not simply use his power to do whatever is right in an absolute sense but must submit himself to the law of the land in which he resides. Despite what some scholars claim,

[150] Commentary on Daniel 3:29 [1561]; CO 40:645–647.
[151] Commentary on Daniel 6:25–27 [1561]; CO 41:30.
[152] Commentary on Genesis 47:22 [1554]; CO 23:574–575. Cf. 47:16; CO 23:572.

Calvin did not believe magistrates should always enforce God's law regardless of constitutional constraints.[153]

Calvin's justification of Joseph's actions lies in tension, however, with his sharp criticism of Protestant princes who justified their caution in religious matters by appealing to the need for stability. Here Calvin's zeal for the kingdom of Christ trumps any appeal to the peace of the political order. The princes charged Calvin with political naivete, such that he did "not understand how kingdoms are to be governed."[154] "They who are desirous to be regarded as prudent and cautious have continually this song in their mouth: 'We must consult the public tranquility; the reformation which we attempt is not unaccompanied by many dangers.'"[155] Calvin chafes at any suggestion that the Reformation promoted sedition,[156] and he agrees that "the public advantage ought always to have the preference."[157] But he reminds his readers that peace is not to be purchased at the price of obedience to God.

> First, we ought to inquire what is the will of God. Next, we ought to follow boldly whatever he enjoins and not to be discouraged by any fear, though we were besieged by a thousand deaths, for our actions must not be moved by any gust of wind but must be constantly regulated by the will of God alone. He who boldly despises dangers, or at least, rising above the fear of them, sincerely obeys God, will at length have a prosperous result.

It makes little sense, Calvin adds, "to appease the world by offending God."[158] The gospel might provoke disorder in the short run,[159] but in the long run there can be no separation between the will of God and the welfare of the commonwealth. "Wherefore, let us learn never to separate what is useful from what is lawful, since we ought not to expect any prosperity or success but from the blessing of God, which is promised not to wicked and rebellious persons who ask assistance from the devil, but to believers who sincerely walk in their ways."[160]

Calvin believed that sincere piety and unity in religion are necessary for the welfare of any society for several reasons. First, meaningful justice requires piety. The second table of the law cannot be separated from the first. "Religion is the best

---

[153] See Ralph Keen, "The Limits and Power of Obedience in the Later Calvin," *Calvin Theological Journal* 27 (1992): 265, 272.

[154] Commentary on Jeremiah 38:1–4 [1563]; CO 39:156–160.

[155] Commentary on John 11:48 [1553]; CO 47:272–273.

[156] Commentary on Micah 3:9–10 [1559]; 43:331. Cf. Commentary on Amos 8:10–13 [1559]; CO 43:127.

[157] Commentary on John 11:49 [1553]; CO 47:273.

[158] Commentary on John 11:48 [1553]; CO 47:272–273.

[159] Commentary on Acts 28:25 [1554]; CO 48:570. Cf. Commentary on Psalm 2:1 [1557]; CO 31:42–43; Dedication of the Commentary on Daniel to the French Protestants [1561]; CO 18:618.

[160] Commentary on John 11:49 [1553]; CO 47:273. Cf. Dedication of the Second Edition of the Commentary on Acts to Nicolaus Radziwil [1560]; CO 18:156.

mistress for teaching us mutually to maintain equity and uprightness towards each other, and where a concern for religion is extinguished then all regard for justice perishes along with it."[161] Piety is the root of charity. Thus "there will never be true charity towards neighbors, unless where the love of God reigns; for it is a mercenary love which the children of the world entertain for each other, because every one of them has regard to his own advantage."[162]

Second, division in religious matters would inevitably give way to division in political matters. As he had written already in 1546,

> where there are jarrings in religion it cannot but be that men's minds will soon afterwards burst forth in open strife. For as nothing is more effectual for uniting us and there is nothing that tends more to draw our minds together and keep them in a state of peace than agreement in religion, so, on the other hand, if any disagreement has arisen as to matters of this nature the effect necessarily is that men's minds are straightway stirred up for combat, and in no other department are there more fierce contendings.[163]

For Calvin this is not necessarily a tendency to be bemoaned. After all, peace should never be purchased at the price of the truth. "For accursed is that peace of which revolt from God is the bond, and blessed are those contentions by which it is necessary to maintain the kingdom of Christ."[164]

Third, like most of his contemporaries, Calvin believed that a commonwealth will be blessed or punished by God in proportion to its measure of faithfulness or disobedience to God's law. In the long run, God would bless faithful magistrates and commonwealths with prosperity. As he puts it in one commentary, "the elements would be serviceable to us were we willingly to obey God, but . . . the heaven and the earth and all the elements will be opposed to us if we pertinaciously resist God."[165] Thus regardless of whether or not the hearts of a people can be changed, "public sins" must be punished, lest the judgment of God fall on that people.[166]

This emphasis on corporate blessing and punishment stands in sharp tension with – if not outright contradiction to – Calvin's more basic insistence that the progress of the kingdom in this age takes place under the cross. The faithful

---

[161] Commentary on Psalm 14:4 [1557]; CO 31:139.
[162] Commentary on Luke 22:39 [1555]; CO 45:608. Cf. Commentary on Jeremiah 22:16 [1563]; CO 38: 387–388.
[163] Commentary on 1 Corinthians 1:12 [1546]; CO 49:315.
[164] Commentary on 1 Corinthians 14:33 [1546]; CO 49:532. Cf. Commentary on Luke 1:17 [1555]; CO 45:17; 12:51; CO 45:292; Commentary on Acts 15:2 [1554]; CO 48:339; Commentary on Colossians 2:2 [1548]; CO 52:99; Commentary on Romans 3:10, 18 [1556]; CO 49:53, 54.
[165] Commentary on Jeremiah 27:11 [1563]; CO 38:551–552.
[166] Commentary on Joel 1:13–15 [1559]; CO 42:526–528. Cf. Commentary on Isaiah 36:20 [1559]; CO 36:613.

should not expect earthly blessing in response to their faithfulness, he so often reminds his readers, but suffering. Anyone who struggles for justice should expect persecution,[167] believers especially. "For though there are common miseries to which the life of men is indiscriminately subjected, yet ... God trains his people in a peculiar manner in order that they may be conformed to the image of his Son."[168] In this respect, the situation of the church is different from that of Israel, for whom blessings pertaining to "this earthly and transitory life" were types of the spiritual kingdom of Christ. The same is true of the Old Testament curses: "now-a-days God does not openly take vengeance on sins as of old." Thus believers should not expect obedience to lead to the earthly blessings that are so prominent in the Old Testament, nor disobedience to lead to such punishments.[169] "God does not appear, as of old, as the rewarder of his people by earthly blessings, and this because we 'are dead, and our life is hid with Christ in God,' and because it becomes us to be conformed to our head and through many tribulations to enter the kingdom of heaven."[170]

Despite such warnings, in practice Calvin often appealed to a theology of blessing and curse, arguing on the basis of 1 Corinthians 11:30 that God still uses "diseases and other chastisements" to discipline his people.[171] As a general rule, when it came to individuals, he tended to emphasize the expectation of suffering and the necessity to rest in hope. When it came to the prosperity of kingdoms, on the other hand, especially when he was lobbying magistrates for political and religious reform, he tended to emphasize Old Testament principles of corporate reward and punishment. The ancient prophets were relevant for Christian societies, he claimed, because "from their histories and examples we ought to make known the judgments of God; ... what he formerly punished he will also punish with equal severity in our own day, for he is always like himself."[172] Calvin believed sixteenth-century Europe was experiencing such corporate punishment. "And yet after all, we wonder how it comes that there are so many wars, so many pestilences, so many crop failures, so many disasters

---

[167] *Institutes*, 3.8.7; Commentary on Matthew 5:10 [1555]; CO 45:164.

[168] Commentary on Matthew 16:24 [1555]; CO 45:481–482. Cf. Commentary on Acts 14:22 [1554]; CO 48: 330–332; Commentary on 1 Thessalonians 3:3 [1551]; CO 52:156; Commentary on Hebrews 12:7 [1549]; CO 55:174.

[169] Commentary on Leviticus 26:3 [1563]; CO 25:13. Cf. Commentary on Isaiah 44:25 [1559]; CO37:124; Commentary on 1 Corinthians 10:11 [1546]; CO 49:460–461.

[170] Commentary on Leviticus 26:3 [1563]; CO 25:14. Cf. Commentary on Zechariah 10:2 [1559]; CO 44:287; Commentary on Jeremiah 33:16 [1563]; CO 39:68.

[171] Commentary on 1 Corinthians 11:30 [1546]; CO 49:493.

[172] Preface to the Commentary on Isaiah [1559]; CO 36:22. See Mark J. Larson, *Calvin's Doctrine of the State: A Reformed Doctrine and Its American Trajectory, The Revolutionary War, and the Founding of the Republic* (Eugene, OR: Wipf and Stock, 2009), 39–40.

and calamities – as if the cause were not manifest! And assuredly we must not expect a termination to our calamities until we have removed the occasion of them by correcting our faults.'"[173]

The irony is all the greater in light of Calvin's conviction that Christ's kingdom flourished most before it was recognized by any political power. For "although the Son of God reigned under the cross, yet amidst the arduous conflicts of persecutions, his glory shone brighter and his triumphs were more splendid than if the church had enjoyed undisturbed prosperity. At length, the haughty loftiness of the Roman Empire, yielding submission to Christ, became a distinguished ornament of the house of God." Calvin likewise believed that it was after it attained this political success that the church fell under the rule of Antichrist. Only now was the Reformation restoring Christ's kingdom, once again under the persecution of the cross.[174] The triumph of Constantine did not fulfill Daniel's famous prophecy about Christ's kingdom because that kingdom is spiritual. "Christ did not utter these words in vain, 'My kingdom is not of this world.'"[175] At a theological level, therefore, Calvin affirmed that temporal prosperity and political power have little to do with the progress of the spiritual kingdom of Christ. At a more practical level, however, he often wrote and acted differently, working hard to ensure that the two progressed hand in hand.

CONCLUSION

Calvin recognized that Old Testament Israel had a typological function that precluded its simplistic use as an example for Christian polities, but he believed that the care of religion that Israel's kings exercised was a central part of the magisterial vocation that transcended their typological status. Calvin defended this position from the Old and New Testaments, but his biblical arguments presupposed more foundational judgments drawn from reason, philosophy, and the laws of nations, all of which he regarded as testimony of natural law.

---

[173] Commentary on 1 Corinthians 11:30 [1546]; CO 49:494.

[174] Dedication of the Commentary on Isaiah to Edward VI [1550]; CO 13:669–674. "Then the kings of the earth and their people voluntarily yielded themselves to the yoke of Christ. Wolves and lions were converted into lambs ... [T]he goodly and unequaled condition of that age, which may be called the Golden Age, clearly demonstrate that she was truly the heavenly kingdom of God ... At the time when she flourished most it was not purple, gold, and precious stones which imparted to her the splendor which invested her, but the blood of martyrs ... In short, her dignity, venerable indeed, but yet spiritual, lay as yet hidden beneath the cross of Christ." Commentary on Psalm 87 [1557]; CO 31: 798–800. Cf. *Institutes*, 4.5.17.

[175] Commentary on Daniel 2:44–45 [1561]; CO 40:605. Daniel prophesied that the future messianic kingdom would be established on the heels of four great kingdoms, destroying the last of them, commonly thought to be Rome.

At the same time, Calvin agreed that the punishment of crimes against the true religion, such as idolatry or false teaching, can only take place in societies where the true religion is acknowledged by public consensus. Although he was not always consistent on this point, and although he was convinced that the establishment of true religion is vital for the health of any society, he recognized that certain contexts preclude a simple magisterial stance toward religion. He also insisted that even in Christian societies, magistrates can only indirectly promote and defend true religion, and then only in its public form. They cannot perform spiritual functions because their office is of the political order rather than of the spiritual kingdom of Christ.

9

Law, Democracy, and Resistance to Tyranny

Although Calvin's commitment to a Christian commonwealth fostered some of the same religio-political intolerance that was pervasive throughout mid-sixteenth-century Europe, I have argued that Calvin's position on the care of religion was determined more by his judgments about natural law (i.e., political philosophy) than it was by his exegesis of scripture (i.e., political theology). This leaves open the possibility that, if interpreted in light of different assumptions about reason and natural law, Calvin's political theology, including his two kingdoms doctrine, might be less alien to a Christian democratic politics than at first seems to be the case.[1]

---

[1] Against the more recent scholarly consensus, Harro Höpfl argues that Calvin paid merely lip service to natural law, but that in reality he was essentially a biblicist who consistently invoked scripture's authority for increasingly specific matters of polity and law. Harro Höpfl, *The Christian Polity of John Calvin* (Cambridge: Cambridge University Press, 1982), 149, 177–179, 188. Höpfl complains that Calvin failed to clarify his philosophical commitments and the way in which they informed his political theology (50–54; Cf. 141–142, 147, 150–151). What of Calvin's discussion and use of natural law? Höpfl doesn't think it is serious: "There is no question of any serious examination of the idea of natural law: Calvin never clearly specified the manner in which it is apprehended, but merely referred to the 'heart' or the 'intellect' or the 'conscience,' and on occasion to 'natural sense' and 'reason'. His appeal to the consent of the ages, or of the Gentiles, to specific articles of the natural law was equally unconcerned with the difficulties of this type of argument. All of which points to the entirely secondary importance of natural law within his thought" (184). This assessment is puzzling. On the one hand, Höpfl admits that Calvin's natural law references are everywhere, and that they are not "peripheral or casual, even if deficient in precision." On the other hand, he claims, "Calvin never allowed to natural knowledge of the moral law any independent adequacy as a guide to moral conduct for Christians; it was always treated as an inferior adjunct to the written divine law, and as unreliable" (180–181). On all the genuinely controversial issues, he insists, Calvin always found the main support for his position in scripture. It is true that, like all orthodox Christian theologians, Calvin placed scripture above natural law. But Höpfl seems to assume that unless Calvin understood natural law to function through systematic reason, perhaps according to the model of Aquinas or the medieval scholastics, his use of it could not have been very serious. But Calvin was quite explicit about his theological conviction that the knowledge of natural law lies in the conscience, in intuition, and in human experience. His method is more general than that of Aquinas, but it is not unconsidered. Furthermore, Höpfl himself admits that Calvin did use natural law in significant ways, especially when it came to matters such as the capital punishment of blasphemy,

In Chapter 9, I extend this argument. I show that despite his practical political conclusions, Calvin's theoretical distinction between the spiritual and civil uses of the law makes possible an appropriation of biblical law that is flexible and readily applicable to a wide range of circumstances, including those of a democratic, pluralistic society. I then turn to Calvin's approach to forms of government, demonstrating that, with respect to institutions and constitutional practices, Calvin's two kingdoms theology encourages pragmatic flexibility and openness to certain democratic practices. Finally, I show that, as expressed in his theory of resistance, Calvin's two kingdoms political theology is conducive toward a theory of limited government appropriate to pluralistic contexts.

Throughout this chapter, I must stress, my argument is not that Calvin supported or would conceivably have supported political pluralism or liberal democracy. Calvin was no liberal, and it is impossible to know what his political predilections would have been had he lived during the twenty-first century. My point, rather, is to show that there are resources in Calvin's two kingdoms political theology for a Christian democratic politics that accepts and respects pluralism.

THE CIVIL USE OF THE LAW

Calvin believed that scripture alone holds authority in matters of faith, but in "matters which concern men" he recognized that "human reasons" hold an important place.[2] To be sure, reason must always be consistent with the teaching of scripture.[3] And Calvin agreed with the other magisterial reformers that the essence of the magisterial task is the enforcement of the outward piety and justice of the natural moral law, which is most clearly revealed in scripture. The law of God is the final criteria for just government.[4]

heresy, and adultery, some of the most controversial political issues of Calvin's tenure in Geneva! In the final analysis, Höpfl has not substantiated his thesis that natural law does not play a major role in the reformer's political theology. This undermines his conclusion that Calvin rejected a "neat parallelism" between the roles of pastors and magistrates according to which pastors find their commission and its content in scripture, while magistrates find the terms of their commission in natural law (albeit subject to scripture) (179). Calvin *was* serious about the importance and authority of natural law and its usefulness in determining what parts of biblical law are normative for contemporary politics and what parts are not. He was quite clear that the relevance of scripture for civil politics must always be interpreted in light of natural law and the limits of politics, and this requires humility in its proclamation on the part of pastors, theologians, and the church. That is why Calvin did not write more about politics than he did.

[2] Commentary on Acts 17:2 [1554]; CO 48:393.
[3] Commentary on Numbers 10:2 [1563]; CO 24:374. Cf. 18:19; CO 24:187–188.
[4] "For Calvin, the law, in its dialectical relation to divine grace, promise, and freedom, is the constitutive structure of Christian spirituality and morality, binding together the civil and ecclesial realms in a single overarching unity of revelation and salvation." Oliver O'Donovan and Joan Lockwood O'Donovan, *From Irenaeus to Grotius: A Sourcebook in Christian Political Thought* (Grand Rapids: Eerdmans,

But for Calvin, this principle was qualified by the fundamental difference between the spiritual and civil uses of the law, and between what is attainable among the regenerate and what is attainable through coercion. Thus while there is an element of truth to the claim that Calvin identified the objective of political order in light of the same ideal of righteousness as he did the spiritual kingdom of Christ, it is crucial to emphasize that, in Calvin's view, whereas the spiritual kingdom is involved in the *restoration of true righteousness* (the spiritual use of the law), the civil order is involved in the *restraint of outward unrighteousness* (the civil use of the law).[5] For Calvin, a decisive feature of the political order is its inherent limitations as a coercive restraint on human sin. The best that civil government can do is to preserve human beings in outward, civil righteousness, so creating the conditions in which the gospel can create true righteousness.[6]

In addition, Calvin believed that the relevance of scripture for civil government is rarely direct. He rejected the claim that a commonwealth must conform to the laws of Moses as being "perilous and seditious," not to mention "false and foolish" (4.20.14). It is the natural and moral law of God, rather, that binds political societies.

> It is a fact that the law of God which we call the moral law is nothing else than a testimony of natural law and of that conscience which God has engraved upon the minds of men. Consequently, the entire scheme of this equity of which we are now speaking has been prescribed in it. Hence, this equity alone must be the goal and rule and limit of all laws. Whatever laws shall be framed to that rule, directed to that goal, bound by that limit, there is no reason why we should disapprove of them, howsoever they may differ from the Jewish law or among themselves (4.20.16).[7]

Calvin reminds his readers that the moral law "prescribes nothing which nature does not itself dictate to be most certain and most just, and which experience itself does

1999), 664. For Calvin, the law of God is what Stevenson calls the "clear, scripturally based criteria for good government." William R. Stevenson, Jr., *Sovereign Grace: The Place and Significance of Christian Freedom in John Calvin's Political Thought* (New York: Oxford University Press, 1999), 94–95. Cf. Ralph Keen, "The Limits and Power of Obedience in the Later Calvin," *Calvin Theological Journal* 27 (1992): 252–276, 264.

[5] Milner is therefore misleading to declare that "Calvin's description of life in the body of Christ is not materially different from his normative conception of the *ordo politicus*." Benjamin Milner, Jr., *Calvin's Doctrine of the Church* (Leiden: Brill, 1970), 188. Cf. Thomas F. Torrance, *Kingdom and Church: Study in the Theology of the Reformation* (Edinburgh: Oliver & Boyd, 1956), 151.

[6] For Calvin, Stevenson claims, "we ought never to assume that civil government can remake the world but only that it might 'provide that a public manifestation of religion may exist among Christians, and that humanity be maintained among men.'" Stevenson, *Sovereign Grace*, 93. "To the extent that government should *try* to remake human beings, spiritually or any other way, it is, as we have already seen, doomed to fail" (94). Cf. Ralph C. Hancock, *Calvin and the Foundations of Modern Politics* (Ithaca: Cornell University Press, 1989), 59–61.

[7] Cf. I. John Hesselink, *Calvin's Concept of the Law* (Allison Park, PA: Pickwick Publications, 1992), 245–249.

not show us to be more profitable or more desirable than anything else."[8] For that reason, Christians can expect to find it reflected in the politics and philosophies of all peoples and nations, not only in scripture.

Certainly Calvin believed the natural moral law is summarized and clarified in the Ten Commandments, beyond which "nothing can be wanted as the rule of a good and upright life." He interpreted the Decalogue representatively, such that moral principles not explicitly mentioned in it were understood to be part of its implicit teaching. But that still left a host of specific rules and regulations in the Mosaic law that had to be categorized either as timeless principles of moral law, ceremonial regulations unique to Old Testament worship, or civil laws potentially useful for, but no longer binding on, Christian commonwealths. In his *Harmony of the Law*, he writes that ceremonial laws, which pertain to the first table of the Decalogue (piety and the worship of God), and political laws, which pertain to the second table (justice and relations between human beings) are to be regarded as supplements that do not add anything to the moral content of God's law but that serve "merely to aid in the observance of the moral law." They are "only helps which, as it were, lead us by the hand to the due worship of God and to the promotion of justice towards men." To put it in Aristotelian terms, "they are not, to speak correctly, of the substance of the law," but are "appendages."[9]

It is true that Calvin was much more sensitive to the error of conflating ceremonial laws with the moral law, which he associated with Judaism, than he was to the danger of conflating political laws with the moral law. In certain respects, Calvin also held to a uniquely dogmatic interpretation of scripture's moral teaching when compared to other magisterial reformers.[10] Still, he repeatedly articulates points at which he finds Israel's civil law to be anachronistic, insufficient, or even counter to natural law.[11] Although he did appeal to the authority of the Mosaic law in arguments about what magistrates should or should not do, he recognized that, taken in isolation, such appeals are insufficient.

The most theologically significant reason Calvin offers why certain laws in the Torah are not binding on all nations is that God gave Israel laws appropriate for its unique mission as God's sacerdotal kingdom.[12] Calvin includes in this category the

---

[8] Commentary on Deuteronomy 10:12 [1563]; CO 24:723.

[9] Preface to Calvin's Harmony of the Law [1563]; CO 24:7–8. See Susan E. Schreiner, *The Theater of His Glory: Nature and the Natural Order in the Thought of John Calvin* (Grand Rapids: Baker Academic, 1995), 78; Guenther Haas, *The Concept of Equity in Calvin's Ethics* (Waterloo, Ontario: Wilfrid Laurier University Press, 1997), 72–75, 84–90.

[10] See John Lee Thompson, "Patriarchs, Polygamy and Private Resistance: John Calvin and Others on Breaking God's Rules," *Sixteenth Century Journal* 25/1 (1994): 3–28.

[11] Cf. Haas, *The Concept of Equity in Calvin's Ethics*, 98.

[12] Such laws include the law about the sharing of manna (Commentary on Exodus 16:17 [1563]; CO 24: 171–172); the law about breaking down altars and images (23:24; CO 24:546); laws pertaining to the chief

laws that called Israel to exterminate the Canaanites and to execute propitiatory judgment on the wicked, but he includes other laws as well. In his commentary on Leviticus 25:23, he notes that Israel's jubilee laws, which guaranteed each Israelite family an inheritance in the land, "can hardly be applied to other nations" because "the land of Canaan was an earnest, or symbol, or mirror of the adoption on which their salvation was founded."[13] The purpose of the law was to preserve liberty by preventing inequality, "lest a few persons of immense wealth should oppress the general body." But the reformer goes on to explain that "we are not bound by this law at present" except with respect to the principle of general equity that requires mercy to debtors and generosity to the poor. "The condition of the ancient people, as I have said, was different. They derived their origin from a single race, the land of Canaan was their common inheritance, [and] fraternal association was to be mutually sustained among them, just as if they were one family."[14]

The same was the case with slavery. God prohibited the permanent involuntary enslavement of Hebrew persons (though tolerating temporary slavery "by indulgence") because he desired that his people be a free people.[15] The design of this law, Calvin argues, was to distinguish Israel from the nations.[16] For "it was yet a very mournful thing for God's children to be the slaves of servants; for they were … a sacerdotal kingdom, and God had so taken them under his protection that their condition was better and more desirable than that of any other kingdom."[17] True, by nature, all people are fundamentally equal and are to be treated in accord with general principles of justice. "Any inequality which is contrary to this arrangement is nothing else than a corruption of nature which proceeds from sin."[18] Christians should therefore continue to prohibit slavery "lest the condition of those who have been redeemed by Christ's blood should be worse among us than that of old of its ancient people."[19] But political laws will necessarily vary based on what is possible and appropriate under particular circumstances. Calvin found slavery abhorrent and lauded its abolition, but he refused to declare that its abolition, or the Mosaic form of its regulation, is binding on all nations.

priest (Commentary on Numbers 3:5 [1563]; CO 24:444–445); the laws on tithes (18:20; CO 24:479–481); laws calling for the extermination of the Canaanites (Commentary on Deuteronomy 7:20–25 [1563]; 24: 553–554); and laws prohibiting alliances with pagan nations (Commentary on Isaiah 30:1 [1559], 15; CO 36:506, 517).

[13] Commentary on Leviticus 25:23 [1563]; CO 24:706.
[14] Commentary on Deuteronomy 15:1 [1563]; CO 24:697–698.
[15] Commentary on Leviticus 25:42 [1563]; CO 24:704.
[16] Commentary on Jeremiah 34:8–17 [1563]; CO 39:86.
[17] Commentary on Lamentations 5:8 [1563]; CO 39:635–636.
[18] Commentary on Genesis 1:28 [1554]; CO 23:28.
[19] Commentary on Leviticus 25:42 [1563]; CO 24:704.

Similar is Calvin's approach to the issue of usury. Long considered one of his most groundbreaking and enduring moral arguments, Calvin's justification of usury presupposes a distinction between political laws unique to Israel's mission as the sacerdotal people of God and the principles according to which Christian polities ought to be governed. The goal of policy, for Calvin, was to approximate the principles of equity to the greatest extent possible in any particular set of circumstances. For practices that were inevitable, such as usury, it was better to bring them under legal regulation and curb excesses than to drive them underground by quixotic efforts to eliminate them entirely.[20]

The key places where Calvin discusses the question of usury are his commentaries on Exodus 22:25, Psalm 15, and Ezekiel 18:5–9, and his letter "On Usury." In his commentary on Exodus, Calvin introduces his discussion of usury by noting that its prohibition was a "political [*politicum*]" law but that the law's application "depends on the rule of charity [*caritatis regula*]." Calvin's logic here is tight: "It is plain that this was a part of the Jewish polity [*politiae iudaicae*], because it was lawful to lend at interest to the Gentiles, which distinction [between Jew and Gentile] the spiritual law [*lex spiritualis*] does not admit." In other words, the law regarding usury must have been political because it did not respect the moral equality of persons. Though Israel was distinct from the Gentile nations, Christian nations are not, and therefore they cannot simply incorporate the Torah's usury law into their own polities. "Moreover, since the wall of partition which formerly separated Jew and Gentile is now broken down, our condition is now different, and consequently we must spare all without exception, both as regards taking interest and any other mode of extortion, and equity is to be observed even towards strangers."[21] Contemporary nations have flexibility with regard to laws concerning interest, but they must observe the principles of equity and charity. "The judicial law [*ius forense*], however, which God prescribed to his ancient people, is only so far abrogated [*abrogatum*] as that what charity dictates should remain, i.e., that our brethren who need our assistance are not to be treated harshly."[22]

[20] On Calvin's approach to usury, see Mark Valeri, "Religion, Discipline, and the Economy in Calvin's Geneva," *Sixteenth Century Journal* 28 (1997): 123–142, 129–131; L. F. Schulze, "Calvin on Interest and Property – Some Aspects of His Socio-Economic View," *Our Reformational Tradition*. South Africa: Potchefstroom University for Christian Higher Education, 1984, 217–230; Jane Dempsey Douglass, "Calvin's Relation to Social and Economic Change," *Church and Society* 74 (1984): 75–81, 79; Haas, *The Concept of Equity in Calvin's Ethics*, 117–121; W. Fred Graham, *The Constructive Revolutionary: John Calvin and His Socio-Economic Impact* (Richmond, VA: John Knox Press, 1971), 77–94, 117–126.

[21] Commentary on Exodus 22:25 [1563]; CO 24:680. Cf. Commentary on Ezekiel 18:5–9 [1565]; CO 40: 425–432. Calvin distinguishes "the political law which God appointed for the Jews in particular [*politica ... lex ... peculiariter Iudaeis*]" and the "common principle of justice which extends to all nations and to all ages." Commentary on Psalm 15:5 [1557]; CO 31:148. Cf. "On Usury"; CO 10:246–247.

[22] Commentary on Exodus 22:25 [1563]; CO 24:680. In his Commentary on Ezekiel, Calvin offers an argument that sheds light on his complicated attitude toward the Torah: "But because God's law

When it comes to working out the principle of charity according to which the charging of interest might be just, Calvin interacts with pagan perspectives, including those of Plato, Aristotle, and Cato.[23] As he puts it, "surely that which heathens even have detested appears to be by no means lawful to the children of God. We know that the name of usurer has everywhere and always been infamous and detested."[24] Calvin outlines three reasons why usury might justly be prohibited. First, as Cato recognized when he compared usury to murder, usurers nearly always have the object of exploiting others. Second, very often usurers neither work nor contribute anything to the community. It is shameful that "while all other men obtain the means of their subsistence with much toil . . . money-mongers should sit at their ease without doing any thing and receive tribute from the labor of all other people." Third, it always seems to be the poor who suffer from usury.[25]

But Calvin adds that this is not all that needs to be said on the matter, for a person might lend at interest without being a professional usurer. The key is to "consider when and from whom a person exacts interest."[26] Calvin rejects Aristotle's argument that usury is unnatural because money is barren. On the contrary, he maintains, a borrower "might make much profit by trading with another man's money, and the purchaser of the farm might in the meantime reap and gather his vintage."[27] The borrower might even be wealthier than the lender and use the money borrowed to grow his wealth even more. "Why should the creditor be deprived of his rights [*suo iure*] when his money brings profit to a neighbor richer than himself?"[28] Finally, there is the case of debtors who would otherwise take advantage of their creditors. "If the debtor has protracted the time by false pretenses to the loss and inconvenience

---

embraces complete and perfect justice we must hold that interest . . . is not altogether to be condemned. Otherwise ignominy would clearly attach to the law of God if it did not prescribe to us a true and complete rule of living justly . . . [W]e shall not find all interest contrary to the law, and hence it follows that interest is not always to be condemned." Commentary on Ezekiel 18:5–9 [1565]; CO 40:430. Calvin's logic here can be reduced to the following syllogism: A) God's law embraces perfect justice; B) God's law permits some charging of interest; C) therefore, charging of interest is not necessarily unjust. The description of the law as embracing perfect justice seems to contradict the reformer's admission that the law tolerated the hardness of human hearts. The only way to make sense of the statement is to assume that Calvin thinks of the law permitting the charging of interest (when it is in accord with charity) as a spiritual law (i.e., the complete and perfect justice), which means that the law prohibiting interest must be a political law. Cf. Sermon on Deuteronomy 23:18–20; CO 28:117–118.

[23] "Methodologically, his argument is as much dependent on philosophical concepts (e.g., prudence, moderation, natural equity, justice, and the publci good) as on biblical injunctions." O'Donovan and O'Donovan, *From Irenaeus to Grotius*, 666.

[24] Commentary on Exodus 22:25 [1563]; CO 24:681. Cf. Commentary on Ezekiel 18:5–9 [1565]; CO 40:431.

[25] Commentary on Psalm15:5 [1557]; CO 31:147–148.

[26] Commentary on Ezekiel 18:5–9 [1565]; CO 40:431.

[27] Commentary on Exodus 22:25 [1563]; CO 24:682.

[28] Commentary on Ezekiel 18:5–9 [1565]; CO 40:432.

of his creditor, will it be consistent that he should reap advantage from his bad faith and broken promises? Certainly no one, I think, will deny that usury ought to be paid to the creditor in addition to the principal to compensate his loss."[29]

There are therefore numerous factors and circumstances that must be taken into account when evaluating the morality of usury, which should be permitted "neither everywhere, nor always, nor [with respect to] all things, nor from all."[30] As he writes in his letter on usury, "we ought not to judge usury according to some certain or particular sentence of God [in scripture], but in accordance with the principle of equity."[31] Calvin is aware that "those who think differently may object that we must abide by God's judgment when he generally prohibits all usury to His people." But the declarations of David and Ezekiel "ought to be judged of by the rule of charity," the "universal rule of justice" "on which hang the law and the prophets – Do not do to others what you would not have done to yourself." According to such principles, not slavish imitation of the laws of Moses, should Christian polities be organized.[32]

A second reason why Calvin believed the political laws of the Torah are not binding on all nations is that Israel's laws tolerated some injustice due to the hardness of human hearts.[33] Calvin argued that the nations are called to follow a higher standard where possible, that of the natural moral law. The exegetical basis for this claim was Jesus' declaration that Moses' law of divorce accommodated human depravity in a way that fell short of God's intent for marriage at creation. Calvin draws an interpretive principle from this declaration, applying it to a broad range of cases revolving around marriage, divorce, violence, and the treatment of slaves and prisoners. In each of these cases, he judges the law in view to be morally deficient in comparison with the natural law of equity, and in each of these cases, he explains the deficiency as a necessary accommodation to the hardness of human hearts.[34] In fact, Calvin argues that this limitation was inherent to all of the Torah's "civil laws [*leges forenses*], the principle of which is not so exact and perfect, since in their enactment God has relaxed his just severity in consideration of

---

[29] Commentary on Exodus 22:25 [1563]; CO 24:682.

[30] Commentary on Ezekiel 18:5–9 [1565]; CO 40:431.   [31] "On Usury"; CO 10:247–248.

[32] Commentary on Exodus 22:25 [1563]; CO 24:682–683. Calvin also uses the rule of equity or charity as the foundation for his interpretation of theft. "This, then, is the rule of charity, that every one's rights should be safely preserved, and that none should do to another what he would not have done to himself." The prohibition of theft implies responsibilities of "liberality and kindness, and the other duties, whereby human society is maintained" (20:15; CO 24:669). Cf. Commentary on Psalm 15:5 [1557]; CO 31:147–148. Cf. Commentary on Genesis 47:20 [1554]; CO 23:573.

[33] God also accommodated Israel in a manner appropriate for a people in its childhood. See Arnold Huijgen, *Divine Accommodation in John Calvin's Theology: Analysis and Assessment* (Göttingen: Vandenhoeck & Ruprecht, 2011), 190–200, 208–236.

[34] See Haas, *The Concept of Equity in Calvin's Ethics*, 99.

the people's hardness of heart [*populi duritiem*]."[35] The same must necessarily be true of all civil laws.

Calvin interprets Jesus' comments on divorce against the backdrop of his criticism of the Pharisees, who he says wrongly interpreted the Torah's accommodation of divorce as an indication that divorce is morally justified. The Pharisees failed to recognize that the law of divorce was a political law rather than a spiritual law. The difference is crucial. "For political laws are sometimes accommodated to the manners of men [*leges politicae interdum ad hominum mores flectuntur*], but God, in prescribing a spiritual law [*legem spiritualem*], looked not at what men can do but at what they ought to do." Jesus therefore challenged the assumption that "what is allowed [*tolerat*] by the political law [*lex politica*] of Moses is on that account considered licit in the sight of God [*protinus licere coram Deo*]."[36] Divorce was permitted because the people were incapable of attaining to a higher legal standard, not because it is just. Yet as Jesus made clear, the true standard of justice is much higher, and it is rooted in the natural law of the created order.[37] "Although what relates to divorce was granted in concession to the Jews, yet Christ pronounces that it was never legitimate [*fuisse legitimum*], because it is directly repugnant to the first institution of God, from whence a perpetual and inviolable rule is to be sought. It is proverbially said that the laws of nature [*iura naturae*] are indissoluble."[38]

Calvin's intent in emphasizing Jesus' logic was not to reduce the rigor of political laws.[39] On the contrary, in a striking display of his own political predilections, Calvin warns magistrates not to use the principle as an excuse for approving injustice. Commenting on Jesus' declaration, "what therefore God has joined together, let not man separate," Calvin writes,

And as he declares that it is not in the choice [*arbitrio*] of the husband to dissolve the marriage, so likewise he forbids all others to confirm by their authority illicit divorces [*ita et aliis omnibus legem edicit, ne sua autoritate illicita repudia confirment*], for the magistrate abuses his power when he gives favor [*gratiam facit*] to the husband to divorce his wife.[40]

---

[35] Commentary on Exodus 22:1–4 [1563]; CO 24:688. See Thompson, "Patriarchs, Polygamy and Private Resistance," 14; Commentary on Genesis 22:19; 26:34 [1554]; CO 23:320, 370; Commentary on 1 Timothy 3:2 [1548]; CO 52:281; Sermon on 1 Timothy 3:2; CO 53:245–249; Commentary on Titus 1:6 [1550]; CO 52:410; Sermon on Titus 1:6; CO 54:423.

[36] Commentary on Matthew 5:31 [1555]; CO 45:180. Cf. Commentary on 1 Corinthians 7:10 [1546]; CO 49:409.

[37] Commentary on Matthew 19:1–9 [1555]; CO 45:528.

[38] Commentary on Deuteronomy 24:1–4 [1563]; CO 24:657–658. Cf. Commentary on Numbers 5:11; CO 24:654; Haas, *The Concept of Equity in Calvin's Ethics*, 100.

[39] As Höpfl observes, Calvin believed the church's duty is "to urge on the magistracy an ever stricter conformity of positive with divine law, and an ever stricter enforcement of obedience to the law." Höpfl, *The Christian Polity of John Calvin*, 196.

[40] Commentary on Matthew 19:6 [1555]; CO 45:529.

Jesus' principle does not justify magistrates' "indolence, if they voluntarily abstain from correcting vices, or neglect what the nature of their office demands." Nor should subjects use legality as an excuse for acting unjustly.[41]

But should Moses have "permitted [*permittere*] what was in itself bad and sinful [*malum et vitiosum*]"? To answer this question Calvin articulates a distinction between what is legally permitted and what is legally approved. "[I]n an unusual sense of the word, he is said to have permitted [*permissum*] what he did not severely forbid [*vetuit*]." As it reads in the French version of the commentary: "strictly speaking, he did not permit [*permis*] it, but in so far as he did not strictly forbid it, he is said to have permitted [*permis*] it." What is the difference? The former connotes approval whereas the latter simply seeks to regulate and mitigate the destructive consequences of what is unavoidable.

> [H]e did not lay down a law about divorces so as to give them the seal of his approbation [*approbaret*], but as the wickedness of men could not be restrained in any other way, he applied what was the most admissible remedy, that the husband should at least attest the chastity of his wife. For the law was made solely for the protection of the women, that they might not suffer any disgrace after they had been unjustly rejected. Hence we infer that it was rather a punishment [*poenam*] inflicted on the husbands than an indulgence or permission [*venia aut permissu*] fitted to inflame their lust.[42]

Calvin reminds his readers that one cannot conflate what is legal with what is moral, and he explicitly appeals to the two kingdoms doctrine as underlying the distinction: for "political and outward order [*politia et externo ordine*] is widely different from spiritual government [*spirituale regimen*]." The law that is moral and spiritual, summarized in the Ten Commandments, demands much more than can be enforced by a human court. It is therefore no surprise that some injustice is "connived at by political laws [*leges politicae*]." As an analogy Calvin observes that civil law allows broader rights of litigation than the spiritual law of charity permits. This is necessary because "the right [of litigation] cannot be conferred on individuals unless there be an open door for demanding it." Freedom to perform what is necessary or loving, in other words, is impossible without the broader freedom to use one's discretion for good or ill. Magistrates cannot micromanage their subjects'

---

[41] Commentary on Matthew 19:7 [1555]; CO 45:529–530. It is only the "wicked forbearance of magistrates" that makes divorce necessary, "because adulterers are not punished" (19:9; CO 45:531).

[42] "Moses conceded [*concesserit*] it on account of their obstinacy and not because he sanctioned it as licit [*licitum probaverit*]." Commentary on Matthew 19:7 [1555]; CO 45:529–530. Calvin's reluctance to use the word "permission" stands in contrast to Jesus' declaraion that Moses "permitted" divorce. In the NASB, Matthew 19:8 reads, "He said to them, 'Because of your hardness of heart, Moses permitted you to divorce your wives; but from the beginning it has not been this way.'"

access to the courts.[43] A magistrate "is constrained to bear many things [*cogetur tamen ferre*] which he does not approve [*probabit*], for we cannot so deal with mankind as to restrain all vices [*cohibeantur omnia vitia*]. It is indeed desirable that no vice should be tolerated [*toleretur*], but we must have a regard to what is possible."[44]

Calvin clearly affirmed the position that it is not always possible for civil government to enforce the moral law, even outwardly. In addition, he affirmed that civil authorities must sometimes regulate unjust actions so as to prevent their worst potential consequences. Yet such toleration and regulation does not constitute moral approval or permission. Faithfulness to God on the part of a magistrate does not require the comprehensive enforcement of biblical morality.

While the law of divorce is the preeminent instance of a political law accommodating the hardness of human hearts, Calvin identifies numerous analogous cases in the Torah. In many of these instances there is nothing in the text to cue him to this interpretation, nor can he appeal to an authoritative statement by Jesus or the apostles. Rather, Calvin judges particular laws as lacking from the standpoint of reason or the law of nations. Take, for instance, the law that permitted Israelites to enslave and marry women captured during war. Calvin argues that such forced marriages should not have taken place at all, but because it was so difficult to restrain the lust of victors in war, "God so tempers his indulgence." There is no ideal law here, only the embarrassing political regulation of libidinous men for whom there was clearly "no room for perfect purity."[45] The Torah likewise outlined a procedure for adjudicating cases in which a man had sex with an enslaved woman who was "assigned to another man." Although adulterers were ordinarily to be put to death, because the woman was a slave the penalty was reduced to a fine and a guilt offering. Calvin points out that in God's eyes there is no difference between slaves and free persons. "Notwithstanding therefore that the crime is worthy of death, still, in consideration of the people's infirmity, the punishment is mitigated," but Christians should not conclude from the "lenity or indulgence of the law that the offense was a trifling one."[46]

Calvin's handling of the law regulating the treatment of male prisoners is even more striking because Calvin explicitly describes it as being deficient in comparison

---

[43] Commentary on Matthew 19:7 [1555]; CO 45:529–530.

[44] "[T]hough it was not punished under the law [*impunitas sub lege*], yet it was not permitted [*permissio*]." Commentary on Malachi 2:16 [1559]; CO 44:456–457. A similar case is the law's toleration of polygamy. Cf. Commentary on Leviticus 18:18 [1563]; CO 24:664; Commentary on Psalm 45:8 [1557]; CO 31:455; Thompson, "Patriarchs, Polygamy and Private Resistance," 15.

[45] Commentary on Deuteronomy 21:10 [1563]; CO 24:353.

[46] Commentary on Leviticus 19:20–22 [1563]; CO 24:649–650.

with the work of heathen writers (specifically Cicero). The law stated that when a city refused to surrender, all of its male inhabitants were to be killed.

> The permission here given seems to confer too great a license, for since heathen writers command even the conquered to be spared and enjoin that those should be admitted to mercy who lay down their arms and cast themselves on the good faith of the general, although the battering-ram may have actually made a breach in the wall, how does God, the father of mercies, give his sanction to indiscriminate bloodshed?

In contrast to Bullinger, Calvin refuses to accept the law as a valid norm for just war. His solution is to concede that the civil law tolerated crimes – in this case murder – that were patently against the law of nature.

> It has already been stated that more was conceded to the Jews on account of their hardness of heart than was justly lawful for them [*iure ipsis liceret*]. Unquestionably, by the law of charity [*caritatis regula*] even armed men should be spared if, casting away the sword, they crave for mercy. At any rate, it was not lawful [*licuit*] to kill any but those who were taken in arms, sword in hand. This permission [*permissio*] therefore to slaughter, which is extended to all the males, is far distant from perfection.

Though the law was imperfect, Calvin suggests, its purpose was to regulate the injustice so as to restrain the Israelites from the even greater cruelty of murdering women and children.[47]

The law of Exodus 21:7–11 actually provided regulations for the event that a man sold his daughter as a slave-wife to another man. If she did not please her master-husband, the law stated, she should be divorced and freed rather than sold to a foreign people. Calvin is appalled. "From this passage, as well as other similar ones, it plainly appears how many vices were of necessity tolerated [*toleranda*] in this people. It was altogether an act of barbarism that fathers should sell their children for the relief of their poverty. Still it could not be corrected as might have been hoped." He infers that the intent of the law was to protect enslaved girls by forcing their masters either to marry or free them.[48] Another law permitted a slave who had the opportunity to win his freedom to divorce his enslaved wife and forsake his enslaved children. Slavery was sufficiently terrible that such a procedure was tolerated, Calvin declares, but "nothing could be more opposed to nature than that a husband,

---

[47] Commentary on Deuteronomy 20:12 [1563]; CO 24:632. On Bullinger, see Mark J. Larson, *Calvin's Doctrine of the State: A Reformed Doctrine and Its American Trajectory, The Revolutionary War, and the Founding of the Republic* (Eugene, OR: Wipf and Stock, 2009), 44–50; Haas, *The Concept of Equity in Calvin's Ethics*, 97–98.
[48] Commentary on Exodus 21:7–11 [1563]; CO 24:650–651.

forsaking his wife and children, should remove himself elsewhere." There was no remedy to "this impious violation of marriage" because if the wife and children were set free "it would have been a spoliation of their lawful master." In this case, the slave's opportunity to win his freedom and the master's right to his slaves equally trumped the sanctity of marriage. But Calvin refuses to consider this procedure just. "The sanctity of marriage therefore gave way in this case to private right, and this defect is to be reckoned among the others which God tolerated on account of the people's hardness of heart because it could hardly be remedied."[49]

The conclusion that Calvin drew from all of these examples, in which God "designedly deviated from the more perfect rule,"[50] was that while Israel's civil laws may be useful for contemporary commonwealths, they are by no means authoritative, nor are they always the best. Calvin's openness to other legal traditions as legitimate expressions of natural law appears from his constant comparisons between the Mosaic law and Roman law.[51] Where the Mosaic law differed from Roman law, he occasionally finds the former to be superior. For instance, Calvin compares the Roman law negatively with the Mosaic law when it comes to the excessive power of life and death that Roman law gave a father over his children. The Mosaic law was superior because it required parents to follow a court procedure.[52] Calvin similarly claims that "both Solon and the Decemvirs have made a change for the worse wherever they have varied from the law of God."[53]

Calvin's own political predilections were clear. He believed magistrates should try to enforce natural law as much as possible. In his commentary on the incest laws in Leviticus 18, he asks whether a magistrate might decide not to enforce such laws of nature. Civil governments might fail to punish certain forms of immorality, he concedes, but they cannot make such actions moral. "It may indeed be decreed that it should be lawful and unpunished since it is in the power of princes to remit penalties. Yet no legislator can effect that a thing which nature pronounces to be

---

[49] Commentary on Exodus 21:1 [1563]; CO 24:700–701. Calvin describes other weaknesses in the Mosaic laws pertaining to slavery as well. See 21:26; CO 24:626. A final set of cases in which Calvin explained the weakness of the law in terms of the hardness of human hearts related to violence. See 21:18; CO 24: 623–624; Commentary on Numbers 35:19 [1563]; CO 24:638–640. In at least one case, Calvin admits that the law of Moses seems to violate natural law, but then proceeds to speculate about the way the law must have been enforced in such a way as to ensure its justice. Commentary on Deuteronomy 23:15–16 [1563]; CO 24:633–634.

[50] Commentary on Exodus 21:18 [1563]; CO 24:623–624.

[51] He offers comparisons on debt slavery (Commentary on Exodus 22:3 [1563]; CO 24:690); theft (22:1–4; CO 24:687–689); the theft of neighbor's landmark (Commentary on Deuteronomy 19:14 [1563]; CO 24:676); just conduct in war (20:10; CO 24:632); the treatment of slaves (Commentary on Leviticus 25:39 [1563]; CO 24:703); contract law (19:35; CO 24:675–676); and laws on incest (18:6; CO 24:661–663).

[52] Commentary on Deuteronomy 21:18–21 [1563]; CO 24:607–608. Cf. Commentary on Exodus 21:20 [1563]; CO 24:624.

[53] Commentary on Exodus 22:1–4 [1563]; CO 24:687–689.

vicious should not be vicious, and if tyrannical arrogance dares to attempt it, the light of nature will presently shine forth and prevail."[54]

Calvin defends this position with appeals to the laws of nations. The classic case is that of capital punishment for adultery. Calvin observes that even before the law was given to Israel,

> by the universal law of the Gentiles the punishment of death was always awarded to adultery. Wherefore it is all the baser and more shameful in Christians not to imitate at least the heathen. Adultery is punished no less severely by the Julian law than by that of God, while those who boast themselves of the Christian name are so tender and remiss that they visit this execrable offense with a very light reproof.[55]

Calvin attributes the Gentile tendency to punish adultery with death to natural law. "This seems to have been done by a divine instinct, that under the direction and authority of nature the sanctity of marriage might be fortified as by a firm guard." To be sure, with respect to various sexual sins the customs of the nations did not always reflect those nations' own best insights. "Truly the world was beguiled by the wiles of Satan when it suffered the law engraven on all by nature to become obsolete."[56] But Christians should follow the nations' better judgments rather than their lapses. The maximum possible enforcement of God's law, within the constraints of wisdom and circumstances, always remains the appropriate objective.

Calvin's ideal political society was a society of Christians, even though he admitted that most baptized persons in Christendom were and always had been hypocrites.[57] But what about a context in which Christians are mixed with pagans? Calvin was conscious that the New Testament was written in just such a context, and he wrestles with the implications when interpreting Paul's instructions to believers in 1 Corinthians 10:5-9-10, "not to associate with sexually immoral people – not at all meaning the sexually immoral of this world . . . since then you would need to go out of the world. But now I am writing to you not to associate with anyone who bears the name of brother if he is guilty [of such sins]." Calvin observes that when Paul wrote these words, Christians lived "mingled with heathens and dispersed among them." The real question, as far as he is concerned, is how Christians should follow Paul's

---

[54] On the sexuality laws of Leviticus 18, Calvin writes, "If any again object that what has been disobeyed in many countries is not to be accounted the law of the Gentiles, the reply is easy, viz., that the barbarism which prevailed in the East does not nullify that chastity which is opposed to the abominations of the Gentiles, since what is natural cannot be abrogated by any consent or custom." Commentary on Leviticus 18:6 [1563]; CO 24:661–663. Cf. Commentary on Exodus 20:14 [1563]; CO 24:641–642.

[55] Commentary on Deuteronomy 22:22 [1563]; CO 24:648–649.

[56] Commentary on Genesis 38:24 [1554]; CO 23:498–499. Cf. Commentary on Leviticus 20:13 [1563]; CO 24:646–647; Thompson, "Patriarchs, Polygamy and Private Resistance," 13.

[57] Commentary on Luke 2:34 [1555]; CO 45:92. Cf. Commentary on Matthew 7:21 [1555]; CO 45:227.

instructions in the era of Christendom, "when all have given themselves to Christ in name."[58]

Calvin does not think that Paul's instructions refer simply to excommunication. Rather, the apostle was urging Christians to avoid "terms of familiarity [*familiariter*]" or "habits of close intimacy [*consuetedine*]" with the wicked.[59] Indeed, he viewed it as a matter of course that they would be "separated [*segregati*]" from unbelievers.[60] Christians must minimize intimate social interaction with them "lest, while we are mingled together in partaking of food and on other occasions, we be defiled by their pollutions and by little and little become profane."[61] People are "gradually infected ... by the vices of those with whom we have intercourse and familiarity." Indeed, "we are more prone by nature to copy vices than virtues."[62] Unbelievers "will always be attempting by all the artifices they can to make a divorce between us and God," and "if we desire faithfully to serve God there ought to be a perpetual quarrel between us and them." Christians who "seek to curry favor with the ungodly" rarely remain uncorrupted.[63]

Calvin clearly assumed that intimacy with unbelievers in a pluralistic society would force intolerable moral compromises. Christians would be forced to offer approval, consent, and even assistance to impiety and injustice. "As however peace cannot be maintained with the ungodly except on the condition of approving of their vices and wickedness, the apostle immediately adds that holiness is to be followed together with peace, as though he commended peace to us with this exception."[64] Christians are to seek peace, but only insofar as it is compatible with the demands of conscience. "In short, we must abstain from giving any consent, or advice, or approbation, or assistance, for in all these ways we have fellowship."[65]

Such comments make Calvin's political theology seem anything but amenable to a context of principled pluralism. But Calvin offers two important qualifications that reopen the possibility. First, he emphasizes the distinction between a corrupting intimacy and "contracts ... which do not at all diminish our liberty." For "As long as

---

[58] Commentary on 1 Corinthians 5:10 [1546]; CO 49:384.

[59] Commentary on 1 Corinthians 5:9 [1546]; CO 49:383–384. Cf. Commentary on 2 Thessalonians 3:6 [1550]; CO 52:212. But Christians should continue to show them humanity, "for it is one thing to withdraw from intimate acquaintance with an individual, and quite another to keep altogether aloof from his society" (3:14; CO 52:215–216). Cf. Commentary on 1 Thessalonians 2:16 [1550]; CO 52:153; Commentary on Acts 13:51 [1552]; CO 48:316; Commentary on Hebrews 12:16 [1549]; CO 55:180.

[60] Commentary on 1 Corinthians 5:10 [1546]; CO 49:385.

[61] Commentary on Colossians 4:5 [1548]; CO 52:129. Cf. Commentary on Philippians 2:15 [1548]; CO 52: 34–35; Commentary on Genesis 47:3 [1554]; CO 23:566

[62] Commentary on Isaiah 30:1 [1559]; CO 36:506. Cf. Commentary on Psalm 1:2 [1557]; CO 31:38–39.

[63] Commentary on Exodus 34:11 [1563]; CO 24:548–549.

[64] Commentary on Hebrews 12:14 [1549]; CO 55:178.

[65] Commentary on Ephesians 5:11 [1548]; CO 51:217–218. Cf. Commentary on James 3:18 [1550]; CO 55:414.

we live among unbelievers, we cannot escape those dealings with them which relate to the ordinary affairs of life."[66] Thus when Paul calls for separation he "does not mean as to food, clothing, estates, the sun, the air ... but as to those things that are peculiar to unbelievers, from which the Lord has separated us."[67] Calvin concedes that in apostolic times Christians and pagans "were even more intermingled, inasmuch as there could scarcely be found a single pious family that was not surrounded on all sides by unbelievers."[68] Christians should not seek to avoid such social interaction.

Second, while observing that the law of Moses prohibited alliances and marriages between Israel and pagan nations, Calvin concedes that "our condition now-a-days is more free."[69] Calvin supported alliances between Protestant and Catholic nations if those alliances were to the advantage of the former, and while he insisted that believers could not knowingly marry unbelievers, he followed the New Testament in maintaining that a Christian already married to an unbeliever should not seek a divorce. "God therefore has called us in peace to this end, that we might cultivate peace with all by acting properly towards everyone."[70]

What is more, Calvin agreed that Christians need not always publicly reprove vice. There are times for silence, even before magistrates, and silence does not always constitute cowardice. Christians are not called to "assert and proclaim what has been given us by the Lord everywhere and always and among all indiscriminately, for the Lord gives his people the spirit of discretion so that they may know when and how far and to whom it is expedient to speak."[71] Christian witness is always to be accompanied by charity for all persons, regardless of merit, because all are made in the image of God. Believers are called to imitate God, not in his judgment of the world (his unique prerogative), but in his "fatherly goodness and liberality."[72] Christ reached out to adulterers and drunkards, and Christians should likewise eschew self-righteousness, associating with sinners even in baptism and the Eucharist.[73] Such qualifications suggest that Calvin does offer theological resources for Christian participation in pluralistic societies.

---

[66] Commentary on Exodus 34:11 [1563]; CO 24:548–549.

[67] Commentary on 2 Corinthians 6:5 [1548]; CO 50:81.

[68] Commentary on Philippians 2:15 [1548]; CO 52:34–35.

[69] Commentary on Exodus 34:11 [1563]; CO 24:548–549.

[70] Commentary on 1 Corinthians 7:15 [1546]; CO 49:413. Cf. Commentary on 1 Peter 3:1 [1551]; CO 55:253.

[71] Commentary on 1 Peter 3:15 [1551]; CO 55:262. Calvin sometimes seems to want to have it both ways. Silence may be appropriate, but Christians need to find a way to communicate their discontent when God is dishonored. Commentary on Isaiah 36:21 [1559]; CO 36:614. Cf. Commentary on Hosea 14:9 [1557]; CO 42:512–514; Commentary on Acts 24:25 [1554]; CO 48:526; Commentary on Matthew 10:32 [1555]; CO 45:291.

[72] Commentary on Matthew 5:45 [1555]; CO 45:189 (Cf. 5:44; CO 45:188).

[73] Commentary on Luke 5:29 [1555]; CO 45:249; Commentary on Matthew 9:12 [1555]; CO 45:250.

That Calvin finds it necessary to qualify the political relevance of biblical law in light of natural law and the inherent limits of civil law is significant. Despite the reformer's own political conclusions, his two kingdoms theology provides the foundation for a legal theory that is conducive toward contexts of democratic pluralism. It suggests that it is not always best for civil government to act with too much rigor, for magistrates must be sensitive to what is possible in particular circumstances involving human beings whose tendency is toward hardness of heart. Calvin's theology also recognizes the difference between the intimacy and friendship of coreligionists, on the one hand, and the sort of interaction necessary for life in political and civil society, on the other. Along with his observations that, in pluralistic contexts, Joseph and Daniel held higher obligations to fairness and legality than to the enforcement of true religion, the reformer's method of determining the relationship between natural, moral, biblical, and civil law suggests the possibility of a Christian democratic politics, despite what his particular political judgments might otherwise lead us to expect.

FORMS OF GOVERNMENT

In the first edition of the *Institutes,* Calvin declared his lack of interest in discussing the best form of government. Owing to the distinction between the two kingdoms, he believed it was his task simply to summarize what scripture teaches about government, not to wander down the path of political philosophy. By God's providence forms of government vary across time and place, and "it is our duty to show ourselves compliant and obedient to whomever he sets over the places where we live" (4.20.8). In the 1536 edition, Calvin left the discussion at that, but in 1543, he began to argue cautiously that one form of government "far excels others": "aristocracy, or a system compounded of aristocracy and democracy." Calvin justified this new position both on the basis of "experience" and by appeal to scripture. Probably thinking of passages like Exodus 18:13–26 and Deuteronomy 1:9–17, which outline dimensions of a system of aristocratic government for pre-monarchical Israel, he proposed that God "willed to keep [Israel] in the best condition until he should bring forward the image of Christ in David." The best government is that in which "freedom is regulated with becoming moderation and is properly established on a durable basis." The happiest people are "those permitted to enjoy this state; and if they stoutly and constantly labor to preserve and retain it, I grant that they are doing nothing alien to this office." The best magistrates are those who "apply themselves with the highest diligence to prevent the freedom (whose guardians they have been appointed) from being in any respect diminished, far less be violated" (4.20.8).

In 1559 Calvin expanded the argument further, noting that "it is very rare for kings so to control themselves that their will never disagrees with what is just and right." As was the case with his reasoning about the civil law, so here too it was Calvin's conviction about human depravity that set the context for his argument about civil government. "Therefore, men's fault or failing causes it to be safer and more bearable for a number to exercise government so that they may help one another, teach and admonish one another, and, if one asserts himself unfairly, there may be a number of censors and masters to restrain his willfulness" (4.20.8).[74]

The same trajectory of thought that marks these successive editions of the *Institutes* appears in Calvin's commentaries. Through the course of his life, Calvin became increasingly cynical about magistrates in general and kings in particular. Yet when he argued that a democratic aristocracy is the best form of government, he stressed that nowhere does scripture prescribe such a system. Where he did see an ideal form of government in scripture, on the other hand, he insisted that this ideal is not binding for the political order.

Paradoxically, Calvin identified monarchy as the ideal form of government chosen by God for Israel. In his commentary on Genesis 49:8, he writes, "when God would institute a perfect state of government among his people, the monarchical form was chosen by him."[75] The establishment of the Israelite monarchy was clouded by the fact that the people sought it too hastily and for the wrong reasons, but it nevertheless reflected the design of God.[76] Israel's prosperity was inseparable from the coming of the promised king. "Hence we gather that its state was not perfect until it began to be governed by the hand of a king."[77] The high point of Israel's history was therefore the monarchy of David and Solomon, both of whom were types of the future king whose government would one day restore the entire world to order.

Of course, Israel's monarchy was designed to be a monarchy under God and under the law. The Torah's law of the king prohibited kings from practicing polygamy or hoarding wealth, and it required the king to maintain and study a copy of the law in order to understand piety and justice. Calvin emphasizes the constitutional significance of the point.

> The royal power is here circumscribed within certain limits, lest it should exalt itself too much in reliance on the glory of its dignity. For we know how insatiable are the desires of kings, inasmuch as they imagine that all things are lawful to them.

---

[74] See Robert M. Kingdon, "Calvin's Socio-Political Legacy: Collective Government, Resistance to Tyranny, Discipline," *The Legacy of John Calvin* (ed. David Foxgrover; Grand Rapids: CRC Product Services, 2000), 112–116.

[75] Commentary on Genesis 49:8 [1554]; CO 23:597. Cf. Höpfl, *The Christian Polity of John Calvin*, 160–161.

[76] Commentary on Deuteronomy 17:14 [1563]; CO 24:368–369.

[77] Commentary on Numbers 24:17 [1563]; CO 25:293.

Therefore, although the royal dignity may be splendid, God would not have it to be the pretext of unrestrained power but restricts and limits it to legal bounds.[78]

Prevented from ruling for their own interest and exhausting the blood of the people in unjust wars, the kings were to be reminded of their fundamental equality with the people, "lest they should imagine that the law of brotherhood was abolished."[79] The prophets were to proclaim this law to the king, and the best kings were exemplary in their submission to the prophetic word.[80]

It is important to pay attention to Calvin's emphasis that magistrates are subject to the rule of law, because a few scholars have claimed the opposite.[81] Even the "philosophers," Calvin writes, have perceived that "as far as possible judges should be restrained by fixed laws, lest, being left free, they should be swayed this way or that by favor or will."[82] The very purpose of "political government" is that "God's tribunal should be erected on earth, wherein he may exercise the judge's office." Magistrates therefore "should not arrogate to themselves a power uncontrolled by any laws, nor allow themselves to decide anything arbitrarily or wantonly, nor, in a word, assume to themselves what belongs to God. Then and then only will magistrates acquit themselves properly: when they remember that they are the representatives [*vicarios*] of God."[83] Government exists on the "distinct understanding" that it is accountable to God and his natural law.[84] Thus those who refuse to acknowledge God deny themselves just title.[85] Not even the "tacit consent of all men" makes a claim to absolute power legitimate.[86]

A good king is characterized by judgment and justice, which Calvin defines in terms of the rendering of rights. "To do judgment means to render to every one according to his right [*pro ius suum cuique reddere*], but when the two words judgment and justice are connected together, by justice we are to understand equity, so that every one has his own right [*cuique ius suum reddatur*], and by judgment is to be understood the execution of due punishment." The primary test of whether or not kings fulfill this function is whether or not they provide justice for the poor and

---

[78] Commentary on Deuteronomy 17:16 [1563]; CO 24:369.

[79] Commentary on Deuteronomy 17:18 [1563]; CO 24:371–372.

[80] Commentary on Isaiah 39:8 [1559]; CO 36:669–670.

[81] See R. N. Carew Hunt, "Calvin's Theory of Church and State," *Church Quarterly Review* 108 (1929): 56–71, 61–63; Hancock, *Calvin and the Foundations of Modern Politics*, 75–78; David Little, *Religion, Order, and Law* (New York: Harper and Row, 1969), 44.

[82] Commentary on Deuteronomy 1:16 [1563]; CO 24:191–192.

[83] Commentary on Exodus 18:15 [1563]; CO 24:187. Cf. Stevenson, *Sovereign Grace*, 90–91.

[84] Commentary on Psalm 82:6 [1557]; CO 31:771. Cf. Commentary on Daniel 6:21–22 [1561]; CO 41: 23–26.

[85] Commentary on Psalm 110:1 [1557]; CO 32:160–161. Cf. 145:10; CO 32:416. Kings only "retain their authority if they keep an intermediate position between God and men." Commentary on Isaiah 37:16 [1559]; CO 36:626.

[86] Commentary on Daniel 5:18–20 [1561]; CO 40:711–713.

defenseless, for strangers, orphans, and widows.[87] Kings are to be characterized by love and compassion for their subjects according to the old proverb, "Mercy is the virtue most suitable for kings."[88] Thus "to cultivate faithfulness and justice and to temper their government with mercy and kindness is the true and solid foundation of kingdoms."[89]

But the particular responsibility of kings to protect the poor from the lawless exploitation of the powerful requires the grace of God and the influence of his Spirit. "[K]ings can keep themselves within the bounds of justice and equity only by the grace of God, for when they are not governed by the Spirit of righteousness proceeding from heaven, their government is converted into a system of tyranny and robbery."[90] This does not mean that all kings must be Christians. Through common grace, the Spirit gives wisdom in justice and righteousness to pagan kings as well. But Calvin is confident that magistrates who self-consciously follow the Spirit's leading as found in the word of God are the most likely to govern in accord with these principles, and it is "a rare virtue for the man who may do as he pleases to exercise such moderation as not to allow himself liberty in any degree to do evil."[91]

Over the years, Calvin became increasingly critical of monarchs with their tendency to exalt themselves above the people and to defy the rule of law.[92] In his commentary on Genesis he argues that in early human history this was not so common.

> [T]he condition of men was at that time moderate, so that if some excelled others they yet did not on that account domineer nor assume to themselves royal power but, being content with a degree of dignity, governed others by civil laws and had more of authority than power ... [S]uch was their moderation that they cultivated equality with their inferiors, who yielded them a spontaneous rather than a forced reverence.[93]

---

[87] Commentary on Jeremiah 22:1–3 [1563]; CO 38:372. See William R. Stevenson, Jr., "Calvin and Political Issues," *The Cambridge Companion to John Calvin* (Edited by Donald K. McKim; Cambridge: Cambridge University Press, 2004), 173–187; Stevenson, *Sovereign Grace*, 97. A magistrate is responsible for "impartially securing to every man the possession of his own rights [*ius cuique suum aequabiliter reddat*], and his manifesting a spirit of humanity ready at all times to succor the poor and miserable, as well as a spirit determined rigorously to subdue the audacity of the wicked." Commentary on Psalm 72:5 [1557]; CO 31:666–667. Cf. 82:4; CO 31:769–770; 101:1; CO 32:56; Commentary on Amos 2:6 [1559]; CO 43:23; Commentary on Isaiah 10:2 [1559]; CO 36:211.

[88] Commentary on Genesis 4:3 [1554]; CO 23:60.

[89] Commentary on Psalm 45:3 [1557]; CO 31:450–451 (Cf. 61:7; CO 31:584).

[90] Commentary on Psalm 72:4 [1557]; CO 31:665–666. Cf. Commentary on Jeremiah 27:6–7 [1563]; CO 38:543–545.

[91] Commentary on Psalm 101:2 [1557]; CO 31:56–57.

[92] Scholars debate just how inherently problematic monarchy was in Calvin's view. See John T. McNeill, "The Democratic Element in Calvin's Thought," *Church History* 18 (September 1949): 153–171, 159–161.

[93] Commentary on Genesis 10:8 [1554]; CO 23:159.

Now, Calvin muses, one can only affirm the old proverb "Great kingdoms are great robberies."[94] Kings are not satisfied with their power "unless they not only flay their subjects but entirely devour them."[95] They "flatter themselves that they are loosed from the laws which bind the rest of mankind, and the pride of this so greatly blinds them as to make them think it beneath them to submit even to God."[96] Modern kings treat their people like slaves. They regard it as "derogatory to their dignity to converse with their subjects and to employ remonstrance in order to secure their submission," displaying "a spirit of barbarous tyranny in seeking rather to compel than to persuade them."[97] Such kings imagine themselves to be "in no respect indebted to their subjects,"[98] imagining that "their pomp and dignity raises them altogether above the common state of man.[99] Kings are often "fools and blockheads,"[100] and their courts are characterized by corruption, not to mention "hypocrisy and servile flattery."[101]

Calvin complains that the princes of Europe found virtually any excuse to wage war, violating treaties and alliances with impunity.[102] So many people were caught up in the folly of it all (Calvin highlights the Spanish and French in particular), being "desirous to have a powerful and wealthy king reigning over them," and yet the result was their own misery.[103] In later years Calvin's rhetoric intensified. He complained that kings "are ashamed to appear humane and devise means only to exercise tyranny."[104] They "cannot contain themselves in the ordinary rank and station of men but wish to penetrate the clouds and become on a level with God."[105] The typical king was "avaricious and rapacious, cruel and perfidious, as well as forgetful of his duties." Given the state of such governments, "we must weep over the state of the world."[106]

---

[94] Commentary on Genesis 10:11 [1554]; CO 23:160.

[95] Commentary on Genesis 47:23 [1554]; CO 23:575.

[96] Commentary on Genesis 2:10 [1554]; CO 23:49–50. Cf. Commentary on Amos 5:10 [1559]; CO 43: 79–80; Commentary on Isaiah 3:14 [1559]; CO 36:89–90; 10:1; CO 36:211; Commentary on Malachi 2:4 [1559]; CO 44:431–433; Commentary on Jeremiah 19:1–3 [1563]; CO 38:322; Commentary on Daniel 4: 28–32 [1561]; CO 40:682–683.

[97] Commentary on Psalm 45:2 [1557]; CO 31:450. Cf. 2:10–11; CO 31:49–50; Commentary on Jeremiah 37:18 [1563]; CO 39:152.

[98] Commentary on Psalm 101:2 [1557]; CO 31:56–57.

[99] Commentary on Psalm 28:9 [1557]; CO 31:286.

[100] Commentary on Psalm 101:2 [1557]; CO 31:56–57.

[101] Commentary on Matthew 14:3–12 [1555]; CO 45:431. Cf. Commentary on Philippians 4:22 [1548]; CO 51:66; Commentary on Jeremiah 15:17 [1563]; CO 38:229; Commentary on Luke 23:11 [1555]; CO 45:753; Commentary on Daniel 2:46 [1561]; CO 40:612–613; 6:12; CO 41:14; Commentary on Exodus 2:10 [1563]; CO 24:25; Commentary on Genesis 42:15 [1554]; CO 23:532.

[102] Commentary on Habakkuk 2:15–16 [1559]; CO 43:554.

[103] Commentary on Isaiah 19:4 [1559]; CO 36:332.

[104] Commentary on Jeremiah 22:15 [1563]; CO 38:386–387.

[105] Commentary on Daniel 6:16 [1561]; CO 41:17. Cf. Commentary on Ezekiel 17:23 [1565]; CO 40:419.

[106] Commentary on Daniel 6:3–5 [1561]; CO 41:2–4. Cf. 11:6; CO 41:227; Commentary on Isaiah 39:1 [1559]; CO 36:665.

As much as monarchy might in theory be the ideal form of government (it is the form of government divinely chosen for Israel and the kingdom of Christ), human depravity makes the system far too susceptible to corruption and tyranny to be ideal for the political order. Given human depravity, few men or women can handle having such tremendous power placed in their hands, and the people inevitably suffer. Indeed, even if a prince is "the best of men," his rule is inevitably tarnished by less admirable counselors and officers. Calvin had seen it all too often. "This has been more than sufficiently demonstrated by experience."[107]

But Calvin identifies a better form of government, one more "reasonable among a free people" and with precedent in the Mosaic law. The book of Exodus describes how when the task of governing Israel proved too much for Moses his father-in-law Jethro suggested that judges be chosen, not on the basis of wealth or rank, but of virtue, to assist in the responsibilities of governance. Calvin notes that Jethro identified four principal qualifications for such judges: "ability in business, the fear of God, integrity, and the contempt of riches."[108] The leaders were to be elected by the people, a feature on which Calvin places his firm stamp of approval. "And this is the most desirable kind of liberty, that we should not be compelled to obey every person who may be tyrannically put over our heads, but which allows of election, so that no one should rule except he be approved of by us."[109]

Calvin specifically contrasts an elective system with hereditary monarchy. "In this especially consists the best condition of the people, when they can choose by common consent their own shepherds. For when anyone by force usurps the supreme power it is tyranny, and when men become kings by hereditary right it seems not consistent with liberty."[110] A republic is also more stable than other forms of government. "If stability is sought for in any kind of government it surely ought to shine forth in a republic, or at least in an oligarchy, in preference to a despotism, because when all are slaves the king cannot so confidently trust his subjects, through their constant fear for themselves." The most stability comes from expanding participation in government as broadly as possible. "But when all unite in the government and the very lowest receive some mutual advantage from their commonwealth, then, as I have said, superior stability ought to be conspicuous."[111]

But Calvin stresses that the republican (or democratic-aristocratic) form of government is not morally required, because there is no scripturally required form of

---

[107] Commentary on Psalm 101:6 [1557]; CO 32:59.
[108] Commentary on Exodus 18:21 [1563]; CO 24:188.
[109] Calvin notes with satisfaction that "nothing was attempted" without the people's consent. Commentary on Deuteronomy 1:13 [1563]; CO 24:190. Cf. Commentary Exodus 18:23 [1563]; CO 24:189.
[110] Commentary on Micah 5:5 [1559]; CO 43:374.
[111] Commentary on Daniel 2:40–43 [1561]; CO 40:599–603.

government. "Jethro then had no wish to establish a law for posterity but points out a remedy for present inconveniences and a provisional arrangement until the people should obtain a peaceful resting-place."[112] Calvin reminds his readers that it is "not conceded to all to elect their judges ... Whether, then, magistrates are appointed by the suffrages of the people or imposed in any other way, let us learn that they are the necessary ministers of God, to confine all men under the yoke of the laws."[113] The political order is not the realm of the perfect but of the imperfect, and systems of government are determined not by theological prescription but by providence.[114]

Scholars continue to debate Calvin's relationship to democracy, but it is important to distinguish the democratic aristocracy that Calvin favored from certain modern theories of liberal democracy.[115] Calvin did not believe that government derives its power from the consent of the governed. Many "inquire too scrupulously by what right power has been attained, but we ought to be satisfied with this alone, that power is possessed and exercised."[116] Those not blessed with republican liberty have no right to seize it for themselves (4.20.8). Nor did Calvin think that a popularly elected government has the right to violate the moral law of God. On the contrary, the foundation of human society is the recognition that human rights and political authority come from God and are regulated by his law. "All sound knowledge and wisdom must commence with yielding to God the honor which is his due and submitting to be restrained and governed by his word."[117]

---

[112] Commentary Exodus 18:23 [1563]; CO 24:189. See Höpfl, *The Christian Polity of John Calvin*, 151–160.

[113] Commentary on Deuteronomy 16:18 [1563]; CO 24:610–611.

[114] See Marc-Edouard Chenevière, *La pensée politique de Calvin* (Geneva and Paris: Labor and Fides, 1937), 181–190. Excerpt translated and published in Robert M. Kingdon and Robert D. Linder, *Calvin and Calvinism: Sources of Democracy?* Lexington, MA: D. C. Heath and Company, 1970.

[115] For a mild defense of Calvin as a proponent of "conservative democracy" see McNeill, "The Democratic Element in Calvin's Thought." Cf. John T. McNeill, "John Calvin on Civil Government," *Calvinism and the Political Order* (ed. George L. Hunt; Philadelphia: Westminster, 1965), 34–38. Robert M. Kingdon and Robert D. Linder have compiled a number of classic readings representing the various sides of the debate in their *Calvin and Calvinism: Sources of Democracy?* Lexington, MA: D. C. Heath and Company, 1970. Arguing that Calvin was a proponent of democracy is Émile Doumergue, *Jean Calvin, Les Hommes et Les Choses de Son Temps* (Lausanne: Georges Bridel and Company, 1917), 5:440, 450–453, 611–614, 701–706. Taking the opposite position is Georges De Lagarde, *Recherches Sur L'esprit Politique de la Réforme* (Paris: A. and J. Picard and Cie, 1926), 66, 453–455. Mediating positions are offered by Chenevière, *La pensée politique de Calvin*, 181–190; Winthrop S. Hudson, "Democratic Freedom and Religious Faith in the Reformed Tradition," *Church History* 15 (1946): 177–194. See also Ernst Troeltsch, *The Social Teaching of the Christian Churches* (trans. Olive Wyon; 2 vols.; Louisville: Westminster/John Knox Press, 1992 [1912]), 2:628–630.

[116] Commentary on 1 Peter 2:13 [1551]; CO 55:244. Cf. Commentary on Jeremiah 38:1–4 [1563]; CO 39: 156–160.

[117] Commentary on Psalm 82:5 [1557]; CO 31:770–771. Cf. Hancock, *Calvin and the Foundations of Modern Politics*, 70.

Thus an elected government, just like a monarchy, must confess that its authority comes from God, and it is bound to submit to his word when it is proclaimed.[118]

This does not mean that in Calvin's view pastors hold personal or discretionary authority over magistrates. Their sole authority is in the word, and where they go beyond scripture or misapply it their authority is nullified. This means that pastors must respect the difference between the natural moral law revealed in scripture and the civil law as applied and enforced by the magistrate. As for their *conduct*, magistrates have no immunity from the word. Pastors are to follow the example of the prophet who "spared neither the king, nor his counselors, nor the princes of the kingdom."[119] Faithful magistrates will feel anything but threatened by this authority of the word.[120] If anything, its proclamation simply makes their task easier by rendering their subjects more just.[121]

One did not have to be a Christian to be a magistrate, in Calvin's view, but in elections Christian magistrates were obviously to be preferred.[122] Like the pastors of the church, magistrates were to be chosen with reference to the "spiritual endowments" by which God "distinguishes and commends those whom he has destined to any exalted office." They are "not duly ordained unless they are placed in the presence of God, nor rightly inaugurated in their offices except when they consecrate themselves to God himself and when his majesty ... acquires their reverence."[123]

Calvin's conditional support for democratic aristocracy was closely related to his distinction between the nature of the kingdom of Christ, foreshadowed by the monarchical yet typological kingdom of Israel, and the realities of temporal politics among sinful human beings. Where Calvin saw scripture affirming the ideal of monarchy, he agreed that this did not mean monarchy is the best form of temporal government. Where he saw scripture affirming the validity of a democratic aristocracy, he embraced that evidence while maintaining that such a system is not

---

[118] "[E]ven kings are not exempted from the duty of learning what is commonly taught, if they wish to be counted members of the Church; for the Lord would have all, without exception, to be ruled by his word." Commentary on Hosea 5:1 [1557]; CO 42:296–297.

[119] Commentary on Hosea 6:10–11 [1557]; 42:335.

[120] Commentary on Micah 3:9–10 [1559]; 43:331. Cf. Commentary on Amos 8:10–13 [1559]; CO 43:127.

[121] Commentary on Micah 3:11–12 [1559]; CO 43:338. Cf. Commentary on Jeremiah 26:17–19 [1563]; CO 38:533.

[122] Josef Bohatec argues that Calvin held to a sort of "Christian heroism," substituting "pneumatic personalities" in place of the "classical ideal personality." Josef Bohatec, *Calvins Lehre von Staat und Kirche* (Breslau: Marcus Verlag, 1937), Excerpt reprinted in Robert M. Kingdon and Robert D. Linder, *Calvin and Calvinism: Sources of Democracy?* (Lexington, MA: D. C. Heath and Company, 1970), 28–29.

[123] Commentary on Numbers 11:16 [1563]; CO 25:171.

commanded. What was non-negotiable for Calvin was the principle that all governments must rule consistent with the moral law of God.[124]

THEORIES OF RESISTANCE

As was described in Chapter 6, Calvin's two kingdoms doctrine guided his approach
to questions of resistance to tyranny in the 1536 edition of the *Institutes*, leading the
reformer to distinguish between the responsibilities of Christians as individuals and
the responsibilities of Christian magistrates. Understanding Calvin's view of resistance sheds light on the way in which his two kingdoms theology could be applied in
contexts without religious uniformity and where the state took a hostile attitude
toward the church. It was a situation faced by Protestants who constituted
a vulnerable minority under the authority of an unfriendly civil government.

Most important to Calvin was the situation in his native country, France. There,
where persecution raged and where the Huguenots veered ever closer to resistance
against the crown, the Frenchman's followers worked out the implications of their
two kingdoms theology in circumstances vastly different from Geneva. Calvin's
lectures on Daniel, published in 1561, were influenced by the rapidly deteriorating
situation. The hostility of the French crown and the independent existence of the
Protestant church seemed to find a powerful analogy in the situation of Daniel and
his fellow exiles in Babylon.[125] In his dedication of the lectures to the French
Protestants Calvin thus rages against those authorities who "put forward the name
of Christianity and boast themselves to be the best defenders of the Catholic faith
[*fidei catholicae optimos defensores*]," while they seek to drive the scepter of Christ's
kingdom away "by threats and terrors, by the sword and flame."[126] The result was
horrific: "[S]ome were slain in their dwellings, and others by the wayside, while the
bodies of your dead were dragged about as a laughing-stock, your women ravished,
and many of your party wounded, and even the pregnant female with her offspring
pierced through and their homes ransacked and made desolate."[127]

The primary lesson Calvin drew from comparing the experience of Protestants in
France to that of the Israelite exiles in Babylon was not that the faithful should rebel
against the government but that they should continue to submit to it, while waiting
patiently for God's sure deliverance. In his lectures on Jeremiah, Calvin,
following Augustine, calls Christians to follow the advice that the prophet gave the

---

[124] Bohatec writes, "It is noteworthy that Calvin sets the establishment of order theologically over that of
his ruling ideal." Bohatec, *Calvins Lehre von Staat und Kirche*, cited in Kingdon and Linder, *Calvin
and Calvinism*, 29. Cf. Keen, "The Limits and Power of Obedience in the Later Calvin," 270.

[125] Dedication of the Commentary on Daniel to the French Protestants [1561]; CO 18:614–624 (620).

[126] Dedication of the Commentary on Daniel to the French Protestants [1561]; CO 18:617–618.

[127] Dedication of the Commentary on Daniel to the French Protestants [1561]; CO 18:620.

Israelites who were going into exile: to build houses, plant crops, marry, and have children "as though they were at home." In the meantime, they were to have their hearts set on their return to the land of Israel in seventy years, not "raising commotions" or undermining the common good in the name of their eschatological hope, but waiting patiently for God to fulfil his promises.[128] Jeremiah called the exiles not only to reject all forms of rebellion but "to do what they could, to exert themselves to the utmost so that no harm might happen to the Chaldean monarchy."[129] The Jews "ought to have deemed their union such as though they were of the same body [with the Babylonians]. For by saying that their peace would be in the peace of Babylon he intimates that they could not be considered as a separate people until the time of seventy years was completed." In seeking Babylon's welfare they were praying for their own associates in happiness and prosperity. Calvin derives from this "a very useful doctrine – that we ought not only to obey the kings under whose authority we live, but that we ought also to pray for their prosperity, so that God may be a witness of our voluntary subjection."[130] Christians should willingly cooperate with those around them in the affairs of the present life, while setting their hope on the future kingdom.

Thus Calvin steadfastly rejected any interpretation of Christian liberty that would undermine the obligations of service in the political order. Christians should be known for their tendency to honor the social order and for the virtues of respect, peaceableness, and friendship. "A regard ought to be had for all, since we ought to cultivate, as far as we can, peace and friendship with all; there is, indeed, nothing more adverse to concord than contempt."[131] Calvin spilled wells of ink insisting that the establishment of the spiritual kingdom occurs without any injury to political powers because the two kingdoms are distinct. Christians are "to cultivate peace with the wicked" insofar as is possible, preferring to "recede from [our] right, [rather] than originate contention by our own fault."[132]

This is the case, Calvin stressed to the end of his life, even in cases of tyranny. Magistrates "often abuse their power and exercise tyrannical cruelty rather than justice," and such were "almost all the magistrates" when the New Testament was written. Nevertheless, even tyrants are to be honored as having been ordained by God, for there has never been a tyranny, "in which some portion of equity has not appeared," and "some kind of government, however deformed and corrupt it may be,

---

[128] Commentary on Jeremiah 29:3–6 [1563]; CO 38:585. Cf. Commentary on Psalm 137:4 [1557]; CO 32: 369–370.

[129] Commentary on Jeremiah 29:7 [1563]; CO 38:586.

[130] Commentary on Jeremiah 29:7 [1563]; CO 38:587–588. Cf. Commentary on 1 Timothy 2:2 [1548]: CO 52:266.

[131] Commentary on 1 Peter 2:17 [1551]; CO 55:247.

[132] Commentary on Genesis 32:5 [1554]; CO 23:438. Cf. Commentary on Acts 17:7 [1554]; CO 48:398; 16:20; CO 48:383.

is still better and more beneficial than anarchy."[133] This emphasis held strong even in Calvin's later lectures on Daniel and Jeremiah. At times he got carried away when depicting the terrors of anarchy (though no more so than did British Prime Minister Winston Churchill when he said he would consider accepting the devil himself as an ally against Adolf Hitler). "It is better that the devil should rule men under any sort of government than that they should be set free without any law, without any restraint."[134] Christians must always fulfil their vocations, yielding even to unjust masters their legitimate rights.[135]

But the two kingdoms doctrine shaped Calvin's understanding of the extent to which Christians should obey tyrants. Whereas Christians are never to yield to tyranny in Christ's spiritual kingdom, in the temporal affairs of the political order, they must be prepared for sacrifice. As Calvin explains in his commentary on Acts, "though the administration of earthly or civil rule [*terreni vel civilis imperii*] be confused or perverse, yet the Lord will have men to continue still in subjection. But when the spiritual government [*spirituale regimen*] degenerates, the consciences of the godly are at liberty and set free from obeying unjust authority."[136] By extension, when civil government invades the spiritual kingdom, such as by commanding Christians to act impiously or unjustly, Christians must disobey. As Peter and John declared to the Sanhedrin, "We must obey God rather than men." Here, Calvin clarifies, we do not really violate the authority of magistrates at all, because the authority they have comes from God.[137] Thus when their commands contradict God's commands they are automatically nullified by the authorizing power. At the point where a magistrate commands one of his subjects to disobey God, he no longer acts as God's representative. "We must obey princes and others which are in authority but in such a way that they do not rob God (who is the chief king, father, and lord) of his right and authority."[138]

In 1559 Calvin added this argument to the *Institutes*. Defending Daniel's disobedience to the Persian king in Daniel 6:22–23, he declares that "the king had exceeded his limits and had not only been a wrongdoer against men, but in lifting up his horns against God had himself abrogated his power" (4.20.32). He makes the point even more explicitly in his lectures, noting that the disobedient prophet claimed he had done nothing against the king. How could Daniel say this? The answer is that he

---

[133] Commentary on 1 Peter 2:14 [1551]; CO 55:245. Cf. Commentary on Psalm 45:6 [1557]; CO 31:451–452.
[134] Commentary on Jeremiah 30:9 [1563]; CO 38:618. Cf. 27:6–7; CO 38:544.
[135] Commentary on Genesis 16:8 [1554]; CO 23:227–228; Commentary on Daniel 4:19 [1561]; CO 40: 665–666.
[136] Commentary on Acts 23:5 [1554]; CO 48:505–506.
[137] Commentary on Acts 5:29 [1552]; CO 48:109.
[138] Commentary on Acts 4:19 [1552]; CO 48:88. This puts the point more narrowly than Keen, who claims Calvin believed that the magistrate no longer acts as a magistrate if he willfully neglects the preservation of law. Keen, "The Limits and Power of Obedience in the Later Calvin," 274.

obeyed the king *insofar as the king held authority over him.* "Daniel was not so bound to the king of the Persians when he claimed for himself as a god what ought not to be offered to him. We know how earthly empires are constituted by God only on the condition that he deprives himself of nothing." This is why the Apostle Peter commanded Christians, "Fear God, Honor the king" (1 Peter 2:17).

> The two commands are connected together and cannot be separated from one another. The fear of God ought to precede, that kings may obtain their authority [*autoritatem*]. For if any one begins his reverence of an earthly prince by rejecting that of God, he will act preposterously, since this is a complete perversion of the order of nature [*naturae ordinem*] ... For earthly princes lay aside their power [*potestate*] when they rise up against God and are unworthy of being reckoned in the number of mankind. *We ought rather utterly to defy than to obey them whenever they are so restive and wish to spoil God of his rights, and, as it were, to seize upon his throne and draw him down from heaven.*[139]

Calvin is not saying here, as some scholars have claimed, that magistrates who rise up against God forfeit their office entirely. He is not saying that usurpation of God's throne is a legitimate cause for full scale rebellion. The point, rather, is that with respect to the case at hand the magistrate has laid aside his authority and may justly be defied.[140]

In such circumstances, subjects are implicated in the impiety of their magistrates if they do *not* disobey them. In his commentary on Hosea, Calvin explains that the Israelites could not shift the blame for their idolatry to the rulers who had led them in it. "The people might indeed have appeared to be excusable since religion had not been changed by their voice, or by public consent, or by any contrivance of the many, but by the tyrannical will of the king alone," but "the prophet shows that all were implicated in the same guilt before God because the people adopted with alacrity the impious forms of worship which the king had commanded." The Protestants in France faced a similar temptation.

> If any one should now ask whether they are excusable who are tyrannically drawn away into superstitions, as we see to be done under the papacy, the answer is ready, that those are not here absolved who regarded men more than God. Nor is terror, as we know, a sufficient excuse, when we prefer our own life to the glory of God, and when, anxious to provide for ourselves and to avoid the cross, we deny God or turn aside from making a confession of the right and pure faith.[141]

---

[139] "*Potius ergo conspuere oportet in ipsorum capita quam illis parere, ubi ita proterviunt ut velint etiam spoliare Deum iure suo, et quasi occupare solium eius, ac si possent eum e coelo detrahere.*" Commentary on Daniel 6:21–22 [1561]; CO 41:25–26. Emphasis added. Cf. Commentary on Luke 2:49 [1555]; CO 45:106. Cf. Commentary on Isaiah 49:25 [1559]; CO 37:213.

[140] See Stevenson, *Sovereign Grace*, 32; Quentin Skinner, *The Foundations of Modern Political Thought* (2 vols.; Cambridge: Cambridge University Press, 1978), 2:219–221.

[141] Commentary on Hosea 5:11 [1557]; CO 42:310–311. Cf. 7:3; CO 42:340–341; 9:15; CO 42:406.

Not only should Christians disobey such tyranny, but they ought to challenge it publicly. "For there is hardly any conduct more offensive or more fitted to disturb our minds than when the worst examples of every sort are publicly exhibited by magistrates, while no man utters a syllable against them, but almost all give their approbation."[142]

Calvin believed subjects have the obligation to criticize and disobey their magistrates when they violate justice, not only when they violate piety.[143] For example, he praises the midwives who defied Pharaoh's decree to kill the male Hebrew children. While Calvin does not believe the midwives should have lied, he endorses their refusal to cooperate with injustice:

> But this doctrine extends still more widely, for many would be more than preposterously wise while, under pretext of due submission, they obey the wicked will of kings in opposition to justice and right [*ius et fas*] ... Yea, to gratify the transitory kings of earth they take no account of God, and thus, which is worst of all, they designedly oppose pure religion with fire and sword. It only makes their effrontery more detestable that while they knowingly and willingly crucify Christ in his members, they plead the frivolous excuse that they obey their princes according to the word of God, as if he, in ordaining princes, had resigned his rights to them, and as if every earthly power which exalts itself against heaven ought not rather most justly to be made to give way.

When a person acts unjustly, it is not a valid excuse that the unjust action has been commanded by a magistrate. Obedience to such unjust laws is "criminal obedience [*scelerati obsequii*]."[144]

These are pregnant words and potentially inflammatory in a revolutionary setting, but it is crucial to interpret them within the parameters of Calvin's broader political theology. All people are called to disobey and resist unjust laws, but each person is to do so in a way *appropriate to her vocation*. For instance, in his commentary on John 2, the story of Christ's cleansing of the temple, Calvin writes,

> let each of us apply to the invitation of Christ, that – so far as lies in our power – we may not permit the temple of God to be in any way polluted. But at the same time,

---

[142] Commentary on Isaiah 3:12 [1559]; CO 36:89. Cf. Commentary on Daniel 4:10–16 [1561]; CO 40: 658–659.

[143] Christians are innocent when they disobey and protest the "impious and unjust edicts of kings." Commentary on Jeremiah 37:18 [1563]; CO 39:152. This is in contrast to the claim of Nicholas Wolterstorff, *The Mighty and the Almighty: An Essay in Political Theology* (Cambridge: Cambridge University Press, 2012), 74; Brandt B. Boeke, "Calvin's Doctrine of Civil Government," *Studia Biblica et Theologica* 11 (1981): 73.

[144] Commentary on Exodus 1:17 [1563]; CO 24:17–18. Unlike Dietrich Bonhoeffer, Calvin did not think a Christian should ever intentionally violate God's law. The midwives took the right action, he argues, but they should not have lied about it (1:18; CO 24:18–19).

we must beware lest any man transgress the bounds of his calling. All of us ought to have zeal in common with the Son of God but all are not at liberty to seize a whip that we may correct vices with our hands, for we have not received the same power, nor have we been entrusted with the same commission.[145]

Calvin makes the same point with reference to Jesus' rebuke of Peter for drawing his sword in defense of his lord. Peter was zealous for a just cause, but he failed to "consider what his calling demands." By offering violent resistance, "he acts the part of a highwayman, because he resists the power which God has appointed."[146] Ordinarily Christians "ought to be prepared for enduring the cross," remembering that "He who strikes with the sword shall perish by the sword." The only exceptions are when institutions and laws provide opportunity for legitimate civil action. "We must also beware of repelling our enemies by force or violence, even when they unjustly provoke us, *except so far as the institutions and laws of the community admit.*"[147]

In fact, Calvin interprets this last clause somewhat flexibly. In his commentary on Matthew he observes that the law sometimes authorizes a private person's use of force [*privatis hominibus . . . usus gladii*], thus making her a public person.

> First, we must make a distinction between a civil forum and the forum of conscience [*civile et conscientiae forum*], for if any man resist a robber he will not be liable to public punishment, because the laws arm him against one who is the common enemy of mankind . . . [However,] in order that a man may properly and lawfully defend himself he must first lay aside excessive wrath and hatred and desire of revenge . . . As this is of rare occurrence, or rather, as it scarcely ever happens, Christ properly reminds his people of the general rule, that they should entirely abstain from using the sword.[148]

Here the two kingdoms distinction explicitly informs Calvin's approach to the question of violence. Christians are called to take up their cross and follow Christ, but just as Christian liberty does not destroy the legitimate authority of the political order, so the call to bear the cross does not nullify the legitimate vocational and civil prerogatives of the political order. It always remains within the prerogative of political officials to resist tyranny to the extent permitted by their vocations (4.20.31).

Calvin did not claim that resistance on the part of lesser magistrates could only take place when God's law is at stake rather than constitutional or secular concerns.[149] On the contrary, he justified the Huguenot cause in the first war of

---

[145] Commentary on John 2:17 [1553]; CO 47:46. Cf. Commentary on Matthew 21:12 [1555]; CO 45:580.

[146] Commentary on John 18:10 [1553]; CO 47:394.

[147] Commentary on John 18:11 [1553]; CO 47:395. Emphasis added.

[148] Commentary on Matthew 26:52 [1555]; CO 45:731.

[149] This is contrary to Keen, "The Limits and Power of Obedience in the Later Calvin," 265, 272.

religion on definitively constitutional grounds. Furthermore, he praised constitutional structures that make rulers accountable to their subjects, and his very emphasis on the magisterial vocation implies a reliance on constitutional considerations.[150] Nor did Calvin forbid lesser magistrates from practicing *active* resistance to tyranny, as his defense of the Huguenot cause demonstrates.[151] Most scholars agree that Calvin affirmed a right of passive resistance on the part of private individuals and a right of active resistance on the part of lesser magistrates.[152] This is true even though Calvin's theory of active resistance was much less defined and his personal proclivities were much more restrained than were the theories of later Calvinist writers.[153]

W. Nijenhuis challenges this consensus, claiming that in sermons Calvin preached during the last few years of his life he began to defend violent resistance to tyranny on the part of Christians who were not magistrates.[154] But the evidence he

[150] See Skinner, *The Foundations of Modern Political Thought*, 2:233–234; McNeill, "The Democratic Element in Calvin's Thought," 164–165; Commentary on Romans 13:4 [1556]; CO 49:251. Cf. Winthrop S. Hudson, "Calvin, a Source of Resistance Theory, and Therefore of Democracy," in Robert M. Kingdon and Robert D. Linder, *Calvin and Calvinism: Sources of Democracy?* (Lexington, MA: D. C. Heath and Company, 1970), 15–24, 23.

[151] This is also contrary to Keen, "The Limits and Power of Obedience in the Later Calvin," 272.

[152] Thompson, "Patriarchs, Polygamy and Private Resistance," 15–18, 27; Stevenson, *Sovereign Grace*, 32–35, 54; Boeke, "Calvin's Doctrine of Civil Government," 67–73; Larson, *Calvin's Doctrine of the State*, 55–60; McNeill, "John Calvin on Civil Government," 38–40; Kingdon, "Calvin's Socio-Political Legacy," 116–120. David Willis-Watkins, "Calvin's Prophetic Reinterpretation of Kingship," *Probing the Reformed Tradition* (ed. Elsie Anne McKee and Brian Armstrong; Louisville: Westminster/John Knox, 1989), 116–134, 126–129; David M. Whitford, "Robbing Paul to Pay Peter: The Reception of Paul in Sixteenth Century Political Theology." *A Companion to Paul in the Reformation* (ed. R. Ward Holder; Leiden: Brill, 2009), 575–606, 597–605; Skinner, *The Foundations of Modern Political Thought*, 2:192–193, 214, 219–221, 232–233. I am unpersuaded by Whitford's and Skinner's claims that Calvin took a more radical stance in his later years. On the implications of Calvin's argument about the lesser magistrates for democracy see McNeill, "The Democratic Element in Calvin's Thought," 163–165; Skinner, *The Foundations of Modern Political Thought*, 2:232–233; H. A. Lloyd, "Calvin and the Duty of Guardians to Resist," *Journal of Ecclesiastical History* 32 (1981): 65–67 and Peter Stein, "Calvin and the Duty of Guardians to Resist: A Comment," *Journal of Ecclesiastical History* 32 (1981): 69–70.

[153] While he supported the Huguenots cause, he did so only because he endorsed their position on constitutional grounds. See Stevenson, *Sovereign Grace*, 140; Skinner, *The Foundations of Modern Political Thought*, 2:192–193; Winthrop S. Hudson, "Calvin a Source of Resistance Theory, and Therefore of Democracy," 21.

[154] According to Nijenhuis, when Calvin declared in a 1560 sermon on 1 Samuel that God often raises up one of his servants with the special vocation of saving his people, it was "the first step on the way to acknowledging the private citizen's right of resistance." W. Nijenhuis, *Ecclesia Reformata: Studies on the Reformation* (Leiden: Brill, 1994), 84. By 1562, he claims, Calvin's ideas on resistance had become "more ambivalent," laying more emphasis on resistance, "even by the private citizen." Thus Calvin believed, "If the honour of God is violated, resistance is required, even armed resistance by the private citizen. For the first time, we now hear the Reformer speaking of two general rules ('reigles générelles'). The first is the one we know already: resistance may be offered only by those into whose hands God has put the sword, that is, the lower magistrates .... But, on 31 July 1562, we find an interesting new accent in Calvin's public pronouncements ... he comes this time to the

musters is not convincing. It is true that Calvin believed God could authorize a person to wield the sword outside of the ordinary channels of his providence and that God did so in Old Testament days through figures like Moses and Phinehas.[155] But Calvin stresses, in a commentary published only a year before he died, that

> private persons [*homines privatos*] would act improperly and would be by no means countenanced by his example if they sought to repress wrong by force and arms. Thus far we should imitate Moses in rendering aid to the suffering and oppressed as far as our means go ... but we must leave it to the judges who are invested with public authority [*publico imperio*] to draw the sword of vengeance.[156]

In fact, even in Calvin's sermons on 1 Samuel, as Keen has shown, the French reformer enjoins obedience to the worst of monarchs and under the worst of circumstances. His rhetoric intensified and his criticism of monarchy grew sharper, but the basic principles of his political theology did not change.[157]

In his lectures on Daniel, Calvin spoke in increasingly dark terms about political powers – monarchs and empires in particular – that oppose themselves to the work of Christ's kingdom. In the Dedication to the French Protestants, he writes that "all earthly power which is not founded on Christ [*quae in Christo fundata non est*] must fall." Those kingdoms that "obscure Christ's glory by extending themselves too much ... shall feel by sorrowful experience how horrible a judgment will fall

formulation of a second 'reigle commune': not only the lower magistrates, but all citizens are called upon to resist an evil ruler so as to protect the poor." Nijenhuis offers the following quote from Calvin's sermon as his chief evidence for this claim: "'[W]e should resist evil as much as we can. And this has been enjoined on all people in general; I tell you, this was said not only to princes, magistrates, and public prosecutors, but also to all private persons.'" Yet he admits that this entails a contradiction within Calvin's thought. "How the two rules could be harmonized is not clear. It seems that life had become stronger than doctrine" (91–92). The only other evidence he offers is a reference to the murder by a 'homo privatus' of Antoine de Bourbon, King of Navarre, as a "reason for thanksgiving to God." Nijenhuis assumes this meant that Calvin approved of the act of murder (93). Yet Calvin had always insisted that God might raise up a deliverer for his people even from among the ranks of the wicked, and that Christians can observe this providence at work with adoration and thanksgiving without approving it. This evidence does not demonstrate that Calvin changed his position in any way. Calvin argued that all people, not only magistrates, should "resist evil *as much as we can*," but that is hardly the same thing as arguing that all people can take up the sword, *regardless of vocation*. The emphasis on vocation is so fundamental to Calvin, as Nijenhuis himself admits, that it requires much more than an ambiguous use of the phrase "resist evil" to demonstrate that he had abandoned it in favor of a position that was inherently contradictory. Cf. Robert M. Kingdon, *Geneva and the Consolidation of the French Protestant Movement 1564–1572* (Madison, WI: University of Wisconsin Press, 1967), 155.

[155] See Commentary on Psalm 106:31 [1557]; CO 32:128. Cf. Commentary on Joshua 2:7 [1564]; CO 25: 441–442. Thompson notes that while Calvin declared that God could raise up exceptional deliverers, he never outlined contemporary circumstances under which this might occur, nor did he ever support such a scenario in practice. Thompson, "Patriarchs, Polygamy and Private Resistance," 27.

[156] Commentary on Exodus 2:12 [1563]; CO 24:27.

[157] Keen, "The Limits and Power of Obedience in the Later Calvin," 254–257, 263. Cf. Willis-Watkins, "Calvin's Prophetic Reinterpretation of Kingship," 125–129.

upon them unless they willingly submit themselves to the sway of Christ [*se Christi imperio subiiciant*]!"[158]

Does this mean the progress of Christ's kingdom would overthrow a kingdom like that of France? Later in the lectures, Calvin wrestles with Daniel's prophecy that the messiah would "break up the political order which we know God approves of and has appointed and established by his power."[159] He answers the question by distinguishing between what is proper to Christ's kingdom and what is accidental to it, or between what Christ's kingdom does directly, and what it does indirectly. Christ does not break such empires "directly [*simpliciter*]," "since all the kingdoms of this world are clearly founded on the power and beneficence of Christ [*fundata esse omnia regna huius mundi in Christi virtute et beneficentia*]."[160] Thus "Christ's kingdom is not contrary to their power." Rather, political empires are broken up "accidentally [*accidentaliter*]" because they oppose themselves to Christ's kingdom.[161] Daniel's prophecy is simply a declaration of "how evanescent and uncertain are all the empires of the world which are not founded in God and not united to the kingdom of Christ [*non fundata essent in Deo, et non coniuncta essent regno Christi*]." Without Christ, political power is "worthless."[162]

There is no doubt that Calvin believed a well-established and prosperous commonwealth is grounded in subservience to Christ, the lord of both the spiritual and the political kingdoms. Although all political rule will one day pass away, during the present age, those that turn themselves against Christ and his gospel will find their power to be particularly fleeting. But Calvin is emphatic that this does not in any way justify triumphalism or rebellion on the part of Christians. True, Christians are called to wage a constant struggle against the Devil and the world, but Calvin warns his readers that this is a spiritual struggle, one waged with the armor and weapons of faith, righteousness, the Spirit, and the word.[163] Focusing on a military or political struggle is a dangerous distraction for Christians because "our difficulties are far greater than if we had to fight with men. There we resist human strength, sword is opposed to sword, man contends with man, force is met by force, and skill by skill, but here the case is widely different." When it is Satan who is attacking us, to struggle against flesh and blood must "not only be useless, but highly pernicious."[164] The Apostle Paul compares Christians to warriors, but "their condition as warriors

[158] Dedication of the Commentary on Daniel to the French Protestants [1561]; CO 18:617.

[159] Commentary on Daniel 2:31–35 [1561]; CO 40:592.

[160] Commentary on Daniel 2:40–43 [1561]; CO 40:601–602. "The kingdom of Christ is said to break up all the empires of the world, not directly, but only accidentally, as the phrase is. [*Dicitur regnum Christi conterere omnia mundi imperia, non simpliciter, sed per accidens, ut loquuntur*]."

[161] Commentary on Daniel 2:31–35 [1561]; CO 40:592.

[162] Commentary on Daniel 2:44–45 [1561]; CO 40:607.

[163] Commentary on Ephesians 6:15 [1548]; CO 51:236. Cf. Commentary on Luke 1:71 [1555]; CO 45:48.

[164] Commentary on Ephesians 6:12 [1548]; CO 51:233–234.

consists not in inflicting evils but rather in patience." Christians demonstrate their mettle through their willingness to suffer.[165]

Thus when critics accused the French Protestants of seeking to overthrow all order and authority, Calvin retorted that the charge was absurd: "as if he who offers a celestial [kingdom] [*coeleste offert*] to the least and most despised of the people would snatch away the empires of the earth from its monarchs [*terrena imperia raperet monarchis*]."[166] He drew attention to his efforts to render Protestants submissive and even claimed credit for the fact that so many spurned rebellion. "It is not necessary for me to relate how strenuously I have hitherto endeavored to cut off all occasion for tumult; ... it is no fault of mine if the kingdom of Christ does not progress quietly without any injury. And I think it is owing to my carefulness that private persons [*privati homines*] have not transgressed beyond their bounds."[167] If the kingdom of France was going to be overthrown, it would be due to its hostility to the gospel of Christ, not the preaching of the reformers or the faithfulness of French Protestants. God could use whatever means he willed, and in the meantime faithful Christians were simply to "obey and suffer." It was therefore God of whom Calvin was thinking when he declared in the second last section of the *Institutes*, "Let the princes hear and be afraid" (4.20.31).[168]

Calvin's two kingdoms theology led him to call Christians to support and submit to the powers that exist, spurning the temptation of religious war, even as he outlined a means by which lesser magistrates could resist tyranny in accord with their vocation. The result was a political theology that prioritized the legitimacy of political order even as it sought to limit that political order through the accountability of law and the authority of multiple levels of magisterial power. Like his theories of law and of forms of government, Calvin's theory of resistance was informed by scripture and fidelity to the lordship of Christ, even as it sought to distinguish the prerogatives of political authorities from the righteousness of the kingdom of Christ. It provided the faithful with a paradigm for following Christ as an oppressed minority under a tyrannical regime.

---

[165]   Commentary on 2 Timothy 2:3 [1548]; CO 52:361.
[166]   Dedication of the Commentary on Daniel to the French Protestants [1561]; CO 18:618.
[167]   Dedication of the Commentary on Daniel to the French Protestants [1561]; CO 18:619–620.
[168]   See Willis-Watkins, "Calvin's Prophetic Reinterpretation of Kingship," 125–129.

Conclusion

Calvin's Two Kingdoms and Liberal Democracy

Calvin was not a political liberal. He died long before anything like liberalism had emerged as a coherent political tradition. Key figures in the genealogy of liberal democracy such as John Milton, John Locke, John Adams, and James Madison were raised in the Calvinist tradition and influenced by Calvinist political thought, and liberalism eventually thrived in lands with a strong Calvinist presence. The orthodox Calvinist and American founding father John Witherspoon even synthesized confessional Calvinism and classical liberalism in a way that became representative of the developing tradition.[1] But it is a vain exercise to speculate how Calvin would have responded to such political and philosophical developments. Indeed, it would be unhelpful even if we could know what Calvin would have thought. Calvin's relevance for contemporary Christian public engagement lies not in his political actions or opinions but in his political *theology*.

True, there can be no doubt that Calvin's theology stands in acute conflict with the Kantian sort of liberalism that makes the human person an autonomous end in herself, let alone with the liberalism of the early John Rawls, with its insistence that religion has no place in democratic politics. For the reformer of Geneva those who find communion with God in the kingdom of Christ necessarily seek to follow God's will in every area of life. As Timothy P. Jackson argues (against the early John Rawls), there can be no Christian acceptance of liberal democracy if the latter demands the rejection of Christ in favor of some other comprehensive doctrine.[2]

---

[1] See Jeffry H. Morrison, *John Witherspoon and the Founding of the American Republic* (Notre Dame: University of Notre Dame Press, 2007).

[2] Timothy P. Jackson, "The Return of the Prodigal? Liberal Theory and Religious Pluralism," *Religion in Contemporary Liberalism* (ed. Paul J. Weitman; Notre Dame: University of Notre Dame Press, 1997), 182–217; Timothy P. Jackson, "To Bedlam and Part Way Back: John Rawls and Christian Justice," *Faith and Philosophy* 8:4 (October, 1991): 423–447; Cf. Timothy P. Jackson, *Political Agape*.

But better versions of political liberalism – even that of the later Rawls – do not demand such religious conversion.[3] Rather, they call each of the various individuals and groups within a pluralistic society to endorse the institutions, practices, and principles of liberalism because of commitments arising from their own comprehensive doctrines. The appropriate commitment to liberalism described by liberals such as Jeffrey Stout is therefore *penultimate* (or *secular*), rather than ultimate.[4] It does not require Christians to leave their faith at the door of the voting booth, legislative chamber, or court, let alone to swear an allegiance that transcends the obligations of one's baptism in Christ. It merely asks that, for the sake of the common good and civic virtue, Christians seek to engage political questions on the basis of arguments and premises that their nonbelieving neighbors can reasonably accept, to propose laws and policies on the basis of procedures that all can regard as just, and to serve together in the building of communities in which Christians and Buddhists, Muslims and Atheists, Agnostics and Spiritualists alike can expect to be treated as equal citizens with equal rights.

The argument of this conclusion is that Calvin's two kingdoms doctrine warrants and guides a commitment to this kind of political liberalism as a faithful expression of the service of Christ. I begin by briefly reviewing Calvin's political theology as analyzed in this book. Though I acknowledge various ways in which Calvin's life and work contradicts a democratic ethos, I argue that the two kingdoms doctrine itself encourages a commitment to political liberalism as the form of government most appropriate for societies characterized by religious, social, and moral pluralism, and that it provides the church with a model for how to fulfill its mission to Christ in light of this commitment. I then identify three general implications of Calvin's two kingdoms theology for contemporary Christian political engagement: America as a secular society, natural law as public reason, and the church as a public church.

Given that this book has focused on Calvin's political theology in its own time and context, any account of what a critical appropriation of that theology might look like for the twenty-first century will necessarily be suggestive. But if my description of the central theological principles of Calvin's thought has been clear and persuasive, I believe the contemporary implications that I draw should make sense to Christians committed to political liberalism as a form of government.

---

[3] See especially Rawls's 1997 essay, "The Idea of Public Reason Revisited," published as Part 4 in John Rawls, *Political Liberalism: Expanded Edition* (New York: Columbia University Press, 2005), 440–490.

[4] Jeffrey Stout, *Democracy and Tradition* (Princeton: Princeton University Press, 2004).

CALVIN'S TWO KINGDOMS THEOLOGY: SUMMARY

In the first half of the sixteenth century, Calvin's two kingdoms theology offered the sharpest distinction between church and commonwealth articulated by a mainstream theologian who did not reject Christian participation in civil government. The papacy claimed that civil government was ultimately subject to the authority of the pope as the vicar of Christ. Luther and Melanchthon distinguished between the two kingdoms but relegated matters of discipline and ecclesiastical order to the civil realm. Zwingli, Bullinger, and the apologists of the royal supremacy in England adopted the caesaropapist position that subjected the church and its discipline to the control of the civil magistracy. And the Anabaptists, when they were not turning toward apocalypticism, separated church and civil government so far apart as to reject Christian participation in civil government. But against his fellow magisterial reformers Calvin insisted on the autonomy of the church from the state with respect to worship, discipline, and poor relief. Against the papacy he rejected claims that the church holds magisterial authority over ecclesiastical or temporal affairs. And against the Anabaptists he insisted on the legitimacy of civil government as an institution in which Christians should participate. He worked hard to implement this political theological vision in circumstances as diverse as Geneva, which could approximate a well-regulated Christian commonwealth, and France, in which the true church was organizationally autonomous and endured the persecution of a hostile state.

Calvin's eschatology led him to argue that human beings were made for communion with God and that creation is destined for a spiritual transformation into the eternal kingdom of Christ. Although the fall into sin disrupted this process, God graciously provided means for the creation's preservation. Through his providence, the influence of natural law, and the political order, God preserves society and its moral order. Christians thus have common ground with nonbelievers with reference to temporal affairs, for a society does not need to be Christian in order to be meaningfully just.

Although Calvin described the kingdom of Christ as a fundamentally spiritual entity, by the word "spiritual," he did not mean that the kingdom is immaterial, otherworldly, or otherwise irrelevant to creation. On the contrary, he insisted that the kingdom of Christ brings about the restoration of the entire material creation. Calvin used the Aristotelian distinction between substance and accidents to distinguish between the temporal affairs of life, which pass away, and the world itself, which will be restored and transformed in accord with its original eschatological purpose. Only through participation in Christ, he argued, can human beings rightfully possess and enjoy the blessings of creation, in hope of this future restoration.

Calvin's eschatological theology thus grounds a paradoxical understanding of the relation between the kingdom of Christ and the present world. On the one hand, Christians should never seek the full realization of the kingdom in temporal affairs, so falling into the dangerous errors of utopianism or triumphalism. On the other hand, Christians should seek the manifestation of the justice and piety of the kingdom in temporal affairs. The church is called to point the world to the gospel that reveals creation's restoration in the kingdom of Christ.

Calvin introduced the two kingdoms doctrine in order to clarify the nature of Christian liberty, given this tension between the "already" and the "not yet." Although Christians are justified by faith alone and sanctified by the Spirit alone, and so ultimately free from all the traditions and laws of human beings, they are nevertheless subject to temporal authorities as necessities of the present life. Government is one means by which human beings serve one another in a fallen world, a vocation necessary to the demands of love. Here again the implications for Christian politics are somewhat paradoxical. On the one hand, Christians should do all within the power of their vocations and the possibility of their circumstances to exhibit the righteousness of Christ's kingdom. Liberty and equality are spiritual ideals worth pursuing as expressions of believers' identity in Christ. On the other hand, love demands that Christians serve one another and sometimes even submit to unjust circumstances for the sake of the common good. Thus Christians should be realistic, never imagining that the temporal versions of liberty, equality, piety, or justice will be ultimately satisfying. Calvin thus distinguished between spiritual (i.e., inward) righteousness and civil (i.e., outward) righteousness and between the spiritual use of the law and its civil use. He contrasted what Christ accomplishes by his word and Spirit to what civil magistrates can accomplish by secular means. This by no means suggests that the civil forms of piety and justice should be despised. On the contrary, such forms are essential to human society. But a government that imagines it can establish spiritual virtue or faith in its citizens is dangerously utopian. Calvin's two kingdoms theology demands humility on the part of those who exercise political power.

Calvin identified the church as the expression of the kingdom of Christ in the present age, both insofar as the church ministers the gospel and insofar as it is the society of those regenerated by that gospel. The church's primary task and chief qualifying mark is to proclaim the word of God – the gospel of restoration and the moral law of piety and justice. Its entire ministry is contained within the word of Christ, and even its sacraments and discipline are merely extensions of that word. Yet when the church faithfully proclaims God's word, it speaks with binding authority to magistrate, citizen, and subject alike. Only the word can point human beings to their ultimate purpose, and only the word and Spirit can restore them to that purpose.

At the same time, as an institution of the present age, the church also contains a temporal or political dimension that must be sharply distinguished from the spiritual kingdom of Christ. The church must enact an order and polity for its worship and life, a process that requires prudence and the use of discretionary authority. But Calvin charged the Roman church with conflating the political and the spiritual by claiming the right to exercise binding spiritual authority over spiritual and political matters alike. In so doing, it invaded the kingdom of Christ, ruling tyrannically over the consciences of believers. Calvin insisted that the church cannot bind consciences in matters of polity which are necessarily subject to circumstances and prudence. The gospel and the moral will of God cannot be conflated with the contextual demands of love and prudence amid the complexities of politics. The faithful church therefore restrains its teaching and discipline to the constraints of God's word, and insofar as it ignores these constraints, it can safely be ignored. The church's spiritual power may not be used to promote or oppose laws and policies that have not been commanded or forbidden by God.

This raises the question of what scripture teaches concerning politics and the obligations of magistrates. The Anabaptists illegitimately sought to transfer gospel standards of righteousness to political life because they failed to take into account human sin and the ongoing need for coercive political institutions, property, and courts of law. Calvin believed, in contrast, that government is ordained by God to fulfill specific temporal objectives, the most important of which are civil righteousness and the outward worship and teaching of true religion. In his early years, Calvin focused on government's secular purposes. He explicitly defended religious liberty for Muslims and Jews, and he clarified that while it is government's task to enforce God's moral law as much as possible, this does not require government to enforce or conform to the laws of Moses. The appropriate laws and polity for a Christian commonwealth are to be determined in accord with natural law, the rule of love, and the virtue of prudence.

Calvin rejected simplistic appeals to the law of Old Testament Israel on the basis of a sophisticated theory of the relation between the various biblical covenants, one that complemented his substantive accounts of law and gospel and of the two kingdoms. He emphasized that although all of the major covenants in scripture were in substance expressions of the one eternal covenant, the forms of the various covenants were different. The Mosaic, or old, covenant differed from the new in that it used outward, temporal, and political forms to point to spiritual realities. In addition, *narrowly* considered, the Mosaic covenant embodied a works principle that promised blessing to the obedient and threatened judgment on the disobedient. Calvin recognized that these dimensions of the old covenant could not be normative for Christians. It was only insofar as Israel and its law reflected God's natural moral law that it could serve as a model for Christian politics.

This principle led Calvin consistently to appeal to natural law in order to prove that what the Old Testament required of magistrates in terms of the care of religion remained binding for Christian rulers. Calvin argued that this position did not contradict the two kingdoms distinction because while magistrates could not convert individuals to faith or make them righteous, they could indirectly promote and defend Christ's kingdom by establishing and defending the ministry of the church and by punishing teachers of heresy. But Calvin emphasized that false teachers could only be punished by death in a society that had embraced the Christian faith by public consent, such that the offender could be said to have knowingly and willingly distorted the truth. Calvin's controversial argument against religious liberty thus rests on two fundamental conditions: 1) that natural law teaches a universally embraced magisterial obligation to care for religion; and 2) that there is a public consensus regarding the true religion.

Calvin acknowledged that in societies with religious diversity, matters would look quite different. He recognized that biblical heroes like Joseph and Daniel had to take nuanced political positions toward false religion because of their obligations to pagan political superiors and to the rule of law. In such circumstances, he recognized the value of government protection of the religious liberty of all persons. On the other hand, whereas with respect to matters of life or sustenance he often used the language of rights, nowhere did he recognize an open-ended right to religious liberty. For Calvin, government is bound by the law of God, and it is always responsible to promote and defend true religion as much as possible in accord with love and prudence.

But Calvin decisively rejected the claim that civil government is obligated to enforce the whole law of God regardless of circumstances. He articulated the fundamental principle that political laws must take into account what is possible given human depravity. Not only is government unable to convert persons to faith or to punish inward vices, but often it must tolerate public injustices as abhorrent as murder, violence, slavery, adultery, divorce, and polygamy. Indeed, it must even regulate such injustice in order to mitigate its most destructive consequences. To be sure, civil government should never affirm unjust conduct, and where it does so, it nullifies its own authority, but it should sometimes tolerate evil for the sake of the greater good.

Calvin's convictions regarding prudence and the nature of human depravity led him to promote a form of government in which authority is distributed among a plurality of virtuous magistrates elected by a free people to serve under the rule of law. To be sure, he never claimed that voting or political participation are human or civil rights. Far more important to him was the obligation of magistrates to rule in accord with God's law. But Calvin believed that where possible, the virtues of love and prudence call for a form of republicanism or aristocratic democracy that reflects principles of freedom, consent, and the rule of law. He raised the rule of law to such a height as to affirm the duty of all persons to disobey government when it commands injustice or impiety and the obligation of lesser magistrates actively to oppose such a government. But he emphasized that ordinarily, Christians are called to submit to government for the sake of the common good, even to the point of suffering, in accord with the example of Christ.

CALVIN'S TWO KINGDOMS THEOLOGY: CONTEMPORARY IMPLICATIONS FOR POLITICAL LIBERALISM

Most Protestant theologians articulated some version of a two realms distinction, but it was Calvin and his followers who insisted most clearly and consistently on the doctrine's implications for an institutional distinction between church and civil government. Later Protestants would clash on just this point, most famously in Heidelberg, where Thomas Erastus gave his name to the Zurich view that the civil magistrate is the lawful governor of the church and its discipline (erastianism), and most enduringly in England, where Elizabeth I's determination to be the supreme governor of the church contributed to the rise of Puritanism with its legacy in the Presbyterian, Congregational, Baptist, and Separatist churches that played such an important role in pushing America toward the separation of church and state.[5] It was no accident that whereas the authoritarian Thomas Hobbes viewed two kingdoms theology as one of the great threats to the sovereignty of the monarchy, the father of political liberalism, John Locke, presented two kingdoms theology as the basis for religious toleration.[6] More than any other Protestant theologian, Calvin founded the model of a church that could operate independently from the state in virtually whatever political and social context it found itself. This model rendered the separation of church

---

[5] Philip Benedict, *Christ's Churches Purely Reformed: A Social History of Calvinism* (New Haven: Yale University Press, 2002), 214–215, 238–254, 395–405.

[6] Thomas Hobbes, *Leviathan* (ed. Edwin Curley; Indianapolis: Hackett, 1994), 210–217; John Locke, "A Letter Concerning Toleration," in John Locke, *Two Treatises of Government and a Letter Concerning Toleration* (ed. Ian Shapiro; New Haven: Yale University Press, 2003), 217–226. Cf. John Perry, *The Pretenses of Loyalty: Locke, Liberal Theory, and American Political Theology* (Oxford: Oxford University Press, 2011); Jakob De Roover and S. N. Balagangadhara, "John Locke, Christian Liberty, and the Predicament of Liberal Toleration," *Political Theory* 36:4 (2008): 523–549; J. Wayne Baker, "Church, State, and Toleration: John Locke and Calvin's Heirs in England, 1644–1689," *Later Calvinism: International Perspectives* (ed. W. Fred Graham. Kirksville, MO: Sixteenth Century Journal, 1994), 525–543.

and state plausible from a Christian political theological perspective and paved the way for the phenomena of denominational pluralism.[7] The obligation of civil government to protect the autonomy of the church and the moral liberty of Christians encouraged the articulation of conceptions of basic rights that were deemed essential to a just society.[8]

There is, then, good *historical* reason to suspect that, his illiberal political commitments notwithstanding, Calvin's political theology offers substantive resources for Christians and churches seeking guidance as they participate in liberal democratic societies. But here I want to make that case on *theological* grounds. My purpose is not to speculate about how Calvin would have worked out the implications of his political theology in twenty-first-century liberal democracies. My purpose, rather, is to suggest how we might appropriate Calvin's two kingdoms theology critically, yet constructively, evaluating and building on its core dimensions in light of scripture, experience, reason, and contemporary challenges.

My proposal presupposes a practical commitment to political liberalism that, regrettably in my view, not all Christians share. I believe the gospel of Christ, in addition to the insights of reason and experience, give us good reasons for such a commitment. Yet even for those who disagree with me, democracy demands our fidelity at least to the degree that it has been providentially ordained by God as the established governing institution (Romans 13). As citizens of a pluralistic democracy, we are called to make sense of our political responsibilities and possibilities in light of the particular officials, bureaucracies, courts, traditions, procedures, laws, privileges and rights – in short, the political system – that we have, regardless of our measure of agreement with them. I believe Calvin's two kingdoms theology offers us good reasons to embrace political liberalism and helpful guidance for what our participation in its practices and institutions might look like. It provides churches and believers with a model for faithfully serving Christ as the Lord of politics, even as we maintain charity, respect, and good faith toward our fellow human beings who do not recognize that lordship.

Here I describe that model in terms of three general principles for contemporary Christian political engagement: America as a secular society, natural law as public reason, and the church as a public church.

---

[7] One need not claim that the origins of democracy or capitalism lie in Calvinism in order to make these claims for its legacy as a factor in the emergence of the separation of church and state. See John Witte, Jr., *Religion and the American Constitutional Experiment* (3rd ed.; Boulder: Westview, 2011), 21–29. For the classic argument, see Ernst Troeltsch, *The Social Teaching of the Christian Churches* (trans. Olive Wyon; 2 vols.; Louisville: Westminster/John Knox Press, 1992 [1912]), volume 2.

[8] John Witte, Jr., *The Reformation of Rights:Law, Religion, and Human Rights in Early Modern Calvinism* (Cambridge: Cambridge University Press, 2007).

AMERICA AS A SECULAR SOCIETY

First, neither America nor any other political society represents Israel or the kingdom of Christ. Coercive political institutions are inherently secular (or temporal), and they exist for fundamentally secular purposes. Their primary purpose is the maintenance of outward peace, justice, and order. This does not mean that government must be irreligious, because the distinction between the two kingdoms is not a distinction between religion and politics. The two kingdoms are not hermetically sealed realms into which life can be neatly divided, nor should they be identified as two of the "spheres" of differentiated human society identified by theorists like Abraham Kuyper, Max Weber, and Michael Walzer.[9] The temporal and the eternal, the spiritual and the political, overlap substantially in the real world, and they are both subject to the lordship of Christ. It is the material world that Christ will transform at the end of the age, and it is in the temporal affairs of the political kingdom that Christians witness to the restoration that is already taking place through Christ's spiritual kingdom. Christians thus seek to confess and practice the righteousness of the kingdom in every sphere of life.

But Christians must distinguish the way in which Christ is establishing his kingdom and restoring human righteousness through the ministry of his word from the preservative and restraining functions for which God has established civil government. Calvin could not be clearer that although civil government has certain responsibilities with respect to religion, it cannot regenerate or sanctify human beings. The task of politics is not to make human beings just or pious in any ultimate sense, but to call them to practices of civil virtue and civil piety conducive of outward peace and justice. Contemporary liberal governments accomplish this by punishing crimes, regulating trade, caring for the poor, ensuring the education of the citizenry, conserving the environment, preserving religious liberty, protecting religious institutions, and a myriad of other ways. But in doing so, they necessarily take into account the limits of government in a fallen world.

Calvin's awareness of the limits of civil law in the face of human depravity complements the liberal aversion to imposing one social group's comprehensive doctrine on others. Moral coercion is intrinsic to the work of government, to be sure, but it requires the support of the public consensus if it is to be deemed legitimate, let alone succeed. Whether the inability to establish such a consensus is lauded as the praiseworthy effect of religious pluralism or mourned as the regrettable consequence

---

[9] Abraham Kuyper, "Sphere Sovereignty," in *Abraham Kuyper: A Centennial Reader* (ed. James D. Bratt; Grand Rapids: Eerdmans, 1998), 461–490; the various essays on vocation by Max Weber in *From Max Weber: Essays in Sociology* (ed. C. Mills and Charles Wright; New York: Oxford University Press, 1946); Michael Walzer, *Spheres of Justice: A Defense of Pluralism and Equality* (New York: Basic Books, 1983).

of humans' hardness of heart, the result is the same: the law must respect the moral pluralism of its subjects if it is to win their allegiance. Calvin argued that even the civil law of Israel, given by God himself, tolerated such abhorrent injustice as the murder of prisoners in war, the forced marriage of captured women, the mistreatment of slaves, polygamy, and casual divorce. For all their frustration at the erosion of traditional morality in the public square in recent decades, contemporary Christians should take comfort from the fact that in many of these areas current law maintains a vastly superior standard to that of Old Testament Israel! Calvin urged his contemporaries to aspire to the higher standard of the natural moral law of God in their politics, and we should do the same. But the political principle remains valid and necessary: as abhorrent as a particular form of injustice might be, it is sometimes necessary to tolerate it.

The point here is not to laud moral and political relativism but to remind Christians of the impressive moral health of contemporary liberal societies while putting the moral failures of such societies in theological perspective. Political liberalism embraces the fundamental rights of the poor, women, and ethnic and religious minorities, rights that Christians should wholeheartedly affirm and promote as requirements of natural law. Liberalism tends to be less admirable in its dismissive attitude toward justice in sexuality and marriage, with deplorable results for children, including the unborn, but also for women and men. Christians should work to heighten moral sensitivities in such areas, building consensus for better laws. But that is precisely the point: They should work to build *consensus* rather than seek to override moral pluralism with brute political force, so undermining the publicly recognized moral authority of the law itself.[10] It is possible for the law to demand too much of persons, thus causing more harm than good. Where it is necessary, compromise is often not the sign of moral weakness but of moral integrity. It can reflect a recognition of the limits of law that arises from the virtues of prudence and love rather than from a merely self-serving pragmatism.[11]

To be sure, sometimes government falls below even a minimum standard of justice. When government acts with blatant injustice, Christians and the church must respond vigorously. When public officials take innocent life, oppress the poor, praise immorality, suppress the worship of God, or prevent the speaking of the truth,

---

[10] Indeed, James Davison Hunter argues that Christians are too quick to view politics as the primary means of social or cultural transformation. James Davison Hunter, *To Change the World: The Irony, Tragedy, and Possibility of Christianity in the Late Modern World* (Oxford: Oxford University Press, 2010).

[11] As the French scholar Jacques Ellul put it, "Our task, therefore, is not to determine what law with a Christian content is; rather, it is to find out what the lordship of Jesus Christ means for law (law as it exists), and what function God has assigned to law." Jacques Ellul, *The Theological Foundations of Law* (trans. Marguerite Wieser; New York: Doubleday, 1960), 13.

the church *must* condemn such injustice. (Mis)interpretations of two kingdoms theology that require political passivity on the part of the church, such as that which was advocated by certain German Christians in Nazi Germany or by some southern churches during the days of racial segregation, are at most an abhorrent distortion of Calvin's (and Luther's) political theology.[12] They ignore the church's obligation to preach the word of God and to discipline Christians guilty of flagrant injustice. Their protests of innocence notwithstanding, they *de facto* aligned the church with injustice. The church must recognize the limits of secular political institutions, but in its teaching and discipline it can never compromise its obligation to proclaim the word of Christ.

The two kingdoms doctrine also leads to what Robert Kraynak regards as the most important practical implication of Augustine's two cities concept: the need for the church to oppose "any political regime that attempts to unify [temporal and spiritual] sovereignty under one head."[13] Both totalitarianism and theocracy make such a Hobbesian attempt. Totalitarianism does so by raising the state and its ideology to the level of a religion, demanding the absolute allegiance of its subjects without regard to God or principles of justice. (Even John Rawls's early theory of justice, which requires all citizens to accept a Kantian comprehensive doctrine, falls into this error.[14]) Theocracy does so by placing the church (or some other religious institution) in the place of God, from whom the state derives its authority (even if via the people), so demanding ecclesiastical control over the state. This is the mistake of churches, pastors, or religious groups who imagine that their own convictions regarding the practical details of politics, policy or law represent the will of God himself, and who therefore attempt to use the church's spiritual power (in word or sacrament) for narrowly political ends. In their messianic and spiritual pretensions totalitarians and theocrats alike reject the claim that the state's purpose is *secular*.

Of course, in Calvin's view the state's purpose included the establishment of religion and the defense of the public honor of God. Yet it is crucial to remember that even here Calvin's concern was fundamentally secular, both in that state's power was limited to the *outward* forms of religion and in that the justification for its religious involvement rested on appeals to natural law and the consensus of nations. It was not only Moses who called for the public establishment of religion,

---

[12] See, for instance, Dietrich Bonhoeffer's criticism of compromised versions of two kingdoms theology throughout his *Ethics* (ed. Clifford J. Green et al.; Minneapolis: Fortress Press, 2009). Against the claims of Green in his introduction to Bonhoeffer's *Ethics*, I follow Patrick Nullens in viewing Bonhoeffer as a two kingdoms theologian in the tradition of Luther. See Patrick Nullens, "Dietrich Bonhoeffer: A Third Way of Christian Social Engagement," *European Journal of Theology* 20:1 (2011): 60–69.

[13] Robert P. Kraynak, *Christian Faith and Modern Democracy: God and Politics in the Fallen World* (Notre Dame: University of Notre Dame Press, 2001), 186.

[14] John Rawls, *A Theory of Justice* (Cambridge: Harvard University Press, 1971).

but Plato, Aristotle, and Cicero. Ironically, following Calvin's political theological method might lead contemporary Christians to quite different conclusions. Why give Moses priority over Jesus? And why give Greek and Roman philosophers more weight than Locke or Stout, whose political reflections take religious pluralism into account? If the experience of medieval Christians taught them that unity in religion is required for public peace, the experience of the religious wars of the seventeenth century and the ideological wars of the twentieth have convinced many contemporary Christians of the opposite. If it was once assumed that the alliance of religion and power increased the credibility of faith among the masses, scholars since Alexis de Tocqueville have observed that in educated, democratic societies it is the *separation* of church and state that works to the advantage of religion.[15] Communitarian political theologians can still make their case that a morally vacuous liberalism needs Christianity, but for many Christians it is just as clear that Christianity flourishes best in the context of a liberal commitment to basic human and civil rights. For such Christians the claim that natural law calls government to care for religion is a hard sell.

No religion should be imposed on a pluralistic society from the top down, but that does not mean, as even the best liberal philosophers have recognized, that civil government should have no concern for religion at all. For Christians, the state is not outside the lordship of Christ, and as Karl Barth pointed out, that means that the state should recognize its subservience to God and protect the free proclamation of the gospel.[16] Yet the relevant question for our time is not, how should the king or magistrate care for, exhibit, and defend true religion, but, how should the bureaucratic, constitutional state recognize its subservience to God and protect the public exercise of religion? Religion continues to hold a prominent place in many contemporary liberal democracies, including Germany and the United Kingdom, where churches remain established, and the United States, where, despite the separation of church and state, there is what Robert Bellah has famously described as America's "civil religion."[17] The very charter of American freedom roots human rights and public authority in the sovereignty of nature's God. The rhetoric of presidents from Washington to Obama, the prominence of religion in the way politicians and intellectuals across the political spectrum debate hot-button issues from immigration to same-sex marriage, the symbolism of public monuments, coins, songs, and the pledge of allegiance, the prominence of chaplains in the military and legislative assemblies, the tax exempt status of religious bodies, and legal

---

[15] See Alexis de Tocqueville, *Democracy in America* (trans. George Lawrence; ed. J. P. Mayer; New York: Harper Perennial, 2006), 287–301.

[16] Karl Barth, *Community, State, and Church: Three Essays* (Eugene, *Wipf and Stock*, 1960), 113–114.

[17] Robert N. Bellah, "Civil Religion in America," *The Robert Bellah Reader* (ed. Robert N. Bellah and Steven M. Tipton; Durham,: Duke University Press, 2006), 225–245.

protection for the religious liberty of both individuals and institutions – all demonstrate that the state does in fact recognize the sovereignty of God and the sanctity of religion, however much particular individuals and groups may object to it. Some Christians question the propriety of certain elements of America's civil religion, but in general they follow ancient and liberal philosophers alike when they laud a salutary public stance toward religion as a healthy expression of human meekness before God. There is still a broad consensus that if the state is to preserve peace, justice, and order, it needs to pay its respect to God; that without God both morality and human rights rest on a shaky foundation.[18]

To be sure, the gospel calls all persons to confess Christ, not simply the generic deity of American civil religion. But America is a pluralistic and democratic society in which the constitutional state represents all citizens, not just those who embrace the gospel. Public power is subject to the rule of written law, to be exercised by public servants occupying offices with defined prerogatives and limits. Thus most appropriate expressions of piety and faith should arise not from officials acting in their public capacity as judges, members of Congress, presidents, bureaucrats, or officers, but from individuals (including those occupying public office) and worshiping communities honest about their motives and faith. (Forms of liberalism that seek to exclude religion from public life are dangerous because they undermine this fundamental right of individual religious expression.) Calvin's two kingdoms theology does not encourage a sharp distinction between private religion and public life, but it does call for a distinction between the personal and the official, between what President Obama does when he offers his Christian testimony at the National Prayer Breakfast and what he does when he authorizes the use of military force to protect Americans from terrorism (however much the latter is informed by his Christian faith). On the one hand, in her public capacity a Christian magistrate is authorized to use the sword to defend justice, even though as an individual she is commanded by Christ not to resist evil but to turn the other cheek. On the other hand, like Joseph and Daniel, a Christian magistrate has no authority to advance a religious agenda regardless of constitutional constraints. As Calvin consistently maintained, each person must serve Christ's kingdom in accord with the limits of her vocation. Christians should promote the righteousness of Christ's kingdom, but they are not above the rule of law.

Calvin also lauded the benefits of making public authority plural and subject to the oversight of a free electorate. True, Calvin did not articulate the liberal notion of a social contract, nor did he affirm a fundamental human right to political participation. He supported aristocratic democracy not because he thought human beings are

---

[18] See, for instance, Michael Perry, *The Idea of Human Rights: Four Inquiries* (Oxford: Oxford University Press, 1998).

naturally good, but because he believed they are depraved. As he saw it, to delegate authority is always to create the possibility for its abuse. Nevertheless, for obvious reasons authority must be delegated. The key is to limit the possibilities of abuse, and Calvin believed that making political power plural and rendering it accountable to the electorate served this function.

But does such a system not expand the opportunities for the abuse of power on the part of the electorate? Interestingly, Calvin pointed out that any just legal system offers persons the opportunity to sue for their rights in court, even though this opportunity is often unjustly abused. A legal system cannot grant liberty for good without also opening up the possibility that it might be used for evil. The only alternative – for government to micromanage its subjects' lives – amounts to tyranny. Calvin thus understood that a person can have a legal right to do something that he has no moral right to do. By analogy, Christians might argue, pushing the democratic strand of Calvin's argument further, we should promote broad political participation despite the possibility of its abuse, because the alternative is worse. We cannot render government accountable to the people without recognizing that the people might err. We should solidify just constitutional and legal constraints, to be sure, but any system that frees people to act for good must also necessarily free them to act for evil. Securing liberty for a people to do good requires the civil protection of freedoms of speech, education, religion, association, trade, and more, even though such freedoms will inevitably be abused.

It is true that Calvin never conceptualized an inherent right to religious liberty. In my view he failed to follow the logic of his own two kingdoms theology to its logical political conclusion on this point. Here Calvin thought he was on firm ground, claiming not only the Mosaic law but also the common consent of the world as evidence for his claim that under certain conditions government should suppress false religion. Yet there are good reasons for Christians to follow Calvin's theology without arriving at his conclusions. Calvin recognized that the peculiar office of Moses was to demonstrate the curse of the law on sinners, and he recognized by extension that Israel's genocide of the Canaanites was a typological expression of God's judgment not to be repeated. But he failed to tie these threads together so as to recognize that Israel's thirty uses of capital punishment (for cases such as idolatry, false teaching, adultery, rebellion against parents, and Sabbath-breaking) were also typological expressions of eternal judgment whose exercise is foreclosed to contemporary political societies. No contemporary nation, no matter how widely its people have publicly embraced the gospel, is in a covenanted relationship with God as Israel was, and Christians have no right to execute the typological judgment of God.

Christians should also go beyond Calvin and defend the right to religious liberty based on the creation of human beings in the image of God. As a bearer of God's image, each human being is called to follow her conscience with respect to the demands of piety, justice, and the truth. Human beings are not *right* when they act impiously or unjustly, but they do have *the right* to exercise agency and responsibility in acting according to conscience. Suppressing this right in the name of preventing its abuse inevitably prevents its right use as well. Calvin should have been more sensitive to the clear teaching of the New Testament that the new covenant of the gospel, in contrast to the old covenant of the law, calls for the building of a voluntary community of faith through the ministry of the word accompanied by the work of the Spirit. The example of Christ and his apostles confirms that Christians should reject the temptation to use political power as a means of spreading the gospel or making human beings righteous. The honor of God is defended not by the willingness of Christians to kill blasphemers, idolaters, or false teachers, but by the willingness of Christians to die for such persons in conformity to Christ's example.

In fact, Calvin's two kingdoms theology, especially his doctrine of the church as Christ's spiritual kingdom, points precisely in this direction. Even though the social context of Christendom limited Calvin's ability to imagine or implement the reality of a voluntary church (what we might identify as the limits of Calvin's "social imaginary"[19]), contemporary Christians are not so limited. To conceive of the church as the body of the faithful gathered around the Lord's Supper and subject to discipline is necessarily to abandon the dangerous ideal of Christendom in which state and church are coterminous. We cannot have it both ways. If the church is a voluntary institution under the free proclamation of the gospel, it cannot also rest on the coercive authority of civil law. Still, we should not forget that it is Calvin who emphasized this differentiation of the church from the broader political realm, and it is Calvin who distinguished the typological kingdom of Israel under the law so sharply from political societies in the time of the gospel.

NATURAL LAW AS PUBLIC REASON

For Calvin, the moral standard for civil government is not the Torah nor is it biblical law. Rather, it is the natural law, which Calvin also identifies as the law of love and the rule of equity. The final authority regarding the content of natural law is scripture, but natural law is also known through reason, the sciences, experience, and the conscience. Indeed, often these sources have much more to say about the various questions that arise in contemporary politics than scripture does. Calvin's emphasis on natural law as the standard for just government, available to believers and nonbelievers alike, offers Christians a basis for public engagement that is

[19] See Charles Taylor, *Modern Social Imaginaries* (Durham: Duke University Press, 2004).

analogous to John Rawls's concept of public reason. As such, it poses a challenge to Christians who assume that scripture offers a blueprint for Christian politics.

John Rawls describes the core concern of his concept of public reason as

> the fact of reasonable pluralism – the fact that a plurality of conflicting reasonable comprehensive doctrines, religious, philosophical, and moral, is the normal result of its culture of free institutions. Citizens realize that they cannot reach agreement or even approach mutual understanding on the basis of their irreconcilable comprehensive doctrines. In view of this, they need to consider what kinds of reasons they may reasonably give one another when fundamental political questions are at stake. I propose that in public reason comprehensive doctrines of truth or right be replaced by an idea of the politically reasonable addressed to citizens as citizens.[20]

Rawls argues that it is essential for religious believers to recognize that their "zeal to embody the whole truth in politics is incompatible with an idea of public reason that belongs with democratic citizenship."[21] He posits public reason as an outworking of the "criterion of reciprocity [which] says: our exercise of political power is proper only when we sincerely believe that the reasons we should offer for our political options . . . are sufficient, and we also reasonably think that other citizens might also reasonably accept those reasons."[22] The point is not necessarily to exclude religion from political culture but to seek a common basis for discussion in the discourse of judges, government officials, and elective politics. Although Rawls's early version of public reason was rightly criticized for its suggestion that political commitments could not be driven by religious reasons or motives, his final version of the concept accepts the legitimacy of religiously motivated political engagement as long as it conforms to shared liberal principles and procedures and seeks to persuade the other members of society on the basis of arguments that are publicly accessible and potentially reasonable (whether or not persuasive) to all. Rawls thus distinguishes public reason, which is compatible with multiple comprehensive doctrines, from what he calls "secular reason," which would require all citizens to be committed to a non-religious comprehensive doctrine. Rejecting the latter, Rawls goes so far as to identify the neo-Thomist natural law theory of John Finnis as a legitimate example of public reason.[23]

Problems remain with Rawls's description of public reason, not the least of which is its ongoing suspicion that religion is a threat to public reason, but it is well-beyond the scope of this conclusion to engage those problems here. My point is simply to

---

[20] Rawls, *Political Liberalism*, 441.　[21] Rawls, *Political Liberalism*, 442.

[22] Rawls, *Political Liberalism*, 446–447.

[23] Rawls, *Political Liberalism*, 451–452. See John Finnis, *Natural Law and Natural Rights* (Oxford: Oxford University Press, 1980).

suggest that Calvin's emphasis on natural law, as a basis for political reasoning that is universal in its scope and accessibility, offers Christians their own form of public reason: a means by which they can participate in moral and political arguments without preaching at nonbelievers or requiring a confession of Christ as a basis for discussion. If Rawls's version of public reason has the virtue of calling us to the "duty of civility,"[24] Calvin's concept of natural law calls us to practice the virtue of charity, in the classic sense of the term.

Christians should not rely *exclusively* on public reason, I would argue, but the *inclusive* use of something like public reason (i.e., a commitment to finding common moral and political ground with persons who are not Christians) is integral to the sort of reciprocal neighbor-love that Christ requires in the command to love one's neighbor as oneself. Christians are called not only to walk as self-sacrificial servants, doing good to the just and the unjust alike (Matthew 5:43–48), but to practice humility, to be reasonable, and to seek peace insofar as it depends on them (Philippians 4:5; Romans 12:18). At the very least, this requires that we work through our political disagreements with nonbelievers (and with one another) in a manner that prioritizes mutual respect and seeks common ground. If Paul could appeal to ideas he shared with Athenian pagans in his evangelistic speech on Mars Hill (Acts 17), surely we ought to do the same when it comes to secular politics. To demand the political normativity of Christian theology or ethics at the expense of peace and order is to undermine the very reason for which civil government was ordained by God. In the name of perfect piety or justice it destroys the possibility of any public peace or justice at all. It reduces politics to a zero-sum game in which participants are driven to the moral extremes, leaving no place for a shared, if imperfect, temporal good.[25]

The reality, as Calvin recognized, is that not even a society of Christians can be ruled with simple reference to a set of biblical proof-texts. Any given commandment, practice, or narrative of scripture must be interpreted in terms of its biblical and covenantal context. Laws must be identified as moral, ceremonial, or civil. If a certain principle is identified as a fundamental principle of justice, it remains to do the hard work of determining whether that principle should be coercively enforced, and if so, how. This process of reasoning depends not only on the careful interpretation of scripture, but on a myriad of factors drawn from extrabiblical

---

[24] Rawls, *Political Liberalism*, 465.
[25] Excellent examples of this are two of the most hot-button issues in contemporary American politics: same-sex unions and abortion. The intransigence of right and left alike on these issues have prevented the enactment of common sense laws that have widespread public support, such as the legalization of civil unions and the prohibition of second and third trimester abortions except where the life of the mother is threatened, leading to outcomes (such as abortion-on-demand and same-sex marriage) for which the lack of public support undermines the integrity of the law.

knowledge and experience, areas in which Calvin recognized that nonbelievers often excel above Christians. In the twenty-first-century world of ever-increasing complexity and social differentiation, this recognition is all the more apt. If Christians are to be faithfully engaged in contemporary political life, we need our nonbelieving fellow citizens and the knowledge and expertise God has given them. To reject this gift is, as Calvin puts it, to reject the Spirit himself.

The point is not that the classic rhetoric and terminology of "natural law" – perhaps weakened due to its abuse over the centuries – must be used. Indeed, it is important to stress that Calvin's account of natural law is not even a systematic epistemological theory (as is that of Thomism, for instance). Though Calvin's use of natural law is sometimes criticized for being casual and unsystematic, in the real world of democratic politics this is actually an advantage. When claiming that a particular moral principle is taught in nature, Calvin appealed to a range of authorities in addition to scripture, including reason, philosophy, human sentiment, the conscience, experience, and the laws of nations, all of which can be described as expressions of what Reformed theology came to call "general revelation." In the twenty-first century, we might compare Calvin's use of natural law to philosophical arguments about human and civil rights, widely embraced moral values, the data of science, history and sociology, or the UN Charter of Human Rights and Freedoms. All of this data should inform and guide Christian engagement in civil affairs, and it provides us with common ground with our nonbelieving neighbors. Both common sense and love require Christians to listen to, learn from, and work with their fellow image-bearers rather than attempt to rule over them.

THE CHURCH AS PUBLIC CHURCH

Finally, the church must be mindful that it is not merely called to a sectarian existence, separated from the world and without regard to the well-being of the world. Rather, expressed in the terms of Robert Bellah and the coauthors of *Habits of the Heart*, the church is called to be a public church, concerned with both the salvation and the temporal welfare of the world.[26] Steven Tipton describes this as

> a "church-like" stance of willingness to engage the society as a whole and wrestle with it dialectically, practically, and structurally, in the cautiously hopeful expectation that such engagement can make the world more humane and just.

---

[26] On the idea of the public church see Robert N. Bellah, et al., *Habits of the Heart: Individualism and Commitment in American Life* (Berkeley: University of California Press, 2008), especially 243–248; Robert N. Bellah, et al., *The Good Society* (New York: Vintage Books, 1992), especially 179–219; Martin Marty, *The Public Church: Mainline-Evangelical-Catholic* (New York: Crossroad, 1981); and Tipton, *Public Pulpits*, 399–442.

It respects yet seeks to press beyond the stance of the sect as a witness community set against the world . . . By arguing across multiple moral languages and visions, the church is willing to engage the larger society more intimately and dialectically than the religious kingdom holding itself at arms length from the political and economic realms.[27]

While Bellah and Tipton describe the model of a public church with reference to Troeltsch's sociological language of sect and church, for further clarity regarding the particular implications of Calvin's two kingdoms theology, I would suggest following Abraham Kuyper's distinction between the church as institution and the church as organism. As an institution defined by its ministry of the word, sacraments, discipline, and the diaconate, the church is called to proclaim the gospel of restoration to the world, while through the organic life of its members in society, the church is called to witness to the righteousness of the kingdom in every area of life.[28]

As an institution, the church's authoritative proclamation is limited to the word and its celebration of the sacraments is limited by discipline. The ministers of the church have no discretionary power over such functions and may not misuse them for the prudentially ordered purposes of politics. But this does not mean the church's vision is sectarian. On the contrary, the church's vision is always universal, its character always public. Its central task is to proclaim the restoration of the world to all who are willing to hear it. This involves a complete proclamation of both law and gospel, embracing God's purposes for human beings in restoring them to communion. The church's proclamation of the word encompasses what scripture teaches about human beings as embodied social creature made in God's image for knowledge, love, justice, and holiness. It is the gospel that provides the only true vision for human flourishing and the ultimate model of righteousness to which human endeavors should aspire. The church seeks to proclaim this gospel as a servant of the word, neither exceeding nor falling short of what it teaches. This is the essential mark of the true church.

That said, Calvin recognized that this task of the church does not give the church authority to find in scripture a blueprint for contemporary politics. The true focus of scripture is the covenantal and eschatological fulfillment of God's promises in Christ, the very word of God incarnate. Thus the church should be wary of moving from a proclamation of the word of God to an authoritative proclamation of policy or politics based on the use of proof-texts. It is well beyond the spiritual authority of the

---

[27] Steven M. Tipton, *Public Pulpits: Methodists and Mainline Churches in the Moral Argument of Public Life* (Chicago: University of Chicago Press, 2007), 436.

[28] I follow this distinction in the broadest sense, without respect to the controversial details of Kuyper's version of it as they have been evaluated and debated for a century now. On the basic distinction see Abraham Kuyper, *Rooted and Grounded: The Church as Organism and Institution* (trans. Nelson D. Kloosterman; Grand Rapids: Christian's Library, 2013).

church in most cases to endorse particular candidates or to call for specific legislation, and insofar as the church transgresses that boundary it ceases to administer the
authority of Christ's kingdom. At this point I draw precisely the opposite implication
from the interplay between Calvin's political theology and modernity, as does André
Biéler. Biéler calls the church to reject the sort of secularization and social differentiation that results in moral pluralism by preaching a holistic ethic that covers
every aspect of life, including politics. "The time has come to put an end to the
alienation of modern men and women, who – in obeying all kinds of different,
frequently contradictory imperatives in their professional political, family and individual behaviour – find their personalities thus chopped into compartments and
their responsibility brought to naught."[29] For Biéler, as for so many other Calvinists
over the years, the legacy of the reformer of Geneva is to be understood in terms of
a comprehensive and expansive worldview that is to be brought authoritatively to
bear in every area of life.

> Too many believers . . . condemn what they call the faith's or the church's meddling
> in political, social or occupational matters. Having lost the fundamentally biblical
> vision of the universal Lordship of Jesus Christ, they take refuge in sentimental
> pietism that allows only a rudimentary part of the individual to be governed by the
> faith . . . For lack of a systematic theological vision of the purposes of society and of
> the appropriate ways for acting, they want to work for their faith but remain
> unconsciously prisoners of the sociological pressures from which they suffer.[30]

Yet Biéler confuses humility with moral confusion. It is not an abandonment of the
lordship of Christ in favor of sociological pressures that makes Christians wary of
dogmatic political theological visions but a refusal to see that lordship compromised.
It is not sentimental pietism that calls for restraint on the part of the institutional
church but a determination not to confuse our own flawed judgments regarding the
complexities of politics with the gospel of Christ's kingdom.

Does this sort of humility negate any possibility of the church's authoritative
prophetic witness? It does not, because the church's prophetic witness does not
consist in particular political statements or policy proposals but in its proclamation of
the gospel and righteousness of God. It is when the church faithfully proclaims that
the love and justice of God require care for the poor and the oppressed, for instance,
that it calls societies to judgment. The Reformed churches of South Africa rejected
the moral authority of apartheid when they declared racism to be a heresy, not
when they offered specific political proposals for its dismantling. Similarly, those
Protestant churches of Germany that were faithful judged the Nazi state when they

---

[29] André Biéler, *Calvin's Economic and Social Thought* (ed. Edward Dommen; trans. James Greig;
Geneva: World Alliance of Reformed Churches, 2005 [1961]), 458.
[30] Biéler, *Calvin's Economic and Social Thought*, 459.

openly proclaimed the unity of Gentile and Jew in Christ and preached the basic demands of the Ten Commandments.[31] The church's uncompromising proclamation of the word renders it prophetic in its witness. There is no need for pastors or denominations to undermine their own credibility by attempting to take up the tasks of think tanks, interest groups, or political parties.

When the church does remain faithful to its mission in the word, sacraments, and discipline, it prophetically shapes its members' understanding of justice. The proclamation of Jesus as the new humanity calls all human beings across race, gender, religion, and socio-economic status to communion in Christ's love, communion that takes vivid expression in the Eucharist. The church's worship testifies to the equality of all of its members, who are called to devote themselves to a political economy of mutual service and the sharing of material possessions. Even here, where the church is arguably at its most "sectarian," the public implications of its gospel ethos are immense.[32] We might think of the obvious principles traditionally emphasized by Christian ethics, such as honor for parents and those in authority, respect for the sanctity of human life, care for the economic, social, and spiritual needs of others, defense of the weak and the oppressed, commitment to the truth, and love and fidelity in marriage. In addition, the church also calls human beings to embody the virtues of Christ, including public virtues like love, justice, peacemaking, generosity, mercy, and compassion, and inward virtues like contentment, piety, and humility. It calls them to embody the self-sacrificial service of Christ toward the suffering and the marginalized, to seek peace and reconciliation among those who are in conflict or at war, and to resist oppressors by all appropriate means. It points toward the appropriate relationship of human beings to the material creation as one of stewardship and care. When the church fails in these areas and when Christians sin, as happens more often than not, the discipline and reconciliation offered through the word and sacraments exhibits the hope of the kingdom of Christ that enables believers to persevere through faith in God. It therefore calls human beings to avoid foisting messianic and utopian dreams upon the state (a burden whose weight so often results in political and moral tragedy), casting their hope on Christ instead.

But the church in Calvin's conception does not only consist of the body of the faithful gathered around the word and sacraments (what Kuyper called the church as

---

[31] Similarly, it was the failure of the Presbyterian churches of the antebellum South to preach the whole word of God, to share the Eucharist with blacks in a spirit of equality, and to discipline their slave-holding members in accord with the word and sacraments, rather than their refusal to offer political proposals, that indicts them for their collusion in racial oppression.

[32] This is the excellent contribution of so many Christian ethicists working from within neo-Anabaptist and liturgical perspectives in recent years. See, for instance, *The Blackwell Companion to Christian Ethics* (2nd ed.; ed. Stanley Hauerwas and Samuel Wells; Oxford: Blackwell, 2011).

an institution). The church also refers to the body of the faithful as they serve Christ and their neighbors in the world, working out the implications of the word and sacraments to the best of their ability, in a spirit of humility, and in accord with their various vocations (what Kuyper called the church as an organism). This service – even when it takes place in the political realm – draws its orientation from the church's ministry of the gospel, for the gospel vision of righteousness is the ultimate prophetic horizon for all of human life. But the church must avoid the temptation to "foreclose public argument" when it comes to the particular questions involved in what Tipton calls the moral argument of public life. This is not only the case because on practical questions the knowledge, expertise, and prudence of individual believers (not to mention that of nonbelievers) often exceeds that of the institutional church, and it is not only the case because these same individual believers often disagree about the implications of the gospel for such practical questions (Here, after all, neither scripture nor natural law usually speaks with perfect clarity). It is also the case because Christ has called individual Christians to freedom and maturity as they witness to the righteousness of the kingdom in their own vocational contexts and according to their own consciences, consistent with the knowledge, expertise, and prudence God has given them. The institutional church thus usurps the unique calling of individual Christian believers when it does not leave them free, within the limits of the church's faithful proclamation, to pursue – and debate – the practical shape that love and justice should take in the times and places to which God has called them.[33]

It is in part through the public words and deeds of the faithful in the political order, therefore, that the church must be content to take up its role as a public church. Here Christians witness, individually and sometimes collectively, to their convictions regarding the justice and love demanded by the gospel. Here it is appropriate for ethicists, farmers, politicians, soldiers, parents, students, or business owners to argue vigorously and thoughtfully for the vision of public righteousness most in accord with their own experience, expertise, and conviction. And here we are in the realm of freedom, each Christian ultimately responsible for her own conduct. To limit the authoritative proclamation of the church in this area is to free the organic church for witness rather than to restrain it. Within the appropriate constraints of a faithful political theology, Christians are free to act according to the best insights of their virtue, character, and conscience.

In his 1967 book *Who Speaks for the Church?* Paul Ramsey warned that a church that abuses its proclamatory function by seeking to overdetermine the political engagement of Christians undermines its own moral authority, tyrannizes consciences, and prevents the body from fulfilling its calling with integrity before

---

[33] See Tipton, *Public Pulpits*, 317, 413–414.

God. In Ramsey's view, the mid-twentieth-century mainline Protestant denominations in America became obsessed with crafting policy statements that confused political positions subject to the judgments of human prudence with the *de jure* prophetic authority of the church. When pastors and theologians address matters of policy, Ramsey observes, they have no more expertise – and they often have less – than the individual Christians in whose vocations and areas of expertise such matters properly lie. The sad reality was that the conservative and liberal wings of the church looked remarkably like "the secular variety of the same opinions."[34] This suggested that the church had lost sight of its true message, the gospel, and was confusing its own political ideologies with the word of God. As Ramsey saw it, "Radical steps need to be taken in ecumenical ethics if ever we are to correct the pretense that we are makers of political policy and get on with our proper task of nourishing, judging, and repairing the moral and political *ethos* of our time."[35]

Calvin's two kingdoms theology suggests that it is only insofar as the church demonstrates that its proclamation is that of Christ, rather than that of a particular ideological movement or agenda, that it maintains prophetic authority. It was the conviction of his hearers that he was prophetically bringing the *gospel* to bear on the injustice of racial segregation, not the creativity of his political proposals, that gave Martin Luther King, Jr., his profound public moral authority. Likewise it was Karl Barth's zeal for the *sovereignty of Christ* in the proclamation of the church that made the Barmen Declaration such an inspiration for the Confessing Church. But we should not forget that for every example of a King and a Barth, there has been a myriad of pastors who claimed prophetic authority for the unjust causes of segregation or Nazism, and it was against such *abuses* of church functions that Barth and King waged their battles. We should not forget that the pulpits of the nations cried out with vitriolic patriotic rhetoric during World War I, just as American clergy have rushed to claim the support of God in every war the United States has fought. When the church so abandons the restraint of the word in the name of short-term political relevance, it is rightly ignored by Christians and nonbelievers alike.

It is Calvin's dual insistence on 1) the authority of the *word* of the kingdom as proclaimed by the church, and 2) the liberty of the *Christian* as she serves Christ in the passing affairs of the present age that makes his two kingdoms theology so useful for our understanding of the mission and public engagement of the church. It frees the church to proclaim a word to the world that is truly prophetic, even as it frees believers for the sort of political engagement that is truly faithful. It keeps the church focused on the priority of the gospel of restoration, even as it reminds the state of its

---

[34] Paul Ramsey, *Who Speaks for the Church?* (Nashville: Abingdon Press, 1967), 21.
[35] Ramsey, *Who Speaks for the Church?*, 15.

temporal mission subject to God. For contemporary Christians, it offers a warning against rejecting political liberalism under the pretense of serving Christ as Lord. Our calling is serve him in *this* place, at *this* time, through *these* people, and through *these* democratic practices and structures that we have been blessed to inherit. Through the prophetic proclamation of the gospel by the church and the public engagement of Christians we convey to our secular communities the immeasurable wealth of Christ's gospel and the wisdom of the moral tradition that flows from it. Christ calls the church to love him and our neighbors with wisdom and faithfulness – being as "wise as serpents" and as "innocent as doves" (Matthew 10:16) – as we inhabit the tension between the present age and the age to come. That is a calling that we should not take lightly.

Index

1 Timothy 2:2, 40, 57, 249, 282, 294, 297, 302, 346

Abrahamic, 259, 268
Academy, 82
  Geneva, 82
  Lausanne, 81
Adam, 34, 53, 92, 94–95, 97–98, 100, 117–119, 128,
  131, 133, 147, 150, 168
adultery, 50, 105–106, 110, 168, 175, 240, 249, 253,
  283, 291, 322, 334, 360, 368
ages, two
  future age/age to come, 94, 102, 122, 128, 132, 147,
    149, 378
  present age, 178
Allen, Claire S., 78, 289
Amboise, Conspiracy of, 87, 89–90
Anabaptists, 1, 9, 19–20, 24, 37–38, 40, 44–45,
  47–53, 56–58, 63, 65–66, 78, 95, 122, 170–172,
  178, 180, 200, 204, 206–208, 228, 231–232, 236,
  246–247, 249–250, 252, 255–256, 295, 297, 357,
  359, 375
anarchy, 31, 36, 78, 172, 180, 241, 245, 347
Aquinas, Thomas, 7, 26, 104–105, 239, 321
aristocracy, 2, 88, 240, 337–338, 342–344, 361, 367
Aristotle, 2, 28, 32, 95, 115, 131, 161, 164, 240, 255, 324,
  327, 357, 366
Armstrong, Brian G., 73, 83–84, 86, 274, 351
ascension, 122, 124–125, 129, 139–140, 147–148,
  192–194
Augustijn, Cornelis, 67
Augustine, 2, 7, 10, 12, 23–24, 34–35, 93, 95, 100,
  136, 206, 209, 237–238, 241, 247, 249, 282–283,
  291, 305, 345, 365

Babylon, 241
  Babylonian Captivity of the Church, 29

Israel's exile in, 205, 241, 292, 303, 345
Backus, Irena, 17, 73, 93, 95–96, 104, 109
Baker, J. Wayne, 45, 52–56, 63, 75, 78–79, 80, 210,
  361
Balagangadhara, S. N., 361
Balke, Wilhelm, 19, 63, 65–66, 78, 95, 122, 171, 200,
  204, 208, 231, 236, 246–247, 249, 295
baptism, 43, 47–49, 50, 52, 54, 65, 73, 76, 186, 192,
  194, 334, 336, 356
Barth, Karl, 103, 281, 366, 377
Battenhouse, R. W., 92
Bavinck, Herman, 14, 101
Bellah, Robert N., 10, 366, 372–373
Benedict, Philip, 17, 19, 46, 62–63, 65, 73, 82–83,
  86–90, 361
Bennett, John, 6
Berman, Harold J., 14, 24, 25
Bernard, of Clairveaux, 187, 190
Berne, 46, 62–63, 65, 78–82
Beza, Theodore, 79, 81–82, 88–90, 244
Biel, Pamela, 54
Biéler, André, 13–14, 205, 374
Bierma, Lyle D., 14, 56, 256, 281
blasphemy, 36–38, 54, 75, 232, 253, 283, 289, 292,
  294, 305, 321, 369
Boeke, Brandt B., 168, 251, 280, 288, 349, 351
Boer, Roland, 142, 168
Bohatec, Josef, 68, 344–345
Bolt, John, 15, 122
Bonhoeffer, Dietrich, 349, 365
Bourbon, House of, 87–88, 352
Bourse Francaise, 77, 225
Brief Instruction, 247–250, 253
Briggs, Charles F., 30–31
Bruening, Michael W., 46, 65, 81–82
Brunner, Emil, 19, 103, 133

Lightning Source UK Ltd.
Milton Keynes UK
UKOW06n0854270817
308030UK00002BA/6/P